Modern
Educational
Measurement

Practical Guidelines
for Educational Leaders

THIRD EDITION

W. James Popham

University of California, Los Angeles

ALLYN AND BACON

Boston • London • Toronto • Sydney • Tokyo • Singapore

Vice President, Editor in Chief, Education: Paul A. Smith
Editorial Assistant: Jill Jeffrey
Marketing Manager: Brad Parkins
Director of Educational Programs: Ellen Dolberg
Editorial Production Service: Chestnut Hill Enterprises, Inc.
Manufacturing Buyer: Megan Cochran
Cover Administrator: Linda Knowles

Internet: www.abacon.com

Between the time Website information is gathered and published, some sites may
have closed. Also, the transcription of URLs can result in typographical errors.
The publisher would appreciate notification where these occur so that they may
be corrected in subsequent editions.

Library of Congress Cataloging-in-Publication Data
Popham, W. James.
    Modern educational measurement : practical guidelines for
educational leaders / W. James Popham. — 3rd ed.
      p.   cm.
    Includes bibliographical references and index.
    ISBN 0-205-28770-0
    1. Educational tests and measurements.   I. Title.
LB3051.P6143 2000
371.26–dc21   99-22345
                                     CIP

Printed in the United States of America

10 9 8 7 6 5 4 3 2 1   RRD-VA   04 03 02 01 00 99

Credits: Cartoons by Joan Orme.

CONTENTS

chapter 9
Selected-Response Items   224

chapter 10
Constructed-Response Items   256

chapter 11
Performance and Portfolio Assessment   278

chapter 12
Improving Test Items   312

chapter 13
Creating Affective Measures   333

part four Using Educational Tests   355

PREFACE

There are revisions of textbooks—and then there are revisions of textbooks. I know. I've revised more than a few textbooks that, in their first editions, I had believed were just this side of perfect. But textbooks, just like a person's wardrobe, often become dated. That's when a significant choice-point arises.

The Robustness of a Textbook Revision

A textbook revision can either be major or mild. *Mild* revisions usually require the author to update the references and toss in a new chapter or two. Thereafter, a brand new copyright date can be affixed to the "revised" textbook and its sales potential substantially rises. Because instructors, and even students, don't like using a textbook that's been written many years earlier, a more current copyright date will often meaningfully prolong the shelf life of any textbook. Mild revisions often work out just fine.

On the other hand, a textbook revision can be *major*. Such revisions take place when the author sets out to re-orient the book substantially. Major revisions represent far more than updating references and preparing a few new chapters. Major revisions are, to the author, a nontrivial pain in the posterior. Major revisions are almost like writing a book from scratch. They're a lot of work.

This textbook, published originally in 1981, was revised once before in 1990. To be honest, that 1990 revision was rather mild. The current version, sporting a nifty new copyright date of A.D. 2000, I assure you, is a major, major revision.

The earliest version of *Modern Educational Measurement* was written chiefly for graduate students who were pursuing educational doctoral degrees in the nation's universities. Because I was a professor in the UCLA Graduate School of Education, I had written a measurement textbook for students who were on their way to becoming professors just like me. That, of course, is a common failing of many university professors. We try to create students in our own likeness. And so it was that the first edition of *Modern Educational Measurement*, and even its mildly revised successor, were measurement textbooks aimed at students who were trodding the traditional doctoral trail traveled by future academics. There were already a fair number of those sorts of books around. I had simply written another one.

A Change of Career Venue

But then, several years ago, I decided to take an early retirement from professoring at UCLA. I'd been there almost 30 years and, therefore, I'd definitely "been there, done that." I had also learned that UCLA emeritus professors could park on campus for free. The temptation was far too enticing.

On retirement, therefore, I found much more time to work with public school educators—real teachers and real administrators—who were wrestling with measurement problems on a daily basis. More often than not, their need to use educational measurement had been brought about by some sort of accountability pressures. The public wanted higher test scores from students, and educators wanted to know how to produce such results. For example, I'd receive a request from a district assistant superintendent to offer workshops for teachers and administrators about "what kinds of tests should be used to show our school board that we're doing a solid job of educating students." Or I'd be asked to give a speech at a district-wide staff development session about "the relationship between testing and teaching." In the past several years, in fact, I've spent an enormous number of hours working with real-world educational practitioners as they attempted to solve measurement-related problems.

To be totally candid, with relatively few exceptions, the educators with whom I worked really didn't know all that much about the kinds of measurement procedures that are called for in today's schools. And why should they? Many of those administrators and teachers had never taken a formal course in educational measurement. And if, sometime during their graduate programs, they had actually completed a course in educational testing, it was usually an all-too-traditional measurement course in which they encountered scads of theoretical content that simply didn't mesh with today's firing-line measurement demands.

More often than not, after I had completed one of those consulting assignments, educators would ask me about recommendations for further reading. Because I had been extolling the notion that measurement, if done well, could play a vital role in improving educational quality, district administrators and teachers often wanted to learn more about the measurement ideas I'd been spouting. And that's when I'd find myself thinking about the second edition of *Modern Educational Measurement*. I could, of course, have suggested that those educators buy a pile of the measurement book I'd revised in 1990. Publishers, of course, respond with enthusiasm to increased sales. And, besides, I'd also pocket some royalty bucks if many of the books were bought.

But I could really never bring myself to push the second edition of this book. Unfortunately, that edition of the book wasn't sufficiently practical to help teachers and administrators all that much. I had written, and revised, a measurement book for aspiring professors. I had not written, and revised, a measurement book for administrators and teachers who wanted to use measurement to improve the quality of schooling.

A Chicago Meeting

And so it was that Nancy L. Forsyth, then Senior Vice President and Education Publisher of Allyn and Bacon, sat down with me over a pair of diet colas at the 1997 Chicago meeting of the American Educational Research Association to decide whether *Modern Educational Measurement* should be revised or, instead, be allowed to expire. When a textbook

goes out of print, of course, it's simply a literary form of euthanasia. She and I both concluded that what was needed was not just a same old, same old minor revision of a measurement textbook originally written for aspiring professors. She, too, sensed the need for
a practical textbook about testing that would address the assessment needs of today's educational leaders. We already had the right modifier in the book's title. It was supposed to
be *modern*. Why not, she proposed, create a revised textbook about modern measurement
for the administrators and teachers who would be leading our schools in the next century?

As she argued persuasively about the need for a thorough reorientation of *Modern
Educational Measurement*, I found myself thinking that I was really going to be obliged to
write almost a brand new book. Oh, I anticipated that from the second edition I could
save a few chapter titles and *all* of the page numbers. But to prepare a measurement book
specifically for folks who were the pivotal, in-the-trenches players in making today's
schools run—that would require a top-to-bottom rewrite. Such a revision would have to
be terribly practical. It would have to deal with what educators really needed to know
about measurement. There could be no "nice to know" content that, although interesting, had no implications for practice. Furthermore, the measurement issues addressed in
such a book would need to be *today's* educational assessment issues—issues that are rarely
treated in traditional doctoral-level measurement books. To write such a book would be
quite a challenge.

However, it was that very challenge that excited me about the prospect of preparing
such a revision. If I could do a decent job of revising *Modern Educational Measurement* so
that it would help educational leaders decide why, when, and how to assess students, I
could supply the kind of assistance that was needed by the many educators with whom
I'd worked in the late nineties. So, in good conscience, I could thereafter recommend a
"for further reading" book that I believed in. And, of course, there were the royalties!

The Revision's Chief Features

Once we'd decided during our two-hour Chicago session (Nancy, being a classy and affluent publisher, picked up the check for the two diet colas) that a thoroughgoing overhaul of *Modern Educational Measurement* would be necessary, we then discussed the format
of the revision. What you'll find in the following pages is remarkably consistent with the
conclusions of that Chicago meeting. Briefly, let me describe what you'll encounter in the
15 chapters that make up this third edition. If you want, you can think of the next few
paragraphs as a "preview of coming distractions."

First, and foremost, this edition has been written with a particular audience in mind,
namely, *educational leaders*. In Chapter 1, I've tried to spell out exactly what I mean by an
educational leader. But, for purposes of this preface, let's say that an educational leader is
an educator—administrator or teacher—whose decisions have an impact on other educators whose activities, in turn, will have an impact on students. The overriding mission
of this third edition is to provide a measurement book that will assist such educational
leaders. The revision, therefore, had to be unrelentingly practical in nature. In preparing
the revision, and in deciding what content to include, my litmus test was always to find
out if a positive answer could be given to the following question: "Do today's educational
leaders *really* need to know what you're writing about?" With only occasional unintended
slip-ups, I've tried to do just that.

Second, the book should be easy to use because educational leaders are invariably busy people. Busy people need a book that's simple to use. Accordingly, you'll discover that each chapter begins with a chapter outline in the form of a small number of *guiding questions* around which the chapter is organized. Whether you regard these questions as an "anticipatory set," or a misplaced and premature end-of-chapter quiz, I hope you'll find each chapter's guiding questions useful. They represent, in a sense, each chapter's instructional objectives. At the end of every chapter, you'll find some succinct answers to each of the chapter's guiding questions provided as a chapter wrap-up. These answers will, when lumped together, function as a chapter summary.

And because you'll most likely encounter some new terminology as you read through the book, I've supplied in the page margins brief definitions of important terms. This in-margin, en route glossary, is provided with the thought that, as you read through the book, you'll mentally be assembling your own glossary regarding the measurement terms that you're apt to encounter in your own work.

At the close of each chapter, you'll also find a set of practice exercises that will help you master the chapter's content. The answers to these practice exercises are provided at the chapter's conclusion, but *after* the exercises themselves. For me to have supplied the answers prior to the exercises themselves would have been pedagogically perverse.

Each chapter is also concluded with a set of discussion questions. You'll find these questions useful in case you attend a cocktail party or staff meeting and run short of conversational topics. You can print the questions on index cards, then whip them out when the conversation lags. There are also some suggestions for further reading if you find that, after having introduced the discussion questions at a cocktail party, you have difficulty supplying answers—any answers. Most chapters also identify some audio or video follow-up resources for those readers who are put off by the printed page.

The final decision that Nancy Forsyth and I made during our 1997 diet cola conference was that the new revision ought to be lively rather than deadly. I've tried to include a variety of features that I hope educational leaders, or educational leaders-in-training, will find interesting and, in some instances, even thought-provoking.

For instance, in most chapters you'll find features called *Educational Leaders Look at Assessment.* In these brief commentaries, real administrators and teachers provide, in their own words, experience-based views regarding one or more topics being considered in that chapter. I'm sure you'll find the views of these educational leaders worth considering. In most instances, there are even pictures of the educators who supplied these views, so you can hook up the words with the face of the person whose views are presented.

In many chapters, you'll find brief inserts entitled *In the News.* These are actually education *squibs.* (The dictionary definition of *squib* is "a short news story.") All of the squibs describe chapter-related content that made the newspapers. After each *In the News* insert, you'll see the phrase, "Your Reaction?" The purpose of the phrase is to encourage you to think through how you respond to the squib's assessment topic. These days, if you didn't already know, educational assessment is definitely a newsworthy issue. The book is peppered with squibs (making it sound like an exotic form of French cuisine) so you'll realize just how important educational measurement currently is.

Finally, the publishers agreed to let me adhere to my fairly irreverent and frequently whimsical writing style. There's no reason that a textbook need be turgid. I've tried to include, via cartoons and verbal levity, enough humor so that you'll not regard the reading of this textbook as an extended penance. If you don't find my attempts at humor to be mirth-inducing, simply frown at any instance of such silliness. There's nothing wrong with feeling superior because you are "above" such absurdity.

This edition of *Modern Educational Measurement* is divided into four parts. Starting off, Part One focuses on the significance of educational assessment to educational leaders. I really think that a person who tries to be an educational leader these days without understanding key concepts about educational measurement will be profoundly disadvantaged. There are two chapters in Part One. Chapter 1 describes why measurement is relevant to the activities of educational leaders and Chapter 2 (a hefty one) supplies you with a way of thinking about what should be measured and how it should be interpreted.

Part Two deals with the evaluation of educational assessments. In Part Two's five chapters, you'll learn how to judge the quality of educational tests created by teachers or sold by publishers. You'll discover that merely because a test is in print does not make it a winning test. Each of the five chapters describes a different factor that educational leaders can use when they're evaluating educational tests.

At the outset of Part Two, readers are also invited to read a separate, optional appendix about some rudimentary statistical procedures needed when educational leaders mess around with measurement. Many readers will want to skip that appendix completely because they already understand elementary statistical notions. Some readers, masochistically inclined, will read the appendix even if they *do* know about statistics. If you're a bit shaky in distinguishing between a mode and a standard deviation, you really ought to wade through the optional appendix.

Part Three includes six chapters intended to help you learn how to construct worthwhile educational assessments. Educational leaders do *not* necessarily need to be test developers. They should, however, understand how a first-rate educational test is developed so that they can determine whether the tests developed by others have been properly constructed.

In Part Three you'll learn how to identify the domain of knowledge, skill, or affect that a test is supposed to measure. There are also chapters dealing with different types of test items and how to improve them. Chapter 11 tackles two of today's significant assessment strategies, performance tests and portfolios. Chapter 13 deals with the assessment of students' attitudes, values, and interests.

Finally, in Part Four you'll find two chapters devoted to the use of educational assessments and, in a sense, to their misuse. Chapter 14 deals with a series of practical problems in the administration, scoring, and interpreting of students' test scores. And the book's final chapter (Chapter 15, if you've been counting) tries to help educational leaders understand why they should not allow standardized achievement tests to be used in judging the quality of education.

Best Wishes

Well, I hope you now have an idea of what's in store for you. If you're using this book in connection with a course, you'll surely want to read the chapters when assigned. Students, after all, should be a docile lot. If, however, you're reading the book on your own, I doubt if you'll be able to put it down. It's not that there's a continuing plot in which an assessment superhero or superheroine successfully overcomes a group of villainous antitest terrorists. Instead, the book's content is so patently important to educational leaders that you'll soon conclude, "I dare not begin another day without knowing this content." (I have always had a rich fantasy life.) Good luck.

I want to thank Nancy Forsyth for initiating this project. She only had to spring for a diet cola to send me down the robust-revision road. That's thrifty publishing. Thanks, too, go to Sean W. Wakely, who took over as Allyn and Bacon's Vice President and Editor-in-Chief of Social Sciences and Education, when Nancy clambered up the corporate ladder. He skillfully "modified" the manuscript's revision during its entire gestation period. Two reviewers for this edition—Catherine McCartney of Bemidji State University and Ralph de Ayala of the University of Maryland—offered helpful comments. Finally, I am deeply appreciative of the word-processing wizardry of Dolly Bulquerin, who transformed my scribbling into sense and made this third edition of *Modern Educational Measurement* a reality. She was wonderful.

W. James Popham
Los Angeles
Late 1999

Why Measure; What to Measure, and How to Interpret What's Been Measured

Whether we will it or not, the sun pops up each morning and nestles behind the horizon each evening for a lengthy siesta. At times it rains; at times it doesn't. The ocean's tides roll in and out on schedule. These occurrences of nature are going to take place even if we tried to stop them.

But educational measurement is not a phenomenon of nature. Educators *voluntarily* created educational measurement. In this first part of the book, you'll find out why. More specifically, you'll encounter two chapters that attempt to answer three questions, namely, why educators measure, what they should measure, and how to make sense out of what has been measured.

If educational measurement doesn't lead to better education for students, then we shouldn't be doing it. In Part One's two chapters you'll learn that the only reason educators ought to assess students is in order to make more defensible educational decisions regarding those students. That's really why educators should be messing around with measurement—*to improve student learning.*

Chapter 1 focuses on what educational measurement is, what educational leaders need to know about educational measurement, and where educational measurement originated. In Chapter 2 you'll deal with the deceptively difficult task of deciding what to measure. Chapter 2 also shows you how educators should be interpreting the results of their assessments. The chapter addresses some difficult choices to be faced by educational leaders. If you master Chapter 2's way of looking at the assessment world, you'll be miles ahead of your educational colleagues in bringing conceptual clarity to the assessment game.

Part One's two chapters set the stage for what's to follow. Educational leaders, or educational leaders-in-training, should give thoughtful consideration to this pair of pivotal, getting-underway chapters.

chapter 1

Measurement's Importance to Educational Leaders

- What is educational measurement?
  Serviceable Synonyms
  A Focus on Inferences

- Who is an educational leader?

- What do educational leaders *not* need to know about educational measurement?
  Exotic Psychometric Concepts or Procedures
  How to Administer or Interpret Individual Aptitude or Personality Tests

- What *do* educational leaders need to know about educational measurement?
  How to Evaluate Educational Quality via Test Results
  How Tests and Test Results Can Improve Instruction

- Where did current educational measurement originate?
  Chinese Civil Service Examinations
  Testing Pioneers in Europe and the United States
  The Powerful Influence of World War I's Army Alpha

2

ever before in the history of schooling have American educational leaders needed to know as much about educational assessment as they need to know at the beginning of the twenty-first century. Because you are currently reading this book, odds are that you are either already one of those leaders or you are preparing to become one. But many readers, possibly including you, may not immediately recognize the absolute *necessity* for today's educational leaders to be well versed in the nuts and bolts of educational testing.

And that's what this first chapter is all about: namely, the importance of educational assessments to educational leaders. I'm even willing to describe Chapter 1's mission with more pedagogical polish: *Having read the chapter, you will be convinced that today's educational leaders—if they are to be genuinely effective—must possess a thorough understanding of the kinds of assessment that impinge on their day-to-day endeavors.* That's correct. This is a chapter designed to *convince.* I am the designated convincer; you are the targeted convincee.

Most readers, of course, will be setting out to read this initial chapter only because they're currently taking a course for which this book (the one you're now holding) is the required text. And when a course instructor says, "Read Chapter 1," most students comply. The bedrock of higher education, arguably, is unquestioning student compliance. Having spent most of my career as a university professor, I regard student compliance as an altogether commendable quality.

But if you really want to become an effective member of the educational leadership community, you'll need to learn about educational measurement not merely because an instructor assigns a chapter in a textbook, but because you recognize that you really can't be a skilled educational leader these days unless you understand the fundamentals of educational measurement.

What's in a Name?

This is a book entitled *Modern Educational Measurement.* And, even though we've all been advised that "You can't tell a book by its cover," there's a corollary axiom that "You shouldn't be reading a book if you don't have at least a foggy idea about what its title means." Looking at the book's title more carefully, I'm sure you're already familiar with *modern* and with *educational*; both words are oft-used modifiers. But *measurement* is the most important of the three words. After all, why would I spend two whole modifiers on it?

A trio of synonyms. Because the three words that will be the most frequent focus of this book are *measurement, testing,* and *assessment,* I'm going to define each word below in an educational context. Look closely for a pattern!

Educational Measurement = A process by which educators use students' responses to specially created or naturally occurring stimuli in order to make inferences about students' knowledge, skills, or affective status.

Educational Testing = A process by which educators use students' responses to specially created or naturally occurring stimuli in order to make inferences about students' knowledge, skills, or affective status.

Educational Measurement, Testing, or Assessment

All three terms describe a process by which educators use students' responses to specially created or naturally occurring stimuli in order to make inferences about students' knowledge, skills, or affective status.

Educational Assessment = A process by which educators use students' responses to specially created or naturally occurring stimuli in order to make inferences about students' knowledge, skills, or affective status.

Now, if you were relatively alert while reading the three definitions, you've probably discerned that the three terms, namely, *measurement, testing,* and *assessment,* are essentially interchangeable. This constitutes first-rate discerning on your part. The three words are, for our purposes, synonyms. In recent years, educators have been tending to use the term *assessment* more frequently than its two semantic siblings because many educators think *assessment* creates a more comprehensive and more palatable image than either *measurement* or *testing.*

Measurement seems to evoke off-putting visions of unsmiling scientists in white lab coats as they employ calipers, slide rulers, or geiger counters. *Measurement,* at least to some, is not a warmth-inducing word. Then there's *testing.* To most educators, a test is a paper-and-pencil instrument usually consisting of multiple-choice, true-false, or essay items. Because most of us have, as students, been on the receiving end of many such traditional paper-and-pencil tests, and because recent years have seen the introduction of a number of alternative sorts of testing approaches, many educators tend to warm up more toward *assessment* than toward *testing.*

These days, if I had to choose only one phrase that might win more friends and create fewer enemies, I'd probably opt for *educational assessment.* That phrase is, at least currently, simply brimming with political correctness. But any upstanding educational leader should realize that, as a practical matter, the words assessment, measurement, and testing are fundamentally synonymous. That's why they'll be used interchangeably in the fun-filled pages that follow. When you're on your own, you have my permission to use whichever descriptor you personally regard as most appropriate.

You'll note that in the repetitive definitions of our three synonymous descriptors, the student must make responses to specially created or naturally occurring stimuli. A specially created stimulus would be, for example, the midterm exam that a teacher constructs. A naturally occurring stimulus, on the hand, might be a routine school assembly in which seating patterns of students are observed to see the extent to which the students volitionally sit with students from other racial groups.

Synonyms in search of an inference. As you'll recall from the preceding one-size-fits-all-three-terms definition, whether educators use the term *measurement, testing,* or *assessment,* an educator's purpose is to make inferences about students' knowledge, skills, or affective status. What is this "inference-making" business all about? Let's see.

First off, educational leaders need to make decisions, lots of them. The kinds of decisions they must make usually revolve around what's instructionally best for students. Educational leaders, of course, will make better decisions if they have an accurate fix on students' knowledge, skills, or affective status. To illustrate, in order to design instructional sequences that would mesh most appropriately with students' current status, educators might need to ascertain:

● **Students' Knowledge,** for example, how many of 500 hard-to-spell words a student can spell correctly from memory.

- **Students' Skills,** for example, a student's ability to make a successful extemporaneous oral presentation to classmates after only forty minutes of preparation time.
- **Students' Affective Status,** for example, students' attitudes toward specific subjects such as mathematics, science, or art.

Suppose, for example, that you were an instructional supervisor who was trying to guide a first-year teacher, Mr. Bevins, as he planned his very first month's worth of instructional activities. Clearly, you'd be in a better position to help Mr. Bevins if you and he had an accurate idea of his students' entry knowledge, skills, and affect. Instructional plans designed for well-understood students are certain to be better than instructional plans designed for mystery-status students.

A problem arises, however, because the measurement of students' knowledge, skill, or affect is much tougher than is the measurement of students' weight or height. With weight, all you need do is drag out a set of bathroom scales and tell students to "Hop aboard!" And with height, all you need do is produce a retractable measuring tape and direct students to "Stand up straight!" while you determine the linear distance between the soles of their feet and the tops of their heads. The weight and height of an individual are sitting there, obvious as can be, yearning to be measured. The kinds of things that educators need to measure, however, are more elusive.

The problem is that the kinds of educational variables educational leaders need to know about are not sitting there, as easy to measure as height and weight. You really can't tell if a child is a good speller merely by looking at the child, even with a magnifying glass. Indeed, you can't determine *any* skill, knowledge, or affect of students simply by visual scrutiny. Instead, you have to collect pertinent evidence, then make evidence-based *inferences*.

Assessment Domain

A particular body of educationally relevant knowledge, skills, or affect.

Here's how it works. Take a look at Figure 1.1 and you'll see on the left an *assessment domain*, that is, a particular kind of student knowledge, skill, or affect in which you're interested. For instance, suppose that the assessment domain in which you're interested is a student's mastery of 200 key U.S. history facts. In order to arrive at a defensible judgment about the extent of a student's knowledge of the history facts, you'll need some evidence. On the right of Figure 1.1 is an assessment such as a 30-item quiz designed to *sample* the 200 facts in the assessment domain. Based on this 30-item representation of the student's knowledge, you can make an *inference* about the students' assessment-domain status. A student's performance on the 30-item quiz is the *evidence* on which you base your inference about the student's mastery of the assessment domain (the 200 key

FIGURE 1.1.

How an assessment domain, representing a domain of knowledge, skills, or affect, allows educators to make inferences about student status with respect to the domain.

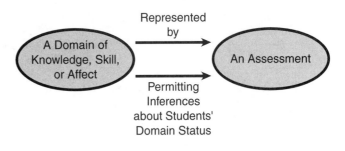

Assessment Inference

An interpretation, based on students' test performance, regarding students' assessment-domain status.

U.S. history facts). If you prefer, you may wish to think of inferences about students' status as *interpretations* regarding students' knowledge, skills, or affect. Most measurement folks use the terms *inference* and *interpretation* interchangeably. The important thing for you to recognize is that all educational measurement revolves around inferences (or interpretations) regarding students' status. Educational assessment is not a bathroom scale and tape-measure game. Rather, it's a game that revolves around collecting domain-representative evidence, then making an evidence-based inference.

But why, you might ask, do we need to sample at all? Why not measure the students' mastery of a total assessment domain? Why not leave sampling to the hoard of pollsters who abound prior to elections but hibernate between elections? The reason educators must sample is the same reason that the election pollsters must sample. The population of people about whom pollsters are making an inference is too large. To conduct pre-election telephone interviews, even a five-minute interview, with *all* the eligible voters in a nation would be prohibitively time-consuming and costly. Similarly, the size of most educational assessment domains is much too large. If educators tried to test the student's mastery of *all* the knowledge, skills, and affect represented by their educational goals, the students would be spending so much time being tested that they'd end up drawing their social security checks before they finished high school.

Most assessment domains are way, way too big. Therefore, when you assess students you'll try to *represent* the assessment domain you're interested in, usually by the use of some sort of sampling. You'll see how the student performs on your representative assessment, then use the evidence resulting from that sample-based assessment to make an inference about the student's status with respect to the assessment domain being represented. Figure 1.1, while appearing to be a seemingly simple graphic representation, constitutes the heart of the educational assessment process. While you'll not need to keep Figure 1.1 constantly in mind as you read every page in this book, it wouldn't hurt for you to think warmly of it—at least every third or fourth page.

In the News

News in Brief: A State Capitals Roundup

Colorado Links Goals, Accreditation

Gov. Roy Romer of Colorado has signed a bill that requires school districts to meet achievement goals to receive accreditation from the state.

The measure is an important step in Colorado's 5-year-old effort to reform its school standards and assessments, the Democratic governor said late last month. Under the law, each district must enter into an accreditation contract with the state board of education. The six-year contracts will define student-achievement standards and goals that the districts must meet.

The state education department will monitor progress and could place a district on probation if it fails to implement a plan. The law also adds some new statewide assessments, including mathematics and science tests for 8th graders, starting in spring 2000, and reading, writing, and math assessments for 10th graders, beginning in spring 2001.

What's your reaction?

Reprinted, with permission, from *Education Week,* June 10, 1998

What You Don't Need to Know

Educational leaders definitely do not need to be psychometricians (a ritzy word for testing specialists). Psychometric specialists derive glee from sending students' test scores through all sorts of statistical gyrations. They have a special affinity for numbers, hence revel in the performance of quantitative wizardry. No, what educational leaders need to understand are the kinds of assessment operations that routinely take place in our schools—often more frequently than many teachers prefer. You do *not* need to know how to administer or to interpret an individually administered intelligence test. You do *not* need to know how to give or interpret projective personality tests wherein examinees attempt to offer their perceptions regarding ambiguous stimuli such as ink blots, federal legislation, or teacher–union contracts. You do *not* need to know how to calculate complicated reliability or validity coefficients for standardized achievement tests, whether national, international, or intergalactic. There is, in fact, a ton and a half of assessment content that educational leaders do *not* need to know anything about. In this chapter, therefore, you'll be looking at the assessment stuff that educational leaders *do* need to know.

Many educators are apprehensive about educational measurement because they believe it is largely a quantitative enterprise in which numbers abound. Actually, that's not true. Instead, educational measurement is primarily a commonsense undertaking. There's never a need to be caught up in a numerical frenzy. As you'll soon see, there's a much greater need for educational leaders to *think clearly* about what they're measuring and what a set of test results signify. Oh, it wouldn't hurt if you can (1) add and subtract single digits or (2) know your multiplication tables up through five times five. But even if you are intimidated by 5×4, you can always ask a math teacher for help. Please don't be put off by fears of the quantitative. You'll soon see that an educational leader's number needs, at least for the purposes of measurement, are really quite modest.

An Educational Leader

Educators whose decisions influence the decisions of others who are responsible for educating students.

Who is an educational leader? Please let me pause, briefly, to let you know the kinds of folks I'm referring to when I talk about *educational leaders.* To me, an educational leader is any educator who holds a position requiring decisions that have an impact on *other* educators and, as a consequence, on the students for whom those other educators are responsible. Some of the leadership positions that immediately come to mind are district-level posts such as those held by superintendents, assistant superintendents, or curriculum specialists. At the school level, of course, principals and assistant principals are also educational leaders. But what about teachers? Can classroom teachers be educational leaders? You bet they can, but only if they make decisions that influence other educators and, therefore, influence the students for whom those other educators are responsible.

To illustrate, for the past several years I've been working with many school-based teams attempting to implement various versions of *school improvement* in their schools. In most of these school-improvement programs, key instructional decisions are made by a school-site team of teachers, administrators, and parents. Those instructional decisions are intended to improve the quality of education taking place at that particular school. For most of the school improvement teams with whom I've worked, the chairperson's position is held by a teacher. Nevertheless, *every* member of these school improvement teams usually has a hand in arriving at decisions that often have a direct impact on the entire teaching staff of the school.

For instance, if a school improvement team decides there will be a schoolwide stress on improving students' written communication skills, and that all of the school's teachers need to bump up the instructional time they devote to "writing across the curriculum," such a decision obviously has an impact on what goes on in every teacher's classroom. Teachers who occupy positions of influence such as holding membership on a school improvement team are, most assuredly, educational leaders.

But what about classroom teachers who nestle hermitlike in their own classrooms, never wishing to influence any colleagues—even a little? What about classroom teachers who only want to teach? Are such classroom teachers educational leaders? Well, by my definition, such classroom teachers are *not* educational leaders. That doesn't mean they're bad educators—or bad people. They're simply teachers who want to teach. Our field needs plenty of those teachers. They should be vigorously applauded and, shortly before their retirement, suitably bronzed.

But this book has been written chiefly for those educators, some of whom may now be classroom teachers, who want to make a bigger dent in the quality of schooling. If you have no aspirations to become such an educational leader, does this mean you should thrust the book violently into a wastebasket, incinerator, or papershredder? Of course not. First, see if you can get a refund where you purchased the book. Failing that, you might simply continue reading. Who knows, by the time you've finished this festive visit to assessmentland, you may have become so captivated with the possibility of *improving instruction via assessment* that you'll totally alter your career aspirations and head toward positions that will make you an educational leader.

What You *Do* Need to Know

Indicators of educational effectiveness. Now, let's turn to the kinds of stuff about assessment that educational leaders really *do* need to know. For starters, you need to recognize that students' test results have become the most widely used *indicator of educational effectiveness*, especially by parents and other citizens interested in the schools. Increasingly, because of the heightened media attention given to students' test scores, the performance of educational leaders is being judged chiefly on the basis of how well students perform on tests. In some instances, in fact, educational leaders have been promoted or demoted solely because of their students' test scores.

In reality, the chain of perceived educational responsibility runs along the lines illustrated in Figure 1.2, where we can see that the caliber of students' test performance reflects, favorably or unfavorably, on teachers, principals, superintendents, and the school board. Ultimately, citizens often decide whether the quality of educational performance *as reflected by student test scores* is satisfactory. At all points along this chain of perceived educational effectiveness, students' tests scores play a pivotal role.

Thus, from an educational leader's perspective, the promotion of reasonable student performances on tests often becomes an imperative. The palpable pressure created by each year's newspaper-published rankings of school districts has actually driven some school administrators to falsify students' test responses so that the school's or district's scores appear

FIGURE 1.2.

A test-score-based chain of perceived educational effectiveness.

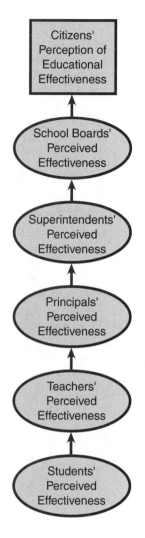

to be more acceptable. A few years ago, for instance, a California school district that annually scored on the annual statewide test in the lowest 5 percent of the state's districts miraculously scored one year in the top 10 percent of state school districts. State-level officials discovered, however, that the "miracle" was attributable to district officials' having altered 1,800 student response sheets so that incorrect answers were erased, then replaced with correct answers. Such incidents, while not widespread, illustrate the pressures that school administrators experience when it comes to student test performance. Everyone, or so it seems, is looking to see how well students perform on educational tests.

Incidentally, by coincidence, I was about to present an afternoon speech in the California "miracle" district to a large group of parents and educators on the very same day the local newspaper's morning edition had proclaimed, in banner headlines, that district educators had been caught, redhanded, in a *Test Cheating Scandal!* At the close of my speech about assessment—a speech I thought was at least a *B+* effort—the question period was devoted exclusively to the district superintendent's answers to audience questions such as, "How's the district fixed for erasers these days?" or "If you were changing the kids' answer sheets, why didn't you go for Number One in the nation?" As I recall, I didn't get a single question about my speech! Perhaps it was a *B–* speech.

Educational leaders, therefore, owe it to themselves, their colleagues, and their pupils to become particularly well informed regarding the ins and outs of educational assessment. Schoolboard members and the public at large must be educated regarding the appropriateness of certain types of test scores as indicators of educational quality. An educational leader who is unfamiliar with the essentials of educational measurement will be unable to inform others about the proper and improper use of test scores as indicators of educational quality.

From time to time, the public's attention has been more strongly directed toward particular test-related issues. More than a decade ago, for example, Dr. John J. Cannell, a physician, argued that because tests were not revised often enough and because accountability-pressured teachers spent too much time "teaching to the test," many of the gains seen in student test scores were actually illusions (*Friends for Education, 1988*). Cannell contended that *all* of the nation's 50 states claimed that, on standardized tests, their students were "above average." More than a few citizens and schoolboard members questioned their local school administrators about the soundness of Cannell's charges. For the most part, school administrators were unable to deal with the Cannell claims.

Distressingly, too few school administrators are as knowledgeable as they need to be regarding the rudiments of educational measurement. Yet, it is almost career-related suicide for today's school administrator to be uninformed about educational assessment's essentials. The ground rules of public education have been fundamentally altered. Educational test results now play a pivotal role in judging the quality of schools. All educational leaders, from assistant principals to chief state school officers, need to understand—thoroughly—the role that assessment results should play in determining the quality of education.

The public's reliance on test results as the overriding indicator of educational effectiveness has even reached the point where some citizens actually *equate* test scores and education. Recently, for example, I was in my car listening to a National Public Radio special on education. During the program, a newly elected schoolboard chairman from an affluent New England school district was interviewed. When asked what his educational priorities would be, the chairman's response was immediate, "Our number one goal in this district is to raise students' test scores!" I can still remember thinking, as I heard the board chairman's remark, he really believes there's no difference between improving test scores and improving education.

But by the time you've finished this book, you'll understand quite clearly why a student's educational accomplishments are not always represented accurately by that student's score on a test. It depends, as you'll learn, on the type of test being used and on the interpretation that's based on the test's results.

To review, the first important understanding educational leaders need is the recognition that test results are now serving as the yardstick by which educational effectiveness is determined. And, accordingly, any skilled educational leader must know about the kinds of test results that should and *shouldn't* be used as measures of educational quality.

Educational Leaders Look at Assessment

Three Decades of Educational Assessment

Rhonda M. Corley, Director
Early Childhood Education
School District of Greenville County
Greenville, South Carolina

After almost 30 years in teaching and administration, beginning as a first-grade teacher, my support for appropriate assessment and accountability has grown stronger. However, my opposition to group-administered paper-and-pencil tests for young children ages 5, 6, and 7 has not faltered. Opposition to this kind of assessment for young children is often perceived as opposition to evaluative measures. Nothing could be farther from the truth. After years of administering state and district programs, I have gained insight into the need for documenting children's progress: (1) to inform teaching, (2) to share with parents, (3) to be good stewards of the funding used, and (4) to justify program continuation.

My journey in understanding the role of assessment has probably taken a familiar route. As a member of the baby boomer set, I began on a road in the early seventies that was strewn with standardized testing that could be used in conjunction with teacher observations to make judgments about children's progress. The late seventies and eighties brought the "back to basics" boulders that good teachers had to maneuver around—national tests, criterion-referenced state tests, monitored checklists, and sub-subskill remediation. In retrospect I realize that the assessment strategies were not the boulders. The obstacles were actually the well-intended but cumbersome policies that the bureaucrats created around the testing programs. I can say this because I was one of those state-level bureaucrats.

My work in the field of early childhood education and my interaction with education leaders and colleagues such as Dr. Samuel Meisels, Dr. Heidi Mills, Dr. Lilian Katz, and Dr. Milly Cowles have strengthened my commitment to alternative assessment strategies for young children. I've also found that most rational people can also see that traditional whole-group paper-and-pencil tests are inappropriate for 5, 6, and 7 year olds. But the current accountability movement blanketing the country has made me fearful that, again, young children may be unduly stressed by our testing frenzy. It may become accountability on the backs of children rather than accountability that involves thoughtful authentic assessment systems developed by knowledgeable adults who know how to support and nurture children's lifelong dispositions for learning. We know that there are better ways to evaluate children's efforts. I hope we can continue to use our professional backbone to demand these appropriate assessment systems for all young children. ●

Assessment as an ally to instruction. The second thing that educational leaders need to know about assessment stems from the powerful impact that assessment, if properly conceptualized, can have on instruction. I realize you may think my suggestion that testing can be a boon to teaching may seem absurd. A seasoned educator may dismiss my suggestion as a valiant, although ineffectual, effort to supply a mite of motivation to readers who might otherwise regard assessment as innocuous, if not deflective.

Let me assure you that I understand such cynicism. I recognize it because, once upon a time when I was a public school teacher, I thought there was only one reason to give tests—and that reason was to award grades to students. My tests, whether they were one-day quizzes, unit tests, or semester exams, were *exclusively* intended to help me determine which students would be receiving *A*s, *B*s, *C*s, *D*s, or *F*s. I was altogether guiltless about my view of testing's role in the classroom. It was a view shared by every teacher in my school, not to mention my first principal, Mr. Ed Doby. (After two years of being my principal, Mr. Doby left education to manage a paint store. I have always wondered about the extent to which my first two years of teaching hastened his career change.)

But the formerly widespread perception of tests as "for-grading-only" tools has been changing in recent years. Increasingly, educational leaders are recognizing that the single, most important dividend of assessment is it can contribute to improved instruction. And that's the second lesson you need to learn about assessment, namely, how assessment can improve the instructional process.

The first way that testing can help teaching is by allowing teachers to get a more accurate idea of their students' current knowledge, skills, and affect. Suppose, for example, Mrs. Ballard requires her brand-new class to complete a preinstruction test to determine her students' entry behaviors. Suppose Mrs. Ballard discovers that an instructional objective she was going to pursue has already been mastered by most students. She can then discard that objective rather than wasting students' time with something they already know. Similarly, teachers can employ tests as en-route monitoring devices to help determine whether students are making suitable progress. And at the close of an instructional sequence, teachers can find out if their instruction really worked by having students complete an assessment covering what was supposed to have been learned.

For all of these uses of testing, the results allow the teacher to make a more informed *instructional* decision. Instructional decisions based on a more accurate picture of students' current status are obviously going to be better instructional decisions than those based on a less accurate picture of a student's status. The more that teachers understand about students' knowledge, skills, and affect, the better will be the instructional decisions that they make. Educational leaders need to know how to help teachers get the most instructional mileage out of the tests their students take.

You'll also be learning, in Chapter 3, about the role that well-conceived educational tests can play in helping the teacher *plan* for instruction. If tests are constructed in advance of instructional planning, but constructed with instruction clearly in mind, those tests can yield planning dividends for teachers. Because such instructionally oriented educational assessments can serve to clarify intended instructional targets, those assessments can really help teachers think more clearly about where they're headed instructionally. And, as a consequence, teachers can plan instructional activities that are more apt to be successful. If educational leaders are going to help classroom teachers supply improved instruction to children, then educational leaders will need to know how tests should be put together if they're going to function in an instructionally facilitative fashion.

Two Assessment Emphases

These two understandings about assessment, then, are needed by successful educational leaders: (1) an understanding of the proper and improper uses of test results as indicators of educational effectiveness, and (2) an understanding of the ways that test results, and tests themselves, can improve the caliber of classroom instruction. When you've finished this book, you'll possess both understandings. Moreover, you'll understand about the bolts and nuts of educational assessment. (In the interest of sequential equity, I think it's time that *bolts* occasionally take precedence over *nuts*.) You'll have acquired many of the boltsy-nutsy *skills* needed to implement your newly acquired knowledge. For example, you'll not only be able to explain to someone why certain tests can benefit teachers' instructional decision-making, you'll probably be able to construct tests that actually help instruction. Or, at the very least, you'll be able to determine the extent to which testing companies' tests and textbook publishers' tests are apt to benefit teachers' instructional decision-making.

As you read on, breathlessly eager to plunge into each subsequent chapter, you're going to be learning about the fundamentals of educational assessment, but always from twin perspectives of (1) improving instruction and (2) evaluating educational quality. You are going to learn what today's educational leaders *must* know about assessment if they're really going to help children learn most effectively.

A Brief, Historical Dip

Educational leaders who are proficient in the use of educational measurement need to understand that today's educational assessment procedures didn't miraculously pop into existence overnight, nor were those procedures created by mysterious quantitative geniuses.

It's fairly obvious that I want you to become an educational leader who is sufficiently knowledgeable about assessment to make a positive impact on the quality of children's education. Putting it another way, I want one of *your* defining professional competencies to be the skill to use educational assessment so that it benefits children. Well, if that's the goal, I don't want you to go galloping into assessmentland not knowing where the horse you're riding came from. I want you to understand, at least in a general way, that people have been tussling with educational tests for centuries. And this educational-test-tussling was undertaken by regular folks who wanted to do a better job in determining students' skills or knowledge. Accordingly, so that you are not totally devoid of knowledge about the roots of what will soon become one of your professional strengths, let's wander very *briefly* down assessment's historical trail.

Going way back. Testing has been around for centuries, for much longer than most people today realize. In biblical times, Jephthah used the term *Shibboleth* as a test word by which to distinguish the fleeing Ephraimites (who couldn't pronounce the *sh*) from his own Gileadites. We are told that those who failed to pass Jephthath's test had their heads lopped off. Phrasing that aversive consequence in suitable educational parlance, you might say that "In relationship to their pretest status, the posttest status of deficit Ephraimite examinees was significantly less cerebral."

Chinese civil service examinations. Formal testing, however, had its origins well before Ephraimites were displaying pronunciation inadequacies. The historian Dubois informs us that as far back as 2200 B.C., Chinese emperors examined their key officials every three years to verify such officials' fitness for office.[1] In fact, for more than 3,000 years the Chinese, who, unlike European nations, had no hereditary ruling class, employed a sophisticated system of competitive examinations to select personnel for government positions.

Every three years, candidates who passed the district examinations gathered in the provincial capitals where, for three sessions, each consisting of three days and three nights, compositions in verse and prose were required. For province-level exams, no credit was given for penmanship because a special bureau of examination copyists, established around A.D. 1000, copied all papers in another person's hand prior to the examination so that it could be read independently by two graders. A third grader received and reconciled the grades from the first two graders. The *failure* rate for these provincial examinations ranged between 90 and 99 percent. It's pretty clear, the provincial examinations were not "a piece of cake."

Finally, for those candidates who survived the provincial tests, similar examinations were held the following spring in Beijing, China's imperial capital. For these Palace examinations the failure rate was 97 percent or higher. Individuals who passed the examinations became mandarins and, as such, were eligible for public office.

A detailed but delightful account of the Chinese civil service examination, published in 1976, is *China's Examination Hell.*[2] In that treatise the author provides a vivid picture of what it must have been like for the nervous young Chinese candidates who, after a can-

non had been fired three times, were admitted to an agonizing examination experience. When today's critics of testing contend that some tests are too long, they might take solace from a consideration of the Chinese system, in which an uninterrupted *seventy-two-hour* bout with an examination was customary.

As the Chinese civil service examinations flourished, certain elements of those examinations became more and more ritualistic. For example, by the time a successful candidate had passed the preliminary exams and reached the prestigious Palace examinations, a prescribed conclusion was to be written by each candidate at the close of the examination: "I, your humble servant, a superficial scholar newly advanced, not realizing where I was, have ventured to state my own views and am so ashamed of offending the Majesty of the Emperor that I do not know where to hide. I respectfully submit my answer."[3] Although this version of abject student humility may seem appealing to certain of today's teachers, they may have to wait a few thousand years before such language starts popping up again at the close of students' exams.

During the sixteenth century, as European contacts with China developed, the Chinese use of written examinations as a way of entering public service was noted and admired by several scholars, including Voltaire, who advocated such a system for France. Early in the nineteenth century the newly established British open civil service examination system was also influenced by diplomats and missionaries who were familiar with the Chinese examinations.

It would seem difficult for today's educators to remain unmoved on contemplating the ancient Chinese examination system. There were the Chinese, centuries before Socrates, wrestling with the same kinds of problems that sometimes cause today's educators to stumble. One is struck with numerous similarities to present-day testing practices, including the use of two independent readers and a third reader who settles differences of opinions.

The idea of locking up students in isolated examination booths all day and all night (see Figure 1.3) might seem particularly appealing to today's teachers for whom students' cheating on examinations poses a problem. To cut down on a classroom's pupil–teacher ratio, of course, selected students could remain incarcerated for an entire semester.

The foregoing account of the Chinese testing exploits was intended to reveal the parallels in the measurement problems faced, for example, by officials of Hunan Province a thousand years ago and educational officials of any U.S. state or Canadian province in recent years. The Hunan officials, like their ancestors hundreds of years before, did the best job they could in devising fair tests, test-administration procedures, and test-scoring schemes. Educators today, like their Chinese counterparts, do the best job they can in devising fair tests, test-administration procedures, and test-scoring schemes. If state or provincial educators make a mistake, then, just as their Chinese predecessors did, they'll revise their testing procedures and try again.

Civil service examinations. Noting the successful experience of a British Civil Service Commission that had been established in the 1850s, several prominent U.S. legislators attempted to create comparable testing operations on this side of the Atlantic in the 1860s. In 1871 a Civil Service Board was established by President U. S. Grant. Although the board went out of existence four years later in 1875, a permanent Civil Service

FIGURE 1.3.

Hundreds of Individual Civil Service Examination Rooms at Nanking, China. © 1927, National Geographic Society. (Photograghed by Maynard Owen Williams about twenty years after testing stopped in 1905.)

Commission was subsequently created in January 1883. Typical of the examination items constructed by the 1871 board and the 1883 commission are the following three items drawn from a twenty-item civil service examination for examiners of trademarks used by the U.S. Patent Office in early 1873:

1. What is a trademark, and to what is it applicable?
2. Who may obtain one?
3. What is the geographical extent of a trademark?

University examinations. We have no records to indicate that any formal examinations existed in Greek and Roman schools or in the cathedral and monastery schools of medieval Europe. (Regardless of records, any sensible person *knows* that if there were teachers, then there were tests!) However, during the later Middle Ages oral examinations became popular in European universities. Among the earliest of these were the law examinations at the University of Bologna that were first given in 1219. Louvain University employed a widely acclaimed competitive examination system in the mid-1400s. In the Louvain scheme, candidates were ranked in four classes: *rigorosi* (honors), *transibiles* (satisfactory), *gratiosi* (charity passes), and failures. Many of today's teachers surely believe they are advancing some of their less able students on what is clearly a *gratiosi* basis.

The Jesuit order, established by St. Ignatius of Loyola in 1540, made extensive use of written examinations for placement and evaluation of students. In 1599 the *Ratio Studiorum*, a set of prescriptions for educational procedures, including the conduct of examinations, was published. Some of the guidelines set forth in that document seem eminently pertinent today. For example, here is one of the test-administration rules from the *Ratio Studiorum*:

> All should be present in the classroom in good time to receive the assignment and instructions, given either by the prefect himself or his substitute, and they must finish the assignment before the end of school. After silence has been enjoined, no one may speak to another, not even to the prefect or his substitute.[4]

Rice, Thorndike, and the origins of standardized testing. An influential pioneer in the U.S. educational testing movement was Joseph Mayer Rice who, in the late 1880s, abandoned his medical practice to find methods of augmenting the efficiency of schooling. After studying psychology and pedagogy, he carried out the first major comparative studies of children's academic accomplishments. In 1897 Rice reported the results of some 33,000 pupils' efforts on a standardized test of spelling. In 1902 he tested 6,000 children with an arithmetic examination, and in 1903 Rice tested over 8,000 students with a language examination. By administering his tests to substantial samples of school children and establishing the average scores to be expected at different grade levels, Rice's work contributed heavily to early thinking about the use of standardized tests in education, especially in the United States.

Rice's efforts greatly influenced the work of E. L. Thorndike, whose insights and creativity helped Teachers College, Columbia University become the early twentieth-century center for the creation of new educational achievement measures. Thorndike and his students not only refined some of Rice's approaches to measurement, but also evolved a host of important technical advances. Many of the standardized achievement tests developed in the early 1900s were created by Thorndike-trained measurement specialists.

Binet's intelligence scales. A giant in the history of educational measurement was Alfred Binet, a French physiological psychologist, who in 1905 created the first successful intelligence scale. His work with young children, featuring the creation of isolated testing procedures as early as 1890, ultimately resulted in the 1905 scale that coalesced thirty of these separate testing approaches into a cohesive, individually administrable intelligence test. The success of Binet's assessment strategies was to prove influential on a number of later measurement specialists and, as a consequence, on education itself.

The impact of World War I on group testing. Given the widely acclaimed success of Binet and his colleagues in devising effective intelligence tests administrable to individuals, it did not take too long until U.S. psychologists began flirting with intelligence tests that were administrable simultaneously to groups of examinees.

Interestingly enough, it was World War I that spurred U.S. interest in group intelligence tests. Even before the United States's entry into the war in 1917, Arthur S. Otis had developed a group intelligence test that could be scored objectively. The Otis test became a prototype for the U.S. *Army Alpha*, the assessment instrument first employed in large-scale testing.

In order for the United States to effectively staff its World War I military endeavors, an efficient procedure had to be developed that would facilitate the identification of likely officer candidates. Robert M. Yerkes, then president of the American Psychological Association, assembled a committee on the psychological examination of recruits in May 1917. This committee of psychologists met at the Vineland Training School in New Jersey and in seven working days, drawing on the prior efforts of Binet and Otis, created ten forms of what they regarded as a group intelligence test, each form consisting of ten different subtests. After several revisions, based on tryouts with fairly small samples of examinees, this test became the famous *Army Alpha*. Examples of the eight subtests included in the *Army Alpha* were Following Oral Directions, Analogues, Arithmetic Reasoning, and Synonym–Antonym.

In all, over 1.7 million men were examined during the World War I army testing program under the direction of Yerkes. Of these, more than one million were tested with one of the five forms of the *Army Alpha* (see Figure 1.4). The testing program was quite sophisticated for its time, with considerable attention being given to technical measurement considerations.

FIGURE 1.4.

Recruits Taking Examination at Camp Lee, 1917. (U.S. Signal Corps photo number 11-SC386 in the National Archives.)

In Texas, the Arrival of Spring Means the Focus is on Testing

by Robert C. Johnston

Talk about ubiquitous: Even 3rd graders in this south Texas town know what "TAAS" stands for.

The Texas Assessment of Academic Skills, given every spring to students in grades 3–10, has come to dominate the lives of students and educators throughout the state.

At a track meet, student athletes swap information about their times, their training techniques—and their scores on the state tests. "I'm proud of how my school has done, and I wonder how others do," said Yvonne Perez, 15, a sophomore and distance runner at the 1,700-student Los Fresnos High School.

The exams are the heart of one of the nation's most comprehensive systems designed to hold teachers, students, and schools accountable for their performance. And with achievement rising statewide, as in Ms. Perez's

small community near the Mexican border, policymakers elsewhere are taking note.

"A grade on the TAAS means the same anywhere you are, and you don't have that in a lot of states," said Heidi Glidden, a researcher with the American Federation of Teachers in Washington. "There's also an embarrassment factor. People don't want to be the worst school in the neighborhood."

Getting tough. The roots of the current Texas system began with get-tough, centralized reforms of the 1980s that included new state assessments and a new curriculum. Lawmakers began in the 1990s to give more authority to individual schools, but at the same time strengthened accountability by creating the more rigorous TAAS in 1993.

Nowadays, springtime signals the eagerly anticipated publication of test results in newspapers and on television. . . .

What's your reaction?

Excerpted, with permission, from *Education Week,* April 29, 1998

Achievement Tests

Assessments of the knowledge and/or skills possessed by students.

The success of the army testing program was unprecedented. The *Alpha*, which featured the first widespread use of multiple-choice test items, stimulated an explosive growth in the number of educational tests that were produced in subsequent years. Whereas only a handful of copyrighted standardized tests existed prior to World War I, after that time the Copyright Office was inundated by newly created standardized tests. Just about anyone who could crank out multiple-choice items and bundle them together, or so it appeared, began publishing group aptitude or achievement tests. The educational testing movement in the United States was definitely underway.

Regular problems, regular people. Clearly, in my rapid-fire race through measurement history, a galaxy of stalwart contributors have been neglected. Those individuals whom I did mention rank among the most prominent contributors, but there were many more. It is important, from your perspective, to recognize that the types of problems these measurement people were dealing with are remarkably similar to the types of problems that today's educators face. Many of the measurement strategies provided by our predecessors were seriously flawed and have long since sunk into the psychometric seas. The surviving measurement schemes, however, constitute our current educational measurement technology. It is not a sacred technology, created without the possibility of modification. Instead, it is a malleable set of improvable tools and rules that are still subject to alteration—maybe by you!

Chapter Wrap-Up

Well, if you've been reading this far, you are just about at the end of Chapter 1. If you recall, early on I indicated that the chief mission of Chapter 1 was to convince *you*, not
someone who might be reading over your shoulder, that today's educational leaders must
master the essentials of educational assessment. I also argued that those essentials are
readily masterable. I hope you're at least convinced of educational measurement's importance. You'll probably need to withhold judgment for a few more chapters to see if I'm
leveling with you about the ease of mastering the measurement content you'll be reading about.

Let's close out the chapter, then, with some pithy answers to Chapter 1's guiding
questions. *Pithy*, in my view, is a significantly underused adjective. I will doubtlessly toss
it in a few more times before you run out of chapters and come face-to-face with the index. The index for this book, incidentally, is peppered with pith.

● What is educational measurement?

Educational measurement is a process by which educators use students' responses to specially created or naturally occurring stimuli in order to make inferences about students'
knowledge, skills, or affective status. Although, in recent years, most educators appear to
prefer the use of educational *assessment* rather than educational *measurement* or educational *tests*, these three descriptors are essentially interchangeable. Whichever descriptive
term is used, the overriding function of educational measurement is to collect evidence
from students so that educators can make inferences about the status of those students.

● Who is an educational leader?

Educational leaders are those educators whose responsibilities call for them to make decisions that influence other educators' activities and, as a consequence, that have an impact on the students for whom those other educators are responsible. Although almost
all district-level or school-site administrators occupy positions of potential educational
leadership, classroom teachers whose activities have an impact on other educators should
also be considered educational leaders.

● What do educational leaders *not* need to know about educational measurement?

Educational leaders do not need to be psychometricians; that is, they don't need to know
how to perform all sorts of complex quantitative procedures that lead to numerical constructs incomprehensible to normal human beings. Nor do educational leaders need to
know how to administer and score individually administered personality or aptitude tests.
Those tasks are the province of school psychologists or guidance counselors. Educational
leaders do not need to know about any assessment concepts or procedures that do not
have a direct bearing on an educational leader's day-to-day activities.

● What *do* educational leaders need to know about educational measurement?

Because students' test results are increasingly being used as the definitive measuring stick
by which educational effectiveness is determined, it is important for educational leaders
to understand the kinds of tests that are needed and the appropriate settings in which stu-

dents' test results *can* serve as an appropriate indicator of educational success. On the flip side, and even more importantly, educational leaders must understand the reasons that, in certain situations, students' test scores should *not* be used as an indicator of a district's, school's, or teacher's instructional quality.

In addition, educational leaders need to know how to help other educators employ assessments so that those assessments benefit *instruction*. Effective educational leaders must be able to help their colleagues use tests that yield instructionally useful information. Effective educational leaders must, therefore, be able to help their colleagues construct or select assessments that illuminate a teacher's instructional decision-making. In short, an educational leader must become really well versed regarding the *instructional* applications of educational measurement.

● Where did today's educational measurement originate?

As early as 2200 B.C., the Chinese employed formal civil service examinations to verify the capabilities of government officials. Several of the procedures employed in connection with those ancient Chinese civil service examinations bear a striking resemblance to the assessment procedures we employ today.

Although there were a number of pioneers in the educational testing field, such as Joseph Mayer Rice in the U.S. and Alfred Binet in France, the development and use of the *Army Alpha* had a particularly powerful impact on educational testing in the United States. The *Alpha*, a group-administrable aptitude test intended to sort out military recruits according to their relative intellectual abilities, became the model for subsequent assessment in the United States, not only of students' aptitude but also of students' achievement.

Practice Exercises

This, the first chapter of the book, was previously billed as a persuasive chapter, that is, a chapter intended to ratchet up your motivational level so that, having recognized the importance of measurement to today's educational leaders, you would read with rigor and relish the remainder of the book. As a result of its heavy focus on convincing you, there wasn't a ton of brand new substantive content included. Yet, there were a few concepts that, if dealt with in the following practice exercises, you'll be more apt to internalize.

Essentially, you're going to be asked to do some classifying of some examples. *After* you tackle these practice exercises, you'll most likely want to consult the *Answers to Practice Exercises* that follow. If you don't need to look at the answer key because you already know you're right, see if I care!

Part A

One of the important distinctions in the chapter was the difference drawn among (a) *assessment domains* of skills, knowledge, or affect; (b) representative *assessments* of students' status with respect to those domains; and (c) the *inferences* derivative from the use of those assessments. Look over the five items below and decide whether each one describes an *assessment domain*, an *assessment*, or an *inference*.

1. A student's ability to write persuasive essays, in other words, essays that can effectively persuade readers to adopt the writer's point of view.
2. A forty-item examination used by a mathematics teacher to determine if students can perform the four basic arithmetic operations, namely, adding, subtracting, multiplying, and dividing.

3. Students in Barton Middle School have a decisively better attitude toward the importance of completing homework than do students in the rest of the district.

4. Frank clearly knows how to write well-organized compositions that possess few, if any, mechanical errors.

5. Students' competence in using and interpreting routinely encountered maps such as city maps or state road maps.

Part B

An attempt was made to distinguish between the kinds of measurement-related knowledge or skills that today's educational leaders need to possess. To give you an opportunity to see if you have a reasonably solid grasp of that distinction, decide whether each of the following five items presents a skill (or a chunk of knowledge) that an educational leader *should* possess (Answer "Should.") or *shouldn't* possess (Answer "Shouldn't.").

6. A more in-depth understanding of the nature of the Chinese civil service examinations that were briefly described in the chapter.

7. Familiarity with the instructional applications and/or instructional limitations of the results of standardized achievement tests.

8. Knowledge of test bias so that teacher-made tests that unfairly penalize students on the basis of gender or ethnicity can be modified.

9. The ability to read, with genuine comprehension, journal articles about advanced educational measurement topics that appear in technical testing journals such as *Psychometrika*.

10. How to judge whether the tests supplied by textbook publishers will prove helpful to teachers as they plan and carry out instruction.

Part C

Although in Chapter 2 we'll take a more thorough look at the difference between aptitude tests and achievement tests, let's see how you do at this point in drawing a distinction between these two types of assessments. Consider each of the tests described below and decide whether it is an *aptitude* test or an *achievement* test.

11. This test was recently developed to predict how well high school students will perform in U.S. colleges even though those students' native language is not English.

12. This examination measures how many "culturally crucial" facts about Western European history are known by students.

13. This traditional and widely used test was designed to gauge students' reading comprehension.

14. This examination is employed to identify students who are having difficulty in writing simple sentences and routine paragraphs.

15. This test must be passed at a specified level by prospective college athletes to indicate that they have a reasonably good chance of succeeding in higher education, hence can be admitted to a suitable four-year college or university.

Answers to Practice Exercises

Part A

1. An assessment domain
2. An assessment
3. An inference
4. An inference
5. An assessment domain

Part B

6. Shouldn't
7. Should
8. Should
9. Shouldn't
10. Should

Part C

11. Aptitude
12. Achievement

13. Achievement
14. Achievement
15. Aptitude

DISCUSSION QUESTIONS

1. Why do you think that in the last few decades there has been such increased attention to student test results as the most important indicator of educational effectiveness?

2. Do you believe that most of the individuals who currently occupy administrative positions in our schools are knowledgeable regarding educational measurement? Why or why not? Should they be?

3. It was contended in the chapter that the *Army Alpha* became the prototype for many subsequent aptitude and achievement tests in the United States Why do you think this occurred? Do you see any problems in using the *Alpha* as a model for *achievement* tests? If so, what are those problems?

4. An educational leader was defined in the chapter as an educator who makes decisions that influence other educators whose activities subsequently have an effect on students. Do you agree with this definition? Why/why not? Can you think of someone who is *clearly* an educational leader? Does this person actually fit the chapter's definition of an educational leader?

5. Based on your own experience, do you think educators currently prefer the term *assessment* rather than *measurement* or *testing?* If so, why? If not, why not? And what about the public in general? When a typical citizen reads about students' once-a-year examination performances, does that citizen think those results came from "assessments," "measurements," or "tests?"

6. If you were asked to give a brief speech to a group of experienced junior high school teachers (who know little about educational measurement) on the topic of *Educational Assessment's Importance*, what would be the chief points you'd try to make in your speech?

SUGGESTIONS FOR ADDITIONAL READING

Arter, Judy. *Assessing Student Performance* (Professional Inquiry Kit, #196214S62). Alexandria, VA: Association for Supervision and Curriculum Development, 1996.

Airasian, Peter W. *Classroom Assessment* (3rd ed.). New York: McGraw-Hill, 1997.

Bennett, Randy Elliot. *A Policy Information Perspective: Reinventing Assessment.* Princeton, NJ: Educational Testing Service, 1998.

Brookhart, Susan M. "A Theoretical Framework for the Role of Classroom Assessment in Motivating Student Effort and Achievement." *Applied Measurement in Education, 10,* 2 (1997): 161–180.

Cunningham, George K. *Assessment in the Classroom: Constructing and Interpreting Tests.* Washington, DC: Falmer Press, 1998.

Educational Testing Service, "Focus," Princeton, NJ: Author, 1997.

McMillan, James H. *Classroom Assessment: Principles and Practice for Effective Instruction.* Boston: Allyn and Bacon, 1997.

Popham, W. James. "Farewell, Curriculum: Confessions of an Assessment Convert." *Phi Delta Kappan, 79,* 5 (January 1998): 380–384.

Rothman, Robert. *Measuring Up: Standards, Assessment, and School Reform.* San Francisco: Jossey-Bass, 1995.

Stiggins, Richard, and Tanis Knight. *But Are They Learning?* Portland, OR: Assessment Training Institute, 1997.

Stiggins, Richard J. *Opening Doors to Excellence in Assessment: A Guide for Using Quality Assessment to Promote Effective Instruction and Student Success.* Portland, OR: Assessment Training Institute, 1997.

Stiggins, Richard J. *Student-Centered Classroom Assessment* (2nd ed.). Upper Saddle River, NJ: Prentice-Hall, 1997.

Wiggins, Grant P. *Educative Assessment: Designing Assessments to Inform and Improve Student Performance.* San Francisco: Jossey-Bass, 1998.

AND FOR THOSE WHO TIRE OF READING

Association for Supervision and Curriculum Development. *ASCD Conference on Teaching & Learning: Assessment* (Videotape: Stock #496274S62). Alexandria, VA: Author, 1996.

Hunter, Madeline. *Teaching and Testing: A Conversation with Madeline Hunter* (Videotape #ETVT-36). Los Angeles: IOX Assessment Associates.

Northwest Regional Educational Laboratory. *A Status Report on Classroom Assessment* [Videotape #NREL-1]. Portland, OR: Author, 1991.

Northwest Regional Educational Laboratory. *Understanding the Meaning and Importance of Quality Classroom Assessment* [Videotape #NREL-2]. Portland, OR: Author, 1991.

Popham, W. James, & Sarah J. Stanley. *Teaching and Testing: A Conversation with Madeline Hunter* [Videotape, #ETVT-36]. Los Angeles: IOX Assessment Associates, 1989.

Popham, W. James. *Title I Assessment: What Educators Need to Know* (Videotape #ETVT-21). Los Angeles: IOX Assessment Associates.

U.S. Department of Education. *Pursuing Excellence: U.S. Eighth-Grade Findings from TIMSS* (Videotape Stock #065-000-01003-8). Washington, DC: Author, 1997.

ENDNOTES

1. For a fascinating account of educational and psychological testing through the ages, see Philip H. Dubois, *A History of Psychological Testing* (Boston: Allyn & Bacon, 1970).
2. Miyazaki, China's *Examination Hell*, trans. Conrad Schirokauer (New York: Weatherhill, 1976). (It should be noted that because this book about China's exams was written by a Japanese scholar and translated into English by someone with a Germanic background, its syntax is delightfully unpredictable.)
3. Ibid., p. 79.
4. W. J. McGucken, *The Jesuits and Education* (Milwaukee: Bruce, 1932).

What to Measure and How to Interpret Results

Now can educators use their choices about decision options and interpretation alternatives to choose appropriate assessment content? Educational leaders, if they wish to contribute effectively to children's educations, must make decisions that increase the likelihood of students' learning. Yet, sometimes, advocating those decisions, because that advocacy may run counter to other people's preferences, will require courage. An effective educational leader, then, usually possesses adequate amounts of spunk, pluck, and/or grit.

In this second chapter, you're going to get an opportunity to apply your personal spunk, pluck, and/or grit as you deal with two of educational assessment's most perplexing problems: (1) determining what *should* be measured, and (2) interpreting the results of what *has been* measured. If you are an attentive reader of chapter titles, of course, you've probably already figured that out.

What to Measure

You might be thinking that I'm trying to frighten you unnecessarily. After all, figuring out what educators ought to measure shouldn't be all that hard. Students are supposed to learn certain things. A teacher is supposed to assess students to see if what they were supposed to learn has, in fact, been learned. So, where's the problem?

Textbooks as a Source

For instance, if a teacher uses Textbook *X*, then it would seem that what should be assessed is already sitting there, nicely nestled between the front and back covers of Textbook *X*. I readily admit that when I was a high school teacher, my exams were almost always spawned by what was in the textbooks my students were using.

But even if teachers adopt a "textbook-please-tell-me" approach when deciding what to measure, there is usually more content in a textbook than a teacher will have time to measure. Remember, every minute that a teacher devotes to *assessing* students is a minute that can't be used for *teaching* them. Some teachers I've spoken to complain that they already must administer so many district-required or state-mandated tests that the time left for teaching is far too brief. So, unless teachers want to abandon teaching totally and have their students take part in a series of measurement marathons, some choices will need to be made about the content in textbooks that really warrants assessment. There's too much stuff in textbooks to assess it all.

Content Standards as a Source

But, in addition to covering what's in a textbook, educators are also under substantial pressure these days to make certain that their students have mastered a set of demanding *standards*. If these standards are thought by educational policymakers to be so important, then standards should surely be influential when educators are deciding what to assess. Let's take a closer look at what most people mean when they talk about "standards."

Actually, there are two kinds of educational standards that frequently get confused. *Content standards* refer to the knowledge and skills educators want students to learn. For example, a content standard that teachers often want students to master is "the ability to communicate effectively in writing." That's a *skill*. Another illustrative content standard would be "the student's ability to recount the important events that led up to the 13 colonies' declaring their independence from Great Britain." That's a body of *knowledge*.

When I was a high school teacher, we referred to such knowledge and skills as the *objectives* we wanted our students to attain. But it is far more fashionable these days to refer to one's objectives as "content standards." And even though many of today's educators fail to add the modifier *content*, when they talk about standards, they're usually referring to the knowledge and skills they want children to learn.

Performance standards, in contrast, refer to the level of proficiency at which students are supposed to master content standards. For instance, if a teacher were using a 50-item test to measure students' knowledge of the historical events preceding the Declaration of Independence, the teacher might decide that students need to answer correctly at least 90 percent of the test's 50 items. For the content standard dealing with students' knowledge of those historical events, therefore, a performance standard would have been established calling for students to answer at least 45 items correctly out of 50. And for a content standard focused on students' writing skill, a performance standard would need to describe the attributes associated with different levels of student writing, for example, what constitutes writing that is "super," "so-so," or "sloppy."

Okay, now that a distinction has been drawn between content standards and performance standards, you can see why confusion will usually result if educational leaders do not tack on a modifier when they refer to standards. If a school superintendent informs the district's principals that "Your standards are definitely too low," is the superintendent talking about (1) the knowledge and skills being sought for students, or (2) the required levels of proficiency that were set for those skills and knowledge?

In many states, officially approved content standards have now been adopted for the state's educators to promote. And if a state's Board of Education decrees that certain content standards in language arts, mathematics, science, and social studies should be pursued by the state's educators, it's fairly obvious that the knowledge and skills embodied in those content standards should play a major role when the state's educators decide what they ought to be assessing.

These state-level content standards are usually based directly on sets of content standards developed at the national level by organizations of educators concerned with particular subject fields. An example of such an organization would be the National Council of Teachers of Mathematics (NCTM). In fact, it was NCTM's 1989 publication of content standards for mathematics that played a catalytic role in stimulating the creation of content standards by many other subject-matter associations.

These national content standards were invariably developed by groups of especially knowledgeable subject-matter specialists. Because of the high stature of the individuals who contributed to the various collections of national content standards, those standards have typically received considerable applause from both educators and laypersons.

Almost all of the sets of national content standards and their state-level siblings are remarkably well-conceptualized documents that reflect extensive analysis and discussion by the leaders of the subject-matter fields involved. The national content standards and

Content Standards

The knowledge and skills students should learn.

Performance Standards

The level of proficiency at which content standards should be mastered.

their state-level counterparts, therefore, would seem to constitute a sparkling source of ideas when educational leaders try to decide what to measure.

Unfortunately, there's a serious problem lurking in most sets of content standards. Those standards were always developed by content *specialists*. And content specialists, with few exceptions, *adore* the content that constitutes their subject field. As a consequence, almost all of the national sets of content standards cover much more content than, as a practical matter, can be taught in the instructional time teachers have available. Subject-matter specialists invariably believe that almost *all* of their field's skills and knowledge ought to be mastered by children. Simply put, there's way too much content in most sets of national content standards to be taught, much less measured, in the time that educators have at their disposal.

In recent years, I've spent a fair amount of time reviewing these national collections of content standards and I'm convinced that if teachers really tried to get students to master *all* of the content set forth by *all* of the subject-matter groups, those teachers would need to teach students twenty-four hours per day until several years after the students had been interred! There's just too much content embodied in most nationally sanctioned content standards for those documents to be readily translated into what should be measured. Educational leaders, if they want to base their assessments on content standards, will almost always need to do some serious prioritizing among content standards. And only the *most* important content standards ought to be assessed.

Teachers' Preferences as a Source

Most of the testing that takes place in our schools, of course, consists of the classroom assessments devised by teachers. In general, classroom teachers create assessments based directly on the instructional objectives they have for their students. And because most teachers' instructional objectives are aimed at the knowledge and skills students are supposed to acquire, it would seem fairly straightforward for teachers to whip out educational tests that help determine whether students have actually achieved the teacher's instructional objectives.

But, as you might have guessed, most teachers face a tough problem when they try to figure out what to measure in their own classrooms. Unfortunately, the full array of skills and knowledge that teachers would *like* students to acquire is typically too extensive to permit tidy assessment, assessment that doesn't impinge too much on the teacher's *instructional* time. Teachers want children to learn, to learn lots *and* lots. But if teachers take time out to *test* even half of that lots *and* lots, then there would only be instructional time left to *teach* only lots. There'd be lots left *untaught*.

And there often isn't a heap of help available from the curricular documents distributed by state or district officials. Whether those curricular guidelines are organized around goals, objectives, aims, expectancies, content standards, outcomes (or whatever synonym for "educational intentions" that's being used by the state's officials), the guidelines still tend to cover too much content, at least for assessment purposes. Just as is the case with most sets of content standards, the curricula recommended by many state and district curricular specialists frequently function as "wish lists," that is, well-intentioned hopes about all the good things children ought to learn. But if educators measured children to see if they had mastered *all* the good things that ought to be learned, there'd be insufficient time left for instructional purposes. Classroom teachers are, therefore, faced with challenging choices when they try to decide what to measure.

Regrettably, I suspect many of today's classroom teachers decide what to measure in the same way I did when I was a teacher. During my first stress-laden year of teaching, I whipped up my tests (quizzes, midterms, and final exams) without all that much careful thought. I grabbed content from the textbooks I was using and from my county's curriculum syllabus. Frankly, I wasn't too concerned about the content of my tests. As I confessed last chapter, the exclusive mission of my classroom assessment during that frantic first year of teaching was to help me assign grades to my students. (Because I had a Catholic upbringing, I understand the therapeutic effects of confession.) As long as my tests were somewhat related to what I was trying to teach, I was satisfied. As a first-year teacher, I was usually scrambling to get ready for tomorrow's teaching. Lesson-planning, not test-construction, was at the top of my priority list. I dreaded, above all dreads, the prospect of a class session in which I simply ran out of things to do.

But, then, when my *second* year of teaching rolled around, I had a much better source for my tests. That source was, obviously, my *first year's* tests. They were already in my locked file cabinet, simply yearning to be reused. So, after receiving only mild massaging, my second year's tests turned out to be near mirror-images of my first year's tests, even though my first year's test-construction thinking had been close to thoughtless. In subsequent years, a similar practice of warmed-over tests was followed. I fear that there are a fair number of today's teachers whose classroom assessments were sired in the same expedient but unsound fashion that I employed during my initial foray into educational measurement.

Where, Then, to Turn?

As I've suggested, the question of "What to assess?" cannot easily be answered by dipping into textbooks, cuddling up to content standards, or using a teacher-knows-best approach. Where, then, is an educational leader to turn in deciding on what to measure? The chief determiner of *what* should be measured rests on *why* you're measuring anything in the first place. If educational leaders initially learn how to respond to the *why* question, they'll find that the *what* question will be more readily answerable.

Later in this chapter, therefore, you're going to consider the most common *purposes* that educators have when they assess students. For each of these assessment purposes, you'll be asked to address the "What to measure?" question head-on. But before doing so, you first need to consider two distinctive ways of interpreting test results. These two interpretive alternatives will be pivotal if, as an educational leader, you're going to think clearly about what to measure. Accordingly, *please, please* (note the reiterated plea) get these two interpretive alternatives down cold.

Two Influential Interpretive Alternatives

You may recall, in Chapter 1, I pointed out that educators measure students in order to arrive at inferences about the status of those students. Educators need to make inferences about students' status because, unlike the measurement of height or weight, the student attributes that educators typically want to know about are covert, not observable. So teachers use a test to measure students' mathematical skills, for instance, in order to arrive at an inference about how mathematically skilled their students are.

An assessment *inference* about the meaning of students' test results is simply another way of describing an *interpretation* of students' test results. Putting it in other words, when an educator arrives at an inference or interpretation about students' test results, that inference or interpretation is simply the educator's way of making sense out of students' test performances.

Test scores, as you probably already know, do not, in and of themselves, make any sense at all. To illustrate, suppose you are a fifth-grade teacher who's given your students a 50-item geography test covering Africa. One of your students, Christine, answers 37 of the 50 items correctly. What does Christine's score of 37 mean? Obviously, it indicates that Christine didn't know all the stuff you dealt with in your African geography test. Perhaps she thought the veldt was a green fabric that covers pool tables. The score of 37 might also indicate that Christine does, in fact, know something about African geography or she probably would have scored lower. But, for *instructional* purposes, those sorts of superficial interpretations aren't especially helpful. What educators need are results-based interpretations that have implications for educational *decisions*. Let's turn, then, to the two major types of assessment inferences that can help educators make such decisions.

Relative, Norm-Referenced Interpretations

A Relative Interpretation

Giving meaning to a test result by comparing it to the results of other test-takers.

The first kind of inference or interpretation that educators can make regarding a student's test results is based on the way the student's results compare to those of other students. For example, remember your imaginary fifth-grade student, Christine, and her performance on the African geography test. If her score of 37 correct out of a possible 50 test items was the *top* score in the class, that would allow you to make a *relative* interpretation of her score, namely, "Christine earned the *highest* score in the class." It is educationally useful to know that Christine outperformed all the other students in the class. You might want to take advantage of her *relatively* superior knowledge of African geography by asking her to do some peer tutoring with some of your less knowledgeable students, many of whom think that Sub-Saharan Africa is some sort of torpedo-shooting underwater boat. (Incidentally, a *top* score of 37 on a 50-item test suggests that your test is either plenty tough or, perhaps, that your teaching about African geography was not Sub-Saharan, but somewhat *subpar*.)

Norm-Referenced Interpretation

Giving meaning to a test result by comparing it to results of other test-takers.

Another, more technical way of characterizing a *relative* interpretation is to describe it as a *norm-referenced* interpretation. A norm-referenced interpretation (or inference) is simply a gussied-up way of describing a relative interpretation because we make sense out of a student's test performance by comparing it to the performances of other students. The other students are called the "norm group," so when we compare one student's test results with that of the students in the norm group, we really "reference" the student's score to that of the norm-group's scores. That's where the term *norm-referenced* comes from. If you consider the in-margin definitions for a "relative interpretation" and a "norm-referenced interpretation," you'll find that they are identical.

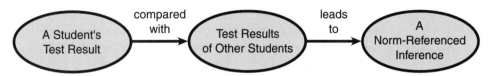

FIGURE 2.1.

A relative interpretation of a student's assessment performance.

In Figure 2.1, you can see a graphic representation of how a relative interpretation, that is, a norm-referenced interpretation, of a student's test result takes place. The *inference* being made is a relative one, namely, how the student's assessment performance stacks up in comparison to the test performances of other students. When educators see that a student's test score was better than the scores of 65 percent of the students in a national norm group, and the educators know the norm group was supposed to be representative of the entire nation, they can reasonably infer that the student's achievement level exceeds the achievement level of 65 percent of the nation's students.

Ordinarily, when educators think about norm-referenced interpretations, what comes to their mind are the interpretations based on one of the several nationally standardized achievement tests used so widely in the United States. Typically, a student (let's call him George and make him a tenth-grader) takes one of these standardized achievement tests, earns a score, then is told how his score stacks up against the scores earned by the many students who constitute the test's norm group. For example, there might have been a national sample of 2,000 tenth-grade students who had already completed the test, and when George's mathematics score on the test is compared with the 2,000-student norm group, it turns out that he outperformed 90 percent of them. His mathematics performance would be interpreted, using a norm-referenced (that is, relative) interpretive framework, as being at the "90th percentile." You can give meaning to George's score by comparing it to scores of those in the norm group.

Actually, when educators make relative interpretations of students' test scores based on national norm-group comparisons, the educators are usually interested in comparing their own students to one another. The national norm group's scores serve as a kind of measuring stick that can be used to allow local student-by-student comparisons such as, "Bill scored at the 85th percentile, but Clyde scored at the 95th!"

Conceptually, there is no difference between (1) the comparison of Christine's 37 score on the African geography test with the scores of her classmates, and (2) the comparison of George's math score with scores of those who constitute the national test's norm group. You can make sense out of a student's performance by comparing that performance to the performances of others who have completed the same assessment. When you "reference" Christine's score back to those of her classmates by saying she "scored highest," you are essentially using her classmates (instead of a national norm group) as the comparative tape measure for your norm-referenced interpretation about Christine.

Because norm-referenced interpretations are most commonly made in connection with nationally standardized tests, many educators, in fact, go so far as to describe these

Percentile

The percent of norm group students who had lower scores than the student being assessed.

national tests as "norm-referenced tests." Technically, a *test* is not norm-referenced. Rather, it is the results-based interpretation you make that is norm-referenced. But, because it's very common in educational circles to refer to nationally standardized tests that yield norm-referenced inferences as "norm-referenced tests," don't be surprised if you, too, start using such descriptions. In your "heart of hearts" (or "head of heads"), you'll still know it is the inference, not the test, that's norm-referenced. Let's turn, now, to the second of the two interpretive alternatives.

Absolute, Criterion-Referenced Interpretations

The second kind of inference (that is, interpretation) you can make regarding a student's test results is not dependent on referencing a student's score to scores of students in a norm group. Norm-referenced interpretations are clearly comparative and, therefore, relative. It is also possible to interpret a student's performance in an *absolute* fashion. An absolute interpretation attempts to describe, as clearly as possible, just what it is that the student can or cannot do. For instance, unlike a relative inference such as "Lee scored at the 46th percentile on a nationally standardized spelling test," an absolute inference would attempt to estimate what proportion of a specified list of words Lee could spell correctly.

An example of how to supply score-based inferences for a spelling test may help clarify the difference between relative and absolute interpretations of assessment results. Let's imagine that the developers of a nationally standardized spelling test for high school students had isolated for each grade level (grades 9–12) a list of 500 words that students most frequently needed to spell. Because there would be some overlap from grade to grade (students, for example, need to spell some of the same words at all grade levels), the 500 spelling words at each higher grade level would always include 300 "new, grade-appropriate words" plus 200 words that had been listed at the two immediately lower level grades.

For each grade level, therefore, a list of 500 spelling words, 300 of which were not found on the tests for previous grade levels, would be the source of a 50-item spelling test. The 50 words to be spelled at each grade level would be randomly drawn from the 500-word list designated for that grade level. In order to make the 50 items on the test as representative as possible, 20 spelling words would be randomly drawn from the 200 lower-grade words and 30 spelling words would be randomly drawn from the 300 "new" words. Technically, this would be a form of *stratified* random sampling.

Let's say the ninth-grade level of the spelling test had been previously administered to a national norm group of 2,500 ninth-graders. As a consequence, the possibility would exist for making norm-referenced interpretations. Assume, then, that Johnny Jergens is a high-achieving ninth-grader who was able to spell correctly 40 of his ninth-grade test's 50 spelling words.

To make a *relative* interpretation of Johnny's 40-correct score (usually referred to as a *raw score*), a teacher would consult the test's norm tables and find that a raw score of 40 correct was equivalent to a score that exceeded the performance of 95 percent of those in the student norm group. So Johnny's test performance would be described as being "at the 95th percentile." Obviously, compared to the students in the national norm group, Johnny Jergens would be regarded as a very good speller.

Absolute Interpretation

Giving meaning to a test result by comparing it with a defined assessment domain.

Raw Score

The "untreated" score earned by a student on an assessment.

In contrast, to make an *absolute* interpretation of Johnny's performance, a teacher would focus on the 500 ninth-grade words that were *eligible* to be tested. Because the 50 words on the ninth-grade test represent the 500 eligible words on the ninth-grade list, the teacher could reasonably infer that Johnny's 40 correctly spelled words out of 50 (that is, 80 percent correct) signified that Johnny "could spell correctly approximately 80 percent of the 500 words on the ninth-grade list."

Each set of 500 grade-level spelling words can be thought of as a target or "criterion." The criterion for each grade level is often described as an *assessment domain.* The nature of an assessment domain was described in Chapter 1. To make an absolute interpretation, you can "reference" the student's score back to the assessment domain. It is for this reason that measurement folks describe such absolute inferences as *criterion-referenced* interpretations.

When educators make a norm-referenced, that is, relative, inference about a student's assessment results, all they really know is how that student's performance compares to the performances of other students. In some instances, as you'll see, such relative interpretations are all that's needed. But teachers who rely exclusively on norm-referenced interpretations really don't have a very clear idea of what it is that their students can or can't do. For instance, if a student scores at the 96th percentile on a nationally standardized achievement test in mathematics, it's pretty obvious that the student knows mountains of math. But, which mountains? The test interpreter, other than knowing that the norm-referenced interpretation is based on mathematical content, has only a weak understanding of what's actually been tested. That is often the case because the content of standardized tests is typically not explicitly described by the companies that distribute

Criterion-Referenced Interpretation

Giving meaning to a test result by comparing it with a defined assessment domain.

"Yes, I know you were qualifed under our former rules, but we've shifted to a norm-referenced admission system."

FIGURE 2.2.

An absolute interpretation of a student's assessment performance.

those tests. For the comparative assessment mission that standardized tests were designed to fulfill, there's really no need for carefully described assessment domains.

If you look at Figure 2.2, you'll see a graphic depiction of how an absolute interpretation, that is, a criterion-referenced interpretation, of a student's test performance takes place. The *inference* being made is an absolute one in the sense that if the assessment domain is well described, you can simply make an inference identifying the proportion of the domain that the student has mastered. For example, if the assessment domain represents knowledge, such as 100 "mental arithmetic facts," then the inference will deal with the percent of those 100 facts that the student appears to have mastered (on the basis of the student's test performance).

Especially for nationally standardized tests, whether achievement tests or aptitude tests, there's no necessity to describe what's measured in great detail. If a test produces student results that allow the students to be accurately compared with the performances of the students in a norm group, then the test will be doing its job well. But the absence of carefully delineated assessment domains obviously limits the possibility of more absolute interpretations.

On the other hand, when educators make a criterion-referenced inference, that is, an absolute interpretation, about a student's assessment results, all they really know is what the student can or can't do. In some instances, as you'll see, such absolute interpretations are all that's needed. But if you make a criterion-referenced interpretation, you really don't know how the student's performance compares to the performances of other students. In some settings, the absence of such comparative information can be a definite drawback.

The most important factor needed in order to make useful criterion-referenced interpretations is a *clearly described assessment domain*. If the assessment domain that the test represents is not well explicated, then it's obviously difficult to pin down what it is that the student's test performance really means. Think back, if you will, to the earlier example about a national spelling test with the 500 eligible words for each grade level actually listed. By carefully sampling from that 500-word assessment domain, the test developers were able to create a 50-item test that would allow educators to make reasonable inferences about a student's mastery of the well-described 500-word assessment domain.

But let's suppose that the test developers of the spelling test had been far more cavalier in their delimitation of an assessment domain. For instance, let's say that they did not actually list the 500 eligible spelling words. Instead, they might have said something vague such as, "Each grade level's 50-item spelling test will be based on words apt to be frequently encountered by students at that grade level."

In the News

In Twist, Consensus Growing on Academic Achievement in Va.

by Kathleen Kennedy Manzo

In the continuing argument over academic standards, disagreement over how they are defined, how rigorous they should be, and how they should be implemented and assessed is all too common.

Yet, in the case of Virginia's "Standards of Learning," now winding down its first year of implementation in more than 1,700 schools throughout the state, an unusual consensus has emerged among many educators, scholars, lawmakers, and parents. They agree that the state's standards for science, mathematics, English language arts, and history and social sciences are clear and concise, rigorous, and heavy on content.

That is not to say that they are uniformly loved—or hated. But the characteristics of the standards are both their strength and their weakness, educators say.

And they are also the reason that the Virginia model is gaining national attention and acclaim as educators and policymakers in at least nine other states look for guidance in crafting their own.

Borrowing freely. Virginia's efforts at writing standards did not come easy. First, they had to be revived by Republican Gov. George F. Allen after his predecessor scrapped an earlier plan amid criticism that the standards were too vague.

Then, hundreds of people flocked to hearings to discuss the standards before their approval two years ago. Debate erupted early, especially over the history and social sciences section, which many parents and teachers feared covered an unrealistically ambitious amount of material. The debate continues in Virginia, where high-stakes tests to measure how well students meet the standards are planned to be rolled out next year. . . .

What's your reaction?

Excerpted, with permission, from *Education Week,* June 11, 1997

Given such a fuzzy description of an assessment domain, can you see how difficult it would be to come up with a meaningful absolute interpretation of a student's test performance? Poorly described assessment domains lead to shoddy criterion-referenced interpretations. For making norm-referenced interpretations, however, less precise descriptions of an assessment domain are often quite sufficient.

Accordingly, educational leaders need to recognize that the usefulness of a criterion-referenced interpretation is dependent on the care with which the assessment domain represented by the test has been described. Many educators, unfortunately, hear the phrase, "criterion-referenced assessment," and automatically assume the assessment will yield educationally useful results. That's just not so. There are many educational tests currently cavorting in criterion-referenced costumes that, upon closer inspection, fail to provide the clear descriptions of assessment domains indispensable for accurate absolute inferences about students' test performances.

Not surprisingly, therefore, if a test is deliberately developed so that it will yield accurate norm-referenced interpretations, it usually (but not always) does. Similarly, if a test is deliberately developed so that it will yield accurate criterion-referenced interpretations, it usually (but not always) does. More often than not, however, if an educational measuring instrument is built to provide norm-referenced inferences, it usually does *not* do a good job in providing criterion-referenced interpretations. And, if an educational measuring instrument is originally built to provide criterion-referenced inferences, it usually does *not* do a good job in providing norm-referenced interpretations.

Two Kinds of Inferences for One Test?

Is it possible to build a test that simultaneously yields nifty norm-referenced interpretations *and* crisp criterion-referenced interpretations? The answer is definitely *Yes*, but only with a quart of qualifiers. If you start with a good criterion-referenced test, one that provides a clear description of the assessment domain that's being represented by the test, then you can subsequently administer the test to a suitable norm group and build normative tables so that relative interpretations will also be possible. For example, a two-for-one interpretation based on such a test might be something such as: "Jolene's test performance indicated she had mastered 65 percent of the scientific procedures contained in the test's assessment domain, and this level of performance was at the 88th percentile." So, given a well-described assessment domain, it is definitely possible to make both absolute and relative inferences about a student's test score.

If the assessment domain being measured by a test is *not* well described, however, as is usually the case with nationally standardized tests, then it is *not* possible to come up with accurate criterion-referenced interpretations of a student's test performance. Given a test that yields good norm-referenced inferences, you can only make accurate criterion-referenced interpretations *if* the test's assessment domain is well defined. More often than not, these sorts of well-defined assessment domains are not created during the construction of nationally standardized achievement or aptitude tests.

Different Ancestries

In Chapter 1 you learned that human beings have been assessing each other for centuries. Most of that assessment has been based on a norm-referenced approach to measurement because, in the main, there was an overriding interest in comparisons such as, "Who is better than whom; or who is worse than whom?"

Criterion-referenced inferences are relatively recent additions to the educator's measurement tool kit. Until someone unearths evidence indicating that the ancient Chinese had stumbled across criterion-referenced inferences a few thousand years ago, I'm going to assume that, with few exceptions (such as Jephthah's Shibboleth test), criterion-referenced interpretations are late arrivals on the measurement scene. Although there are a few allusions to such inferences in earlier times, credit for drawing our attention to criterion-referenced interpretations goes to Robert Glaser. In 1963, Glaser authored a brief but provocative essay on testing entitled "Instructional Technology and the Measurement of Learning Outcomes: Some Questions." Stemming from his concerns regarding the impact of more effective instructional techniques on traditional measurement tactics, Glaser introduced the concepts of norm-referenced and criterion-referenced measurement.[1]

Although a period of several years' dormancy followed, in the early seventies educational interest in criterion-referenced measurement increased dramatically. *Criterion-referenced* was the fashionable word among avant-garde educators who applied it in adjectival form to just about every unescorted noun in the neighborhood. We saw workshops, speeches, and conferences on such topics as *criterion-referenced testing, criterion-referenced evaluation,* and *criterion-referenced instruction.* It is reported that one group of librarians even staged a seminar on *criterion-referenced references.* Criterion-referencing was way up on the popularity charts.

Popular notions, of course, attract all sorts of followers. Soon we saw the emergence of a small but vocal cult of criterion-referenced assessment devotees who, with the characteristic zeal of recent converts, totally repudiated any preexisting objects of adoration (norm-referenced inferences) in favor of a new assessment deity. "Criterion-referenced inferences," these proponents of a new assessment order often enunciated, "are education's only salvation."

I'm overdramatizing a mite, but it is true that in the seventies many educators were admonished to abandon norm-referenced inferences altogether. Criterion-referenced interpretations were being touted as an answer to every educator's measurement requirements.

Some of the contestants in this educational measurement debate engaged in wholesale rejection of the other folks' testing tools. Sweeping castigations such as the following found their way onto the podium and into print: "Norm-referenced inferences, having outlived their usefulness, should be abandoned completely." Or, "Criterion-referenced inferences must, of necessity, deal only with piddling outcomes." Or, with greater vigor, "Critics of norm-referenced (or criterion-referenced) inferences were born under conditions of debatable legitimacy." The latter allegation was often phrased in a somewhat more earthy manner.

These disputations about the relative virtues of norm- and criterion-referenced inferences were marked by more heat than light. (That's a *relative* assertion.) However, after the partisan struggle diminished to some extent, a fundamental truth was recognized by most of the testing debate's contestants, namely, that both norm-referenced and criterion-referenced interpretations are needed if educators are to accomplish the full range of necessary purposes.

Cognitive Assessment

Measurement of students' knowledge and/or intellectual skills.

Three Kinds of Outcomes

Let's briefly consider the major categories of outcomes in which classroom teachers and school administrators are interested, namely, *cognitive, psychomotor,* and *affective* outcomes. *Cognitive* tests attempt to tap a student's knowledge or intellectual skills, such as one's capacity to solve verbal or mathematical problems. *Psychomotor* tests attempt to measure a student's physical competencies, either small-muscle skills (such as using a keyboard) or large-muscle skills (such as pole-vaulting). *Affective* tests attempt to gauge students' attitudes, values, and interests, such as what is measured by a test of one's self-esteem.

Tests in the cognitive realm are often focused on a student's *current knowledge and/or intellectual skills.* These tests are usually referred to as *achievement* tests. But tests of a cognitive sort may also be focused on a student's *potential* to perform well subsequently. These tests are referred to as *aptitude* tests.

Psychomotor Assessment

Measurement of students' small-muscle or large-muscle skills.

Most educators are far more familiar with cognitive than psychomotor tests, having been reared on a steady diet of cognitive aptitude and achievement tests since they sauntered through the kindergarten door. Educators have less frequently encountered psychomotor tests unless they were the exams taken in a keyboarding class (it used to be called "typing") or the performance tests required of us in a physical education class. For both cognitive and psychomotor tests, teachers ordinarily are concerned with measuring *optimal performance,* that is, getting an answer to such questions as, "How well can you perform this skill?"

**Affective
Assessment**

Measurement of
students' attitudes,
interests, and/or
values.

For affective measures, however, educators are more eager to get a fix on a student's *typical performance*. Educators are less interested in the question, "What *can* you do?" and more interested in the question, "What *will* you do?" To secure a reasonable idea of a student's attitudes toward school, for example, you'd need to find out how the student typically feels about school. You don't really want to know if students have the ability to *create* positive or negative impressions about school (unless they're in a drama class). Instead, you want to know how students *truly* feel about school.

For affective measures, therefore, the conventional distinction between aptitude and achievement makes little sense. What educators usually want to do when assessing in the affective realm is to snare an idea of students' current affective status in order to determine what students' future actions are apt to be. To illustrate, social studies teachers may wish to assess students' current *attitudes* regarding government so that reasonable predictions can be made concerning students' future *behaviors* regarding government (after school has been completed) such as voting or participating in the political process.

Three Kinds of Decisions

Let's review what's been dealt with so far in this chapter. First, it was suggested that deciding what an educational test should measure is a tougher task than might be thought. No matter whether it's a teacher who is deciding what content to include in a final exam, a district curriculum specialist who is deciding what content to include in a districtwide achievement test, or a state department of education staff member who is deciding what content to include in a statewide high school graduation examination, there are no easy answers to the question, "What to measure?"

Next, two fundamental interpretive alternatives were described for making sense out of students' test results, namely, relative (norm-referenced) and absolute (criterion-referenced) interpretations. The amount of attention given to the distinction between norm- and criterion-referenced interpretations was intended to reflect the significance of these two fundamental ways of assigning meaning to students' test performances.

But in order to determine which of these two kinds of interpretation is needed, it is necessary to identify the *purpose* that the educational measurement is supposed to accomplish. Only then can educators really determine what should be measured. The purpose of any educational assessment device, whether the assessment is a commercially published standardized achievement test or Miss Wakefield's weekly quiz for her 26 fourth-grade students, is to help educators make better decisions. In fact, *the decisions to be based on students' assessment results should be the chief determiners of what should be measured.*

To close out the chapter, you're going to look at three different categories of decisions that educators can make more defensibly if they have access to students' test performances. An educational leader who understands the important distinctions among these three types of decisions will be better able to select one of the two interpretive alternatives previously discussed. Then, based on that interpretation, what's actually included in the assessment instrument can be more sensibly selected.

In Figure 2.3, this three-step sequence is represented graphically. As can be seen in that figure, the three steps are: (1) identifying the decision at issue, namely, the decision

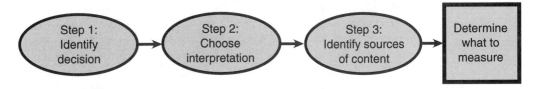

FIGURE 2.3.

A three-step approach to the determination of what should be measured.

to be influenced by students' test performances; (2) choosing the appropriate type of inference, namely, whether a relative or absolute interpretation of student's measurement results is required; and (3) determining an appropriate source of content, namely, the place or places where what's needed for potentially suitable items or exercises can be found.

Let me pause, briefly, to offer you a bit of in-chapter encouragement. This is a fairly hefty chapter, and some of its content might be somewhat off-putting because it looks too complicated. But educational leaders have to deal with a complicated world. So, please hang in there. Think hard about what you're reading. If you do, it will become crystal clear by the chapter's conclusion. Or it won't.

Let's look at the three most common categories of educational decisions that can be better made by considering students' test performances. Those three types of decisions consist of *selection*, *evaluation*, and *instruction*. A description of each decision type, along with appropriate interpretations and likely content sources, will help you to use the three-step formula (in Figure 2.3) for determining what should be assessed.

Selection Decisions

Teachers and administrators are frequently faced with the necessity to make *selections* among students. For example, decisions must be made about which students should be admitted to college or to other sorts of advanced training programs. At the other end of the spectrum, decisions must be made about which poorly performing students warrant special remedial instruction. It's difficult to imagine a week in a typical school that wouldn't be suitably sprinkled with decisions involving the selection of students. However, there are two quite different settings in which such choices are made, and the nature of those settings should determine whether educators opt for norm- or criterion-referenced interpretations.

Fixed-quota settings. One type of selection decision occurs in situations where there are more applicants than openings. For example, let's say a prestigious law school has only 100 openings for its next year's class, yet the law school is deluged with over 500 applicants for those slots. Even though there are numerous candidates, there is a *fixed quota* of openings. Accordingly, decisions must be made among the candidates so that only 100 of the more than 500 applicants are admitted to the law school.

In this type of fixed-quota setting, it is necessary to sort out individuals according to their relative abilities. Therefore, norm-referenced interpretations are needed. Indeed, most tests that yield norm-referenced inferences for such selection situations have typically been polished aplenty so they perform precisely this sort of "spread-them-out-and-spot-the-best" function. In the same way, if an educator were trying to make selections at the low end of the ability continuum, for instance, when teachers attempt to identify the most instructionally needy students from a group of learning-impaired children, then norm-referenced interpretations would again be more appropriate than criterion-referenced interpretations. In these situations, relative contrasts among students are needed.

To illustrate, let's suppose our fictitious prestigious law school had used an admissions test that had been constructed to provide criterion-referenced, rather than norm-referenced, inferences. For the sake of argument (they argue a lot in law schools), let's assume that almost 150 of the 500 applicants attained extremely high scores, so high that the scores were essentially the same (that is, within a point or two of each other). Because the test had not been deliberately constructed to detect variability in applicants' levels of functioning, this type of result is quite possible. Yet, because the law school's quota was fixed at 100 and the law school's faculty was unable to distinguish among the *150* highest scoring applicants, an admissions test designed to yield absolute interpretations failed to permit a sensible sorting job. A test specifically constructed to provide norm-referenced interpretations would have done the job better.

Requisite-skill/knowledge settings. In addition to fixed-quota contexts, there are other settings in education where the decision revolves around not who is best or worst but, rather, who is *qualified*. For example, let's say a medical school has just put the finishing touches on its preparation of a flock of fledgling physicians. Before the medical school faculty releases these successors of Hippocrates, it is decided to give the students a comprehensive "everything-a-patient-would-like-you-to-know" examination. On the basis of the exam's results, some students will receive their ceremonial white coats and stethoscopes while others will be required to continue training until they improve their medical moxie.

In such a setting, norm-referenced inferences would not be appropriate. An example of such an inappropriate decision would be "to certify the best 25 percent of this year's students." If this year's collection of medical students was truly inferior, the medical school would be sanctifying the best of an unqualified lot. Would you want your appendix excised by a slow-witted surgeon who was licensed by virtue of being at the 75th percentile among a class of incompetents? No, this would be an instance where the *requisite skills* needed by an individual should be identified, then measured, so that criterion-referenced inferences could be drawn. Only those candidates who display the requisite medical knowledge and skills should be certified to practice.

The same sort of logic applies when one approaches the licensing of educators. Children deserve truly qualified teachers and school administrators, not the best of a weak group of prospective educators. Criterion-referenced inferences that accurately reflect a student's mastery of the necessary knowledge and/or skills should be employed in requisite-skill/knowledge situations.

Dominant score interpretations. So, depending on the context, a test that's needed for selection purposes may require inferences of a relative nature or an absolute nature. The majority of tests designed to make a selection decision are used in fixed-quota con-

News in Brief: A State Capitals Roundup

Mich. Adopts New Terms for Proficiency Testing

After months of deliberation, the Michigan state school board has adopted a new scale for rating juniors who take the state's controversial high school proficiency test.

The board voted May 7 in favor of a plan to create four achievement levels of test performance. The levels will be represented by numeric rankings on students' transcripts.

The first three levels will also be a state endorsement that tells college officials and others who see the transcripts that the students have acquired at least basic education skills.

The four levels are: 1, endorsed, exceeded Michigan standards; 2, endorsed, met Michigan standards; 3, endorsed, basic level; and 4, not endorsed.

State policymakers were forced to change the test after hundreds of parents refused to let their children take the exam last year, arguing that it was too punitive and vague. The old test rated students as proficient, non-proficient, and novice.

"Anything that wasn't proficient was reported as failing, which wasn't the intent," said Kathleen Straus, the president of the state board.

"We're hoping this will be clearer," she added.

What's your reaction?

Reprinted, with permission, from *Education Week*, May 20, 1998

---

texts. As a consequence, for the measurement devices that provide evidence used in selection decisions, norm-referenced interpretations are usually most appropriate.

However, if the selection decision hinges on a student's possession of certain knowledge or skills, then an absolute interpretation makes more sense. Although these situations are far less common than fixed-quota settings, educational leaders need to recognize the difference between the two kinds of situations. For selection decisions, it is clear that the type of inference to be made depends directly on whether a fixed-quota or requisite-skill/knowledge setting is involved.

Content sources. As you just saw, the kind of interpretations to be made in connection with selection decisions depends on whether the selection is to be made in a fixed-quota or requisite-skill/knowledge situation. Such is also true with respect to the content to be included in an assessment instrument. And in this regard, *content* refers to the major ingredients actually contained in a measuring device. To illustrate, the content of a reading achievement test might be the set of reading passages and test items (linked to those passages) that constitute the test. The content of a biology test might be the diagrams, pictures, and test items that constitute the test. For a psychomotor test, such as an assessment of someone's keyboarding skill, the content of the test might be the stimulus materials, printed or oral, that the student must input, via a keyboard, into a computer's memory. For an affective assessment device, the content might consist of the series of statements to which the student anonymously registers agreement or disagreement. Assessment content, in short, is the substance of the tasks that make up the test.

Returning to the two kinds of selection decisions, you'll see that there are key differences in the content sources for fixed-quota and requisite-skills/ knowledge settings. *For fixed-quota contexts*, such as deciding which students to choose for admission to a highly selective future educational program, the content that should be selected is "whatever works" to make the best predictions about students' future success. *Empirical predictiveness*,

Test Content

The substance of the tasks contained in an assessment instrument.

therefore, is the important attribute of content for selection tests that are to be used in fixed-quota situations.

Empirical, that is, experienced-based, predictiveness simply means that in choosing the content for measurement devices to be used in fixed-quota situations, you need to find out what content actually predicts accurately, irrespective of whether it intuitively appears to be the "proper" content. To illustrate, suppose you were trying to develop a new measurement device to predict who would be successful in a graduate program in engineering. If you discovered, by some fluke, that the way students answered a question about their favorite kind of low-fat yogurt was, in fact, predictive of whether they would do well in the graduate engineering program, then you would definitely want to include the yogurt item in your prediction test. Even though the content of that item might seem peculiar, responses to the yogurt item are empirically predictive of students' future engineering success. Accordingly, the item should be retained in a test designed to help make selection decisions in a fixed-quota context.

Obviously, in devising a good measurement instrument for this kind of predictive purpose, the test developers would not select a load of loony content. Rather, test developers would try, using the best logic they can muster, to come up with content that would, indeed, predict how well someone will do in a graduate engineering program. But, in the final analysis, empirical predictiveness is the factor that must determine test content for selection tests used in fixed-quota settings.

For selection in requisite-skill/knowledge settings, the content of an assessment instrument is ordinarily determined by experts who make their best judgment about the skills and/or knowledge that an individual must possess in order to be selected. These experts will often rely heavily on their own experiences and expertise in order to identify what they believe to be the critical knowledge or skills needed if someone is to be selected for a particular function. For instance, suppose you were to take part in the creation of a new teacher licensure examination to be used to issue teaching certificates for prospective teachers. To isolate the truly critical skills and/or knowledge needed by first-year teachers, you might call on experienced educators, and especially those who supervise first-year teachers, so you could garner ideas from them regarding what knowledge and/or skill must truly be possessed by an effective first-year teacher.

The more important the stakes associated with the test's results are, the more pronounced should be the competence of the individuals doing the content selection. It is for this reason that national licensure examinations for any professional specialty are invariably built only after a panel of nationally recognized experts has had a thoroughgoing opportunity to propose the test's likely content. To reiterate, the most appropriate content source for tests used in connection with selection decisions for fixed-quota contexts is empirical predictiveness; for requisite skill/knowledge contexts, it is expert judgment.

Evaluation Decisions

A second category of educational decisions that can be informed by assessment results deals with *evaluation*. In this instance, *evaluation* refers both to the evaluation of instruction and to the evaluation of students. Let's start off with the evaluation of instruction.

Evaluation of instruction. When an educator engages in *instructional evaluation*, an attempt is being made to determine the effectiveness of an instructional endeavor. The instruction might be what's provided by a *teacher* in that teacher's classroom, or the instruction might be a full-blown language arts *program* complete with printed materials for students, manuals for teachers, audiovisual aids, and a galaxy of suggested instructional activities.

When educators carry out instructional evaluation, there are really three decision options available to them. First, the instruction being evaluated, if it is regarded as effective, can be retained "as is." It's working, so don't alter it. If the language arts *program* is a clear winner, then it should be used in the future. If a particular *teacher* is judged to be effective, then the teacher should be encouraged to stick with whatever instructional procedures the teacher is using.

A second decision option arises if the instruction is determined to be only somewhat successful. In such instances, the appropriate decision would be to modify the instruction so that it works better. For instance, if a language arts *program* seems to help children learn how to read, but appears to fall down in teaching them how to write, there might be supplemental exercises in written communication added to the program. And if a *teacher* seems to be only partially successful, then the decision should be to look for deficits in the teacher's instruction that can be remedied.

Finally, if the instruction is determined to be downright dismal, the instruction ought to be terminated. In the case of our illustrative language arts *program*, this would mean the program ought to be jettisoned and replaced by another program that, in turn, should then be evaluated to determine its effectiveness. With respect to *teachers*, if a given teacher is simply unable to teach effectively, and all sorts of assistance hasn't worked to boost the teacher's skill, then it will be in children's best interest to insist that the teacher look for an alternative line of work.

To reiterate, when educators evaluate instruction, the three decisions to be made are: (1) retain it as is, (2) modify it, or (3) discard it. Now, what about the kind of assessment and the interpretations that are needed to help an educational leader make one of these three decisions?

First off, it should be recognized that although students' assessment results should play a major role in arriving at evaluative judgments regarding instruction, there are usually other factors to consider, such as the instruction's costs or its unintended side effects. But, overridingly, if any instructional activity is to be judged successful, it should clearly have a positive impact on students.

Let's imagine, for instance, that a school district's administrators have purchased an expensive new program focused on helping children be more effective oral communicators. We'll call our fictitious new program *Speakwell* and assume that it consists chiefly of videotaped practice activities whereby students engage in videotaped oral communication exercises, then review the videos with the assistance of critiques by teachers and other students. Now, let's suppose that at the start of the school year, before *Speakwell's* installation, all students gave three-minute videotaped impromptu speeches. These videotaped speeches were intended to serve as a pretest. (We'll suppose that the improvement of students' skill in delivering impromptu speeches was a major emphasis in the *Speakwell* program.) Then, at the end of the school year, another round of three-minute impromptu speeches was given by the same students, but on a set of different topics, as a posttest.

Then, through the magic of electronic video-editing equipment, random samples of the pretests and posttests were mixed together so that it wasn't possible for a judge to tell *when* a particular videotaped speech had been given, that is, as a pretest or posttest. Thereafter, 10 speech teachers from a nearby school district were asked to judge each of the videotaped speeches and rate it on a five-point scale ranging from *dazzling* (5 points) to *dreadful* (1 point). Then, after all the speeches were rated, the average ratings for the pretest speeches and posttest speeches were computed by a staff member who knew which of the videotaped speeches were pretests and which were posttests.

Now, let's imagine that there was absolutely no difference between the averages of the pretest ratings and the posttest ratings. In other words, after a full year of using the expensive *Speakwell* program, students didn't appear to be one bit more skilled in their ability to deliver impromptu speeches than they were at the start of the year. Based on this assessment-produced evidence, it would be likely that the educational leaders who need to deal with *Speakwell's* future in the district would most likely arrive at a well-warranted "dump-it" decision.

It is quite sensible to employ students' assessment results as a major factor in evaluating instruction *if the assessments employed are appropriate.* Later on, in this book's final chapter, you'll learn that the use of standardized achievement tests to evaluate instruction is *not* appropriate. You'll see that, although students' achievements are genuinely important when educational leaders evaluate instruction, nationally standardized achievement tests do not provide accurate evidence by which to judge instruction's effectiveness.

For evaluating the quality of instruction, the most appropriate assessment-based inference educators should make is an absolute one, that is, a criterion-referenced interpretation. In determining whether students have learned what they should have learned, it is more helpful to get an accurate fix on the knowledge and skills that students do or don't possess than it is to see how students compare with one another.

Evaluating students. Another kind of evaluation-based decision facing educators involves the awarding of grades to students.[2] This time-honored activity, of course, has historically been heavily based on students' test performances. Teachers wish to affix a suitable label to a student's accomplishments, so those who perform well on classroom assessments get high grades while those who perform poorly on classroom assessments get low grades. This sort of performance-dependent grading has probably been going on since Socrates was dishing out oral exams to Plato and other Greek-letter guys.

Typically, teachers' grade-giving is an altogether unsystematic, even unpredictable, undertaking. Some teachers dispense grades on a totally relative basis, that is, the best of this year's students get high grades while the worst of this year's students get low grades. This sometimes takes place no matter how able this year's crop of students really is. Other teachers use a relative approach to grading, but establish a sort of mentally recollected "norm-group" based on memories of how well their past students have performed over the years.

Then there are teachers who employ a more absolute approach to grading, so if the teacher has determined that a given level of student performance warrants an *A*, then all students who achieve that level, no matter how many, will receive an *A*. Just as there are norm-referenced and criterion-referenced interpretations of students' assessment results, there are also norm-referenced and criterion-referenced approaches to grade-giving.

The grade-giving picture is complicated still further by the tendency of some teachers who, when deciding on grades, try to include some attention to the native ability that a student possesses. If, for instance, a given student is thought by the teacher to be decisively less than super smart, but the student performs fairly well on tests, the teacher may give the student a high grade because, "in view of the student's potential, a commendable level of achievement has been attained."

Still other teachers try to take account of student *effort* as they distribute grades. If Clyde works really diligently, but scores lower than Claude, who didn't work as hard, some teachers might reward Clyde's effort with a higher grade than the grade given to Claude.

Clearly, the grading practices of classroom teachers vary enormously. With few exceptions, however, students' test results figure prominently in a teacher's grade determinations. And, as we have seen, the assessment-based inferences that teachers make about students' test performances will vary depending on how the teacher approaches the grading process.

Dominant score interpretations. As noted earlier, for evaluating instruction, the most useful kind of interpretation to be drawn from test results will ordinarily be a criterion-referenced interpretation because, more often than not, educators are interested in the degree to which students have learned particular knowledge and skills.

For the evaluation of students, that is, the assignment of grades, teachers vary substantially in the rationales they employ for grade-giving. Although, historically, relative conceptions of grading have predominated, recent years have seen much greater reliance on more absolute approaches to grade-giving. The most accurate characterization of current grading practices would be to describe it as a markedly mixed bag. As such, it is difficult to say which kind of assessment-based inference will be more prevalent in the grading of students.

If teachers favor a relative conception of grading, then relative interpretations of students' test results are most appropriate. If teachers favor an absolute approach to grading, then it would be most sensible to come up with absolute interpretations of students' test results. In short, the grading rationale should be identical to the type of results-based interpretations that the teacher uses.

Content sources. If instructional evaluation is taking place, then the content of the assessments needs to reflect, "What *should* be taught to students at this age?" If the evaluation is focused on judging the effectiveness of a commercially distributed instructional program, for example, then it is important that the content of a test that's used to evaluate the program not only represent the content addressed by the program's developers, but also the content deemed appropriate by a nonpartisan group of experts. This means that the content for a test being used to evaluate an instructional program must usually be chosen by a panel of subject-knowledgeable teachers and/or curriculum specialists.

What these subject-matter experts should try to do is lay out the content, for example, the knowledge, skills, or affect, regarded as age-appropriate for the students receiving the program. To make such judgments, the subject-matter experts should rely on their own experience plus all the relevant curricular recommendations of concerned state and national curricular groups. If a test already exists that covers much of this age-appropriate content, then it should be chosen for the evaluation. If no such test exists, then it will need to be developed. If you tried to evaluate an instructional program covering Objectives *X, Y,* and *Z* with a test covering Objectives *Q, R,* and *S,* you'd be a curricular klutz.

The focus on content that *should* be taught also applies to the evaluation of teachers. Teachers need to be appraised on the basis of whether they are helping students attain what students at that age should attain. If a teacher who was to be evaluated tried to "play it safe" by pursuing low-level instructional objectives—objectives so simple that students were almost certain to achieve them—the teacher would deserve no applause. Instead, those engaged in evaluating teachers must deal with the content that students *ought* to be mastering. As with program evaluation, the determination of what content a teacher should be assessing is best rendered via the professional judgment of subject-matter knowledgeable educators.

Turning from the evaluation of instruction to the evaluation of students, the key question here is not "What *should* be taught to students of this age?" Instead, the appropriate question to ask is "What *has* been taught to these students by this teacher?" It is clearly unfair to base students' grades on content that has not been taught. In fact, there is a landmark 1979 ruling by a Federal Appellate Court (Debra P. v. Turlington, 1979) that if a property right (such as a high school diploma) is denied to a student on the basis of a test whose content has not been taught to the student, this denial constitutes a violation of the student's property rights guaranteed by the U.S. Constitution!

Without wishing to intimidate teachers by invoking FBI scrutiny regarding unconstitutional testing, it should be apparent that fundamental fairness requires teachers to construct grade-determining tests covering only what the teacher has attempted to teach the students. Accordingly, the content of grade-determining tests should reflect, insofar as the available testing time permits, the content covered during the teacher's instruction.

Instructional Decisions

The third and final member of our "big three" decisions to be influenced by students' test results focuses on the choices that educators make regarding the instructional activities they provide for students. Although such instructional decisions can take place at any level, that is, at the classroom, the school district, or statewide, the closer the decision is to the student, the more impact the decision will have on what the student learns. For this reason, the classroom teacher's instructional decisions are apt to be the most influential ones, so let's consider in particular the relationship between assessment evidence and the instructional decisions that classroom teachers make.

What to teach? One decision that every teacher needs to make involves a choice about what to teach. This is an especially vexing problem when a new school year starts, and the teacher receives an unfamiliar collection of students, students whose skills and knowledge are unknown to the teacher. Few teachers, of course, select their instructional objectives at random. A skilled teacher will typically make such instructional decisions by using evidence from preassessments that identify the skills and knowledge (or, possibly, attitudes) with which the students enter the class. If the teacher discovers that most students have already mastered a skill the teacher was intending to teach, then it would obviously be redundant to provide much instruction aimed at such an already mastered skill. (Clearly, preassessments need to be administered at or near the beginning of instruction if they are to provide teachers with instructional guidance.)

On the flip side of preassessment results, suppose a teacher were planning to promote students' mastery of a particular advanced skill, such as a high level mathematical skill based on solving simultaneous equations, and assumed that students' entry behaviors included mastery of the *enabling* mathematical skills needed to grapple successfully with the equation-solving skill. But, to the teacher's surprise, a preassessment administered during the first week of the school year reveals that this year's students have not already achieved the necessary enabling skills. In such a situation, the teacher's decision should surely be to help students master the needed enabling skills first before tackling the advanced skill. (Students will usually have trouble solving simultaneous equations if they can't add or subtract.)

How long to teach? A second kind of decision that can be beneficially influenced by students' assessment results concerns the duration of instruction. How long should the teacher continue to teach toward a given instructional objective? In some instances, the teacher will make that decision for a whole class. For instance, a planned three-week instructional unit on "How a president is elected" might be appropriately wrapped up in only two weeks if almost all of the students display, on a progress-monitoring quiz, that they've really mastered the important ingredients of the presidential-election sequence.

The teacher's decision to halt instruction aimed at a particular objective might also be made on a student-by-student basis. For instance, imagine that Miss Melville, an English teacher, is promoting her students' ability to compose paragraphs that not only "sparkle" from a communication perspective, but are also not "laden with errors in spelling, punctuation, and mechanics." If, via occasional en-route assessments, Miss Melville spots individual students who have already mastered this paragraph composition skill, she may choose to send those students trooping down some sort of enrichment road while keeping the rest of her students on the straight-and-narrow paragraph path.

Progress-monitoring assessments, because they typically provide teachers with better evidence than might be obtained from the teacher's casual observations, will often help classroom teachers decide more accurately when to stop instruction that's focused on a particular educational objective.

Dominant score interpretations. For purposes of instructional decisions of any kind, the teacher will invariably want to make absolute, criterion-referenced interpretations of students' assessment performances. This will be the case because, if teachers are trying to decide what to teach, how to teach it, or how long to teach it, they'll need to get the most accurate fix possible on what it is that students can or can't do. For instructional decision-making, relative inferences about students are of much less use. The problem with relative interpretations is that the referent group of students (the group to whom comparisons are being made) often shifts or is unknown. Whereas a given teacher's current class may be weak, the previous year's class may have been wonderful. But a student who scores "at the top of this year's class" may, one year earlier, have scored near the bottom of that more able group. The teacher really doesn't know what students can or can't do if score-based inferences are exclusively relative.

Norm-referenced, that is, relative, interpretations simply let a teacher know how students compare with one another. Such interpretations do not allow the teacher to make accurate inferences about the knowledge or skills that students possess. Absolute inferences are needed if the teacher is going to make good instructional decisions.

Even though almost all classroom instructional decisions ought to be based on criterion-referenced interpretations of test results, there are occasional instances when a teacher is facing a fixed-quota situation and wants to sort out the best or worst student achievers. In those cases, a relative inference would be preferable. But the need for such norm-referenced interpretations in most classrooms is usually quite rare.

Content sources.   The content that teachers decide to incorporate in their tests will often prove influential in determining what the teacher will emphasize instructionally. Later, in Chapter 3, I'll be recommending that, while teachers should not "teach to the test" in the sense that the teacher is directing instruction toward a particular set of test items, the teacher *should* teach toward the assessment domain of skills, knowledge, or affect represented by the test.

The assessment domains that teachers identify, therefore, should coincide with the *most important* of the teacher's instructional objectives. Teachers teach students tons of things. Teachers seek increases in students' skills, knowledge, and/or affect, but there are so many things that most teachers teach, there is insufficient time in the school day to assess students' status with respect to all that's taught. Accordingly, the teacher should select a modest number of the *most significant* instructional objectives, then assess student status with respect to those pivotal objectives.

If you are getting the idea that I don't think teachers need to measure students' mastery of everything they teach, you are 100 percent correct. (If you scored less than 100 percent correct, try harder.) Some educators become bitten by the testing bug and believe that teachers need to test everything they teach. That is a practical impossibility, unless teachers want to dramatically reduce what they teach so there's time available for all the assessment that would be required. But that would be silly.

If the results of student assessments are really going to influence the instructional decisions that teachers make, then the teacher should not be overwhelmed by too much assessment data. Teachers who collect too much assessment evidence are likely to be influenced by none of it. Think about a zealous elementary school teacher who has the instructional responsibility for students' growth in all subjects. Now let's suppose that our zealous elementary teacher tries to assess student mastery of about 10 objectives in each of the following subjects: language arts, mathematics, social studies, science, art, music, and physical education. That would be about 70 objectives, each of which should be represented by a reasonably well-described assessment domain. And students' status with respect to each of those 70 assessment domains would need to be measured, in a given year, for each of the teacher's students. That's much too much measurement. That amount of measurement could move an otherwise mentally healthy teacher into psychotic la-la land.

Even if a hyper-compulsive teacher assesses students with respect to all 70 objectives, it's unlikely that the teacher would be able to make any *instructional sense* out of the assessment evidence. These would be excessive evidence; the teacher would be cerebrally swamped. It is much more reasonable for the teacher to isolate only a *small* number of

Curriculum

The ends, that is, the learning objectives sought for students.

the most important objectives per subject area, then assess students with respect to those objectives. Teachers will be instructionally influenced by test results that they can intellectually digest. With too many assessment domains, teachers will soon discover that an oversupply of assessment is undigestible.

In determining what to teach, teachers will usually rely on their own subject-matter expertise as well as the subject-matter expertise of others. At this point the teacher is

Educational Leaders
Look at Assessment

Test Scores and Educational Decisions

W. Richard Bull, Jr.
Assistant Superintendent of Administration & Human Resources
Accomack County School Board
Accomac, Virginia

Student performances on educational tests influence a school administrator's decisions in a number of areas. One of these is *student scheduling.* Low student test scores may require more remedial courses, while high student test scores may necessitate additional advanced placement courses. Test scores can also dictate if a course is taught as a semester-course or as a year-long course. Test scores also influence whether a course needs to be offered in summer school or at night. The sequencing of courses may also be affected by student performance on assessments.

Curriculum is a second area affected by test scores. Course content must often be adjusted to meet the state testing mandates. What's covered in those tests needs to be addressed in our curriculum. Our instructional strategies must also be reviewed after analyzing test scores because the use of too much lecture or too little conceptual thinking will adversely affect student performance.

Instructional material decisions are also based, at least to some extent, on students' test performances. Low scores may require the purchase of a new textbook series and related materials. The current emphasis on technology requires additional "state of the art" computer labs. We need to align our technology with what's to be assessed.

Personnel decisions are sometimes related to the student performance on educational assessments. A lower pupil-teacher ratio may be beneficial for a teacher who is having instructional difficulties as reflected by students' test scores. Low test scores may emphasize the need for providing staff development, especially for teachers who work with heterogeneous and remedial classes.

Finally, there's the effect that students' test performances have on *budgetary decisions.* All of the aforementioned areas significantly impact a school division's budget. Additional instructional personnel, new textbook adoptions, and technology are expensive. In fact, any of these areas may have such a large impact on a budget that a phase-in over several budget years is often necessary.

It's no stretch of reality to say that students' test performances can have an impact on almost everything that goes on in a school district. That's certainly true in our district. ●

engaging in the determination of *curriculum*, that is, the isolation of the learning objectives or *ends* to be sought for children. It is through *instruction*, that is, the means designed to accomplish those ends, that the teacher hopes students will learn.

Instruction

The means, that is, the teaching activities, intended to accomplish curricular ends.

Now, when selecting curriculum, that is, age-appropriate instructional objectives, skillful teachers will turn to a variety of sources such as state or district curricular documents, the content standards devised by national organizations, or the recommendations of thoughtful individuals such as the Core Curriculum advocated by E. D. Hirsch and his associates.[3] It's even okay for the teacher to review the sorts of outcomes that are aimed at by textbooks. But, after sifting through the various recommendations of others, the teacher will still need to decide what instructional objectives to pursue once the classroom door has been closed. Again, I urge a "less is more" assessment approach wherein only small numbers of genuinely salient objectives are assessed. Just because a curricular expert thinks teachers need to teach "everything," that doesn't mean teachers need to do so, and it surely doesn't mean teachers have to test even half of "everything."

It is possible, then, to build pretests that cover (1) key assessment domains based on the chosen high import objectives, and (2) any prerequisite *en route* or *enabling* skills and/or knowledge that students will need for those objectives. Similar progress-monitoring assessments can be devised so that, along the way, students can be measured to see at what point the teacher can stop instructing toward a given objective. Any project-monitoring assessments, clearly, must be based on the objectives currently being pursued by the teacher.

The major instructional yield from properly formulated assessment domains, as will be described in Chapter 3, will be the clarity they can provide to the teacher regarding where the instruction ought to be heading. A well-described assessment domain, and the test that represents it, serve to *operationalize* an instructional objective that, otherwise, might be too ambiguous for effective instructional decision-making.

Putting It All Together

Decisions, Interpretations, and Content

As you have seen, there are three major steps that must be taken in deciding what to assess and how to interpret assessment results. First, educators must determine what sort of decision is at issue. Three kinds of decisions were considered in the chapter, namely, decisions focused on selection, evaluation, and instruction. Second, educators must decide whether a relative or absolute interpretation of students' test results will be most useful. Finally, likely content sources for an assessment must be considered so that tasks eliciting students' knowledge, skills, and/or affect can be incorporated into the assessment instrument.

The manner in which the second step (determining the type of interpretation) and the third step (determining content) interact should be briefly mentioned. If a norm-referenced interpretation is to be made, then there is less need for tight definition of assessment domains than would be the case if criterion-referenced interpretations are to be made. Because criterion-referenced interpretations depend so directly on a clear explication of what students can or can't do, well delineated assessment domains are a must. But for norm-referenced interpretations, as long as the assessment domain is

Educational Leaders Look at Assessment

What Students Should Learn—And How Well?

Rebecca S. Christian
Director of Student Assessment
Louisiana Department of Education
Baton Rouge, Louisiana

On a Spring evening not too long ago, I watched a television interview with Louisiana State University baseball coach, Skip Bertman. The sportscaster questioned the team's ability to deliver on a winning season. Coach Bertman responded by saying, "I have high expectations and will not accept a low reality." I jotted down those words which communicated his belief in the team that would later become the winners of the collegiate world series. For me this statement articulated the philosophy that all Louisiana educators must endorse as we complete the task of establishing standards for the 21st century. High expectations for our students must be adopted despite the reality of statistics that rank our state at or near the bottom (e.g., a high percentage of school age children in poverty, low scores on the State Comparison National Assessment of Educational Progress).

In Louisiana, setting expectations is a multi-step process. First, teachers must collaboratively identify curricular expectations in order to initiate more rigorous content standards. Once these standards have been established, advisory committees of classroom teachers and curriculum specialists play an instrumental role in test development by reviewing test and item specifications for accuracy. The test specifications are used to create the actual test items and advisors are asked to react to this test development process by reviewing the items for content bias and making recommendations to improve the questions. Teachers' committees are involved in finalizing the item banks after field test data are reviewed and ultimately participate in setting the performance standards or passing scores for the test.

While other groups may also participate in determining the standards, the expectations of educators will always be a critical consideration. These expectations must not be based on low reality issues but, instead, on the belief that all students should be able to meet 21st century Standards. A decade ago when

Louisiana educators established standards for the Graduation Exit Exam, they defined reasonably difficult content parameters for the test, but low expectations influenced the passing scores. Much of the data used to recommend the standard was based on teacher perception data. At the time of the field test, teachers were asked to record their perception of each student's expected performance. This information was used to plot scores for attainer and non-attainer groups as identified by the teacher perception data. A statistical determination of the most efficient point with which to separate the two groups resulted in establishing a common cutoff score to be consistent from one test administration to another. Predictions of student attainment rates indicated that up to 35 percent of students would fail one or more components of the Exam at that standard of performance. Policymakers, concerned about high failure rates, agreed with the Department's recommendation that the low passing scores be adopted for the interim on the basis that the standard be revisited within a two to three year period.

The momentum that accompanies high stakes testing resulted in teachers' emphasizing important skills with carefully designed strategies and students' being receptive to learning because of the significance of a passing score on all components of the Exam as a graduation requirement. Due to the positive impact, scores for the initial year of testing were far better than predicted by the teacher perception data. A review of the standards never occurred, because a legal challenge was filed regarding the constitutionality of the test requirement for public school students. The State Board was reluctant to make changes until legal issues were resolved. By that time, plans were being developed to redesign the entire state program including the Graduation Exit Exam.

Certainly the process for establishing teacher levels of expectations can be improved upon. As performance standards for the 21st century assessments are determined, the following recommendations will be incorporated:

- Involve a cross-section of citizens in all steps of the process
- Use operational test data rather than field test data to set the cut scores
- Apply several standard setting approaches to determine the accuracy of the standard
- Adopt a schedule for periodically revising cut scores

In the final analysis, the standard-setters and policymakers may find the key to a successful state-level effort is high expectations on the part of educators and their refusal to accept a low reality. ●

reasonably congruent with what is being assessed, sensible comparisons can be made among students' test scores. And that's what's really important for such relative interpretations. Thus, content selections should always be influenced not only by the decision at issue, but by the kind of score-based interpretation to be made.

A Tabular Representation

High-Stakes Tests

Assessments used to make important decisions about students or reflect the effectiveness of educators.

In an attempt to help you synthesize the mound of stuff that's been addressed in this chapter, I've tried to represent the whole works in Table 2.1. As you can see, for each major decision focus there are two subcategories, and each of these subcategories is associated with the interpretation most likely to be made about students' status. For each of these interpretative alternatives, there is a likely content source that can be used to help identify the knowledge, skills, or affect that the actual assessment will contain. Take your time in figuring out how to use Table 2.1. It's the only table in the chapter, and it will feel unloved if you don't lavish a bit of attention on it.

Clearly, the level of effort that is devoted to the determination of what should be measured is directly linked to the importance of the uses to which the test results will be put. If the purpose of the assessment is exclusively to help a classroom teacher try to do a good instructional job, then there would need to be far less attention given to the isolation of tested content than would be required for a *high stakes* test, such as a state-level test to be used for diploma-denial.

Chapter Wrap-Up

It's time to conclude this chapter by providing responses to the chapter's guiding questions. Because each of those guiding questions was addressed at nontrivial length in the chapter itself, authorial compassion requires the wrap-up answers to those questions to be accurate, *but terse*. And, come to think of it, a terse and accurate answer to a question is, by definition, a *pithy* answer. Hence, prepare for a bit of chapter-ending pithiness.

TABLE 2.1. Factors to consider in deciding what to measure		
DECISION FOCUS	**DOMINANT INTERPRETATION**	**CONTENT SOURCE**
Selection		
Fixed-Quota	Relative	Empirical Predictors
Requisite Skill/Knowledge	Absolute	Expert Judgment
Evaluation		
Instructional Evaluation	Absolute	What *Should* Be Taught
Student Grading	Relative or Absolute	What *Has* Been Taught
Instruction		
What to Teach	Absolute	Age-appropirate Objectives
How Long to Teach	Absolute	Current Objectives

What should educators measure?

When determining the content to include on a test, that is, the items and/or exercises designed to measure the knowledge, skills, or affect to be assessed, educators can be guided by a consideration of what's treated in textbooks, what's recommended in sets of content standards or curriculum guides, and the teachers' own content knowledge. However, because such sources will usually yield substantially more potential content than can realistically be assessed in the time available for instruction and assessment, the determination of content to be assessed by a test is considerably more difficult than many educational leaders recognize. If students' performances on tests are to yield accurate inferences about students' status with respect to the assessment domains represented by those tests, considerable care must be expended on the selection of appropriate content. Educational leaders, having recognized the difficulty of identifying what tests should measure, must devote sufficient time and resources to this important undertaking.

How should educators interpret assessment results?

A *relative* interpretation of students' test results requires educators to make a comparative or *norm-referenced* inference about a student's performance. For such an inference, a given student's score is contrasted with the performances of students in a comparison group. An *absolute* interpretation of students' test results requires educators to make a *criterion-referenced* inference about a student's performance. For such an inference, a given student's score is described according to the proportion of the assessment domain (represented by the test) that the student has mastered.

Educational leaders must understand that the nature of the inference to be made about students' test performances will usually play a key role in determining what kinds of content should be included in the test itself. Although there are a limited number of instances in which students' test performances can be interpreted in both an absolute and relative manner, more often than not one of these two interpretive alternatives should be chosen.

What kinds of educational decisions should be influenced by assessment results?

Three prominent types of educational decision should be influenced by students' assessment results. First, there are *selection* decisions in which some students must be chosen from a larger group of students. One kind of selection decision occurs in a *fixed-quota* setting where there are more applicants than openings. Another form of selection decision takes place in a *requisite-skill/knowledge* setting where those students selected must possess either skills and/or knowledge thought to be necessary.

A second type of educational decision to be influenced by students' assessment results focuses on *evaluation. Instructional evaluation,* one form of evaluative decision-making, involves a determination of the effectiveness of instructional programs or teachers. A second form of evaluative decision-making occurs when *student grading* takes place.

Decisions regarding the day-to-day particulars of *instruction* constitute a third type of educational decision that can be better made by consulting students' test performances. Although there are numerous ways that classroom teachers can use students' assessment performances to make more defensible instructional decisions, two of the most prominent kinds of instructional decision-making occur when the teacher attempts to decide *what to teach* and *how long to teach it.*

How can educators use their choices about decision options and interpretation alternatives to choose appropriate assessment content?

The actual content of an assessment instrument, that is, the tasks to which students must respond, can best be determined by a three-step process in which educators (1) identify the decision at issue, (2) choose the appropriate way to interpret students' assessment results, and (3) identify likely sources of content. A tabular scheme to assist in this three-step process was provided in Table 2.1. The importance of the purpose(s) underlying the assessment should play a major role in determining how much attention must be given to the determination of what should be measured. Because educational measurement calls for educators to make inferences about the assessment-domain status of students based on how these students respond to the content of educational tests, it is apparent that educational leaders need to focus ample attention on the question of "what to measure."

Practice Exercises

Part A

Let's get underway with some relatively straightforward exercises in which you must identify what kinds of assessment interpretations are being made by fictitious educators. (Fictitious educators are al-

ways the best kind. They sue less.) Read each of the following items, then decide whether that item's make-believe educator has arrived at (a) an absolute interpretation, (b) a relative interpretation, (c) both a relative and an absolute interpretation, or (d) neither a relative nor an absolute interpretation.

1. Harry Higgins, affable sixth-grade teacher, has given his students a major social studies examination covering a semester's worth of social studies content. On reviewing his students' test results, he calls one of his students, Marvin, to his desk and informs him, "Your test performance, Marvin, was truly magnificent; you appear to know more than 97 percent of the social studies content I taught this year." (*a, b, c,* or *d?*)

2. H. C. Hoover, meticulous midwest high school math teacher, has reviewed his students' mathematics scores on the spring administration of the *Iowa Tests of Basic Skills.* He tells Melinda, one of the students he thought was quite weak, "You scored at the 48th percentile on the *ITBS* math section, Melinda. That means your math performance is as good as approximately half the math students in the United States. From now on, I'm going to expect stronger performances from you in my class!" (*a, b, c,* or *d?*)

3. Coretta Kline teaches remedial mathematics in a suburban middle school. She gives weekly 10-item quizzes in her class, then urges students to add together, over the course of a semester, the number of items they have answered correctly. (Although some students, especially those who can't add, have difficulty with this summation activity, most students like to see how they have performed cumulatively on the weekly quizzes.) Last week, Coretta took one of her students aside and said, "You scored high on this week's quiz, Jonathan; you answered all 10 items correctly!" (*a, b, c,* or *d?*)

4. The Assistant Superintendent for Instruction at the district office, Marvella Mergins, has spent considerable time reviewing students' test performances on a district-developed achievement examination in elementary school science. She supplies each of the district's 14 elementary school principals with an individualized report similar to the following: "The average performance of students in your school on the district's 50-item science test was 31.2 items correct. That score was equivalent to a districtwide school-by-school percentile of 78.

The mean score indicates that your students have mastered slightly more than 60 percent of the scientific skills and knowledge constituting the assessment domain covered by the district science test." (*a, b, c,* or *d?*)

5. Felipé Fogosto, a high school English teacher, has prepared an extensive list of 50 common mechanical errors often made by students when they engage in written communication. Although Felipé assesses his students' composition skills by having them write actual essays, letters, and so on, he also wants students "to know the 50 errors." His test calls for students to state, from memory, either in writing or orally, as many of the "Fifty Writing Foul-Ups" as students can remember. Felipé tells Gerald about the results of last week's written test: "Gerald, you were able to describe 45 of the 50 mechanical foul-ups; you've mastered 90 percent of the eligible content." (*a, b, c,* or *d?*)

Part B

This second set of exercises is intended to give you practice in coupling an educator's intended use of test results with the kind of interpretation that should be made of students' test performances. For each of the following situations, decide whether a norm-referenced or criterion-referenced interpretation would be better. You'll need to focus on the specific kind of decision that's at issue, then choose an appropriate interpretive alternative. If you need to, a quick review of Table 2.1 before undertaking this set of exercises wouldn't be all that inane.

6. A special magnet high school emphasizing science and mathematics has been constructed in your district. The school's dazzling new building, loaded with all sorts of scientific whistles and bells, unfortunately, can only accommodate 400 students. Yet there are 1,400 students whose parents have signed up their children for the new magnet school. Admissions to the school will be chiefly determined on the basis of student performances on a state-developed

math–science examination administered to all the state's eighth-grade students. What kind of results-based interpretation would be best?

7. A federal funding program has awarded your district with $250,000 to be used in *one* elementary school (as stipulated in the federal authorizing legislation) to bolster children's reading skills. The program calls for the district to select the lowest performing school based on whatever nationally standardized achievement test is currently used in the district. In your district, the School Board has decided that the *Stanford Achievement Tests* will be administered to all students each spring. What kind of interpretation should be given to each school's reading comprehension performance on those standardized tests?

8. Suppose you are a principal of an elementary school that has been directed to accept nearly 100 students from an adjacent school district that's been closed down by a state-appointed school-closure commission. Because students' records from the old district are pretty skimpy, you ask your teachers to give each of the students a pretest, early in the school year, to identify the entering students' current achievement levels. How should you guide your school's teachers in the interpretation of the new students' performances? In other words, what kind of score-based inferences should you encourage your school's teachers to make?

9. Your school district has created an elaborate new computer-based social studies program that students can complete at their own pace. The program features heavy use of historically based films and videos. Students love the new program and try to be assigned to it. However, before any student is permitted to enroll in the new program, a computer proficiency test must be passed to demonstrate that the student can profit educationally from the program. The proficiency test is partly paper-and-pencil and partly performance-based whereby students must display their computer skills while being observed by a computer-skilled parent aide. What kind of interpretation should be made about students' performances on the computer proficiency test?

10. Your school district's governing board has adopted the voluntary content standards and performance standards developed by your state's department of education. One of the key content standards calls for students to be able to write effectively. A detailed scoring scheme has been developed by the state to be used in judging the quality of students' written communication skills. Near the close of each school year, all students are obliged to compose a piece of writing, on a particular topic, that is addressed to a specified reader. Students are allowed three class periods for this activity so that there are opportunities for prewriting activities as well as for revisions of drafts.

What the district school board really wants to see is a striking increase in the number of students who achieve a rating of at least 4.0 on a five-point, that is, 1.0 (low) to 5.0 (high) scale. What sort of interpretation should be given to the students' end-of-year written compositions?

Answers to Practice Exercises

Part A

1. Harry's score interpretation is clearly an absolute one. You should have chosen *a*. But if Harry really wanted to make an accurate inference, he should have informed Marvin that he "appeared to have learned 97 percent of the social studies content represented by the examination." As suggested in the chapter, most exams represent less than 100 percent of everything that teachers teach. If teachers spell out clearly what is in the assessment domains their

tests are supposed to represent, then the absolute inferences they make regarding the meaning of students' test performances will be more illuminating. And, of course, if teachers spell out clearly what is in their assessment domains, this set of "What's *eligible* to be assessed" information can yield instructional dividends if communicated to students prior to or during the instructional process.

2. Mr. Hoover was making a relative inference regarding Melinda's test performance when he stated his conclusion about her performance compared with that of the national norm group. If you didn't choose *b*, your performance on this exercise-item was *absolutely*, not *relatively*, klucko.

3. Coretta's interpretation was really nothing more than telling Jonathan what his raw score was. There really wasn't an interpretation beyond that. She didn't relate the 10 out of 10 to any kind of assessment domain. You should have chosen *d*. (This was a tough practice item because there's no inference being made—none at all.)

4. Marvella provided the district principals with both a relative interpretation (78th percentile) and an absolute interpretation (about 60 percent of the assessment domain mastered). You should have opted for *c*. This item, although fraught with fictionality, illustrates how tests representing well-described assessment domains can yield useful norm-referenced *and* criterion-referenced interpretations.

5. Felipé's test-based inference was an absolute, criterion-referenced one. You should have chosen *a*.

Part B

6. This would be a fixed-quota setting in which norm-referenced interpretations are needed. Hopefully, the students who get into the math–science magnet school will, among other things, spend a bit of time studying magnets.

7. This is another case in which norm-referenced interpretations would be preferable. What is needed is a decision about the single, worst performing school. That's an instance of a fixed-quota situation, and one in which relative interpretations of each school's average test scores should be made.

8. Because the school's teachers will, for purposes of making instructional decisions, need to know the precise nature of the new students' knowledge and skills, what's needed in this situation is a set of criterion-referenced interpretations.

9. This is a requisite-skill/knowledge selection setting and, as such, criterion-referenced interpretations are most appropriate.

10. This is an instance of instructional evaluation. The district school board members should be more interested in the actual level of students' writing skills rather than in how students compare to one another. What's called for here, then, are criterion-referenced interpretations of students' written compositions.

DISCUSSION QUESTIONS

1. One of the key concepts dealt with in the chapter revolved around the distinction between norm-referenced (relative) and criterion-referenced (absolute) interpretations of students' test performances. Calling on your personal understanding of these two interpretive alternatives, think about classroom teachers, district superintendents, and local school board members. For each of these three positions, which (if either) of the two interpretive alternatives should be used more frequently?

2. Assume that you've been called on, during an evening meeting of elementary school parents, to explain to parents the difference between norm- and criterion-referenced test interpretations. (I could have asked you to give your explanation to a group of high school parents at an evening meeting, but you might end up talking in an empty room!) Using the kind of language that would be *understandable to laypeople*, how would you explain the difference between norm-referenced and criterion-referenced test interpretations?

3. What kinds of educational assessments require that only modest energy be devoted to identifying suitable content for the assessments? Can you give examples? What kinds of educational assessments require substantial energy in identifying suitable content for the assessments? Can you give examples?

4. In the chapter, it was contended that educators typically won't be able to choose what's to be measured in their tests simply by relying on the sets of content standards developed by national subject-matter specialists. Do you agree or disagree? If so, why? If not, why not? (If you don't have a position on this issue, get one.)

5. Suppose you are an elementary school principal who wants to work with your school's teachers to help them decide, more defensibly, what to measure in their assessments. Before you begin, however, you try to find out what sources your school's teachers currently rely on when they're trying to isolate assessment content. What do you think you'd find? Would you encounter any differences if you were a high school principal and you were working with high school teachers?

SUGGESTIONS FOR ADDITIONAL READING

Berk, Ronald A., (Ed.). *Criterion-Referenced Measurement: The State of the Art.* Baltimore: Johns Hopkins University Press, 1980.

Cunningham, George K. *Assessment in the Classroom: Constructing and Interpreting Tests.* Washington, DC: Falmer Press, 1998.

Flanagan, Dawn, P., Judy L. Genshaft, and Patti L. Harrison (Eds.). *Contemporary Intellectual Assessment: Theories, Tests, and Issues.* New York: Guilford, 1997.

Glaser, Robert. "The Instructional Technology and the Measurement of Learning Outcomes: Some Questions." *American Psychologist, 18,* 7 (August 1963), 519–521.

Glaser, Robert. "Instructional Technology and the Measurement of Learning Outcomes: Some Questions." *Educational Measurement: Issues and Practice, 13,* 4 (Winter 1994): 6–8.

Hirsch, E. D., Jr. *The Schools We Need: And Why We Don't Have Them.* New York: Doubleday, 1996.

Impara, James C., and Barbara S. Plake (Eds.), Linda L. Murphy (Managing Ed.). *13th Mental Measurements Yearbook.* Lincoln, NE: Buros Institute of Mental Measurements, 1998.

Impara, James C., and Barbara S. Plake (Eds.), Linda L. Murphy (Managing Ed.). *Tests in Print V.* Lincoln, NE: Buros Institute of Mental Measurements, 1999.

Jervis, Kathe, and Joseph McDonald. "Standards: The Philosophical Monster in the Classroom." *Phi Delta Kappan, 77,* 8 (April 1996): 563–569.

Linn, Robert L., and Norman E. Gronlund. *Measurement and Assessment in Teaching* (7th ed.). Upper Saddle River, NJ: Prentice-Hall, 1995.

Marzano, Robert J., and John S. Kendall. *A Comprehensive Guide to Designing Standards-Based Districts, Schools, and Classrooms.* Aurora, CO: McREL (Mid-Continent Regional Educational Laboratory), 1996.

McMillan, James H. *Classroom Assessment: Principles and Practice for Effective Instruction.* Boston, MA: Allyn and Bacon, 1997.

Shepard, Lorrie. *Measuring Achievement: What Does It Mean to Test for Robust Understanding?* In "William Angoff Memorial Lecture Series." Princeton, NJ: Educational Testing Service, October 1997.

AND FOR THOSE WHO TIRE OF READING

Association for Supervision and Curriculum Development. *On Multiple Intelligences & Education with Howard Gardner* (Audiotape: Stock #295056S62). Alexandria, VA: Author, 1995.

Association for Supervision and Curriculum Development. *Multiple Intelligences Series* (Videotape: Stock #495003S62). Alexandria, VA: Author, 1995.

Northwest Regional Laboratory. *Seeing with New Eyes* (Videotape #NREL-17). Los Angeles: IOX Assessment Associates.

Popham, W. James. *Criterion-Referenced Measurement: Today's Alternative to Traditional Testing* (Videotape #ETVT-35). Los Angeles: IOX Assessment Associates.

Popham, W. James. *Norm-Referenced Tests: Uses and Misuses* (Videotape #ETVT-32). Los Angeles: IOX Assessment Associates.

Popham, W. James. *A Parent's Guide to Standardized Tests* (Videotape #ETVT-34). Los Angeles: IOX Assessment Associates.

ENDNOTES

1. Although Glaser used the expression *criterion-referenced measurement* for the first time in a chapter coauthored one year earlier with David Klaus, it was his 1963 article that caught the attention of the educational community. The earlier coauthored piece was Robert Glaser and David J. Klaus, "Proficiency Measurements: Assessment Human Performance," in *Psychological Principles in Systems Development,* ed. Robert M. Gagne (New York: Holt, Rinehart and Winston, 1962), pp. 419–474. The 1963 essay that stimulated the interest in criterion-referenced measurement was Robert Glaser, "Instructional Technology and the Measurement of Learning Outcomes: Some Questions," *American Psychologist,* 18 (1963), 519–521. Because of its landmark qualities, the diligent reader should consult Glaser's 1963 remarks. It is a widely reprinted essay, for example, in W. James Popham, ed., *Criterion-Referenced Measurement: An Introduction* (Englewood Cliffs, NJ: Educational Technology Publications, 1971), pp. 5–14.

2. Technically, the "awarding" of grades makes it sound as though teachers are dispensing some sort of prizes or honors when they dish out grades. I can recall giving students a good many Ds and Fs. But in no case do I remember the recipients of those low grades believing they were being given *awards.*

3. Core Knowledge Sequence: Content Guidelines for Grades K–8, Core Knowledge Foundation, Charlottesville, VA, 1998.

How to Evaluate Educational Assessments

Educators these days, it seems, are almost surrounded by tests. Tests appear to be lurking around every educational corner.

Some of these tests are good ones. If good tests are used by educators, then students will usually benefit. However, not all the tests out there are good ones. And bad tests, if used by educators, will not benefit students. This second part of the book is intended to help educational leaders distinguish between assessments that are beneficial and those that are not.

There are five chapters in Part Two. Each chapter focuses on an important factor to use if an educational leader wants to evaluate an assessment device. And that's likely because today's educational leaders will often find it necessary to judge the merits of a given measurement instrument.

In a traditional measurement textbook, a consideration of what to look for in an educational test would almost always be initiated by an explanation of *validity* and *reliability*, the twin towers of traditional psychometries. There's no question about the importance of validity (Are test-based interpretations accurate?) or reliability (Is the measurement consistent?). But before dealing with validity in Chapter 4 and reliability in Chapter 5, you're first going to deal in Chapter 3 with a more educationally relevant factor that educational leaders should employ when evaluating tests, namely, the *instructional contribution* of an assessment device. The placement of instructional contribution as the leadoff factor in the following five chapters is intended to emphasize its importance. Tests that don't help children learn better are tests that shouldn't be used.

The final two chapters in Part Two deal with *absence of bias* and *comparative data*. Test bias is a key consideration in the appraisal of all assessments, educational or otherwise. Finally, the quality of the comparative data accompanying a test is especially important when educators need to make norm-referenced interpretations.

The five chapters in Part Two are really important ones (he said, trying to add a bit of motivational muscle). Educational leaders will need to evaluate the assessments that they'll encounter almost daily. Part Two's five chapters will help you do a defensible job of appraising these tests. Based on the five evaluative factors described in the next five chapters, an educational leader could come up with a readily usable five-factor framework for evaluating educational tests. Certain of the factors always apply. Certain of the factors apply only in certain situations. You won't know which are which until you've read with diligence Chapters 3 through 7.

Part two

An Invitation to an Appendix

On several occasions as you read through Part Two's five chapters, you'll encounter the use of some basic statistical notions such as means, standard deviations, or correlation coefficients. Even though in this book's 15 chapters I've tried to reduce such number-nudging to an absolute minimum, there will always be a few instances in which an educational leader is likely to run into such statistical concepts.

Frankly, because many people are intimidated by statistical calculations, even if those calculations are no more complicated than determining the midpoint of a set of test scores, I'd prefer to leave any sort of statistical stuff out of this book. Statistical concepts constitute only a teensy-weensy part of what an educational leader needs to know about educational measurement. Unfortunately, that teensy-weensy segment of the measurement game, if not understood at all, can sometimes lead to confusion.

So, I've tried to dodge this dilemma by providing you with an *absolutely optional* Appendix commencing on page 427. The Appendix describes the rudimentary statistics needed to evaluate educational tests. You don't need to read the Appendix as far as I'm concerned. (If you're using this book in a course and the instructor says, "Read the Appendix," I suspect you'd best comply. After all, I'm not giving out course grades.)

The Appendix attempts to provide readers with an intuitive understanding of (1) graphic data displays such as bar graphs, (2) indicators of central tendency such as the median, (3) indicators of variability such as the standard deviation, and (4) indicators of relationship such as the correlation coefficient. Now, if you've already completed an introductory statistics course, there's probably no need to even flip through the Appendix, unless you need a quick review. But if you've never completed an introductory statistics class, you really ought to wade through the wonders of the Appendix. Let me explain why.

As you've probably already discerned, I believe that educational leaders dare not allow assessments to be carried out exclusively by assessment folks. The decisions resulting from the use of educational tests impinge too directly on educators' activities. But if educational leaders create a world in which anything statistical is, to them, "off limits," then there will be times when those educational leaders will simply have to accept, without comprehension, the choices made by "statistically literate" measurement specialists. That situation is unacceptable.

At least at an intuitive level, today's educational leaders need to understand the purpose of such statistical indices as correlation coefficients and means. Educational leaders need to know that a normal distribution is not a distribution without need of psychotherapy. As indicated earlier, at several points in Chapters 3 through 7, you'll find that statistical concepts pop up. To get the most out of Part Two, there'll be times when you really ought to understand the basic statistical ideas now waiting patiently for you in the Appendix.

The need for intuitive understandings about a small set of statistical concepts does not signify that educational leaders will ever actually have to calculate a correlation coefficient or compute a standard deviation. It's perfectly acceptable for educational leaders to get other, more numerically nimble folks to perform such calculations. But educational leaders really ought to be comfortable in *understanding* what's meant when a school board member raises a question about "the correlation between students' test results and results on the district-adopted standardized tests."

So, I suggest that you page through the Appendix located between page 427 and page 456. If you find that its contents are incomprehensible, study the Appendix as if it were a main-line chapter. If you find the contents are decisively old hat, then skip that puppy altogether. One of the most charming aspects of optional book parts is that you can exercise your option.

chapter 3

Instructional Contribution

- Are all educational assessments instructionally relevant?

- How have educational assessments usually been evaluated?

  The Perspective of Measurement Traditionalists

  Impact of the Accountability Movement

  An Altered Role for Educational Leaders

- How can educational assessments make an instructional contribution?

  Target Instructional Domains and Educational Assessments

  Focusing Instruction on the Domain Being Assessed rather than the Assessment

- Should assessments be developed before or after instructional planning?

- What kinds of test-preparation activities are appropriate and what kinds aren't?

Ⓐll educational tests, if they are worth using, should make a contribution to the quality of education that children receive. In fact, *most* educational tests should make a direct contribution to the *instruction* children receive. In other words, most educational assessments really ought to help teachers do a better job of teaching.

Let me clarify what I mean about testing's contribution to *education* versus its contribution to *instruction*. There are some assessment instruments that are supposed to help educators make better decisions about students, but decisions that are not instructional in nature. For instance, a high school counselor might want to get a fix on a student's vocational interests in order to supply that student with more astute advice regarding what kind of job to seek when school's finished. The counselor could have the student fill out some sort of vocational interest inventory in order to better counsel the student. Now the vocational interest inventory, if it is any good, may make a contribution to the student's overall *education*—perhaps by helping the student choose more job-relevant courses in high school—but the vocational interest inventory would not, strictly speaking, make a contribution to the classroom *instruction* that the student receives.

Another example of an educationally relevant but instructionally irrelevant assessment would be a legislatively mandated statewide test that is to be used by policymakers in the awarding of extra funds to the state's schools. As educational leaders carry out their educational leading, they might encounter a small number of assessment instruments that, although educationally relevant, really have no bearing on the day-to-day instruction that's provided to children.

But suppose you were somehow magically able to stack up all the tests that a mythical graduating high school senior had been obliged to take since strolling into kindergarten. And, because you are already into a magical and mythical mood, imagine that you could actually stack all those tests into a single, high, subtly swaying, but sufficiently stable pile. I'd be willing to argue that more than 95 percent of that tottering tower of tests could have made a direct contribution to the classroom *instruction* that your mythical student received. In short, I believe that all but a few educational measuring instruments *should* have a direct and positive impact on classroom instruction.

And if I'm correct, or even if I'm only half correct, this means that one evaluative factor by which educational leaders ought to judge tests is by the contribution those tests make to the quality of instruction that teachers provide. And that, unsurprisingly, is what this chapter is about.

A New Test-Evaluation Factor

After excluding the small proportion of educational assessments that are not supposed to make a direct contribution to instruction, I suggest that educational leaders make a test's *instructional contribution* the most important factor to be used in judging the test's quality. The degree to which an assessment will help teachers design and deliver better instruction should become your *dominant* consideration when appraising an educational assessment. If an educational assessment will help a teacher's instructional decision-making, that assessment passes this new litmus test; if it doesn't help a teacher's instructional decision-making, the assessment flops.

What you need to realize is that this recommended emphasis on a test's instructional contribution does not mesh with the customary way that educators have been told to evaluate tests—far from it. Traditionally, measurement experts have directed educators to appraise tests chiefly on the basis of two psychometrically sanctioned factors, namely, *validity* and *reliability*. Validity refers to the accuracy of test-based interpretations and reliability refers to the consistency of measurement. Both of these concepts are important. Both need to be understood by educational leaders. You'll learn all you need to know about validity and reliability in the next two chapters. But validity and reliability are *not* the most important factors by which to appraise educational tests. The most important factor by which to judge educational tests is the instructional contribution those tests are likely to make.

You need to recognize that what's being advocated here is a mild form of measurement heresy. Measurement specialists have been touting the importance of validity and reliability for so many years that most educators, when asked about how to judge a test's quality, will almost knee-jerkishly respond that validity and reliability are at the top of the test-evaluation list. Indeed, if you are reading this book as part of a graduate program intended to qualify you for a position of educational leadership, you can be almost certain that most already established educational leaders, if they learned how to evaluate assessments in a traditional measurement course, will have been directed to use conventional ways of evaluating assessments. And conventional ways of evaluating educational assessments place *no importance* on an assessment's instructional contribution. Let me explain why.

A measurement maven's perspective. The individuals who created our current assessment technology were a talented group of people—most of whom had a decidedly quantitative bent. Many of today's psychometric superstars—let's think of them as measurement mavens—actually appear to derive some sort of perverse pleasure from dwelling among numbers. (I know many of today's educational measurement experts, and at least 65 percent of them are, otherwise, normal.)

Educational measurement experts, tracing back to World War I's *Army Alpha*, have been consumed by the drive to create assessment instruments that accurately and consistently determine an individual's skill, knowledge, or affect. That was the mission of educational measurement specialists: They wanted to do a wonderful job of measuring. When they'd measured whatever they were measuring, they'd turn the results over to educators whose job it would then be to use those results for whatever purpose seemed suitable. In a real sense, the measurement specialist's task was to *measure*, not *use* the results of that measurement. Accordingly, we've had several generations of educational measurement mavens who perceived their responsibilities to cease as soon as accurate and reliable measurements had been made.

I am not faulting educational measurement specialists. They did their job superlatively, and to this day continue to refine the assessment techniques by which educators can secure ever more precise inferences about students' knowledge, skills, and affect. But, you must understand—really understand—that, for the most part, educational measurement people really have not been attentive to the instructional impact of the assessment devices they were creating. That was someone else's job. As far as educational measurement experts were concerned, measurement folks measured; teacher folks taught. To be truthful with you, most measurement experts don't know squat about instruction. It's no wonder that they scurry away from a test's instructional implications.

The game changes. But then, in the 1970s, state legislative bodies began to enact laws requiring students to pass tests in order to demonstrate that the state's students possessed sufficient knowledge and skills. Often, important contingencies were tied to these legislatively required tests. Sometimes, for example, students had to pass particular tests before being awarded a high school diploma or before being promoted to the next grade. The era of *educational accountability* had definitely rumbled onto the scene.

The key feature of the educational accountability movement was the installation of state-mandated student testing. The purpose of this testing was patently clear. Legislators did not believe that public school educators were doing their job effectively. There were too many reports of high school graduates who couldn't fill out job application forms or read a grocery list. State legislatures, one by one, enacted laws calling for mandated student testing. The legislators wanted *evidence* that students were learning as well as they should be learning.

Thus, educational assessments that, for a half-century, had simply been used to identify students' skills or knowledge were soon transformed into *quality-monitoring tools*. If a state's students performed well on these state-imposed tests, usually administered annually, the state's educators were regarded as successful. If a state's students performed poorly on the tests, the opposite conclusion was reached.

Educators definitely were not the originators of these accountability tests. Rather, accountability tests were imposed on the education profession by an incredulous citizenry, that is, a citizenry doubtful about whether its tax dollars were being well spent on schools. Sometimes off-the-shelf standardized achievement tests were employed to satisfy a state's

Educational Accountability

The imposition of required student tests as a way of holding educators accountable for the quality of schooling.

News in Brief: A National Roundup

In the News

Many Fail New Nevada Tests

Although one-third of Nevada's 11th graders may have failed new proficiency exams now required for graduation, state education officials plan to make the test even harder next year.

The state school board this month set this year's passing scores for the new, tougher tests at 61 percent for math and 70 percent for reading.

Preliminary results later released by the education department showed that based on those cutoffs, 33 percent of the juniors failed the math test and about 20 percent failed the reading test.

The students, who first took the exams last month, will have four more chances to pass them as seniors next year.

State board members said the failure rates shouldn't discourage them from maintaining high standards.

In fact, board members said they would consider raising the passing scores to 70 percent in math and 75 percent in reading over the next two years.

What's your reaction?

Reprinted, with permission, from *Education Week*, May 27, 1998

accountability testing laws. Sometimes a state created a brand new test intended to yield criterion-referenced interpretations. Sometimes a state created a new test that was intended to yield state-level norm-referenced interpretations.

Most of the state-developed accountability tests, unfortunately, measured fairly low-level student knowledge and skills. It was common to refer to these assessments as "minimum competency tests" because, in general, they were thought to measure very basic skills and knowledge that students were supposed to achieve. Actually, a good many of the early state-developed accountability tests could have been better described as the "most minimal imaginable competency tests" because they assessed extraordinarily low-level student skills and knowledge. To be candid, too many educators who took part in the design of these early accountability tests tried to play it safe by adopting assessment targets that teachers could readily promote. Those test designers feared that, if too many students failed the state's accountability test, the state's educators would appear to be ineffectual. Fortunately, more recent revisions of statewide accountability tests attempt to assess higher level student outcomes.

Irrespective of the quality of the student outcomes being assessed by the accountability tests of the seventies, because of the significance of the tests' consequences, those tests were instantly transformed into *curricular magnets*. Whatever skills and knowledge were assessed by statewide accountability tests began to receive greater emphasis in local school curricula. And the accountability tests soon attained even higher visibility when local newspapers began to publish results of statewide test scores, ranking performances of the state's districts and even the schools within those districts.

Increasingly, accountability assessments became *high-stakes* tests in the sense that they produced either (1) important contingencies for the student test-takers or (2) evidence that was used by the public to rate the quality of schools and districts. And, not surprisingly, high-stakes tests soon began to influence educators. Because educators, quite understandably, wanted their students to perform well on these significant tests, whatever

Research Notes

In the News

Assessment Payoff

Maryland's 4-year-old assessment program has been a force for change in schools that have shown big improvements in student achievement, according to a team of University of Maryland researchers.

The researchers studied 10 schools where students made bigger gains on the tests than expected given their socioeconomic status, and five schools where students were doing worse than expected. As part of their state-financed study, the researchers spent time observing classes in the schools and interviewing teachers and administrators. A 5th grader and a teacher at each of the schools also wrote about their experiences at their schools.

In the big-gaining schools, the researchers found, the Maryland State Performance Assessment Program, or MSPAP, had become a focus of instruction. The assessment is among a new generation of tests in a number of states that go beyond traditional multiple-choice questions to ask students to show what they can do with what they know.

"A lot of teachers said this was the spark that really began to help schools recognize that there were things in the instructional process that they needed to be attending to," said Francine Hultgren, a professor of educational policy, planning, and administration at the university and a study author. Her research partners were William D. Schafer, Willis D. Hawley, Andrew L. Abrams, Carole C. Seubert, and Susan Mazzoni.

But the tests were among a web of factors that the researchers identified as key to the improvements at the more successful schools. One overwhelming factor was having principals who took the lead in changing the instruction that went on in their schools.

"And that was related to collaborative problem-solving," Ms. Hultgren added. "In the more successful schools, teachers were trusted to address their classroom concerns and there was a feeling that it was all right to take a risk."

Professional development in those schools was also more focused. The teachers and administrators jointly decided on the topics for staff seminars, and teachers were expected to use what they learned throughout the year.

Having clear goals, adequate support services, and a curriculum aligned with the state testing program were among other factors the investigators identified as contributing to achievement gains.

The study has not yet been published, but the researchers are sharing their findings now with school districts throughout the state.

—Debra Viadero <dviadero@epe.org>

What's your reaction?

the tests measured began to occupy more importance in the curriculum. Educational tests that, for decades, had whirled innocuously in educational space had, almost overnight, begun to play a key role in the day-to-day decisions made by educators. The educational measurement game had changed—profoundly.

New games call for altered plays. I am not going to mince words—or pies. I want you, an educational leader or someone preparing to be such a leader, to realize that the impact of educational assessment has become so significant in recent years, educators dare not leave the creation and interpretation of educational measuring instruments to the measurement specialists. There was a time when the world of education and the world of educational testing didn't intersect all that meaningfully. But today's educational leaders would have to be genuinely impaired if they continue to allow measurement folks to run the educational assessment game in private. The impact of educational assessment on the educational process is far too substantial.

Educational Leaders
Look at Assessment

Believable *Evidence of Improvement*

Toni Bowling
Curriculum Director
Unified School District #244
Burlington, Kansas

Improved student achievement is of utmost importance for Kansas Schools. The Kansas school accreditation process (Quality Performance Accreditation) requires that schools prove that student achievement is on the rise. Reliable assessment instruments are extremely important when this level of accountability is placed on our schools. And so is a sensible data-gathering design.

Keeping this in mind, the staff of Burlington Middle School recently committed to piloting an instructionally oriented pretest-posttest performance assessment technique. The areas the staff tested were reading comprehension and math problem-solving. The difficulty with past pre- and post-assessments was determining improvement over time. We were always unsure of the meaning of the results, especially on performance assessments. If the scores improved greatly, was it because the spring task was not as difficult as the fall task? Or was the improvement due to students' familiarity with the pretest? Or, on the other hand, if the scores did not improve, was it because the spring task was more difficult than the fall task? When using pre- and post-assessment scores to determine improvement, these questions must be eliminated.

To pilot this assessment technique for math problem-solving, the teachers developed *two* multi-step problem-solving tasks on which students could utilize a four-step process while solving. The task for the pretest was administered in late October. For the pretest, half the students performed one task while the other half performed the other task. Students were instructed not to date their papers. Codes that only the teacher knew were placed on the papers to identify that the responses were pretests. For instructional purposes, the teacher went ahead and scored the papers using a predetermined rubric. The papers were then stored away until after the posttest.

In the meantime, the entire staff at Burlington Middle School implemented various strategies to teach using the communicating problem-solving processes across the curriculum. The problem-solving processes rubric was used by all teachers at least twice each semester. In March the posttest was administered. The tasks were reversed so that all students performed both tasks. For instance, those students who got Task A in the fall were given Task B in the spring and those students who got Task B in the fall were given Task A in the spring. The posttests were also coded, then mixed with the previously coded pretests.

An unbiased team of teachers blind-scored both sets of performance tasks in the spring. Names were covered in order for teachers to score the papers objectively. Because of the codes, the scorers were not aware of which papers were pretests and which were posttests. The same rubric that the students had been using in classroom instruction was used to score the assessments. After the papers were scored, the codes were revealed in order to compare pre-posttest results. Comparisons of the same forms of the tests were used to show growth.

The results were very interesting. The average increase was 10 percent for both tasks. On both occasions, the scores for Task A were much lower than the scores for Task B. This tells us that Task A is much more difficult than Task B. But because we only compared the scores of the same forms from fall to spring, we believe that the 10 percent growth is a reliable indicator of improvement.

▶

The reading comprehension assessment was administered in the same way using two samples of authentic literature. Results of the reading assessment were similar to the problem-solving. Although the total group showed improvement, scores for one of the passages were lower than the other.

Throughout this process we have identified many things that we need to do *instructionally* to better ensure improvement in the areas of math problem-solving and reading comprehension. Most of the problems are in making sure that the assessments are instructionally friendly. At this time we see no problems with the novel data-gathering design we used.

We plan to repeat this assessment technique throughout the remainder of our accreditation cycle to use as a local indicator of improved student achievement. We believe that this assessment is closely aligned to the instruction in the middle school classroom and will provide us with reliable data to prove that student achievement is rising. ●

In the past, most educational leaders would simply defer to whatever words were written or spoken by measurement experts. This deference was justified on the grounds that measurement experts were, after all, experts. Moreover, many educational leaders considered the field of educational measurement, bristling with numbers and formulae, as more than a little intimidating. Can any field run by psychometricians be comprehensible to mere mortals?

Well, the time to be put off by psychometricians has, like the filmstrip projector, vanished completely. The era of psychometric-off-put evaporated as soon as accountability testing and its high-stakes assessments began to influence what went on in classrooms. Anyone who is going to be a genuine educational leader today *must* understand the rudiments of educational measurement. If you understand what's in this book, you'll know more than enough to be able to *influence* what's to be tested and to *interpret accurately* the results of educational tests. Actually, what educational leaders need to know about assessment is not all that esoteric. On the contrary, the really important elements of educational measurement simply embody common sense.

Surely, some of that common sense gets wrapped in language or numbers that could easily intimidate an educational leader. Strip away the psychometric trappings and you'll invariably discover that the underlying notions are quite sensible. You dare not be intimidated by what you'll encounter in subsequent chapters. For example, the next two chapters deal with *validity* and *reliability*. Most educational leaders, at least the normal ones, have not spent much time thinking about such concepts. Validity and reliability, it was thought, are best dealt with by measurement specialists. This is not true!

You need to understand what the essence of validity is and, beyond that, why there are several sorts of reliability evidence. *You* need to arrive at such understandings because there's a new assessment game in town and, if you're going to be an effective educational leader, *you* must learn how to play it.

Instructional Contribution as an Evaluative Factor

Deciding whether the evaluative factor applies. In deciding whether to judge an educational test according to its likely contribution to instruction, you first need to decide whether the test under consideration should, in fact, be helping educators make better instructional decisions. If the test's use is intended to benefit *education* but not *instruction*, then don't judge it on the basis of its instructional contribution. If, however, use of the test can lead to more defensible instructional decisions, then the test's instructional contribution becomes a significant factor by which you should evaluate its quality.

Let's consider for a moment the types of educational assessments that, if they are properly chosen or constructed, can have an impact on instructional decision-making. Presented below are several examples of such tests and explanations of why it is that the tests are likely to have an impact on instructional decisions.

- *A classroom teacher's preassessments*—because, on the basis of students' performances, the teacher can determine what content to emphasize instructionally. If the students appear to have already mastered an objective that the teacher was planning to pursue, the objective can be dropped. If students do not appear to possess the entry skills and knowledge the teacher assumed to be present, instructional attention must then be given to such skills and knowledge.
- *A classroom teacher's progress-monitoring tests*—because, based on how well students are mastering the knowledge, skills, or affect being emphasized by the teacher, decisions can be made by the teacher about whether to continue or cease instruction related to what was assessed.
- *A statewide diploma-denial examination*—because teachers will not want their students to be denied a high school diploma, whatever knowledge and skills are assessed by the statewide examination are apt to receive instructional attention in the state's classrooms.
- *A classroom teacher's end-of-year final examination*—because students' performances on culminating examinations such as this can suggest to teachers whether alterations should be made in the instruction they will supply during the following year.
- *A countywide school-ranking examination*—because, if schools are to be ranked on the basis of a countywide examination, such as a commercially produced standardized achievement test, attempts will be made by many teachers and administrators to improve the test scores of their school's students.

To repeat a point made earlier, there are a small number of educational assessments that have no impact on the instructional decisions made by classroom teachers, school-site administrators, or district-level administrators. Such tests, albeit *educationally* relevant, are not *instructionally* germane. There are not many of these tests that you're apt to encounter. But, before attempting to judge an educational assessment on the basis of its instructional contribution, *first* think through whether the assessment really can have an impact on instructional decision-making. If that impact is possible, as an educational leader you then must realize that a factor in the test's appraisal should be the test's instructional contribution.

Determining whether a test does make an instructional contribution. Once you've decided that an educational assessment *should* make an instructional contribution, your next task is to decide whether the assessment *does* make an instructional contribution.

In order to tackle that assignment, you must first recognize that the instructional process is invariably intended to help students acquire certain knowledge, skills, or affect.

Teachers' instructional approaches vary, of course, with some teachers opting for direct instructional strategies while other teachers prefer less direct instructional strategies. But, variations in instructional strategies notwithstanding, teachers want their students to attain certain kinds of objectives. In the previous chapter, those intended instructional outcomes were described as the *curriculum*.

In determining a test's instructional contribution, it is helpful to focus on the instructional objectives that teachers (or state/district/school officials) are attempting to accomplish. In a sense, these objectives represent *target instructional domains*, that is, the domains of knowledge, skill, or affect that the teacher wants students, as a consequence of instruction, to accomplish. In Figure 3.1 such a target instructional domain is depicted. Examples of such target instructional domains in language arts would be a student's:

- knowledge of standard conventions of spelling, punctuation, and pronunciation;
- one-on-one oral communication skill; or
- increased enjoyment of volitional reading.

Let me be up-front with you. (It is often endearing when an author preannounces an upcoming instance of honesty.) The reason I'm describing an intended instructional outcome as a "target instructional domain" instead of using a more common descriptor such as an "instructional objective" is that, in subsequent chapters, you'll see that a target *instructional* domain is really identical to an *assessment* domain. And, because we use tests to get a fix on students' status with respect to assessment domains, it will be easier for you to make that transition. (Not only am I honest, I am thinking of *your* well-being. Such consideration is touching, don't you think?)

Target Instructional Domain

The cognitive, affect, or psychomotor outcomes that are to be promoted instructionally.

Target instructional domains, if they are too numerous, will render teachers irrational. I know of more than a few former teachers who are now heavily medicated as a result of the well-established neurosis known as "instructional-objective-overload." Thus, to preserve a semblance of sanity, teachers would be wise to focus on a small number of truly important target instructional domains. But even what's contained in a truly important target instructional domain is usually far too much to be measured in its totality. For example, if a teacher's target instructional domain were something such as "students' skill in composing persuasive essays," there is an almost infinite number of different persuasive essays that a student could be asked to compose. Because it would obviously take too long to have students tackle all those persuasive essay tasks, what we do is *represent* the persuasive essay writing domain with a test that samples the domain, then we arrive at a test-based inference about a student's domain status.

Consider Figure 3.2, in which you'll see that an assessment is depicted as representing a target instructional domain. Note that the assessment oval is thin-lined while the instructional domain's oval is thick-lined. This is intended to indicate that the assessment

FIGURE 3.1.

The knowledge, skill, or affective instructional objective that the teacher intends to promote.

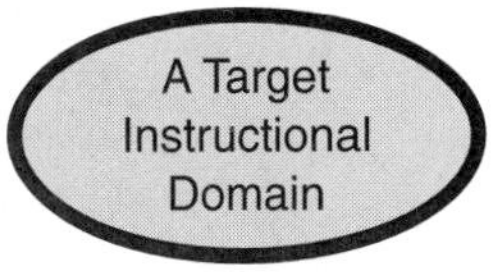

A Target Instructional Domain

FIGURE 3.2.

How an assessment that samples a target instructional domain is used to determine students' status with respect to that domain.

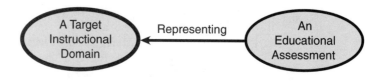

is only a sample-based *representation* of the instructional domain itself. It is the assessment's sample-based representation of the target instructional domain that educators use in order to make inferences about students' status with respect to the domain. Educators should not care all that much about students' performance on a *test* as such. Rather, educators should use students' test performances to make inferences about *students' domain status.* That's what educational measurement is really all about.

Now, with this distinction having been drawn between instructional domains and educational assessments, let's consider the pivotal question that must be answered affirmatively if a test is going to make an instructional contribution:

> Will the test, and/or the descriptive information accompanying it, help a teacher make sensible decisions about how to promote students' mastery of the target instructional domain represented by the test?

There's no need for the interpretation of this question to be very complicated. For example, if you were a classroom teacher who was planning a two week unit of instruction on Topic *X*, would a consideration of a particular test and/or the descriptive materials accompanying it help you make better instructional plans for the unit? If the answer is Yes, then the test (and/or its descriptive information) makes an instructional contribution. If the answer is No, an instructional contribution is lacking.

If a test (and/or its descriptive information) can help a teacher plan a more effective lesson for tomorrow, the test makes an instructional contribution. These contributions are not abstract, theoretical contributions. On the contrary, they are very practical. They help answer the question of *"What should the teacher do next.?"*

Domain descriptions. If you've been alert as you've been reading the last few paragraphs, you'll note that in order to make sensible instructional decisions, a teacher can rely on either the test itself *and/or* the descriptive information accompanying the test. Let's see why, in certain situations, educators may or may not require descriptive information beyond an assessment itself.

Sometimes a teacher can look at the test and figure out quite easily what domain is being represented by the test. For instance, let's say a school's site-based management committee has decided to see if there are improvements in students' school-related attitudes over the course of the year. The committee has selected a 20-item self-report inventory to be completed anonymously by students. By looking at the items on the assessment device, a teacher can readily see that four attitudinal foci are being measured. The inventory has four sets of five items, each dealing with students' (1) self-esteem as

"Well Miss Jones, according to this year's new rating scale, on a 10-point scale you earned a minus 17!"

learners, (2) perceived safety at school, (3) enjoyment of reading, or (4) interest in mathematics. Those four affective domains, then, are being assessed by the self-report inventory. Teachers who wish to promote students' more positive affect on one or more of those four dimensions will have a reasonable idea about where they are to head and, therefore, can devise instructional schemes to promote modifications in student affect. (Later, in Chapter 13, we'll dig more deeply into affective assessments.)

Let's consider another example in which an educator's review of an assessment instrument will prove sufficient to make appropriate instructional decisions. Suppose you were an English teacher who had been directed by your district's central office to administer a districtwide multiple-choice test entitled "Mainstream Mechanics of Writing." The test is to be administered each spring to all of the district's secondary school students. As you consider the 30-item test, you see that it deals exclusively with the kinds of grammatical errors made most frequently by teenagers. For instance, there are several items dealing with subject–verb disagreement as well as with faulty pronoun reference. A review of the test itself conveys to you a reasonably clear idea about the target instructional domain that the test is attempting to represent. With such an understanding of the domain that you need to get students to master, you can often plan a sensible *on-target* instructional sequence for your students.

But sometimes a review of the test itself provides insufficient clues regarding the nature of the target instructional domain the test represents. If that's the case, then you'll need to see if there is supplemental descriptive material that will help understand the instructional domain more clearly. For instance, let's say you're a sixth-grade classroom teacher who's been asked to administer a standardized achievement test that, in its language arts section, contains 20 items dealing with the correct spelling of 20 words. You realize that your seventh-graders need to spell many more than 20 words correctly, so you're eager to find out what words are contained in the complete target instructional domain represented by the standardized achievement test's 20 words. However, when you consult all of the descriptive materials that are provided with the tests, there is no listing of the spelling words that are *eligible* to be tested. From an instructional perspective, you do not have a sufficiently clear notion of the target instructional domain represented by the 20 items on the test.

This shortcoming illustrates the need for clarity regarding the target instructional domain represented by an assessment instrument. Teachers should design their instruction so that it promotes students' mastery of the target instructional domain, not merely a batch of test items representing that domain. In Figure 3.3 you can see this distinction represented graphically. As you will note, the teacher's instruction should focus on the target instructional domain. The teacher's instruction should *not* focus merely on the test itself. Tests *represent* domains of knowledge, skill, or affect. Teachers should teach toward these domains, not toward the assessments that represent those domains.

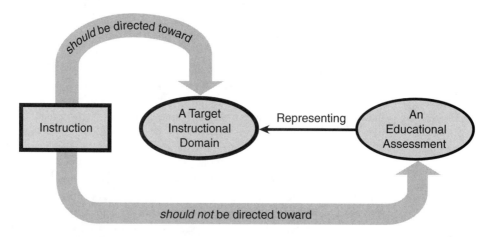

FIGURE 3.3.

Appropriate and inappropriate directions for instruction.

It is because teachers should be promoting their students' achievement of *what a test represents* and not what the test's specific items contain that clarity of the instructional domain is so important. Indeed, if you can't really get an accurate idea of what the domain is, then you can be quite confident that the assessment's instructional contribution will be minimal.

Ideally, measuring instruments that are deliberately developed to yield criterion-referenced interpretations would always be accompanied by crisp descriptions of the domain(s) represented by those measuring instruments. Unfortunately, there are a large number of so-called criterion-referenced tests that are accompanied by domain descriptions far too fuzzy to be of much help in instructional decision-making. Educational leaders must recognize that many assessments proudly touted as "criterion-referenced" may, in fact, provide domain descriptions too sketchy to help teachers make appropriate instructional decisions.

The chief attribute of an educational assessment that will make an instructional contribution is clarity of the domain of skill, knowledge, or affect being assessed. Without such clarity, teachers won't be able to design on-target instructional activities for students.

An Instructional Cup that Runneth Over

Earlier in the chapter, I urged educational leaders to become far more involved in the development and interpretation of the educational tests that are increasingly being used to evaluate educational quality. Consistent with that involvement would be a relentless push for clarity of domain definition. There is ample evidence that teachers will be able to design more effective instructional sequences only if they have a clear idea about where the instruction should be heading. If educators are going to be held accountable for their students' performance on educational assessment instruments, then it is only fair that teachers be thoroughly familiar with the target instructional domains being measured by accountability tests. Educational leaders who wish to judge a test by its instructional contribution will, as a point of departure, immediately look for clarity of the test's domain description.

But what if educational tests were built specifically with instructional implications in mind? What if educational tests were built not exclusively by measurement specialists, but by measurement specialists working in collaboration with educators *who understand instruction?* If such tests were at hand, their positive impact on the instructional process would be considerable.

What I'm suggesting, quite simply, is that educational leaders should make sure instructionally astute educators play a prominent role in the original generation of the measurement instruments that are now so influential. If educational leaders insist, for example, high-stakes tests always be developed in such a way that instructionally knowledgeable individuals have input into the development process, odds are that the resultant assessment devices will be able to make a decisively positive contribution to instruction. What every test-development team needs is a *teachers' advocate* who continually challenges test developers to show how the skill or knowledge measured by a test can actually be taught by regular, not angelic, teachers in typical, not optimal, classrooms.

If educational leaders sit back passively, believing that they dare not intrude onto the terrain of the testing folks, then educational leaders will deserve what they get when test results are, often inappropriately, used against them.

The Relationship between Testing and Teaching

Historically, educators have designed instruction in an effort to achieve the instructional intentions that constitute the curriculum. After the curriculum had been determined, then instruction was planned. After instruction was delivered, then assessment took place. Traditionally, therefore, educators had what might be referred to as *instruction-influenced assessment*. But, although that curriculum–instruction–assessment sequence is traditional, it is often dysfunctional. Let's see why.

A comparison between the more traditional educational approach in which instruction influences assessment and the kind of assessment-influenced instruction being described here can be seen in Figure 3.4.

In a traditional approach to instructional design, an approach in which instruction influences assessment, the teacher (1) is guided by the curriculum that's been adopted by the state and/or district, (2) plans instructional activities to promote the educational objectives set forth in that curriculum, and (3) assesses students. In an assessment-influenced approach to instructional design, also indicated in Figure 3.4, the teacher still (1) starts with the educational objectives set forth in the curriculum, (2) then moves to create assessments based on those goals, and (3) only thereafter plans instructional activities intended to promote students' mastery of the knowledge, skills, and/or attitudes that are to be assessed. In both approaches, curriculum is the starting point. Educational intentions still govern the entire process. But in the two contrasting approaches, the sequence of instructional planning and assessment development is reversed.

Instruction-Influenced Assessment

Assessment-Influenced Instruction

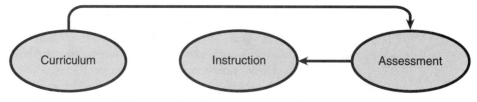

FIGURE 3.4.

Traditional instruction-influenced assessment versus assessment-influenced instruction, both of which are governed by curricular considerations.

Educational Leaders
Look at Assessment

Assessment's Educational Impact: Some Bad, Some Good

Robin R. Hunter
Principal
Simi Valley Unified School District
Simi Valley, California

Educational testing can make a tremendous impact on the instructional process in both a positive or a negative manner. The direction of this impact is determined by both the nature of the assessment and how the resulting information is used. As is required in many states and in conjunction with certain categorical programs, nationally normed tests provide a broad view of how our students perform in relation to other students across the nation. This information is politically sensitive as all school boards want their students to "show" well. Unfortunately, if these test scores become the driving goal of the district, then the test becomes the classroom curriculum as we chase our tails attempting to teach everything that is tested. This process very effectively drives right around district and state curriculum and results in a very fragmented classroom instructional program.

On the other hand, standardized achievement tests can be a thermometer to show how our students (including data on all subgroups) do competitively and to identify areas of strength and weakness. For instructional decisions in the classroom, however, other assessments are more appropriate for driving teaching in a cohesive curriculum. Assessments based upon district content standards may have a very positive impact on the classroom program. These assessments, adminis-

tered frequently throughout the year, give teachers accurate data on student learning that should guide their daily instructional decisions. This type of instructional decision making is different and far more effective than making these decisions based upon what comes on the next page in the textbook. It is based on teaching students as learners rather than "covering" material. Our school uses assessments in mathematics, writing and reading that allow teachers to flexibly group and regroup students for instruction. Much as a cook frequently tastes his or her cooking to adjust seasonings, classroom assessment should be an ongoing process to adjust teaching. When you have clear content standards, assessment provides the avenue to consistent school-wide progress toward attaining those standards. Assessment that occurs as a perfunctory event at the end of teaching is of little value to the teaching/learning process. ●

Assessment-influenced instruction rests on the assumption that, in many instances, what is to be assessed *will* influence the teacher's instructional decisions. Consequently, if the assessment can be created prior to the teacher's instructional planning, the resultant clarity provided to the teacher will help the teacher make more appropriate instructional choices.

For instance, when teachers develop their own assessments *before* instructional plans are made, the teachers are meaningfully *clarifying* the curricular objectives that are being pursued. In other words, the assessment serves as the exemplification of whether an objective has been achieved. That clarity provides far more insight for teachers when they make their instructional plans.

It is important to remember that, as indicated earlier, educational assessments *represent* the domain of knowledge, skills, or affect being promoted. Teachers should *never* teach toward the classroom test itself. Instead, teachers should teach toward the knowledge, skills, and/or affect that are sampled by the classroom test. But, when teachers construct classroom assessments prior to instructional decision-making, those teachers will have a markedly better understanding of what the objectives really are because the objectives will have been operationalized. And, of course, the more clearheaded that teachers are about curricular *ends*, the more skillfully they can select suitable instructional *means* to accomplish those ends.

If tests are devised prior to a teacher's instructional planning, the increased clarity regarding the nature of the objectives being promoted will yield all sorts of instructional-planning benefits. Here are a few of the more prominent dividends that classroom teachers will receive:

- *Accurate task analyses.* Because teachers will know more clearly what the terminal results of an instructional sequence are supposed to be, teachers can better pinpoint the enabling or *en route* knowledge/skills that students must acquire before mastering what's being taught.
- *On-target practice activities.* Because teachers know better what kinds of end-of-instruction outcomes are being sought for students, they can make sure to select guided-practice and independent-practice activities that are more accurately aligned with the target outcomes.
- *Lucid expositions.* Because teachers understand more clearly what's to be assessed at instruction's conclusion, during the instruction they can provide clearer explanations to their students about the content involved and where the instructional activities are heading.

Instructional planning will benefit most fundamentally from teachers' early familiarity with educational assessments because teachers will better understand what it is hoped that their students will be able to do when instruction has been concluded.

Assessment-influenced instruction, although it is a concept that many educators will view as unusual, can have big payoffs for children. Remember, if educational assessment doesn't help children learn better, we shouldn't be doing it. Assessment-influenced instruction, especially if the assessments are fashioned with the input of instructionally knowledgeable educators, can have a profound and positive impact on instruction. It is for this reason that you are being urged to employ an educational test's instructional contribution as a salient factor in deciding whether the test is a winner or loser. As indicated at the outset of the chapter, there is a small number of educational tests that really aren't supposed to make all this much instructional difference. But for at least nine out of ten educational assessments into which you bump, the evaluative factor of *instructional contribution* will be importantly relevant.

Let's close out the chapter with a brief consideration of an unfortunate consequence of the preoccupation with getting students to score well on tests. That unfortunate consequence is *inappropriate test preparation*.

Test Preparation

An educational achievement test is employed in order for educators to make a reasonable inference about a student's status with respect to a domain of knowledge and/or skills it represents. Ideally, of course, an achievement test will sample the assessment domain representatively so that the level of a student's performance on the achievement test will serve as a reasonably accurate reflection of the student's status with respect to the assessment domain. The nature of this relationship is illustrated in Figure 3.5, where it is indicated that a student who answered correctly 80 percent of the items in an achievement test would be expected to have mastered about 80 percent of the content in the domain of knowledge and/or skills that the test was measuring. The relationship between a student's test performance and that student's mastery of the assessment domain represented by the achievement test, as will be seen later, is a key factor in establishing the appropriateness of test-preparation practices.

Two Test-Preparation Guidelines

Two guidelines can be employed by educational leaders who wish to ascertain the appropriateness of given test-preparation practices. Taken together, the two guidelines provide teachers with a useful way of thinking about the suitability of particular test-preparation activities. Here, then, is the first guideline: the *professional ethics guideline*.

> *Professional Ethics Guideline:* No test-preparation practice should violate the ethical norms of the education profession.

The professional ethics guideline obliges teachers to avoid any test-preparation practice that is unethical. Ethical behaviors, of course, are rooted not only in fundamental morality but also in the nature of a particular profession. For example, physicians should

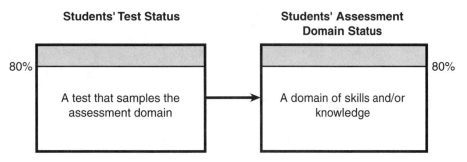

Students' Test Status   **Students' Assessment Domain Status**

80%   A test that samples the assessment domain   →   A domain of skills and/or knowledge   80%

FIGURE 3.5.

The inference-illuminating relationship between a test and the assessment domain it samples.

be governed not only by general ethical principles dealing with honesty and respect for other people's property, but also by ethical principles that have evolved specifically for the medical profession. Similarly, teachers should not engage in test-preparation practices that involve violations of general ethical canons dealing with theft, cheating, lying, and so on. In addition, however, teachers must take seriously the ethical obligations that they undertake because they have agreed to serve *in loco parentis*. Teachers who serve "in place of the parent" take on an ethical responsibility to serve as models of moral behavior for children.

It is also true that when teachers engage in test-preparation practices which, if brought to the public's attention, would discredit the education profession, such practices may be considered professionally unethical. This is because, in the long term, such practices can erode public confidence in our schools and, as a result, diminish financial support for the schools. Consequently, this erosion of public support renders the education profession less potent.

Thus, according to the professional ethics guideline, teachers should not engage in test-preparation practices that involve such behaviors as violating state-imposed security procedures regarding high-stakes tests. A growing number of states have enacted regulations so that teachers who breach state test-security procedures can have their credentials revoked. Accordingly, teachers should not engage in unethical test-preparation practices because there are both potential personal repercussions (for example, loss of credentials) and professional repercussions (for example, reduced citizen confidence in public schooling). Most importantly, teachers should avoid unethical test-preparation practices because such practices are *wrong*.

Let's look, then, at the second of our two guidelines—the *educational defensibility guideline*.

> *Educational Defensibility Guideline:* No test-preparation practice should increase students' test scores without simultaneously increasing students' mastery of the assessment domain tested.

This second guideline emphasizes the importance of engaging in instructional practices that are in the educational best interest of students. Teachers should not, for example, artificially increase students' scores on a test while neglecting to increase students' mastery of the domain of knowledge and/or skills that the test is supposed to reflect.

An appropriate test-preparation practice raises not only students' prepreparation-to-postpreparation performance on a test, but also raises students' prepreparation-to-postpreparation mastery of the assessment domain being tested. This situation is illustrated in Figure 3.6, where you can see that a 20 percent prepreparation-to-postpreparation jump in students' mastery was seen both on the test and on the assessment domain it represents.

Conversely, an inappropriate test-preparation practice raises students' prepreparation-to-postpreparation performance on the test, but not students' mastery of the assessment domain itself. This situation is illustrated in Figure 3.7, where students' test performances increase, but their assessment domain mastery doesn't.

Appropriate Test Preparation

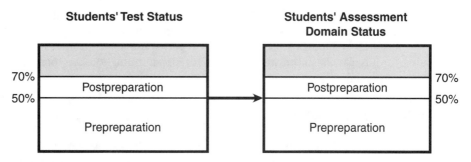

FIGURE 3.6.

Appropriate test preparation based on the criterion of educational defensibility.

The result of such inappropriate test-preparation practices is that a deceptive picture of students' achievement is created. The test results no longer serve as an accurate indicator of students' status with respect to an assessment domain. As a consequence, students who in reality have not mastered a domain of content may fail to receive appropriate instruction regarding such content. The students will have been instructionally short-changed because inappropriate test-preparation practices led to an inflated estimate of their content mastery. Such test-preparation practices, because they rob students of needed instruction, are educationally indefensible.

Using these two guidelines, educational leaders can help teachers determine what sorts of test-preparation activities are appropriate and what sorts are not. In recent years, I've spent a considerable amount of time talking with teachers about test preparation. I'm convinced that the vast majority of teachers will avoid inappropriate test-preparation

Inappropriate Test Preparation

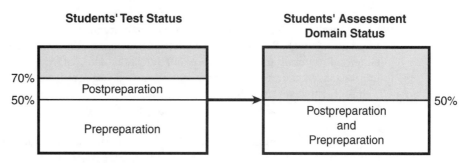

FIGURE 3.7.

Inappropriate test preparations based on the criterion of educational defensibility.

practices if they give any thought to that issue. Many teachers, unfortunately, have never seriously considered what kinds of test preparation are nifty and what kinds are nefarious. If you, as an educational leader, use the two guidelines given here to help teachers discuss this issue, you'll find that very few teachers will really want to shortchange children by supplying inappropriate test preparation. But teachers need to think about what it is that constitutes *appropriate* test preparation and how that form of test preparation differs from *inappropriate* test preparation.

Chapter Wrap-Up

This is the first of Part Two's five chapters intended to assist educational leaders as they evaluate tests. It dealt with an evaluative factor highly relevant to the work of educators, namely, the instructional contribution that a test can make. The chapter will be concluded with our now traditional review format. (After all, it's been used in the first two chapters, and I have remarkably lenient standards when it comes to tradition-establishing.) Each of the guiding questions posed at the chapter's outset will be pithily answered.

● Are all educational assessments instructionally relevant?

Although the vast majority of measuring instruments used in education have the potential to make contributions to teachers' instructional decision-making, there are a few educational tests that really don't bear all that heavily on the day-to-day drama of instruction. Assessments used by school guidance personnel to counsel individual students, for example, frequently do not impinge all that directly on the instructional process. But, because teachers' classroom assessments surely represent the most common kind of educational measurement device, and all of these classroom tests have instructional implications, it is apparent that an enormous proportion of educational tests, at least potentially, are *instructionally* relevant.

● How have educational assessments usually been evaluated?

In the past, educational tests were routinely evaluated by measurement specialists, and only by measurement specialists. Educators played little, if any, part in the appraisal of educational tests. Measurement specialists, in carrying out their appraisals of educational tests, relied exclusively on traditional psychometric evaluative factors such as reliability and validity. A test's instructional impact was *never* considered.

With the dawning of educational accountability in the 1970s, however, educational tests began to make a difference in what teachers taught. High-stakes tests were those that either led to important decisions about students or, alternately, were employed to form impressions of educators' effectiveness. Educators, eager to have their students perform well on high-stakes tests, began to supply instructional attention to whatever the high-stakes tests measured. The tests, therefore, functioned as a sort of curricular magnet. Whatever was tested was taught.

Because of the importance of students' test performance, educational leaders were encouraged to abandon their perennially passive role regarding educational assessments. Instead, educational leaders were urged to join forces with measurement personnel so that collaboratively created assessment instruments would prove more beneficial to children.

● How can educational assessments make an instructional contribution?

After first deciding whether an educational test *should* be instructionally relevant, the question must be raised about whether a test, and/or the descriptive material that accompanies the test, will help teachers make sensible instructional decisions. Educational assessments are, in reality, only representative samples of a target instructional domain of skill, knowledge, or affect. The test, if it is to make an instructional contribution, will help teachers decide how best to provide instruction that promotes students' mastery of the domain of knowledge, skill, or affect represented by the assessment. A test that, perhaps abetted by accompanying descriptive material, helps teachers make better day-to-day instructional decisions will provide teachers with clarity regarding what the test measures. Then teachers can, as a consequence, make more astute instructional choices. It is imperative, however, that teachers focus their efforts on students' mastering the target instructional domain rather than the educational test representing that domain.

● Should assessments be developed before or after instructional planning?

In recognition of the impact that educational tests often have on teachers' instructional decisions, it is recommended that instructionally relevant educational assessments be created prior to instructional planning. The resulting assessment-influenced instruction will benefit because of more accurate task analyses, more on-target practice activities, and more lucid expositions from the teacher. Although assessment-influenced instruction may not always be possible, its benefits to teachers can be substantial.

● What kinds of test preparation activities are appropriate and what kinds aren't?

Two guidelines were provided in the chapter to help educational leaders think about the appropriateness of test-preparation practices. The *professional ethics guideline* stipulated that no test-preparation practice should violate the ethical norms of the education profession. The *educational defensibility guideline* contended that no test-preparation practice should increase students' test scores without simultaneously increasing students' mastery of the assessment domain tested.

Practice Exercises

Part A

For this first set of five items, decide whether each of the following educational assessments can appropriately be appraised, at least in part, on the basis of the assessment's *instructional contribution*. If the assessment can, respond *Yes* (or some suitably synonymous answer such as "You bet!" "Darn right!" or "Yup!") If the assessment really ought not be judged using instructional contributions as an evaluative factor, think up your own variation of *No*.

1. This midterm exam is used by Mr. Shavers in his ninth-grade biology classes. Although he's used revised versions of the same examination for several years running, he thinks the current 50-item form is quite praiseworthy.

2. This districtwide test of 10th-grade students' ability to write narrative essays has been administered each May for the past five years. Each high school's relative ranking among the district's 11 high schools is publicized in local newspapers after all students' essays have been scored at the district office.

3. How about a standardized achievement test that's administered at four different grade levels in all schools in a state? After students in grades 4, 6, 8, and 10 take the test each spring, the state's school districts are ranked according to results, as are the schools within those districts.

4. This is a college-predictor test that is employed to forecast which students will succeed in college and which ones won't. It is administered three times each year by a national testing organization.

5. This 10-item quiz is always employed by Mrs. Blevens in the middle of her four-week instructional unit for eighth-graders on "Australia: Its Life through Its Literature." Mrs. Blevens uses the test results to determine her students' *en route* mastery of the unit's objectives.

Part B

Here's a somewhat trickier challenge. Look at the five descriptions below and decide whether each represents (a) a target instructional domain or (b) an educational assessment that might represent a target instructional domain. You have to opt for *a* or *b*—there can be no *a* ½ answers.

6. The student's ability to deliver effective 10-minute extemporaneous speeches after only 90-minutes' preparation.

7. The student's construction of a pair of wooden bookends in the woodworking class.

8. The student's original composition in response to the following prompt: "Write an essay of 500 words or more describing the most unforgettable person you know."

9. The student's ability to spell (aloud or in writing) 25 "spelling demons" randomly chosen from a previously distributed list of age-appropriate but hard-to-spell words.

10. The ability to solve previously unencountered word problems requiring at least two of the following arithmetic operations: addition, subtraction, multiplication, and division.

Answers to Practice Exercises

Part A

1. This kind of classroom test is clearly one that should be judged on the basis of its contribution to Mr. Shavers's biology instruction. You'll learn later about other evaluative factors to use with such tests, but instructional contribution is surely one factor to use with this test. You should have answered *Yes.*

2. This is another case where an affirmative answer wins and a negative answer should lead to your rereading the chapter. This test of students' essay-writing skills is certainly a test that should be scrutinized according to its instructional payoffs.

3. Once again, a *Yes* answer wins. Such high-stakes tests, because they have the potential to influence instruction beneficially (or adversely) should definitely be evaluated by the use of factors including instructional contributions. As you'll learn in Chapter 15, distressingly, most standardized achievement tests fail to satisfy this evaluative factor.

4. Although this test is clearly educational, its instructional implications are negligible. You should have come up with a solid *No* for this practice item. Most of these academic aptitude tests caution teachers not to try to teach to the specifics measured by the tests. Too much direct instruction toward the test's items would often lead to inaccurate estimates of students' academic aptitude.

5. Here's a solid instance of an instructionally relevant test. A *Yes* answer from you would have been highly commendable. By the way, when I was a student teacher, I taught a four-week unit on the same Australian topic as Mrs. Blevens. At the end of four weeks, I found myself even cursing in Australian.)

Part B

6. This is an instructional domain; *a* is correct.
7. Here's an assessment of a youngster's word-working skills; *b* wins.
8. Measuring students' writing skills is a widespread assessment undertaking these days. This is a test *item*, however, and not the target instructional domain. The target instructional domain is students' descriptive writing skill. This test elicits a sample of that skill; *b* is the right answer.
9. This is a nicely identified domain description that, clearly, depends on the previously distributed list of age-appropriate but hard-to-spell words. The correct answer is *a*.
10. Here's another case in which an *a*-answer will give you an *A* grade. For this target instructional domain, you would need to build assessments to measure students' mastery of the mathematical skill being assessed.

DISCUSSION QUESTIONS

1. How important do you think a test's *instructional contribution* really is? Do you believe most educational leaders would agree with you? Why or why not?
2. If you were asked by a group of teachers in a middle school to explain to them the difference between "teaching to test items and teaching to the domain represented by those items," what would you say to the teachers?
3. Do you think that tests should be developed prior to instructional planning? What are the arguments in favor of, and opposed to, your position on this issue?
4. What sorts of test-preparation practices do you think teachers should employ? What sorts of test-preparation practices do you think are *verboten*? Should the use of *verboten* be *verboten*?
5. Do you believe that educational leaders have been too passive over the years with respect to the creation and interpretation of educational tests? Why?
6. Can you think of a half-dozen educational tests that do *not* have instructional implications? Are there any features that these tests have in common or are they all different kinds of measurement devices?
7. If you were the chair of a local school board, and you wanted your district's high-level administrators to become more proactively involved in educational assessment, what kinds of arguments (or mechanisms) would you use to persuade the administrators?

SUGGESTIONS FOR ADDITIONAL READING

Allalouf, Avi, and Gershon Ben-Shakhar. "The Effect of Coaching on the Predictive Validity of Scholastic Aptitude Tests." *Journal of Educational Measurement, 35,* 1 (Spring 1998): 31–47.

Brookhart, Susan M. "A Theoretical Framework for the Role of Classroom Assessment in Motivating Student Effort and Achievement." *Applied Measurement in Education, 10,* 2 (1997): 161–180.

Linn, Robert L. *Assessment-Based Reform: Challenges to Educational Measurement.* In "William H. Angoff Memorial Lecture Series" (ED 393 875). Princeton, NJ: Educational Testing Service, August 1995.

Niyogi, Nivedita S. *The Intersection of Instruction and Assessment: The Classroom, A Policy Issue Perspective (Policy Information Center Publications* Catalog, ED 388 724). Princeton, NJ: Educational Testing Service, March 1995.

Northwest Regional Educational Laboratory. *Assessment Strategies to Inform Science and Mathematics Instruction: It's Just Good Teaching.* Portland, OR: Author, 1997.

Northwest Regional Educational Laboratory. *Improving Classroom Assessment: A Toolkit for Professional Developers (Toolkit 98).* Portland, OR: Author, 1998.

Stiggins, Richard J. *Opening Doors to Excellence in Assessment: A Guide for Using Quality Assessment to Promote Effective Instruction and Student Success.* Portland, OR: Assessment Training Institute, 1997.

AND FOR THOSE WHO TIRE OF READING

Hunter, Madeline. *Teaching and Testing: A Conversation with Madeline Hunter* (Videotape #ETVT-36). Los Angeles: IOX Assessment Associates.

Kline, Everett, and Grant Wiggins. *Curriculum and Assessment Design* (Audiotape: Stock #295191S62). Alexandria, VA: Association for Supervision and Curriculum Development, 1995.

Popham, W. James. *Improving Instruction Through Classroom Assessment* (Videotape #ETVT-25). Los Angeles: IOX Assessment Associates.

Popham, W. James. *Test Preparation Practices: What's Appropriate and What's Not* (Videotape #ETVT-31). Los Angeles: IOX Assessment Associates.

The Validity of Assessment-Based Interpretations

In this chapter you're going to be looking at a second evaluative factor that educational leaders can use to tell if an assessment device is woeful or wonderful. The evaluative factor is *validity*. It's doubtful if any educator who possesses even a smidgen of experience has not heard somebody talk about "test validity" or the "validity of tests." But most educators, unfortunately, assume that concepts such as *validity* and *reliability* ought to be the concerns of measurement experts, not in-the-trenches educators. That assumption, especially if made by an educational leader, is absolutely *invalid*. Let me explain why.

As has been suggested in the three earlier chapters, students' test performances are increasingly being used as the chief indicator by which educators' quality is judged. Because that's so, educational leaders dare not permit gaps to exist in their understanding of what makes educational tests tick. And validity, as you'll see, is truly tick-central. If you don't grasp what's going on with this key evaluative factor, you'll never genuinely understand why many educational tests are currently being misused.

As you read on in Chapter 4, you'll encounter some terminology that, at first glance, may seem somewhat off-putting. Don't be put off. You need to know this stuff. If you think for a moment about the different kinds of validity evidence you'll be encountering, you'll discover that there's nothing exotic about these ideas, and there's nothing that's too complex to understand. Rather, the central concepts in this chapter are all rooted in commonsense ways of telling whether the tests that educators use are being used properly. Sure, the descriptive terminology may be unfamiliar to you, but the commonsense notions to which that terminology applies will be readily understandable. Remember, validity and reliability are not the exclusive province of psychometricians. Educational leaders—and that means you—must also master these concepts.

Inferences and Interpretations

Educators use tests in order to draw inferences about the individuals being tested. Another way of saying the same thing is to say that educators use tests in order to make interpretations about the individuals being tested. As noted in Chapter 1, measurement specialists use the two terms *inference* and *interpretation* interchangeably. That's what I'll be doing in this and all other chapters, namely, using those two terms interchangeably. (The availability of a synonym can so spice up one's writing!)

Classroom teachers arrive at measurement-based interpretations about students' accomplishments after administering final examinations to find out how much knowledge or how many skills their students have acquired. Similarly, when a school counselor administers a vocational-interest inventory to students, the counselor hopes to draw inferences about the vocations in which those students are interested. (That, after all, is the kind of inventory it is.)

When educators employ tests, whether a paper-and-pencil achievement test or some kind of attitudinal inventory, the student who completes the test typically earns a score. Based on that score, educators draw an *inference* or *interpretation* regarding the student's status.

A score-based inference will usually be fairly straightforward, for it must necessarily deal with the student's status regarding the assessment domain represented by the test or inventory being used. To illustrate, if a student earns an almost-perfect score on a test measuring mathematical computation skill, the resulting inference might be that "this student appears to have mastered the computation skills in the assessment domain represented by the test." Conversely, a student who stumbled seriously on the mathematics computation test, concluding that $6 \times 6 = 66$, might evoke an inference such as "this student's mastery of the computational skills reflected in the test is remarkably close to the square root of zero."

From these score-based inferences, educational leaders often arrive at *second-level inferences* such as, "The district's mathematics program is not working." The legitimacy of second-level inferences, of course, usually depends on a number of factors other than the simple, score-based inference about whether students are skilled at mathematical computation. Later on, in Chapter 15, you'll see that standardized achievement tests can be used to make valid inferences about whether students can master the knowledge and skills represented by the test. Yet, when that *first-level inference* is the basis of a *second-level inference* that "these schools with low standardized test scores are ineffective," serious difficulties arise.

In educational assessment, validity refers to the accuracy of inferences based on students' responses to assessment devices such as tests, inventories, and so on. Measurement validity does not extend to second-level inferences in which first-level, score-based inferences are employed to arrive at a subsequent conclusion.

The Importance of Validity in Educational Measurement

The concept of validity is one of the most important ideas that educational leaders will be working with when they use educational tests. It is a concept that, in spite of its pivotal importance in educational measurement, is often misunderstood. For example, many educators and more than a few measurement specialists mistakenly refer to "the validity of a test." A test is merely a tool that we use in order to make inferences. If we misuse the tool by employing it in the wrong situation, it is not the tool that's defective. It's the tool-user.

For instance, if you were a kitchen buff intent on creating an elegant caramel frosting, you might frequently rely on a tablespoon. Tablespoons are nifty measuring tools. They allow us to determine with accuracy how much of a given ingredient to toss into an emerging culinary masterpiece. But suppose you tried to use the tablespoon to take the temperature of the frosting mix. You might infer that the frosting mix is hot enough, turn it off, and watch with surprise as it turns into an unassailable lump of caramel-colored sugar. Indeed, any inferences about the temperature of the frosting based on the use of a tablespoon would, in all likelihood, be inaccurate. Rather than a tablespoon, you should have employed a candy thermometer to determine the frosting's temperature. But that doesn't render the *tablespoon* invalid. Rather, it was the tablespoon-based *inference* about the frosting's temperature that was invalid. And anyone who would make such a wacko inference should be forcibly excluded from any kitchen on earth.

In the same way, a language arts achievement test that can allow a school superintendent to draw valid interpretations about tenth-graders' punctuation skills would not yield valid interpretations about first-graders' abilities to speak Russian. If the superintendent were silly enough to try to use the language arts test in such a situation, it would

Second-Level Inferences

Inferences that are drawn from score-based inferences about students' status with respect to an assessment domain.

Educational Leaders
Look at Assessment

Inferences: Valid and Valued

Liz Dunham
School Improvement Specialist
Department of Defense Schools
(DoDDS)
United Kingdom District

Our system-wide school improvement process, which was implemented three years ago, includes guidance on determining goals based on data, and gathering "evidence of success" data to determine progress and to provide the basis for future decisions. When I became the district school improvement specialist last fall, it was clear that, in spite of systemic guidance, few educators in our thirteen district schools were using data to drive their school improvement decisions. Thus, it became my job to determine why teachers and administrators were *not* using data, and then to provide any support they needed to help them make some progress in this area. I will briefly recount what I found and the actions we took as a district staff to support the schools and to help them to move forward.

To be successful in planning and implementing school improvement, educators need to have an understanding of basic assessment principles such as the importance of standardizing conditions and using assessment tools that match the target goal. Without this understanding, it is unlikely that educators will be able to gather useful data or ever get to the point of making valid inferences from the data. It's fair to say that some of our educators lack this understanding; however, in our district, it appeared that this was not the problem. Instead, there has been an affective rather than a cognitive obstacle to the school improvement process.

When the school improvement process was introduced three years ago, like many schools and school districts, our educators faced "top down" guidance and many restrictions about how to write and implement their school improvement plans. Early implementation was not smooth; communication was poor; the paperwork was substantial; the computer template for the planning form was flawed; deadlines were difficult to meet. Thus, the process was not viewed by many as worth the effort. Our district staff adopted the view that until inferences about the success of school improvement strategies are *valued*, educators will not put

forth the effort to make the inferences *valid*. And because the inferences involved can't possibly be valid if the other parts of the process are flawed (such as using an assessment tool that produces data irrelevant to the target goal), then until educators value the process, few inferences, either valid or invalid, are likely to be made. This is why our district staff worked hard this year on our educators' affect toward the school improvement process.

All members of the district's professional staff shared *active* responsibility for district-wide school improvement. We ruthlessly reduced paperwork requirements related to school improvement. We set up mechanisms to encourage more school-level ownership of that school's improvement plans. We tried to focus on positive school-improvement "success stories" in district schools. And we made certain that all district principals were thoroughly familiar with all district-level attempts to promote school improvement. To find out whether all these efforts made any difference, each October we now administer an anonymous, self-report affective inventory about school improvement to all district educators.

As a result of all these efforts by the district team, it appeared by the end of the school year that the affect toward the process was improving. Also during this last school year, educators began to be critical of their own process and often identified areas that needed improvement. For example, at several schools they recognized that they had not replicated their con-

▶

ditions on their pre- and posttests and, at others, they realized that their assessment instruments did not match their target goals.

We're not there yet, but after this year, educators appear more likely to see the value of the school improvement process in which they are involved. Because of this, they tend to be more concerned about using appropriate assessment tools that will enable them to gather data and to make inferences about their progress. In our district, before we could deal with examining whether inferences and decisions were *valid*, we had to consider whether the process itself was *valued*. By spending the time on educators' affect toward school improvement this last year, listening to our educators, and dealing with their concerns, we feel that they are more likely to work together and to put forth real effort in a process that is designed to improve student achievement. ●

be the *interpretation* about first-graders' abilities to speak Russian that would be invalid, not the test itself.

Messick states it succinctly when he observes that "one validates, not a test, but an interpretation of data arising from a specific procedure."[1] Linn echoes that point when he asserts that "questions of validity are questions of the soundness of the interpretation of a measure."[2] As you can see, a measurement tool, when employed, simply yields data—typically, test scores. The *interpretation* of those test scores is the operation that may or may not be valid. Thus, the concept of validity in educational measurement deals with *the validity of score-based interpretations.*

Some measurement writers define validity as "the degree to which a test measures what it purports to measure." What they imply with such a definition is that the test yields a score from which valid score-based inferences can be drawn. As you proceed through this key chapter, however, it will be important for you to understand that tests themselves are never valid. Rather, the concept of validity is linked to the interpretations that educators draw based on the use of tests.

As you will see, there is not a simple on/off determination of whether a score-based inference is valid. Rather, you must make *judgments* regarding the validity of score-based inferences. In order to make those judgments as defensibly as possible, educators assemble one or more types of *evidence of validity*. This chapter deals with the different sorts of validity evidence that educational leaders might have at their disposal.

Acceptable and Unacceptable Descriptive Terminology

In a field such as education, where educators face numerous situations in which score-based inferences are at issue, it is only natural that different people would come up with different ways of thinking about validity. By the 1950s, matters were really getting out of hand, with all sorts of exotic validity types and validity terms finding their way into the measurement literature. People were writing about "intrinsic" validity, "extrinsic" validity, "divergent" validity, "convergent" validity, "face" validity, and, in all likelihood, "two-faced" validity.

To quell this confusion, the professional associations most concerned with the quality of educational tests attempted to establish some order in the assessment field. In 1954 the American Psychological Association (APA) published *Technical Recommendations for Psychological Tests and Diagnostic Techniques.* One year later the American Educational Research Association (AERA) and the National Council on Measurements Used in Education (NCME) collaborated to publish (through the National Educational Association) *Technical Recommendations for Achievement Tests.* Later, in 1966 and 1974, these three organizations (APA, AERA, and NCME) joined forces to publish (through APA), revised *Standards for Educational and Psychological Tests and Manuals.* In 1985 those standards were revised again by a committee of measurement experts representing the three organizations and published by APA as *Standards for Educational and Psychological Testing.* A new revision of the *Standards* is scheduled to be published in, approximately, the year 2,000.

Now, why all the fuss about professional associations and their attempt to reduce the terminological chaos with respect to such concepts as test validity?

Well, as any student of language will tell you, the meanings we attach to words are basically conventions. We fly in an *airplane* and write at a *desk* because the terms *airplane* and *desk* have, through convention and custom, become widely accepted ways of describing things we fly in and write at.

In a technical field such as education where precision of communication is imperative, it makes sense to rely on widely used conventions. Otherwise, educators will be employing all sorts of aberrant expressions to describe technical phenomena, with the result that confusion, rather than clarity, ensues. As a consequence, it will be strategically sensible for us to rely on the terminology conventions most recently sanctified by APA, AERA, and NCME, and this means the terminology endorsed in the *Standards.*[3] Those

N.C. Gets First School-by-School Performance Results

by Kathleen Kennedy Manzo

While many North Carolina school administrators and teachers are winning praise and cash for meeting or exceeding performance expectations on state tests, others are starting the school year scrambling to respond to their students' low achievement.

In the state's first-ever school-by-school performance assessment, some 56 percent of North Carolina's public elementary and middle schools met or exceeded expectations on state tests in reading and mathematics, according to a report on more than 1,600 schools released in August.

The report also identified 7.5 percent of the schools as low performing. High schools will be included in the program next year.

In releasing the assessment, North Carolina joins a rising number of states that divvy up rewards or impose penalties for districts and schools based on student performance on state tests.

North Carolina's testing initiative already has sparked two lawsuits and won both praise and criticism from educators and parents. State officials tempered their satisfaction with the results with vows to boost the performance of more than 700 schools that did not meet their goals.

"The first-year report shows us that while a great number of our schools are making tremendous progress, we have to do more to make sure all of our students are getting the best education possible," Gov. James B. Hunt Jr., a Democrat, said in a statement. . . .

What's your reaction?

Excerpted, with permission, from *Education Week*, September 3, 1997

who wish to become particularly conversant with the ins and outs of validity would do well to read relevant sections of the most current APA–AERA–NCME *Standards*.

In passing, I should note that, because of the high stakes associated with many educational tests these days, such as receiving a high school diploma or being admitted to various sorts of training programs, the technical adequacy of educational tests is often being challenged in court. In these courtroom challenges regarding the acceptability of educational tests, substantial deference is given by jurists to the *Standards*. In fact, because of the potential likelihood that certain tests will be the focus of litigation, many test developers are trying to adhere to the guidelines embodied in the *Standards*. They don't want their tests to be seen as inconsistent with professional test-development and test-evaluation guidelines.

In the remainder of this chapter, therefore, you'll consider the three categories of validity evidence endorsed in the *Standards*, that is, *content-related evidence of validity*, *criterion-referenced evidence of validity* (predictive and concurrent), and *construct-related evidence of validity*. The rest of the chapter is organized so that each of these three types of validity evidence is described. If there are any special considerations associated with the collection of validity evidence for tests to be used when arriving at absolute versus relative interpretations, those considerations will be briefly identified.

At first blush, people making their initial pilgrimage to measurementland might legitimately wonder why it is that we are going to be talking about different sorts of validity evidence. As indicated earlier, it's because various types of evidence can be useful in reaching a judgment about the validity of a score-based inference.

Choosing an example from another field, suppose you were trying to judge how effective a new automobile was. You might conceive of "effectiveness" as: (a) the auto's fuel-consumption ration, (b) an index of the auto's power under stress conditions, or (c) the auto's mechanical longevity. Each of these alternative perspectives deals with an aspect of the new automobile's effectiveness. Viewed together, they provide you with a richer notion of the auto's effectiveness than if you had focused only on one aspect of the auto's capabilities. In like manner, when you really think hard about the validity of a measurement-based interpretation, you'll discover that there are related, but substantially different, ways of conceptualizing whether a test measures what it is supposed to measure.[4] Now let's look at three varieties of evidence bearing on the validity of score-based inferences.

Content-Related Evidence of Validity

How would a reasonable person approach the task of deciding whether a score-based interpretation is valid? Well, one of the first questions that might come to someone's mind, particularly someone who was thinking about achievement tests (such as a test of one's mathematical skills), would be the following: "Does the test deal with the *content* it's supposed to be measuring?" For example, does a test supposedly measuring someone's knowledge of Asian history cover the important particulars of history in Asia, rather than the history of Argentina or Greece? Because of this very sensible concern about the adequacy with which a test taps the topics it should tap, one form of validity evidence is known as *content-related evidence of validity*.

A definition. Let's start our consideration of content-related evidence of validity with the definition of such evidence supplied in the *Standards:*

> In general, content-related evidence demonstrates the degree to which the sample of items, tasks, or questions on a test are representative of some defined universe or domain of content.[5]

All right, you might respond, that's a pretty sophisticated way of saying, "Does the test cover the content it's supposed to cover?" But how can we determine whether a test covers the appropriate content? As you will soon see, the key ingredient in securing content-related evidence of validity is *human judgment*.

To gather content-related evidence of validity, however, you need to do far more than merely ask experts to judge whether the test *seems* to be based on appropriate content. This type of superficial judgment regarding whether the test *appears*, on the face of it, to be relevant for a given purpose, is sometimes referred to as *face validity*. Face validity is not a *Standards*-approved form of validity evidence and should not, therefore, be employed by educational leaders. Indeed, it was to extinguish the proliferation of such expressions as *face validity* that the *Standards* were originally produced.

Unlike face validity, which often rests on a single judgment of the match between a test's appearance and its intended use, content-related evidence of validity is produced by a set of (1) test-development operations designed to secure suitable content representativeness, and (2) subsequent appraisals of the resulting content.

Content-Related Validity Evidence

Evidence indicating that an assessment suitably reflects the content domain it represents.

Now what are these "operations" that must be carried out properly if a test's content is to be representative of a defined domain of content? Well, one of the first things that must be done in order to collect content-related evidence of validity is to define, in clear and unambiguous language, the domain of content that a test is supposed to represent. In Figure 4.1 you can see how a test is supposed to function as a representation of a defined content domain of skills, knowledge, or affect. Note that the educational assessment depicted in Figure 4.1, as you saw in the previous chapter, is bounded by a thinner circle than the content domain it is supposed to represent. That's simply because in any educationally worthwhile content domain there will almost always be so much content that an assessment can only *sample* what's contained in the content domain.

The content definition should, of course, be influenced by the purpose for which the test is intended to be used. For instance, if an algebra teacher's midterm examination is supposed to represent all of the course content covered during the first half of the course, then the universe of content to be represented by the test could be defined by listing all of the algebraic knowledge and skills treated before the midterm exam. To choose another example, suppose you were building a new test to measure the skills and knowledge needed by those who repair laptop computers. If you could set forth, in sufficient detail, the body of skills and knowledge that laptop computer repair personnel need in order to function satisfactorily, then you would have defined the universe of content that the new test should represent.

The key term in thinking about content-related evidence of validity is *representativeness*. A test should *represent* a defined domain of content. Because of the breadth of many content fields, it is impossible for a test to measure *exhaustively* the domain of content involved. Thus, for a test to represent a domain of content properly, the test must usually sample the major aspects of that domain.

There are two basic strategies that can be applied, separately or in concert, to secure content-related evidence of validity. First, an attempt to incorporate suitable content on the test can be carried out (and documented) *during test development* itself. The test's developers, calling on additional content experts as necessary, can exercise their best judgments in an effort to build a test that satisfactorily represents a desired domain of content or behavior.

The second strategy to follow in gathering content-related evidence of validity is to send a test through a series of *post facto judgments* about the representativeness of it content. For example, a panel of independent experts can be asked to review a test, item by item, to see if the test's items satisfactorily represent the domain of content or behavior involved. You'll consider both of these alternatives shortly.

For classroom teachers, the typical approach to gathering content-related evidence of validity would be to judge, *during development*, which content should be included in a test. If the *post facto judgment* approach were to be employed, the teacher might ask other teachers to review the content-appropriateness of a test's items.

FIGURE 4.1.

How an educational assessment represents a central domain of skills, knowledge, or affect.

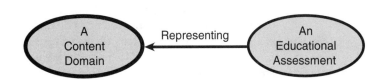

Whether Content Equals Behavior

The attentive reader will have noted that in the previous paragraphs your amiable author has been playing a bit fast and loose with two concepts, namely, "content" and "behavior." I've been focusing, of course, on content-related evidence of validity. But measurement experts, when dealing with content-related evidence of validity, often rely on such phrases as "the behaviors demonstrated in testing" and "the performance domain." Doesn't this sound as if they should be describing something called "behavior-related evidence of validity" or "performance-related evidence of validity" instead of "content-related evidence of validity"?

Well, here is where history confuses us a bit. At the outset, content-related evidence of validity was a notion applied almost exclusively to *achievement* tests and, as such, made a good deal of sense. Did the content, that is, the knowledge and skills on a test, adequately represent the subject-matter content it was supposed to sample? However, that rather limited conception of content coverage doesn't work so wonderfully when educators start talking about tests dealing with students' attitudes or physical skills. In those sorts of assessment situations, educators are more directly concerned with student behaviors rather than with subject-matter content. This, of course, is where confusion can fester. (It can fester faster than you'd think. Indeed, early confusion about behavior and content can foster faster festering.)

It is likely that, when the various measurement experts who produced early versions of the *Standards* wrestled with this problem, they decided to use the phrase "content validity"[6] but to define it more broadly so that the focus was also on student behaviors, rather than only on content. In the case of achievement tests, particularly tests of knowledge, the emphasis will still probably be on content. With many other types of tests, however, it will make more sense to think of content-related evidence of validity as an umbrella covering behavior as well as content.

Interpretation Influences

When assembling content-related evidence of validity, there are some differences in the approaches that should be employed if an assessment device is to be chiefly used for relative (norm-referenced) interpretations versus absolute (criterion-referenced) interpretations. Let's start off with the impact that a quest for relative interpretations can have.

Relative interpretations. Tests that are used to make norm-referenced interpretations, especially standardized achievement tests, have been around for half a century or more. With half a century of experience, one would surmise that for most standardized achievement tests the quantity and quality of evidence regarding content-related evidence of validity would be pretty impressive. Sadly, it isn't.

For most commercially published tests, there is a technical manual of some sort that offers information and evidence regarding validity, reliability, and other psychometric considerations. In almost no instance will one find a really first-rate assembly of content-related evidence of validity for a standardized achievement test.[7]

What is typically found in the technical manuals of most such tests is a description of how the test's developers attempted to make sure that all of the crucial content was included in their test. For example, the manual will describe the qualifications of the subject-matter experts who helped decide what content should be included. The manual might also set forth how the test developers surveyed the content included in widely used textbooks or, perhaps, in the content standards or curriculum syllabi of states and major school districts. These days, there will almost always be a description of the attention given to the relevant content standards developed by national subject-matter groups. In essence, the thrust of most standardized achievement test manuals is to describe the *process by which the test's content was selected*, then assume that such a description adequately handles the matter of content validity. This casual treatment of such an important topic is regrettable.

There are undoubtedly a number of reasons why standardized achievement test developers have given only modest attention to content-related evidence of validity. One reason is the absence of any generally accepted procedures for assembling content-related evidence of validity. In spite of the efforts of the *Standards* writers to illuminate what is meant by content-related evidence of validity, the *Standards* do not provide much in the way of step-by-step guidance regarding how test developers should gather such evidence.

In the same vein, there have been no agreed-on schemes to depict the content-related evidence of validity in a quantitative manner. Other types of validity evidence, to be described later in the chapter, can be represented by tidy quantitative indicators. This is not so with content-related evidence of validity. Perhaps the absence of these pithy numerical indicators has dissuaded standardized test constructors from getting heavily involved in the assembly of content-related evidence of validity.

Another reason that creators of standardized achievement tests may have been a bit relaxed in their efforts to secure content-related evidence of validity is the dominant reliance on normative interpretations of a student's performance. As long as the test covers the *content* of concern (for instance, reading) in a general way, then to use the test effectively it is ordinarily sufficient to identify the student's relative status in relationship to that of the normative group. Accordingly, less attention need be given to the test's content boundaries.

Absolute interpretations. Turning to absolute score interpretations, because the purpose of a criterion-referenced interpretation is to provide a clear picture of what it is that a student can or can't do, it is only natural that, for criterion-referenced interpretations, content-related evidence of validity should be a matter of paramount importance. Because, as you saw earlier, the focus of content-related evidence of validity is on the content and behaviors being sampled by a test, the challenge in assembling evidence regarding a test's content coverage is to make sure that the *description* of the test's measured assessment domain is sufficiently accurate so that precise interpretations can be drawn from a student's test performance.

A Need for Quantification

Whenever possible, those assembling content-related evidence of validity should try to report their results quantitatively. For example, when documenting the role of subject-matter experts in identifying the content for a to-be-developed test, the test's developers should indicate *how many* experts were selected from what sort of original list of invitees, *how many* opportunities those experts had to review the proposed content for the test, *what proportion* of the experts supported each content category on the test, and so on. Any important circumstances associated with the experts' content recommendations should also be described, for instance, whether the content experts provided by-mail advice or engaged in face-to-face discussions before offering content recommendations.

Post facto judgmental procedures to gather content-related evidence of validity are particularly appealing because such evidence can be gathered quite systematically. A panel of knowledgeable individuals can be asked to decide (1) whether each item represents the designated assessment domain, and (2) the extent to which the assessment domain's important components have been measured by the test's items. I'll illustrate such a two-stage procedure by using a statewide high school graduation test in mathematics as an example.

Suppose you were attempting to assemble content-related evidence of validity for such a test. You might follow a scheme along these lines:

1. Assemble a panel of fifteen to twenty individuals who are knowledgeable regarding the kinds of mathematical skill and knowledge needed by high school graduates.
2. Ask such panelists to review independently every item on the test, by supplying a *Yes* or *No* for all test items in response to a question such as the following:

> *Item Relevance.*   In order to receive a high school diploma in this state, should a student possess the mathematical knowledge or skill measured by this test item?

3. Compute the percentage of *Yes* responses to each item, then determine the average percentage of *Yes* responses for all of the test's items. This index reflects the test's *item relevance.*
4. Ask each panelist to respond independently to a question such as the following:

> *Content Coverage.*   Having first considered the entire range of mathematical content (knowledge and skills) that should be possessed by a high school graduate in this state, what percentage of that range of mathematical content is represented by this test's items?

5. Compute the mean percentage of all panelists' content-coverage percentage estimates. This index reflects the test's *content coverage.*

The data from steps three and five constitute useful evidence regarding a test's content-representativeness. For example, if (in Step Three) panelists, on average, determine that 85 percent of the test's items should be mastered by a high school graduate and (in Step Five) that over 90 percent of the total range of needed mathematical content is represented by the test's items, those are impressive figures. If, however, Step Three yielded an item-relevance index of only 55 percent positive panelist responses and Step Five re-

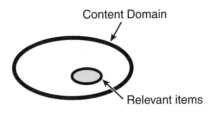

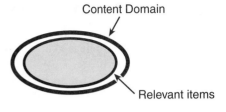

FIGURE 4.2.
Two levels of content coverage for items judged relevant to the content domain.

sulted in a content-coverage index of only 60 percent, then the content-related evidence for the test would not be compelling.

It's important to secure judges' reactions to questions about item relevance *and* content coverage, for if only the item-relevance judgment is required, then panelists might find that all of a test's items were relevant to the designated content domain but that only a small portion of the domain was represented on the test. This situation, illustrated in Figure 4.2, would arise if the relevant items (on the left in Figure 4.2) were redundant, that is, measured the same, limited aspects of the assessment domain. In the situation at the right of Figure 4.2, the test's items cover the assessment domain's content more representatively.

Before bidding farewell to content validity, it must be stressed one final time that test developers should give much more systematic and intense attention to this important, but characteristically underemphasized, form of validity evidence.

Criterion-Related Evidence of Validity

Instead of talking about a second approach to validity, it's bonus time; you will soon learn about *two* forms of *criterion-related evidence of validity*. Actually, the two variants of this type of validity evidence differ only in a temporal manner. Accordingly, measurement specialists simply lump them under a simple generic heading. Let's see what the *Standards* say about criterion-related evidence of validity.

> Criterion-related evidence demonstrates that test scores systematically relate to one or more outcome criteria. In this context the criterion is the variable of primary interest, as is determined by a school system, the management of a firm, or clients, for example. The choice of the criterion and the measurement procedures used to obtain criterion scores are of central importance. Logically, the value of a criterion-related study depends on the relevance of the criterion measure that is used.[8]

As you see, criterion-related evidence of validity is based on the extent to which a student's score on a test allows you to infer the student's performance on a criterion variable. The most common example of criterion-related validity evidence occurs when educators employ a verbal aptitude test, administered in high school, to predict what kind of grades (the criterion) students will earn in college.

Predictive and Concurrent Validity Evidence

If you administer the predictor test (in the previous paragraph's example, this was a verbal aptitude test) in high school and wait, say, two years, until students earn a two-year grade point average (the criterion), the relationship between students' grade point averages and their scores on the verbal aptitude test will bear on the test's *predictive criterion-related evidence of validity*. With predictive-validity studies, it is requisite for a substantial time interval to occur between administration of the predictor test (being evaluated) and the gathering of criterion data (by which to judge the predictor test's predictiveness).

With *concurrent validity* studies, no such time interval is present. For instance, let's say you administered a verbal aptitude test to college sophomores *on the same day* they receive information about their two-year grade point averages. Even though the aptitude test was designed for high school students, not college sophomores, the resulting correlation coefficients between college students' test scores and their grade point averages does provide you with some, admittedly weaker, criterion-related evidence of validity. For instance, if there were only a 0.21 correlation coefficient between predictor (the test) and criterion (grade point averages), then that trivial relationship would certainly cast doubt on the predictive inferences about college grades that one might draw from scores on the aptitude test.[9]

In the practical world of education, you'll typically want to make future predictions, for instance, about the chances that a high school student has for academic survival in college. That being the case, you might ask why educators don't always gather criterion-related validity evidence of the predictive sort, because it so obviously coincides with the real world's requirements. The most common reason for gathering concurrent-validity information, rather than predictive-validity information, is that people can't afford to wait.

While predictive inferences based on concurrent studies must be made most cautiously, it's better to make such inferences on the basis of concurrent-validity evidence than on the basis of no validity evidence whatsoever. Test developers sometimes adopt a strategy of creating a new test and disseminating it on the basis of concurrent studies, hoping to carry out predictive studies at a later point. Given the practicalities of real-world test development, this is often a sensible strategy.

Quality of the Criterion

When a test has been developed chiefly to make predictions regarding how someone will perform in a subsequent situation, then criterion-related evidence of validity is the most appropriate approach. The student's performance in the subsequent situation is typically indicated by some sort of variable referred to as the *criterion* variable. Indeed, it is because educators want to see how the test being validated relates to this criterion variable that this type of validation data is referred to as *criterion-related evidence of validity*.

It should be apparent, therefore, that the legitimacy of the criterion variable itself is pivotal in this validation approach. If test developers merely adopt the most convenient criterion measure at hand, the resulting validation effort will typically be of little worth. Great care must be taken to establish that the criterion variable itself is legitimate. For example, if you want to see how well students perform academically in college or high school, then a grade point average (GPA) is a sensible indicator. However, let's say the test

Criterion-Related Validity Evidence

Evidence demonstrating the systematic relationship of test scores to a criterion variable.

Criterion Variable

An external variable that serves as the target for a predictor test.

developers were in a hurry, so that rather than gathering official GPAs from the school's records, they relied on students' *self-reported* GPAs. Obviously, student recollections tend to be somewhat inaccurate (and typically inflated), so the self-reported GPAs would constitute a less defensible index of academic achievement than would GPAs based on official transcripts.

Instead of going to the official records or asking students for self-reported GPAs, what if the test developers had asked parents to estimate how well (on a ten-point scale) their children were doing in school? While it would certainly be possible to compute a correlation coefficient between students' scores on a predictor test and these highly partisan parental ratings—with the resulting r carried out to three or four decimal points—the coefficient would certainly contribute less to criterion-related evidence of validity for the test than would a study involving a less biased criterion variable. Selection of a criterion measure on the basis of opportunism should obviously be avoided.

Quality of the Validation Study

What sort of criterion variables are educators usually interested in when they attempt to secure criterion-related evidence of validity, either of the predictive or concurrent variety? Well, grade point averages or teacher ratings often serve as criterion measures when someone is trying to supply validity evidence for a test that's predictive of one's academic performance. For predicting vocational success, educators sometimes use comprehensive skill tests as a criterion, such as an end-of-school exam. Supervisory ratings of on-the-job performance are also employed.

Sometimes you can employ less obvious, but indisputably sound, criterion variables. For instance, a colleague of mine was validating a predictor survey being used to screen potential waiters and waitresses for a national restaurant chain. He chose as a criterion variable the size of tips given on credit card receipts as his criterion measure. Although he recognized that many tips were given in cash, so would not be recorded, he inferred that the tips reported on credit card receipts would reflect customer satisfaction with the waiters and waitresses.

Had my colleague administered the predictor survey to already employed personnel and then correlated their performance on the test with the past month's tips, this would have been an instance of *concurrent* criterion-related validity evidence. Had he administered the test to newly hired personnel, then waited six months to gather the information on tips, it would have been a case of *predictive* criterion-related validity evidence.

Because criterion-related validity evidence is needed if you want to be confident of the legitimacy of your predictive inferences about someone's performance on a criterion variable, you must be certain that the individuals involved in the validation investigation are similar to those people for whom you wish to make predictions. The less similarity there is between those in the validation sample and those for whom you wish to make predictions, the more tentative your predictions should be.

By the same token, the conditions surrounding the validation study (or studies) should be comparable to the conditions surrounding the situation in which you want to make predictions. If these situations are markedly dissimilar, your predictions should be made with cartons of caution.

Interpretation Influences

As you will doubtlessly recall from Chapter 2's discussion of relative, that is, norm-referenced interpretations, the chief mission of a good norm-referenced interpretation is to distinguish among students so that meaningful comparisons can be made between, for example, Billy and Bertha. The most typical situation in which educators find need of such comparative information is when they select individuals in a *fixed quota* situation.

For any *aptitude* test, criterion-related evidence of validity is the most useful sort of validation data because these tests are invariably used for predictive purposes. Even standardized *achievement* tests are sometimes used to make predictions about students, such as when educators employ a test of a student's reading achievement levels in the lower grades to predict the student's reading achievement levels in higher grades. In such cases, of course, criterion-related evidence of validity would be of great value in judging the test's potential value for this sort of predictive purpose.

It is not surprising, therefore, that the vast majority of validation studies carried out on educational tests during the last half century have been of a criterion-related nature. Because the bulk of published tests available to educators were intended to permit norm-referenced interpretations, and because these tests were typically used to make predictions in fixed quota settings, it was only natural that measurement personnel would become preoccupied with criterion-related evidence of validity.

Because in most cases a test that's constructed to permit criterion-referenced interpretations is employed to get a fix on what the student can do *now*, not predict what a student will do in a later setting, there are relatively few instances in which criterion-related evidence of validity bears focally on the worth of such tests. There are, of course, situations in which educators might wish to ascertain a student's current status with respect to a well-defined assessment domain, yet also use that current-status information to make predictions about the student's future status. For such situations, educational leaders should approach the assembly of criterion-related evidence of validity in much the same way as their colleagues who wish to make norm-referenced interpretations.

Construct-Related Evidence of Validity

Being a compassionate textbook author, I have saved the most complicated category of validity evidence for the last. Besides that, I feared that if I embarked on a discourse on *construct-related evidence of validity* too early, you might never have forged ahead to discover the raptures of content-related and criterion-related validity evidence.

We can begin by seeing what the committee preparing the *Standards* had to say when they described construct-related evidence of validity.

> The evidence classed in the construct-related category focuses primarily on the test score as a measure of the psychological characteristic of interest. Reasoning ability, spatial visualization, and reading comprehension are constructs, as are personality characteristics such as sociability and introversion. Endurance is a frequently used construct in athletics. Studies of leadership behavior often refer to constructs such as consideration for subordinates (giving praise, explaining reasons for action, asking opinions) and initiating structure (setting goals, keeping on schedule). Such character-

istics are referred to as *constructs* because they are theoretical constructions about the nature of human behavior.[10]

Explaining Construct-Related Validation

Here's how construct-related evidence of validity evidence is assembled. (Oh yes, please read this and the next few paragraphs slowly, because the ideas presented therein are apt to be foreign to your experience. Indeed, they are apt to be foreign to anyone's experience.) First the test developer conceives of the existence of some *hypothetical construct*, such as "love of animals." Typically, the creation of this hypothetical construct is based on prior research or plenty of experience. Second, a test is developed that supposedly measures this construct. Let's say you have whipped up a thirty-item test entitled the Animal Lover's Inventory (ALI, for short). High test scores on the ALI are said to indicate that the examinees love animals, and low test scores are said to indicate that the examinees find animals repugnant.

Now, with the ALI in hand, you want to see if we can assemble construct-related evidence of validity. Based on your knowledge of what this construct is, you then design an investigation in which you predict that if the ALI does what it's supposed to do, individuals should obtain particular kinds of scores on the test. For instance, let's say one prediction is that if you administered the ALI to individuals entering and exiting the City Dog Pound, those people *leaving* the pound with a dog or cat in their arms would get higher ALI scores than those who are *entering* the pound with a dog or cat. This study would be based on the idea that animal lovers would tend to rescue pets from the pound where pets are apt to be "put to sleep," while those who are dropping off animals at the pound are not doing so because the animals need a nap.

If you could get ALI scores on the two groups of examinees, that is, pet leavers and pet getters, and found that your hypothesis was confirmed (ALI scores of pet getters being significantly higher than ALI scores of pet leavers), you have produced evidence, not only regarding the validity of ALI-based inferences, but also of the legitimacy of the construct itself.

If the hypothesis had not been confirmed, then doubt is cast on (1) the validity of ALI-based inferences, (2) the legitimacy of the construct on which the test was based, or (3) both of these. In situations where the predicted results do not occur, it is the task of the test developers to determine whether there are defects in the construct, the test, or perhaps in the design of the construct-validity study that was carried out. Construct-related evidence of validity is *not* satisfactorily produced by a single study; rather, construct-related evidence of validity should be based on an accumulation of research studies. Actually, all varieties of validation evidence ought to be gathered via several studies, not only one data-gathering effort.

Construct-Validation Strategies

There is no single way to gather construct-related evidence of validity. The kinds of empirical data that can bear on the quality of a test (and the construct on which it is based) are truly myriad. The only limiting factor is the ingenuity of the construct validator.

More often than not, construct-validation studies are of the following sorts:

1. *Intervention Studies:* Attempts to demonstrate that students respond differently to the measure after receiving some sort of treatment.
2. *Differential-Population Studies:* Efforts to show that individuals representing distinct populations score differently on the measure.
3. *Related-Measures Studies:* Correlations, positive or negative depending on the measures, between students' scores on the test and their scores on other measures.

Let's briefly illustrate each of these approaches to the assembly of construct-related validation evidence. There are, of course, many others.

To illustrate the *intervention studies* approach, we might be evaluating a new inventory measuring a person's text anxiety, that is, the extent to which people become anxious before taking tests. From 100 prospective college students taking a mathematics test, we randomly select fifty and inform them that their scores on the approaching test will be "crucial." We tell the other fifty students that the test will be "no big deal." Then we give all 100 people our test-anxiety inventory prior to their taking the mathematics test. Our prediction is that the fifty students who receive the "crucial" treatment will display greater test anxiety on our inventory than the other fifty students.

Turning to an illustration of the *differential-population* approach, let's imagine that you have created a self-report questionnaire designed to measure people's preoccupation with their own skin quality. You then administer the new test to (1) 100 adolescent boys and girls besieged by acute acne attacks, and (2) residents of a retirement community, all of whom are at least seventy years old. Your prediction, not surprisingly, would be that the teenagers would display higher scores (reflecting greater preoccupation with skin quality) than would the senior citizens. Had your inventory dealt with "skin wrinkles," of course, the prediction would have been reversed.

Finally, to illustrate a *related-measures* approach, you might predict that scores on a newly developed problem-solving test would be negatively correlated with scores on a rigidity test. That is, better problem solvers would display less rigidity while weaker problem solvers would tend to possess stronger perseveration tendencies. As this example illustrates, the notion of the predicted conclusion can be positive or negative, depending on the measures involved.

There is one validation evidence that is often confused by educators, and it occurs when someone correlates a new test of, for instance, intellectual aptitude with a previously established test of that same attribute. Suppose, for example, that you had developed a nifty new aptitude test that was culturally unbiased and delightfully inexpensive and could be administered in less than 6.5 minutes. Now if you had 100 students tested with your new aptitude test, named the *Shorty* for obvious reasons, then related these *Shorty* scores to student scores on the widely accepted *Stanford-Binet Intelligence Scale*, what sort of validity would you have?

Well, too many people think that this scenario constitutes an instance of criterion-related evidence of validity. It doesn't. It's an example of construct-related evidence of validity, because you're assuming that the *Stanford-Binet* already has been established as a measure of intellectual aptitude and you're simply trying to piggyback on the established test's assessment of the construct your new test is trying to measure. It is *not* an instance

---

Construct-Related Validity Evidence

Empirical evidence that (1) supports the posited existence of a hypothetical construct, and (2) indicates that an assessment device does, in fact, measure that construct.

of criterion-related validity evidence because the *Stanford-Binet* is not an index of a criterion behavior which you wish to predict. Why, after all, would someone go to the trouble of whomping up a test of Construct *X* merely to predict someone's score on another test of Construct *X*? If the previously established test of the construct is good enough for you to use in your validation study, it's probably good enough to already measure the construct in which you're interested. Intellectual aptitude tests are created in order to predict how individuals will perform later in some criterion situation, such as in college or on the job. Aptitude tests are not created to predict one's scores on another aptitude test.

Thus, whenever for purposes of gathering validity evidence educators attempt to correlate two measures of the same attribute, we are adopting a construct-related validity evidence strategy. It is typically a fairly weak form of construct-related evidence because the creators of the new test are accepting the established test's virtues. If that established test's score-based inferences are less than satisfactorily valid, as will often be the case, then evidence based on the use of the established test to gather construct-related evidence of validity is less powerful.

What measurement folks are attempting to do when they try to assemble construct-related evidence of validity is to build a network of key relationships and understandings so they have confidence that their test legitimately taps the attribute they're trying to measure. To establish such networks is a vexing business. The more elusive the attribute being measured is, the more vexing the task is. One does not satisfy the need for construct-related evidence merely by churning out a correlational study or two.

Eligible Targets for Construct Validation

Measurement experts usually opt for construct-related validation strategies when they are attempting to assess elusive attributes such as those found in the affective domain, for example, anxiety, self-concept, and locus of control. For more routine tests, such as a student's ability to read, we rarely see full-blown efforts to assemble construct-related evidence of validity. Yet it is only because we are more comfortable in our belief that an individual possesses "skill in reading" that we fail to employ construct-related strategies here too. There is no fundamental difference between the constructs of (1) a student's self-confidence, and (2) a student's ability to perform double-digit multiplication. Neither of these entities is observable. Both must be inferred. As a consequence, test developers would do well to assemble the necessary network of relationships and data needed to establish the legitimacy even of a skill as prosaic as "the ability to read with understanding."

Interpretation Influences

We have a long history of gathering construct-related evidence of validity for tests intended to yield norm-referenced interpretations, particularly in efforts to evaluate the kinds of measuring instruments used for clinical work with individuals. These investigations, because of the admitted elusiveness of the constructs being assessed, have often been marked by considerable care on the part of those carrying out the studies. As indicated earlier, however, less attention has been given by standardized achievement test developers to assembling construct-related evidence of validity for traditional tests designed to measure skills and knowledge.

As you will see in a subsequent chapter, developers of tests intended to provide criterion-referenced interpretations often select one particular measurement strategy from several contenders, then describe this measurement strategy in great detail so that test items congruent with the strategy can be created. For norm-referenced interpretations, the attributes being assessed are often broader and described more generally. For developers who are focused on criterion-referenced interpretations, therefore, a clear choice among assessment strategies usually must be made. For instance, should a student's ability to write be assessed by (1) a multiple-choice test dealing with the rules of usage, (2) a completion-type test in which partial sentences are to be completed, or (3) a requirement that the student compose an original essay? If one of these three assessment strategies is selected as an index of the student's "ability to write," then construct-related evidence of validity should be drawn regarding the score-based inferences to be drawn from the test to see if the assessment strategy that was selected turned out to be appropriate.

Relationships among the Three Types of Evidence

The three types of evidence that have just been described should be regarded as convenient categories for accumulating data regarding the likelihood that test-based inferences will be valid. But, as the *Standards* authors assert, "the use of the category labels does not imply that there are distinct types of validity or that a specific validation strategy is best for each specific inference or test use."[11] Rigorous, nonoverlapping distinctions among the categories of validity evidence really aren't possible. For instance, evidence of the content-related or criterion-related varieties are also related to the construct-related category.

The *Standards* authors sum up the situation nicely when they stress the importance of all three types of validity evidence:

> An ideal validation includes several types of evidence, which span all three of the traditional categories. Other things being equal, more sources of evidence are better than fewer. However, the quality of the evidence is of primary importance, and a single line of solid evidence is preferable to numerous lines of evidence of questionable quality. Professional judgment should guide the decisions regarding the forms of evidence that are most necessary and feasible in light of the intended uses of the test and any likely alternatives to testing.[12] Having dealt with the topic of validity in some detail, you will be turning in the next chapter to a consideration of reliability.

Consequential Validity

In recent years, those who frequent the literature of educational measurement have encountered, with ever-increasing frequency it seems, the expression *consequential validity*. Acceptance of this concept has been fostered chiefly by the attention given to the consequences of test use in Samuel Messick's influential validity chapter in the third edition of *Educational Measurement* (1989).

Although every right-thinking educator ought to be concerned about the consequences ensuing from a test's use, it does not follow that test-use consequences need to be linked to the now widely held view that *validity* is rooted in the accuracy of inferences educators derive from students' test performances. I believe, therefore, that the reification of consequential validity is apt to be counterproductive. It will deflect educators from the clarity they need when judging tests *and* the consequences of test use.

Consequential Validity

A concept, disputed by some, focused on the appropriateness of a test's social consequences.

A clear conception of validity.   Because I've been involved with educational measurement since the time the earliest versions of the *Standards* were available in the mid-1950s, and have observed the way that different versions of the *Standards* dealt with validity, I regard the 1985 *Standards* treatment of validity to be a striking advance over earlier conceptualizations of validity. For one thing, the authors of the *Standards* don't equivocate regarding the paramount significance of validity. Their treatment of validity starts off with the assertion that "validity is the most important consideration in test evaluation." The *Standards* then go on to make clear that validity refers to test-based inferences, not the test itself:

> A variety of inferences may be made from scores produced by a given test, and there are many ways of accumulating evidence to support any inference. Validity, however, is a unitary concept. Although evidence may be accumulated in many ways, *validity always refers to the degree to which that evidence supports the inferences that are made from the scores* (AERA, APA, NCME, 1985, p. 9, emphasis added).

The *Standards* assert that various types of evidence—namely, construct-related evidence, content-related evidence, and criterion-related evidence, can be brought to bear when someone is making a judgment about the validity of a score-based inference. Because, in the field of education, we are typically trying to get an accurate estimate of a student's status with respect to desired instructional aims such as the student's mastery of certain skills or domains of knowledge, an educator's instructional decisions are obviously apt to be unsound if that educator's score-based inferences about student status are invalid.

Yet, even though the 1985 *Standards* sets forth a lucid definition of validity, most of our teachers and school administrators have, at best, only a murky notion of what validity really is. Having spent the past decade or so in trying to sharpen teachers' classroom assessment skills, I have encountered relatively few American educators who understand that validity depends on the accuracy of score-based inferences and is not a property of a test itself.

When teachers finally grasp the significance of "validity-focused-on-inferences" rather than "validity-focused-on-tests," they really begin to understand that assessment instruments do not invariably, or even frequently, yield results leading to incontestably accurate inferences. A test is only a measuring instrument, an instrument far less precise than most practitioners believe. Such instruments should be used to arrive at inferences about students' status with respect to the domain of knowledge, skills, or affect represented by the test. And, because educational tests do not represent with unflawed perfection those domains, the resultant score-based inference will often be less than completely accurate. But because educational tests typically yield *numerical* results, and because human beings usually ascribe excessive accuracy to numbers, many educators regard the results of educational tests with unwarranted deference. If educators think that the measuring instrument is valid, they'll also tend to regard its numerical results as "valid," that is, as accurate. The emphasis on the validity of inferences makes it clear that the validation of inferences depends on the *inferer's judgment* rather than on numbers. That view sends a solid signal to those many educational practitioners who currently kowtow to the numerical precision of assessment instruments.

Cluttering instead of clarifying. I think that when the advocates of consequential validity attempt to make social consequences an integral part of validity, they do a disservice to clarity. They are asking a crisp concept, that is, *validity as the accuracy of score-based inferences,* to take on additional complexities. As a result of this excessive complicating, few educators will really understand what the essence of validity truly is. Note, for example, the multiple foci that Messick wants validity to embrace:

> Validity is an overall evaluative judgment of the degree to which empirical evidence and theoretical rationales support the *adequacy* and *appropriateness* of *interpretations* and *actions* based on test scores and other modes of assessment. (Messick, 1995, p. 5)

Messick's conception of validity, the cornerpiece of his 1989 chapter about validity in *Educational Measurement* (Messick, 1989), goes way beyond the notion that validity refers to the accuracy of inferences based on the results of testing. Messick, of course, agrees with most writers, and with the *Standards,* that validity is not a property of the test itself. Rather, he says, it is a property of the meaning of the test scores. But such meaning, he contends, must be derived not only from test items and stimulus conditions, but also from the examinees and the context of the assessment. Where Messick's conceptualization of validity opens the door for social consequences is when he asserts that "in particular, what needs to be valid is the meaning or interpretation of the scores as well as any implications for action that this meaning entails" (Messick, 1995, p. 5).

Messick wants the social consequences of a test's use to become an important part of his validity framework. As he says,

> what is needed is a way of cutting and combining validity evidence that forestalls undue reliance on selected forms of evidence, that highlights the important though subsidiary role of specific content- and criterion-related evidence in support of construct validity in testing applications, and *that formally brings consideration of value implications and social consequences into the validity framework* (Messick, 1989, p. 20, emphasis added).

I think Messick's 1989 validity framework did, indeed, cut and combine evidence so that social consequences became a key "facet" of validity. It's just that the price to be paid for doing so is far too high. Educators will need to give up the fundamental clarity that the architects of the 1985 *Standards* carved out when they asserted that validity refers to score-based inferences.

There is, for most of us, solid satisfaction in encountering a simply stated, compelling truth. When the educational measurement community arrived at its 1985 *Standards* consensus that validity refers to the accuracy of score-based inferences, many educators were gratified. Here was a potent notion that could be communicated to practitioners. Here was a way to get teachers and administrators to focus their attention on the adequacy of the *evidence* that was used to support a score-based inference about a student's status. But the clarity of "validity-as-score-based-inferences" is being threatened by those who would require the concept of validity to shoulder theoretical baggage that, though focused on an issue of importance, does not really bear on the accuracy of score-based inferences.

Let me use a simple example to illustrate this problem. Suppose that you want to make educational placement decisions about middle school students in an affluent school district. Let's assume that a mathematics achievement test has been carefully developed over a three-year period by district educators and external consultants. The mathematical knowledge and skills to be promoted by the district during grades 6 through 8 are carefully delineated, then reviewed rigorously by a committee of district educators, parents, and independent mathematics consultants. Varied types of selected-response and constructed-response test items are employed in the test. The items are reviewed for content representativeness and potential bias, field-tested, revised, then reviewed and revised, again and again. *Everyone* who scrutinizes the test and the definitions of the assessment domain it was created to represent reaches the same conclusion. This is a test from which valid inferences can be drawn regarding the levels of a middle school student's mathematics achievement.

Schematically, the mathematics test is depicted in Figure 4.3 by the rectangle at the right while the content domain of mathematics skills and knowledge it represents is seen at the left. Based on efforts to produce varied forms of evidence regarding the validity of inferences about student mathematical status based on the students' test results, everyone involved concludes that the test allows the district's educators to make accurate inferences about students' mathematical achievement levels.

Now, having established that the new test adequately represents the mathematics assessment domain, and assuming that there are no major contextual factors (such as insufficient testing time) that confound any inferences, it is reasonable to assume that the district's educators can use students' test scores to make valid inferences about the mathematics achievement levels of the district's middle school students. With few exceptions, students who score well on the test will possess most of the mathematics skills and knowledge circumscribed by the assessment domain. With few exceptions, low-scoring students won't possess the knowledge and skills set forth in the assessment domain. Two such *valid* score-based inferences (Valid Inference A and Valid Inference B) are depicted in Figure 4.4. Clearly, there may be exceptions to the validity of score-based inferences in the case of particular students. Joselyn Jones may have had the flu on the day of the test and, therefore, might have scored lower than she otherwise would have. Billy Barton may

FIGURE 4.3.

An achievement test as a representative sample of an assessment domain in middle school mathematics.

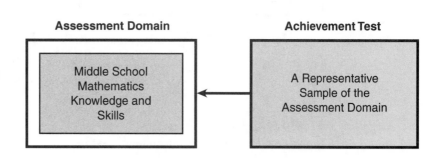

Assessment Domain

Middle School Mathematics Knowledge and Skills

Achievement Test

A Representative Sample of the Assessment Domain

In the News

Mo. Bill Would Crack Down on Fraudulent Test-Taking

by Jessica L. Sandham

Any student caught cheating on a college-entrance exam faces immediate cancellation of his test scores and typically needs to take the exam again to meet college-admissions requirements.

But if a third party contributes to the exam fraud by taking the test for another person, he or she often goes unpunished. Missouri state Sen. Steve Ehlmann would like to change that.

The Republican legislator has introduced a bill that would, in part, make it a legally punishable misdemeanor in his state for a person to take an official examination, such as the SAT or ACT, in place of someone else.

"If another student does the cheating, a school can expel them both," Mr. Ehlmann said. "But if the person taking the test illegally is not a student, there's no way to punish them."

Of the roughly 1.8 million students who take the SAT I: Reasoning Test every year, fewer than 200 are found guilty of exam fraud, said Kevin Gonzalez, a spokesman for the Princeton, N.J.-based Educational Testing Service, which administers the test.

Out of that group, the most common form of cheating is copyrighting, not impersonation, he said.

If Missouri lawmakers approve Mr. Ehlmann's bill, the state will become the 17th to pass a law addressing academic dishonesty, according to Amy Cook, a policy analyst at the Education Commission of the States, based in Denver. It is unclear how many of these laws would apply to cheating on the SAT or ACT, Ms. Cook said. . . .

What's your reaction?

Excerpted, with permission, from *Education Week*, April 15, 1998

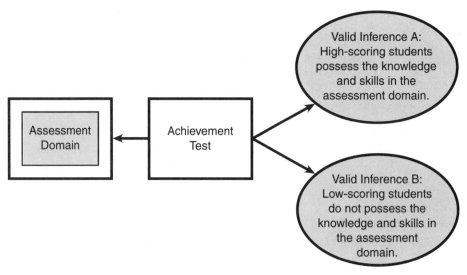

FIGURE 4.4.
Two valid inferences based on students' test results.

have, during the evening prior to the test's administration, used his mail-order "pick-a-lock kit" to gain access to the teacher's locked desk, memorized most of the answer key before the test was administered, and thus scored higher than he really should have. But, because of the care with which the test was developed, valid score-based inferences will generally be made from almost all students' performances. And, because of those valid inferences, students will be assigned to the appropriate computer-delivered mathematics programs.

Now, let's suppose in this imaginary affluent school district that a new, strong-willed school board is elected. For the sake of this illustration, imagine that the new board members enact some genuinely bizarre policies regarding the use of students' scores on the district's new mathematics test. For example, the board requires that any *girl* who scores below the overall median will be (a) prohibited from engaging in any extracurricular activities, (b) prevented from taking any art or music courses, and (c) required to take at least two mathematics courses per semester. All boys who scored below the median would be expelled. If the boys scored *really* low, they would first be publicly beaten. Such absurd decisions, while deplorable, do not alter one whit the *validity* of the test-based inferences about students' mathematics achievement. Those inferences are just as accurate as they were before the board made its ludicrous test-use decisions.

Messick and the other proponents of consequential validity will, I fear, make it impossible for educators to understand what measurement validity is *really* about. By asking the concept of validity to carry more conceptual freight than it should, advocates of consequential validity will have eroded the lucidity of what's meant by assessment validity.

Addressing test-use consequences. Without exception, advocates of consequential validity believe the social consequences of test use should be considered when judging whether a test's use is appropriate. So do I. But whereas the proponents of consequential validity would intertwine that consideration with validity by using Messick's 1989 validity framework, I would keep social consequences separate.

Reliability, after all, is regarded by measurement specialists as an important consideration when evaluating tests. But that doesn't mean we need to make reliability a "facet" of validity. Attending to the social consequences of test use should be an important task of test developers, test distributors, and test users. But such attention should be given *separately* from the assembly of evidence regarding the accuracy of score-based inferences.

I want test developers and users to assemble as much evidence as is feasible about the likely or potential consequences of test use. And, after a test has been in use for some time, I'd like to see solid scrutiny of any *unintended* effects, positive or negative, of the test's use. Shepard (1993) offers some useful advice about how to regard the intended and unintended effects of test use.

I believe that the proponents of consequential validity are striving for something good. Their concern is on target. Their mistake, I believe, is in trying to tie social consequences into a validity framework. Such a wedding of related but distinctive concepts will not be symbiotic, it will be septic.

Reporter's Notebook

In the News

Annual Conference Spotlights Trends, Key Issues in Research

Despite early-childhood experts' warnings against testing young children, most school districts give students some kind of standardized reading assessment before they leave 3rd grade, according to Chrys Dougherty, an assistant professor from the Lyndon B. Johnson School of Government at the University of Texas at Austin. He surveyed 251 U.S. districts between 1993 and 1995.

He found that 90 percent of them gave primary-grade children some kind of formal test that included assessment of reading skills.

Since the late 1980s, groups such as the National Association for the Education of Young Children have cautioned against excessive testing of any kind for young children. Mr. Dougherty said he was stunned by his findings indicating that educators are not heeding that advice.

But he viewed district's testing practices as positive.

"If children are not reading by the end of first grade, that's a risk factor for their future reading achievement, and it seems incumbent upon school districts to pay attention to that," he said.

—Debra Viadero & Steven Drummond

What's your reaction?

Reprinted, with permission, from *Education Week*, April 29, 1998

Chapter Wrap-Up

The chapter summary will be woven, as usual, around the chapter's guiding questions.

● What is validity?

In educational assessment, validity refers to the accuracy of the inferences (or interpretations) that are made based on students' performances on measurement devices. Because inaccurate inferences will lead to unsound decisions, many measurement specialists regard validity as the single, most important factor by which to judge the quality of an educational test. Through the years, a conventional terminology for describing validity-related notions has been sanctioned by measurement professionals in the form of the *Standards* developed by the American Psychological Association, the American Educational Research Association, and the National Council on Measurement in Education. The *Standards* identify three different forms of evidence that can be employed to determine the validity of score-based interpretations.

● What is content-related evidence of validity?

One form of validity evidence focuses on the extent to which the domain of knowledge, skill, and/or affect that a test is supposed to represent is, in fact, adequately represented. Because of the origins of standardized achievement tests, when it was imperative for a test to represent appropriate subject-matter content, this form of validity evidence is described as "content-related," even though in some cases the assessment domain ostensibly being represented by a measuring instrument may deal more with affective factors, skills, or behaviors than with what educators usually think of as "subject-matter content." Even though much content-related evidence of validity is based on human judgment, there is still a need to quantify such judgments if possible. Although content-related evidence of validity is extremely important if educational leaders wish to be assured that test-based interpretations are valid, one encounters few instances where a rigorously assembled set of such evidence accompanies tests, even in the standardized achievement tests distributed by major testing companies.

What is criterion-related evidence of validity?

Criterion-related evidence of validity consists of the degree to which students' test performances are related to an external criterion such as subsequent grades earned in school. Predictive validity evidence of this type involves the collection of assessment data, then correlating the data with students' scores on the criterion variable after a substantial period of time has elapsed. Concurrent validity evidence of the criterion-related variety focuses on the correlation between predictor-test scores and a predicted criterion, but data regarding the predictor and criterion are collected without any time delay. Because of the significance of the criterion variable to this form of validity evidence, great care must be given to the selection of a truly defensible criterion. Similarly, care must be given to the specifics of the validation study, whether predictive or concurrent, in which data are collected regarding the relationship between students' test scores and their performance on the criterion variable. Because many standardized academic aptitude tests are specifically designed to permit test-users to make predictions about students' performances in subsequent criterion situations, criterion-related evidence of validity is especially important to the developers and users of such academic aptitude tests.

What is construct-related evidence of validity?

Construct-related evidence of validity is, in a sense, the most comprehensive form of validity because, if one wished to, it would be possible to consider the other two varieties of validity evidence as forms of construct-related validity evidence. Construct-related evidence is based on the accumulation of empirical evidence that (1) the hypothetical construct being measured actually exists, and (2) the assessment device in use does, in fact, measure that construct. Three kinds of empirical data-collection studies are often relied on in the collection of construct-related validity evidence. Intervention studies try to show that students will, as predicted, respond differently to a measure after receiving some sort of treatment. Differential-population studies attempt to find out if, as predicted, individuals representing distinct groups respond differently to a measuring device. Related-measures studies center on whether predicted relationships between students' scores on a test and other similar or dissimilar tests are actually present. Although it is generally believed construct-related evidence of validity is most suitable for elusive psychological constructs such as one's fear of heights, almost all educational variables actually represent covert, unobservable entities. Accordingly, if educational leaders have any meaningful doubt about the legitimacy of a construct such as "reading ability" or "the ability to see mathematical connections," construct-related validation studies are very much in order.

Is "consequential validity" a useful concept?

Although *consequential validity* has been advocated since an important 1989 analysis of validity by Messick, it was argued in the chapter that the concept of consequential validity is not only unsound, but also apt to deflect educators from the idea that assessment validity is rooted in the accuracy of score-based inferences. It was stressed that the social consequences of using a test are tremendously important in judging the appropriateness of the test's use, but the consideration of a test's consequences should remain separate from validity. The "consequential validity" of tests should not be employed by educational leaders.

Practice Exercises

There were four types of validity evidence described in the chapter (if you'll allow me to split up the two variations of criterion-related validity-evidence). To give you some practice in distinguishing among them, see if you can decide in each of the following ten vignettes whether a (a) *content-related*, (b) *predictive criterion-related*, (c) *concurrent criterion-related*, or (d) *construct-related* evidence-gathering strategy is being employed.

1. A test of high school study habits and attitudes, supposedly predictive of how well high school students will perform academically, is administered to twelfth-graders during the same week that their cumulative grade point averages in high school are made available. The resulting "validity coefficient" is .56.
2. A group of college English professors judge the adequacy of coverage of a newly developed test of students' knowledge of grammar and syntax. The professors conclude that the coverage is "excellent."
3. Scores on a new version of the *Miller Analogies Test* (MAT) taken during college students' senior year are correlated with their grades in graduate school two years later. The MAT versus GPA correlation is .49.
4. Scores on a sixth-grade achievement test in basic skills are used as a predictor of high school achievement as reflected by high school teach-

ers' rankings of students. The rank–order correlation coefficient between these two variables is .55.
5. Scores on a newly developed self-esteem test are correlated with scores on the widely used *Coopersmith Self-Esteem Inventory*. The correlation between the two sets of scores was quite high ($r = .84$).
6. Teachers who will ultimately be using results of a newly developed math test review it, item by item, to make sure that all of the key topics have been tested. They are divided in their opinions.
7. A test publisher predicts that the firm's new vocational interest test will show that those scoring high on various subscales (such as "clerical" or "sales") are more likely to hold "real life" positions in those job categories than are those scoring low on such subscales.
8. A screening test administered to applicants for medical school correlates .63 with end-of-program grades earned by medical students.
9. A new quantitative aptitude test is administered to high school juniors two days before they take the district-wide test of mathematical skills. The resulting correlation between the two measures is .71.
10. A group of content specialists judges the contents of a new test in history and concludes that its content coverage was so splendid that they are "thoroughly contented."

Answers to Practice Exercises

1. This would be an instance of criterion-related validity evidence of the concurrent type.
2. Content-related evidence.
3. Criterion-related (predictive) evidence.
4. This is another case of predictive criterion-related evidence.

5. This is a case of construct-related evidence of validity. If it caused you any problems, reread the section dealing with *construct* validity evidence of this type (page 000).
6. Content-related evidence.

7. Construct-related evidence.
8. Predictive criterion-related evidence.
9. Concurrent criterion-related evidence.
10. This was a tough one: content-related evidence.

DISCUSSION QUESTIONS

1. If you were asked to explain in jargonless English the three basic categories of validity evidence for educational tests to a group of citizens on a school advisory council, how would you do it?
2. Which of the three types of validity evidence do you think is most important for norm-referenced interpretations? Why?
3. Which of the three types of validity evidence do you think is most important for criterion-referenced interpretations? Why?
4. Which of the various types of validity evidence is the most expensive for a test publisher to gather? Why do you think so?
5. What is the conceptual relationship, if any, among the three types of validity evidence? Can you think of situations in which all three types of validity evidence should be gathered?
6. From the perspective of an educational leader, which (if any) of the three types of validity evidence should be most important? Why?

SUGGESTIONS FOR ADDITIONAL READING

Airasian, Peter W. *Classroom Assessment* (3rd ed.). New York: Mc-Graw Hill, 1997.

Baglin, Roger F. "A Problem in Calculating Group Scores on Norm-Referenced Tests." *Journal of Educational Measurement, 23,* 1 (Spring 1986): 57–68.

Benson, Jeri. "Developing a Strong Program of Construct Validation: A Test Anxiety Example." *Educational Measurement: Issues and Practice, 17,* 1 (Spring 1998): 10–17, 22.

Burger, Susan E., and Donald L. Burger. "Determining the Validity of Performance-Based Assessment." *Educational Measurement: Issues and Practice, 13,* 1 (Spring 1994): 9–15.

Carey, Lou M. *Measuring and Evaluating School Learning.* Boston: Allyn & Bacon, 1988.

Code of Fair Testing Practices in Education. Prepared by the Joint Committee on Testing Practices. Washington, DC: American Psychological Association, 1988.

Crocker, Linda. "Assessing Content Representativeness of Performance Assessment Exercises." *Applied Measurement in Education, 10,* 1 (1997): 83–95.

Cunningham, George K. *Educational and Psychological Measurement.* New York: Macmillan, 1986.

Delandshere, Ginette, and Anthony R. Petrosky. "Assessment of Complex Performances: Limitations of Key Measurement Assumptions." *Educational Researcher, 27,* 2 (March 1998): 14–24.

Gronlund, Norman E.. *Measurement and Evaluation in Teaching* (5th ed.). New York: Macmillan, 1985.

Haney, W., and G. Madaus. "The Evolution of Ethical and Technical Standards for Testing." In R. K. Hambleton and J. Zaal (Eds.), *Handbook of Testing.* Amsterdam: North Holland Press, 1988.

Hanson, Ralph A., Robert F. McMorris, and Jerry D. Bailey. "Differences in Instructional Sensitivity between Item Formats and between Achievement Test Items." *Journal of Educational Measurement, 23,* 1 (Spring 1986): 1–12.

Linn, R. L. "Educational Assessment: Expanded Expectations and Challenges." *Educational Evaluation and Policy Analysis, 15,* (1993): 1–16.

Linn, Robert L., and Norman E. Gronlund. *Measurement and Assessment in Teaching* (7th ed.). Upper Saddle River, NJ: Prentice-Hall, 1995.

Linn, Robert L. "Evaluating the Validity of Assessments: The Consequences of Use." *Educational Measurement: Issues and Practice, 16,* 2 (Summer 1997): 14–16.

Madaus, G. F. "Minimum Competency Testing for Certification: The Evolution and Evaluation of Test Validity." In G. F. Madaus (Ed.), *The Courts, Validity, and Minimum Competency Testing.* Hingham, MA.: Kluwer-Nijhoff, 1983.

Mehrens, William A., and Irvin J. Lehmann. *Using Standardized Tests in Education.* New York: Longman, 1987.

Mehrens, William A., and S. E. Phillips. "Sensitivity of Item Difficulties to Curricular Validity." *Journal of Educational Measurement, 24,* 4 (Winter 1987): 357–370.

Mehrens, William A. "The Consequences of Consequential Validity." *Educational Measurement: Issues and Practice, 16,* 2 (Summer 1997): 16–18.

Messick, S. "Validity." In R. L. Linn (Ed.), *Educational Measurement* (3rd ed.), pp. 13–103. Washington, DC: American Council on Education & National Council on Measurement in Education, 1989.

Messick, S. "Standards of Validity and the Validity of Standards in Performance Assessment." *Educational Measurement: Issues and Practice, 14,* 4 (Winter 1995): 5–8.

Moss, P. A. "Themes and Variations in Validity Theory." *Educational Measurement: Issues and Practice, 14,* 2 (Summer 1995): 5–13.

Moss, Pamela A. "The Role of Consequences in Validity Theory." *Educational Measurement: Issues and Practice, 17,* 2 (Summer 1998): 6–12.

Popham, W. James. "Consequential Validity: Right Concern—Wrong Concept." *Educational Measurement: Issues and Practice, 16,* 2 (Summer 1997): 9–13.

Shepard, Lorrie A. "Evaluating Test Validity." In L. A. Darling-Hammond (Ed.), *"Review of Research in Education, 19* (1993): 405–450." Washington, DC: American Educational Research Association.

Shepard, Lorrie A., "The Centrality of Test Use and Consequences of Test Validity." *Educational Measurement: Issues and Practice, 16,* 2 (Summer 1997): 5–8.

Standards for Educational Psychological Tests. Prepared by a joint committee of the American Psychological Association, American Educational Research Association, National Council on Measurement in Education. Washington, DC: American Psychological Association, 1985.

Taleporos, Elizabeth. "Consequential Validity: A Practitioner's Perspective." *Educational Measurement: Issues and Practice, 17,* 2 (Summer 1998): 20–23, 34.

Yalow, Elanna S., and W. James Popham. "Content Validity at the Crossroads." *Educational Research, 12,* 8 (October 1983): 10–21.

AND FOR THOSE WHO TIRE OF READING

Williams, Reed. *Test Reliability and Validity* (Audiotape). Tape recording from the 1988 session of the American Educational Research Association (AERA). Available at AERA, 1230 Seventeenth St., N. W., Washington, DC 20036.

ENDNOTES

1. Samuel A. Messick, "The Standard Problem: Meaning and Values in Measurement and Evaluation," American Psychologist, 30 (1975), 955–966.
2. Robert L. Linn, "Issues of Validity in Measurement for Competency-Based Programs," (Paper presented at the Annual Meeting of the National Council on Measurement on Education, New York, 1977).
3. Standards for Educational and Psychological Testing. Prepared by a joint committee of the American Psychological Association, the American Educational Research Association, and the National Council on Measurement in Education (Washington, DC: American Psychological Association, 1985).
4. As an undergraduate philosophy major, I discovered that St. Thomas Aquinas loved to conclude his philosophical analogies with "in like manner." I've always resisted the temptation to emulate him; that is, I resisted until now.
5. Standards for Educational and Psychological Testing, p. 10.
6. Until the 1985 version of the Standards, the phrase used to describe what we've been considering was *content validity* rather than *content-related evidence of validity*.
7. I have obviously not read all the technical manuals for all the standardized achievement tests in the world. (Even if I had, I'd be ashamed to admit it.) However, I've read a good many of these manuals. I have never found a truly compelling set of content-related evidence of validity.
8. Standards for Educational and Psychological Testing.
9. Remember, if you find the use of phrases such as "correlation coefficient" intimidating, take a dip (or even an extended swim) in the Appendix that starts on p. 427.
10. Ibid.
11. Standards for Educational and Psychological Testing.
12. Ibid.

5 Reliability of Assessment Devices

chapter

- What is reliability?

- What is stability reliability evidence?
  When Needed
  How Collected

- What is alternate-form reliability evidence?
  When Needed
  How Collected
  Stability and Alternate-Form Evidence
  Post Facto Form Equating
  Separate Field-Testing versus Embedding

- What is internal consistency reliability evidence?
  Split-Half Technique
  Kuder–Richardson Formulae
  Coefficient Alpha

- What is the standard error of measurement?

Validity and reliability are the meat and potatoes of the measurement game. In the previous chapter educational leaders received a fairly hefty serving of meat; now it's potato time.

From the chapter on validity you learned that the concept of validity evidence is not unitary. There are different sorts of validity evidence, depending on what functions a test is designed to serve. Not surprisingly, reliability is also a multimeaning concept. There are different sorts of reliability, depending on the way the reliability evidence is gathered. In general, when educators think about the reliability of a test, they focus on the *consistency* with which the test is measuring whatever it's measuring. Most educators probably conceive of consistency as *consistency over time*. In other words, if you asked a run-of-the-mill group of educational leaders to to tell you what is meant by a test's reliability, odds are they'd respond with something like this: "Test reliability indicates whether students would get essentially the same scores if they took the test at different times." The sort of reliability these folks are talking about is referred to as *stability*, and it constitutes an important type of reliability. Later, you'll look carefully at ways of securing stability estimates, as well as several other types of reliability. Before doing that, however, let's spend a moment or two considering the relationship between reliability and validity.

Can Validity Find Happiness If Reliability Is Unfaithful?

If a test yields valid inferences, must it also be reliable? If a test is reliable, does that mean its inferences are valid? If a test is not reliable and yields no valid inferences, should it be cherished or fed to a paper shredder?

Answers to these and similar questions depend on the relationship between reliability and validity. That relationship can be set forth succinctly: *Test reliability is a necessary, but insufficient, condition for valid score-based inferences.*

In order for a test to yield valid score-based inferences, it must be reliable. Unreliable tests cannot possibly yield valid score-based inferences. The mere fact of a test's reliability, however, does not guarantee the validity of inferences based on its use. Let's see why this is so.

First, please recall the discussion at the outset of the previous chapter in which I described a test whose scores yielded perfectly valid inferences when used in the setting for which it was designed (to assess tenth-graders' punctuation skills) but yielded absurdly invalid inferences when used in a setting for which the test was patently inappropriate (to assess first-graders' abilities to speak Russian). In much the same way, you can think of a test that produces delightfully reliable scores but whose results might be employed in drawing zany and incorrect inferences. Such a test, while reliable, would not yield valid inferences. To illustrate, suppose you prepared a fifty-item vocabulary test that yielded very consistent scores, even if students took the test again several weeks after their initial encounter with it. Thus, of course, the test possesses reliability of the stability sort. However, let's say you used students' scores on the vocabulary test to draw inferences about their aptitude to pole-vault. Clearly, those inferences would be invalid. Even if you had the fifty-item test entitled in boldfaced letters at the top, *A Really Swell Pole-Vaulting Aptitude Test,*

Assessment Reliability

The consistency of results produced by measurement devices.

the test would not permit valid inferences regarding one's future pole-vaulting prowess. A test can be reliable without necessarily leading to valid score-based inferences.

But how about tests that yield valid score-based inferences? Do they *really* have to be reliable? Well, think of a newly created aptitude test for which you're gathering criterion-related concurrent evidence of validity. Let's say you are attempting to correlate scores on the new aptitude test with 200 students' current grade point averages. You administer the aptitude test, then calculate the grade point averages, and are just about ready to compute the correlation coefficient between these two sets of data when a violent but remarkably selective tornado bursts through the door, swoops up only the aptitude test scores, and carries them off to the Land of Oz. Distressed by these developments, although cooled by the breeze, you readminister the tests to the 200 students. Now you once more sit down to crank out the correlation coefficient, only to discover that in the meantime the guilt-ridden tornado has swooped back and redeposited the original aptitude test scores. Pleasantly surprised by the beneficence of Mother or Father Nature, you glance at the two sets of aptitude test scores and discover, to your surprise, that students' scores fluctuate wildly. Gwendolyn, who earned a high score on the first testing, earned a low score on the second; and Tulliver, who earned the top score on the initial test administration, only scored near the mean on the second test administration. A cursory consideration of the remaining test scores confirms your suspicion: The test is not reliable.

Now can you see that if you ran the correlation between grade point averages and the first batch of aptitude test scores, you would get a correlation coefficient that would be radically different from the one you would get you used the second set of aptitude test scores? Unreliable, that is, inconsistent, test scores can never yield a consistent relationship with a criterion variable. A test that is unreliable can rarely yield valid score-based inferences.

There's always a chance that, for a number of examinees, unreliable tests could result in valid score-based inferences. For instance, if a classroom teacher were using a totally unreliable final examination, it's always possible that some of the more able students would, as a result of mere chance, score well. The teacher's inferences about those few students might be valid, but the inferences would be accurate because of raw chance, not because of the evidence created by the teacher's flawed final examination.

Hopefully, the points made in past few paragraphs will help confirm my original contention that reliability is a necessary, but insufficient, condition for valid score-based inferences. To establish a test's worth, we need evidence relevant to both reliability *and* validity.

As indicated before, there are different ways of securing evidence regarding the reliability with which a test measures whatever it's measuring. We now consider the three most commonly used approaches to test reliability and, as a consequence of those considerations, assume that the reader will come to the inescapable conclusion that different approaches to test reliability yield substantially different ways of viewing the consistency with which the test measures whatever it's measuring. The three approaches to reliability which are described are *stability*, *alternate-form*, and *internal consistency*. As with the previous chapter's discussion of types of validity, after describing each of these three approaches to reliability in general, we point out any differences that might arise if we were attempting to establish the reliability of tests focused on norm-referenced or criterion-referenced inferences.

Stability Reliability

Already alluded to, *stability* estimates of reliability are based on the consistency of a test's measurement *over time*. In the most common way of determining a test's stability, educators administer a test to a group of examinees, wait for a reasonable interval (say two or three weeks), then readminister the test to the same examinees. By correlating examinees' scores on the two occasions, the educators secure a reliability coefficient, in this case a stability coefficient (often called a *test–retest* coefficient). If the coefficient is high, for instance, .80 to .90, then the test developer and test user can take some solace in the fact that individuals will apparently obtain comparable scores on the test even though it is administered at different times.

This sort of stability information would be of interest to a test user if, in fact, it was likely that the test might have to be administered to individuals at different times. Suppose, for example, that a high school graduation test was being administered by a school district under such strict security conditions that, if a student were absent, that student would be obliged to wait three weeks until the test was readministered. Under such circumstances, educators should definitely be interested in the test's stability.

The length of the interval between the two testing occasions is, of course, an issue of significance. If you wait only minutes or seconds to readminister the test, the students' second test performance is likely to be influenced by the initial testing experience. Too short a between-testing interval is obviously unsound. At the other extreme, if you wait a decade or two between testings, all sorts of intervening events in the lives of the students will act to mess up the resulting correlation between the two sets of test scores. The selection of the between-testing interval's length should be made so as to reduce the influence of the first testing on the second, but also to reduce the likelihood that intervening events in the lives of the students will distort the second set of test results. Between-testing intervals of several days or a few weeks are common when establishing the stability reliability of achievement tests whose results might be influenced by intervening instruction. Longer between-testing intervals are often the case with aptitude tests because such measuring devices are thought to be less influenced by instructional interventions.

A problem with the stability approach to reliability determination is that teachers and students often view the *readministration* of a test as a less than superlative use of their time. Students who are instructed to "retake the same old test" will often score lower on the second testing merely because they view the activity as meaningless. Care must be taken to create an atmosphere in which students will devote comparable zeal to both test administrations. That's easier said (I just said it) than done.

For many widely distributed standardized achievement tests, one does not see efforts to secure evidence of stability reliability, chiefly because of the costs involved. Large samples of students are usually employed to secure normative data for such tests. Hence, the costs of logistical difficulties of readministering tests to large numbers of students often incline standardized test developers toward other reliability strategies.

Sometimes, however, only samples of the normative population are readministered the test in order to secure a stability estimate. With well-developed standardized achievement tests and a reasonably short between-testing temporal interval, the stability coefficients often range between .70 and .90. In some instances, tests of verbal aptitude have

Stability Reliability

The consistency of assessment results over time.

been readministered after an interval of one or two years and yield stability coefficients as high as .80.

As with other approaches to reliability, the longer the test, the more reliable the test tends to be. A one- or two-item test is obviously subject to chance error, while a test of 100 items will yield a much more representative estimate of a student's performance. Most standardized tests, because they typically deal with somewhat general skills, knowledge, or aptitudes, are relatively long instruments and, therefore, tend to yield relatively high reliability coefficients.

Users of locally developed assessments, such as teacher-made classroom tests or district-developed exams, are often concerned about the stability with which their tests are measuring. There are settings, however, in which educators who wish to make criterion-referenced interpretations are fearful that students' scores on their tests will not be sufficiently variable to produce reasonable reliability coefficients. When the *variability* present in a group of test scores is low, it is much less likely to secure a high correlation (with *any* other variable) involving those test scores than if the test scores displayed considerable variability. Users of many locally developed tests often hope that, as a consequence of effective instruction, most students will earn high test scores. If instruction were successful and oodles of students earned high scores, the resulting *range restriction* would make it impossible to secure the sorts of reliability coefficients that one would obtain with tests in which there is considerable score variability.[1]

Even though this fear of range restriction and its consequent depression of the magnitude of reliability coefficients has been a subject of discussion among educators and measurement experts for well over a decade, the experience of most educators is that, sadly, instructional interventions are rarely sufficiently effective to get most students up to mastery. As a consequence, whenever there is a reasonable degree of score variability present, traditional correlational methods can usually be employed to secure an index of a locally developed test's stability over time.

Classification Consistency

Because locally developed tests are often employed in connection with impending decisions about students and/or instructional programs, it has been proposed that a *classification-consistency*, rather than a score-consistency, approach to reliability might be sensibly employed with such tests. For instance, suppose you were placing low-scoring students in a remedial reading program if they earned a score of less than 60 percent correct on a reading test. If Griselda earned a score of 55 percent correct on the test, she would go into the remedial class. She would go in the remedial class if she only scored 40 percent or even 59 percent. Now, one way of conceptualizing a district-developed test's stability is to categorize students according to the *decisions* made about them in order to find out, if the test were administered at a different time, how many students would be classified in the same manner.

To illustrate this *classification-consistency* approach, let's use the example of the reading test with 60 percent correct being used as the cutoff score. Assume that the test was administered to 100 youngsters in early February and that 72 percent earned a score on the test of 60 percent or better, so that the remaining 28 percent would be targeted for the remedial class. Then in mid-February the test was readministered, and students were once more assigned according to the 60 percent correct standard. Let's say that, of the 28 percent who originally scored below the designated cutoff, all but five youngsters still scored below 60 percent correct. Of the 72 percent who hit 60 percent correct or better on the initial test, however, seven students fell below that standard on the second test administration. Thus, for 88 percent of the youngsters, consistent classifications were made. That is, 23 percent of the students fell below the standard both times and 65 percent were above the standard on both testing occasions.

Classification Consistency

A representation of the proportion of students who are placed in the same category on two testing occasions or two test forms.

In using the classification-consistency approach to the determination of test reliability, it is important to note that the extent of classification-consistency is strongly dependent on *where the performance standard is* (that is, where the cutoff score is which will be used to make decisions) *in relationship to the average performance of the group.* This point can be illustrated by considering the two situations depicted in Figure 5.1. In which of these two situations would you be likely to get a higher test–retest percentage of classification consistency?

Consideration of the two situations should allow you to see that in Situation Z there would be a greater degree of classification consistency because there are fewer scores close to the cutoff point (45); thus, the predictable score fluctuations that would occur with the second test's administration would find few students crossing over the cutoff score. In Situation X, however, the proximity of the mean (25) to the cutoff score (27) would indicate that more students would fluctuate around the cutoff score merely because there are more students close to that point. The lesson to be drawn here is that the proximity of the distribution's mean to the cutoff score will play a significant role in determining the magnitude of classification consistency. In general, test developers who employ a classification-consistency approach would do well to provide classification-consistency percentages based on several different (but likely) performance standards.

A final point about the reliability of tests depends on the *length* of these tests in comparison to the traditional standardized tests with which most educators are familiar. Because locally developed tests will sometimes have only ten to twenty items per measured

FIGURE 5.1.

Two fictitious distributions of test scores with equal means and standard deviations, but dissimilar cutoff scores.

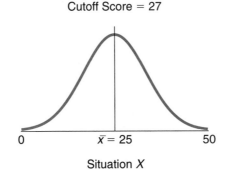

Cutoff Score = 27

$\bar{x} = 25$

Situation X

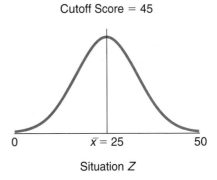

Cutoff Score = 45

$\bar{x} = 25$

Situation Z

content domain, you can expect lower reliability coefficients than would be found if longer tests were being employed. If, for example, test users have come to expect stability coefficients of .80 or better for traditional standardized tests of 50 to 100 items, those test users should alter their expectations when the test–retest reliability coefficient of a ten-item, teacher-constructed classroom test is being reported. Although educators do not yet have the experience with short-test reliability coefficients to establish reasonable expectations for such reliability coefficients, it is certain they will dip well below the .80 to .90 levels.

False positives, false negatives.   There are two kinds of *misclassifications* that educators can make when they are making inferences focused on students. If you were to classify a student as having mastered a given skill or knowledge domain, but the student actually had not, this is referred to as a *false positive*. Conversely, if you were to classify a student as *not* having mastered a skill or knowledge domain, but the student really had mastered it, this is referred to as a *false negative*.

Clearly, there are occasions when educators will find one of these types of misclassifications more significant than the other type. Classroom teachers, for instance, ought to worry more about false positives because teachers may then move students on to more advanced content when, in fact, they need to spend more time on the current content. If students are classified as false negatives, then they'll end up getting more instruction than they really need. But, as anyone knows who's been in a classroom, that sort of mistake often happens. Some teachers contend, in fact, that "too much overlearning" is a contradiction. I personally don't share that view.

Alternate-Form Reliability

A second form of reliability is associated with the use of two or more forms of the same test. Because it is generally hoped that the two or more forms will yield consistent information regarding students, there is a necessity to secure information regarding *alternate-form* consistency.

In the most straightforward manner of securing alternate-form reliability, you simply administer two forms of the same test, then correlate students' scores on the two test forms. The resulting coefficient is referred to as an *alternate-form coefficient of reliability*.

Typically, publishers of standardized tests will supply information regarding the extent to which two or more forms of the test are parallel with respect to the content or skills they cover. These comparable forms of the test can either be presented by publishers as content-parallel, meaning they supposedly cover the same content, or as difficulty-parallel, meaning both forms of the test are equally difficult. Information will usually be supplied regarding each test form's mean and standard deviation (often based on an administration to students used during the norming of the test). Finally, the correlation between students' performances on the two forms will typically be supplied.

Evidence of the equivalence of different test forms is needed whenever multiple forms are being employed as essentially interchangeable tools. This is often the case when

---

False Positive

Classifying a student as having mastered what's being measured when, in fact, the student hasn't.

False Negative

Classifying a student as not having mastered what's being measured when, in fact, the student has.

Alternate-Form Reliability

The consistency of measured results yielded by different forms of the same test.

N. C. Kindergarten Standard Set

This year, for the first time, academically gifted 4-year-olds will be allowed to enter kindergarten in North Carolina under the new eligibility standards the state school board set last month.

After approving a policy to allow children who turned 4 as late as April 16 to enter kindergarten this fall, education officials scrambled to set rigid guidelines for screening those children.

Without the standards, which require the children to score in the 99th percentile on aptitude tests, as many as 5,000 4-year-olds could have been eligible to start kindergarten this school year. Under the new standards, state officials say only about 500 children will qualify to start kindergarten a year earlier than the previous law allowed.

In addition to their performance on the aptitude tests, prospective pupils will be judged on samples of their work and interviews with the children and their parents. Parents must pay for the testing. Principals who approve the children for early entry can rescind the decision within 90 days if they discover the youngsters are not academically ready or mature enough for school.

What's your reaction?

Reprinted, with permission, from *Education Week,* September 3, 1997

educators use tests for making important decisions about individuals and there is the need for *test security.* For example, the *Miller Analogies Test* (MAT) is a widely used test of one's verbal aptitude, typically employed as a screening test for those students applying to graduate schools. Because students are permitted to retake the MAT on different occasions, it is either necessary to have different forms of the MAT or to count on a student's forgetting everything about the first administration of the test prior to the second test administration. However, as every graduate school professor will attest, although graduate students are a forgetful lot, they aren't *that* forgetful. Obviously, multiple MAT forms are requisite. Furthermore, just as requisite is information regarding the extent to which an individual taking two different MAT forms is apt to earn consistent scores on the two forms. Sometimes, typically because of limited financial resources, multiple test forms are made available, but *only* assertions such as the following are found in the test's technical manual: "Content-parallel test forms are available." Now, although educators should applaud efforts to develop test forms possessing content that is parallel, assertions about content similarity will not suffice. Correlational evidence is also needed regarding how students perform on the two test forms. In addition, students' means and standard deviations on the two forms are needed.

You can get a strong, positive r between two test forms, yet one form can be much more difficult than the other. For instance, let's say you gave fifty youngsters a 100-item test, then pretended you were administering a much more difficult second form of the test by knocking off ten points from each student's score. If you ran a correlation between the two sets of scores (that is, the original scores and the set of "scores minus ten points"), the resulting correlation coefficient would be 1.00. It is for this reason, that is, to check for *difficulty disparities,* that you also need descriptive statistics on the two forms, such as the test-form means. The alternate-form reliability coefficients for most well-established standardized tests, as was the case with such tests' stability coefficients, tend to hover between .80 and .90. Some alternate-form reliability coefficients of standardized tests even get as high as .95.

Educational Leaders
Look at Assessment

Reliability of Diagnostic Tests

Dr. Sheila O. Kahrs
Assistant Principal
Barrow County Schools
Winder, Georgia

In order to know what is going on inside a student's mind or to know how much information is being processed by students, we use diagnostic assessment tools. These tools, much like a doctor's blood test, are just that.

Tests are diagnostic in nature and indicate the performance of a student regarding a certain criterion or standard. Test results confirm knowledge of information and skills, the ability to analyze, draw conclusions, understand inference, and think in analogies. In order for assessment to serve its purpose as a diagnostic tool, the results must be consistent.

If a teacher were to readminister the very same classroom test to the same group of students after a few days, I believe the individual students' scores would be very close to each other. The only difference that would occur is if there was a review and reteaching of the material between the two testing occasions. Certain physical or emotional factors could also influence testing results and would influence the overall score if they were strongly affecting the student.

If two different forms of the same test were used, it is possible that wording differences would assist individual students in one form over the other and would render a higher score in one version over the other. ●

One substantial difference between test developers who plan to make norm-referenced or criterion-referenced interpretations is the rigor with which a test's assessment domains are described. Whereas those seeking norm-referenced inferences typically provide only rather general descriptions of what these tests are measuring, developers of tests for which criterion-referenced inferences are sought usually set forth detailed descriptions of the rules employed to generate the tests' items. This increased rigor of description, typically taking the form of test-item specifications, makes it easier to create truly equivalent forms of a test.

Think of it like this: a set of specifications for a test makes explicit the item-generation rules that define a content domain of to-be-tested student behavior. By using these item-generation rules, you can theoretically create an almost unlimited number of test items to tap the behavior thus defined. To get equivalent forms of such a test, in theory, all you need do is randomly sample from the item pool.

However, theory, in measurement as elsewhere, is often messed up by practice. So even with tests that spring from delightfully detailed test-item specifications, you'll still need to garner the customary empirical data regarding alternate-form reliability.

As you saw in the treatment of stability reliability, this information is often best represented in the form of classification-consistency data. If possible, classification-consistency data along with more traditional correlational data should be presented.

Stability and Alternate-Form Reliability

Stability and Alternate-Form Reliability

The consistency of measured results over time using two different test forms.

Measurement people sometimes combine the two previously discussed forms of reliability evidence. They have the need to secure such reliability information when they administer different forms of a test after a time delay. In Figure 5.2 you'll see the reliability approaches depicted that have been described so far. Of the three approaches, the lowest reliability coefficients will arise from a combination of stability and alternate-form reliabilities because there are two factors (the time delay and any differences between the two forms) that operate to reduce the consistency of measurement. Thus, whereas standardized test developers strive for .80 to .90 reliability coefficients when dealing with stability or alternate-form approaches, they may be well satisfied with a solid .70 or so when they combine stability and alternate-form reliability.

Before turning to the third and final form of reliability, that is, *internal consistency*, let's deal with a special problem that arises as a consequence of assessment situations in which students may need to take different forms of the same test. As indicated earlier, such situations are becoming particularly common in education.

Post Facto Form Equating

For most educators there is rarely the need to create truly equally difficult test forms. If Mrs. Billings, veteran chemistry teacher, creates a new final examination every term, she may attempt to make each new form essentially as difficult as its predecessors. But Mrs. Billings simply does the best job she can in creating items similar in difficulty to those earlier examinations. She doesn't lose sleep if her final exams aren't *perfectly* equal in difficulty.

There are, however, settings in which teachers and administrators must interpret the results of student performances on tests for which bona fide equal difficulty is necessary. Take, for example, the use of competency tests as a requirement associated with high school graduation. Different forms of the same test are typically employed. (If different forms weren't employed, an oft-failing student would be apt to pass, finally, merely because of familiarity with the test's items.) In such settings, where significant contingencies hinge on student test performance, it is important to have each form of the test constitute an equal challenge to students. After all, how fair would it be to alter the difficulty of the test forms used on different occasions? Students might pass or fail the test,

FIGURE 5.2.

Three commonly employed approaches to determining the reliability of educational tests.

(1) Test + Time Delay vs. Retest	=	*Stability*
(2) Form A vs. Form B	=	*Alternate-Form*
(3) Form A + Time Delay vs. Form B	=	*Stability and Alternate-Form*

not because of what they knew, but because by chance alone they were given an easy or a tough form of the test.

Test forms of dissimilar difficulty constitute an open invitation to those who would legally challenge a testing program's legitimacy. And educational leaders, increasingly in today's litigious environment, need to know how to make sure that tests are *legally* defensible. If test forms of different difficulties are used in a testing program, those who operate the program are almost certain to lose if challenged in court. As a consequence, measurement specialists have given substantial attention to the problem of how to equate the difficulty of different test forms. And the equidifficulty of test forms, of course, bears significantly on alternate-form reliability.

Two approaches to determining item difficulties. Before describing the approach used most often these days to deal with the problem of test forms that are unequal in difficulty, it is necessary to describe, quite briefly, the two chief ways that the relative difficulties of test items are determined. The most important determinant of item difficulty, of course, is the way in which the test item is written in the first place. If you set out to create an easy and a tough test item in, say, world history, you'll probably be able to do so merely by focusing on historical topics that are well known, for example, *How many ships did Columbus use in his voyage to the Americas?* or on topics that are obscure, for example, *Who was the general who fought Julius Caesar most effectively in Gaul?* (If you're a trivia buff, it was Vercingetorix.)

But beyond the obvious disparities in difficulty that are built into items at the moment they're born, it is necessary to get a more accurate fix on item difficulty so that, insofar as possible, we can create equally difficult test forms. The two procedures that test developers employ to determine the difficulty are (1) *field-testing* new items pools, and (2) *embedding* new items in operational test forms. Let's consider each approach briefly.

When test developers field-test new items, they set up a separate administration of items to individuals similar to those for whom the test will ultimately be used. For instance, if a new statewide achievement test in fifth-grade mathematics is to be created, the developers might create large numbers of mathematics items, then administer those items in a formal field test so that several hundred fifth-graders respond to each item. As a consequence of such field tests, it is possible to determine the difficulty level of each item, then configure a number of operational forms of the test so that, in aggregate they are equal in difficulty.

One problem with such separate field tests is that they are often disruptive because they characteristically intrude on the ongoing instructional programs in schools. A second difficulty stems from the seriousness with which students participate in the field test. Younger students, in general, respond to any test, real test or field test, with seriousness. Older students, however, sometimes do not expend the same effort on a field test that "doesn't count." Thus, for instance, responses of high school seniors to items on a non-counting field test may be substantially different than would have been the case if the test really had a significant impact on those seniors. The effect of the sometimes unmotivated performances of field-test students is to mislead test developers about the actual difficulty of the items being field-tested. As a consequence, instead of equally difficult test forms, the test developers end up with forms of differing difficulty. The less similar that the field test's conditions are to those of the real test, the less accurate will be the item-difficulty estimates derived from the field test.

As indicated, a second approach to the determination of item difficulties involves the embedding of new test items in regularly administered versions of an ongoing testing program. For example, imagine a statewide testing program that routinely tested all of the state's children at each of three grade levels each year with a sixty-item test. By adding room for, say, four extra items on each test form, officials of the testing program could try out a large number of items per year. Suppose, for instance, that there were approximately 20,000 pupils per grade level. By creating twenty different "subforms" of the test, each of which contained four *different* embedded items, the testing program's staff could try out eighty new items per year by having about 1,000 students respond to each item.

The embedded-items approach to determining item difficulties is not without its problems. First, there are nontrivial costs associated with the printing and scoring of different "subforms." In addition, there are ethical considerations associated with asking students to complete items that are not scored. What happens, for example, if a defective embedded item so upsets students that they answer other regular items incorrectly. Should students be warned that there are trial, uncounted items in the test they take? If so, what are the consequences? Sentiments regarding the use of embedded "trial" items run so strongly in some quarters that legislation has been introduced in some states to prohibit the use of embedded field-test items.

Regardless of which of these two item-tryout methods is used, that is, a separate field test or embedding, the resulting item difficulties are useful to test developers as they attempt to create equally difficult test forms. However, given the imprecision of such estimates, it is still possible that different test forms will vary in the challenge they present to students. To create challenges that are equally difficult for students, irrespective of the test form used, measurement specialists now use a procedure that we will briefly preview in this chapter, then describe in more detail in Chapter 7. That procedure involves the use of *scale scores.*

Scale scores. Scale scores are derived from raw scores but employ a new numerical system. For example, on a test containing seventy-five items, a student's raw score could range from zero to seventy-five correct. However a scale-score system could be established for that same test so that a student's "score" could range from 500 to 1,000. As we shall see in Chapter 7 scale-score systems have some useful characteristics. For purposes of creating equally difficult challenges for students on difficult test forms, it is possible to use a scale-score system to *equalize* test forms of different difficulty *statistically.*

To illustrate, let's say that on a scale-score system of 500 to 1,000, a student needs a score of 800 to pass a seventy-five-item test. On an especially difficult form of the test, a raw score of fifty-five items correct might be equal to the (passing) scale score of 800. On an especially easy form of the test, a raw score of sixty items correct may be needed to achieve a passing scale score of 800.

This *post facto* form equating permits students to face a genuinely equally difficult task on different forms of a given test. As such, *post facto* form equating by use of statistical adjustments provides students with equitable challenges irrespective of the test form employed. In Chapter 7, you'll dig more deeply into the nature of scale scores.

Internal Consistency Reliability

The final type of reliability you must consider represents a substantial departure from the two reliability strategies treated previously. In those strategies, the basic task was to relate an examinee's scores on two tests (or two test forms) administered with or without a temporal delay. This final form of reliability is known as *internal consistency* and, as the label suggests, it focuses on the consistency of a test's internal elements, namely, its test items.

The previously treated methods of estimating reliability all require data from two testing sessions. Internal-consistency methods of calculating reliability can be used with data from only a single test administration. Internal-consistency estimates should be thought of as revealing the extent to which the items on the test are internally consistent with one another, that is, the extent to which the items are homogeneous. Such methods should not be used with *speeded* tests in which students only have a limited amount of time to complete the test.

The *split-half* technique for establishing a test's internal consistency consists of dividing a test into two equal halves, ordinarily by treating the odd, then the even, items as though they constituted separate tests. The entire test is administered to a group of individuals; then their two subscores (derived from the odd and the even items) are correlated. The resulting correlation coefficient is considered an estimate of the degree to which the two halves of the test are performing their functions consistently. Because longer tests are more reliable than shorter tests, it is then necessary to apply the Spearman-Brown prophecy formula which, using the correlation between the two half-tests, estimates what the reliability would be on the full-length test—that is, including both odd and even items. The procedure works as follows:

$$\text{Reliability on full test} = \frac{2 \times \text{reliability on half-test}}{1 + \text{reliability on half-test}}$$

The simplicity with which the Spearman-Brown formula can be used is illustrated in the following example, in which the half-test correlation coefficient is .60:

$$\text{Reliability on full test} = \frac{2 \times .60}{1 + .60} = \frac{1.20}{1.60} = .75$$

As you can see, use of the Spearman-Brown formula will always increase the magnitude of the reliability estimate (unless the half-test $r = 0$).

A widely used index of the homogeneity of a set of dichotomously scored test items (that is, items that can be scored as right or wrong) is the *Kuder-Richardson* method, particularly formulae 20 (K-R20) and 21 (K-R21). Now please, unless you really get enthused by formulae such as the following and need a subtle shot of algebra, don't get intimidated by the K-R procedures. You need to have a general idea of how these internal consistency approaches work, but it's not necessary to become intimate with the innards of either K-R20 or K-R21.

The K-R21 formula is somewhat less accurate than the K-R20 formula, but it is so simple to compute that it is the most frequently employed estimate of internal consistency. One version of the K-R21 formula is the following:

$$\text{K-R21 reliability coefficient} = \frac{K}{K-1}\left(1 - \frac{M(K-M)}{Ks^2}\right)$$

where K = number of items in the test
   M = mean of the set of test scores
   s = standard deviation of the set of test scores

The K-R20 formula, for which K-R21 is a reasonable approximation in most situations, follows:

$$\text{K-R20 reliability coefficient} = \frac{K}{K-1}\left(1 - \frac{\Sigma pq}{s^2}\right)$$

where K = number of items in the test
   Σpq = sum of the variance of items scored dichotomously (right or wrong)
   s^2 = variance of the total test

A p Value

The proportion of students who answer a test item correctly.

Both of these formulae can be thought of as representing the average correlation obtained from all possible split-half reliability estimates. The K-R20 formula is used less frequently than K-R21 because it requires far more computation. Typically, a computer is employed when one seeks a K-R20 estimate. The K-R21 formula is an algebraic derivation of K-R20 that assumes the p values of all items (that is, the proportion of students who score correctly on an item) are identical. If that assumption is not satisfied, and it almost never is, then K-R21 will yield a slightly lower estimate of reliability than will K-R20. Although both formulae are used by large-scale test publishers (who have access to computers and lots of electricity), local educators would ordinarily rely on the K-R21 formula.

What's the common-sense rationale of the K-R procedures? Simply put, these approaches rest on the notion that, if a test's items are relatively homogeneous, there will be lots of variance on the test because, for example, on a knowledge test, students who know the subject well will get very high scores because most of the items are measuring the same thing. Similarly, students who don't know much will do very badly because they'll fail across the board on similar sorts of items. The K-R21 formula, for example, incorporates this sensible notion by stressing the impact of test-score variance although making a couple of adjustments for test length, $\frac{K}{K-1}$, and the possibility of getting a large standard deviation, M(K − M). If you have substantial difficulty in comprehending how the K-R formulae work (and if you really want to), you'll find it helpful to play number-plugging for a bit. For instance, set up a few fictitious numbers in the K-R21 formula, then juggle the size of the standard deviation, or the size of the mean, or the number of items in the test. See how these differences affect the size of K-R21.

The Kuder-Richardson method, as is the case with all internal consistency estimates, focuses on the degree to which the items in the test are functioning in a homogeneous fashion. *Coefficient alpha*, developed by Cronbach, is a more generalizable estimate of the internal-consistency form of reliability and can be used with test items that yield other than binary scored responses.[2]

Coefficient alpha can be used, for instance, to compute the internal consistency of a set of test items (short-answer or essay) in which each of the items could receive a range

"I think it's a case of inconsistent internal consistency!"

APTITUDE TEST X

of points, not just be scored as correct or incorrect. Such multipoint items are said to be scored *polytomously*. (Now, don't tell me you haven't learned at least *one* new word in this book!) For example, student essay-writing assignments are often scored 4, 3, 2, 1, or zero. The formula for coefficient alpha is

Polytomous Items

Test items to which responses are given more than two score-points.

$$\alpha = \frac{K}{K-1}\left(1 - \Sigma\frac{s_i^2}{s_x^2}\right)$$

where K = number of items on the test
s_x^2 = varience of the total test
s_i^2 = the sum of the variances of individual items

As indicated earlier, internal-consistency estimates are commonly computed by publishers of standardized tests. Because, as you have seen, these estimates are heavily dependent on a test's variance, this is one reason that publishers of standardized tests strive to produce tests with considerable score variance. After all, if a potential purchaser of two standardized achievement tests is choosing between two tests that are identical in all respects except that one has a K-R20 of 0.74 and the other has a K-R20 of 0.93, the latter test will typically be purchased.

It should be noted, however, that internal consistency of tests is sometimes, ever so subtly, proffered for more than it is. Internal-consistency estimates tell us very little about a test's stability or the equivalence of different test forms. It is only what it says it is, a reflection of the extent to which items on the test are internally consistent.

The Standard Error of Measurement

The three different methods of estimating a test's reliability have chiefly focused on the consistency of a group of students' scores on a test. What about the consistency of an *individual's* score? Suppose, for example, you have determined that the stability r on a test was .82 and its K-R21 was 0.89. What would you be able to discern about the consistency (accuracy) of Larry Jones's score of 65 correct? Well, except in a general way, very little. To provide an index of the consistency of an individual's test performance, we use an index referred to as the *standard error of measurement.*

The standard error of measurement can be thought of as a reflection of the variability of an individual's scores if the test were administered again and again. However, because it is not practical to readminister tests interminably to an individual (the student becomes fatigued, annoyed, or senile), measurement folks estimate the variability of an individual's test scores based on data from a group. The formula for the standard error of measurement is the following:

$$s_e = s_x \sqrt{1 - r_{xx}}$$

where s_e = standard error of measurement

s_x = standard deviation of the test scores

r_{xx} = the reliability of the test

Standard Error of Measurement

The consistency of an individual's test performance.

"Mr. Huff, as a first year math teacher you have created tests with a <u>perfect</u> reliability — they yield scores that are consistently meaningless."

Educational Leaders
Look at Assessment

"Consistent" Classroom Assessments

Lynn Winters
Assistant Superintendent
Research, Planning & Evaluation
Long Beach Unified School District
Long Beach, California

Hmmm. Now why would a teacher want to give the very same classroom test to a group of students after a few days? I can only imagine two occasions when a teacher would actually take the time to give the very same test to a group of students within a short period of time: (A) she expected cheating had occurred, or (B) she is asking students to "master" really critical material.

(These days that can mean fourth-grade math facts.) In Case A, suspected cheating, she would want the scores be *similar* on both occasions for the students who had actually studied the material and *different* for the "cheaters." In Case B, she would want the scores to be *similar* for students who had "mastered" the content, that is, equally high, and *different*, hopefully improved, for students who did not do so well on the first occasion. In neither case would she expect all scores to be "similar." In both instances, *she expects similar scores from students who really knew the answers* and different scores for students who guessed at or didn't know the answers.

There may be one scenario in which administering the same test twice within a few days might become a routine classroom practice. This situation is actually the general case of the above scenarios, namely, the teacher gives the same test twice in order to verify student scores because the scores are going to have serious consequences for students. While it is currently rare that one teacher-made test would ever be used for such high-stakes decisions as graduation, promotion, or placement, in this era of "teaching to standards," classroom tests have potentially higher stakes than in the past. In our district, for example, teachers use two classroom running record assessments to decide which children will attend remedial summer school or be retained in the third grade. These two assessments follow a series of similar tests given throughout the year. Children who consistently "pass" the reading tests but "fail" the final placement test are assigned to remediation, where they are assessed again. If the scores aren't consistent,

that is, students who "failed" are then found to have "passed," parents have the option of removing their children from the remedial reading program. In the two years we have had the summer reading program, not one parent has elected to remove a child due to an "unreliable" score. The benefits of the program outweighed the negative consequences of "failing" the reading test. Our experience is a good example of how important it can be to have consistent classroom assessments. It is also an example of how impossible it is to have perfectly reliable assessments. When tests are used for high-stakes decisions, you need to compensate for reliability. In our district, further assessment opportunities and "revocable consequences" (parents may withdraw children from remedial programs) provide a backup for unreliable (and perhaps invalid) judgments.

Perhaps the most intriguing question about the reliability of classroom assessments is: What does it mean for a classroom test to be reliable? Traditional notions of reliability, test–retest, alternate form, and internal consistency of items presuppose repeated administration of the same or parallel tests. This makes no sense in the classroom in terms of time and cost. I think we need to make a shift from psychometric definitions of consistency to more conceptual ones when we talk about classroom assessment. In classroom assessment, the teacher is the instrument. The teacher's criteria for adequate performance define standards for students. If students don't have a clear picture of what they are shooting for and how high they must aim, their chances

▶

▶ of success are wobbly at best. And if the target keeps shifting (standards aren't consistent) then even straight shooters may miss the mark. All too often, in my experience, students perceive classroom tests (including my own) to be moving rather than fixed targets.

Consistency in classroom assessment is inextricably linked to the validity of teacher decisions about students. Consistency or reliable classroom assessment requires teachers to have a good handle on what content and skills are most important for students to know and *how well* students need to know the material. Consistency means that teacher judgments about content acquisition, otherwise known as "content and performance standards," remain stable over time, despite changes in the curriculum, the student population, or the political zeitgeist. This consistency isn't inflexible or unchanging. Classroom tests may look very different from year to year. Passing scores may change from test to test. But the decision rules that teachers use to select assessment topics, write appropriate questions, and evaluate the quality of student work remain constant. And, in the best of all possible worlds, these teacher expectations are clearly communicated to students and parents. ●

To illustrate the use of the formula, suppose you were working with a test that had a standard deviation of 7.5 and a reliability coefficient of .91. You would substitute in the formula and solve as follows:

$$s_e = 7.5\sqrt{1 - .91}$$
$$= 7.5\sqrt{.09}$$
$$= 7.5(.3)$$
$$= 2.25$$

Now, what does this 2.25 signify? Well, and this is based on some special properties of the normal curve that you'll investigate in Chapter 7, you can use a value of ±2.25 to make some assertions about the accuracy of an individual's test score. Suppose a student earned a score of 37 correct on a test. You could then say that your student's 37 lies plus or minus one standard error of measurement (2.25) of that individual's *true* score, that is, the individual's score if there were no errors of measurement whatsoever associated with the test score, 68 percent of the time. Similarly, within plus or minus two standard errors of measurement of the observed score (37), you would know that the individual's true score fell 95 percent of the time.

Thus, you could build a 68 percent *confidence band* by adding 2.25 and subtracting 2.25 from the score of 37. In other words, you could be 68 percent certain within the limits of 34.75 and 39.25.[3] A 95 percent confidence band would be ±2s_e or 32.50 to 41.50.

Standard errors of measurement work just like the opinion polls displayed almost daily on television news programs. When you watch such a TV poll and see that it reports a "margin of error of ± 3%," that 3 percent functions in the same way that a standard error of measurement does.

The authors of the 1974 APA–AERA–NCME *Standards* were particularly supportive of the standard error of measurement, as you can see from the following remarks:

Reliability coefficients have limited practical value for test users. The standard error of measurement ordinarily is more useful; it has great stability across populations since it is relatively independent of range of talent, and it may be used to identify limits that have a defined probability of including the true score. Test users may use reliability co-efficients in comparing tests, but they use standard errors of measurement in inter-preting test scores. Information in a test manual about a standard error of measurement may often be more important than information about a reliability coefficient.[4]

You will note that the formula for the standard error of measurement is influenced by the standard deviation of the test scores and the reliability of the test. But, as you have seen, there may be more than one index of a test's reliability. Which reliability coefficient should be used in computing the standard error of measurement?

Generally, if there are substantial differences in the sizes of the reliability coefficients available, you should probably compute more than one standard error of measurement so that test users will see that confidence-based assertions about a student's score will vary depending on the standard error of the measurement being used.

What's Really Necessary

Looking back at what's been treated so far about reliability, as an educational leader you ought to be saying something such as, "All right, this measurement business about con-sistency is all well and good, but what does it have to do with the real world of what goes on in schools?" It's a good question, and the answer is "often, not much."

Classroom teachers, for example, should rarely be messing around with the kinds of reliability procedures considered in this chapter. What normal teacher would spend time calculating K-R21 coefficients for classroom exams, even important classroom exams? However, educational leaders need to be on the lookout for pertinent reliability evidence whenever the consequences of a test's use are important. And, of course, the kind of re-liability evidence you look for should match the requirements of the situation in which any testing is to take place.

For example, if you were a school principal and you'd been supplied with two forms of a district-developed competency test, you'd want to be looking for evidence of alternate-form reliability. If the district office staff tried to ladle some evidence of stability reliability for one of the test forms, or attempted to use internal consistency coefficients to support the equal difficulty of the two forms, you need to know why the district office staff is wrong.

In short, educational leaders need to know what reliability is, and that it comes in sev-eral forms. But, depending on the importance of the use to which test scores will be put, more often than not there's no need for reliability evidence in the day-to-day world of schooling. When, however, test reliability does become an issue, as an educational leader you should be familiar with the key features of the various kinds of reliability evidence.

Chapter Wrap-Up

As is our now well-established custom (after all, this is Chapter 5), the chapter summary will take the form of pith-laden responses to the chapter's guiding questions.

● What is reliability?

When educators think of *reliability*, they ought to automatically think of its synonym, namely, *consistency*. Assessment reliability refers to consistency of measurement. In everyday language, if an assessment device is reliable, it measures with consistency. There are, however, several different ways to look at consistency of measurement, that is, stability evidence, alternate-form evidence, and internal-consistency evidence. If a test is unreliable, that is, if it measures whatever it's measuring with inconsistency, there is little likelihood that educators can make valid inferences about the meaning of students' test performances.

What is stability reliability evidence?

Stability estimates of a test's reliability are based on the consistency of measurement *over time*. If students' test results from two administrations of the same test—separated by a meaningful between-testing interval—turn out to be positively correlated, then the test is said to possess stability reliability. In situations where students who are absent on an initial testing occasion must take the same test later, there should be test–retest evidence gathered to show that the test represents a similar challenge even if administered on separate occasions. Typically, educators simply administer a test to a group of students, wait a few weeks or so, then readminister the same test to the same students. The correlation between the two sets of scores is referred to as a stability reliability coefficient. In some educational settings, instead of computing a correlation coefficient, it makes sense to determine how many students would be classified the same way (for example, masters or nonmasters) on the two testing occasions. Such classification-consistency approaches also yield a sensible way to look at a test's consistency over time.

What is alternate-form reliability evidence?

Alternate-form reliability evidence is collected when the same group of students completes two forms of the same assessment device, and their performances on the two forms are correlated. Such evidence is needed whenever educators wish to employ two or more forms of the same assessment device. Because developers of nationally standardized tests often must make available multiple forms of a test, there is usually much attention given to alternate-form reliability evidence by such test-makers. In addition to correlations between students' performances on the two tests, however, it is also necessary to make sure that the two test forms are equally difficult. This can be done simply by contrasting the means of the two test forms. Indices of alternate-form reliability can represent a correlational or classification-consistency approach.

If you want to take two different forms of a test and administer a different form to the same individuals after a three-week delay, you will be able to collect reliability evidence of the stability *and* alternate-form variety. Because of the two potential sources of inconsistency, namely, the two different forms as well as the time delay between testing, coefficients for this type of *reliability* evidence are usually lower than is seen for either stability or alternate-form approaches.

Because equally difficult test forms are so pivotal in the collection of alternate-form reliability evidence, test developers frequently try out test items to establish their difficulty, then constitute different forms so that the item difficulties of the two forms are similar. Sometimes these item difficulties are determined via separate field tests; sometimes they are determined by embedding a small number of trial items in an operational form of a test.

● What is internal consistency reliability evidence?

The focus of an internal-consistency approach to reliability is the homogeneity of the set of items that constitute a test. If the items are functioning in a similar fashion, then the test is said to be internally consistent. In earlier times, the most common way to determine a test's internal consistency was to split the test into two halves, correlate students' scores on the two halves, then adjust the resulting coefficient higher to take account of the fact that the split-half tests were only 50 percent as long as the original test. More recently, internal-consistency estimates developed by Kuder and Richardson (especially K-R20 and K-R21) are commonly employed to gauge a test's internal consistency. For test items that may be assigned several scores (as opposed to a simple right or wrong test item) internal consistency is usually determined via use of Cronbach's coefficient alpha.

● What is the standard error of measurement?

Whereas the several ways of getting at test reliability described in this chapter obviously represent different ways of thinking about assessment consistency, they all provide an index about the consistency of a *group* of test scores or test items. The standard error of measurement, in contrast, provides an estimate of the consistency of an *individual* test-taker's performance. The standard error of measurement functions much like the plus or minus error margins now widely reported with any kind of sampling-based opinion polls. As with those error margins, the smaller the standard error of measurement, the more consistency educators can ascribe to a student's test performance.

Practice Exercises

For the following five exercises, decide whether the reliability approach described is chiefly one of *stability, alternate-form,* or *internal consistency.*

1. Clyde Collins builds a test for his history class, then computes a split-half coefficient which, because he recently completed "a top-drawer course in measurement" at a nearby college, he adjusts upward using a Spearman-Brown prophecy formula.

2. Julie Jones gives an end-of-unit sixty-item exam to her fourth-graders, then readministers the exam two weeks later, and correlates her students' scores on the two test administrations.

3. A commercial test publisher creates three forms of a test and administers the three different forms to the same students on three consecutive days. The correlations among Forms A, B, and C are all quite high.

4. A test-development agency calculates K-R20 estimates on all of its standardized achievement tests.

5. Developers of a new aptitude test create three forms of a new test, then determine the correlation coefficients among the three forms. Those *r*'s were the following: A *vs.* B = .82, B *vs.* C = .79, A *vs.* C = .90.

Answers to Practice Exercises

1. Internal Consistency
2. Stability
3. Alternate-Form
4. Internal Consistency
5. Alternate-Form

DISCUSSION QUESTIONS

1. What issues regarding assessment reliability should be of most concern to an educational leader. Why?
2. What is your opinion of the respective merits of reliability coefficients *versus* the standard error of measurement?
3. If you were obliged to explain the meaning of the standard error of measurement to a group of lay citizens, how would you go about it in the most lucid fashion?
4. Can you describe different kinds of decision settings in which each of the three types of reliability estimates would be particularly helpful?
5. Assume that you were the president of a test-development firm that was attempting to compete for sales against major commercial test publishers. How much of your development resources would you spend on obtaining reliability evidence as opposed to evidence of validity?
6. Do you think educational leaders will find classification-consistency approaches to reliability more useful than correlational approaches? Why?
7. If you were obliged to determine the technical properties of newly developed test items, would you favor separate field-testing or embedding? Why?

SUGGESTIONS FOR ADDITIONAL READING

Airasian, Peter W. *Classroom Assessment* (3rd ed.). New York: McGraw Hill, 1997.

Brennan, R. L, and M. T. Kane. "An Index of Dependability for Mastery Test," *Journal of Educational Measurement, 14*, 3 (Fall 1977): 277–289.

Carey, Lou M. *Measuring and Evaluating School Learning.* Boston: Allyn & Bacon, 1988.

Cunningham, George K. *Educational and Psychological Measurement.* New York: Macmillan, 1986.

Cunningham, George K. *Assessment in the Classroom: Constructing and Interpreting Tests.* Washington, DC: Falmer Press, 1998.

Feldt, Leonard S., and Robert L. Brennan. "Reliability." In Robert L. Linn (Ed.). *Educational Measurement* (3rd ed.). New York: Macmillan, 1989.

Kane, Michael T. "The Role of Reliability in Criterion-Referenced Tests." *Journal of Educational Measurement,23*, 3 (Fall 1986): 221–224.

Linn, Robert L., and Norman E. Gronlund. *Measurement and Assessment in Teaching* (7th ed.). Upper Saddle River, NJ: Prentice-Hall, 1995.

McMillan, James H. *Classroom Assessment: Principles and Practice for Effective Instruction.* Boston: Allyn & Bacon, 1997.

Mehrens, William A., and Irvin J. Lehmann. *Using Standardized Tests in Education.* New York: Longman, 1987.

Reckase, Mark D. "Portfolio Assessment: A Theoretical Estimate of Score Reliability." *Educational Measurement: Issues and Practice, 14*, 1 (Spring 1995): 12–14, 31.

Skaggs, Gary, and Robert W. Lissitz. "IRT Test Equating: Relevant Issues and a Review of Recent Research," *Review of Educational Research, 56*, 4 (Winter 1986): 495–529.

Standards for Educational Psychological Tests. Prepared by a joint committee of the American Psychological Association, American Educational Research Association, National Council on Measurement in Education. Washington, DC: American Psychological Association, 1985.

Subkoviak, Michael J. "A Practitioner's Guide to Computation and Interpretation of Reliability Indices for Mastery Tests." *Journal of Educational Measurement, 25*, 1 (Spring 1988): 47–55.

Wainer, Howard. "Can a Test Be Too Reliable?" *Journal of Educational Measurement*, *23*, 2 (Summer 1986): 171–173.

Wainer, Howard, and David Thissen. "How is Reliability Related to the Quality of Test Scores? What is the Effect of Local Dependence on Reliability?" *Educational Measurement: Issues and Practice*, *15*, 1 (Spring 1996): 22–29.

AND FOR THOSE WHO TIRE OF READING

Williams, Reed. *Test Reliability and Validity* (Audiotape). Tape recording from the 1988 session of the American Educational Research Association (AERA). Available at AERA, 1230 Seventeenth St., N. W., Washington, DC 20036.

ENDNOTES

1. See, for example, W. J. Popham and T. R. Husek, "Implications of Criterion-Referenced Measurement," *Journal of Educational Measurement*, (1969), *6*, 1, 1–9.

2. Lee, J. Cronbach, "Coefficient Alpha and the Internal Structure of Tests," *Psychometrika, 16* (1951), 297–334.

3. Although this is not mathematically precise, it constitutes the usual way of interpreting confidence bands.

4. *Standards for Educational and Psychological Tests*. Prepared by a joint committee of the American Psychological Association, the American Educational Research Association, and the National Council on Measurement in Education (Washington, DC: American Psychological Association, 1974), p. 50.

6 Absence of Bias

chapter

- What is assessment bias?
  Offensiveness and Unfair Penalties
  Assessment Bias versus Instructional Shortcomings

- Do "culture-fair" tests avoid assessment bias?

- How should bias in test items be identified?
  Judgmental Review
  Empirical Analyses

- How should bias in test administration be identified?

- How should bias in test interpretation be identified?

- What is the best way to deal with the assessment of LEP students, that is, those who possess limited English proficiency?

143

I've entitled this chapter *absence of bias* (rather than simply *bias*) because I'd like you to think about absence of bias as a positive factor to be used when evaluating tests, just as you regarded instructional contribution, validity, and reliability as positive test-evaluation factors. Bias is a bad thing. *Bias*, as defined by *The American Heritage Dictionary*, describes a "preference or inclination that inhibits impartial judgment." That, of course, is why wise people will avoid bias. It messes up judgment. *Absence* of bias is a good thing.

A Look at Assessment Bias

In connection with educational testing, bias exerts its typical nastiness. Biased tests yield results that are likely to be misinterpreted. It is interesting that, although we have had many decades of educational testing in the United States, it is only during the past decade or two that educators have become sensitized to the possibility that our traditional testing procedures may be bursting with bias.

The kinds of bias that may be encountered in tests ranges wide. You can find instances of gender bias, religious bias, geographic bias, linguistic bias, and just about any other bias in the ballpark. Perhaps the most insidious form of bias in educational testing is ethnic or racial bias, because testing practices that are ethnically or racially biased tend to stifle the attainments of individuals who have often already been served up more than their share of social inequities. There are so many factors, economic, historical, and social, that operate to oppress people from minority groups that it constitutes a major educational tragedy when the progress of minority youngsters is stultified because of bias in testing.

Robert L. Williams, a black psychologist who created an intelligence test biased *in favor* of black people, the *Black Intelligence Test Counter-balanced for Honkies*, or the *Black Intelligence Test of Cultural Homogeneity*, makes the point eloquently as he points out how African Americans have been systematically penalized by white-oriented tests:

> May I ask, "Is it more indicative of intelligence to know Malcolm X's last name or the author of Hamlet?" I ask you now, "When is Washington's birthday?" Perhaps 99% of you thought February 22. That answer presupposes a white norm. I actually meant Booker T. Washington's birthday, not George Washington's. "What is the color of bananas?" Many of you would say, "Yellow." But by the time the banana has made it to my community, to the ghetto, it is brown with yellow spots. So I always thought bananas were brown. Again, I was penalized by the culture in which I live. "What is the thing to do if another child hits you, without meaning to do it?" The frequency of the response is determined by the neighborhood lived in. In my community, to walk away would mean suicide. For survival purposes, children in Black communities are taught to hit back; however, that response receives zero credit on current intelligence tests such as the Stanford-Binet (Form L-M). Thus, the test items are no more relevant to the Black experience than is much of the curriculum. Black children will naturally do worse on tests which draw items from outside their culture.[1]

African Americans, Hispanic Americans, and most other minority groups have often suffered from educational testing practices that are unquestionably biased in favor of in-

News in Brief: A National Roundup

Seniors Denied Graduation Walk for Failing Alabama State Test

No pass, no walk. That was the message affirmed by the Montgomery County, Ala., school board, which has voted 4–3 to keep students who haven't passed the state's graduation exam from walking across commencement-ceremony stages.

Two board members had introduced a resolution on the issue on behalf of the parents of 60 seniors countywide who have completed the 22 course credits required for graduation but have not passed the long-standing 8th-grade-level exam.

Parents of two seniors from Sidney Lanier High School also filed a federal lawsuit last month against county and state officials, arguing that the test is racially biased—56 of the 60 students are black—and that the students were not given enough notice of the consequences of failing the exam.

The case continues to move forward even though the plaintiffs failed late last month to get a federal judge to allow the students to take part in graduation exercises.

What's your reaction?

Reprinted, with permission, from *Education Week*, June 10, 1998

dividuals from the majority culture. Educational tests have typically been written by white, middle-class Americans; tried out on white, middle-class students; and normed on white, middle-class students. Is it any wonder that youngsters from other ethnic groups or lower socioeconomic strata would fare more poorly on such tests than children of the white, middle-class types who spawned those tests?

It should be noted, however, that no allegation is made here of malevolence on the part of test developers or test users. No, it has been less a case of maliciousness than a case of freewheeling *ignorance*. Test developers have ignorantly assumed that a white, middle-class item writer could generate items that would provide all students with an equal chance to get a correct answer. Far too often that assumption was unwarranted.

At an obvious level, let's say test items contain words or phrases that are common to the white, middle-class experience but foreign to, for example, Chicano children from the barrios of East Los Angeles. Those barrio children, unable to understand the vocabulary of the test items, will perform less well on the test than they would have if they had comprehended the vocabulary.

At a less obvious level, think about the subcultural value evidenced in the previous quotation from Williams. If an African American ghetto child has been forced to embrace a "fight-when-attacked" value, that child should not be penalized on a test by items that are looking for a "turn-the-other-cheek" response. Ghetto and barrio children must often avoid cheek-turning if they are to survive.

Test bias is operative whenever there are qualities in (1) a test itself, (2) the way in which the test is administered, or (3) the manner in which the test's results are interpreted that unfairly penalize or give an advantage to members of a subgroup because of their membership in that subgroup. This sort of definition of test bias has been bouncing around in measurement circles for a decade or two, but it is really more complicated to define test bias than it appears at first.

First, note that the test-bias sword chops in both directions. If members of a subgroup are penalized by a test because of their membership in that subgroup, the test is obviously biased. Most of the examples that come to mind when educators think of test bias are of such a negative sort. However, a test is equally biased if it gives *advantages* to members of a subgroup, thus penalizing other subgroups. Let's say you whipped up a new aptitude test that drew so heavily on notions derived from the Orient that Asian Americans would perform dazzlingly, while all others would perform dismally. Such a test, though not penalizing a particular group, would also be unfair.

Assessment Bias *versus* Instructional Shortcomings

Disparate Impact

When the test scores of different groups are decidedly different.

Every time that members of a minority group score lower on a test item than members of the majority group, does that mean the test item is biased? Think hard about that question before you answer. Now, if you are entitled to continue reading by having followed my advice and devoted hard thinking to your answer, here's the correct response: absolutely not! Although such a test item *may* be biased, it may also be totally unbiased and may merely be detecting deficits in the instruction received by minority children.

In the late seventies and early eighties, a number of states established minimum competency testing programs that called for high school students to pass competency tests, usually in reading, writing, and arithmetic, prior to being awarded a high school diploma. When these tests were administered on a statewide basis, it was often discovered that a sizably larger proportion of minority students failed the tests than was the case with white students. The tests were, clearly, having a *disparate impact* on certain kinds of students. However, that fact *does not automatically indicate that the competency tests were biased*. What it may indicate is that the instructional program in that state has failed to provide the state's minority children with the kinds of competencies they should have acquired in order to pass the prescribed tests.

In some states, for example, the state department of education staff members computed separate p values, that is, the proportion of students answering an item correctly, for majority and for minority students. Any item for which there was a substantial disparity in p values was automatically considered biased and, therefore, was excised from the test. No effort was made to see if, indeed, there was something in the test item that might have rendered it biased. The mere fact that more minority youngsters answered an item incorrectly was automatically considered proof that the item was biased.

However, subsequent analyses of some of the discarded items revealed no ingredients whatsoever that could be considered to penalize unfairly any minority group. The alternative hypothesis, therefore, appears far more tenable, namely, that the minority youngsters did poorly on those items because they had been badly taught. By tossing out such items merely on the basis of differential p values, the very items were eliminated that could reveal the skills and knowledge that the minority youngsters lacked.

While it is perfectly sensible to employ empirical schemes, such as looking for disparate p values between, for example, the scores of children from high versus low socioeconomic strata, any items thus identified *should then be judged* to see whether they possess features that constitute bias against low socioeconomic status youngsters. If the items do indeed possess such elements, then the items should obviously be modified or jettisoned. If no biasing elements can be identified, however, the alternative hypothesis seems likely, namely, that the low socioeconomic status youngsters were not well taught with respect to the content covered in those items.

If, for instance, you asked children to come up with the result of adding two plus two and a group of minority students happened to answer the item incorrectly more often than majority students, you obviously wouldn't toss out the item. Everybody ought to know how to add two plus two. (After all, our entire mathematics edifice is predicated on the fundamental truth that two plus two equals approximately four.) However, when the test item deals with a less obvious skill or a more exotic bit of knowledge, some folks let differences in p values take the place of sensible judgment.

Culture-Fair Tests

In an effort to circumvent the problems associated with tests that yield different scores for different groups, efforts were made to create *culture-fair* testing instruments. Typically, these tests were largely nonverbal in nature. Some of the better known of these instruments are Cattell's *Culture-Fair Intelligence Tests*, *Raven's Progressive Matrices*, the *Leiter International Performance Scale*, and the *Davis-Eells Test of General Intelligence*.

The David-Eells test, often referred to as the prototype of culture-fair tests (even though insufficient sales failed to warrant its continued publication), was predicated on the general strategy of trying out items and eliminating those on which children from lower socioeconomic or different cultural backgrounds scored significantly worse than others. The test consists of problems thought to be common to the experience of all urban children and is entirely pictorial, except for the directions, which are read aloud by the test administrator. The test was designed for children in grades one through six.

The following are sample items from the test.[2] One type of problem is referred to as "probabilities." A picture is presented showing a situation, and the student is given (having been read aloud by the test administrator) three possible explanations. The test taker's task is to pick the most likely explanation.

Another type of item in the *Davis-Eells Test of General Intelligence* is called "analogies." These items present a pictured relationship between two objects in an example, then a new object and three pictorial options. In each case, the relationship between elements in the example is suggested or made clear by the test administrator before the student is required to choose the appropriate analogue for the new object from the three options.

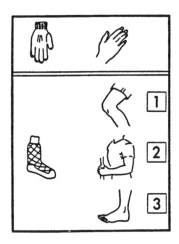

Culture-Fair Tests

Assessment devices designed to eliminate bias by employing only stimulus materials common to all cultures.

Another part of the test is called "best ways" and presents pictorial problems with three possible solutions depicted. The student's task is to select the picture that shows the best way to solve the problem.

The Davis-Eells test received a great deal of research attention, and some encouraging validity evidence was gathered. For instance, Davis-Eells test scores correlate around .50 with the *Otis Quick-Scoring Mental Ability Tests* and approximately .40 with standardized achievement tests in reading, language, and arithmetic. On the whole, however, the Davis-Eells test failed to fulfill its promise as a genuinely culture-fair test.[3]

Cattell's *Culture-Fair Intelligence Tests* employed a somewhat different approach to the creation of unbiased testing instruments. Four different types of items are found in the tests. Series items oblige the student to select a choice that completes a series. Classification items require students to choose something that does not belong in a set. Matrices items require students to find a choice that completes a pattern. In the conditions items, a dot must be placed in one of the choices that coincides with the conditions present in a boxed figure.[4]

Three levels of this test are available, aimed at ages four to eight, eight to thirteen, and ten to sixteen. As seen in the sample items, the tests are essentially perceptual and nonverbal, because directions are read aloud to students so that they understand the task. Several studies have been reported that indicate that economically disadvantaged children, both whites and African Americans, score slightly higher on the Cattell tests than they do on more traditional aptitude tests.[5] These results have been used to demonstrate the greater fairness of the Cattell approach, in contrast to the more heavily verbal orientation of typical aptitude and achievement tests. Nevertheless, when one considers the entire array of available evidence regarding the *Culture-Fair Intelligence Tests,* a negative conclusion must be drawn regarding their utility.[6] Although the tests do not appear to be intrinsically unfair to any culture, it is not true that groups from one culture or subculture score as well on the tests as groups from another culture or subculture. Indeed, even nonverbal tests may be biased against (or in favor of) certain subgroups because there is research evidence to suggest that certain subcultures include more pictures, puzzles, and other nonverbal stimuli than do other subcultures.

In general, interest in developing culture-fair tests has definitely declined. In part, this reduction of interest was due to the lack of success among those who pioneered the creation of culture-fair tests. In part, it was also recognized that if human development is viewed as a process dependent on an interaction between inherited qualities and environmental factors, assessment instruments must tap the effects of those environmental forces. Only by focusing on dimensions of lesser significance can test developers, therefore, create assessment devices that will be fair to those from substantially different environments. Oakland and Matuszek conclude that "psychologists generally agree that one test cannot be universally applicable and fair to persons from all cultures and still assess important psychological characteristics."[7]

The general strategy employed in most so-called culture-fair tests involves the avoidance of heavy dependence on verbal material. Most attempts to develop culture-fair aptitude tests, therefore, have yielded nonverbal instruments. Ebel dismisses the utility of these instruments:

> But there is no good reason to believe that these nonverbal tests get any closer to the basic nature of intelligence than do the verbal tests. Ability to do well on them can also be learned. And since verbal facility is so important an element in school learning, and in most areas of human achievement, what the nonverbal tests succeed in measuring seems to have little practical usefulness.[8]

An Introduction to IPAT
CULTURE FAIR INTELLIGENCE TESTING

NOTE: The present notice is intended only as a brief first exposure to IPAT Culture Fair Intelligence Tests, from which, it is hoped, the reader will go on to study much more complete evidence and information in the Manuals and Technical Handbooks for the scales. They cannot effectively be evaluated or used without this fuller study.

Do the following sample problems:

ANSWERS

SERIES

Which of the five choices would complete the series?

CLASSIFICATION

Which one is different?

MATRICES

Which of the five choices would look right in the empty box?

CONDITIONS

In which of the five numbered boxes could a dot be put inside the circle but outside the square, as in the box at the left?

INTRODUCTION: You have just been introduced to an IPAT Culture Fair Intelligence Test, much as an examinee would be; that is, you have started taking the test. The examinee, however, has several examples of each type to work through, in the process of discovering what is required in the test proper. Also, such supplementary explanation as is necessary, oral or written, is given him in his primary language, whatever that is: English, Spanish, German, Italian, French, Japanese, Hindi, etc. This includes telling him the answers to examples, after he has worked them for himself (in this case, alternatives 1, 4, 1, and 3, respectively).

© IPAT, 1949, 1957.

Evaluating for Test Bias

From the preceding discussion, it should be evident that eliminating test bias constitutes a nontrivial measurement problem. Perhaps the best approach that educators can currently employ is to exercise the best evaluative judgments that they can muster in reviewing the test itself, the procedures used to administer it, and the interpretations made from the test's results.

Reliance on a judgmental approach to detecting and, once detected, eliminating test bias forces you immediately to a consideration of "who will render the judgments?" Suppose, for example, that you're trying to see whether Puerto Rican youngsters in New York City are being unfairly penalized by items on a test of reading achievement. Should you have the test items reviewed by a panel of white, middle-class school teachers? Obviously not. But how about a panel of Spanish-speaking teachers? Well, maybe yes or maybe no. What if the Spanish-speaking item-reviewers are middle-class Chicanos from San Diego? Is the ability to speak Spanish sufficient to qualify one to judge the suitability of test items for any Spanish-speaking group? Of course not. Similarly, the experience of African Americans in the rural South may not coincide at all with that of African Americans who were raised in the urban North.

The implication of the question-and-answer business in the previous paragraph is that those who will be doing the judging of items must be truly conversant with student population for whom the tests are designed. If tests for Puerto Rican youngsters are involved, then Puerto Rican judges should be used to review the test items. If tests are to be used for large groups of students, say for a national test, then the use of a judgmental approach to the detection of test bias starts to get really difficult.

Testing, as indicated earlier, is big business. Businesses must sell their wares if they're going to stay in business. This means that they must set their prices at a competitive level if they are going to be successful in selling their merchandise. If you were going to buy a battery-powered electric bagel slicer and were choosing between two models, one of which cost twice as much as the other, you'd probably opt for the less expensive choice. On the other hand, anyone who is sufficiently bizarre to want a battery-powered electric bagel slicer might go for the more costly model.

Bagel slicers aside, it is apparent that if publishers of national tests wanted to do a superior job in having their instruments reviewed by panels representing all minority groups with whom the test might be used, the costs (of paying the reviewers and revising the test based on their comments) could be substantial. These substantial costs would in many cases boost the price of the test beyond what was commercially competitive. Thus, even well-intentioned test publishers find themselves in a financial bind when it comes to the elimination of test bias. What is morally praiseworthy may be economically imprudent.

Some test publishers deal with this dilemma by adopting a flagrantly tokenistic strategy. For instance, I've seen one published standardized achievement test in reading that had all of its items reviewed by *one* white, *one* African-American, and *one* Hispanic-American reviewer. Any item judged to be biased *by all three judges* was removed from the test. Surprise of surprises, not too many items were tossed out.

However, it's easier to snipe at questionable practices than it is to propose constructive solution strategies. If users of educational tests become so sensitized to the perils of biased tests that they *demand* full-scale bias-reduction operations prior to purchasing a test, all test publishers would soon comply with these demands. Moreover, because this would result in an across-the-board increase in the price of tests, no one test publisher would need to forsake that necessary competitive edge. To reiterate a point that has and will be made often in this book, the production of high-quality educational assessment is not inexpensive. Decisions made on the basis of inexpensively produced tests, however, will typically result in errors that are both humanely and socially more expensive than one realizes.

Detecting Bias In Test Items

As suggested, the determination of whether a test item is biased against any group of students is chiefly dependent on human judgment. Shortly, you will consider two judgmental strategies for detecting bias in test items. First, however, you need to deal with two dimensions that may render a test item biased, namely, the extent to which the item *offends* or *unfairly penalizes* a group of students on the basis of personal characteristics such as gender, ethnicity, or socioeconomic status. Test items that offend or unfairly penalize students because of personal characteristics must be identified so that they can be excised from tests.

Offensiveness

A test item is offensive when it contains elements that would insult any group of test takers on the basis of their personal characteristics.

Offensiveness.   An example of a test item that might *offend* certain students would be an item in which members of a group are portrayed in a stereotyped manner. To illustrate, if minority youths were depicted in an item as members of rowdy gangs while majority youths were not, then the item should be judged to be biased because it might offend minority students. Another example of an offensive test item would be one that depicted members of a minority group as dull-witted or implied that females could not succeed in "the hard world of business." Test items that offend students are apt to have an adverse effect on those students' scores because an offended student will often be distracted when completing subsequent items and will, therefore, perform more poorly on those items. Think of how you would be likely to perform on an examination if some of the test's items seriously disparaged your own ethnicity, religion, or parental background.

Unfair penalties.   A test item that would *unfairly penalize* a particular group of students would be an item on which those students performed less well than another group of students, even though both groups were at the same achievement level with respect to the knowledge or skill being tested. This difference could be caused, for example, by dissimilar interests of the two groups. It could also be caused by differences in the two groups' mastery of a skill (or knowledge) that was irrelevant to what was being tested. To illustrate, suppose a test item required students to draw a conclusion from a reading selection about cosmetics. It is possible that males would perform less well on such an item than females, *not* because they are less able to draw conclusions (the skill being tested), but because, as a group, they may be less interested in and have less knowledge about cosmetics.

It should be noted that a biased test item *unfairly* penalizes a student. If test items are well constructed, they may very properly penalize students who *ought* to be penalized.

In the News

Minn. Board Gives Tentative Nod to Rule Targeting 'Diversity' Gaps

by Ann Bradley

After more than two years of deliberation, the Minnesota state school board has tentatively approved a policy change that would focus new attention on closing the achievement gaps between students of different races, ethnic backgrounds, and genders.

The proposed "educational diversity rule," endorsed this month by the board and scheduled for public comment this fall, is scheduled for a final board vote next spring. It would replace a 1998 rule that requires districts to address race, gender, and disability in their curricula.

At the same time, the board is also overhauling graduation standards and updating its policies on desegregation. The diversity policy is meant to complement the other efforts.

The proposed changes come as Minnesotans are grappling with the results of the state's new basic-skills test, which students must pass in order to graduate. In the Twin Cities, the home of many of the state's nonwhite students, the results have been disappointing.

Under the diversity rule, districts would be required to establish advisory committees and write plans specifying whether any achievement gaps exist.

Districts must also state their goals and time lines for reducing the disparities.

In addition, districts would have to explain how they would write curricula that were "culturally responsive" and "multicultural, gender fair, and disability aware," the proposed rule states.

It would be up to districts themselves to monitor their compliance with the plans, the rule says, but the documents should spell out what actions school boards would take if a school or program fell short of the goals.

Districts that fail to file plans with the state education commissioner could have their funding withheld. Those that fail to act on their plans could receive technical assistance from the state, be required to participate in an audit, or see their state aid reduced. . . .

What's your reaction?

Excerpted, with permission, from *Education Week*, September 24, 1997

Classroom teachers who create crackerjack quizzes may discover that their able but nonstudying students are penalized because they possess insufficient knowledge. That's not an unfair penalty. It is sweet justice!

Unfair Penalization

Test items unfairly penalize test takers when there are elements in an item that would inequitably disadvantage any group because of its personal characteristics.

Bias Eradication

In order to eliminate test items that offend or unfairly penalize students because of personal characteristics, two related but different approaches have been employed with high-stakes tests in recent years. Educational leaders ought to know about each.

Even though classroom teachers will not ordinarily be inclined to devote the same level of procedural effort to bias eradication, you will see that the dual foci of the following bias-eradication procedures are applicable even to the assessments employed by teachers.

Judgmental reviews. One approach to detecting (and eliminating) test items that offend or unfairly penalize students is to subject all potential items to a stringent review by a specially constituted *bias-review panel*. Members of such a bias-review panel should be dominantly or exclusively members of minority groups. To make sure that the panel considers potential gender bias as well, reasonable proportions of female and male reviewers are usually asked to serve as panelists. The number of reviewers constituting a bias-review panel typically varies, depending on the importance of the test involved. I have moderated bias-review panels with as few as eight members in some settings and with as many as thirty-five members in other settings.

The panelists are first provided with an orientation in which the nature of test bias is considered. For example, if items are to be reviewed regarding whether they offend *or* unfairly penalize, then both of these two concepts should be described and, if necessary, discussed by the panelists.

It is not always the case that both of these two item defects will be considered in the bias review. For example, until recently, one of the nation's leading test-development organizations asked bias-review panelists only to review test items on the basis of whether the items would offend minority students, not unfairly penalize those students.

After an orientation, then, all panelists would be asked to supply, individually, a Yes/No answer to a question such as the following for each test item:

> Might this item offend or unfairly penalize any group of students on the basis of personal characteristics such as sex or ethnicity?

Typically, if panelists consider an item to be biased, they are asked to describe in writing, briefly, the reason that they believe the item to be biased. (This procedure allows those who subsequently consider panelists' bias judgments to eliminate negative but irrelevant item judgments such as "This item was too easy.")

Bias-review panel sessions can be operated so that panelists review all items independently, at their own speed, then simply submit their item-review forms when finished. As an alternative, panelists might be asked to review independently a set of items at a time, say 10 to 15, then discuss each other's responses to the set of items. Panelists would be permitted to alter their per-item judgments after these intermittent group discussions.

At the close of the review session, a percentage of positive panelists' judgments for each item is calculated. At this point, items are typically deleted if a specified segment of the reviewers judged the item to be biased. Although, typically, a minimum percentage of negative reviews is established, such as 10 percent, it is possible that only one reviewer, but a perceptive one, isolates a clear shortcomings in an item. In such cases, irrespective of the numbers of reviewers who spotted the bias defect, the item should be discarded or modified.

All procedures to be used in the conduct of bias-review panels are, of course, important. For instance, the phrasing of the question that panelists must respond to is particularly significant. Note that in the previously cited question (in the box), the initial word is *might*. Let's say you substituted the word *would* for *might*. Do you think the *would*-version or the *might*-version is apt to lead to more items' being discarded as biased? Hopefully, you thought that the *might*-version would lead to more biased items, because when we ask reviewers to respond that an item *would* offend or unfairly penalize students, we force the bias reviewers to be much more certain regarding the item's shortcomings than if we only ask whether the item *might* have such an adverse effect.

If, however, a bias-review panel is carefully selected, oriented, and assisted during the review process, most biased items can be identified and eliminated. In today's atmosphere about the potential inequity of educational tests, it is difficult to imagine a high-stakes test that should be developed without reliance on a bias-review panel.

Empirical analyses. A second major approach to the detection of biased items involves *empirical analyses* of the differences between groups of students based on actual adminis- trations of the test items. Typically, these analyses are based on field tests of the items in advance of the items' inclusion in an operational form of the test. This approach permits defective items to be jettisoned before they are used in an actual test.

The logic operative in such empirical analyses is fairly straightforward. If it turns out that particular groups (minority or gender) perform appreciably lower on certain test items than other groups, then such items are "flagged" as potentially defective items. For instance, suppose that the following *p* values were obtained for two different test items based on field-test results:

ITEM NO. 24	*p* VALUES
African-American students	.48
Hispanic-American students	.46
White students	.86

ITEM NO. 37	
Males	.92
Females	.59

Item No. 24 would most likely be identified as a *potentially* biased item because the white students so substantially outperformed their African-American and Hispanic- American counterparts. Item No. 37 would be flagged as a *potentially* biased item because of the disproportionately weak performance of females.

There have been a variety of statistical schemes devised in recent years to detect po- tentially biased items based on empirical tryouts. The fundamental approach, however, is well illustrated by the previously supplied *p*-value differentials. In essence, one is at- tempting to isolate test items for which certain groups score lower (or higher) than what one would predict on the basis of probabilities.

Once an item has been identified by such empirical means, a choice point has been reached. Either the item is *automatically* regarded as biased because of differences in stu- dent performances, or the item is earmarked for *additional judgmental review*. I strongly recommend the latter approach because, as indicated earlier in this chapter, the automatic discarding of such items sometimes eliminates test items covering the very content that minority students most need to be taught. Advocates of the automatically biased ap- proach, however, have sometimes succeeded in establishing procedures in which any flagged items (for which *p*-value disparities of a given magnitude exist) are not permitted to be used on tests.[9] If judgments are to be made regarding items flagged as potentially biased, then those judgments should be rendered by individuals representing the groups who would be offended or unfairly penalized.

An increasingly popular approach to the detection of potentially biased items is referred to as *differential item functioning* (DIF). In a DIF analysis, two or more subgroups are identified (for instance, ethnic or gender subgroups) and then the difference between each group's *actual* item-performance and the group's *expected* item-performance is determined. A group's actual performance is based on how many students in that group answered the item correctly. A group's expected item performance is based on the group's overall performance on the entire test. For example, let's say that a particular minority group scored 15 percent lower on the total test than the majority group. On any given item, therefore, you might expect a lower performance on that item by the minority students (because of their overall lower test performance).

A DIF analysis compares the difference between the actual and expected performance on each item for each group involved in the analysis. If the expected and actual *p*-value for any group differs by a predetermined amount, then a check is made of the expected and actual *p*-value differences on that item for all other groups. If the difference on an item for one group is significantly larger than for the other groups, that item is flagged for further scrutiny by judges to discern if there are apparent biasing elements in the item. If so, of course, the item is discarded.

A combination of approaches.   Clearly, if resources permit, it is advantageous to use both of the two bias-detection strategies just described. If (1) item writers can be sensitized to the importance of writing items free of bias, (2) items can be reviewed by a bias-review panel, and (3) empirical group differences can be employed in an effort to detect biased items that might have been overlooked, the vast majority of biased test items can be removed from educational tests.

How about the Classroom Teacher?

Educational leaders influence teachers. One form of influence that's definitely needed is advice to classroom teachers that they, too, need to be attentive to the detection and elimination of bias in their own classroom assessments.

Classroom teachers need to know that assessment bias exists. Assessment bias in educational tests is probably less prevalent than it was a decade or two ago because most measurement specialists, having been sensitized to the presence of assessment bias, now try to eliminate such biases. However, for the kinds of teacher-developed assessment procedures seen in typical classrooms, systematic attention to bias eradication is much less common.

All classroom teachers *routinely* need to use absence-of-bias as one of the evaluative criteria by which they judge their own assessments and those educational assessments developed by others. For instance, if a teacher is ever called on to review the quality of a high-stakes test such as a district-developed or district-adopted examination whose results will have a meaningful impact on students' lives, the teacher should be sure that suitable absence-of-bias procedures, both judgmental and empirical, were employed during the examination's development.

But what about a teacher's own tests? How much effort should teachers devote to making sure that their tests don't offend or unfairly penalize any of their students because of personal characteristics such as ethnicity or gender? My answer is that teachers really do need to devote attention to absence-of-bias for *all* of their classroom assessment procedures. For the least significant of teachers' assessment procedures, I suggest that teachers simply heighten their consciousness about bias eradication as they generate the test items or as they review the completed test.

For more important examinations, teachers should try to enlist the assistance of a colleague to review their assessment instruments. If possible, teachers should secure the help of colleagues from the same subgroups as those represented in their students. For instance, if many of a teacher's students are Hispanics (and the teacher isn't), then the teacher should try to get a Hispanic colleague to look over the test's items to see if there are any that might offend or unfairly penalize Hispanic students. When teachers enlist a colleague to help them review their tests for potential bias, they might carry out a miniversion of the bias review panel procedures described in this chapter. Briefly, teachers can describe to their coworkers how to define assessment bias, give the coworkers a succinct orientation to the review task, and structure their colleagues' reviews with absence-of-bias questions such as those seen earlier in this chapter.

Classroom teachers rarely have an opportunity to scrutinize items based on empirical analyses because, for the most part, fairly large student samples are required to make such analyses work well. For the most part, then, classroom teachers must rely on judgmental rather than empirical approaches to the detection of biased items.

Most importantly, if educational leaders can help teachers personally to realize how repugnant all forms of assessment bias are, and how assessment bias can distort certain students' performances even if the assessment bias was inadvertently introduced by the test's developer, teachers will be far more likely to eliminate assessment bias in their own tests because in education, as in any other field, assessment bias should definitely be *absent*.

Detecting Bias in Test Administration

Besides the test items themselves, another likely source of bias is associated with the procedures employed in the administration of the test. The actual administration of a test constitutes a complex interaction among examiner variables, student variables, and situational variables. Suppose, for example, that a large group of African-American adolescents was being tested in a stuffy, poorly lit cafeteria by a white examiner whose surly manner would arouse hostility in white saints, much less minority teenagers. Suppose also that these African-American youngsters had previously performed rather badly on tests similar to the one being administered in an uncomfortable room by a borderline bully. Is it any wonder that these minority students might perform less well than they might have in other test-administration settings?

Examiners. Without question, the behavior displayed by an examiner during the test's administration can be influential in determining the way that students will perform on the test. While research assembled thus far does not indicate that examiners need to be of the same race as students,[10] there is some tendency for adult and older adolescent African Americans to prefer working with African-American psychologists and counselors, rather than whites with comparable training.[11]

More important than racial match is the demeanor of the examiner as perceived by the test-takers. If the examiner is a cold, aloof individual who is convinced that the students being tested will perform badly on the test, those sentiments will often be sensed by students. Test administrators (and that includes classroom teachers) should systematically sort out any stereotypic expectations they have regarding particular types of students. Either they should get these expectations under control or replace themselves with less offensive test administrators.

So much for the negatives. Now, on the positive side, it is desirable to use examiners who understand the verbal and nonverbal behavior of the individuals being examined. Examiners who are attentive to student reactions will be able to sense when certain actions may be warranted, such as restructuring a situation in which students appear to be displaying less-than-satisfactory motivation to do well on the test.

In the same vein, Tidwell recommends that "tangible actions should be taken to motivate examinees to perform at their optimal achievement levels.[12] She argues that many minority youngsters, having experienced previous failures in such examinations, may be anxious to "check out" psychologically from the exam as soon as they encounter a question or two they can't answer. To heighten the attentiveness of minority youngsters, Tidwell recommends that such students should be urged often to do their very best work when being tested. Minority students should also be informed that they will be confronted with difficult test items and that, *just like other groups of students*, they are not expected to answer all or even most of the items correctly. This kind of proactive stance is advocated in order to counter a minority child's response that on stumbling over a few tough items, might be, "I can't do well on this test like all those white kids." The child would then cease to expend the necessary energy on subsequent items. To head off such defeatist dispositions, test administrators will obviously have to be on their toes.

Students. All students should be equally familiar with the nature of the test being taken. Some youngsters, particularly those who come from other nations, are less familiar with typical U.S. testing situations than they need to be in order to perform well on tests. Such youngsters (indeed, any youngsters who are intimidated by the nature of the test itself) should be given ample practice opportunities to become accustomed to the *form* of tests being used.

Educational leaders should attempt to make sure that minority students acquire the same degree of "test wiseness" that we often encounter in white, middle-class students who may answer an item correctly because of their familiarity with testing practices, not their knowledge of the content being tested (for example, "always choose the longest answer in a multiple-choice test—it's more likely to be correct than the shorter options").

In particular, considerable attention should be directed to reshaping the expectations of minority children who have a history of unsuccessful performance on examinations. Such youngsters should be given successful test experiences in less threatening situations, then encouraged to bring heightened motivation and aspirations to any high-stakes testing situation.

The setting. For any student it is important to provide a comfortable test administration setting that is conducive to promoting the student's best efforts. For a minority student such settings may be *imperative*. For example, suppose that you are a seasoned, white test-taker. You might be able to do well on a test if it was administered in an outhouse during a hurricane. However, suppose you're a minority test-taker who has often flopped on tests. If the setting is less than comfortable, that might be just the straw that snaps the camel's back. (I am told that the backs of especially weak-backed camels can be induced to crumple if even a half-straw is employed.)

Detecting Bias in Interpretations

To the extent that educators employ criterion-referenced interpretations, rather than norm-referenced interpretations, there is somewhat less concern about biased interpretations, because the focus is on whether or not the student can (does) display a behavior of interest. With norm-referenced interpretations, however, the strong possibility exists that educators may make a biased interpretation of a student's score because they use an inappropriate set of normative data on which to base their inferences regarding what the score signifies. This possibility leads to an interesting and important issue regarding whether educational leaders should advocate the gathering and utilization of separate normative data for particular groups of minorities, for example, African Americans, Asian Americans or Hispanic Americans.

In the first place, it is necessary for any large-scale normative samples to be *drawn* on a stratified basis so that, for instance, with national norms, a representative proportion of African Americans, Hispanic Americans, Native Americans, and Asian Americans will be included. Obviously, if the normative sample's percentages of minority students are at variance with those in the population at large, it would be misleading to employ those normative data in interpreting an (underrepresented) student's test results.

However, even if the national norms are sufficiently representative, in some cases minority students will still be disadvantaged. For instance, if you're using the *Graduate Record Examination (GRE)* as a screening test to select students for graduate school, it may turn out that minority applicants may systematically be excluded if you merely select applicants on the basis of the highest *GRE* scores.

This has led some educators to propose that separate norms for minorities be created in addition to national norms. Oakland and Matuszek, for example, contend that "the availability of both national and localized norms, particularly when reported by various social class and racial-ethnic groups, provides for greater accuracy and clarity in interpreting test scores."[13] A number of those who have addressed themselves to the test-bias issue share this point of view.

On the other side of the argument, however, there is the danger that by establishing separate normative tables for minority subgroups, we thereby authenticate the notion that these groups are essentially different from the majority, that is, less able than the majority, and that those differences are unalterable. There is a strong spirit of second-classism that surrounds the advocacy of separate norms for minorities. Although there is little doubt that, at the present, greater "accuracy and clarity in interpreting test scores" might be

UC Urged to Drop SAT

Members of the University of California board of regents may consider eliminating the SAT as an admissions requirement for the university system, after hearing recommendations from a task force assigned to evaluate how continued use of the test would affect minority-student enrollment.

"The SAT is not a good tool to use for a high-stakes decision like this," said Eugene Garcia, the chairman of the system's Latino Eligibility Task Force and the dean of the graduate school of education at the university's Berkeley campus.

Dropping the SAT would increase eligibility rates for Hispanic students by 59 percent and would also help African-American applicants, the task force concluded.

The regents, who voted two years ago to eliminate racial preferences in admissions to the university, seemed receptive to the recommendations, Mr. Garcia said.

"I think they have a notion of fairness," he said. "And the question is, 'Is this a fair test?'"

What's your reaction?

Reprinted, with permission, from *Education Week,* October 1, 1997

Educational Leaders
Look at Assessment

Cracker-Box Learning

**Joe G. Frésquez,
Director**
Bilingual Education Program
Española Public Schools
Española, New Mexico

Educational assessment has been a part of my life since I started school in first grade. I recall written examinations and oral interrogations were the first types of educational assessments I was exposed to as a student in the public school system.

Written examinations were also known as essay questions; this type of assessment was uniform for all students who were expected to answer the same question(s) but permitted a wider coverage of the content, which was based on the student's recall of the subject matter under question and the ability to express his/her thoughts in written communication.

A number of years later, oral interrogations and written examinations were still used to test my competency and proficiency for my Master's Degree in Spanish from New Mexico Highlands University and my Master's Degree in Guidance and Counseling from the University of New Mexico.

My first experience with objective multiple-choice tests was when I was in about the 10th grade. I remember to this day the anxiety and frustration I suffered with this type of test. I don't know which standardized test it was, but the test had to be sent away for scoring. To make matters worse, my science teacher and advisor was very disappointed with me and my test results. He could not believe I scored so low on the test because I was an A and B student and was always on the honor roll. In those days my peers and I spoke only Spanish, but I missed the multiple-choice item response for the meaning of the word *saltine*. My advisor could not understand how I selected the wrong response if I knew the meaning of the word *salt* in Spanish which is *sal* and very similar in spelling and pronunciation in both Spanish and English except for the letter *t*.

To this day, I have not done well on multiple-choice item tests. I wanted to attain a Ph.D. back in the 1970s, but I was too scared of failure if I did not do well on the GRE (Graduate Record Examination) and the MAT (Miller Analogies Test). ●

gained, there is the long-run danger that we shall never promote an educational system in which ethnicity is not a dominant factor if we continue to employ ethnic variables in our test interpretations. I find myself lined up with the opponents of separate norms.

Some believe that, whenever the use of national normative data results in the selection of students in such a way that the ethnic composition of those selected is markedly different from the total population, a quota system should be employed. This sort of quota scheme would work as follows: If there are 22 percent black students in a given age group, then the twenty-two highest-scoring black children should be selected. Such quota schemes have been the subject of considerable controversy, both educational and legal, with claims of "reverse racism" being leveled by white applicants who have been excluded because of such procedures. Others, advocating a form of "compensatory justice," argue that such quota schemes are requisite in order to correct for prior social inequities. An increasing number of state legislatures have enacted laws precluding the use of quota systems in vocational and educational settings.

It is clear from the foregoing discussion that many issues relative to test bias are far from resolved. We do no yet possess a tidy tool kit by which we can unbias any potentially biased testing device. However, perhaps most importantly, modern educators are far more cognizant of the possibility of test bias than were their predecessors. Vigilance against test bias can help us isolate and then excise biased testing practices. Even with our best efforts, some test bias will surely slip by. Without our best efforts, minority and low socioeconomic youngsters are certain to be unfairly treated. This is unacceptable.

The LEP Dilemma

As more and more youngsters whose native language is not English enter our schools, educational leaders find themselves facing a new assessment issue, one not present a generation ago. Foreign-born students, more often than not, when first attending U.S. schools, possess *limited English proficiency* (LEP). The assessment issue that's causing considerable turmoil in many settings these days is "how should LEP students be assessed, in their native language or in English?"

Although Spanish is the dominant non-English first language of most LEP students in the United States, there are many other first languages of LEP students in this country. Several assessment directors from metropolitan school districts have told me that in their schools there are more than 100 first-born languages and dialects spoken by their district's LEP students.

Now it is altogether obvious that if a child, let's say he's a fourth-grader named Raul, came to the San Diego Unified School District from Mexicali two months ago, there's a strong chance that an English-language test is going to prove baffling. Assuming Raul is only beginning to fathom the fundamentals of English, how valid would our inferences about Raul's mathematical skills be if we based those inferences on a test featuring story problems all written in English?

Some educators, recognizing the near certain invalidity of score-based inferences if written tests are presented in languages that students can't understand, have urged that parallel versions of all assessments be developed in languages familiar to LEP students. As appealing as that proposal may initially sound, the cost of developing translated tests for *all* languages and dialects used by LEP students would be financially prohibitive. It costs much more than one imagines to develop a good alternate-language version of any test. To do so for even a handful of languages represents a daunting task. But if an educational leader opted only to develop Spanish-language versions of key tests, is this not patently unfair to the non-Hispanic *minority* LEP students who, unlike their Spanish-speaking classmates, must still struggle with a test written in a language they do not understand?

Then there's the special problem of measuring a student's ability to read English. Operating on the assumption that in a nation whose official language is English, educators want all students to be able to communicate in English, how *educationally* appropriate do you think it would be to translate an English-language reading test into Vietnamese? Could an educator make valid inferences about Vietnamese students' ability to read English if those students were never obliged to comprehend passages in English?

The LEP issue, of course, represents a very tangible form of the absence-of-bias problem. A number of state-level laws and numerous court rulings are beginning to clarify just what represents a fair and unbiased approach to the assessment of LEP children. As an educational leader, if you find yourself in a position that has anything to do with the testing of LEP students, I urge you to consult recent reviews of the legal issues associated with this thorny problem. Dr. Susan Phillips of Michigan State University, an educational measurement specialist *and* an attorney, recently suggested at a national assessment meeting that federal laws and federal court rulings will soon clarify how educational leaders should proceed in trying to avoid bias in the assessment of LEP students so that those students are as well measured and as well taught as is possible, but to do so within the realm of what is financially and practically possible. Her advice to educational leaders is to keep abreast of relevant new laws and new case law related to the education and assessment of LEP students. It is good advice.

Chapter Wrap-Up

To supply you with a thoroughly unbiased summary of this chapter about assessment bias, the chapter wrap-up is, as always, fashioned with profound pithiness around the chapter's guiding questions.

● What is assessment bias?

Assessment bias can be present in a test's items, in the way a test is administered, or in the way that the test's results are interpreted. Assessment bias occurs in any of these instances if a group of students might either be offended or unfairly penalized on the basis of personal characteristics such as gender, religion, race, ethnicity, or socioeconomic status. If minority students are outperformed on a given test item by majority students, however, this disparate impact does not *necessarily* signify that the item is biased against minorities. Instead, such a performance disparity may indicate (and often does) that the minority students have simply not been properly taught.

● Do "culture-fair" tests avoid assessment bias?

Although the 1950s and 1960s saw considerable attention being given to the creation of measuring devices that were intended to minimize assessment bias by providing more neutral stimulus material in test items, these so-called culture-fair tests never achieved their intended goal. It became clear that insofar as human development represents a link between a student's inherited qualities and the student's environment, the only way to avoid environmental (cultural) particularism was to focus on cultural dimensions of less significance. Little developmental work has been done on culture-fair tests in recent years. These tests did not solve the assessment-bias problem.

● How should bias in test items be identified?

The two most frequently traveled avenues for identifying biased test items are judgmental reviews and empirical analyses. Judgmental reviews focus on item-by-item answers to such questions as: "Might this item offend or unfairly penalize any group of students on the basis of personal characteristics such as sex or ethnicity?" Empirical analyses focus on field-tested items' difficulty-level differences between gender groups or groups of majority and minority students. Classroom teachers can review their own test items on the basis of these two dimensions, although judgmental reviews are more likely in view of the large samples of students needed for empirical analyses.

A widely used empirical analysis for bias detection these days is called *differential item functioning* (DIF). This approach attempts to flag potentially biased items on the basis of differences among subgroups' expected versus actual performances on test items.

● How should bias in test administration be identified?

Even if a test's items are totally free from bias, those bias-free items can be administered in such a way as to render certain students' performances inaccurate because of assessment bias. Test administrators must be particularly attentive to avoiding all forms of verbal or nonverbal conduct that might cue students to the belief that the examiner believes the students are not sufficiently capable. On the flip side, skillful examiners can do much proactively to assure students that they should continue to expend effort on a test even if a few items are missed. Students should all, irrespective of their group status, be familiar with the *form* of the assessment being used. Modest practice for students in dealing with any unfamiliar item types is highly appropriate. A comfortable test-administration setting is always desirable.

● How should bias in test administration be identified?

Some writers believe that, in order to render more accurate interpretations of the performances of students from a given group, separate norms should be established for such groups. The argument of this separate-norms point of view is that a persistent perception of second-class status is apt to be generated by creating lower expectation norms for distinct subgroups. The use of test results to establish quota systems for minority students has been the subject of hot debate in recent years. Many states have adopted laws prohibiting the use of test-based quotas.

● What is the best way to deal with the assessment of LEP students, that is, those who possess limited English proficiency?

The assessment of students with limited English proficiency (LEP) constitutes a substantial measurement issue for many educational leaders. It was recommended that educational leaders become particularly attentive to LEP-relevant legislation and court decisions because there is apt to be legislative and judicial clarification of how best to assess LEP students.

Practice Exercises

Suppose that you are a member of a bias-review panel responsible for judging a set of test items for a high school graduation test. Five sample test items have been provided below. You are to answer the following question for each of the five items:

> Might this item offend or unfairly penalize any group of students on the basis of personal characteristics such as sex or ethnicity?

If you believe that there are elements in a test item that might offend or unfairly penalize any group of students, then mentally answer "Yes" for that item. If you believe that a test item would not offend or unfairly penalize members of a particular group, then mentally answer "No." If you answer "Yes," that is, if you believe an item might be biased, try to identify, mentally, the nature of that bias.

After reviewing and making judgments about all of the sample items, read the comments in the Answers to Practice Exercises that follow the items. Please don't examine those comments until after you've judged all five items. The comments provide observations regarding how one might think about potential bias in each sample test item.

SAMPLE ITEMS

Sample Item 1

> With five minutes left in the championship football game, the score was tied at 20. North High School then scored a touchdown but missed the extra point. West High School then took the kickoff and scored a field goal just before the game ended.

What was the final score of the game?

A. North High: 25; West High: 22
B. North High: 27; West High: 24
C. West High: 25; North High: 23
*D. North High: 26; West High: 23

Sample Item 2

> Many birds will live in urban areas if they can find nesting places similar to those in their natural habitats. Cardinals and mockingbirds often build nests in low trees or shrubs. Blue jays and robins nest in shade

> trees. They also build nests under the edges of roofs and in mailboxes. Ruby-throated hummingbirds prefer trees, especially those close to flower gardens. The house sparrow, one of the most common birds, will nest in almost any small opening. They are a familiar sight in the downtown areas of big cities.

Which kind of bird builds nests in mailboxes?

*A. robins
B. ruby-throated hummingbirds
C. blue jays
D. house sparrows

Sample Item 3

Given $f(x) = \setminus x \setminus$ and $g(x) = 3\sin(x)$, what is the range of $f(g(x))$?

A. $0 < f(g(x)) < 1$
B. $-1 < f(g(x)) < 1$
*C. $0 < f(g(x)) < 3$
D. $-3 < f(g(x)) < 3$

Sample Item 4

> Carlos needs a new jacket. The jacket he wants costs $22.50 (including tax), but he only has $7.50. To earn the money, Carlos gets a job as a busboy at a local restaurant. If he earns $2.50 per hour (after taxes are deducted), how many hours will he have to work before he'll have enough money to but the jacket?

A. 4 hours
*B. 6 hours
C. 9 hours
D. 10 hours

Sample Item 5

[1] Dear Mr. Scott

[2] I understand that you sometimes help young inventors market their inventions. [3] I have invented a tool that makes washing windows faster and easier. [4] Enclosed is a working model of this invention. [5] Please let me know if you will be interested in working with me.

[6] Sincerely yours,

[7] Chris Weathers

In which part of this letter, if any, is there an error in *punctuation*?
*A.   Part [1]
B.   Part [3]
C.   Part [6]
D.   None of the above

Answers to Practice Exercises

Sample Item 1: This item appears to be biased against female students because it depends on specific information associated with the game of football. The answer to this item cannot be determined without knowing the point value of a touchdown and of a field goal. Although we might wish it were otherwise, it is probably true that females are, in general, less likely to have this knowledge than are males. If so, females would be more likely to miss this item than males, even if they had the same level of mathematical competence.

Sample Item 2: This item does not appear to be biased. It does, however, have a serious flaw. The pronoun they in the fourth sentence seems to refer to both blue jays and robins. If that were true, then the item has two equally correct answer choices: A and C. This flaw does not make the item biased against a particular group of students. *All* students would be penalized by this faulty item. Defective items such as this should be identified and modified or eliminated at earlier points in the test-development process.

Sample Item 3: This item does not seem to be biased. Although some groups of students, for example, females or minorities, may not have had the opportunity to learn the knowledge and skills needed to answer this item correctly, the item itself does not appear to have elements that might offend or unfairly penalize such groups. Unlike the first sample item, this item does not require skills or knowledge that are (1) irrelevant to the skill or knowledge being tested, and (2) more likely to be possessed by an identifiable group of students.

Your task as a bias-review panelist is to judge whether *items* are biased, not whether students' prior educations have been equally effective. Substantially different performance by groups on a test item may reflect deficiencies in the education of a particular group of students; it does not necessarily indicate that the *item* is biased.

Sample Item 4: This item appears to be biased. It portrays an Hispanic male in a stereotypical manner. Carlos is poor, and he takes a menial job. This would probably be offensive to Hispanic students.

Sample Item 5: This item does not seem to be biased. There appear to be no elements in the item
that would offend or unfairly penalize any group of
students on the basis of personal characteristics
such as sex, race, or ethnicity.

DISCUSSION QUESTIONS

1. If you were an educational leader who was trying to encourage the faculty of a middle school to be more attentive to the isolation and elimination of assessment bias,
   what would be your most effective arguments?
2. Imagine that you are a newly appointed superintendent of a large metropolitan
   school district. Can you identify typical district operations in which assessment bias
   might be present? What could you do to reduce such bias?
3. Suppose you were hired to head up the test-discrimination subgroup of a major test
   publishing house. What sort of procedures would you install to reduce the presence
   of bias in your firm's operations?
4. Do you believe that there should be separate racial group norms for tests? Why?
5. If you were obliged to choose between the use of (1) a bias-detection panel or (2) a
   group difference field-test approach to the detection of test items, which would you
   select? Why?
6. If a colleague of yours expressed the view that, "if there's a disparate impact of testing, you can be sure that there's bias lurking somewhere," how would you respond?

SUGGESTIONS FOR ADDITIONAL READING

Bond, Lloyd. "Disparate Impact and Teacher Certification." *Journal of Personnel Evaluation in Education, 12,* 2 (June 1998): 211–220.

Benson, Jeri. "Detection Item Bias in Affective Scales." *Educational and Psychological Measurement, 47,* 1 (Spring 1987): 55–67.

Cole, Nancy S., and Pamela A. Moss. "Bias in Test Use." In Robert L. Linn (Ed.), *Educational
   Measurement* (3rd ed.). New York: Macmillan, 1989.

DeMars, Christine E. "Gender Differences in Mathematics and Science on a High School Proficiency Exam: The Role of Response Format." *Applied Measurement in Education, 11,* 3
   (1998): 279–299.

Duran, Richard P. "Testing of Linguistic Minorities." In Robert L. Linn (Ed.), *Educational Measurement* (3rd ed.). New York: Macmillan, 1989.

Educational Testing Service. *Diversity among Asian American High School Students.* Princeton, NJ:
   Author, January 1997.

Educational Testing Service. *Reaching Standards: A Progress Report on Mathematics* (Policy Information Reports). Princeton, NJ: Author, 1995.

Fennema, Elizabeth, Thomas P. Carpenter, Victoria R. Jacobs, Megan L. Franke, and Linda W.
   Levi. "New Perspectives on Gender Differences in Mathematics: A Reprise." *Educational
   Researcher, 27,* 5 (June–July 1998): 19–21.

Fuchs, Douglas, and Lynn S. Fuchs. "Test Procedure Bias: A Meta-Analysis of Examiner Familiarity Effects." *Review of Educational Research*, 56, 2 (Summer 1986): 243–262.

Keenan, Jo-Anne Wilson, and Anne Wheelock. "The Standards Movement in Education: Will Poor and Minority Students Benefit?" *Poverty & Race*, 6, 3 (May–June 1997): 1–3, 7.

Klein, Stephen P., Jasna Jovanovic, Brian M. Stecher and Dan McCaffrey, Richard J. Shavelson and Edward Haertel, and Guillermo Solano-Flores and Kathy Comfort. "Gender and Racial/Ethnic Differences on Performance Assessments in Science." *Educational Evaluation and Policy Analysis*, 19, 2 (Summer 1997): 83–97.

Linn, Robert L., and Fritz Drasgow. "Implications of the Golden Rule Settlement for Test Construction." *Educational Measurement: Issues and Practice*, 6, 2 (Summer 1987): 13–17.

Lott, Juanita Tamayo. *Asian Americans: From Racial Category to Multiple Identities*. Walnut Creek, CA: Alta Mira Press, 1998.

Montagu, Ashley. *Man's Most Dangerous Myth: The Fallacy of Race (6th ed.)*. Walnut Creek, CA: Alta Mira Press, 1997.

National Center for Fair & Open Testing. *FairTest Examiner* (Quarterly Journal). Cambridge, MA: Author, 1998.

Northwest Regional Educational Laboratory. *Assessment: A Development Guidebook for Teachers of English Language Learners*. Portland, OR: Author, 1998.

Oakland, Thomas, (Ed.). *Psychological and Educational Assessment of Minority Children*. New York: Brunner/Mazel, 1977.

Popham, W. James. "Teacher Competency Testing: The Devil's Dilemma." *Teacher Education & Practice*, 1, 1 (Spring 1984): 5–9.

Prassee, David P., and Daniel J. Reschly. "Larry P.: A Case of Segregation, Testing, or Program Efficacy?" *Exceptional Children*, 52, 4 (January 1986): 333–346.

Rooney, J. Patrick. "Golden Rule on 'Golden Rule'." *Educational Measurement: Issues and Practice*, 6, 2 (Summer 1987): 9–12.

Rooney, J. Patrick. "A Response from Golden Rule to ETS on 'Golden Rule'." *Educational Measurement: Issues and Practice*, 6, 4 (Winter 1987): 19–23.

Scheuneman, Janice Dowd. "An Experimental, Exploratory Study of Causes of Bias in Test Items." *Journal of Educational Measurement*, 24, 2 (Summer 1987): 97–118.

Sharma, Sarla. "Assessment Strategies for Minority Groups." *Journal of Black Studies*, 17, 1 (September 1986): 111–124.

Shepard, Lorrie A. et al. "Validity of Approximation Techniques for Detecting Item Bias." *Journal of Educational Measurement*, 22, 2 (Summer 1985): 77–105.

Standards for Educational Psychological Tests. Prepared by a joint committee of the American Psychological Association, American Educational Research Association, and the National Council on Measurement in Education. Washington, DC: American Psychological Association.

Valdés, Guadalupe, and Richard Figueroa. *Bilingualism and Testing: A Special Case of Bias*. Greenwich, CT: Ablex Publishing, 1994.

ENDNOTES

1. Robert L. Williams, "Black Pride, Academic Relevance, and Individual Achievement," in *Crucial Issues in Testing*, eds. R. W. Tyler and R. M. Wolf (Berkeley, CA: McCutchan, 1974). Reprinted with permission of the publisher.

2. Sample items from the *Davis-Eels Test of General Intelligence*, copyright © 1952, 1953 by Harcourt Brace Jovanovich, Inc. Reproduced by special permission from the publisher.

3. For example, see Victor H. Noll, "Relation of Scores on Davis-Eells Games to Socioeconomic Status, Intelligence Test Results, and School Achievements," *Educational and Psychological Measurement, 20* (Spring 1960), 119–129.

4. Sample items from the Cattell *Culture-Fair Intelligence Test*, copyright © 1949, 1957 by the Institute for Personality and Ability Testing, Champaign, IL. Reproduced with permission.

5. For example, see Keith Barton, *Recent Data on the Culture-Fair Scales*, Information Bulletin 16 (Champaign, IL.: Institute for Personality and Ability Testing, 1973).

6. See, for instance, the reviews of these tests in O. K. Buros, Ed., *Fifth and Sixth Mental Measurements Yearbooks* (Highland Park, NJ: Gryphon Press, 1959 and 1965).

7. Thomas Oakland and Paula Matuszek, "Using Tests in Nondiscriminatory Assessment," in *Psychological and Educational Assessment of Minority Children*, ed. T. Oakland (New York: Brunner/Mazel, 1977), p. 62.

8. Robert L. Ebel, *Essentials of Educational Measurement*, 3rd ed. (Engelwood Cliffs, NJ: Prentice-Hall, 1979), p. 350.

9. For example, in the Golden Rule Settlement (Lloyd Bond, "The Golden Rule Settlement: A Minority Perspective," *Educational Measurement: Issues and Practice*, 6 [Summer 1987], 18–20.) and an Alabama State Board of Education agreement regarding that state's teacher certification tests.

10. Oakland and Matuszek, "Using Tests in Nondiscriminatory Assessment," p. 60.

11. J. Sattler, *Assessment of Children's Intelligence* (Philadelphia: Saunders, 1974).

12. Romeria Tidwell, *Guidelines for Reducing Bias in Testing* (Los Angeles: IOX Assessment Associates, May 1979), pp. 15–16.

13. Oakland and Matuszek, "Using Tests in Nondiscriminatory Assessment," p. 56.

7

High-Quality Comparative Data

In this chapter, you're going to learn about something that, as an educational leader, you'll not always need. Such a revelation by your bound-to-be-honest author might incline you to skip Chapter 7 and scurry on to Chapter 8. After all, what time-conscious educational leader wants to dawdle over a topic that sometimes won't be necessary?

The problem with such an efficiency-oriented analysis is that *sometimes you will need what's in this chapter.* To be ready for those occasions, and they're often important, no chapter-dodging is allowed. More specifically, you'll be learning about a fifth and final evaluative factor by which to judge the caliber of tests. In this instance, however, that evaluative factor should only be applied to tests from which relative, that is, norm-referenced, interpretations are to be made. Because norm-referenced interpretations will only be as good as the *comparative data* on which those relative interpretations are based, the quality of a test's comparative data is the last of Part Two's five factors that can be used to gauge the caliber of educational tests.

Three of those evaluative factors, namely, *validity*, *reliability*, and *absence of bias*, should always be applied when educational tests are being evaluated. For two of the five evaluative factors, however, it depends. For assessment devices that are apt to have a meaningful impact on teachers' instructional decision-making, then the evaluative factor of *instructional contributions* should definitely be applied. In such instructionally relevant contexts, you'll find that Chapter 7's evaluative factor, that is, *high-quality comparative data*, may not apply all that often. Actually, because the assessment devices in most instructionally oriented settings are intended to provide criterion-referenced rather than norm-referenced inferences, comparative data are often not even relevant. However, in any kind of educational context in which norm-referenced interpretations are to be made, educational leaders should definitely apply this final evaluative factor, namely, *high-quality comparative data*.

A Call for Comparisons in Competitive Contexts

We live in a society that, many in many aspects, is remarkably competitive. People are constantly being compared with one another regarding appearance, wealth, intellectual prowess, and so on. This competitive orientation gets a substantial boost in the nation's schools where, in the earliest grades and ever after, educators are constantly attempting to compare students with one another so that the best and worst students can be identified. Although most clinical psychologists decry this preoccupation with competition because of its adverse impact on emerging self-concepts, there is little likelihood that our schools will soon be transformed into noncompetitive, idyllic gardens of cooperation.

While excessive emphasis on student-versus-student comparisons can obviously be harmful, there is a sense in which comparisons are indispensable if we are to make much sense out of an individual's performance. For instance, suppose you are a teacher who has just completed a brand new two-week instructional unit dealing with an aspect of ethics, and you want to find out whether your unit was a winner. Assuming you had developed a completely new (and, as far as you know, unique) forty-item test measuring students' knowledge and attitudes about the ethical issue being studied, how would you interpret the postinstruction performance of your class? Let's say the mean performance of your class on the test was 29.9. Is this good or bad? Was your unit on ethics a triumph or a disaster?

It's only when you are able to compare scores of individuals, or groups of individuals, that you begin to get a fix on answering the question "How good is this performance?" Getting back to the ethics example, you can see that if you had access to the performance of similar but uninstructed students on your forty-item test and discovered that their mean performances were all around 15.0 or so, your students' performance of nearly 30 would look pretty impressive. Let's say you also tried out your test on a group of philosophers specializing in ethics (a national philosophy conference fortuitously being held at a nearby hotel), and their mean score was 32.0, barely two points higher than your students. All of a sudden, you'd get fairly ecstatic about your two-week ethics unit. You'd apparently been able to pick up where Aristotle left off. Ethics instruction would definitely appear to be your calling.

Please note in the foregoing example that insights regarding the meaning of a group's test performance are possible as a consequence of comparing that group's performance with the performance of other groups. Similarly, the interpretation of an individual's test score can be appreciably enhanced by having data available regarding the performance of other individuals.

With norm-referenced interpretations, for example, if no normative data were available by which you could make comparisons, there would be little sense that you could make out of a score of, say, 83 items correct. If you consult a normative table, however, and discover that a score of 83 items correct is higher than the scores earned by 97 percent of nearly 1,000 students who had previously taken the exam, then the score of 83 starts to take on some meaning.

Now, although it is true that, where comparisons are made, an invidious spirit of competitiveness often follows, this need not be the case. If educators can employ comparative data adroitly, in order to reach the sorts of conclusions about individuals and groups of individuals that *without such comparative data would be impossible*, yet resist the temptation to pin eternal "winner" and "loser" labels on students, educators can pick up the dividends of comparative data while dodging the deficits of unbridled competitiveness.

In this chapter you will encounter a variety of concepts associated with the use of comparative data for educational tests. For instance, you'll delve into the properties of the *normal curve* because it is employed so frequently for comparison purposes. You'll also consider the various sorts of specially devised numerical schemes that are used to represent a student's test performance in comparative terms. Finally, you'll take a hard look at the kinds of normative data that serve as the central comparative framework for relative test interpretations, that is, where normative data come from and how such data should be most effectively displayed. In order to evaluate a test on the basis of its comparative data, you'll obviously need to evaluate that comparative information itself. This chapter supplies the information you'll need in order to make these sorts of appraisals.

Later in this chapter, you'll be learning about some different ways of making relative comparisons among students' test performances. Do educational leaders need to become super-skilled at calculating these comparative score-reporting methods? Probably not. But, as an educational leader, you'll need to have a rough idea of how these sorts of comparative score-reporting methods function. If a school board member tells you that "the district's mean NCE was well below acceptable," you do not want to be in a position where you ask the board member to respell NCE. Accordingly, don't be put off by the

Educational Leaders
Look at Assessment

Test Scores:
Deity or Devil?

Stephen Sexton
Superintendent of Schools
Fremont Public Schools
Fremont, Nebraska

A brilliant young lad has been newly employed by Data Du Jour. He jauntily walks into the office of the CEO of a major hardware chain and promises if the chain uses the new UR2 software, his firm will guarantee the CEO that the program will tell him what the content of his stores are within 25 to 50 percent accuracy. For any given store, if the actual inventory level is 70 percent, the young man promises without fail the software will tell the CEO if the store is stocked between 61 and 70 percent. Should the CEO be thrilled? Would you?

And yet we depend on achievement tests to be the "be all" by which schools are judged, teachers are evaluated, and careers made or broken. Who is responsible? We are! From day one, the educational community has allowed standardized achievement tests to be used as the means of judging student performance and, unwittingly, instruction in their schools. Educators should know these examinations are congruent with a maximum of 25 to 50 percent of the local curriculum at best.

There is strange news on yet another front, if my reading of the literature is accurate. We have districts swearing that by using international examinations and related data and materials, they are now "world class" in performance. As a result of these articles appearing in reputable journals, other boards are rushing to the train that will lead their district to world class schools. According to one national expert in assessment evaluation, use of the international examinations to judge local performance is nothing short of "frightening."

Prior to accepting employment seven months ago in my present district, I was superintendent in two systems in which the board placed total and unyielding confidence in raising test scores. It didn't matter what the scores measured, with whom kids were compared, or if the kids could actually "do" anything with whatever it was they learned. As one board member put it, "We don't know what we want, but we want *something*."

Outcomes were marginally more popular than the plague. Test scores went up. Why did they go up? Teachers and administrators may be a lot of things, but dumb isn't necessarily on the list. Raising test scores artificially just isn't that tough. It can be done, but what of the ethics? I have friends who have been superintendents of major school systems, systems whose names would be recognized by anyone not living on Pluto. My friends have lost their jobs for one reason and one reason alone, their district's test scores did not rise.

In a society consumed with the "Les Izmore" philosophy of finance and how schools should be run, it isn't likely that the swing away from the infatuation with standardized achievement tests is likely to decrease. We are seeing more and more the motto, "Let data drive your schools" being the platform for legislators. What this means to most legislators and the public in general is, "Let achievement tests drive your schools."

If there is a solution to the current craving for norm-referenced test data, it may rest in a pyramid design that would include norm-referenced results for gross comparisons, criterion-referenced results to gauge instructional effectiveness, and performance assessment to determine students' actual application skills. The major problem, at least based on my own experience, is getting the public to buy a multiple-assessment strategy in the face of national media pressure that seemingly points in the opposite direction. ●

Illinois Scores at Odds with Perceptions of Capabilities

by Kathleen Kennedy Manzo

Illinois teachers and students feel confident about their knowledge of science and math, but that confidence is at odds with the state's lackluster performance in an international comparison.

The chasm has led a state task force to recommend extensive teacher training and curriculum development to ensure that Illinois students meet world-class standards in those subjects.

In its report on the state's middling ranking on the Third International Mathematics and Science Study, a panel of math and science educators told the state school board last month that proper implementation of national standards and the state's frameworks in math and science is critical to becoming more competitive.

Training called key. "It shows us that our curriculum is such that we are not teaching things that other countries are teaching," said Richard J. Wylie, the president of the Illinois Council of Teachers of Mathematics and a task force member. "The standards are only as good as the implementation, but they have the potential to give us

good guidance if we provide sufficient professional development in instruction and curriculum."

Despite steady improvements on state tests, Illinois' 8th graders, like students nationwide, did not measure up to their international counterparts on the TIMSS test. A national sample of participants was selected for the U.S. assessment. Illinois, along with Colorado and Minnesota, chose to expand its sample of participating schools so test data could be used to compare their students' performance with that of students in other countries. Illinois paid more than $100,000 to be part of the study.

The sample of 2,000 Illinois students scored on a par with American students in general, but significantly lower than peers in 25 other countries in math and 16 other countries in science. Representative samples of 8th graders from 41 countries took the test last fall. Fourth graders from 26 countries also took the test, but those state-level data have not yet been released. Singapore, Korea, and Japan turned in the top performances....

What's your reaction?

Excerpted, with permission, from *Education Week,* October 1, 1997

number-based reporting schemes you'll soon be reading about. Instead, try to gain a general, intuitive understanding of how these reporting procedures can be used in arriving at norm-referenced interpretations. That's the level of understanding an educational leader really needs.

The Normal Curve

As you know (or, if you don't know, as you can learn in the Appendix), it is possible to represent a distribution of test scores graphically. There is a statistically derived distribution, *the normal curve,* that is particularly useful in helping educators as they compare a student's score with the scores earned by other students. Before describing how the normal curve can be used for such purposes, let's consider its chief characteristics.

The normal distribution is a symmetrical, bell-shaped curve whose mean, median, and mode are identical. In addition, a normal curve has some other alluring qualities that make it useful. Consider, for example, Figure 7.1, in which the normal curve is displayed. You will note that along the base line of the curve, ordinates (vertical lines from the curve to the base line) have been erected at distances of one standard deviation unit, plus and minus three standard deviations from the mean. Because of the properties of the normal curve, these ordinates always divide the distribution into predictable proportions. For instance, notice that between the mean and plus one standard deviation there is 34.13 percent of the distribution. Remember, that because the area under the curve line represents the proportion of scores in the distribution, if you had a set of test scores distributed in a perfectly normal fashion, then 34.13 percent of those scores would fall between the mean and plus one standard deviation. Similarly, the area between plus and minus one standard deviation from the mean would contain 68.26 percent of the scores.

In most statistics textbooks there are detailed tables that indicate precisely what proportion of the normal curve is bounded by ordinates erected at any point along the base line in terms of standard deviation units. To illustrate, by consulting one of these tables you would discover that a test score that was 1.30 standard deviation units above the mean would exceed 90.32 percent of the scores in a normal distribution. In other words, an ordinate erected at a point 1.30 standard deviation units above the mean of the normal curve would enclose an area (to its left) that represented .9032 of the normal curve.

By becoming familiar with a table of the normal curve, you will be able to find out, for example, that the area plus *and* minus one-half standard deviation from the mean of a normal distribution includes nearly 40 percent of the distribution (19.15 percent of the distribution on either side of the mean).

As I indicated earlier, the normal distribution is really a statistically generated theoretical distribution. In the real world of education—a world filled with student-thrown chalkboard erasers, tardy pupils, and PTA meetings—do educators ever encounter any variables (such as a particular kind of test score) that are distributed in a totally normal fashion? Probably not.

However, it is the belief of most educational measurement specialists that a good many educational variables are distributed in an *approximately* normal manner. Now, if you're dealing with an educational variable, such as one's measured aptitude to solve geometric problems, and you discern that the variable seems to be fairly normal in its distribution among individuals, then you can take advantage of the properties of the normal curve in interpreting students' performances. Even though your interpretations are approximations, you will be able to say that a person whose academic aptitude score turns out to be −1.0 standard deviation units from the mean has less academic aptitude than about 84 percent of all students (see Figure 7.1).

Normal Curve

A unique test-score distribution whose properties are helpful in making relative interpretations of students' performance.

FIGURE 7.1.

Percentages of the normal curve enclosed by ordinates erected at standard deviation points.

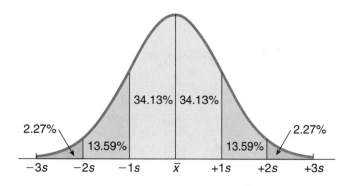

Later in the chapter you will see some interesting applications of the normal curve in transforming a set of raw scores from a nonnormal distribution into a fictitious normalized form. The normal curve is really quite a nifty tool for those educators who muck about with tests and students' test scores.

In review, the normal distribution provides a convenient way to describe students' test performances if the data distributions you are working with turn out to be arranged in an approximately normal fashion. Because you can describe different students' performances according to this normal curve framework, you can thereby compare their performances. For instance, if John's score were 0.2 standard deviation units below the mean and Harry's score were 1.3 standard deviation units above the mean, you could compare their two performances by discovering the proportions of the normal curve that is bounded by ordinates erected at those two points on the base line. The base line of the normal curve, divided into whole and fractional standard deviation units, becomes a sort of interpretive yardstick for contrasting different students' test performances. A standard deviation's distance is the unit of measurement you use on that base line to aid in your norm-referenced interpretations.

Percentiles

A particularly popular technique for comparing different individuals' test scores is to express them as *percentiles*. As this term is employed by most educators, a percentile is a point on a distribution below which a certain percent of the scores fall. For example, if you discover that Juanita has a test score that is equivalent to the 47th percentile, you can therefore assert that Juanita's score topped 47 percent of other students. That's essentially accurate.

Percentiles are sometimes described as *centiles*. The 25th percentile is often referred to as the *first quartile*, that is, the percentile below which 25 percent of the distribution's scores fall. The 50th percentile, which is also the median, is occasionally referred to as the *second quartile*. The 75th percentile is also called the *third quartile*.

A good many educators misuse the term *quartile* because they will say something such as the following: "Most of the students scoring in the first quartile were boys." This statement is in error because a quartile is a *point*, not a range of scores. It would be proper to say that most students who scored *below* the first quartile were boys. Those who misuse the term *quartile* mistakenly equate it with a *quarter* of the distribution. However, a quarter is not the same as a quartile.[1]

Standard Scores

Another useful technique for comparing students' test scores is referred to as a *standard score*. Whereas a percentile only tells us how a student's test score stacks up relative to test scores of other students (in percentage terms), a standard score tells us in *standard deviation units* where a student's score is with respect to the mean of the distribution. For a number of purposes, standard scores can prove most useful to measurement specialists. Although classroom teachers and school administrators will have less direct need to use standard scores, such scores do pop up now and again when standardized test results are released. Like most vegetables these days, there are several varieties of standard scores.[2] There are several commonly used types of standard scores.

z Scores

If you recall the earlier description of the normal curve, you'll remember that, by using the base line of that distribution as a sort of "standard deviation unit yardstick," you were able to make some useful statements about the proportion of scores exceeded by a score falling at a particular point on the distibution's base line. The most fundamental of standard scores, the z score, relies on the same standard deviation unit yardstick. A z score tells you *in standard deviation units* how far a raw score is above or below the mean of its distribution. A z score of +1.5 would be one and one-half standard deviation units *above* the mean. A z score of –2.5 would be two and one-half standard deviation *below* the mean.

Careful consideration of the formula used to compute z scores will help you understand what a z score represents:

$$z = \frac{X - \overline{X}}{s}$$

where X = a raw score
$\overline{X}$ = the mean of the distribution
s = the standard deviation of the distribution

Let's use a simple example to show how this formula works. Suppose the mean of a distribution was 32.8 and the standard deviation of that distribution was 2.2. Now if a student gets a raw score of 35, you can see that the student scored one standard deviation above the mean. You can toss the necessary numbers in the formula and solve it s follows:

$$z = \frac{35 - 32.8}{2.2}$$

$$= 1.0$$

You'll realize that a z score of 1.0 lets you know that the raw score from which it was derived falls one standard deviation unit above the mean of the raw score distribution.

In a normal curve, because plus and minus three standard deviation units account for most of the scores, z scores will range from –3.0 to +3.0 and account for all but a minuscule proportion of the distribution's scores. For any kind of distribution, normal or not, if all of the raw scores are converted into standard scores by our clever trick of subtracting the mean and then dividing by the standard deviation, the resulting distribution of z scores would have a mean of zero and a standard deviation of 1.0.

In Figure 7.2, you see what happens to a distribution when its raw scores have been zapped into z scores. Notice that the shape of the raw score distribution has not been altered one bit. If it was negatively skewed going in after all the raw scores have been converted to z scores, it will still be negatively skewed. Only the means and standard deviations have been altered. Given a person's z score along with the mean and standard deviation of the original raw score distribution, it is easy to reverse the process and find out what that individual's raw score is. For instance, if someone has a z score of –2.0 when

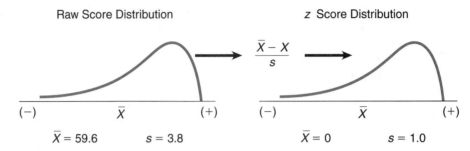

FIGURE 7.2.

The effects of transforming a raw score distribution into a z score distribution.

the original mean and standard deviation were 78 and 6 respectively, then you can use the z score conversion formula and obtain the raw score as follows:

$$z = \frac{X - \overline{X}}{s}$$

$$-2.0 = \frac{X - 78}{6}$$

$$X = 66$$

A disadvantage of z scores is that they contain decimals and minus values. Most people, educators included, find decimals and minus values troublesome to work with. Accordingly, measurement specialists have devised a scheme to dodge decimals and un-minus the negative numbers. You can refer to such standard scores as *transformed.*

T Scores

A *T score* is simply a transformed z score that has been multiplied by 10 (to get rid of the decimals) and had 50 added to it (to get rid of the minus values). The formula for the calculation of a *T* score, then, is

$$T = 50 + 10z \qquad \text{or} \qquad T = 50 + 10\left(\frac{X - \overline{X}}{s}\right)$$

As a consequence of these two operations, that is, adding a constant and multiplying by a constant, the resulting distribution of *T* scores has a mean of 50 and a standard deviation of 10.

Let's see how a *T* score is computed. Suppose you have a distribution of test scores in which the mean is 64.6 and the standard deviation is 8.4. If a student earned a score of 60.4 on the test, you would calculate the *T* score for that raw score as follows:

$$T = 50 + 10\left(\frac{60.4 - 64.6}{8.4}\right)$$

$$= 50 + 10(-.5)$$

$$= 45$$

When encountering a *T* score of 45, you'll instantly know that the raw score it represents is one-half standard deviation below the mean of the raw score distribution in which it is located. Similarly, a *T* score of 60 would represent a raw score one standard deviation unit above its mean.

Some people refer to *T* scores as *transformed standard scores* because, of course, the original *z* scores have been transformed. Other individuals use the expression *Z scores* instead of *T* scores. Because there is, as a consequence of so many different labels, the possibility of confusion when folks are talking about *T* scores, be sure that everyone is referring to the same creatures when you're engaging in a discussion about standard scores.[3]

That discussion can get even more confusing, indeed, when you discover that there are *normalized z* and *T* scores that are also used to describe a student's test performance. Let's turn now to a consideration of these normalized standard scores.

Normalized Standard Scores (Normal Curve Equivalents)

Normal Curve Equivalent (NCE)

A standard score that, based on a raw score's percentile, indicates the raw score's standard-deviation distance from a distribution's mean if the distribution had been normal.

Please put a pair of notions together that you've encountered so far and see how, in combination, they can provide you with yet another way to describe a student's performance in relationship to that of other students. You have seen that if scores are arranged in a perfectly normal fashion, you can state precisely what proportion of the distribution's scores are exceeded by a score at a particular point along the base line of the curve. For example, a raw score that is plus one standard deviation distance above the mean in such a normal distribution of scores exceeds 84.13 percent of all the scores. To take maximum advantage of the normal curve's interpretive assistance, however, you must express a raw score in standard deviation units according to its distance and direction (above or below) from the mean of the distribution.

In addition, you've seen that *z* scores and *T* scores provide you in a single number, a raw score's location in relationship to the mean based on standard deviation units. Now, *if* a distribution of scores were distributed normally, you could readily combine these two notions, because a *z* score of +1.0 or a *T* score of 60 would also tell you that the raw score being represented was one standard deviation above the mean, and thus exceeded 84.13 percent of the distribution's scores. By coupling *z* or *T* scores with the normal curve's established proportions, accurate interpretations of a raw score's relative position could be readily rendered. However, distressingly, not all distributions of test scores are arranged in a normal manner. Nature has, as usual, foiled a straightforward interpretive framework.

Unruffled by Mother or Father Nature's capriciousness, measurement people have devised a scheme for using standard scores with nonnormal distributions. They merely act *as if* the distribution were perfectly normal. To illustrate, let's say you had gathered a set of test data for a new test and you discovered that the data were distributed in a markedly nonnormal fashion. Perhaps you really believe that the underlying attribute being measured was arrayed normally in the real world but that the test being used had produced the nonnormal scores. Under these conditions, for ease of interpretation, you could convert the raw scores into *normalized standard scores*. A normalized standard score is a standard score (*z* or *T*) that would be equivalent to a raw score *if* the distribution had been perfectly normal.

TABLE 7.1   Normalized z Scores and Percentile Equivalents

z SCORE	PERCENTILE	z SCORE	PERCENTILE
3.0	99.9	−0.1	46.0
2.9	99.8	−0.2	42.1
2.8	99.7	−0.3	38.2
2.7	99.6	−0.4	34.5
2.6	99.5	−0.5	30.9
2.5	99.4	−0.6	27.4
2.4	99.2	−0.7	24.2
2.3	98.9	−0.8	21.2
2.2	98.6	−0.9	18.4
2.1	98.2	−1.0	15.9
2.0	97.7	−1.1	13.6
1.9	97.1	−1.2	11.5
1.8	96.4	−1.3	9.7
1.7	95.5	−1.4	8.2
1.6	94.5	−1.5	6.7
1.5	93.3	−1.6	5.5
1.4	91.9	−1.7	4.5
1.3	90.3	−1.8	3.6
1.2	88.5	−1.9	2.9
1.1	86.4	−2.0	2.3
1.0	84.1	−2.1	1.8
0.9	81.6	−2.2	1.4
0.8	78.8	−2.3	1.1
0.7	75.8	−2.4	0.8
0.6	72.6	−2.5	0.6
0.5	69.1	−2.6	0.5
0.4	65.5	−2.7	0.4
0.3	61.8	−2.8	0.3
0.2	57.9	−2.9	0.2
0.1	54.0	−3.0	0.1
0.0	50.0		

There are two steps in calculating normalized z scores. First, convert each of the raw scores in the distribution to its percentile equivalent (as described earlier in the chapter). Second, consult a table of the normal curve (available in most statistical texts) to discover what the equivalent z score would be for each percentile. In Table 7.1 an abridged set of z values and percentile equivalents is presented for this purpose. A full-blown table of the normal curve would contain a more fine-grained breakdown of percentile equivalents than Table 7.1, but this abbreviated version will illustrate how this game is played. To compute a normalized T score, simply multiply the tabled z score by 10 and add 50. As with nonnormalized standard scores, many people prefer to work with normalized T scores instead of normalized z scores because of the absence of decimals and minus values.

Let's see how to obtain a normalized T score for a given score. Suppose you wanted to convert a raw score to a normalized T. You'd first find out, in its own raw score distribution, what percentile that raw score represented. Let's assume it turns out to be on the 92nd percentile. Then you'd go to Table 7.1 and look up a percentile of 92 in the percentile column, discovering that the closest percentile is 91.9 and that its equivalent z score is 1.4. You'd multiply 1.4 by 10 and add 50 to obtain a normalized T score of 64.

Now even though you have learned how to compute normalized z and T scores, it may strike you that you've acquired a technical skill for coping with fantasy. After all, a distribution is either normal or it isn't. If it isn't, then it just doesn't seem fair to massage it by means of number nudging so that it appears to be normal. After all, things ought to be represented the way they are.

Well, while your leanings toward authenticity are to be applauded, you will discover a few instances in which measurement people do have need of normalized standard scores. For instance, sometimes there are statistical analyses that need to be conducted, requiring the scores to be in a normal shape. In such cases there may be an advantage in transforming a set of skewed raw scores into normalized standard scores. There are also techniques for comparing persons' scores on two different tests by using *normal curve equivalents* as the comparative device. In the late seventies the normal curve equivalent (NCE) received considerable attention because the federal government proposed a scheme to dispense federal education dollars that relied heavily on NCE conversions.

There are a number of solid technical reasons why the use of NCE conversions to compare scores from different tests constitutes an unsound procedure. Accordingly, there is substantial disagreement over the legitimacy of using NCEs in this fashion. If you find yourself faced with a decision to use or not use NCEs for comparative purposes, be sure to look further into this topic.[4]

From an educational leader's perspective, however, it is more important for you to realize that there are normalized z and T scores floating around in measurement land, usually referred to as NCEs, and that some test publishers use these sorts of scores to describe students' test scores. You must be alert to the possibility that *normalized*, rather than routine, z and T scores are being employed. Be sure to find out which is which, because merely by looking superficially at a table of standard scores it is not all that apparent whether you're dealing with normalized or nonnormalized scores. Although it may seem a metaphysical impossibility, a z is not a z is not a z. For that matter, a T is not a T is not a T.

Stanines

Stanine

A normalized standard score based on dividing a distribution into nine units of one-half standard deviation distances.

A *stanine* is a normalized standard score based on dividing the normal distribution to nine intervals along the distributions's base line. Indeed, its very name, *stanine*, is formed by combining the *sta* of *sta*ndard and *nine*. Stanines are normalized in much the same fashion that you can obtain normalized *z* and *T* scores. But because the stanine scale is a rather gross scale consisting of only nine values, it is simpler to determine the stanine values that correspond to given raw scores.

In Figure 7.3 the positions of the nine stanine values of the normal curve are represented. Note that, with the exception of the first and ninth stanines, all of the stanines are of an identical size, namely, one-half standard deviation unit. The middle stanine, therefore, extends plus and minus one-fourth standard deviation unit from the mean. A distribution of stanine scores has a mean of five and a standard deviation of approximately two stanine score units.

Stanines provide educators with a rough approximation of a student's performance relative to that of others. Because you determine an individual's stanine by identifying the

FIGURE 7.3.

Stanine units represented in approximate percentages of the normal curve.

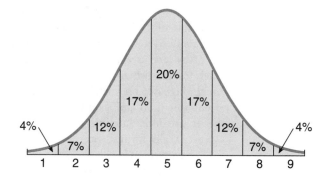

percentile to which that person's raw score would be equivalent, then, using percentages given as in Figure 7.3 to locate the proper stanine, it is clear that stanines are *normalized*. Even if the original raw score distribution is decisively nonnormal, you need to follow the customary scheme for normalizing a score. To illustrate, if Rapunzel Jones earned a raw score that was (in her raw score distribution) equivalent to a 33rd percentile, then you would know that Rapunzel's score was in the middle of the fourth stanine, so you'd assign her a stanine score of four.

Because of the fact that you're losing a substantial degree of precision when you employ only nine values to represent a wide range of scores, some educators avoid the use of stanines. On the other hand, a good many educators rely heavily on stanine scores precisely *because* they constitute a grosser way of describing a student's score. Recognizing the imprecision of educational measurement, more than a few educators prefer to use gross descriptors in communicating test results and thus not misrepresent the precision of the data-gathering devices. Stanines, particularly in some geographic regions and for some test publishers, remain a popular way of describing a student's performance.

Scale Scores

You have looked, now, at z and T scores, both transformed and untransformed. You've also considered stanines. Traditionally, these sorts of scores are referred to as *standard scores*. More recently, however, educators are encountering score-reporting schemes referred to as *scale scores*. Whereas the sorts of standard scores you have considered thus far are predicated on the use of standard deviations in relation to a score-distribution's mean, there are other kinds of scale scores that are not based on the standard deviation. Let's now take a look at some of these scale scores.

A scale score constitutes yet another attempt to give meaning to students' test performances. Scale scores are being used with increasing frequency these days to report results of nationally standardized tests as well as results of state-level student testing programs. Although scale scores are not typically used in reporting test results to parents, scale-score reporting systems are often employed in describing group test performances at the state, district, and school level. Because of the statistical properties of scale scores, such scores can be used to permit longitudinal tracking of students' progress. Scale scores

Scale Score

Based on the conversion of raw scores to a new numerical scale, a student's relative performance is reported on the converted scale as a scale score.

can also be used to make direct comparisons among classes, schools, or school districts. The statistical advantages of scale scores are considerable. As a consequence, educational leaders need to become familiar with their main features.

Any *scale* used for test scores refers to numbers, assigned to students on the basis of their test performances, that reflect increasing levels of achievement or ability. Such a scale might be based on a set of raw scores so that each additional test item correctly answered yields one more point on the raw score scale. As you have seen, raw scores, all by themselves, are difficult to interpret. Therefore, measurement specialists have devised different sorts of scales for test-interpretation purposes. Scale scores are converted raw scores that use a new, arbitrarily chosen scale to represent levels of achievement or ability.

In essence, a scale-score system is created by devising a brand-new numerical scale that is typically very unlike the original raw score scale. The students' raw scores are converted to this brand-new scale so that, when score interpretations are made, those interpretations are drawn from the converted scores based on the new scale. Such converted scores are called *scale scores*. For example, in Figure 7.4, you see an original raw score scale and a converted score scale. You will note a range of raw score points from zero to 40 for a forty-item test. Below the raw score scale, you see a converted scale ranging from 500 to 900. For a number of reasons, some of which I'll go into shortly, it is sometimes preferable to use a scale-score reporting scheme rather than a raw score reporting scheme. Thus, a student who achieved a raw score of thirty items correct might be given a scale score of 800.

One of the reasons that scale scores have become popular in recent years is the necessity to develop several *equidifficult* forms of the same test. For example, a basic skills test must sometimes be passed before high school diplomas are awarded to students. Those students who initially fail the test are, typically, given other opportunities to pass it. The different forms of the test that are used for such retake purposes should, in fairness, represent equidifficult challenges for students.

However, because it is almost impossible to create test forms that are *absolutely* identical, scale scores can be used to help solve the problem. Scores on two test forms of *differing* difficulty levels can be statistically adjusted so that, when placed on a converted

FIGURE 7.4.
A student's test score represented in raw score and scale-score units.

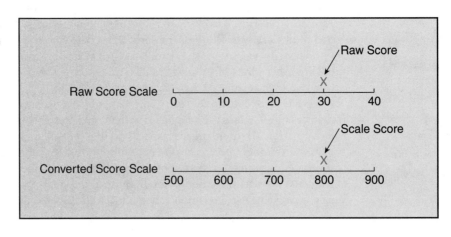

score scale, the new scale scores represent students' performances *as if* the two original test forms had been equidifficult.

There are mistakes often made in interpreting scale scores because some educators assume that all scale scores are somehow similar. For example, when the *Scholastic Assessment Test (SAT)* was initially administered over fifty years ago, the average scale score on the verbal section was 500. This does not signify that the average scale score on the *Scholastic Assessment Test today* is 500 or that other tests using scale scores have an average score of 500. Scale-score systems can be constructed so that the average score is 600, 700, or even 1,000.

Item-Response Theory

Many of the more popular types of scale-score systems are based on what measurement specialists refer to as *item-response theory*, or IRT. Item-response theory was, in the past, sometimes referred to as *latent-trait theory*. IRT scale-score reporting systems are distinctively different from raw score reporting systems because IRT scale scores take into consideration the difficulty and other technical properties of *each* item on the test. Some test publishers have reproduced IRT-based scale scores for their tests that range from zero to 1,000 across an entire K–12 grade range. At each grade level, there is a different average scale score. For example, the average scale score for third-graders might be 585, and the average scale score for tenth-graders might be 714.

These IRT-based scale scores can, when constructed carefully, yield useful interpretations *if one can reference them back to some notion of relative student performance*, such as

percentiles. If *average scale scores* are provided at different grade levels, this can also aid in the interpretation of scale scores.

Let's consider, more carefully, the essential features of scale scores based on item-response theory. One of the limitations of standard scores such as z and T is that they assume that all items are equal to each other. As students answer each additional test item correctly, it is assumed that a constant increment of ability is represented. Realistically, however, it is never the case that test items are truly equidifficult. Thus, to the extent that test items vary in difficulty as well as other qualities, traditional standard scores can misrepresent students' test performances.

There are several approaches to the creation of scale scores via item-response theory. Two of the most popular are the *Rasch model* (also known as the *one-parameter model*) and the *three-parameter model*. Whereas the Rasch model is focused solely on the single parameter of an item's *difficulty*, the three-parameter model is based on an item's (1) difficulty, (2) discrimination among students, and (3) susceptibility to student guessing. Some test publishers also use a *two-parameter model* focused on an item's difficulty and its susceptibility to guessing.

Item-Response Theory (IRT)

A scale-score system that, by using considerable computer analyses, creates a new scale based on the properties of each test item.

IRT assumptions. All item-response theory approaches are based on three important assumptions. The first of these assumptions is that a *unidimensional* trait is being measured, in other words, that all of the items measure the same attribute. It is for this reason that IRT approaches are sometimes referred to as latent-trait models because they are designed to measure an assumed (latent) trait. A second assumption is that item *independence* is present. Phrased differently, the independence assumption simply means that one item will not influence how a student answers other items. The final assumption of all IRT approaches is that the items on a test are assumed to adhere to an *item-characteristic curve* consonant with the IRT model being used. In general, this assumption means that, as a student's ability increases, a greater probability exists for the student to answer the item correctly.

There are ardent proponents of various IRT approaches. Each IRT approach has its advantages and disadvantages. However, for most educators, the Rasch (one-parameter) model is easier to understand. So, without implied advocacy of the Rasch model, I'd like to delve a bit more deeply into its innards so that you can see what's involved in one of the more popular IRT schemes.

Rudiments of Rasch. The Rasch model was developed some years ago by the Danish mathematician Georg Rasch. (His first name does not end with an *e*, so I've spent many hours deleting the *e* from word-processors who want to make a *George* out of *Georg*.) Here's how Rasch's approach works. First, test items are administered to a reasonably large group of examinees. Rasch experts differ as to how many responses per item they think are needed, but somewhere between 200 and 500 responses are required for each item. Then all of the items are analyzed to see if they "fit" the Rasch model, that is, to see if an item's item-characteristic curve is constant with what the Rasch model would predict. In general, this means that an item is supposed to be answered correctly more often by students who perform well on the total test than by students who do badly on the total test. In this regard, the Rasch approach is similar to the traditional item-analysis operations used by most test-developers.

All items that fit the model (and most properly constructed items typically do) are then *calibrated* on a new scale. That is, they are assigned values on a new difficulty scale called the *logistic* scale. The unit of this scale is the *logit* (pronounced low-jit). The logistic scale has logit values that usually range from –3.0 to +3.0. The new scale is at the heart of the Rasch approach because the newly calibrated logit difficulty values will be subsequently employed to build equivalent tests. Let's see how this calibration business works.

First, assume you have found that the first five items on your test do, indeed, fit the Rasch model. Their *p* values (that is, the proportion of students who answer an item correctly), based on administering the test to 300 students, are given below.

ITEM	p VALUES
1	0.73
2	0.91
3	0.44
4	0.51
5	0.76

After sending the items through a Rasch computer routine that almost endlessly coaxes, kicks, and cuddles them, you can also obtain each item's value on the logistic scale. Note below that the more difficult an item is, the higher is its score on the logistic-difficulty scale. This is the reverse of the traditional *p* value scheme in which higher values indicate easier items.

ITEM	p VALUES	LOGIT VALUE
1	0.73	–0.2
2	0.91	–1.6
3	0.44	1.1
4	0.51	0.8
5	0.76	–0.4

Each item, then, is assigned a logit value. Different forms of a test can be composed of items with different logit values, yet because you know what the logit values of the different tests were, you can derive an *ability estimate* for students irrespective of which form of the test they were given. Using Rasch analytic techniques, you can come up with a defensible estimate of how a student would have performed on a test form *as though* the form had been identical in difficulty to another test form. In essence, IRT approaches to the creation of scale scores allow educators to adjust students' ability estimates statistically so that those estimates represent how well a student would have performed had all forms of the test been perfectly equidifficult.

IRT scale-score adjustments. Here's how scale scores are used to make statistical adjustments so that, regardless of the difficulty of the test form that students take, those students can be presented with an equidifficult challenge. In In essence, scale scores take the raw scores earned on different test forms, then place those raw scores on a converted scale so that raw scores on a more difficult test are adjusted upward and the raw scores on a less difficult test are adjusted downward. This process is illustrated graphically in Figure 7.5 in which three sets of scores based on three different forms of the same test are represented. Note that below each set of raw scores there is a new (converted) scale that has been used to adjust for the different difficulties of the three forms. In this illustration the raw scores are based on a seventy-five-item test form, and the scale scores range between 400 and 1,000 with a mean of 700. If a Rasch approach had been employed, these scale scores would be obtained from students' ability estimates.

FIGURE 7.5.

An illustration of scaled-score adjustments of scores based on test forms of differing difficulty.

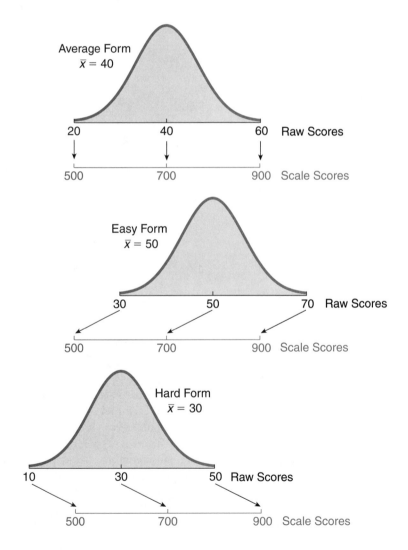

Note that on the test form of *average* difficulty a mean raw score of 40 is converted to a mean scale score of 700. On the *easy* test form, however, a mean raw score of 50 is also converted to a mean scale score of 700. Similarly, on the *hard* test form, a mean raw score of 30 ends up as an identical scale score of 700. As can be seen, therefore, no matter how difficult or how easy the test form, statistical adjustments can be made so that (1) students who take an easy test form are not unfairly advantaged, and (2) students who take a hard test form are not unfairly penalized.

Although IRT scale scores are not something that the typical classroom teacher or school administrator will have any wish to whip up on a dull weekend, it seems clear that educators will be forced to understand something about such score-interpretation methods. What educational leaders *do* need is a general understanding of how these sorts of scale scores come into existence. Hopefully, by pondering the preceding paragraphs, you've gained an insight or two into how IRT approaches work. (Frankly, I'd be happy if you picked up even half an insight.)

The relationship among stanines and percentiles, as well as the other scale and standard scores you've been considering, can be seen in Figure 7.6, in which a widely used depiction of the normal curve, percentiles, and standard scores is presented. This figure, distributed initially by the Psychological Corporation in 1947, has been used through the years in a host of measurement and statistical texts.

Grade Equivalents

Grade-Equivalent Score

Score-reporting estimates of how a student's performance relates to the average performance of students in a given grade and month of the school year.

Another frequently used technique for describing a student's score is to express that score as a *grade equivalent* (GE) or a *grade-equivalent score*. If a test has been administered to a large number of students so that it is possible to estimate what the median student will score on entering the fourth grade in September, then whatever that raw score value is would be considered to be a grade-equivalent score of 4.0. By dividing a school year into ten months, you can represent a student's score as, for example, 4.3, to indicate that the student's performance was equal to that of the median student three months into the fourth grade (December).

Grade equivalents are used for interpretive purposes because they seem so blessedly simple to understand. After all, if a youngster gets a test score on a nationally standardized achievement test that can be represented as 5.9 grade-equivalent score, then it seems obvious that the child is functioning just below (by one month) the beginning of sixth-grade level. Unfortunately, there are some serious problems with grade-equivalent scores that should be well understood by educational leaders who are inclined to use them.

For one thing, no test publisher has the financial resources to do an across-the-board testing of youngsters, grades K through 12, on a month-by-month basis. Such an enterprise would be enormously costly to the test publisher, not to mention the intrusion it would make on students' instructional programs. As a consequence, test publishers usually test at a few grades, establish a relationship between test scores and grades, then use the relationship line to *estimate* the various grade-month points needed for all the rest of the scores that students at various ages will receive. However, these estimates are made by extrapolation and are often made on really shaky assumptions. For example, it is assumed that whatever is being tested is studied by students consistently from year to year. It is also

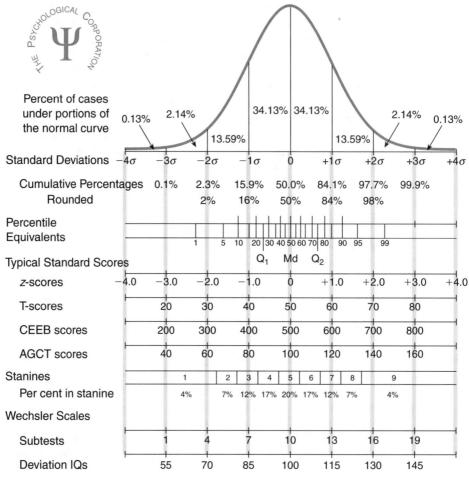

FIGURE 7.6.

Relationship among normal curves, percentiles, and frequently used standard scores.
(Reproduced and adapted by permission. All rights reserved, © 1947, 1952, © 1959,
1963, 1966, 1968 by the Psychological Corporation, New York, N.Y.)

assumed that a student's increase in competence is essentially constant over the years. It is
further assumed that the test reasonably samples what is being taught at all of the grade
levels for which scores are being reported. These assumptions are almost never satisfied.

A troublesome problem with grade-equivalent scores is that they yield no clues as to
an individual's percentile standing, a key comparative ingredient you've been able to snag
from most of the previous score-representation schemes you've considered so far. To illustrate, a student might get a higher grade-equivalent score on a reading test than on a

mathematics test, yet have a substantially lower percentile rank on the reading test than on the mathematics test.

The most serious deficit with grade equivalents is that they're so frequently misinterpreted. To illustrate, if a fourth-grade student gets a grade equivalent of 7.5 in mathematics, it is *not* accurate to say that the fourth-grader is doing well in seventh-grade mathematics. It is more appropriate to say that a grade-equivalent score of 7.5 is an estimate of how an average *seventh-grader* would have performed on the fourth-grade mathematics test. Obtaining a 7.5 grade-equivalent score doesn't mean that the fourth-grader has any of the mathematics skills taught in the fifth, sixth, or seventh grades because these skills were probably not even measured on the fourth-grade test.

But what happens when grade-equivalent scores are *below* the actual grade level tested? Let's say a fifth-grader earns a mathematics grade-equivalent score of 2.5. It doesn't make much sense to say that the fifth-grader is doing fifth-grade math work as well as a second-grader, because second-graders obviously aren't given fifth-grade math work. About the best you can say is that in mathematics achievement the fifth-grader appears to be lagging several years behind grade level.

A final problem with grade-equivalent scores is that unsophisticated people automatically transform what is to what *should* be. For instance, the raw score that is equivalent to the grade-equivalent score for a beginning eighth-grade student may be 112 items correct on a test. Many people may demand that all beginning eighth-graders should earn a score of 112 or higher. "After all," they assert, "isn't that what a beginning eighth-grade student should be doing?" Such misguided folks lose sight of the fact that it was the *median* eighth-grade performance that led to the grade-equivalent score and that *by definition* 50 percent of the examinees will fall below this score. It's something like a school board president who criticizes the district superintendent because half of the district's pupils continue to fall below the median of their own students' annual examination performances. In the same vein, if you're a teacher or administrator whose test scores are reported as grade equivalents, you can be quite certain that more than a few parents will want their children promoted a grade or two because their youngsters' grade-equivalent scores "indicated that the child should be working at a higher grade level."

For a number of reasons, therefore, grade-equivalent scores should be used only with considerable caution and with plenty of accompanying disclaimers. Because grade-equivalent scores are often misinterpreted, some districts have adopted formal policies precluding their use. It is often helpful, if grade equivalents must be employed, to accompany them with some of the other score-interpretation schemes that were treated in this chapter. Personally, I think grade-equivalent scores should be shunned by educational leaders. One gets so few opportunities in life to shun. Grade-equivalent scores are well worth shunning.

You have considered, now, a number of different techniques for representing a student's raw score performance. Many of them rely on the availability of comparative data before they can be used. If a teacher administers an achievement test and wants to secure percentile-equivalent performances for students, that teacher will typically want to base those percentiles on *national* normative data, rather than on the performance of the thirty-three students in that particular class. Let's turn, now, to a consideration of the sorts of normative data that will lead to defensible use of the various comparative score descriptors I've been fussing over.

Norms

In educational measurement educators frequently encounter such expressions as *norms, norm groups,* and *normative tables.* In general, normative notions are based on the assembled performance summaries of a group of individuals who have been administered a particular examination. For instance, before developers of a new norm-referenced reading test publish their test, they will almost certainly administer that test to a large number of students (thereafter called the *norm group*), then summarize the results of those students' test scores in tabular form. These norm tables permit those using the test to identify the percentile equivalent for any student's raw score. In making sense out of a student's raw score, such norm tables are of immense assistance.

Let me pause briefly in my explanation of normative data to draw attention to a frequent misuse of the term *norm* because there are some educators, and far too many lay citizens, who think of norms, just like grade equivalents, as representing what *should* be. In the sense that test developers gather normative information, they are merely assembling data regarding the current status of students' performance. To equate what *is* with what *ought* to be is an instance of thoroughgoing wrongheadedness. People who are confused on this score assume that a *norm* is a synonym for *standard*. Such is not the case.

In Chapter 14 you will delve into the problem of standard setting. At this point, however, it should be recognized that, while normative data, may, and should, influence the performance standards educators set, the two notions are certainly not identical. To illustrate, let's say you're a teacher who discovers that your pupils perform far below national norms on a test of history knowledge. Should you be concerned? Probably you should. Apparently, youngsters across the nation know more about history than your pupils do and you may want to spruce up your history instruction or simply spend more time on historical content. But what if your pupils are average or slightly above average on national norms? Can you now sit back complacently and assume that your students know enough about history? Absolutely not.

The historical knowledge of the entire norm group may be well below what it *should* be. Maybe pupils throughout the country are learning less than they *should* about George Washington, Abraham Lincoln, and Sacajawea (Lewis and Clark's Native American guide). The point is that normative data merely let us know how students are currently performing. Although such information is very helpful, it should not be mixed up with notions about what a realistic expectation of students' performance should be.

Again, if you're interested in making relative inferences based on students' test performances, one of the evaluative factors you can use to appraise an educational test is whether or not the test is accompanied by comparative data and, if so, what the quality of the comparative data is. I'll conclude the present chapter by highlighting some of the things you should be looking for when you scrutinize the quality of a set of normative data. If a test for which you want to make norm-referenced interpretations is not accompanied by comparative data, of course, you can instantly check it off as deficient on that count.

National and Local Norms

Most test publishers of instruments designed for nationwide use attempt to assemble a set of national norm data. They will administer the test to as large a sample of students

Norm Group

The group of test-takers whose scores are used to make relative interpretations of others' test performances.

as they can reasonably afford, attempting to cover, at least on a geographic sampling basis, the entire nation. If possible, they'll gather a sufficiently large set of test scores so that they can break down their normative tables according to sex, geographic region, type of school setting (for example, urban, suburban, rural), and so on. To create truly comprehensive normative data is a very, very costly business. For most test publishers, the accumulation of extensive normative data is reserved for those tests that seem apt to sell well enough to justify the major financial investment in the readying of first-rate normative information.

With tests less likely to sell in large volume, test publishers must be realistic about gathering of normative information, and it is this sort of normative data, in particular, that should be rigorously evaluated when one considers such tests for possible adoption.

In the process of gathering a decent set of national normative data, there are seemingly endless administrative details to be handled. School districts must be identified that will cooperate in the norming. Recalcitrant school officials must be persuaded that the testing's intrusion into the ongoing instructional program is worthwhile. (In passing, it should be noted that, because of the recent upsurge in testing of all kinds, many school people are becoming justifiably resistant to extra testing of any sort. In such a setting, securing the necessary number of schools to cooperate in the norming is sometimes a minor miracle.)

There are numerous decisions to be made along the way during the assembly of normative data. For example, one of the factors that sells tests is the *size* of the normative sample. An educator choosing between two tests, which on other counts appear to be of equal quality, will often choose the test that has the larger (therefore more "respectable") norm sample. Accordingly, there is a continuing temptation for supervisors of normative data gathering to go after the largest, most convenient sample at hand. Such *samples of convenience*, however, often fail to satisfy a number of other requirements needed in a good normative sample.

There are also subtle choices that must be made regarding *when* the normative testing should be done. It is in the commercial interest of test publishers *not* to have their tests be widely perceived by educators as "too tough." Because local school officials generally don't want their pupils to look like dullards on nationally standardized achievement tests, such officials would certainly tend to avoid the adoption of tests that seemed certain to show that local students did not perform well according to national norms. Local school officials would tend, instead, to buy a test that gave their pupils a more reasonable chance to succeed.

Accordingly, if you are in charge of a norming operation and plan for a spring "end-of-academic-year" normative testing, would you want to test most of the youngsters in your norm group in April, May, or June? Well, because kids will have learned more by June than April, you might want to do your norm gathering earlier in the spring. Thus, if local educators subsequently contrasted their pupils' end-of-academic-year performance with that of pupils in your test's national norm group, the local youngsters would come out looking better than if you'd done your norm gathering later and thus allowed your test's norm group pupils to become as knowledgeable as possible. In reporting the time at which the normative tests were administered, therefore, it would be misleading if you indicated that "normative testing took place during April–June" when, in fact, the bulk of that normative testing took place in April.

Educational Leaders
Look at Assessment

Assessments as
Curricular Support

Robert R. Tryon
Superintendent of Schools
DoDDS Brussels District
Brussels, Belgium

As I prepared to eat my French fries at a local cafe, I was approached by a woman who asked me two questions. I assumed that she was a parent. The first question was, "How many planets are there in our galaxy?" I tore my eyes from my piping hot French fries, and responded, "Nine." Then she asked, "Which is larger, the moon or the sun?" I responded, "From where I view the moon from time to time, it looks smaller than the sun." She said, "These are just some of the questions that many children cannot answer in school. Aren't they covered in your curriculum?"

With those questions on the table, and my fries beginning to cool, I put on my best full-faced smile and began to prepare internally the very best answer I could give this person. She went on to ask, "Why do science teachers constantly teach about dinosaurs and volcanoes every year?" I wanted to leave her with no doubt about what the purpose of schooling is and that the curriculum is the foundation for all learning in the classroom. Here's roughly what I told her.

Yes, there is a stated curriculum that follows the national standard set by our school system. It is not driven by textbook and materials, but such materials are used to augment and supplement the curriculum each teacher is to impart. Curriculum documents are mammoth publications, and to expect every facet of the curriculum to be covered in every discipline is expecting too much. This is where the abilities and the talents of teachers come into play. They sort and select through curricula to determine which information is critical for *their* children to know. And that's where assessment comes in.

Teachers pretest children to find out how knowledgeable the children are in required areas of the curriculum, and they teach a mastery of what's needed.

Students who need additional help are provided interventions; while other students, who are more capable, have their learning extended to cover the curriculum in depth.

Teachers, then, are held accountable to teach to this curriculum utilizing the latest research-based teaching strategies. To find out if they've been successful, teachers use a variety of assessment instruments. They utilize standardized tests, alternative assessments, short-term assessments, and long-term assessments, all of which are used to improve the instruction that is occurring in the classroom. This requires assessment skills and knowledge on the part of the teacher.

I always reinforce the importance of communication with parents in the home. Parents are the first-line teachers of their children. They, too, can light up the eyes of inquisitiveness in their children when they sit with books or materials referring to the stars and galaxies. It is truly a partnership in this day and age, and we will continue to keep a commitment on fostering a quality curriculum, utilizing effective assessment-adjusted teaching strategies, and being accountable for our results through the use of a variety of assessment instruments.

Having finished this diatribe, I looked away from the parent and back at my fries. They were frigid. ●

The foregoing comment is not intended to suggest that test publishers are deceitful in their accumulation or presentation of normative data. To my knowledge, no such instances of deliberate data falsification by reputable test publishers have ever been recorded. It is just that educational testing in our nation is big, big business. Because the financial stakes are high, the possibility of subtle, self-serving commercial decisions exists. As an evaluator of educational tests, you must be alert to the nuances as well as the major evaluative factors when appraising a set of national normative data.

Many educators believe that their test interpretations are markedly enhanced if they prepare a set of local norms to be used, perhaps, in concert with national norms. Local norms can often prove highly helpful to local educators whose day-to-day decisions can be illuminated by comparing individual student performances to those of a more similar group than is typically true with the groups that provide national norm data. Sometimes, because national tests may not be accompanied by suitable normative data for the particular local group of students, it will be necessary to prepare local norm tables.

To illustrate, suppose your school system is in the southwestern part of the United States and that your schools serve a predominantly Spanish-speaking student population. Let's say you discover, however, that in the sample of pupils who constituted the national norm group, few Spanish-speaking youngsters were represented. In such a case it may be necessary for your school system to garner local norms.

It is important, of course, if both local and national norms are available, not to confuse the two. To say that one of your students "scores at the 59th percentile" would be insufficient. You'll have to add the phrase, "on local norms." You may discover that local and national norms are substantially different. Clarification regarding which norms are involved is, accordingly, necessary.

Criteria for Judging Normative Data

What sorts of factors should be considered when reviewing a set of comparative data? In the first place, of course, whether comparative information exists or not can be readily answered. However, assuming that there are normative data at hand, what should you be looking for in deciding whether the data are adequate? Here are a few points to consider:

Sample size. Is the sample in the norm group large enough to assure a reasonable degree of stability in the data base from which educators must draw interpretations?

Representativeness. Is the sample drawn in such a way as to represent the kinds of students for whom interpretations must be made?

Recency. Were the normative data gathered in the last few years or is the information out-of-date because it was collected too long ago?

Description of procedures. Are the procedures associated with the gathering of the normative data sufficiently well described so that those procedures can be properly evaluated?

Let's deal, briefly, with each of these four points. First, educators would prefer that test publishers employ as large a sample as possible because of the obvious resulting stability in the quality of the interpretations that educators will reach. Other factors being equal, if one normative sample has only fifty students per grade level and another has 1,000 students per grade level, the larger sample will be preferable.

However, size is not enough. And, although this is not the place to engage in an extensive discussion regarding sampling procedures, it is apparent that a normative sample will be more useful if it can be stratified so that all relevant subgroups have been included in it. For example, if there is reason to believe that boys perform differently from girls on a particular test, the normative data should be collected so that educators can split out separate norms for boys and girls.

As indicated in the previous chapter, the issue of whether to develop supplemental normative tables for particular minority groups is a troubling one. On the other hand, separate forms, for example, for Hispanic youngsters, would permit better interpretation of Hispanic children's test performance, particularly if there is a substantial difference between the Hispanic students' scores and those of the total population. On the other hand, the creation of separate ethnic norms tends to perpetuate the belief that certain minority groups are less able (even if their lower test performance arises because of previous instructional inferiorities). In general, we are faced with a dilemma of risking long-term deficits (by having separate ethnic norms) or risking short-term deficits (by lumping all ethnic groups together). It is an issue to be considered most carefully, particularly by test developers, but also by those evaluating tests.

If all of the major factors that are related to test performance can be taken into account when the test norms are prepared, this would be ideal. Typically, limitations of resources preclude most test publishers from doing so to the extent that they would wish. The job of an educational leader who must evaluate tests will be to weigh the overall adequacy of the normative data's representativeness.

Typically, publishers of most widely used nationally standardized tests update their normative data every half-dozen years or so. For some kinds of tests this is more crucial than others. For instance, if the content of a field is shifting rapidly, as was the case several years ago in mathematics and language arts, then it is important to renorm the tests because it would be unfair to compare today's students to those who were taught with dissimilar curricular emphases. In other content or attitudinal areas, where there is more stability in the expectations educators have of students, you can be a bit more relaxed with any requirements for test-norm recency. You will have to decide whether you're working with any measured knowledge, skill, or affect that is apt to get out of date fairly rapidly. In any event, it would obviously be better to have norms assembled in recent, rather than medieval, times.

For all the foregoing reasons, it is necessary that explicit descriptions be provided of the procedures employed in assembling the normative data in the technical information that accompanies the test's norm tables. That description should leave little to the imagination regarding the key details of how the tests were administered, to whom, when, under what conditions, and so on. For example, in this era of rampant "overtesting" of students, in some instances test publishers have been forced to select fourth-choice or fifth-choice school districts for the norm sample because the initially invited districts declined their invitation to the norming party. When a test's technical information fails to provide a well-documented description of the various procedures used to secure normative data, a test evaluator should view such data with some suspicion and even a dash of disdain.

News in Brief: A State Capitals Roundup

Indiana to Pay for PSAT

Gov. Frank L. O'Bannon has set aside $630,000 of existing state funds to pay for Indiana students to take the Preliminary SAT free of charge.

The Democratic governor wants to make sure that the $8.73 cost to take the PSAT doesn't keep any students from signing up for the exam. But even more, said Phil Bremen, Mr. O'Bannon wants to send a message to students that the PSAT is important.

The test, which will be given in October, is a practice test for the SAT college-entrance exam. Indiana students who take the PSAT before the SAT typically score 12 or 13 percentage points higher on the SAT than students who don't take the preliminary test, according to information provided by the College Board to the state's

commission for higher education. A similar trend is also true nationally, the Board said.

Mr. Bremen said students who improve their SAT scores stand a better chance of being accepted by the colleges of their choice and receiving scholarships.

In April, Gov. O'Bannon set aside $5 million for remedial instruction for high school sophomores who did not pass the ISTEP-Plus, the Indiana Statewide Testing for Educational Progress assessment. Students must pass the test before graduation.

What's your reaction?

Reprinted, with permission, from *Education Week*, May 20, 1998

Chapter Wrap-Up

As in previous chapters, this end-of-chapter summary is firmly rooted in the chapter's guiding questions. Given this chapter's focus, if you prefer to think of the first half-dozen chapters as a "norm," then this chapter's summary is simply trying to fit in.

● **What is the normal curve and how is it used to make relative test-score interpretations?**

The normal curve is a bell-shaped, symmetrical curve whose mean, median, and mode are the same. By employing a score distribution's standard deviation as a sort of measuring stick along the baseline of a normal curve, vertical lines (ordinates) erected along the baseline cut off specified portions of the normal curve distribution. For example, an ordinate erected at a distance of one standard deviation from the mean isolates 34.13 percent of the distribution between that ordinate and an ordinate erected at the mean. As a consequence, more than two-thirds of the scores on a normal distribution fall within plus or minus one standard deviation distance from the normal distribution's mean. By knowing the distance of an individual's raw score from a normal distribution's mean (distance, that is, in standard deviation units), it is possible to identify the proportions of the normal distribution that fall both above and below the individual's raw score. To use the properties of the normal distribution to make such interpretations, of course, the set of scores with which one is dealing must be arranged in an approximately normal fashion.

● What score-reporting techniques are used to make relative test-score interpretations?

Numerous ways exist for describing the relative nature of the test performance of an individual or group of individuals. Each of those treated in the chapter will be briefly described in this chapter wrap-up.

Percentiles, the most commonly used way of describing students' relative test performances, indicate the point in a distribution of test scores below which a certain proportion of the scores fall. To illustrate, if you were to learn that a student had a score equal to the 65th percentile on a nationally standardized achievement test, you would know that the student had outperformed 65 percent of the students in the test's norm group.

A *standard score* indicates in standard deviation units how far a student's score is from the mean of the distribution of test scores. A *z score* distribution of scores has a mean of zero and a standard deviation of 1.0. So, a z score of 2.0 would indicate that the raw score represented by that standard score was two standard deviations above the distribution's mean. A *T score* distribution is a transformed standard score based on z scores that have been multiplied by 10 and had 50 added to them. A *T* score of 40 would indicate the raw score was one standard deviation distance below the distribution's mean.

Normalized standard scores, also referred to as *normal curve equivalents* or NCEs, represent the location of a student's score on the baseline of a distribution *if* that distribution had been arranged in a perfectly normal fashion. To find the location of a raw score's normal curve equivalent, you need to determine the score's percentile rank, then consult a table to find out where that percentile would be on the baseline of a normal curve. A normalized z distribution has a mean of zero and a standard deviation of 1.0; a normalized *T* distribution has a mean of 50 and a standardized deviation of 10.

Stanines are normalized standard scores that provide educators with a rough approximation of how a student's test performance compares with that of other students. This is done by dividing a normal distribution into nine segments of one-half standard deviation distance each. These nine segments (the nine stanines) contain the following percentages of a normal distribution: Stanines 1 and 9 = 4 percent each; Stanines 2 and 8 = 8 percent each; Stanines 4 and 6 = 17 percent each; and Stanine 5 (which is centered at a distribution's mean) = 20 percent. Thus, high standard test performances would be reflected by stanines 8 or 9; low student test performances would be reflected by Stanines 1 and 2.

Scale scores are being increasingly employed to report students' test performances, not often to parents but frequently to educational policymakers. A scale-score system is created by employing a brand-new numerical scale that has little to do with students' original raw scores. Students' raw scores are then converted to the new scale. Many educators are familiar with academic aptitude tests that have means of 500 and standard deviations of 100. If properly conceptualized, scale scores can be treated statistically in ways that raw scores cannot.

Item-Response Theory (IRT) *Scores* are another variety of scale scores. IRT scores, through the magic of computers, are based on a scale that is created after taking into consideration the difficulty and, sometimes, other technical properties of every item in a test. By employing an IRT approach in the creation of scale scores, it is possible to adjust the difficulty levels of different forms of the same test so that the challenge provided to students on varying test forms is essentially identical. Several varieties of IRT approaches are employed in the field of educational measurement, for example, the one-parameter Rasch model, the two-parameter model, and the three-parameter model. Each model is based on different aspects (parameters) of test items such as their difficulty, their susceptibility to guessing, and their ability to discriminate among students. Currently, no consensus exists about which IRT approach best serves the needs of educators.

A *grade-equivalent score* provides educators with an intuitively appealing but often inaccurate estimate of the level of a student's test score in terms of years and months of the school year. For example, a fifth-grade student whose raw score on a standardized achievement test was assigned a grade equivalent of 6.2 would have performed at the same level as a beginning sixth-grade student who had received two months of sixth-grade schooling. Grade-equivalent scores are so frequently misinterpreted that increasing numbers of school districts have abandoned them as a score-reporting technique.

● How should the quality of normative data be judged?

Assuming that you are interested in using a test in order to make relative interpretations of students' scores, and thus are concerned about the quality of a test's normative data, four criteria were identified to help appraise the caliber of normative data. The norm group's *sample size* should be large enough to ensure reasonable stability. The norm group's sample should have been drawn in such a way that the sample's *representativeness* of various kinds of student subgroups is acceptable. *Recency*, of course, is another consideration when judging the adequacy of a set of normative data. Any norm group constituted during the Pleistocene Period should be regarded as somewhat out-of-date. Finally, a clear *description of procedures* that were employed to assemble the normative data should definitely be provided so that the adequacy of those procedures can be ascertained.

Because local norms are frequently established in addition to national norms, educational leaders must be alert to the possibility that students' scores might be interpreted according to local rather than national norms. Often, the interpretive differences between local and national norms are considerable.

Practice Exercises

Standard scores and scale scores are really easy to work with, once you get the hang of them. For the ten questions in this chapter's self-test, you are free to use any of the tables or formulae in the chapter.

1. A student who scored in the 61st percentile would be in which of the following stanines?
   a. Fourth
   b. Fifth
   c. Sixth
   d. Seventh

2. What is the T score of a student whose raw score is 17 when the mean of the test-score distribution is 20 and the standard deviation is 2.0?
   a. 55
   b. –1.5
   c. 35
   d. 20

3. What is the T score equivalent of a z score of 3.0?

4. A normalized T score of 30 is equivalent to which of the following percentiles?
   a. 2nd
   b. 30th
   c. 16th
   d. 40th

5. Which of the following test items, based on the logit value of each, is most difficult?
   a. Item 20, logit value = 1.16
   b. Item 27, logit value = zero
   c. Item 36, logit value = 2.12
   d. Item 43, logit value = −.89
6. If a distribution of test scores is essentially normal, what approximate percentage of the scores would a person exceed whose T score was 60?
   a. 60%
   b. 84%
   c. 34%
   d. 15%
7. Given a fairly normal distribution of test scores, in which stanine would a student's score fall whose z score was −1.1?
   a. Fifth
   b. Fourth

c. Third
d. Second
8. If a distribution of test scores is decisively skewed, to what percentile (approximately) will a T score of 60 be equivalent?
   a. 84th
   b. 60th
   c. 98th
   d. Uncertain
9. A student scoring in the fifth stanine could have which of the following percentiles?
   a. 55th
   b. 50th
   c. 45th
   d. All of these
10. What is the normalized T score equivalent of a student's score at the 16th percentile?

Answers to Practice Exercises

1. C
2. D
3. 80
4. A
5. D

6. B
7. C
8. D
9. D
10. 40

DISCUSSION QUESTIONS

1. In the chapter, four criteria were given for judging the adequacy of normative data, namely, *sample size, representativeness, recency,* and *description of procedures.* How would you rank these according to their importance? Why?
2. Do you believe that separate norms should be supplied for different racial groups? If so, why? If not, why not?
3. What is your own view regarding the appropriateness of grade-equivalent scores? Why?
4. Which of the standard scores or scale scores treated in the chapter do you think is the most useful to a parent? How about to educational leaders? Why?
5. Can you identify any educational variables that you would consider to be decisively normal and/or nonnormal in the manner in which they are distributed? If so, what are they?

6. If you were called on by a group of classroom teachers to describe the reasons that item-response theory approaches to scale scores have become more popular, what would your main points be?

SUGGESTIONS FOR ADDITIONAL READING

Cannel, John J. "Nationally Normed Elementary Achievement Testing in America's Public Schools: How All 50 States Are Above the National Average." *Educational Measurement: Issues and Practice*, 7, 2 (Summer 1988): 5–9.

Carey, Lou M. *Measuring and Evaluating School Learning.* Boston: Allyn & Bacon, 1988.

Cunningham, George K. *Assessment in the Classroom: Constructing and Interpreting Tests.* Washington, DC: Falmer Press, 1998.

Ebel, R. L., and D. A. Frisbee. *Essentials of Educational Measurement*, pp. 267–286, 288–299, 301–315. Engelwood Cliffs, NJ: Prentice-Hall, 1986.

Hambleton, Ronald K. "Principles and Selected Applications of Item-Response Theory." In Robert L. Linn (Ed.), *Educational Measurement* (3rd ed.). New York: Macmillan, 1989.

Hambleton, Ronald K., and H. Swaminathan. *Item-Response Theory: Principles and Applications.* Higham, MS: Kluwer-Nijhoff, 1985.

Hoover, H. D. "The Most Appropriate Scores for Measuring Educational Development in the Elementary Schools: GE's." *Educational Measurement: Issues and Practice*, 3, 4 (Winter 1984): 5–7.

Linn, Robert L., and Norman E. Gronlund. *Measurement and Assessment in Teaching* (7th ed.). Upper Saddle River, NJ: Prentice-Hall, 1995.

Lloyd, Brenda H. "Implications of Item-Response Theory for the Measurement Practitioner." *Applied Measurement in Education*, 1, 2 (1988): 135–143.

McMillan, James H. *Classroom Assessment: Principles and Practice for Effective Instruction.* Boston, MA: Allyn & Bacon, 1997.

Mehrens, William A., and Irvin J. Lehmann. *Using Standardized Tests in Education.* New York: Longman, 1987.

Peterson, Nancy S., Michael J. Kolen, and H. D. Hoover. "Scaling, Norming, and Equating." In Robert R. Linn (Ed.), *Educational Measurement.* New York: Macmillan, 1989.

Popham, W. James. "Normative Data for Criterion-Referenced Tests?" *Phi Delta Kappan, 57,* 9 (1976): 593–594.

Yen, Wendy M. "The Choice of Scale for Educational Measurement: An IRT Perspective." *Journal of Educational Measurement, 23,* 4 (Winter 1986), 299–325.

AND FOR THOSE WHO TIRE OF READING

Popham, W. James, and Sarah J. Stanley. *A Parent's Guide to Standardized Tests* (Videotape #ETVT-34). Los Angeles: IOX Assessment Associates.

Popham, W. James, and Sarah J. Stanley. *Making Sense Out of Standardized Test Scores* (Videotape #ETVT-33). Los Angeles: IOX Assessment Associates.

Surveying the Influence of IRT on Testing Practices. Ronald K. Hambleton, University of Massachusetts. Tape recording from the 1988 session of the American Educational Research Association (AERA). Available at AERA, 1230 Seventeenth Street, N.W., Washington, DC 20036.

ENDNOTES

1. If you're a district administrator who discovers that a school board member misuses the term *quartile*, you should rarely attempt to provide the board member with a crash course in appropriate measurement terminology. Unless, of course, you're planning on a shift in careers.

2. It is now genetically possible to grow purple tomatoes and blue carrots, although why one would wish to do so eludes me.

3. If you find yourself having a lively discussion with someone about standard scores, you should probably try to broaden your interests.

4. See, for example, R. L. Linn, "Validity of Inferences Based on the Proposed Title I Evaluation Models," *Educational Evaluation and Policy Analysis, I,* 2 (March–April 1979), 23–32.

Creating Educational Tests

This textbook has 15 chapters and an optional appendix about statistics. Because you've already finished Chapter 7, using a baseball metaphor, you're rounding second base and heading into third. If you read Part Three's six chapters carefully, you'll be heading for home with no chance of being called "out."

The first chapter in Part Three (Chapter 8) deals with the sticky problem of describing what you're going to assess and, having done so, how to do so in a way that helps educators do a better instructional job. Chapters 9 and 10 look at selected-response and constructed-response items and will supply you with a series of practical guidelines about how to create sparkling renditions of those items. In Chapter 11, you'll be dealing with performance testing and portfolio assessment. Because students' responses to both of those forms of assessment are typically judged with the use of a scoring rubric, in Chapter 11 you'll also learn about how to distinguish between rubrics that are rapturous and those that are rancid.

In Chapter 12, you'll learn about ways of improving test items. Unfortunately, educators rarely construct perfect items on their first try. Chapter 12 describes both judgmental and empirical ways of sprucing up the items that constitute educational assessments.

Finally, Part Three is concluded by Chapter 13, which treats the assessment of student affect. You'll learn in that chapter about how to first generate suitable affective assessment instruments, then how to make appropriate inferences from students' responses to those instruments.

Part Three, as you can see, deals chiefly with the actual assessment instruments that educational leaders need to know about if they're going to be assessment-knowledgeable educational leaders. And, of course, all educational leaders want that.

Part three

Tying Down the Assessment Domain

Circumscribing What's to Be Measured

As has been frequently indicated during the initial chapters of this entrancing text about testing, educators employ assessments in order to make inferences about the status of students. More specifically, a test is employed in order to make an inference about students' status with respect to the assessment domain represented by that test. Valid inferences about students' status regarding the knowledge, skill, or affect set forth in the assessment domain will allow educators to make better decisions about how to educate children. (If I appear to be strumming the same old guitar chord again about assessment-based inferences, the reason is that the chord is important and, to me, quite melodious.)

All right, if the validity of score-based inferences hinges on a test's accurate representation of an assessment domain, then it's pretty clear that educational leaders need to know something about assessment domains. Clearly, you can't know if an assessment instrument adequately represents an assessment domain if you don't know what the assessment domain is. And that's what this chapter is about, namely, how to tie down what's in an assessment domain. That tying-down is necessary not only for those who are constructing an assessment device, but also for those who are trying to interpret students' performances on the assessment device after it's been used.

Traditional Tying-Down Techniques

Through the years, educational measurement folks have come up with numerous techniques for circumscribing an assessment domain. Many of those approaches have been devised chiefly to suit the needs of measurement personnel. That's to be expected. If measurement specialists must develop standardized achievement or aptitude tests, the domain-definition procedures those specialists create ought to help develop better versions of such tests. We'll take a look at some of the more traditional schemes used to identify what's contained in an assessment domain.

As you might suspect, teachers characteristically expend far less effort in spelling out what's embodied in the assessment domains that their classroom tests represent. After all, busy teachers are lucky just to churn out one or two good tests. Rarely do teachers have time to describe the assessment domains their classroom tests are supposed to represent. But, even so, you should consider the kinds of procedures that some teachers have employed to isolate what their classroom tests are supposed to represent.

So far, the phrase I've been using to describe what tests are supposed to represent is *assessment domains.* But there are certainly other synonymous descriptors that, as an educational leader, you're likely to encounter. For instance, even in this remarkably consistent book I have varied my own enchanting descriptors on occasion. If you doubt the accuracy of this confession regarding inconsistency, take a gander in Chapter 3 at Figure 3.3 on page 76. You'll see I've referred to what a test represents as a "target instructional domain." That switch in descriptors was not intended to induce confusion on your part. (I have had, as you will agree, many subsequent opportunities to induce confusion after Chapter 3.) No, I referred to what a test represents as a *target instructional domain* because, at that point, I was focusing on an instructional issue (whether to teach toward a test or toward the domain it represented). You'll also find folks referring to an assessment domain as a

Test-Item Specifications

The rules governing the construction of a test's items.

content domain (even though some tests are focused less on content mastery than they are on students' mastery of cognitive skills or on student affect).

Historically, those developing large-scale assessments such as statewide tests or nationally standardized achievement tests describe assessment domains as "test specifications," "test-item specifications," or "test blueprints." There's no compelling reason to use any one of these fundamentally synonymous descriptors. What educational leaders need to do, however, is to make sure that they understand what's being implied when these different descriptors are employed. To illustrate, many test-developers employ the phrase "test-item specifications" to refer explicitly to the rules for generating the items on a test, but use the phrase "test specifications" to signify a document that dictates how many items of certain types should constitute a test form.

Although most of the labels employed to describe assessment domains are largely interchangeable, alert educational leaders (they're much better than lethargic ones) should always seek clarification when a colleague uses any descriptor intended to indicate the set of knowledge, skills, or affect ostensibly represented by an assessment instrument. Before turning to the details of how an assessment domain might be described, let's first dabble for a moment or two in a few practicalities.

Practical constraints. Imagine for a moment that you've decided to abandon educational leadership as a career, and have chosen, instead, to become an educational test developer for an educational measurement company. Imagine further (once you're on an imagination roll, don't stop) that your company's president has directed you to head up the development of a high school basic-skills test in mathematics. After six months, you've polished and repolished the test until it simply sparkles with psychometric splendor. Alas, it takes most youngsters at least 120 minutes to complete the test. Some youngsters take almost 200 minutes to finish the test. Because most high school class periods are 45 to 55 minutes in length, you have created a test that would require at least three, and maybe even four, class periods for its administration. Because most school folks are usually reluctant to toss a four-period exam at their students, you have produced a test whose likelihood of use would be decisively limited. More careful advance practical planning might have headed off such a calamity.

Besides the length of time available for testing, there are other rather routine concerns of a practical nature to which test developers need attend. For instance, with large-scale tests, will the nature of the test be such that hand or machine scoring is possible? In many large school districts, it is a necessity that tests yield student responses capable of being optically scanned (by electronic scanning machines or an unemployed Cyclops). If this is so, it would be a serious error to create a test consisting of short-answer items that would have to be handscored by human beings or visiting extraterrestials.

Even with classroom tests, teachers must also concern themselves about test length and the problems of scoring. For instance, essay tests may be simple for teachers to create, but are time-consuming to score. Teachers must be realistic about how many out-of-school hours they're willing to devote to test-scoring.

Then there's the problem of test security. Will it be necessary to develop an entirely new form of the test in subsequent years, or can this year's test be reused? Both teachers and commercial test developers must face this question. The extent to which new forms

Test Specifications

The rules governing the allocation of certain kinds of items in a test.

of the test will be needed and the degree to which equivalent difficulties on these forms will be required can dictate how many items must be developed.

Is the test to be a time-limited test (a speeded test) in which students are given a finite amount of time to complete the test? Will the students require any resources during the completion of the exam, such as dictionaries, electronic calculators, or laptop computers? Will accommodations for disabled students be required, such as for those who are visually or auditorily impaired?

These kinds of considerations should lead you to recognize that there are practical requirements associated with the test's administration and scoring that often constrain the nature of the test itself. Such constraints should be foreseen and accommodated in subsequent decisions about what sorts of assessment domains can actually be measured.

A Range of Assessment Options

All right, let's say that, in deciding on an assessment domain, you've given reasonable attention to the sorts of practical constraints just described. How should you go about figuring out what types of items will actually be in the assessment domain? Well, there's a high probability that inexperienced assessors will gravitate too quickly toward the sorts of tests with which they are most familiar. Because most of us grew up by taking endless numbers of multiple-choice tests, there is a likelihood that test developers will initiate—and conclude—their thoughts about a multiple-choice assessment domain without seriously considering other measurement options.

In the next several chapters, you'll have an opportunity to review many different types of assessment techniques. Some of these assessment procedures are of a paper-and-pencil sort. Others involve observations of students in action. Others focus on the appraisal of student-generated products, such as an art student's ceramic vase or a home economics student's banana cream pie. Still others are based on portfolio collections of student-produced work.

Now, in a very real sense, some of these diverse assessment strategies constitute their own "test items." The necessity to produce a yummy banana cream pie is a test item in a homemaking class. However, it is obviously not a multiple-choice test item. Unfortunately, many educators do not think of diverse measurement approaches when they set out to delimit their assessment domains.

Even if the decision is made to create a paper-and-pencil test, there are all sorts of choices still open to the creative assessor. For example, in addition to the omnipresent multiple-choice item, you can use short-answer items, matching items, binary-choice items, essay items, or variations and combinations of these item types.

What you'll first need to do is get a reasonably good idea of what sort of attribute you wish to measure, for example, what skill or attitude you have in mind. To illustrate, let's say you're a speech teacher and you want to see how well your students can "organize their prespeech plans." With this general idea in mind, you should then review *all reasonable contenders* for the task of finding out how well your students can plan their speeches. You should think of paper-and-pencil approaches, such as whether students can, under examination circumstances, write a respectable organizational outline on a speech topic that you would supply. Perhaps, as a variant of that approach, you could construct test items that would require students to choose among alternative outlines for speeches, some of the outlines having deliberately been made more defensible than others. You should also consider oral-assessment schemes, such as having students describe aloud their plans for a speech on a preassigned topic. Ingenious test planners could come up with still other assessment options. The important point here is that *premature closure* on particular test strategies, particularly of the traditional multiple-choice variety, is to be eschewed. (Actually, use of the word *eschewed* should be eschewed.)

Let's briefly consider the kinds of domain-definition approaches that, as an educational leader, you're apt to encounter. We'll start with the models most often employed by measurement personnel in test-development agencies, then see how some classroom teachers have simplified those approaches.

Two-way grids. One of the most popular domain-definition strategies employed by test-development firms is a *two-way* grid in which one dimension reflects the *content* to be covered in the test and the other dimension describes the kinds of student *cognitive be-*

Two-Way Grids

An assessment-domain definition citing content according to the cognitive level measured and the number of items for each.

havior to be assessed on the test. In its most typical form, the two-way grid consists of content categories at the left and cognitive behavior categories across the top, such as the two-way grid presented in Table 8.1, where the numerals in the center of the grid reflect the number of items dealing with each of the topics at one of the four levels of student cognitive behavior (in this instance drawn from the first four levels of Bloom's widely used *Taxonomy of Educational Objectives*).[1] In the illustration in Table 8.1, you can readily see how the fifty items in this examination have been allocated to both content topics and cognitive-behavior levels.

If the developers of a test are distressed that there are only about half as many items calling for student analysis as opposed to the items calling for knowledge or comprehension, then this situation can be altered by replacing some knowledge or comprehension items with analysis items. If the test developers are distressed that Topic 4 has too few items, then this deficiency can also be rectified. Clearly, two-way grids such as this can be helpful in apportioning items on tests so that those constructing a test can avoid inadvertent overemphases or underemphases.

The rows and columns on such grids can be made more fine-grained or less fine-grained than those seen in Table 8.1. For example, one could describe students' cognitive behavior on test items as only "recall" or "beyond recall," as presented in Table 8.2, where there is also a more detailed breakdown of content than was seen in Table 8.1's two-way grid. In Table 8.2 you'll see an evenly distributed allocation of 100 items across both content and cognitive-level categories. Again, if any substantial disproportionalities are revealed, these can be modified.

It is possible, of course, to add additional dimensions so that you really end up with three-way or four-way grids. To illustrate, suppose you were developing an achievement test in which you not only were attentive to content and cognitive behavior (as in the

TABLE 8.1   A Typical Two-Way Grid Used to Define An Assessment Domain.

	NUMBER OF TEST ITEMS FOR EACH COGNITIVE LEVEL				
	KNOWLEDGE	COMPREHENSION	APPLICATION	ANALYSIS	TOTAL
Topic 1	3	2	2	4	11
Topic 2	4	3	3	2	12
Topic 3	3	5	5	0	13
Topic 4	2	3	0	0	5
Topic 5	3	2	2	2	9
Total	15	15	12	8	50

TABLE 8.2 **A Two-Way Grid with Detailed Content Categories and Only Two Levels of Cognitive Behavior.**

	ITEMS PER COGNITIVE LEVEL		
CONTENT OF ITEMS	RECALL	BEYOND RECALL	TOTAL
Topic A	12	14	26
Subtopic A_1	4	5	(9)
Subtopic A_2	5	3	(8)
Subtopic A_3	3	6	(9)
Topic B	10	11	21
Subtopic B_1	5	6	(11)
Subtopic B_2	5	5	(10)
Topic C	14	11	25
Subtopic C_1	7	3	(10)
Subtopic C_2	7	8	(15)
Subtopic C2a	3	4	(7)
Subtopic C2b	4	4	(8)
Topic D	14	14	28
Subtopic D_1	6	7	(13)
Subtopic D_2	8	7	(15)
Total	50	50	100

previous two examples), but also wanted to make sure that the test items were equally balanced on dimensions such as sex (of those individuals who are described in the items) or item type (multiple-choice or true-false). These features would be added as third or fourth dimensions to a grid that would, of course, be more difficult to depict in a simple table. You could use parentheses, brackets, or some other scheme to represent the additional dimensions. The sorts of two-way grids you have just considered would be more aptly described as test specifications rather than as test-item specifications because they are not addressed to the particulars of what the test's items should be like.

The key question is *when* should an assessment domain's specifications be created for an educational test: before or after the test is written? The answer, without question, is *before* the test is put together. Two-way grids, as you have seen, can be useful in-process checks of whether there are too few or too many items of a particular kind. However, if the domain-description is really going to guide the creation of a test (and if it isn't, then the test might as well be developed without forethought), the domain-description should govern the item-generation process.

A review of the item grids presented in the technical manuals of some standardized achievement tests, because of the almost anarchic pattern of item allocations found there, suggests that such grids sometimes are actually after-the-fact appendages that have exercised little influence over the production or selection of the test's items.

Content/Skill Listings

An assessment-domain definition listing the assessable knowledge or skills along with the number of items for each.

Content or skill listings. Another specifications technique used for large-scale assessments is to list the content categories in the test, along with the number of items per category. Perhaps, the objectives (or skills) covered by the test are listed along with the number of test items per objective (or skill). You can see such a scheme depicted in Table 8.3, in which an actual state-level test is broken down according to items per skill.

By inspecting a domain description such as Table 8.3, you can see that the test developers apparently set a minimum number of items per skill, namely, four. The reason that certain skills are assessed by five, six, or seven items is not clear, although in some instances these minor anomalies might arise merely because of the form of the item itself (such as an item structure that really requires multiple answers per item from students).

You can also note that the level of skill descriptions in such tables is often insufficient to really tie down the explicit nature of the items themselves. For example, note the many mathematics skills cited in Table 8.3 that read somewhat as follows: "Solve problems involving comparison shopping." Well, that leaves a shopping-cart load of latitude regarding what might be in the actual items. The items could include very subtle comparison-shopping problems in which two jars of peanut butter must be contrasted according to weight, cost, and crunchiness. Alternatively, the problems could be so obvious that even a mathematical incompetent could solve them: "If two cans of candied okra are equal in quantity and quality, but Can A costs 50 percent more than Can B, which should you buy?" More importantly, of course, why would anyone wish to buy candied okra—even if it is a bargain?

However, the level of the detail in the content descriptors of specifications for many large-scale tests is such that the item writer is constrained only generally in the creation of items. To illustrate, because standardized achievement tests are chiefly intended to permit norm-referenced comparisons among students with respect to rather loosely defined attributes such as "knowledge of algebra," the imprecise level of descriptive rigor employed in the specifications for most standardized achievement tests is usually quite sufficient for such norm-referenced contrasts.

Teacher simplifications. Few classroom teachers have time to develop complex test blueprints that thoroughly delineate assessment domains for most of their classroom tests. There aren't enough hours in the day.

So, if there were serious attempts by teachers to tie down an assessment domain, those attempts often turn out to be substantial simplifications of the kinds of two-way grids or skill/content listings seen in Tables 8.1, 8.2, and 8.3. And that's just fine! Educational leaders need to establish realistic expectations for their in-the-classroom

TABLE 8.3   **Number of Skills and Items in a State's Eleventh-Grade Functional Literacy Test**

SKILL NO.	BRIEF DESCRIPTION OF FUNCTIONAL LITERACY SKILL	NO. OF ITEMS
	Mathematics	
17	Determine elapsed time between two events.	4
24	Determine equivalent amounts of money.	4
30	Solve problems involving whole numbers.	5
32	Solve problems involving decimal numbers and percents.	4
33	Solve problems involving comparison shopping.	5
34	Solve problems involving a rate of interest.	5
35	Solve purchase problems involving sales tax.	5
36	Solve purchase problems involving discounts.	4
37	Solve problems involving measurements.	4
38	Solve problems involving the area of a rectangle.	4
39	Solve problems involving capacity.	4
40	Solve problems involving weight.	4
41	Find information in graphs and tables.	7
	Mathematics Total	59
	Communication Skills–Reading	
11	Infer main idea of a selection.	6
12	Find specific information in a selection.	5
16	Infer cause or effect of an action.	5
20	Identify facts and opinions.	4
21	Identify an unstated opinion.	5
26	Identify source to obtain information on a topic.	5
28	Use index cross-references to find information.	5
29	Use highway and city maps.	6
	Reading Total	41
	Communication Skills–Writing	
32	Include necessary information in letters.	7
33	Complete a check and its stub.	5
34	Complete common application forms accurately.	5
	Writing Total	17
	Functional Literacy Test Total	117

Kansas Board Members Compromise, Keep Assessment

by Millicent Lawton

Kansas elementary and secondary school students will continue to take a statewide assessment—albeit in a modified format—thanks to a compromise by state board of education members.

For two months this summer, a deadlock on the state board left the fate of Kansas' student testing program hanging in the balance.

But finally last month, the board voted to give the assessment system another year of life by renewing the state's annual testing contract with the University of Kansas.

In adopting the delicately brokered compromise, each side in the standoff gave something up.

Conservative Republican board members who had argued for the demise of the current testing system allowed it to continue.

And moderate Republican and Democratic board members agreed to changes, including the removal of "performance" testing school items from the assessment.

The revisions to the assessments begin this school year, with more significant alterations due for 1998–99 and beyond.

Many in the state greeted the compromise with relief. "I'm pleased to see the taxpayers' investment in these tests will not be wasted," Gov. Bill Graves, a Republican, told reporters after the vote.

And John Koepke, the executive director of the Kansas Association of School Boards, said the most important consequence of the plan was the knowledge "that the two sides can work together in spite of ideological differences. . . ."

What's your reaction?

Excerpted, with permission, from *Education Week*, September 3, 1997

colleagues. Whereas the measurement specialists in test-development companies may have the time and inclination to carve out highly detailed domain-descriptions, most teachers have neither the time nor the inclination to engage in such activities. But any clarity that a teacher can give to the assessment domain being promoted will almost always help the teacher think more clearly about what's to be taught.

Assessment Domain Definitions as Instructional Facilitators

Educational leaders will find that tests, if properly conceptualized, with instruction in mind, can prove enormously helpful in *promoting more effective teaching*. The chief reason for that instructional payoff is the clarity associated with what's being measured. This point is depicted graphically in Figure 8.1, in which it can be seen that two factors, (1) importance of results and (2) clarity of assessed content, typically have an impact on instruction. Consideration of Figure 8.1 will reveal, however, that even a high-stakes test is likely to have no instructional impact if there is no clarity regarding what's being assessed.

In the case of achievement tests, that is, tests of students' knowledge or cognitive skills, there are three obvious dividends from well-defined assessment domains. (These dividends were initially identified in Chapter 3.) First, a teacher who understands where students are ultimately heading will be better able to carry out an *accurate task analysis* and,

FIGURE 8.1.

Instructional impact of tests based on the importance of test results and the clarity of content being assessed.

Clarity of Assessed Content

		Clear	Unclear
Importance of Results	High Stakes	Substantial Impact	No Impact
	Low Stakes	Meaningful Impact	No Impact

as a consequence, provide students with the necessary en route knowledge and skills they need. Second, a teacher who understands where students are ultimately heading will be better able to provide more on-target practice, that is, *relevant guided and independent practice activities.* Finally, a teacher who understands where students are ultimately heading will typically be able to supply *more effective explanations* to those students. In short, there are substantial instructional benefits derivative from crisply defined assessment domains.

In Chapter 3 it was suggested that one of the evaluative factors educational leaders should employ when appraising assessment instruments is an assessment's likely instructional contribution. What's being suggested now is that if an assessment instrument is not accompanied by a well-defined assessment domain, that assessment instrument is unlikely to be of much instructional assistance.

But when does a well-defined assessment domain become *too* well defined? This is a concern that you, as an educational leader, need to keep in mind. If the attempt to define an assessment domain is so elaborate that it is seen as daunting by most teachers, then there's little likelihood that the assessment will help instruction. This is the time when you'll have to use your best professional judgment and remember that in the delineation of assessment domains, most teachers will applaud a make-it-palatable approach. An instructionally catalytic assessment instrument should have the domain it represents well defined, but not in so much detail that the domain definition will be dodged by teachers.

To sum up the instructional role of assessment domains, they provide teachers with targets, that is, the educational outcomes it is hoped the teacher's students will attain. A domain of skill, knowledge, or affect sets forth what the teacher is responsible for promoting. An assessment is supposed to be a representative sample based on the defined domain. That's why teachers should orient their instruction toward the assessment domain rather than the test representing that domain.

Assessment Domains for Diverse Instructional Outcomes

Briefly, let's consider how assessment domains should be defined for different kinds of intended instructional outcomes. We'll look at domains for (1) cognitive skills measured by either performance tests, (2) cognitive skills measured by selected-response tests, (3) knowledge measured by either selected-response or constructed-response tests, and (4) affect measured by students' anonymous responses to self-report inventories.

Performance Test

An assessment of students' skill or knowledge by requiring them to respond to a task eliciting a behavior or product.

Rubric

A scoring guide to be used in evaluating students' constructed responses, typically used with performance tests or portfolios.

Cognitive skills assessed via performance tests. If students are attempting to master genuinely high-level cognitive skills, such as the ability to write narrative essays, make effective oral presentations, or solve complex mathematical problems, one of the best assessment approaches to use is a *performance test*. Performance tests present students with a task (such as a directive to write a narrative essay on a particular topic), then judge the adequacy of students' performance of that task. In some cases, the student provides a product such as an essay. In other cases, the task will call for some student behavior that must be evaluated as it takes place (such as when teachers judge the quality of students' oral reports).

In either case, the two critical components of an assessment-domain description for a performance test are (1) a delineation of the kinds of tasks that students may be asked to carry out, and (2) the evaluative procedures that will be used to judge the quality of students' responses to whatever task or tasks they are given. These evaluative procedures are typically referred to these days as scoring *rubrics*. In Chapter 10, you will learn much more about rubrics because, if crafted with instruction in mind, rubrics can provide considerable instructional insight for teachers.

But, in a nutshell, to tie down the assessment domain for cognitive skills that are to be assessed via performance tests, it is necessary to spell out the important features of the tasks that students will need to perform and the key elements of the scoring rubric that will be used to judge the quality of students' responses to those tasks. Teachers who review these task descriptions and scoring rubrics should have a sufficiently clear idea about where to head instructionally so that on-target and effective instructional planning can follow.

Cognitive skills assessed by selected-response tests. Another common kind of cognitive skill is one that can be assessed via a *selected-response test*, such as a test containing multiple-choice items. For example, a test might present the students with a previously unencountered example of propaganda, and the students would be required to select, from four options, the type of propaganda presented.

For these sorts of tests, a decently described assessment domain would provide teachers with a clear idea of what a test item might be like, that is, the stimulus section of an item as well as its potential response options. Again, the purpose of the domain definition is to help teachers obtain a reasonably accurate picture of what's expected of students. The more clearly that teachers understand what constitutes an *eligible* test item, the better that the teacher can plan to have students achieve what those test items are attempting to assess.

In the 1980s, measurement specialists who were attracted to the virtues of criterion-referenced interpretations sometimes produced sets of test specifications (and accompanying test-item specifications) so lengthy and overwhelming that teachers simply avoided them. The lesson from that experience, of course, is that the level of detail embodied in the definition of an assessment domain must be sufficient for reasonable clarification of what's to be assessed, but not so detailed that teachers will be repelled. To carve out suitable definitions of assessment domains so those domains achieve this middle-of-the-road level of detail calls for more than a little assessment artistry.

So an instructionally helpful assessment domain for the kinds of skills that could readily be assessed via paper-and-pencil test items, either of the selected-response or constructed-response variety, will usually consist of (1) the defining attributes of correct and incorrect skill-applications, and (2) an indication of the type, or types, of test items that can be used to see if students possess the skill.

For example, suppose you were trying to see if a teacher's students could determine which two of the five following statistics would best describe a set of test scores given to students: the mean, median, mode, standard deviation, or range. The domain definition would need to spell out, as succinctly as possible, the kinds of data for which someone should and shouldn't use each of the five statistics. Then the kinds of test items that might be used should also be identified. The resulting domain definition should give teachers a solid idea of the skill being promoted and how that skill might be assessed.

Knowledge assessed by selected-response or constructed-response tests. There's nothing wrong with knowledge. Even though it ranks at the bottom of most cognitive taxonomies, and even though it only calls for students to memorize information, knowledge is a good thing to have. Indeed, having knowledge usually beats the alternative decisively.

So, what does a domain of knowledge look like? Well, one example would be a list of vocabulary words that teachers might like their students to be able to define (from memory). Another domain of knowledge would be a spelled-out set of the most important facts that teachers would like students to remember about the Revolutionary War. Or a chemistry teacher might want students to know, from memory, a set of "key chemistry concepts." These examples will, hopefully, give you an idea about the chunks of relatively homogeneous information that educators would like students to be able to recall.

Now, how do teachers usually go about testing students' knowledge? Well, teachers usually dream up a few questions that are based on the teacher's general idea of the knowledge domain under consideration, then see how well students do when answering those questions. Typically, the questions are presented in the form of multiple-choice, true-false, or short-answer items. There's nothing wrong with these sorts of items; they usually do a knowledge-assessing job quite well. Unfortunately, a teacher's understanding of the content domain's boundaries is frequently limited. More often than not, teachers have less than a lucid idea of the full range of content that their knowledge-tests supposedly sample.

Yet, if a test's assessment domain is going to supply teachers with the clarity they need to devise more appropriate instruction, that assessment domain must stake out *all* of the content constituting that domain. If teachers know all of the content that's eligible to be assessed, then their instruction can realistically be directed toward that complete domain rather toward a few knowledge-focused questions.

Besides, if an assessment domain clearly lays out the collection of knowledge that the student should master, then astute teachers will make that collection of knowledge available to the students during the instructional process. Knowledge to be memorized by anyone should not be knowledge kept secret.

So, an instructionally useful assessment domain will typically consist of (1) a listing of all the facts, information, concepts, or terms that constitute the content students should know, and (2) a brief description of the kinds of test items that might be on a test intended to ascertain a student's level of knowledge.

Affect assessed by student self-report inventories. In addition to the promotion of students' knowledge and skill, some teachers try to promote certain kinds of affective outcomes, such as students' more positive attitudes toward certain subjects. Later in this book, in Chapter 13, considerably more attention is given to the assessment of students' affect.

For purposes of tying down an affective assessment domain to be represented by some kind of assessment device, let's assume you're using an anonymous self-report inventory containing positively and negatively phrased statements to which students register agreement or disagreement. What the assessment domain would need to contain, therefore, is a description of the pivotal concepts that would be addressed in the inventory's items (statements). For instance, if the inventory were dealing with students' attitudes toward reading, the assessment domain might list the kinds of reading-related activities or student sentiments about which statements for the inventory could be generated, such as "student's personal enjoyment of voluntary reading" or "student's perceived confidence as a skillful reader." Thereafter, a variety of statements would be generated about those activities or statements such as "I like to read when I have free time" or "I am really not a very good reader."

After listing the central concepts on which statements in a self-report inventory could be based, all that's missing in the definition of an affective assessment domain is a brief description of the form of the items in the inventory, for instance, the kinds of response options to be used (for instance, "agree and disagree," *versus* "strongly agree, agree, uncertain, disagree, and strongly disagree").

With this kind of assessment-domain description in hand, teachers will have a sufficiently clear idea about where they're heading instructionally so that they can devise suitable activities to help students acquire the desired affect.

Clarity of intention as the key. You've just had an opportunity to see how a reasonably well-described assessment domain can provide teachers with the kind of clarified expectations that, almost invariably, lead to better instructional planning. The more clearly that teachers understand the kinds of outcomes they seek for students, the more likely it is, therefore, that effective instruction will be provided to those students.

Because a suitably tied-down assessment domain can supply teachers with such clarity, assessment domains should always be generated *prior* to the teacher's instructional planning. If the teacher's tests are developed at the end of instruction, as instructional afterthoughts, it's clear that those tests will have little impact on the instruction itself. Accordingly, early assessment planning is imperative.

But because teachers should be directing their instruction toward assessment *domains* rather than assessment *devices*, educational leaders must encourage their colleagues to use or develop tests that spring from well-defined assessment domains.

Focusing on Assessment-Based Inferences

As educators attempt to circumscribe the assessment domains on which their tests are based, there's a devious danger lurking. The danger, simply put, is that too much specificity in a domain definition may lead to reliance on a *unitary* type of test item. Such an overemphasis on a single type of item in assessments may incline teachers to devote excessive instructional attention to the specific kind of item employed in the test. As a consequence, students will be less able to *generalize* their skills and knowledge in different contexts.

In the 1970s and 1980s, many of the early attempts to create assessments that would yield criterion-referenced interpretations led to assessment domains defined with so much labyrinthian detail that few teachers had the patience to wade through them. Even worse, most of those elaborately described assessment domains ended up with only one item format being permissible, for example, a particular type of five-option multiple-choice item. As a consequence, too much teacher time was devoted to the student's mastering only the item-type defined in the assessment domain. The student's likelihood of generalizing was, at best, modest.

An abbreviated domain description. As an antidote to this sort of instructionally unsound assessment thinking, especially for cognitive tests, I recommend that you focus your descriptive efforts exclusively on the score-based inference that you wish to make. First, you must identify the nature of that inference in a reasonably clear fashion so that you have an intuitive understanding about what you're trying to measure. In educational terms, you need to try to "get inside the student's head" so that you understand the *essence of the intellectual operations that the student must perform in order to satisfactorily complete the tasks represented in the test's items.* And a test item, in this instance as in most others, signifies a wide range of performance tests as well as the more traditional paper-and-pencil testing formats. What you need to focus on are the various kinds of test items that will help you make accurate inferences about students' status with respect to a particular kind of cognitive ability.

A description of the "intellectual essence" required by the test's items is then provided, as a paragraph or two, at the outset of the assessment domain's description. This is necessary so that item-writers can get a satisfactory fix on what they need to present as tasks (test items) in order to find out if the student can display the cognitive ability being sampled by the test. I suggest that this boiled-down general description of what's going on in the successful student's head be accompanied by a set of varied, *but not exhaustive,* illustrative items. Variety and nonexhaustiveness are critical here because such a descriptive strategy will oblige teachers to promote generalizable cognitive abilities if they wish their students to perform well on a test that's based on such an assessment domain. Given the announced diversity of the kinds of items that *might* be invoked to assess the student's mastery of Skill *X*, a teacher who wished to boost student performance on a high-stakes test would be a fool to focus only on a single assessment variation of that skill. An example of the assessment-domain description I'm proposing is presented in Box 8.1.

The general description of the score-based inference to be made, plus a diverse array of illustrative test items, taken in concert, will provide both item-writers and teachers with a solid enough idea of what's at stake so both groups can proceed with their distinctive endeavors. The teacher will know, at a sufficient level of clarity, what kind of cognitive ability is to be promoted in students. The item-writer will know, at a sufficient level of clarity, what kinds of tasks must be presented to students.

BOX 8.1 An illustration of an assessment domain that fosters students' generalized abilities.

An Assessment Domain Description

Comprehending Central Messages

General Description

Items can be phrased in a variety of ways, but they all *must require the student to have recognized or intended the central message of the selection* or a designated part of the selection. Items may call for students to create or choose the most accurate summary of the selection or part of the selection, to identify or state the topic of all or a part of the selection, or to identify or state the main idea or central point of a selection or part of that selection. Items may or may not require the student to make an inference in order to select or construct the appropriate answer.

Illustrative, Nonexhaustive Items

- What is this selection mainly about?
- Write a brief paragraph describing the theme of this passage.
- Describe, in one sentence, the passage's central message.
- What is the main point of this essay?
- Orally, indicate what the main idea is of the passage's fourth paragraph.
- Select the *best* statement of the essay's central message about human development:

  A. Nature is much more important than nurture.
  B. Nurture is much more important than nature.
  C. Nature and nurture are equally important.
  D. Neither nature nor nurture are all that significant.

A verification procedure. But even well-intentioned item-writers can fail to hit the mark, particularly if they're given the interpretive latitude I'm proposing here. It is imperative, therefore, that *for high-stakes tests* you add a new stage to test development, namely, a verification of the extent to which newly constructed test items do, in fact, elicit the kinds of student responses from which one can infer accurately what the student "can or can't do."

I suggest that for high-stakes tests the verification procedure take the form of the panel-review procedures so widely used now in assembling content-related evidence of validity for high-stakes assessments such as diploma-sanction tests. In these procedures, a panel of 10 to 20 qualified judges renders a series of item-by-item judgments regarding whether a test's items are content-appropriate. For instance, panelists often focus on such questions as whether an item "appropriately measures a skill or knowledge that is necessary for high school graduation."

For the verification procedure I'm proposing here, all you need to do is modify that panel-review methodology slightly so panelists must render individual judgments regarding "whether a student's response to this item will contribute directly to an accurate inference about whether the student possesses the cognitive ability measured by the test." That cognitive ability, of course, would have been communicated to the reviewers in the form of the general description referred to earlier and seen in Box 8.1. Panelists' judgments would then be transformed into the percentage of positive judgments per item and, thereafter, to a mean per-item index for the entire test. The higher the panelists' mean per-item judgments for a test's items, the more confidence that test-users can have in the score-based inferences associated with the test.

Precursive Item Constraints

The attempt, through the use of detailed assessment-domain definitions, to limit the nature of items before they are written.

**Postcursive
Item Review**

The attempt to
verify the validity
of a score-based
inference by judging
the degree to which
a test's items
contribute to that
inference.

What I am proposing is that educators shift any quest for assessment clarity from a *precursive* to a *postcursive* emphasis. Heretofore, educators have attempted to attain clarity by spelling out in great detail, prior to item-construction, just what the item-writers are permitted to do. In my experience, that strategy was initially appealing but has revealed itself to be *instructionally* disadvantageous. It either fosters nongeneralizable instruction by teachers or proves too onerous to serve as genuine clarification for most teachers. For these reasons, I believe a procedure that emphasizes postcursive verification will prove more serviceable. I am not suggesting that developers of educational tests have ignored the test's items once those items had been created. Rather, I am asking for a far more systematic postcursive scrutiny of items than has been undertaken in the past.

Obviously, educational leaders would not be urging classroom teachers to expend the elaborate attention to postcursive item-review I've been suggesting here. No, that kind of item scrutiny ought to be devoted only to genuinely high-stakes assessments. But, for those sorts of important tests, educational leaders should be on the lookout for evidence that any intended assessment-based inferences are, in fact, valid. The scheme just described is one way of tackling that issue.

To repeat, if educational assessment is ever going to make a bona fide contribution to *education*, then the development of clarified descriptions of assessment domains is a must. Assessment domains really do need to be tied down.

Chapter Wrap-Up

As usual, in summarizing this chapter an attempt will be made to answer the chapter's three guiding questions. Because I made up the guiding questions, you'd think I'd know the answers. Yet, because I once took a workshop in humility, I'll let you be the judge of whether the answers are accurate. (I can be genuinely obsequious when inclined.)

● What is an assessment domain?

An assessment domain is a description of the body of skills, knowledge, or affect to be represented by an assessment device. Putting it another way, when a testing device is used with a student, the student's performance allows educators to make an inference about the student's status with respect to the assessment domain represented by the testing device.

Because test-based inferences about students center directly on their status in relation to the assessment domain represented by a test, it is important to circumscribe with care just what an assessment domain contains. It is the key to an educator's arriving at a valid score-based inference about the meaning of students' performances.

Traditionally, assessment domains have been described as specifications, test blueprints, or content domains. Irrespective of the label being employed, these approaches have attempted to circumscribe what a test is supposed to represent. In some cases, the level of detail associated with domain definitions has been relatively modest. Such is often the case when norm-referenced interpretations of students' status are sought. Among the most common domain-definition strategies for such tests are two-way grids (that is, content *versus* levels of cognitive behavior) and skill or content listings. In other cases, considerable effort has been devoted to the item-generation rules associated with tests. These highly detailed efforts at domain definition have traditionally been used more frequently by those who wish to arrive at absolute, that is, criterion-referenced, interpretations of students' performances.

How can assessment domains function as instructional facilitators?

Even though it is generally believed *high-stakes* educational tests are the most powerful variable when it comes to influencing teachers' instructional practices, much more important is the *clarity* with which a test's assessment domain is defined. More clearly described assessment domains increase the likelihood that teachers will (1) carry out more accurate task analysis, (2) provide more relevant practice opportunities to students, and (3) supply more effective explanations. Clarity regarding assessment permits more astute instructional planning by teachers. High-stakes tests with ill-defined assessment domains are likely to have a negligible impact on the instructional process.

For different types of instructional objectives, suggestions were offered in the chapter regarding how an assessment domain ought to be structured. Generally speaking, there should be some attempt to circumscribe the content to be assessed as well as an indication of the eligible types of test items that might be employed to ascertain the status of students with respect to the assessment domain.

How should an instructionally helpful assessment domain be focused?

In order to get the most instructional yield from an assessment domain, it should be oriented around the inference to be drawn from the student's test performance. Although an illustration was supplied in the chapter about drawing an inference about a cognitive skill, the inference-focus approach should also be employed for affective assessment and even psychomotor assessments. Educational leaders will find it helpful as they deal with assessment issues if they habitually try to isolate the test-based inference to be drawn and, thereafter, the decision(s) that will be based on that inference.

Care must be taken to build assessment-domain descriptions so that they encourage teachers to promote students' generalized mastery of the knowledge, skill, or affect the teacher is attempting to promote. An abbreviated model for an inference-focused (and generalizability-inducing) domain description was supplied in the chapter. Because of the brevity of such domain definitions, however, it was suggested that *for high-stakes tests* considerable attention be given to the postcursive review of a test's items to make sure they do contribute to a valid score-based inference about the meaning of a student's performance.

Practice Exercise

This was a chapter intended to help you see how to construct an instructionally beneficial assessment domain. There's only one practice exercise for this chapter. See if you can develop a new assessment-domain description somewhat akin to the sample supplied in Box 8.1 on page 219. As you can see from that example, the domain description need not be all that lengthy. The most important consideration, of course, is that you spell out the nature of the inference that hinges on students' assessed performances.

Oh yes, because the illustration in Box 8.1 deals with students' ability to comprehend the central messages in what they read, it would be sporting of you to select some *other* skill or knowledge. Otherwise, scurry to a copy machine.

Answer to Practice Exercise

Because it is impossible to foresee the kind of skill, knowledge, or affect you might have tackled (I have allowed my membership dues to lapse in Psychometric Psychics Associated), I really can't dish out any very specific feedback on this exercise.

You might compare your domain definition with the one in Box 8.1 to make sure you've spelled out the inference you hope to make in unequivocal terms. In Box 8.1, the inference revolves around a student's ability to recognize or infer central messages of reading selections. Your assessment domain's inference should be as readily identifiable.

Another way you can gauge the quality of your practice exercise domain definition would be to ask someone else to review the illustrative item types you're designated to see if, using each of these item types, a valid inference could be made about the knowledge, skill, or affect that's allegedly being measured.

DISCUSSION QUESTIONS

1. Considerable attention was given in the chapter to the importance of well-described assessment domains in arriving at valid interpretations of students' knowledge, skill, or affect. Do you think that all this attention to domain definition is necessary, or can educators simply review a test, then arrive at a valid inference regarding the meaning of students' test performances?
2. In the chapter, it was recommended that the assessment domains for tests of student knowledge incorporate a detailed and exhaustive list of all eligible content. If this were done, how would a test be generated from that delineated content? How might a teacher make use *instructionally* of such an assessment-content *universe?*
3. Why do you think some assessment-domain definitions might limit the student's generalized mastery? How important is a student's generalized mastery of knowledge or skills?
4. Some writers have contended that a well-defined assessment domain serves to *operationalize* (or exemplify) a teacher's instructional intentions. How do you think this takes place?
5. Do you see any fundamental difference between the kinds of assessent domains required for absolute test-based inferences *versus* those required for relative test-based inferences? If so, what might those differences be?
6. If you were a district superintendent who was meeting with a group of middle school teachers to help them with their classroom assessments, how much emphasis would you recommend that the teachers give to the definition of assessment domains?

SUGGESTIONS FOR ADDITIONAL READING

Airasian, Peter W. *Classroom Assessment* (3rd ed.). New York: McGraw-Hill, 1994.

Linn, Robert L., and Norman E. Gronlund. *Measurement and Assessment in Teaching* (7th ed.). Upper Saddle River, NJ: Prentice-Hall, 1995.

McMillan, James H. *Classroom Assessment: Principles and Practice for Effective Instruction*. Boston, MA: Allyn & Bacon, 1997.

Martin, Jane Roland. "There's Too Much to Teach: Cultural Wealth in an Age of Scarcity." *Educational Researcher*, *25*, 2 (March 1996): 4–10, 16.

Rothman, Robert. *Measuring Up: Standards, Assessments, and School Reform*. San Francisco: Jossey-Bass, 1995.

Stiggins, Richard J. *Student-Centered Classroom Assessment* (2nd ed.). Upper Saddle River, NJ: Prentice-Hall, 1997.

AND FOR THOSE WHO TIRE OF READING

Kline, Everett, and Grant Wiggins. *Curriculum and Assessment Design* (Audiotape: Stock #295191S62). Alexandria, VA: Association for Supervision and Curriculum Development, 1995.

Popham, W. James. *A Parent's Guide to Performance Assessment* (Videotape #ETVT-26). Los Angeles: IOX Assessment Associates.

Wiggins, Grant, and Richard Stiggins. "Tape 1—Traditional Tests" (Videotape: Stock #614237S62) in *Redesigning Assessment Series*. Alexandria, VA: Association for Supervision and Curriculum Development, 1992.

ENDNOTE

1. Benjamin S. Bloom, and others, *Taxonomy of Educational Objectives, Handbook I: The Cognitive Domain*. New York: D. McKay, 1956.

chapter 9
Selected-Response Items

- What is the difference between selected-response and constructed-response test items?

- Do certain weaknesses in item-writing apply to all test items?

- What are the important features of binary-choice items?
  Dividends and Deficits
  Item-Writing Guidelines

- What are the important features of matching items?
  Dividends and Deficits
  Item-Writing Guidelines

- What are the important features of multiple-choice items?
  Dividends and Deficits
  Item-Writing Guidelines

In this chapter you're going to be reading about the raptures of constructing actual assessment items. "But, why," you might ask, "does an educational leader need to know how to construct test items?" After all, educational leaders should be leading, not testing. (That's a reasonable question. If you happened to be thinking it, you get an A-plus.)

First off, educational leaders really need to know the practical ins and outs of assessment, not just the theoretical stuff about three varieties of validity evidence. Only if an educational leader really understands measurement—from the time a test is born until its results are interpreted—will other educators really ascribe assessment competence to that educational leader. Ideally, educational leaders will have spent some "time in the testing trenches," rather than simply having read about testing in textbooks, even a textbook as illuminating as this one.

There's a second reason that you, as an educational leader or a leader-in-training, need to know about the practicalities of test-item construction. Educational leaders often find themselves working with teachers whose classroom assessment instruments need major surgery. Many teachers simply "test as they were tested themselves" and, as a result, end up with many poor tests. If you are familiar with the ground rules for generating various types of test items, you'll obviously be in a better place to help those teachers spiff up their classroom tests. And that's a good thing to be doing.

An Either/Or Split

There is something intrinsically heartwarming about being able to categorize anything into two tidy categories. For example, objects are either animate or inanimate and most people, prior to surgical adjustment, are either men or women. Yes, two-way classifications restore our confidence that the world, at least some parts of it, isn't all that complex.

In the field of educational measurement, at least as I've been treating it so far, I seem to be answering a number of questions with an altogether equivocal, "It depends." Such a wishy-washy response, for instance, is wholly suitable when responding to such queries as: "How many test items per skill should a test contain?" or "How high does a reliability coefficient *really* have to be?" or, finally, "What is the maximum permissible size of a standard error of measurement?"

With so much indeterminacy abounding in measurement, it may be comforting to encounter one solid, honest-to-goodness, two-way split that does a decent classification job. Fortunately, it's a fundamental one. *All of the test items employed in educational assessment devices call for students to make either a selected response or a constructed response.* Students make selected responses when they choose among the options on a multiple-choice test or when they opt for true, rather than false, in a true–false test. Students make constructed responses when they whip out a series of essay answers or when they respond to short-answer test items.

However, our happy little two-category scheme holds up even when you're dealing with more exotic types of student responses. For instance, when students present an extemporaneous speech in a public-speaking class, the speech constitutes a constructed response. When a student creates a ceramic bowl in a pottery class or a pair of bookends in a woodworking class, those are also constructed responses. When student choices of magazines are monitored during a free-reading period (that is, to see which types of magazines the students choose) as an indication of the students' interests in certain types of literature, this is an instance of a selected response.

It is impossible to find student responses that don't fit the *selected- versus constructed-response* classification scheme. It is an *exhaustive* classification scheme. However, as any lover of classification schemes might ask, is it also *mutually exclusive?* Well, fortunately, the selected- *versus* constructed-response category scheme is also mutually exclusive. A given student's response is always either selected (as from among options) *or* constructed (as in oral, written, or manual-production activities).

Now one could, of course, combine both sorts of responses into a single item. The most common instance of this occurs when teachers ask students to first answer a true–false item (a selected response) and then correct any false items by writing out a modified statement that is true (a constructed response). What you have in such items is a two-part test item, one part of which demands a constructed response and one part of which demands a selected response. The two types of student responses are not merged (thus casting doubt on our delightful two-category system); they are only juxtaposed.

In this and the next chapter, you will be considering the most common kinds of paper-and-pencil test items, and the advantages and disadvantages of relying on a particular item type, that is, selected- or constructed-response items. Each of the two chapters then treats the most common paper-and-pencil test items of its category. A later chapter deals with such procedures as performance assessment and portfolio assessment. In this, the selected-response chapter, you'll look at *binary-choice items, multiple-choice items,* and *matching items.* In Chapter 10, the constructed-response chapter, you'll consider *short-answer items* and *essay items.* For each type of item, the dividends and deficits of that item-type are described. In addition, a set of explicit item-writing guidelines is presented for each type of item. Most of the item-writing guidelines are accompanied by illustrative test items that violate or adhere to that particular guideline. Because the bulk of educational testing consists of paper-and-pencil assessment instruments, it's only natural to lavish more attention on how to construct winning test items of a paper-and-pencil variety.

The Necessity of Practicality

If you are an alert reader, you may have noted in the previous paragraph that this and the next chapter are apt to be terribly applied. You will learn all sorts of details about how to prepare decent test items. You have, indeed, moved from the somewhat theoretical thrills of Part Two (evaluating educational tests) to the practical task of constructing educational tests.

However, theory unimplemented is theory in a vacuum. You now need to consider how one takes all those lovely ideas of reliability, instructional contributions, validity, and so on, then blends them into first-rate tests. And there's the rub. Test developers, whether classroom teachers, staff members in a commercial testing agency, can have mastered all the psychometric niceties treated earlier, yet turn out tests that are abominable.

If you're going to go to the trouble of gauging a test's technical quality, or developing a set of norm-tables for it, be sure that the items themselves are as good as you can

"All right, Jones, for your final Ph.D. oral exam we have a single question: TRUE or FALSE...."

make them. That's the purpose of this and the next chapter, namely, to provide the sort of guidance that will permit you to avoid obvious errors in the construction of test items.

Obstacles to Good Item-Writing

Irrespective of whether teachers have decided on a selected- or constructed-response item format, there are still a number of silly mistakes that can be made as test items are written. Because silliness, once isolated, is a bit easier to avoid, let's consider five *general impediments to good item-writing:*

1. Unclear directions
2. Ambiguous statements
3. Unintended clues
4. Complicated syntax
5. Difficult vocabulary

Unclear directions. All of the foregoing list of impediments are particularly pertinent to classroom tests. For openers, take the matter of writing directions that explain to

Educational Leaders
Look at Assessment

What about Teachers' Judgments?

Whenever the topic of teacher assessment of student achievement comes up, I think of a particular faculty meeting where we were discussing instructional improvement plans and the need for supporting data.

Teachers of required subjects in our district enjoy the support of a sophisticated testing system. Data from this system is abundant! These teachers could consider, for example, the performance of students taking algebra at one school and compare this with students' performance levels from across the entire district. They could review the collective student performance in any given classroom in any given school and also identify any individual student's performance. This made the identification of areas needing to be addressed by instructional improvement plans rather easy in departments where the district-required testing occurred.

Teachers in the "non-tested" curriculum areas were unable to address the instructional-improvement task with the same volume of supportive data. I asked those individuals to participate in a little exercise. Their challenge was to consider the curriculum that they would teach in the next few weeks and identify the

Dr. Frederic W. Skoglund
Assistant Superintendent
Educational Services
Mesa Unified School District
Mesa, Arizona

concept(s) that *students would find most difficult*. Teachers from such departments as Art, Business, Music, and Physical Education were all able to quickly accomplish the task. We then discussed, as an entire faculty, our professional obligation to improve the effectiveness of our instruction in areas where students were experiencing difficulty. Instructional improvement plans were viewed in a different light after that meeting.

A high quality testing system is a great source of data *but so is the knowledge of an experienced teacher*. Even though such teacher-judgment measurement is statistically imperfect, the intuitive observations made by a dedicated and thoughtful teacher are often the very best method of assessing student achievement. ●

students how to go about responding to the items. All too often such directions are added belatedly, just before the test is put together in its final form. After all, the teacher who has been grinding out all of the test items will surely have a clear idea of how a student is supposed to respond. Unfortunately, that kind of knowledgeable teacher sometimes imputes too much insight to the student and thus writes test directions that are too sketchy. Test developers must assume that test-takers are a truly primitive lot. Accordingly, the test's directions should be developed with much care.

For instance, sometimes the directions for a set of matching items do not make it clear whether the student can use a response for more than one "match." If students think they can, but the teacher thought they couldn't, an obvious problem will result, not to mention lower-than-warranted test scores for the students. Directions should really be tried out in advance on a few students to make certain that these directions accurately communicate the teacher's intent. Writing test directions for very young children, say first-graders, is particularly difficult. There are the numerous ways in which little tots can evade our best efforts to constrain them. I have personally been outwitted by five-year-old children more than a few times as I've tried to assess those tiny squirmers. Ideally, the directions for a set of test items should be written prior to or at least during the preparation of the items. Last-minutery in the creation of test directions is a definite no-no.

Most classroom teachers, of course, will churn out oodles of tests during the course of an academic year. If a teacher relies a good deal on a particular sort of test item, for example, the quality of the directions for the items should be reviewed in early tests so that, if found wanting, the directions can be spruced up for future tests.

Ambiguous statements. Ambiguous writing is almost always to be avoided, unless one is a politician, a member of the diplomatic corps, or the contract negotiator for a teacher's union. In test items an ambiguous statement is particularly reprehensible because students may, as a consequence of that ambiguity, come up with an incorrect response even when, in reality, they know the correct answer. For example, consider the following true–false item, and note how the *faulty reference* of the relative pronoun renders the statement ambiguous.

An Ambiguous True–False Item

There is substantial research evidence that many teachers become hostile toward certain students because of their low self-concepts.

Suppose you were a student who had to provide a true or false response to this question. Your dilemma would stem from the fact that *their* can refer to the *teachers'* low self-concepts or the *students'* low self-concepts. Given the present form of the item, there's no way to tell whose low self-concepts are referred to by *because*. If, as a student, you were to get a continual stream of such ambiguous items, you can be pretty sure that your own self-concept would sink a little during the test.

The difficulty with the sort of faulty references commonly seen when teachers employ relative pronouns, such as *his*, *her*, and *their*, is that the teachers themselves have an abundantly clear idea *in their own heads* regarding who the pronoun's referent is. Unfortunately, the student is not privy to that information. A teacher will often fail to recognize such problems because, to the teacher, the pronoun's referent is obvious. Good item-writers will, however, remove *any* possibility of ambiguity from their items.

Unintended clues. A third obstacle to the creation of stellar test items arises when a teacher inadvertently tosses in clues that permit students to come up with correct answers to items they couldn't answer correctly without those unintended clues. If there are many of these unintended clues in a test, the test's quality will surely be impaired.

To illustrate, many inexperienced item writers of multiple-choice tests will make the correct answer twice as long as the other response alternatives. The testwise student will often opt for the longer answer in such a situation and, of course, will often be right.

Writers of true–false items often give away the correct response by adding the qualifier, such as *never* or *always*, to an item. Because most students realize there are very few absolutes in the world, the astute answer to such items is invariably "false."

Still other teachers provide unintended grammatical clues to the correct answer. A common item-writing error of this sort is seen in the following item in which the correct answer to a multiple-choice question is given away by the article *a*, which is the concluding word in the item's initial phrase.

A Grammatically Cued Multiple-Choice Test Item

The annual award received by a musical recording artist for outstandingly successful recordings is called a

a. Oscar
b. Emmy
c. Obie
d. Grammy

Because three of the response options are words that start with vowels, and one should use the article *an* (not *a*) immediately before such words, the choice *Grammy* stands out. Because teachers themselves will often be unable to spot unintended clues that they might leave in items, it is particularly helpful to have another teacher review one's items with the charge to look for fairly blatant give-away elements in the items.

Complicated syntax. A fourth obstacle to effective item-writing occurs when items are written that incorporate convoluted syntax. Use of many clauses is to be avoided. Writers such as James Joyce or Thomas Hardy are known for their labyrinthine sentence structures. Some of their clause-laden meanderings extend almost forever. Joyce and Hardy would probably have made poor item-writers. Note the following item, and you'll see how the use of introductory clauses, appositive clauses, and gratuitously tossed-in clauses can make the task of the test-taker unbelievably difficult.

A True-False Item with Snarled Syntax

Having slain Hector, the feared Trojan warrior, Achilles, who was considered by all to be the most valiant of the Greeks, was destined to perish because of a flaw which, incurred while he was being immersed in the River Styx as an infant, he possessed.

If you find teachers writing items such as the preceding (the item happens to be *true*), try to get them to take a workshop in "lean sentence structure." If a teacher's sentences contain so many *whos* and *whiches* that they resemble an Annual Pronoun Convention, then strike a blow for simplicity. Many students won't be able to wade through such syntactical gyrations.

Difficult vocabulary. Anyone, given the inclination and a copy of the *Oxford English Dictionary*, can write sentences with words that others can't understand. Whereas such a writing style may enhance a neurotic writer's self-esteem, it has no place in the preparation of educational test items.

The use of polysyllabic terminology in test items is particularly reprehensible because it does not penalize students evenhandedly. In dealing with such items, students get a break if they come from highly verbal families in which dinnertime conversations seem sustained by a thesaurus. Students from less verbal environments will surely stumble over exotic terms. The use of hypersophisticated vocabulary, then, isn't merely confusing; it's also unfair. This kind of unfairness, of course, was the focus of my Chapter 6 treatment of absence-of-bias.

In review, I have briefly considered five general obstacles to good item-writing that, distressingly, pop up in educational tests all too frequently. Whether the items are of a selected-response or constructed-response sort, these five flaws should be avoided.

Let's turn now to the first of the three types of selected-response items to be treated in this chapter, that is, the *binary-choice item*.

Binary-Choice Items

Binary-Choice Items

Test items requiring students to choose from only two options.

A *binary-choice item* provides only two responses and directs the students to select one. The most common form of binary-choice item is the true–false test, but this item category also includes any kind of item in which the student is given a statement or question, then asked to respond yes–no, right–wrong, agree–disagree, and so on. When educators are working with any subject matter that breaks down into two discrete categories, they can also employ binary-choice items by presenting several examples of two categories, then asking the student to go through each example and decide whether it is logical or illogical, animate or inanimate, and so on.

Without a doubt, the most common use of binary-choice items is to measure a student's ability to identify the correctness of factual statements or definitions. The following are some examples of typical binary-choice items.

Directions: Read each of the following statements and, if the statement is true, place a T before it; if the statement is false, place an F before it.

___ 1. During the 1990s we saw a decline in U.S. space exploration activity.
___ 2. A peace treaty between Egypt and Israel was ratified by both nations in 1979.
___ 3. President Bill Clinton was often referred to as "The Comeback Kid" because of his rapid-fire ability to supply verbal retorts.

Directions: Circle the Y (for *Yes*) or the N (for *No*) to indicate whether the following statements accurately describe you.

Y N 1. I would rather play with my friends than go to school.
Y N 2. I never try to be tardy to class.
Y N 3. I become restless as the school day wears on.

"You have your choice of weapons, sir: pistols, swords, or meringue pies!"

AN EARLY AMERICAN SELECTED-RESPONSE TEST

Dividends and Deficits

Due to the typical brevity of binary-choice items, many people believe that such items, particularly of the true–false variety, can be cranked out almost mindlessly. There are thousands of true–false items being used this very minute that support such a contention. To create a good true–false item is not a simple task, however, and the most widespread weakness in these items is that insufficient attention is given to their development.

Because binary-choice items can be written so tersely, it is possible to cover a wide content range with them. Typically, this is the most frequently cited advantage for such items. Well, perhaps it is simple to generate any kind of binary-choice item, but to create a *good* item of this type takes a considerable amount of effort and time.

Perhaps the overriding weakness of the binary-choice item is the ease with which students can guess the correct answer. By chance alone, a student who knows nothing about an exam ought to be able to get a 50 percent correct score. Given the inadvertent clues that sometimes are found in most sets of test items, the skillful guesser's score rises even higher. There really isn't a good way of circumventing this deficiency, so the user of binary-choice items will have to recognize that even a middle ability gorilla who is able to choose between two options ought to get about half the items right.

It should be pointed out, however, that even if "random guessing" (as opposed to "informed guessing") is taking place, its influence on test scores diminishes as the length of the test increases. Whereas the random guesser has a 50 percent chance of getting a single true–false item correct, the chance of getting a perfect score on a five-item test shrinks to 3 percent and on a ten–item test to one-tenth of one percent. Reasonably long true–false tests of, say, 100 items are capable of securing reliability coefficients in the .85 to .95 range, thus suggesting that there's something being measured more consistently than the student's luck.

When true–false items are used, they often encourage students to engage in verbatim memorization of statements from the text or teachers' remarks. Most teachers, of course, do not wish to promote such memorization behavior. Even so, by lifting statements from the text or adroitly inserting a *not* into a textbook's positive statement, teachers obviously set conditions in which rote memorization pays off.

Another difficulty with the true–false item is that it presents as its options two extremes that rarely match up with the real world. In the real world, you'll usually find that things are *relatively* true or *relatively* false. In the true–false item there is no place for gradations of truth or falsity. How many times have sophisticated test-takers yearned for response options such as "somewhat true" or "pretty largely false."

Some teachers have tried to salvage the true–false item by modifying it so that, for instance, a student is supposed to correct a false statement. Of course, such modifications move this item partially into the constructed-response category and thus create the problems of objectivity in scoring that accompany such items. Frankly, most of these makeshift remedies fail to ameliorate the inherent weaknesses of the true–false item.

However, lest you think that the measurement community in its entirety finds true–false items repugnant, it should be noted that Robert L. Ebel, one of educational measurement's recognized leaders, was a stalwart proponent of the true–false item. Ebel mounted a powerful argument supporting the virtues of the true–false item.

The basis of Ebel's advocacy of true–false items is summarized in the following four propositions that he defended with verve:

1. The essence of educational achievement is the command of useful verbal knowledge.
2. All verbal knowledge can be expressed in propositions.
3. A proposition is any sentence that can be said to be true or false.
4. The extent of students' command of a particular area of knowledge is indicated by their success in judging the truth or falsity of propositions related to it.

There is little doubt that if teachers are truly attentive to the potential deficits of binary-choice items, such as those mentioned in the preceding paragraphs, reasonably decent items of this sort can be generated. One place where the astute test-maker should employ them is in situations in which the subject-matter content being tested breaks down naturally into two categories. For instance, if a chemistry teacher is testing whether students can distinguish between organic and inorganic compounds, a binary-choice test format may be the only sensible one to employ. If so, however, the teacher should be particularly careful not to provide unintended clues to the correct answer, because coping with student guessing already presents a serious problem.

Multiple binary-choice items. A variation of binary-choice items is the *multiple binary-choice item* in which a cluster of items is presented to students requiring a binary response to *each* of the items in the cluster. Usually, but not always, the items are related to an initial statement or set of statements. Multiple binary-choice items are often formatted so that they look somewhat like traditional multiple-choice tests. But in a multiple-choice test, the student must choose one answer from several options. In a multiple binary-choice test, the student must make a response for each statement in the cluster. Presented below is an example of a multiple binary-choice item.

Imagine that a dozen of your advanced students completed a 10-item Right–Wrong quiz and earned the following number-correct scores:

$$5, 6, 7, 7, 7, 7, 8, 8, 8, 8, 9, 10$$

Now, indicate whether each of the following four statements is true or false:

5. The range of the students' scores is 5.0. (True)
6. The mode for the set of scores is 8.0. (False)
7. The median for your students' scores is 7.5. (True)
8. The median is different than the mean. (False)

Multiple Binary-Choice Items

Test items presenting a group of binary-choice items linked to a single, usually somewhat lengthy stimulus.

David Frisbie (1992) reviewed the available research regarding such items and concluded that multiple binary-choice items are (1) highly efficient for gathering student achievement data, (2) more reliable than other selected-response items, (3) able to measure the same skills and abilities as multiple-choice items dealing with comparable content, (4) a bit more difficult for students than multiple-choice tests, and (5) perceived by students to be more difficult but more efficient than multiple-choice items. When teachers construct multiple binary-choice items, they must be attentive to all of the usual considerations in writing regular binary-choice items.

In support of multiple binary-choice items, I have found them useful in the fairly lengthy midterm and final examinations I employed for years at UCLA whenever I taught the course in educational measurement for which this book was chosen as a text. (I am particularly biased toward the virtues of textbooks that I write.) My exams provided brief fictional vignettes about measurement followed by five binary-choice items based on each vignette. Because the midterm examination consisted of fifty binary-choice items and the final examination consisted of 100 binary-choice items, I was confident that students could not "guess" their way to excellent examination performances. Well-constructed multiple binary-choice items, if there are enough of them, can prove a useful ally to classroom teachers.

Item-Writing Guidelines

The chief problems in creating binary-choice items are to avoid ambiguity and to formulate items that don't contain inadvertent clues. Adhering to the following guidelines will be of considerable value in dodging these deficiencies. These and other guidelines, incidentally, refer exclusively to items for *cognitive*, not *affective*, assessments. I'll deal with affective inventories in Chapter 13.

1. *Conceptualize binary-choice items in pairs, not singly.* If you recall that binary-choice items work best when two discrete categories are being sampled (such as *true* and *false*), it should be apparent that if there is a good statement to reflect one of the two categories, there is usually an opposite version of that statement reflecting the other category. For example, relying on some concepts treated in earlier chapters, the following pair of true–false items is presented.

True Version

As a test's reliability increases, the likelihood of the test's yielding valid inferences increases.

False Version

As a test's reliability increases, the likelihood of the test's yielding valid inferences decreases.

Unless a parallel but opposite version of a statement can be produced, the statement is usually not a good contender for a true–false item. Although only one of the two statements will actually be used on the test, the practice of conjuring up both versions, at least mentally, often helps teachers identify potential shortcomings in binary-choice items, particularly of the true–false variety.

2. *Phrase the item so that a superficial analysis by the student suggests a wrong answer.* If the test items are designed to test students, and not merely be give-away items, then one way to heighten the difficulty of the test is to phrase items in such a way that a casual reading of the statement will lead the student to the wrong answer. Note, for example, the following right–wrong item which, at first glance, sounds pretty commendable.

Right-Wrong

Because of the inherent diversity of human beings, most classroom teachers and instructional psychologists recommend an individually designed instructional sequence for each learner. (Wrong)

This statement really reeks of goodness, because of such heart-warming phrases as "the inherent diversity of human beings"; thus, students might be willing to bestow a hasty *right* on such an item. More careful analysis, however, suggests that most classroom teachers, particularly those who have been teaching for more than one week, would recognize the considerable impracticality of whipping up a truly individualized instructional sequence for each student. A more careful consideration of the statement, therefore, should indicate to a student that the winning answer is "wrong."

3. *Rarely use negative statements, and never use double negatives.* It is often difficult for students, particularly with true–false items, to agree that a negative depiction of a phenomenon is accurate. However, when a true–false statement contains a double negative, then matters really get perplexing. For instance, consider how you would respond to the two statements below if you were to encounter them as part of a true–false test on the history of South America:

Too Many Negatives

    T   F   In 1911 Hiram Bingham, who became a U.S. senator and governor of Connecticut, did not discover the lost Inca city, Machu Picchu, because of his considerable disinterest in antiquity.

Better

    T   F   In 1911 Hiram Bingham, who became a U.S. senator and governor of Connecticut, discovered the lost Inca city, Machu Picchu, because of his considerable interest in antiquity.

The initial phrasing of the question about Machu Picchu contains two negatives which, of course, cancel out each other. Some people like to pepper their tests with such double negatives. Well, although we can allow teachers a bit of literary license now and then (after all, the financial rewards of teaching aren't that super), we should permit them no such liberties when it comes to double negatives for true–false items. Moreover, triple negatives, obviously, are an abomination. For example, try this one:

True-False Negativity

None of Britain's recent prime ministers was unaware of the absence of sufficient energy resources in the British Isles themselves.

---

4. *Don't include two concepts in one statement.* When a teacher treats two ideas in a single statement, it is possible that the first idea is false, the second idea is false, or the relationship between the two ideas is false. Clearly, some students will have a tough time sorting out which of these situations is present. The previous Machu Picchu item illustrated this point. In the following statement, what should guide the student in coming up with an overall judgment about the statement's truth or falsity?

Educational Leaders
Look at Assessment

Matching Objectives and Items

In my opinion, there are few educational objectives that cannot be measured via a selected-response test. It is important to note that teachers must incorporate a variety of assessment tools in order to best facilitate learning. Teachers tend to use multiple-choice or binary-choice items because they can be machine-graded and take relatively less time to administer and evaluate than multi-formatted assessments.

As we have learned from the learning styles and brain research, it is important that students have the opportunity to learn and express themselves in a variety of ways. Selected-response test items are a significant and important part in the assessment process, but

Dr. James R. Kahrs
Principal
Gwinnett County Public Schools
Lithonia, Georgia

full reliance on one type of assessment is inappropriate. The most important criterion is that the assessment accurately reflect the educational objective and what is taught. ●

Weak

   T   F   Tournament badminton players use feathered shuttlecocks because goose feathers are more bulky than hummingbird feathers.

While both of the main ideas in the sentence are correct—that is, tournament badminton players do, indeed, use feathered shuttlecocks, and goose feathers are surely heftier than hummingbird feathers—it is the *because* that renders the statement false. The best idea is to avoid these kinds of complexities by sticking with a single idea per statement.

5. *Have an approximately equal number of items representing the two categories being tested.* If teachers are working with right–wrong, true–false, or animate–inanimate, they should try to provide items so that roughly half will represent one of the two categories. Some students have what is called a *response set* so that they tend to guess *true* more often than *false* or they'll guess *wrong* more often than *right*. So that such students will not be unduly penalized, teachers should avoid having a heavy proportion of items reflecting only one of the two categories being used. It is, incidentally, unwise to create *exactly* half the items of one sort and *exactly* half of another, because some test-wise students will then be aided as they try their way through the unknown items in the test.

If teachers are eager to get test items to discriminate among students, as would be the case if the teacher were hoping to make norm-referenced interpretations, then it is wise to employ somewhat more false than true statements in the test. A few researchers have identified what they call an *acquiescent response set* among students. The way the response set works is that if students have no certain knowledge of a statement's falsity, they are more willing to accept such an assertion as true. In practice, this means that, in cases of doubt, they'll tend to mark more false statements as true than true statements as false.

6. *Keep similar the length of items representing both categories being tested.* Teachers tend to make true statements longer, particularly in true–false tests, because of all the qualifiers that must be inserted to make such items indisputably true. Cunning students can, therefore, guess at *true* for a long item and *false* for a terse one. More generally, therefore, no matter what the two categories are, for example, acceptable–unacceptable, there should be no systematic length bias in favor of either of the two types of answers.

Matching Items

A *matching item* consists of two lists of words or phrases that require the student to match items in one list with the appropriate items in the second list. Items in the list for which a match is sought are referred to as *premises*, and items in the list from which selections are made are called *responses*. Typically, the student is directed to match items from the two lists according to a particular kind of association indicated in the test's directions. For example:

Directions. On the line to the left of each military conflict listed in *Column A*, write the letter of the U.S. president in *Column B* who was in office when that military conflict was concluded. Each name in *Column B* may be used no more than once.

Column A

___ 1. World War I
___ 2. World War II
___ 3. The Vietnam Involvement

Column B

a. Clinton
b. Johnson
c. Nixon
d. Reagan
e. Roosevelt
f. Truman

Because matching items, such as these, invariably call for the student to relate two things that have some factual or logical basis for association, this type of item can be applied in only a small number of situations.

The preceding example illustrates a common feature of well-constructed matching items. Note that the lists in each column are *homogeneous*, that is, all of the items at the left deal with different military conflicts, whereas all of the items on the right consist of names of U.S. chief executives. This type of homogeneity is desirable in such items because it contributes to the plausibility of all matching possibilities, hence minimizes the extent to which unknowledgeable students can guess correctly.

In addition, observe that there are more items in Column B than in Column A. This illustrates an *imperfect match*, a quality that increases the effectiveness of matching items because students who know most (but not all) of the pairs in the item cannot easily guess the last few on the basis of elimination.

Matching items are typically used for detecting the student's knowledge of simple association, such as the relationships between famous people and their accomplishments. Because of its brevity, the matching item is an efficient way of measuring one's knowledge of such associations.

Dividends and Deficits

The major advantage of a matching item is its compact form, thus making it possible to tap a good deal of information while taking up little testing space on a printed page. Such items can also be efficiently scored. As with true–false items, however, this kind of item can often promote a student's memorization of low-level factual information at the expense of higher-level cognitive skills. An additional advantage of such items is that they are relatively easy to construct (although not as simple as most people think). The main trick in generating a good matching item is to come up with two homogeneous sets of things to be associated. Because teachers should often crank out extra options to list in the response column, it is sometimes difficult to generate enough *plausible* responses.

Matching items, if well written, encourage students to cross-reference and thus integrate their knowledge because of the necessity to refer to the relationships among members of the listed responses and premises. On the other hand, matching items do not work well if teachers are trying to test unique ideas, because matching items need pools of related ideas.

The main weakness of the matching item is that it is restricted to assessment of mere associations, typically of a fairly factual sort. Such items are particularly susceptible to the inclusion of unintended clues that enhance the student's chances of guessing correctly. And, of course, if a student is successful on a test because of guesswork alone, there will be an invalid inference made about the student's status with respect to the assessment domain represented by the test.

Classroom teachers often find that they can profitably allocate a segment of their examinations to matching items because, in contrast to short-answer or essay items, matching items are relatively easy to score.

It is typically impossible to devise an *entire* test of matching items. Usually, therefore, you'll find teachers devoting only a part of an exam to such items. As indicated, the potential applications of matching items outside the classroom are few, but even so there are several rules that should be followed when employing this sort of assessment approach.

Matching Items

Test items requiring students to associate items from two lists as directed.

Premises

A matching item's listed elements (on the left) for which a match is sought.

Responses

A matching item's listed elements (on the right) from which matching selections are made.

Item-Writing Guidelines

The major considerations when creating matching items should be to set them up so the students can respond quickly, without confusion, and unabetted by clues that lead to correct guesses.

    1. *Use relatively brief lists, and place the shorter words or phrases at the right.* For the student, brief sets of premises and responses are much easier to work with than lengthy, apparently interminable lists. By the time that students have sorted through a lengthy list of responses, for instance, they may have forgotten the premise for which they were seeking a match. From the teacher's point of view, shorter lists make it easier to develop homogeneous sets of premises or responses.

    By placing the shorter words or phrases on the right, the student is encouraged to complete the matching item efficiently by reading the lengthier premises first and then scanning the response column until the correct answer is, hopefully, detected.

    2. *Employ homogeneous lists in a matching item.* As indicated earlier, in any matching item it is important to make sure that the set of premises is composed of similar sorts of elements. In the same way, the set of responses for any matching item should be homogeneous. For example, if the student is called on to match famous women and their accomplishments, then the list of accomplishments (because each accomplishment's description is sure to be lengthier) will be on the left and the list of woman's names on the right. All statements in the premise list should be descriptive of a particular woman's accomplishments. For example, none should simply list the birthdate of a woman in the response list. Similarly, only women's names should appear in the response list.

    The following is an example of a matching item that violates this guideline. Neither the set of premises nor responses is homogeneous. Note that it is impossible to come up with a cohesive description for either the list at the left or the one at the right. They are heterogeneous, not homogeneous, clusters.

Heterogeneous Lists

Directions. Match the letters of items in the list at the right with the phrases in the list at the left. Each letter may be used once, more than once, or not at all.

____ 1. Formerly ruled by czars	a. The Great Wall
____ 2. Site of the Valley of the Kings	b. America is discovered.
____ 3. The People's Republic of China	c. U.S.S.R.
____ 4. 1776	d. Great Britain
	e. Egypt
	f. A nation is created.

    Next is an example of a matching exercise that adheres to this guideline. Note that the list of premises consists exclusively of descriptions of former professional basketball players, whereas the list of responses includes only the names of former basketball players.

Homogeneous Lists

Directions. On the line at the left of each description, place the letter of the name of the professional basketball player who fits the description. Each player in the list at the right may be used only once.

Description

___ 1. A Los Angeles Laker guard from West Virginia know as "Zeke from Cabin Creek."

___ 2. A towering center who played college basketball at the U. of Kansas and once scored 100 points in a pro game.

___ 3. Having led the University of San Francisco to the NCAA championship, this 6'10" center dominated pro basketball for many years with the Boston Celtics.

___ 4. As one of Indiana's most famed high school players, this 6'5", all-star played for the University of Cincinnati before becoming what many consider to be one of the finest guards ever to play professional basketball.

Player

A. Elgin Baylor
B. Wilt Chamberlain
C. Michael Jordan
D. Oscar Robertson
E. Bill Russell
F. Jerry West

3. *Include more responses than premises.* To eliminate the likelihood that the student who knows most of the answers will be able to guess correctly at the last few responses, teachers should be sure to toss in a few extra response options. In the previous examples about U.S. presidents and basketball players, note that there are more responses than premises.

4. *List the responses in a logical order.* To avoid unconsciously giving the student extra clues, such as when some teachers unthinkingly list all the correct responses first and only toss in a few wrong answers at the end of the response list, teacher's should list the responses alphabetically or in some logical order for example, chronologically. The U.S. presidents and the basketball players in the previous examples were listed alphabetically.

5. *Describe the basis for matching and the number of times a response may be used.* In the directions at the beginning of a matching item, teachers should set forth in clear language just what the student should use as the basis for attempting to match responses to premises. Also, teachers should indicate whether a response can be used once, more than once, or not at all. The phrase, "Each name on the list at the right may be used once, more than once, or never," is commonly employed. Such directions, as with several of my other guidelines, reduce the likelihood that the wily student will be able to outguess the wily teacher.

6. If possible, *place all premises and responses for a matching item on a single page.* Merely to make students' responses to an item more efficient and to avoid the noisy flap of oft-flipped pages, it is sensible to put all of the premises and responses for a matching item on one page.

Multiple-Choice Items

Multiple-Choice Items

Test items requiring students to choose a response from three or more options.

Without a doubt, one of the most popular forms of test item is the *multiple-choice item*. As the most widely used selected-response type of item, it is applicable to a number of different testing situations. It can be used to assess mere recall of factual knowledge, really powerful sorts of intellectual skills, or significant attitudinal dispositions. The most common kind of multiple-choice item presents the student with a question along with four or five possible answers, from which one is to be selected. Nevertheless, the stimuli to which the student makes responses need not be merely verbal nor, for the matter, simple. Educators can measure truly sophisticated sorts of student-response options if they are clever enough.

The initial part of a multiple-choice item will typically be a question or an incomplete statement. This section of the item is known as the *stem*. The stem could, of course, be a map, an illustration, a graph, or some other sort of printed or audio presentation. In essence, it is the stimulus to which the student makes a response. The possible answers are referred to as *alternatives*. In the set of alternatives there are several wrong answers and at least one correct answer. The wrong answers are called *distractors* because it is their mission in life to distract the unknowledgeable or unskilled student from too readily guessing the right answer.

Item-Stem

The stimulus segment of a multiple-choice test item.

Test-makers also have a choice between the *direct-question* and the *incomplete-statement* format for multiple choice items. Usually the direct question is preferable when used with younger students but the incomplete-statement form is more concise. It is best to employ the direct-question format unless the item-writer can maintain the stem's clarity while effecting a substantial shortening of the stem. Both of these formats are illustrated next. At the same time, an example is given of a *best-answer* and *correct-answer* type of multiple-choice item.

Direct-Question Form (best-answer approach)

Which state is generally thought to have the most effective state-operated environmental protection agency?
a. Wyoming
b. Pennsylvania
c. Ohio
d. Montana

Incomplete-Statement Form (correct-answer approach)

The capital of Florida is
a. Miami
b. Tallahassee
c. Tampa
d. Fort Lauderdale

**Item
Alternatives**

The answer options
in a multiple-choice
test item.

Observe that the top example calls for the student to select the best of the four alternatives, whereas the bottom example asks for the one correct answer. There are many kinds of situations for which more than a single correct answer exists. There may be several correct answers, but one of them is the best—that is, the *most* correct—answer. The alternatives for a multiple-choice test item can be built so as to incorporate these relative degrees of correctness. This is one of the most appealing features of the multiple-choice item because it can call for the student to detect subtle gradations in the quality of contending alternatives.

There is another reason to favor the *best-answer* approach over the *correct-answer* model. It is often difficult for the teacher to come up with a correct-answer alternative so precisely phrased that all authorities will concur with its correctness. It is much easier to build alternatives, one of which will, in the view of all acknowledged experts, be better than the other alternatives.

Dividends and Deficits

One virtue of the multiple-choice item is its considerable flexibility. It can be applied to the assessment of many different sorts of cognitive and affective outcomes. As a selected-response type of item, it can be objectively scored, thus leading to tests with greater reliability and ease of scoring. For instance, if you compare a multiple-choice item with even a short-answer type of constructed-response item, you will see that the multiple-choice form leads to far simpler and more consistent scoring. Because students often can't figure out what the teacher is searching for in a short-answer item, they may come up with all sorts of exotic responses. In the multiple-choice item, the response options are circumscribed.

Ambiguous Short-Answer Item

Recent research suggests that political success is most often due to _____

Unambiguous Multiple-Choice Item

Recent research suggests that political success is most often due to
a. the candidate's charisma
b. financial resources of the candidate
c. the parental training of the candidate
d. the whims of the electorate

Another advantage of multiple-choice items, particularly over binary-choice items, is that the increased alternatives make it more difficult for students to guess the correct answer, thereby increasing the reliability of each item and its contribution to an assessment-based inference about students' status.

From an instructional perspective, there is yet another plus for multiple-choice items. Because there are several alternatives, it is possible to build in distractors that reflect particular kinds of wrong answers, thereby allowing a teacher to use students' item responses diagnostically by spotting the categories of incorrect responses that students make. Teachers can then follow up with additional instruction based on the most common sorts of errors made by an individual student or a group of students.

Multiple-choice items are also relatively unaffected by students' *response sets*—tendencies on the part of students to respond in particular ways, such as when students favor "true" responses in true–false tests. It is possible, of course, that somewhat strange students may display response sets toward the choice of certain letters (choice *b*, for instance). Fortunately, few of these students exist.

A major weakness of multiple-choice items is that, when a series of alternatives is presented to students, they can often *recognize* a correct answer that, without assistance, they could never *construct*.

An additional weakness, one shared by all selected-response items, is that the student has no opportunity to synthesize thoughts, write out creative solutions, and so on. Another weakness, encountered particularly by beginning teachers, is that it is sometimes difficult to generate a sufficiently large set of plausible distractors. Thus, a beginner's multiple-choice item sometimes looks as much too obvious as the following example.

Undemanding Distractors

Mickey Mouse's two nephews are

a. Huey, Dewey, and Louie
b. Clarabelle Cow
c. Morty and Ferdy
d. Abbott and Costello

Any genuine devotee of Mickey Mouse would know that Morty and Ferdy are, although among the least honored of the Disney mice-people, Mickey's legitimate nephews. The other distractors, on all sorts of counts, are obviously wrong.

Item-Writing Guidelines

Because of the popularity of multiple-choice items, there are more guidelines for their creation than for any other type of selected- or constructed-response item. Here are the most important of these rules, illustrated when necessary.

1. *The stem should present a self-contained question or problem.* The student should be able to read the stem, discern what the question or problem is, then go about selecting the correct answer from the alternatives. A badly constructed multiple-choice item sometimes presents only a word or phrase in the stem, forcing the student to read through all of the alternatives before figuring out what the item is really about. To avoid this weakness, the teacher ought to be confident that the item's stem, framed either as a direct question or as an incomplete statement, is meaningful in itself. Some teachers check to see if an item stem is self-contained by attempting to read it without any of its alternatives, then seeing if it is complete enough to serve as a short-answer item. If so, the stem is usually sufficiently complete. Consider the following two examples, and note that the top item does, in fact, include a self-contained stem. The bottom item's stem is essentially meaningless. Observe also that the top item is a *best-answer*, rather than a *correct-answer*, item.

Praiseworthy

President Franklin Roosevelt's most significant domestic accomplishment during his presidential years was
a. terminating the Great Depression.
b. creating the CCC.
c. unifying the Democratic Party.
d. rotating his vice-presidents.

Reprehensible

President Franklin Roosevelt
a. lived for some years after the death of his wife, Eleanor.
b. was originally governor of California before becoming president.
c. was a swimmer in the Olympic Games prior to becoming a politician.
d. died in office during World War II.

---

2. *The stem should contain as much of the item's content as possible.* Multiple-choice items should be written so that the student can quickly scan the alternatives after considering the stem. All alternatives ought to be pithy, even though some will contain the wrong pith. If, however, teachers load the alternatives with many words, rapid scanning is obviously impossible. This rule cannot always be followed, because in order to assess certain kinds of learning outcomes, the teacher may have to set up a series of lengthy alternatives. However, if it is not imperative to create lengthy alternatives, teachers should stuff an item's stem with most of the item's relevant content.

3. *If possible, avoid negatively stated stems.* The problem with negatively formulated stems is that such phrasing can confuse students who, if the stem were phrased positively, would readily choose the correct alternative. Most of the time, with a little brain bending, a teacher can come up with a way to transform a negatively stated item into its positive counterpart. In the following example, you'll see two items that attempt to assess the same knowledge. The top item will surely confuse those students who fail to note the *not* in the item. The bottom item would only be confusing to students who think the Mississippi River is in New Jersey.

Crummy

Which one of the following cities is not located in a state west of the Mississippi River?
a. Los Angeles
b. Cleveland
c. Denver
d. Reno

Yummy

Which one of the following cities is located in a state east of the Mississippi River?
a. Los Angeles
b. Cleveland
c. Denver
d. Reno

Incidentally, notice that both of the items in the example are *correct-answer* versions of multiple-choice items.

However, there are some situations in which teachers might be interested in having the student spot something that should *not* be done. For example, suppose the teacher was constructing a test of a student's ability to supply first-aid assistance to heart attack victims. Perhaps the teacher wants to be sure that the students would *not* make any serious error that would jeopardize the victim's survival until more competent medical assistance arrived. In such cases, the teacher might wish to list sets of alternative actions, some of which should never be taken. For these kinds of situations it is quite acceptable to use negatively framed stems, but the teacher should call the students' attention to the negative formulation by capitalizing, underscoring, or otherwise dramatizing the *not* or *never*.

4. *Be sure that only one alternative represents the correct or best answer.* Teachers will sometimes erroneously write an item that contains two or even more correct answers. Most experienced teachers who write their own multiple-choice tests have experienced numerous postexam confrontations as their more able students do battle over whether the teacher's scoring key is correct. Care must be taken not to include more than one right answer. This can be done sometimes by having colleagues or a supersmart student review all alternatives carefully in a draft version of the test.

Dismal

Which of the following U.S. presidents is regarded as the Democrat who introduced the greatest number of domestic *social improvement* programs?
a. Johnson
b. Clinton
c. Reagan
d. F. Roosevelt

> *Delightful*
>
> Which of the following U.S. presidents is regarded as the Democrat who introduced the greatest number of domestic *social improvement* programs?
> a. Johnson
> b. Ford
> c. Nixon
> d. Reagan

In the preceding two items we see that one could reasonably argue whether Lyndon Johnson or Franklin Roosevelt had introduced the greatest number of domestic social improvement programs. In the second version of the item, by replacing Clinton with Gerald Ford and replacing Roosevelt with Richard Nixon in the second version of the item, the choice of Johnson becomes less debatable.

Sometimes a teacher, vexed with the fact that more than two alternatives to a multiple-choice item seem plausible, will alter the directions to the items so that more than one alternative may be chosen. The following is an example.

> *A Modified Binary-Choice Format*
>
> Which, if any, of the following geometric figures necessarily contains at least one right angle? You may choose one, more than one, or none of the alternatives.
> a. Parallelogram
> b. Rectangle
> c. Rhomboid
> d. Square

There is nothing wrong with using such items, but the teacher should recognize that a multiple-choice item is no longer being employed. What you now have is a multiple binary-choice item. The student is obliged to make an on–off decision for each alternative because there may be one, more than one, or no correct answers.

5. *Each alternative should be grammatically consistent with the item's stem.* If you can recall the early-in-the-chapter treatment of inadvertent clue-giving, you'll remember the poor item that had a stem ending in *a* and only one alternative (Grammy) that began with a consonant instead of a vowel. Clearly, such item-writing mistakes give away the correct answer to one and all. There are similar kinds of grammatical oversights, such as seen in the following example, in which the teacher unconsciously points students to the top item's correct answer.

Laughable

In the commercial publishing of a book, *galley proofs* are most often used
a. page proofs precede galley proofs for minor editing.
b. to help isolate minor defects prior to printing of page proofs.
c. they can be useful for major editing or rewriting.
d. publishers decide whether the book is worth publishing.

Laudable

In publishing a book, *galley proofs* are most often used to
a. aid in minor editing after page proofs.
b. isolate minor defects prior to page proofs.
c. assist in major editing or rewriting.
d. validate menus on large ships.

Notice that, in the top item's stem, the only alternative that meshes grammatically with the stem is choice *b*. Only a grammatical goon, therefore, would choose *a*, *c*, or *d*. In the bottom item you'll see that all alternatives are grammatically consonant with the stem, hence are eligible contenders to be the correct answer, at least on syntactical grounds.

6. *Avoid creating alternatives whose relative length provides an unintended clue.* Teachers want to write an item that helps them arrive at a valid inference about students' status with respect to a skill, knowledge, or affective domain. A multiple-choice item in which most of the alternatives are terse, but one resembles an epistle from St. Paul to the Romans, may incline the unknowledgeable student to go for the epistle-length alternative. After all, one gets so much more for one's choice. To counter this error, of course, all teachers need to do is write alternatives that are relatively similar in length. In the following examples, to shape up the out-of-balance alternative *d* in the top item, the teacher merely shortened it in the bottom item to coincide with the length of the other choices.

Reprehensible

Epistemology is that branch of philosophy dealing with
a. the nature of existence.
b. morality.
c. beauty.
d. the nature and origin of knowledge, that is, the manner in which human beings sense and process external stimuli in the form of knowledge.

Virtuous

Epistemology is that branch of philosophy dealing with
a. the nature of existence.
b. morality.
c. beauty.
d. the nature of knowledge.

Another type of inadvertent give-away clue in multiple-choice items occurs when teachers use a distinctive word in the item's stem, then employ a different form of that word in one of the alternatives. For example, suppose the teacher employed the word *appellation* in the stem, and then used the word *appellate* in one of the alternatives. Some students might opt for that alternative merely because of the verbal similarities. Try to avoid such verbal associations unless there is an important reason for using them.

7. *Make all alternatives plausible.* Even an item's distractors should appear alluring to the unknowledgeable student. Teachers should not write items so that there is only one obviously correct alternative and several *chump choices*. Each distractor's plausibility should be carefully considered. If any of them appear to be ludicrously wrong, they should be replaced.

In certain instances this rule is easier to dispense than to follow. It's often devilishly tough to come up with a large enough number of reasonable contenders as distractors. Sometimes this takes more time than creating a genuinely super stem. In the previous example about Mickey Mouse's nephews, you saw an extreme example of one reasonable alternative and *three* chump choices. With just a bit of massaging, the Morty and Ferdy choice could have been surrounded by more plausible distractors. Even "Forty and Merdy" would have been better than "Abbott and Costello."

Incidentally, although there hasn't been any previous discussion about the *number of alternatives*, now might be a good time. You'll notice that all of the multiple-choice examples used so far in the chapter have had four alternatives. Generally speaking, most measurement specialists recommend four or five alternatives because that number cuts down sufficiently on student guessing. If teachers go with only three alternatives, for instance, the student has a 33 percent chance of coming up a winner due to chance alone. If a teacher started using up to six or seven alternatives, however, the reading requirements for each item would begin to bulge. Consequently, if there are no compelling reasons to the contrary, a set of four or five alternatives per item would seem appropriate. I have used only four choices here in order to conserve trees (more likely, a sapling or two).

8. *Randomly use each alternative position for correct answers in approximately equal numbers.* I have previously described students' response sets, such as tending to mark all doubtful true–false items as true. Well, teachers have their item-writing response sets also. If all the four-alternative, multiple-choice items ever written on earth were assembled into a gigantic examination, what alternative do you suppose would be used most often for the correct answer. Would it be *a*, *b*, *c*, or *d*? You'd go to the head of the test-construction class if you chose *c*.

Teachers, even seasoned ones, being for the most part a fairly normal lot, are loath to give away the right answer too soon, and thus tend to avoid choices *a* or *b*. Yet they fear designating the last answer—that is, *d*—as the correct choice too often. Consequently, if you're ever faced with a life-or-death multiple-choice test and must guess wildly, go with choice *c*.

To avoid this weakness, of course, teachers merely need to set up the correct answers so that they will bounce around among the alternative positions roughly the same number of times. It's easy to count the number of times that, in a given test, each of the alternatives has been used for the correct answer. If you've overbooked on any answer option, do some letter-switching. In other words, simply spread the wealth.

9. *Unless important, avoid alternatives such as "none of the above" or "all of the above."* In many instances, teachers employ phrases such as "none of the above" for their multiple-choice items because they've run out of ideas for plausible distractors and want to create a final option. Although there are some situations in which a "none of the above" response works suitably, the *"all of the above" option is never appropriate.*

A major problem with the "all of the above" alternative is that a student may read alternative *a*, recognize that it is correct, mark the answer sheet, and never consider choices *b, c,* or *d.* Other students who realize that two of the alternatives are correct will, even without knowing anything about the third alternative, naturally choose the "all of the above" alternative. Both sorts of problems can be avoided by eliminating the "all of the above" response as an option.

When teachers rely on "none of the above" as an alternative, they are forcing the item into a correct-answer rather than best-answer form, because if teachers ask the student to identify a best answer of several rather poor alternatives, it's still possible to pick the best among poor choices. Consider the voter's dilemma in many elections!

A correct-answer rather than best-answer structure, of course, robs teachers of the possibility of creating alternatives with gradations of correctness. And that is definitely one of the most appealing features of the multiple-choice item.

Nevertheless, there may be significant sorts of outcomes that can be conceptualized in such a way that the "none of the above" response forces the student to consider the item's other alternatives more carefully. Use of the "none of the above" alternative makes a test more difficult than when it is not used. This occurs because the "none of the above" option creates the possibility that there may be no correct answer among the other alternatives. In such cases it would seem more suitable to use the "none of the above" response as a fifth choice in a five-alternative, multiple-choice item. Be sure to call the student's attention to the possibility that none of the initial alternatives may be correct and that, in such instances, the "none of the above" option should be selected.

A Really Rotten Item

A cure for tension headaches is
a. aspirin
b. codeine
c. relaxation
d. none of the above
e. all of the above

The preceding item is a genuine loser on several counts. First, it violates our ninth guideline by using *both* a "none of the above" and an "all of the above" response. Second, although the teacher apparently wanted choice *e* to be the correct answer, because *a, b,* and *c* can all reduce tension headaches, when the student chooses *e*, that also includes choice *d.* Because choice *d* (none of the above) negates the correctness of *a, b,* and *c*, the student is in trouble city. The item is, as indicated, one that should be shipped to the nearest compost heap.

The Allure of Multiple-Choice Items

Because multiple-choice items are employed so prevalently in teacher-made and commercially developed tests, many beginning teachers gravitate immediately to this form of testing. As indicated before, the multiple-choice item is loaded with advantages. It's versatile, objectively scoreable, and not too subject to guessing. Besides that, because it has its separate alternatives, teachers can try out an item, gather empirical data regarding how each of its components works, and spruce the item up until it's an object for assessment adoration.

However, there *are* other legitimate forms of testing, some involving selected responses and some involving constructed responses. Teachers dare not forget these other approaches. Besides that, depending on what teachers are trying to measure, they can remold the classical multiple-choice format so that it better suits their purposes. For instance, teachers can create two-stage items involving both selected and constructed responses (in which students must, for example, choose an answer, then improve it). In other words, beware of the multiple-choice item's seductive appeal. Classroom teachers and school administrators need other weapons to do battle effectively with the numerous assessment problems they face.

There is no doubt that, of the selected-response options you've been considering, the multiple-choice item has some particularly appealing features and few of the drawbacks associated with binary-choice and matching items. In Chapter 11 you will see how to shape up selected-response test items once they have been born. However, even though there are dandy empirical schemes for improving the quality of selected-response test items, by adhering to the guidelines given here, teachers will be more apt to produce test items that need only a bandaid, not invasive surgery.

Chapter Wrap-Up

Let's close out the chapter, as usual, with my effort to provide glib answers to the chapter's five guiding questions. Because, for three of those guiding questions, there's a substantial chunk of content, I'll probably have trouble being simultaneously succinct and accurate. You can decide if the summary sacrifices accuracy or succinctness. You can even see if my summary is pithy.

● What is the difference between selected-response and constructed-response test items?

Sometimes, thankfully, the nature of a phrase makes it transparently clear what the phrase means. And that's the case with respect to selected-response and constructed-response test items. When an assessment instrument uses a selected-response test item, students must select their answers from the response options provided to them. When an assessment uses a constructed-response test item, the student must generate a response rather than choosing it from options. All test items are either selected-response or constructed-response in nature.

- ## Do certain weaknesses in item-writing apply to all test items?

  Regardless of whether students select or construct their responses to test items, there are weaknesses in item construction that should be avoided. In the chapter, the following five obstacles to item writing were identified: (1) unclear directions, (2) ambiguous statements, (3) unintended clues, (4) complicated syntax, and (5) difficult vocabulary.

- ## What are the important features of binary-choice items?

  Binary-choice test items, the most common of which is the true–false item, give students only two options between which to choose. Binary-choice items, because of their brevity, can be used to cover a wide range of content. The most serious drawback of binary choice items is *not* that the student can guess a correct answer, because the inclusion of a reasonable number of binary-choice items in a test reduces the guessing factor appreciably. Rather, the most serious drawback of binary-choice items is that, if not developed with care, such items can foster mere memorization on the part of students. A useful variation of this item type is the multiple binary-choice item in which several binary-choice items are based on a single, usually more lengthy, set of stimulus materials.

  The chapter's item-writing guidelines for binary-choice items were, in abbreviated form, the following: (1) conceptualize items in pairs, (2) make students' superficial analyses lead to incorrect answers, (3) avoid negative statements, (4) have only one concept per item, (5) use equal content representing the two categories, and (6) keep the length of each category's items similar.

- ## What are the important features of matching items?

  A matching item presents two different lists to students, then asks the student to match appropriate items from the two lists. As with binary-choice items, matching items can assess a substantial amount of information because of their compact form. The downside of this item type is that it typically taps only the low-level associations that are required when someone must match content from two lists.

  In abbreviated form, the chapter's item-writing guidelines for matching items were these: (1) use short lists and place the shorter words or phrases at the right; (2) make sure each list contains homogeneous content; (3) use more responses, listed on the right, than premises, listed on the left; (4) list responses in logical order; (5) describe the basis for matching and the number of times a response can be used; and (6) place all premises and responses on a single page.

- ## What are the important features of multiple-choice items?

  Multiple-choice items commence with a question or incomplete statement called the stem, then present three or more options from which students are to choose either the correct answer or the best answer. A major advantage of the multiple-choice item is its considerable flexibility for use in measuring students' status with respect to both cognitive and affective assessment domains. Especially when using a best-answer form of this item type, it is possible to incorporate in a test item the requirement that students make subtle distinctions in determining the relative correctness of several answer options.

  In brief, the chapter's 9-item-writing guidelines for multiple-choice items were the following: (1) the stem should be self-contained, (2) the stem should contain most of an item's content, (3) negatively stated stems should be avoided, (4) only one option should be the correct or best answer, (5) all alternatives should be grammatically consistent with the stem, (6) alternatives should be similar in length, (7) all alternatives should be plausible, (8) correct answers should be divided about equally among alternatives, and (9) "all of the above" should never be used while "none of the above" should be used only to increase an item's difficulty.

Practice Exercises

Items of the type discussed throughout the chapter are presented here. Each item will contain at least one deliberate violation of the item-writer's guidelines associated with that type of item. The items may also display one of the five general obstacles to good item writing presented early in the chapter.

Before undertaking these practice exercises, spend a moment or two reviewing all of the item-writing guidelines and the five obstacles. Then see if you can spot the most salient flaws in the following items.

1. *True or False:* America's literary circles became preoccupied with Adolf Hitler in the 1960s as a direct result of the 1960 publication of *The Rise and Fall of the Third Reich* by Robert Payne.

   Flaw(s)? _____

2. *Right or Wrong:* Current rules of etiquette suggest that it is not considered improper for a man to avoid helping a woman into an automobile.

   Flaw(s)? _____

3. *Matching:* Match the invention on the left with the inventor on the right.
   ___ 1. Telephone   a. Bell
   ___ 2. Electric light bulb   b. Edison
   ___ 3. Phonograph   c. Franklin
   ___ 4. Waxed paper   d. Marconi

   Flaw(s)? _____

4. *Multiple Choice:* Good writing is
   (a) predicated on the eschewing of obfuscatory verbiage.
   (b) the culmination of a euphoric and ethereal procreation.
   (c) the residue of relentless, onerous effort.
   (d) all of the above.

   Flaws(s)? _____

5. *Multiple-Choice:* One of the chief ingredients in the Greek dish, moussaka is an
   (a) eggplant.
   (b) carrot.
   (c) melon.
   (d) brussels sprout.

   Flaws(s)? _____

Answers to Practice Exercises

1. This binary-choice item violates guideline four, "Don't include two concepts in one statement." Not only are there two ideas and a statement of causality present, but the volume referred to was authored by William L. Shirer. Robert Payne wrote *The Life and Death of Adolf Hitler* in 1975. It is this sort of trivial concern

with facts and details that often spurs criticisms of true–false items.

2. This binary-choice item violates guideline three about the inclusion of double negatives. There are so many negatives in the practice item that a student's head would swim. Phrasing it negatively, it is unlikely that the

student's head would remain in a nonswimming state.

3. This matching item has two chief problems. First, it violates guideline three because there are not more responses than premises. Second, it fails to describe the basis for matching (guideline five), so that the unsuspecting student will fail to realize that Edison invented everything except the telephone.

4. There are several problems with this multiple-choice item. For one thing, one of the five obstacles to good item-writing seems to be present, namely, the use of a difficult vocabulary. Many of the terms employed are far too obscure and could have been replaced with simpler and more comprehensible words. A second defect of the item is that it violates guideline one, which calls for the stem to be a self-contained question or problem. This stem isn't. The stem should also contain as much of the item's content as possible (guideline two). This stem doesn't. Besides that, there's a violation of guideline nine because we find an "all of the above" option. In sum, it's a pretty putrid item.

5. This multiple-choice item violates guideline five, which calls for each alternative to be grammatically consistent with the item's stem. Of the four alternatives, only *eggplant* meshes with the article *an*.

DISCUSSION QUESTIONS

1. If you were trying to present the *relative* advantages of binary-choice, multiple-choice, and matching items to a group of elementary school teachers, how would you go about it? What would the major points of your presentation be?
2. How would you contrast the merits of selected- *versus* constructed-response test items?
3. Which of the three types of selected-response test items treated in the chapter would take the most time and effort to produce?
4. Are any of the three types of selected-response items more appropriate for the needs of classroom teachers? Why?
5. Drawing on your own experience, how skilled do you think most classroom teachers are in constructing selected-response test items? Why do you think that is so?

SUGGESTIONS FOR ADDITIONAL READING

Carey, Lou M. *Measuring and Evaluating School Learning.* Boston: Allyn & Bacon, 1988.

Cronbach, L. J. *Essentials of Psychological Testing* (4th ed.). New York: Harper & Row, 1984.

Cunningham, George K. *Educational and Psychological Measurement.* New York: Macmillan, 1986.

Downing, Steven M., and Thomas M. Haladyna. "Test Item Development: Validity Evidence from Quality Assurance Procedures." *Applied Measurement in Education, 10,* 1 (1997): 61–82.

Frisbie, David A. "The Multiple True–False Format: A Status Review." *Educational Measurement: Issues and Practice, 11,* 4 (Winter 1992): 21–26.

Gay, L. R. *Educational Evaluation and Measurement: Competencies for Analysis and Application* (2nd ed.). Columbus, OH: Charles E. Merrill, 1985.

Gronlund, Norman E. *Measurement and Evaluation in Teaching* (5th ed.). New York: Macmillan, 1985.

Mehrens, William A., and Irvin J. Lehmann. *Using Standardized Tests in Education.* New York: Longman, 1987.

National Center on Education and the Economy and the University of Pittsburgh. *Performance Standards, Volume 1: Elementary School.* Washington, DC: Authors, 1997.

National Center on Education and the Economy and the University of Pittsburgh. *Performance Standards, Volume 2: Middle School.* Washington, DC: Authors, 1997.

National Center on Education and the Economy and the University of Pittsburgh. *Performance Standards, Volume 3: High School.* Washington, DC: Authors, 1997.

Roid, G. H., and T. M. Haladyna. *A Technology for Test-Item Writing.* New York: Academic Press, 1982.

Schrock, T. J., and D. J. Mueller. "Effects of Violating Three Multiple-Choice Item-Construction Principles." *Journal of Educational Research*, 75, 5 (1982): 314–318.

Shepard, Lorrie, Sharon Lynn Kagan, and Emily Wurtz (Eds.). *Principles and Recommendations for Early Childhood Assessments.* Washington, DC: The National Education Goals Panel, February 1998.

AND FOR THOSE WHO TIRE OF READING

Phillips, S. E. "Legal Corner: Calculator Accommodations." *National Council on Measurement in Education*, 6, 1 (January 1998): 2.

Popham, W. James. *Assessing Mathematics Learning* (Videotape #STVT-26). Los Angeles: IOX Assessment Associates.

Popham, W. James. *Creating Challenging Classroom Tests: When Students SELECT Their Answers* (Videotape #ETVT-23). Los Angeles: IOX Assessment Associates.

Wiggins, Grant, and Richard Stiggins. "Tape 1—Traditional Tests" (Videotape: Stock #614237S62) in *Redesigning Assessment Series*. Alexandria, VA: Association for Supervision and Curriculum Development, 1992.

ENDNOTE

1. Robert L. Ebel. *Essentials of Educational Measurement*, 3rd ed. (Englewood Cliffs, NJ: Prentice-Hall, 1979), Chap. 7.

Constructed-Response Items

- What are the relative merits of selected-response and constructed-response items?

- What are the important features of short-answer items?
  Dividends and Deficits
  Item-Writing Guidelines

- What are the important features of essay items?
  Item-Writing Guidelines
  Item-Scoring Guidelines

Constructed response tests are those that call for the student to *produce* something instead of merely choosing between two or more alternatives. There are many settings in which educators wish to know whether students can produce satisfactorily. In some of these settings, it makes no sense to rely on anything other than a constructed-response testing strategy.

In the most commonly cited instance of this sort, English teachers typically want their students to be able to prepare satisfactory written compositions, for instance, essays, personal letters, or business letters. In order to get a solid fix on whether a student can whip out an acceptable paragraph or two, the only truly sensible way of gauging that skill is to have the student actually author some paragraphs. Even if a teacher discovers by means of selected-response test items that the student knows all the rules of spelling, punctuation, and usage, there is no assurance, *on the basis of the selected-response test alone*, that the student can actually produce an acceptable paragraph.

Sometimes, a selected-response measurement strategy is recommended when it is believed that for some practical reason (such as cost) a constructed-response approach to assessment is not feasible. A selected-response test is used as a *proxy* for a constructed response, hoping that the student's performance on the selected-response test will serve as an acceptable *surrogate* for the constructed response. There are many instances in which this strategy works beautifully. Indeed, in some studies in which efforts have been made to verify the legitimacy of a proxy selected-response test, the correlation between individuals' scores on a constructed-response test and their scores on a proxy selected-response test is as high as .95.

This is understandable, of course, because in many situations both a selected- and constructed-response test are really tapping a fundamental skill or knowledge that manifests itself equally well under the two conditions. For example, in a UCLA graduate class that I often taught on educational evaluation, students had to complete a final examination that had two major sections, one consisting of thirty multiple-choice questions. A second, longer section of the exam consisted exclusively of constructed-response items. Over the years it became apparent to me that students who scored well on the multiple-choice items would usually score well on the essay sections of the test, and those who scored low on the multiple choice items were apt to score low on the constructed-response section. Just for kicks a few years ago, I went back over my grade books for the last few years and discovered that the correlation between students' scores on the two sections was almost .90. In view of the fact that for each exam paper it took me about ten minutes to score the essay section and only twenty to thirty seconds to score the multiple-choice section, I was sorely tempted (in classes of thirty or so) to skip the essay responses completely. I could have saved myself about five hours of test scoring. Besides that, because my exams were similar from year to year, I got tired of reading essentially the same kinds of responses. But, of course, I resisted the temptation. After all, if graduate students devote four hours to completing an exam, they expect the professor to at least browse through their efforts.

However, there are situations in which educators do not have much confidence that a selected-response test will serve as a proper proxy for the constructed-response behavior in which they are interested. For example, suppose you were a speech teacher and you wanted to assess the end-of-year skill of your would-be orators. There is just no way that a selected-response test, even a genuinely exotic one, can tell you whether your students can deliver an effective impromptu or extemporaneous speech. To see if students can give effective speeches, you must let them speak. Demosthenes didn't display his eloquence on a true–false test.

If you think about it for just a moment you will realize that all of the examples I have been using for constructed-response test items fall nicely into one of two types. Either the student is constructing some sort of *product*, as in the case of an essay exam, or some sort of *behavior*, as in the case of an impromptu speech. This two-part classification scheme takes care of all student responses, and it is particularly useful when thinking about constructed-response tests.

For instance, how would you classify the following sorts of student responses? Are these instances of tests in which a *product* or *behavior* is yielded?

Student Response	*Product or Behavior?*
A. Builds an end table in woodshop class	_____
B. Runs the 100-meter dash in a P.E. class	_____
C. Creates an oil painting in art	_____
D. Dances the waltz in a ballroom dancing class	_____

Well, *A* and *C* represent student products, and *B* and *D* constitute student behaviors. One of the interesting aspects of this distinction between products and behaviors is that, when educators employ behaviors in an educational measurement situation, the educators must make certain that the student's behavior is *recorded*. Unlike student products, such as the oil painting and the end table, that can be subsequently appraised with respect to their quality, student behaviors disappear once they occur. Suppose, for instance, that a female pole-vaulter was practicing by herself at the college track stadium. Let's say that she put together an incredible vault and soared over the bar at 22 feet! However, sadly, if nobody recorded that spectacular pole vault, there is no way to verify that it ever occurred. Thus, whether one employs videotape, film, audiotape, or relies on a judge's recording (such as when a speech teacher grades a student's speech), educators must make certain that for measurement purposes there is a recording made of behavioral responses, as opposed to those yielding products.

Relative Merits of Selected-Response and Constructed-Response Items

There are, of course, other ways of dividing the test-item world than whether the items require the student to select or construct answers. For instance, some measurement folks distinguish between *recognition* and *production* types of test items. Other people classify test items according to whether they are *subjectively* or *objectively scoreable*. Others talk about *short-answer* or *long-answer* sorts of items. However, in most of these systems there is a certain degree of confusion about short-answer items. Such tests, for example, a fill-in-the-blank kind of assessment, are surely not as easy to score objectively as a true–false test, yet they are not as subjectively scorable as essay exams. Similarly, how *long* can a short-answer item be before it becomes a *long-answer* item? With the selected-response versus constructed-response division, no such overlap exists.

The most crucial attribute of any well-developed educational assessment is that it permits valid score-based interpretations about students' abilities. However, beyond that fundamental consideration, there are additional factors to which educators should attend. Among these are the pros and cons of using various kinds of test items. To illustrate, it is possible to contrast selected- and constructed-response items according to their merits on several dimensions. Let's examine a few of these, indicating whether selected-response or constructed-response items come out ahead.

Types of outcomes measured. To assess the student's knowledge of factual information, the selected-response test item is clearly the winner. Many selected-response items represent a far more efficient way of assessing such knowledge than, for example, one or two essay-type constructed-response items. Selected-response items, however, can be used for many more purposes than merely to gauge students' factual knowledge. Such items can also be used to measure their possession of complex intellectual skills, not to mention their attitudes, interests, and so on. The most important ingredient in a selected-response item is the stimulus material that provides the setting for which the student selects a response. If the stimulus material merely calls for the student to choose among alternatives reflecting factual knowledge, the item is obviously focused only on the assessment of such knowledge. On the other hand, if the stimulus material presents a complex situation in which the student must make choices that require the use of fine-grained and sophisticated discriminations, the item is clearly destined for a more ambitious measurement mission.

Selected-response items are not appropriate for measuring students' abilities to synthesize ideas, to write effectively, or to perform certain types of problem-solving operations. Although not efficient for measuring a student's factual knowledge, constructed-response items constitute the only reasonable way of assessing students' abilities to write, to combine concepts, or to perform certain kinds of complex intellectual operations that call for originality. If you want to find out how well a student can write an original essay, for instance, you'll be unable to find any kind of a selected-response item that even comes close to assessing such a skill.

Item preparation. Even though it usually takes longer to prepare good constructed-response items than is thought, less time is typically required to turn out a few essay items than is needed to develop a large number of selected-response items. This time requirement is reversed, however, when it comes to scoring students' responses.

Item scoring. When an exam is over and the last students have turned in their test papers, teachers have to face the arduous task of scoring the tests. For the educator who uses selected-response items, a job is in store. For the educator who uses constructed-response items, a tough job is in store. Anyone who has speedily scored a series of student responses to multiple-choice items will report that the task can be completed pretty quickly. For constructed-response items that elicit lengthy student responses, however, the task sometimes seems to go on interminably.

Besides the time required to score the tests, there is another substantial scoring difference between these two testing approaches. Selected responses can be scored with impersonal objectivity. Constructed responses—even short-answer items, but particularly long essay answers—are subjectively scored. Subjective scoring typically results in inconsistency that, in turn, yields unreliable test results.

Form of student's response. With a selected-response item, the student is forced to deal with the kinds of responses made available. Students can recognize or even guess the correct answers to selected-response items. Constructed-response items, on the other hand, provide less structure for the student, thus permitting (encouraging?) frequent flights of verbal fancy. Crafty students, particularly those with writing ability and a fair amount of smarts, can overwhelm the inattentive teacher with reams of irrelevant rhetoric. Such baloney, of course, cannot be employed in responding to selected-response items. (I have personally been conned by verbally facile students more than a few times.)

Instructional impact. The structure of tests tends to shape the nature of students' learning. Thus, if constructed-response tests are typically employed by a teacher, that teacher's students will tend to be concerned with broader kinds of subject-matter considerations and with the ability to organize and present ideas carefully that such tests typically require. Selected-response tests, on the other hand, tend to encourage students to master a more comprehensive collection of factual information or to acquire the kinds of intellectual skills measured by the particular kinds of items employed.

Item-types to use. In reviewing the various advantages and disadvantages of selected- and constructed-response items, it is apparent that there is no simple victor. Although you can pick up certain advantages by choosing a constructed-response format, you also acquire a number of liabilities, and vice versa. Because the practical problems of scoring many students' exams is an important one, and because of the subjective scoring problems associated with constructed-response tests, selected-response items have been used with greater frequency. Often, by employing creative forms of a multiple-choice test, one can measure really high-level student competencies. If either selected- or constructed-response items will do the assessment job to be accomplished, the selected-response form is often chosen on practical grounds alone.

Yet there are instances when only a constructed-response test format will really get at the student skill to be measured. There is no other way to determine how well a child can write cursively than by having the youngster write cursively. To use a selected-response item as a substitute would surely be inappropriate. There are times when your first thought may be to use a constructed-response format, but further consideration might allow you to identify a selected-response scheme that would serve as a suitable surrogate. Clearly, the initial decision you make about which of these two testing approaches to employ will influence your subsequent test-development activities.

The allure of alternative assessment. In the 1990s, educators saw a number of state policymakers install statewide testing programs that incorporated a substantial number of constructed-response items. The architects of these new assessment programs were eager to have students *create* their responses rather than merely select responses from multiple-choice items.

More often than not, the new statewide assessment programs were said to represent *alternative assessment* approaches because, quite clearly, they constituted an alternative to the more traditional selected-response tests. In some instances, the altered statewide testing programs of the 1990s ended up being called *authentic assessment* programs because there was an effort to make the programs' constructed-response test items more closely resemble the kinds of tasks that students would encounter "in real life" when they left school.

But, whether dubbed "alternative" or "authentic," most of the widely heralded new statewide testing programs of the 1990s were obliged to retrench dramatically after only a few years. Large-scale assessment programs that included substantial numbers of constructed-response items proved to be immensely expensive. And, because most of the 1990s were not fiscally fabulous for most state governments, many of the more exciting of these new state-level assessment programs had to scale back their constructed-response aspirations dramatically. In many instances, it was not instructional considerations or psychometric imperatives that led to those retrenchments. It was simply a matter of money.

Let's turn now to the first of the two constructed-response items you'll be considering in this chapter, namely, the short-answer item. In Chapter 11, you'll look at two more recent constructed-response assessment approaches, that is, those based on performance tests and portfolios. As you'll see, those two forms of assessment are, in several ways, substantially different from short-answer items and essay items.

Educational Leaders
Look at Assessment

Constructed Responses
in the Classroom

Our thinking about the use of assessment and the elements of quality assessment has evolved as a result of our experiences and work in the area of school improvement. As classroom teachers, our testing procedures were automatic and shaped by limited knowledge about effective assessment practices. "Constructed-response" was not even a part of our vocabulary. Multiple-choice and essay were the terms and formats we used for the construction of our teacher-made tests. These tests were designed for grading purposes and usually as an afterthought to the instructional process. We followed the traditional cycle of classroom life: teach-test-grade, with little thought given to planning assessments that would impact on our instruction. Consequently, our tests, constructed-response or otherwise, were very limited in terms of "payoffs" for increasing student learning. We were victims of the mantra, "testing for evaluation's sake."

As we began working with schools in the area of school improvement, we found that we were not alone in our provincial view and knowledge of classroom assessment. Our experience with most teachers regarding classroom assessment is that they have limited understanding of how to design quality constructed-response tests. Often items are written with no understanding of the essential learning being assessed. In addition, the items are usually developed with no criteria for judging the demonstration of the essential learning. Decisions about how to score and grade responses are arbitrary and determined as the teacher graded the items. We found that, although these assessments yielded numbers and grades, there was no substance in terms of illuminating student learning.

Through our continued interactions with classroom teachers, we also found that there was little understanding of the importance of linking curriculum, assessment, and instruction as interdependent pieces. "Testing" (assessment) was an end in and of itself and

Rosanna M. Currier
School Improvement Liaison
DoDDS-Wuerzburg District
Germany

Beverly A. Erdmann
School Improvement Liaison
DoDDS-Wuerzburg District
Germany

had no direct link to specific student outcomes. As long as this remained the pervasive belief about and purpose of assessment, there was little incentive to identify either the essential learning and/or desired student outcomes prior to instruction. Testing (assessment) would remain an end product rather than a guide to instruction and desired student learning.

In our quest to assist schools in the collection of assessment data to document student progress, we learned that, if we could assist educators in the development and selection of quality assessment instruments, student learning would also be significantly enhanced. Over the past several years, as we have worked with school improvement leadership teams, we have continued to make assessment and documentation of student learning our priority. We feel quite confident in referring to the old adage, "nothing suc-

▶

▶ ceeds like success." As teachers have worked to increase their understanding, expertise, and knowledge in the area of assessment, their efforts have been supported and improvement evidenced by increased student learning. Educators have begun to experience a shift in their thinking, which has led to a successful formula for developing/selecting assessments that guide instruction and result in helping all students achieve. ●

Short-Answer Items

Short-answer items oblige a student to supply a word or phrase in response either to a direct question or in order to complete an incomplete statement. A short-answer item can be contrasted with the essay examination chiefly because of the brevity of the response that the short-answer item solicits. When short-answer items call for a very extensive response on the part of the student, they should be considered essay items and treated as such. The following are examples of short-answer items.

Completion. The name of the individual (saint) who invented fudge brownies is

_____.

Direct Question. What was the name of the individual (saint) who invented fudge brownies?

_____

Short-Answer Item

A test item eliciting a brief response, usually a word or phrase, from students.

Short-answer test items are particularly suitable for measuring relatively simple types of learning outcomes, such as a student's knowledge of factual information. For example, a teacher might present a complex geometric figure for the student's consideration, then ask a series of short-answer questions about several of the figure's features and how they are related. Although short-answer items are typically used for the assessment of simple kinds of learning outcomes, it is possible to present very complex questions so that the student's brief response reflects a high-level intellectual operation.

Dividends and deficits. Because a short-answer item often deals with relatively unsophisticated sorts of learning outcomes, it is considered to be one of the easiest to construct. However, as you have seen with other apparently simple sorts of items, the short-answer item also requires considerable care on the part of the teacher to make sure that a satisfactory item is produced.

A key advantage of short-answer items is that they require the student to create an answer rather than merely to recognize it. With any sort of selected-response items, alert students have access to the correct answer. Their task is to spot it. With constructed-response items, however, it is necessary for students to *produce* the correct answer, not merely choose it. Thus, the kind of partial knowledge that might enable a student to snag a correct answer in a selected-response test will often be insufficient for responding correctly to a short-answer test item.

The principal weakness of short-answer items is the difficulty teachers have in scoring student's responses. Because it is possible that students will construct a variety of responses, such as using synonyms for the answer intended by the teacher, it is sometimes difficult to determine whether a given answer is correct. Furthermore, there is the problem of legibility. Some students may produce a correct answer that is literally undecipherable by even the most astute cryptographer. Beyond that, how should a teacher deal with grammatical foul-ups or misspelled words? Should full or partial credit be given?

It is also much more time-consuming to score short-answer items than it is to score selected-response items. If large numbers of selected-response answer sheets are involved, they can usually be scored by optical scanning equipment, which "reads" the test papers and scores them. Short-answer items, however, require a human scorer to render a judgment on each of the responses. This takes time, plenty of time.

There have been recent advances in computer-scoring of students' responses not only to short-answer items but also to essays. Given the enormous sophistication of today's computer programmers, it will not be surprising if tomorrow's computers can simultaneously (1) score a scad of students' constructed-response exams and, at the same time, (2) bake a flawless pineapple upside-down cake. For the immediate future, however, it appears that teachers will need to be scoring their students' answers to short-answer items (and baking their own pineapple upside-down cakes).

Item-writing guidelines. Although it is thought that the short-answer item is one of the easiest kinds of items to construct, there are still potential deficiencies in the way that teachers prepare such items. I'll now review some of the more salient of these pitfalls.

1. *A direct question is generally preferable to an incomplete statement.* Particularly when an examination is designed for young children, but even for older students, the direct-question format should be preferred. This is a more familiar form to youngsters and, therefore, is less apt to induce confusion. In addition, the direct question usually forces the teacher to phrase the item in such a way that less ambiguity is present. It is astonishing how many times a teacher will create an incomplete-statement type of short-answer item that turns out to be ambiguous. Because the teacher clearly has in mind what should complete the sentence, it is assumed that the student will think along those same lines. This assumption is often unwarranted. Teachers must try to come up with questions or incomplete statements for which there is one, and only one, reasonable answer. It is sometimes helpful for the teacher to think first of the intended answer, then build a question for which that answer is the *unique* appropriate response.

2. *Structure an item so that the required response should be concise.* Responses to short-answer items, whether they consist of direct questions or incomplete statements, should be brief phrases, words, numbers, or symbols. By providing clear directions at the beginning of the test and by phrasing questions carefully, it will be clear that the students' response should be brief. If the response is brief, cogent, and accurate, then it will also be *pithy.* However, the quest for brevity in a response should not supersede the phrasing of the item so that the kind of response called for is clear. Note, for instance, in the following examples that both teachers who wrote the items wanted the response "biped." Yet the top item will surely produce a galaxy of reasonable responses. The bottom item, by the addition of the phrase, "is technically classified as a," reduces the item's ambiguity.

Dismal. An animal that walks on two feet is _____.

Defensible. An animal that walks on two feet is technically classified as a/an

_____.

Incidentally, for computational problems in mathematics it is wise to specify (perhaps in parentheses) the degree of accuracy required, such as how many places beyond the decimal point are necessary.

3. *Place the blank near the end of an incomplete sentence or in the margin for a direct question.* If blanks are placed at the beginning of an incomplete sentence, the student may have forgotten what is sought by the time that the sentence has been read. (Students have such annoyingly brief attention spans!)

Troublesome

The _____ is the legislative body that constitutionally must ratify all treaties with foreign nations signed by the president of the United States.

Terrific

What is the legislative body that constitutionally must ratify all treaties with foreign nations signed by the president of the United States?

_____

In these examples we see that even the student who knows that the U.S. Senate must ratify foreign treaties might get a bit lost with the top item in which the blank occurs near the beginning of the sentence. The bottom item, in addition to the fact that it is a direct question, permits much more efficient scoring than if the teacher has to visually dip in and out of sentences to check answers. With answers lined up in a list, the teacher needs only to scan the answers to see whether they're correct or incorrect.

4. *For incomplete-statement types of items, restrict the number of blanks to one or, at most, two.* When the teacher employs too many blanks in an incomplete statement, the ambiguity index of the item rises dramatically. Note, for instance, the following example, and try to decide how you would respond to it. When items have so many blanks as the following, they are sometimes referred to as *Swiss cheese items.* It should be apparent why.

Swiss Cheese Item

After heroic struggles, in the year _____, _____ and _____ discovered _____.

5. *Blanks for answers should be equal in length.* Beginning teachers often vary the length of the blanks for short-answer items consistent with the length of the expected answer.

This practice, of course, results in providing unintended clues as to what answer is sought. And that, of course, reduces the validity of a test-based interpretation about the student's status with respect to the assessment domain represented by the test. The length of item blanks should be identical throughout the test so as to avoid this problem.

6. *Provide sufficient answer space.* Though it is true you are considering the short-answer item, teachers need not make them skimpy-answer items. In the following example, you'll see that the student would be in trouble when trying to write out the name, "The Gettysburg Address," in the space available. A little more generosity on the teacher's part is warranted. (I suppose it would be worse if the teacher had asked the student, from memory, to write out the entire Gettysburg Address in the teensy space provided.)

An Excessively Frugal Answer Space

What is the name of the famous address by Abraham Lincoln that commences with the phrase "Fourscore and seven years ago?" _____

The Essay Item

By all odds, the most common type of constructed-response test item is the essay question. The essay question can be used to measure complex as well as simple types of learning outcomes, but, because its primary application involves the student's ability to write, synthesize, and create, let's focus on the item as a vehicle for assessing these higher levels of cognitive outcomes.

Restricted and Extended Responses

Essay Item

A test item eliciting a response of one or more paragraphs from students.

It is often thought that the teacher exercises no control over the student's freedom of response in essay items. To the contrary, however, such test items can be structured so that the student is obliged to produce a very short answer, almost resembling a short-answer response, or an elaborate and lengthy answer. The two types of test items that reflect this distinction are referred to as *restricted-response items* and *extended-response items*.

A restricted-response item distinctively limits the form and content of the student's response. Content is typically restricted by limiting the scope of the topic to be treated in the response. The form of the response, such as its length, is restricted in the way the question is phrased. Two examples are presented below.

Restricted-Response Items

Describe, in a paragraph of no more than fifty words, the three most common causes of HIV infection among teenagers.

List, in brief statements, three similarities between the United States's involvement in the Vietnam and Gulf War conflicts.

Restricted-Response Item

An essay item that markedly limits the form and content of a student's response.

Another technique for restricting the student's response is to provide a certain amount of space on the test paper and require the response to be made within the confines of that space. The problem with this tactic, however, is that some students typically employ a tiny handwriting style, whereas others use large, bold handwriting. The former writers might be able to squeeze a small novella into the provided space; the large-penmanship people might be able to scrawl out only a few sentences or, perhaps, a lengthy clause.

Limiting students' responses to restricted-response essay items makes the scoring of those items more straightforward and reliable. Such items, however, are characteristically less valuable as measures of learning outcomes that require the student to display organization and originality.

Extended-response questions provide the student with far more latitude. The student typically produces a longer answer and is less constrained regarding the nature of that answer. Two examples of extended-response items follow.

Extended-Response Items

Explain the meaning of the two phrases *formative evaluation* and *summative evaluation*, and then describe the relationship between these two concepts.

Critically evaluate the impact on American life of the economic crises of the early 1990s, particularly with respect to the alteration in Americans' expectations regarding the role of government.

Extended-Response Item

An essay item that gives students few constraints in how they are to respond.

There is general agreement that extended-response items call for more sophisticated responses on the part of the student, but there is doubt as to whether these complex responses can be as satisfactorily scored. In a few paragraphs I'll describe some of the guidelines that can be employed to score more accurately student's answers to such extended-response items. However, you should recognize that, generally, the more extended the response called for in the question, the less consistently those responses can be scored.

Dividends and Deficits

As a tactic to assess kinds of complex learning outcomes, the essay item is indisputably the best approach. Because this kind of item can require a student to put together ideas and to express them in original ways, there is no way of simulating that kind of requirement in a selected-response item or, for that matter, even in a short-answer item. Moreover, a constructed-response item, such as the essay question, requires the student to *produce*, rather than merely recognize, a correct answer, thus rendering the essay question a far more demanding kind of test item.

Essay items are also popular because they provide an opportunity for students to improve their composition skills. In recent years an increasing amount of criticism has been leveled against public schools because of the poor quality of student composition. Essay questions provide an additional opportunity for students to practice their composition skills.

It is often believed that essay items are easy to create, yet you will see that this advantage is more apparent than real. Although most teachers can, while strolling toward class, dash off a series of essay questions, those questions characteristically will be rather abysmal. To create essay questions that do a decent assessment job, far more test-construction time is required.

The deficits of the essay test are sufficiently significant that, were it not because essay items get at really worthwhile kinds of learning outcomes, such items might never be used. Without a doubt, the essay item's most serious deficiencies are (1) the time that's required to score students' responses, and (2) the unreliability of scoring. Many investigations have shown that essay questions are often scored differently by different judges and that this variability in scoring, of course, markedly reduces reliability. If you will recall Chapter 5's discussion of reliability, a test that is unreliable cannot yield valid inferences. The use of well-constructed scoring procedures, however, can markedly reduce the unreliability of scoring student essays.

Another problem with the essay item is the amount of time necessary to score students' answers. If the scoring is done conscientiously, an enormous number of hours will have to be spent in scoring the tests. Faced with the prospect of spending an endless number of hours in scoring, some teachers restrict their judgments to superficialities, thus reducing the quality of the assessment effort.

Any experienced teacher can tell you that the essay question also provides a marvelous opportunity for the cunning student who knows little, but can dazzle the teacher with clever writing and a compelling vocabulary. Many students bluff their way effectively through essay questions without knowing much about the subject matter treated in the question. Too many teachers who score essay tests become impressed with the student's general verbal ability or writing style, rather than focusing on the student's responsiveness to the teacher's question.

A final deficit derives from the fact that relatively few essay questions can be answered (because they require so much student response time). As a consequence, subject-matter content cannot be sampled comprehensively. Only a few questions can usually be employed in a single test, and this often leaves gaps in the content coverage of the examination.

Item-Writing and Item-Scoring Guidelines

Because, with essay questions, the pivotal problems are associated both with the writing of items and with the scoring of the tests, I'll consider rules for writing essay items and for scoring essay responses.

1. *Frame questions so that the student's task is explicitly defined.* At a silly extreme, you might think of an unlucky student who encounters a nebulous essay question, such as, "Insightfully, discuss truth." Obviously, the student's task is ill defined, and different students will interpret the question variously. Teachers should try to add a sufficient amount of detail to the question so that the focus of the intended response is clear. In the following examples, one of the questions clearly supplies insufficient guidance to the student. Can you pick out the putrid item?

> *Outlandish.* Discuss democracy in Canada.
>
> *Outstanding.* Describe how the system of "checks and balances" built into the U.S. Constitution was designed to preserve the democratic system envisioned by the Constitution's architects.

As limitations to the questions are added, the teacher obviously moves toward the restricted-response form of an essay question. Even with extended-response kinds of items, however, it is necessary to add sufficient guidance for students so that the general thrust of the question is apparent.

2. *Specify the point value and an approximate time limit for each question.* Although the teacher usually knows how much time should be used for each question's response, students will be less certain. It is helpful, therefore, to provide some rough estimates of how long the student should spend on each question.

If the examination is to be used for classroom-grading purposes, it is also desirable to supply the student with an idea of the weighting—for example, number of points—to be given to each item. Sometimes item weightings appear to be identical as far as the student is concerned, yet a teacher will have in mind that the last two questions are the really pivotal ones and will be weighted more heavily. The student, unaware of this well-kept secret, may emphasize the early part of the examination and give the last few questions short shrift, or even medium-height shrift, thereby producing an unsatisfactory examination performance.

3. *Employ a larger number of questions that require relatively short answers rather than only a few questions that require long answers.* This guideline suggests that, by using many restricted-response essay questions, one can do a better job of content sampling. With only a few questions on an essay exam, there is so much emphasis on a limited number of content areas that if, in a three-question essay test, for example, a student has overlooked one of the three topics, there goes one-third of the exam down the drain. Thus, it is preferable to have a good many items requiring responses of half a page rather than to have two or three items that demand responses of several pages in length.

4. *Do not employ optional questions.* Even though it is a routine practice to provide several essay questions, then allow the students to choose questions that suit them, this is an unwise procedure. An examination, for example, may include five essay questions and require the student to respond to only three of them. The students, of course, enjoy this procedure because they can select the questions that they can respond to best. Yet, except for its beneficial effects in reducing student anxiety, the use of optional questions has little to recommend it.

When students respond to different questions, they are actually taking different tests. Therefore, the possibility of evaluating their achievement on a common basis disappears. It is also possible that if students are aware that the optional-question procedure will be employed, they can prepare several answers in advance and attempt to plug them into certain questions on the examination.[1]

In most instances, the use of optional questions on an examination reflects the teacher's uncertainty about what it is that the examination should really be measuring.

The more equivocal the teacher is about the importance of the examination's contents, the more likely that optional questions are to be employed. Optionality, at least of this sort, should be avoided.

5. *Verify a question's quality by writing a trial response to the question.* Anyone who is fashioning an essay question ought to be able to conjure up a pretty good answer for the question. If the teacher can't produce a solid answer, then it is more than likely that the question has some problems. These problems, certain to be encountered by the students later on, can be spotted and rectified on the basis of the teacher's trial response.

Too many times an essay question is drummed up in a hustle by a teacher who assumes that there are no substantial problems with the question. Only during the exam itself, with all sorts of pressures on students, are the flaws in the item discovered. That's too late. A trial response can help teachers detect defects in their essay questions.

6. *Prepare a scoring guide in advance of considering students responses.* Any kind of scoring key prepared in advance will usually need to be modified to some extent as the actual papers are scored. Sometimes students will interpret questions a bit differently than the teacher had in mind or may come up with different insights than were anticipated. Yet it is extremely helpful to prepare a scoring key in advance of scoring essay exams. The advance scoring key should list the major evaluative criteria that would be looked for in an acceptable response or, on the contrary, the major defects that might appear in an unsatisfactory response.

Without advance evaluative criteria for judging responses, the grading of student papers often becomes a guessing game. Different teachers bring their own criteria to bear in judging students' responses. Under such circumstances many students win. Many lose. Some of the winners should be losers, and vice versa. Advance scoring keys would help reduce this anarchic situation. Moreover, even though the creation of such scoring keys may oblige teachers to devote more effort to the exam process than has been their custom, the ensuing accuracy and fairness of the examination process will make it well worth the effort.

7. *Score all answers to one question before scoring the next question.* Too many teachers try to score an entire examination at one time, one question after another, then turn to the next student's paper. This is a particularly unsound practice because the student's response to one question can influence the teacher adversely or positively, regarding the scoring of the next question. A far more consistent evaluation occurs if all of the answers to the first question are scored together, then all of the answers to the second question, and so on. In scoring the responses to different questions, the order of the papers should also be altered.

8. *Make prior decisions regarding treatment of such factors as spelling, penpersonship, and punctuation.* Because factors that are irrelevant to the major learning outcomes being measured can sometimes influence a teacher's scoring, it is important to decide in advance how to treat them and not leave this decision to the exigencies of the moment as a particular student's test paper is being graded. In some cases, of course, these very considerations will form a major focus of the essay examination, as in instances when a social studies teacher is having students produce essays about social-studies topics that also reflect their essay-writing skills. In such instances, the teacher may be legitimately concerned about spelling or punctuation. Often, however, the essay will focus on different factors than spelling and syntax. The teacher should give careful *advance* consideration to the extent to which sloppy syntax and stumbling spelling should influence the score. There are no hard-and-fast rules regarding such matters, so the teacher will have to decide whether these kinds of factors are sufficiently relevant to the student's general learning prowess that they should be included in the scoring scheme.

   9. *Evaluate essay responses anonymously.* Because a teacher's knowledge of a particular student will sometimes becloud an appraisal of that student's response, it is particularly important not to look at the student's name prior to grading the paper. A teacher, for example, can have students place their names on the reverse side of the last page of the examination, thereby permitting the examinations to be graded anonymously.

   Obviously, after a teacher has worked with students' responses for a month or two, in many instances it's impossible to avoid knowing that a given scrawling handwriting style was spawned by sloppy Sam or that a left-hand leaning writing style (with petite circles over all lower-case i's and j's) was authored by stylish Sally. But many students' responses, if names are not readily observable, will not be easily recognized, Sam's and Sally's styles notwithstanding.

   10. *Score essay responses via analytic or holistic rubrics.* These days, a scoring guide to be used in judging the quality of students' constructed responses is usually referred to as a *rubric*. (In the next chapter, you'll be shown rubrics that can have a decisively positive effect on instruction.) Essay answers can be scored in two ways. Both of these may require the use of a scoring guide, such as was described in guideline six. The first of these scoring approaches is referred to as an *analytic* scoring strategy. In an analytic scoring approach, a student's response is assigned a given number of points on each evaluative criterion separately. For example, suppose in a government class the teacher had created an essay question for which the ideal response focuses on four distinct problems in a current political crisis. The teacher develops a rubric that gives students up to five points for each of these four problems, that is, twenty points for a perfect response. For each of the four problems, the teacher assigns one point if the student's response mentions the problem, one or two additional points if the problem is well described, and one or two more points if the problem's possible solution is described. Thus, an analytic rubric something like the illustrative rubric in Figure 10.1 could be employed.

FIGURE 10.1.

An illustrative analytic rubric for an essay examination in a government class.

ANALYTIC RUBRIC

Problem Area	Identified (1 point)	Described (1–2 points)	Solution (1–2 points)
Local Control	1	2	1
Federal Support	1	1	
Legal Constraints	1	2	2
The Media	1		

Student's Name   Joe Hill

Total Points   12

Educational Leaders
Look at Assessment

When Students Must
Generate Answers

Educators are in the business of continually monitoring and adjusting their instruction based on emerging evidence. Teachers use many forms of assessment to gain information regarding student achievement. Based on my experience, both in the classroom and as a teacher support and resource, I've seen firsthand the wide range of adeptness at using and creating constructed-response classroom tests.

Some teachers have not received much formal training in the use or design of constructed-response test items. As a result, these teachers select assessment formats that mirror their own experience as students using traditional evaluation techniques such as multiple-choice and/or true–false designs.

Other teachers, my first grade team for example, have received some training in alternative assessment techniques and are in the process of designing their own constructed-response test questions. Having the support of colleagues facilitates the creation of test questions and provides a collaborative setting for generating scoring criteria reflecting instructional objectives.

Kim Thoman
Instructional Strategies Specialist and Coach
Manhattan Beach USD
Manhattan Beach, California

I have found that constructed-response classroom tests can be useful in any curricular area and provide the perfect way of gathering insight into a student's understanding and application of important concepts. While scoring a constructed-response classroom test takes more than scoring a multiple-choice test, the information I am able to extract regarding my students' thinking and reasoning has been invaluable. My students' responses provide a wealth of information about their thought processes and understanding of key instructional objectives. This information has been extremely useful in terms of communicating with parents and planning future instruction. ●

A scoring rubric, such as the one illustrated in Figure 10.1 can be used by the teacher to supply feedback to the student. This is one of the more significant advantages of an analytic scoring approach, because a low-scoring student can be informed in a relatively detailed manner just what deficiencies need to be corrected.

In contrast to an analytic scoring approach, the teacher can grade essays on a *holistic* basis. As its name implies, the holistic approach views the essay response as a whole, and the teacher renders a single overall score or grade. Holistic scoring should not be thought of as a necessarily crude, judgmental scheme whereby the teacher plucks a global judgment from the air. A scoring rubric, not unlike the previously described analytic rubric, can be used to help structure the expectations of the teacher. However, unlike the analytic method, in which point-by-point allocations for each evaluative criterion are made, the holistic scorer considers all evaluative criteria, but renders final judgments in one big blob. ("Blob," incidentally, is not a widely employed psychometric descriptor.)

Holistic scoring schemes can be quite cavalier or amazingly careful. In particular, holistic scoring of student essays, paragraphs, and other sorts of written compositions, has been refined over the years. By employing some of these refinements, holistic scores have been able to come up with amazingly high interjudge agreements, that is, when different judges scoring the same essays produce remarkably consistent scores.

The advantage of the holistic approach to scoring student compositions is, of course, that it really saves time. The disadvantage, however, particularly if the examination is being used in connection with an instructional program, is that the student gets only global, not particularized, feedback.

If there is to be additional instruction for the student, then it seems clear that an analytic scheme is preferable. For instance, if a student has prepared an inferior composition in an English class, it does that student little good to know that the composition was "flawed." What the student really needs to know is the detailed reasons that the composition was a loser. The particulars having been isolated, the student can then get cracking to eliminate those sorts of deficiencies.

Clearly, then, the choice between analytic and holistic scoring approaches is sometimes a difficult one. It depends on the purpose of the examination, the scoring resources available, the permissible turnaround time (that is, how much time can be allowed for scoring), and a host of similar factors. In some cases, both a holistic and analytic scoring scheme can be adopted.

In some districtwide and state-level testing programs, for example, student compositions are scored holistically, but those compositions considered failures on the basis of the holistic scoring are then scored analytically. Because only a fraction of the papers are deemed failures on the basis of the holistic scoring, this two-step scheme saves considerable time and money.

During the eighties, a number of statewide assessment programs were installed in which students' composition skills were measured by requiring students to create an original composition, that is, a writing sample. In some instances, these assessment programs required that many thousands of student compositions be scored each year. In Texas, for example, well over a million student compositions were scored annually. Although in many cases these statewide composition assessment programs were scored in-state by state-trained teachers, the magnitude of the scoring requirements typically led to the use of test-scoring agencies specializing in large-scale scoring of student compositions.

Typically, some form of holistic scoring is employed to score these thousands of student compositions. The compositions are usually scored by two trained raters on a multiple-point basis, such as four points for an excellent response, three points for an acceptable response, two points for a barely acceptable response, and one point for an unacceptable response. The evaluative criteria that are used in rendering these holistic judgments are often communicated to the state's educators so that instructional programs in the field of writing can be aligned with the state-operated scoring program. In most instances in which state-level composition tests have been installed, there has been a substantial increase in the amount and quality of composition instruction in the schools.

A Final Admonition

Most of today's educators grew up in educational settings in which constructed-response tests were churned out almost unthinkingly by teachers. Because these educators have been the victims of such instant assessment schemes, they may be inclined to think that constructed-response tests, although time-consuming to score, can be conjured up in the twinkling of an eye. However, as this chapter has attempted to stress, creation of constructed-response tests is not fool's play. Great pains should be taken to create the items. No less attention should be given to the scoring procedures.

In the next chapter, you'll be considering two forms of constructed-response items that are merely logical extensions of the kind of guidelines you've encountered in this and the previous chapter. That chapter will focus on performance assessment and portfolio assessment. As you read that chapter, then, try to see the special relevance of this chapter about constructed-response items to these newer, more popular forms of educational assessment.

Chapter Wrap-Up

Before bidding adieu to this chapter about two commonly employed constructed-response items, I am compelled to *construct* a summary based on the chapter's guiding questions. "Construction," it seems, is in the air.

● What are the relative merits of selected- and constructed-response items?

If educators must choose between selected- and constructed-response items for their assessment devices, that choice will usually revolve around the types of outcomes measured, the ease of item preparation, and the ease of item-scoring. In general, constructed-response items will permit assessment-based inferences about students' status with respect to higher level cognitive outcomes than would usually be possible with selected-response items. Even though this is true *in general*, it is still possible to devise selected-response items that can elicit high-level cognition from students. Item generation is typically easier for constructed-response items than for selected-response items, although the creation of good selected-response items usually takes more time than most teachers think. Item-scoring of students' responses is much easier for selected-response items than for constructed-response items. It was the substantial costs of storing students' constructed responses that forced many states in the 1990s to abandon or markedly reduce the movement toward greater reliance on constructed responses in their statewide achievement tests. An educator's final choice between selected- and constructed-response items is sometimes quite difficult to make. It is likely that, unless computerized scoring of students' responses reduces scoring costs dramatically, a blend of the two item-types will be necessary.

● What are the important features of short-answer items?

When test items call for students to generate a word, phrase, or number in response to a question or incomplete statement, these are referred to as *short-answer items*. Short-answer items are especially useful in assessing students' status with respect to domains of knowledge, that is, factual information. However, because students are being asked to generate their responses rather than to choose a response from alternatives that are presented, it is often easier to tap higher level cognitive behavior from students if a teacher is reasonably skillful in item-construction.

The item-writing guidelines for short-answer items were, in abbreviated form, the following: (1) prefer direct questions to incomplete statements, (2) solicit concise responses, (3) place the blanks for students' answers carefully, (4) restrict the number of blanks for incomplete-statement items to one or two, (5) use equal-length blanks, and (6) provide adequate answer space.

● What are the important features of essay items?

A distinction was drawn in the chapter between essay items that solicit restricted (shorter) versus extended (longer) responses. There is a clear relationship between the length of the response sought and the difficulty of scoring students' responses consistently. Essay items, popular since medieval times, have historically been employed to measure a variety of higher level cognitive outcomes. A serious drawback of essay items is the time requirement associated with scoring students' responses. Another problem is the potential unreliability of scoring, although this can be reduced considerably with the use of well-devised scoring rubrics.

The item-writing guidelines for this type of assessment item, briefly, were these: (1) define the student's task explicitly, (2) indicate point values and time limits for each item, (3) employ more questions with short answers than fewer questions with long answers, (4) do not allow students to choose among questions, and (5) write a trial response to each question to verify the question's quality.

For scoring students' responses, the following guidelines were recommended: (1) prepare a scoring guide prior to scoring, (2) score all answers to one question before moving to another question, (3) decide in advance about the importance of factors such as writing mechanics, (4) evaluate responses anonymously, and (5) score responses using analytic or holistic rubrics.

Practice Exercises

Before tackling these practice exercises, please review the guidelines for short-answer and essay items provided in the chapter. *Then* go through each of the following items, and see if you can spot which guideline is violated. You will start with three short-answer items, then close with a pair of essay items. Remember, look for the violated guidelines in each of the following five items.

1. *A short-answer item.* What were the underlying causes of World War I?

_____

_____

_____

_____

_____

_____

_____

2. *A short-answer item.* _____ was the vocation of nine of the fifty-six original signers of the U.S. Declaration of Independence.

3. *A short-answer item.* _____ _____, one of Quebec's greatest _____, created _____ during the _____ century.

4. *An essay item.* In whatever depth you consider suitable, discuss the evolution of humankind.

5. *Directions for an essay test.* Directions to students: Choose two of the following three items, each of which will be worth fifty points.

Then write for approximately sixty minutes on the two items chosen.

Answers to Practice Exercises

1. This item violates guideline two, which calls for the item to be phrased so that the required response should be *concise*. The question, as currently phrased, could reasonably be answered by students for at least a week or two. It elicits an essay-type response, not a short-answer response.

2. This short-answer item runs counter to guideline three, which suggests that blanks be placed near the end of an incomplete sentence. You could have flipped the statement around or turned it into a direct question to improve it. Incidentally, the vocation of nine of the fifty-six original signers of the U.S. Declaration of Independence was farming (or agriculture). There's just no telling when you'll next be asked to supply this knowledge nugget.

3. This is a classic Swiss cheese item and, as such, violates guideline four. Even Canadians who live in Quebec would have a tough time answering the item.

4. This item is clearly not a restricted-response type of essay item. On the contrary, it supplies no restrictions at all. It violates guideline one, because the student's task is not explicitly defined. It is also inconsistent with guideline two, because no value or time limit has been provided. Not only has no time limit been set, the student is told to write in "whatever depth you consider suitable."

5. This test violates guidelines three and four. First, as optional selection of items is permitted, this is clearly contrary to guideline four. Then only two long-response items are used, rather than more short-response items. This is a violation of guideline three.

DISCUSSION QUESTIONS

1. After having reviewed the pro and con sides of both selected- and constructed-response items, what factor would induce you as an educational leader to recommend one or the other item-types to teachers?

2. Try to think of at least a half-dozen types of constructed-response test items including (1) student behaviors, then (2) student products. Are there any similarities in the kinds of items you have identified?

3. Although it is clear that for constructed-response items one can isolate instances of student behavior *versus* student products, could this also be said for selected-response items? If so, how?

4. What is your own view regarding the relative virtues of holistic versus analytic scoring of student compositions? How about the scoring of responses to an essay examination in a history course; would your opinion change?

5. Why do you think that essay exams, in spite of considerable criticism of those exams during earlier years, remain relatively popular among teachers?

SUGGESTIONS FOR ADDITIONAL READING

Breland, Hunter M. *Writing Skill Assessment: Problems and Prospects: A Policy Information Perspective* (ED 401 317). Princeton, NJ: Educational Testing Service, April 1996.

Bryant, Deborah, and Mark Driscoll. *Exploring Classroom Assessments in Mathematics: A Guide for Staff Development* (Stock #198187M48). Alexandria, VA: Association for Supervision and Curriculum Development and National Council of Teachers of Mathematics, 1998.

Carey, Lou M. *Measuring and Evaluating School Learning.* Boston: Allyn & Bacon, 1988.

Cronbach, L. J. *Essentials of Psychological Testing* (4th ed.). New York: Harper & Row, 1984.

Downing, Steven M., and Thomas M. Haladyna. "Test Item Development: Validity Evidence From Quality Assurance Procedures." *Applied Measurement in Education, 10,* 1 (1997): 61–82.

Gay, L. R. *Educational Evaluation and Measurement: Competencies for Analysis and Application* (2nd ed.). Columbus, OH: Charles E. Merrill, 1985.

Gronlund, Norman E. *Measurement and Evaluation in Teaching* (5th ed.). New York: Macmillan, 1985.

Meredith, Vana H., and Paul L. Williams. "Problem Identification and Control." *Educational Measurement: Issues and Practice, 3,* 1 (Spring 1984): 11–15.

Miller, Wilma H. *Alternative Assessment Techniques for Reading & Writing.* West Nyack, NY: Center for Applied Research in Education, 1995.

Mullis, Ina V. S. "Scoring Direct Writing Assessments: What Are the Alternatives?" *Educational Measurement: Issues and Practice, 3,* 1 (Spring 1984): 16–18.

National Center on Education and the Economy and the University of Pittsburgh. *Performance Standards, Volume 1: Elementary School.* Washington, DC: Authors, 1997.

National Center on Education and the Economy and the University of Pittsburgh. *Performance Standards, Volume 2: Middle School.* Washington, DC: Authors, 1997.

National Center on Education and the Economy and the University of Pittsburgh. *Performance Standards, Volume 3: High School.* Washington, DC: Authors, 1997.

Page, Ellis B., and Nancy S. Petersen. "The Computer Moves into Essay Grading: Updating the Ancient Test." *Phi Delta Kappan, 76,* 7 (March 1995): 561–565.

Roid, G. H., and T. M. Haladyna. *A Technology for Test-Item Writing.* New York: Academic Press, 1982.

AND FOR THOSE WHO TIRE OF READING

Popham, W. James. *Assessing Mathematics Learning* (Videotape #STVT-26). Los Angeles: IOX Assessment Associates.

Popham, W. James. *Creating Challenging Classroom Tests: When Students CONSTRUCT Their Responses* (Videotape #ETVT-24). Los Angeles: IOX Assessment Associates.

Popham, W. James. *The Role of Rubrics in Classroom Assessment* (Videotape #ETVT-18). Los Angeles: IOX Assessment Associates.

ENDNOTE

1. During a June 1998 national conference in Boulder, Colorado, Robert Linn presented evidence from approximately 30,000 students indicating that, when students choose the items to which they will respond, there are nontrivial differences created in the difficulty of the now "different" tests.

11

Performance and Portfolio Assessment

In this chapter you'll be considering two variants of constructed-response assessment, but they're sufficiently different from short-answer and essay items that they deserve a special chapter. You'll be looking at *performance assessment* and *portfolio assessment*. Because there are strong advocates of both these versions of constructed-response measurement and, therefore, because both assessment approaches are often being recommended these days, educational leaders need to understand the key features of both assessment approaches.

Consistent with this book's emphasis on the need for educational measurement to make a bona fide contribution to *education*, I'll attempt to familiarize you with ways that both performance assessment and portfolio assessment can make meaningful contributions to the quality of students' learning.

You'll be looking at performance assessment, rubrics (in more detail than in the previous chapter's brief consideration of essay-scoring), and portfolio assessment. Because rubrics should be employed to judge students' responses for both performance assessments and portfolio assessments, the role of rubrics will be pivotal to either form of assessment.

Performance Assessment

Let's first consider performance assessments or, as they are often called, *performance tests*. Although all educational tests require students to perform in some way, when most educators talk about performance tests, they are thinking about assessments in which the student is required to construct an original response. Often an examiner (such as the teacher) *observes* the process of construction so that an observation of the student's performance and a judgment about that performance are required. Actually, the distinction between performance assessments and more conventional tests is the degree to which the examination simulates the criterion situation—that is, the degree to which it approximates the assessment domain about which educators wish to make inferences.

For instance, suppose that a teacher who had been instructing students in the process of collaborative problem-solving wanted to see whether students had acquired that skill. The *inference* at issue revolves around the extent to which each student has mastered the skill. The *educational decision* on the line might be whether particular students need additional instruction or, instead, whether it's time to move on to other instructional objectives. The teacher's real interest, then, is in how well students can work with other students to arrive collaboratively at solutions to problems. In Figure 11.1, you will see there are several assessment procedures that could be used to get a fix on a student's collaborative problem-solving skills. Yet, note that the two selected-response assessment approaches (Assessment Choices 1 and 2) don't really ask students to construct anything. For the other three constructed-response assessment options (Assessment Choices 3, 4, and 5), however, there are clear differences in the degree to which the task presented to the student coincides with the class of tasks constituting the assessment domain of collaborative problem solving. Assessment Choice 5, for example, is obviously the closest match to the behavior called for in the objective. Yet, Assessment Choice 4 is surely more of a "performance test" than is Choice 1.

Performance Assessment

Students are given a demanding task, then asked to respond to it orally, in writing, or by constructing a product.

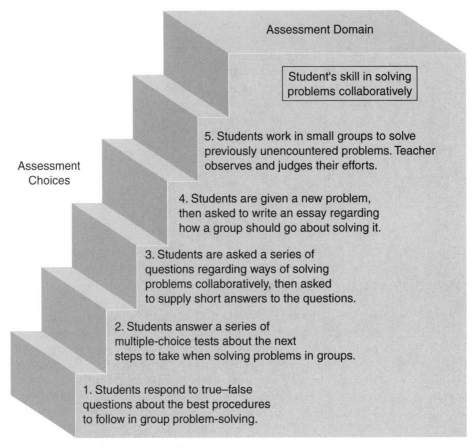

FIGURE 11.1.

Assessment choices that vary in the degree to which the student's task approximates the desired assessment domain.

Educational leaders, therefore, must realize that different educators will be using the phrase *performance assessment* to refer to very different kinds of assessment approaches. Many educators, for example, are willing to consider short-answer and essay tests as forms of performance assessment. In other words, they essentially equate performance assessment with any form of constructed-response assessment. Other educators establish more demanding requirements in order for a measurement procedure to be described as performance assessment. For example, some performance assessment advocates contend that genuine performance assessments must possess at least three features:

● *Multiple evaluative criteria:* The student's performance must be judged using more than one criterion. To illustrate, a student's ability to speak Spanish might be appraised on the basis of the student's accent, syntax, and vocabulary.

● *Prespecified quality standards:* Each of the criteria on which a student's performance is to be judged is clearly explicated in advance of evaluating the quality of the student's performance.

● *Judgmental appraisal:* Unlike the scoring of selected-response test in which electronic computers and scanning machines can, once programmed, carry on largely without the need of real people, performance assessments depend on human judgments to determine the acceptability of a student's performance.

Look back at Figure 11.1 and you'll see that, if the foregoing three requirements were applied to the five assessment options supplied, Assessment Choice 5 would qualify as a performance test, and Assessment Choice 4 probably would as well, but the other three assessment choices wouldn't be regarded as performance assessments under a definition that requires the incorporation of multiple criteria, prespecified quality standards, and judgmental appraisals.

Authentic Assessment

Performance assessment in which the student's task resembles real-life tasks.

"To test your scripture – copying skills, Brother Thomas, we'd like you to whip out a few old testaments during the next three months."

Educational Leaders Look at Assessment

Beyond Multiple Choices

Joe G. Frésquez, Director
Bilingual Education Program
Española Public Schools
Española, New Mexico

In retrospect, it's funny how I learned the meaning of the word *saltine* after selecting the wrong choice for a meaning in a standardized multiple-choice test. Having grown up in an isolated Spanish community where my family made a living off the land, I had never gone to a supermarket where I could have seen the word *saltine* printed on the label of a box of Saltine Crackers. Only when my science teacher and advisor, who was also Spanish, used the results of the test and my cultural knowledge of the word *sal* did I learn that *sal + tine = saltine*. Later on in life, when I left Peñasco, New Mexico and saw the word on a box of crackers, I felt like I had made a really big discovery! Until then I had "memorized" that *sal + tine = saltine*, but with that box of crackers staring at me in the face, I knew that I had found a real word I could chew on!

If I had continued to live in the deprived, isolated environment that I grew up in, I would have probably forgotten my science teacher's word formula. Just learning this formula, even after my teacher advisor's help, didn't mean I could show what I could do with the word and how to apply it. I still needed that box of crackers to show me and to help me put real teeth into it.

I have been an educator for the last 27 years and I still believe very strongly in oral interrogations and written examinations. I also believe very strongly in the use of *performance assessment*. Educators need to know how to use such assessments in order to determine whether students possess productivity skills and whether students are able to use what they have learned by producing products and giving performances.

To determine whether a student possesses the necessary productivity skills, educators must know how to design and use rubrics that will help them assess a student's abilities to work well with others, to be a productive thinker, and to be responsible and produce quality work. Educators thus must be able to develop tasks and assignments where productivity will be rated

and that can be used to determine the student's outcome or grade.

Educators *must* be able to design and use rubrics to determine students' skills. Modern-day educators *should* know how to design performance assessments (select outcomes, determine end products, and identify thinking skills).

Performance assessment, in my opinion, should be used as an alternative to standardized multiple-choice tests. This does not mean I recommend performance assessment as complete replacement for the CTBS or ITBS. Norm-referenced tests such as the CTBS and ITBS, however, should always be supplemented with other evaluations of the student's performance.

To determine whether students possess the necessary knowledge and skills for a course, teachers must be able to use multiple-choice tests, essays, teacher interviews/observations, and other forms of assessment.

As an elementary school principal for seven years and a high school principal for ten years, I worked with many teachers who worried about standardized achievement test results. In our school district, as well as in other school districts in New Mexico, scores from standardized achievement tests will be used to determine how schools are ranked and which schools will receive state department of education accreditation. Principals and teachers in our school district are now more frightened than ever because they are afraid of losing their jobs. Every spring, standardized achieve-

▶

▶ ment tests are given to our students, and the results continue to be low. From the teachers' point of view, these standardized achievement tests assess only the students' knowledge of isolated facts. Knowledge that is short-term and that students quickly forget after the test. Our students' poor results on these multiple-choice tests not only discourage teachers and principals, but also fail to motivate students to study.

What we need in our schools are curricular embedded assessments that can be used to motivate students. If we want our students to exhibit quality performance and products, we must give them examples of what quality is. We cannot expect students to complete a hundred-piece jigsaw puzzle without providing them with the whole picture. We cannot expect students to produce a quality essay without giving them an example of an outstanding essay. Students need to see examples of the finished product. Well-conceived performance assessments, accompanied by numerous examples of students' high-quality responses, can move educators in appropriate instructional directions. ●

Many advocates of performance assessment would prefer that the tasks presented to students be more *authentic* in the sense that the tasks represent real-world rather than school-world kinds of problems. Other proponents of performance assessment would be elated simply if more school-world measurement represented constructed-response tests rather than selected-response tests. In short, performance assessment enthusiasts often advocate different approaches to measuring students on the basis of how those students perform. What's "performance" to one educator may not qualify as "performance" to another.

Educational leaders will sometimes encounter educators who use other phrases to describe performance assessment. For example, educators may use the phrase *authentic assessment* (because the assessment tasks more closely coincide with real-life, nonschool tasks) or *alternative assessment* (because such assessments constitute an alternative to traditional paper-and-pencil tests). Later in the chapter, you'll be considering portfolio assessment, which is a particular type of performance assessment and should not be considered a synonymous descriptor for a performance-assessment approach to educational measurement.

The Rationale for Performance Assessment

The proponents of performance assessment base their support of performance assessment on a number of factors. Mehrens (1992) has identified several reasons why educators advocate performance assessment. Presented below are descriptions of three influences that he believes contribute to the support for performance assessment.

● *Disillusionment with selected-response tests.* Advocates of performance assessment believe that because multiple-choice and binary-choice tests call only for *recognition* on the part of the students, those tests fail to tap higher-order thinking skills such as whether students can solve problems, synthesize, or think independently. Although selected-response tests are sometimes criticized as being biased or as dealing with unimportant content, the most frequently voiced criticism of selected-response tests is, not surprisingly, that the student need only *select* a response.

● *Impact of cognitive psychology.* Cognitive psychologists believe that students must acquire both content knowledge and procedural knowledge. Such psychologists argue that all cognitive tasks require both kinds of knowledge. Because particular types of procedural knowledge are simply not assessable via selected-response tests, some cognitive psychologists have been calling for increased use of performance assessment in education to accompany what they believe should be an increased instructional emphasis on students' acquisition of procedural knowledge.

● *Negative influence of conventional tests.* As the stakes associated with an educational test rise, many teachers emphasize instructionally the content embodied in the test. Because many educators recognize that high-stakes tests will most likely continue to influence what a teacher teaches, they argue that performance assessments will constitute more worthy instructional targets than traditional paper-and-pencil tests. As a consequence of more appropriate high-stakes assessment targets, it is believed teachers' instructional activities will move in appropriate directions.

Although there are other arguments that can be mustered in favor of performance assessment, Mehrens (1992) has nicely captured the major motivations of those who advocate the widespread installation of performance assessments. Mehrens, incidentally, is highly supportive of the use of performance tests by classroom teachers because he believes significant instructional improvement will flow from such assessments. He is skeptical, however, about the use of performance tests for purposes of educational accountability, that is, for determining whether teachers (individually or aggregated at the school/district level) are providing effective instruction for their students.

To review, a performance test presents a demanding task to a student, then asks the student to respond to the task in writing, orally, or by constructing some type of product, for example, composing a narrative essay on a given topic. Educators ordinarily use performance tests when they want to determine a student's status with respect to a significant skill. Based on the student's level of achievement on a performance test, educators make an inference about the degree to which the student has mastered the skill that the test represents. Excellent results on the performance test imply that the student has mastered the skill; poor results suggest the opposite.

Performance Assessment Tasks

There are two critical components of a performance test, namely, the *task* the student must attempt to carry out and the *rubric* (scoring guide) used to judge the adequacy with which the student has done that carrying out. Let's focus first on a performance assessment's task.

It is the skill a performance test measures, of course, that will govern the nature of the tasks to be used. And it is in connection with the selection of those skills that an educational leader can have a positive impact on educational assessment. What you must recognize is that *performance assessment takes time*. It takes time to generate suitable tasks. It takes time to devise a scoring rubric. It takes time to score students' responses. And, because performance assessment does take so much time, educational leaders should make sure that performance tests are selected judiciously. If too many performance tests

Performance Assessment Tasks

The constructed-response assignment that a performance test presents to the student.

are imposed on teachers, you can be assured that teachers will rebel. There is already considerable concern on the part of teachers that too much teaching time is being diverted to testing. If teachers are called on to carry out a ton of performance tests, it's almost certain that performance assessment will suffer a premature demise. And most teachers will be cheering at the funeral.

Accordingly, if an educational leader has only a limited number of assessment chips to wager on performance testing, then those chips ought to be bet with wisdom aplenty. To illustrate, think about a fourth-grade teacher who has the responsibility of promoting students' growth in a variety of subjects such as language arts, science, and the arts. How many performance assessments *per subject area* do you think this fourth-grade teacher is going to be willing to undertake each year? Well, if I were that fourth-grade teacher, I'd guess that anywhere from one to three performance tests per subject would fill my assessment plate quite nicely. And if my guess is accurate, this means that performance assessment will most often need to be used in assessing students' mastery of the *most* significant skills, such as their ability to communicate orally, to read with comprehension, or to solve everyday mathematical problems. It would be assessment folly to devise and implement a performance test devoted exclusively to the student's skill in identifying the appropriate form of pronouns to employ when modifying gerunds. Such a modest skill is unworthy of the energy required by first-rate performance assessments.

A performance assessment, therefore, must measure *a truly powerful skill* that students need, in school and/or after their schooling has been completed. A skill such as "being able to communicate effectively in writing" would qualify as such a powerful skill. Incidentally, many of our educational insights regarding performance tests have been based on the work of language arts specialists who, for more than two decades, have been assessing students' composition skills. In the performance tests used to collect students' "writing samples," the tasks given to students are typically described by language arts educators as *prompts*. A skill such as "being able to discern subject–verb agreement" would not.

Second, a performance assessment must measure *a truly teachable skill*, in other words, a skill that teachers can effectively promote in their classes. Unfortunately, some performance assessments, as clever and "innovative" as can be, strive to assess a student's inborn intellectual capacity. Smart kids will do well on such performance tests; unsmart kids won't. The skill being measured by the performance test is fundamentally unteachable.

Educational leaders are apt to encounter situations in which too many low-level skills are supposed to be assessed by a plethora of performance tests. This, too, is educationally unsound. If you can focus on *skill-importance* and *skill-teachability*, you'll usually end up with suitable skills to be assessed by performance tests.

Performance assessment typically requires students to respond to a small number of more significant tasks rather than to a large number of less significant tasks. Thus, rather than answering 50 multiple-choice items on a conventional physics examination, students who are being assessed via performance tests may find themselves asked to perform an actual experiment in their physics class, then write an interpretation of the experiment's results and an analytic critique of the procedures they used. From the physics teacher's perspective, instead of seeing how students respond to the 50 "mini-tasks" represented in the multiple-choice test, an estimate of each student's status must be derived from a student's response to a single, complex task. Given the significance of each task that is used in a performance-testing approach, it is apparent that great care must be taken in the selection of such tasks. Generally speaking, classroom teachers will either have to (1) generate their own performance test tasks, or (2) select performance test tasks from the tasks that are available elsewhere.

Tasks and Skill-Focused Inferences

Consistent with the frequently asserted message in this scintillating measurement book, the chief determinants of how teachers ought to assess students are (1) the inferences that teachers want to make about their students, and (2) the decisions the teachers will base on those inferences. For example, suppose you're a history teacher and you've spent a summer at an oceanside bungalow meditating about curricular matters (which, in one luxurious setting or another, is the public's perception of how most teachers spend their summer vacations). After three months of heavy curricular thought, you have concluded that what you really want to teach your students is to be able to apply historical lessons of the past to the solution of current and future problems that, at least to some extent, parallel the problems of the past. You have decided to abandon the week-long, 2,000 item true–false final examination that your stronger students refer to as a "measurement marathon" and your weaker students refer to by using a rich, if earthy, vocabulary. Instead of true–false items, you are now committed to a performance assessment strategy and wish to select tasks for your performance tests that will help you infer how well your students can draw on the lessons of the past to illuminate their solutions of current and/or future problems.

In Figure 11.2, you will see a graphic depiction of the relationships among (1) a teacher's instructional objective, (2) the inference that the teacher wishes to draw about each student, and (3) the task for a performance test intended to secure data to support the inference that the teacher wants to make. As you will note, the teacher's instructional objective provides the source for the inference, and the assessment tasks yield the evi-

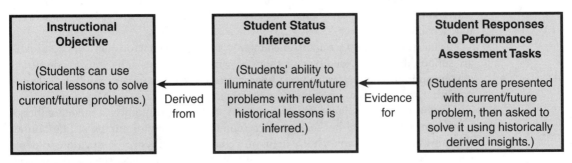

FIGURE 11.2.

Relationships among a teacher's instructional objective, the assessment-based inference derivative from the objective, and the performance assessment task that will provide evidence for the inference.

dence needed for the teacher to arrive at a defensible inference regarding the extent to which students can solve current or future problems using historical lessons. To the degree that students have mastered the instructional objective, the teacher will make a decision about how much more instruction, if any, is needed.

The Generalizability Problem

Perhaps the most serious psychometric shortcoming of performance assessment is that, because students respond to fewer tasks than would be the case with conventional paper-and-pencil testing, it is often more difficult to generalize accurately about what skills they possess.

Let's say, for example, that a teacher is trying to get a fix on students' ability to multiply pairs of double-digit numbers. If, because of the teacher's instructional priorities, the teacher can devote only a half-hour to assessment purposes, the teacher could require the students to respond to 20 such multiplication problems in the 30 minutes available. (That's probably more problems than the teacher would need, but I'm trying to draw a vivid contrast for you.) From a student's responses to 20 multiplication problems, the teacher could get a pretty fair idea about what kind of double-digit multiplier the student is. As a consequence of the student's performance on a *reasonable sample* of items drawn from the assessment domain, the teacher can conclude that "Juan really knows how to multiply those sorts of problems," or that "Bill really couldn't multiply double-digit multiplication problems if his life depended on it." It is because the teacher has sampled well the domain of student performance (from which the teacher wishes to make an inference) that the teacher can more confidently make inferences about students' abilities to solve similar sorts of multiplication problems. With only a 30-minute assessment period available, however, if the teacher moved to a more elaborate kind of performance test, the teacher might only be able to have students respond to *one* item. For example, suppose the teacher presented a multiplication-focused mathematics word problem involving the use of manipulatives, and wanted students to derive an original solution, then describe that solution in writing. The teacher would be fortunate if students could finish the task in a half hour. Based on this single task, how confident would the teacher be in making inferences about students' abilities to perform comparable multiplication tasks?

This, as I hope you now see, is a major problem with performance testing. Because students respond to fewer tasks, the teacher is put in a trickier spot when it comes to making inferences about their skills. If a teacher uses only one performance test, and a student does well on the test, does this signify that the student *really* possesses the skill the test was designed to measure, or did the student just get lucky? On the other hand, if a student messes up on a single performance test, does this signify that the student *really* doesn't possess the assessed skill, or was there a feature in this particular performance test that misled the student who, given other performance-test tasks, might have performed wonderfully?

Teachers are, therefore, faced with two horns of a classic measurement dilemma. Although performance tests often measure the kinds of student abilities that teachers would prefer to assess (because those abilities are in line with worthwhile instructional aims), the inferences that teachers make about students on the basis of their responses to performance

Test Violations Uncovered

The Kentucky Department of Education is lowering an elementary school's state achievement test scores after finding that employees there engaged in "inappropriate test practices."

State school officials concluded in a report last month that, for the past two school years, some 4th grade teachers and the former principal at Louisa Elementary School in Lawrence County violated state test rules by typing students' writing portfolios—a key component of the state test—and by improperly asking parents to assist their children with the portfolios.

A July 16 letter from education Commissioner Wilmer S. Cody to Lawrence County school officials states that the elementary school may have to hand over the $112,037 in reward money it received for raising its 4th graders' test scores.

What's your reaction?

Reprinted, with permission, from *Education Week*, August 6, 1997

tests must be made with increased caution. As with many dilemmas, there may be no perfect way to jump the dilemma's two horns. But there is, at least, a way of dealing with the dilemma as sensibly as possible. In this instance, the solution strategy is to devote great care to the selection of the tasks embodied in performance tests. An important consideration in selecting such tasks is to choose those tasks that optimize the likelihood of accurately generalizing about students' skills. If teachers really keep generalizability at the forefront when they select/construct performance-test tasks, they will be able to make the strongest possible performance-based inferences about their students' capabilities.

A Formidable Assessment Tool: Rubrics

During the late 1990s, *rubrics* became enormously fashionable. It was difficult to attend an educational conference without running into relentless support for the educational payoffs of rubrics. Indeed, the term itself seemed to evoke all sorts of positive images. Rubrics, according to their backers, were incontestably good things.[1]

But for many educators, rubrics inspire a series of questions. What are rubrics, and where did they come from? What is an educationally appropriate role for rubrics? Why do so many current rubrics fail to live up to their promise as guides for both teachers and students? What should educational leaders do to make rubrics better?

Components of a Rubric

As used today, the term *rubric* refers to a scoring guide used to evaluate the quality of students' constructed responses, for example, their responses to a performance test's tasks. A rubric has three essential components: evaluative criteria, quality definitions, and a scoring strategy.

Evaluative criteria are the factors that are used to distinguish acceptable responses from unacceptable responses. The criteria will obviously vary from rubric to rubric, depending on the skill involved. For instance, when evaluating written compositions, teachers often use such evaluative criteria as a composition's organization, mechanics, word choice, and supporting details. If you were to judge a student's skill in making an oral presentation, however, you might be looking at evaluative criteria such as eye contact or posture. Evaluative criteria can either be given equal weight or they can be weighted differently. (In passing, I must confess that because I completed five years of Latin in high school and college, I feel compelled to use a word or two of Latin at least on a semiannual basis. Thus, be aware that the Latin word *criterion* is singular and *criteria* is plural. Unfortunately, so many educators mix up these two terms that I don't even become distraught about it anymore. However, now that you know the difference, if you find any of your colleagues erroneously saying "the criteria is" or the "the criterion were," you can make an ever so subtle, yet altogether condescending smirk.)

The evaluative criteria for judging students' responses to performance tests have been called many things, for example, *rubrics, scoring guidelines*, and *scoring dimensions*. Regardless of the label employed, the criteria used to score students' responses identify the factors to be considering when determining the adequacy of a student's performance. Putting it another way, what are the attributes that a student's acceptable response will possess and that an unacceptable response won't?

Quality definitions describe the way that qualitative differences in students' responses are to be judged. For instance, if *mechanics* is an evaluative criterion, the rubric may indicate that, to earn the maximum number of points for mechanics, a student's composition should contain no mechanical errors. The rubric must provide a separate description for each qualitative level that can be used in judging students' performances. This means that, if four different levels of quality are assigned to a written composition's organization (with different numerical or verbal labels for each level), the rubric must provide descriptions for each of those levels.

A *scoring strategy* may be either holistic or analytic. Using a holistic strategy, the scorer takes all of the evaluative criteria into consideration but aggregates them to make a single, overall quality judgment. An analytic strategy requires the scorer to render criterion-by-criterion scores that may or may not ultimately be aggregated into an overall score. This difference in the application of evaluative criteria was described earlier (Chapter 10) in the context of scoring students' essay responses.

The original meaning of rubric had little to do with the scoring of students' work. The *Oxford English Dictionary* tells us that in the mid-15th century, *rubric* referred to headings of different sections of a book. This stemmed from the work of Christian monks who painstakingly reproduced sacred literature, invariably initiating each major section of a copied book with a large red letter. Because the Latin word for 'red' is *ruber*, rubric came to signify the headings for major divisions of a book.

A couple of decades ago, rubrics began to take on a new meaning among educators. Measurement specialists who scored students' written compositions started using the term to describe the rules that guided their scoring efforts. They could have easily employed a more readily comprehensible descriptor, such as *scoring guide*, but *scoring guide* lacked adequate opacity. (Specialists in any field, it seems to me, apparently adore opacity.) *Rubric* was a decisively more opaque, hence technically attractive, descriptor.

Evaluative Criterion

A standard on which a quality judgment may be based.

Typically, educators don't use rubrics unless the constructed response being judged is fairly significant. Thus, teachers rarely use rubrics to judge students' responses to short-answer tests. And, of course, rubrics are unnecessary for scoring students' performances on selected-response tests. With a few exceptions, teachers use rubrics to judge the adequacy of students' responses to performance tests.

Rubricity Wrongdoing: Three Flaws

Although the rubrics of the nineties received almost universal applause from educators, the vast majority of those rubrics were instructionally fraudulent. They were masquerading as contributors to instruction when, in reality, they had no educational impact at all. Here are three flaws that are all too common in teacher-made and commercially published rubrics, flaws that render rubrics instructionally useless.

Flaw 1: Task specific evaluative criteria. A rubric's most important component is the set of evaluative criteria to be used when judging students' performances. The criteria should be the most instructionally relevant component of the rubric. They should guide the teacher in designing lessons because it is students' mastery of the evaluative criteria that ultimately will lead them to skill mastery. Moreover, a teacher should make the rubric's evaluative criteria available to students to help them appraise their own efforts.

But what if the evaluative criteria in a rubric are linked only to the specific elements in a particular performance *task?* Unfortunately, I've run into a flock of such task-specific rubrics, especially in nationally standardized achievement tests that call for constructed responses from students.

A Task-Specific Rubric

A rubric whose evaluative criteria deal only with a particular task rather than the skill represented by that task.

Consider, for example, a task I encountered in a standardized achievement test that presents a cross-section picture of a vacuum bottle, then calls on students to identify the materials that had to be invented before vacuum bottles could be widely used. Such tasks are interesting, often inventive, and may even be fun for students to do. But the test's accompanying rubric contains evaluative criteria that are totally task-specific. Each evaluative criterion in the rubric was linked to the student's proper interpretation of the features of the *particular* picture that accompanies the *particular* item on the standardized achievement test. Each one of the rubric's evaluative criteria was exclusively based on the specific vacuum-bottle task.

How can such task-specific evaluative criteria help guide a teacher's instructional planning? How can such criteria help students evaluate their own efforts? Perhaps commercial test publishers are eager to install task-specific evaluative criteria because such criteria permit more rapid scoring as well as a much greater likelihood of between-scorer agreement. But such evaluative criteria, from an instructional perspective, are essentially worthless. Teachers need evaluative criteria that capture the essential ingredients of the *skill* being measured, not the particular display of that skill evoked by a particular task. Task-specific rubrics don't help teachers teach better.

Flaw 2: Excessively general evaluative criteria. Just as task-specific evaluative criteria render a rubric instructionally useless, so too do excessively general evaluative criteria. Numerous rubrics contain evaluative criteria so amorphous that they are almost laughable.

Many commercially published rubrics provide several qualitative levels so that teachers can ostensibly distinguish among students' performances. The highest level of student performance is designated as "advanced," or some synonymous label, then described as "a superior response to the task's chief components, thoroughly complete in all respects." A second, lower level of response is described in slightly less positive terms, and so on. In essence, these overly general evaluative criteria allow both teachers and students to conclude that really good student responses to the task are, well, really good. And, of course, really bad student responses are, you guessed it, really bad.

I'm exaggerating a bit, but not much. Many rubrics now being billed as instructionally useful provide teachers and students with absolutely no cues about what is genuinely significant in a student's response, and they offer teachers no guidance regarding the key features of the tested skill. How can teachers plan an instructional sequence of a skill if the distinguishing characteristics of skill-mastery are nonexistent?

What the rubric's designers have attempted to do is create a "one-size-fits-all" scheme for scoring students' responses to very different sorts of tasks. But the final result of that effort, typically, is little more than a redefinition of an A, B, C, D, F grading scale.

Flaw 3: Dysfunctional detail. Another shortcoming in many rubrics is excessive length. Busy teachers won't have anything to do with super-lengthy rubrics. If educational leaders want rubrics to make a difference in classroom instruction, they'll need to make sure rubrics are available that teachers will actually use. Lengthy, overly detailed rubrics are apt to be used only by teachers who have completed staff-development workshops on the joys of compulsivity.

Many of the rubrics being circulated these days are lengthy and laden with details. After all, most of the earliest rubrics were created for use in large-scale, high-stakes assessments. If a state's high school diploma was linked to how well a student functioned on an important statewide performance test—a writing sample, for instance—the architects of the accompanying rubric understandably might have leaned toward detailed scoring rules. In general, the more detailed and constraining a rubric's scoring rules, the greater the likelihood of between-rater agreement. For high-stakes tests, detailed rubrics are common.

When some educators and textbook publishers introduced rubrics for classroom use, the models being recommended were often based on rubrics from these earlier large-scale assessments. But such lengthy, excessively detailed rubrics almost invariably turn teachers off—an unfortunate effect, because a properly fashioned rubric can really improve the caliber of instructional activities.

In contrast to a brief rubric, detailed rubrics will, of course, spell out more precisely how to ascertain the quality of a student's response. A one- or two-page rubric will be subject to wider interpretation than will a six-page, "lay out all the scoring rules" rubric. But the practical choice comes down to this: (1) should educators build short rubrics that offer less than stringent scoring guidance but *will* be used by teachers? or (2) should educators build lengthier rubrics that provide stringent scoring guidance but *won't* be used?

Happily, in almost all instances, lengthy rubrics probably can be reduced to succinct but far more useful versions for classroom instruction. Such abbreviated rubrics can still capture the key evaluative criteria needed to judge students' responses. Lengthy rubrics, in contrast, will usually attract dust.

Task-Mastery *versus* Skill-Mastery

Some teachers, unfortunately, equate a performance test with the skill itself. This problem stems less from rubrics themselves than from an error made by rubric-users. A particularly prevalent misunderstanding occurs when rubric-users become so caught up with the particulars of a given performance test that they begin thinking of the *test* as the skill itself. For example, if the performance test calls for a student to display mathematical problem-solving skills by carrying out a specific multistep solution, too many teachers become fixated on the student's mastery of that particular multistep solution as the target of their instructional efforts. These teachers are promoting test mastery rather than skill mastery.

Realistically, any really worthwhile skill can probably be measured by an array of tasks that could be embodied in different performance tests. For example, to determine a student's ability to give an extemporaneous speech, a teacher might allow a student to choose from many topics for the "speech" performance test. As a practical matter, of course, teachers don't have time for students to display a single skill through a dozen different performance tests. Although the more performance tests a student completes, the more accurate will be teachers' inferences about skill mastery, teachers usually rely on one or two efforts by a student on a performance test.

Teachers must, however, instruct toward the *skill* represented by the performance test, not toward the *test*. Test-focused instruction, especially if it mimics the test in every detail, will often inhibit the student's general mastery of the skill. Students may, indeed, learn how to do well on a *particular* performance test, but if asked to tackle a different performance task, a task derived from the same skill, they may stumble. Teachers must keep in mind that performance tests represent skills. The tests are not the skills themselves.

Skill-Focused Rubrics

Skill-Focused Rubric

A rubric whose evaluative criteria are conceptualized according to the skill being assessed.

Having maligned various kinds of instructionally noxious rubrics, it's time for me to get constructive. What would a rubric look like that not only helped teachers judge the quality of students' responses to a performance test but also assisted those teachers in helping students acquire the skill represented by that test?

For openers, such a rubric would contain *only* three-to-five evaluative criteria. It is tempting to a rubric's designer to lay out all of the possible criteria that could be used to judge students' responses; but rubric developers should remember that their efforts should guide teachers, not overwhelm them. In rubrics, as in most realms of life, less is definitely more.

Second, each evaluative criterion must represent a key *teachable* attribute of the skill being assessed. Each criterion must be teachable in the sense that teachers can help students increase their ability to use the criterion when tackling tasks that require the use of the skill being assessed. For example, many teachers are quite competent in helping students learn how to compose essays that embody skillful organization, effective word choice, appropriate mechanics, and suitable supporting detail. Each of these criteria is eminently teachable. Effective teachers of composition can share these criteria with students to help those students master essential writing skills. Because the students have access to the teacher's evaluative framework, many students will adopt that evaluative framework for the evaluation of their own efforts.

All of the rubric's evaluative criteria should be applicable to *any* task employed to gauge a student's skill-mastery. Ideally, each of the evaluative criteria will be given a concise descriptive label to help teachers and students identify it. I've seen numerous rubrics that really do contain all of the features I've described here, but the rubrics are so badly laid out that it's very difficult for anyone to tell what's really most important. Well-formed rubrics ought to be teacher- and student-friendly.

I do not want to suggest that the isolation of teachable evaluative criteria for rubrics is fools' play. It isn't. But I have seen many rubrics containing teachable evaluative criteria. Educational leaders must insist on the use of such rubrics.

The more quickly educators abandon both task-specific and excessively general rubrics, the more likely it will be that teachers will employ rubrics that actually enhance instruction. In addition, for routine use, relatively short rubrics must be the rule. If educational leaders want teachers to focus their instructional attention on the evaluative criteria embedded in rubrics, rarely should a rubric exceed one or two pages. With any rubric intended for classroom use, a sheaf of papers held by a staple should be regarded as the enemy.

Rubrics represent not only scoring tools but also, more importantly, they serve as instructional illuminators. Appropriately designed rubrics can make an enormous contribution to instructional quality. Unfortunately, many rubrics now available to educators are not instructionally beneficial. If these flawed rubrics are not rapidly replaced with instructionally helpful ones, then the educational promise of rubrics will surely not be realized. Educational leaders who understand what a good rubric is and what a bad rubric is can help teachers identify those that will improve children's learning.

An Illustrative Instructionally Oriented Rubric

To provide you with an example of a rubric that satisfies all the suggestions I've been ladling out, I want you to consider the following performance task in history (Box 11.1) and its accompanying skill-focused rubric (Box 11.2). The performance test was developed for the Department of Defense Dependents Schools in Hessen, Germany. The skill being assessed is, as you will see, genuinely high level. (This is the skill, incidentally, that was briefly depicted in Figure 11.2.) If parents discovered that their children could accomplish the skill being assessed, you'd surely see a clear case of parental awe. Even though the skill is truly demanding, the educators who devised the skill believed it was a skill that—over time—could definitely be taught. See what you think, because in the chapter's practice exercises, you'll have an opportunity to suggest how this history skill *could* be taught.

BOX 11.1 A Performance Test

Using History's Lessons

Skill Description:

Students will be able to draw on the lessons of history to predict the likely consequences of current-day proposals. More specifically, students will be presented with a current problem setting and a proposed solution. The student must then (1) identify one or more historical events that are particularly relevant to the problem setting and proposed solution, (2) justify those selected, (3) make a history-based prediction regarding the proposed solution's likely consequences, and (4) defend that prediction on the basis of historical parallels.

ing proposed as a solution to the problem. Students will be asked to write an essay in which they (1) identify, from a prespecified timeline of major events in U.S. history, one or more historical events that are relevant to the proposed solution; (2) justify the relevance of the identified event(s); (3) make a defensible prediction of the probable consequences of the proposed solution based on the identified historical event(s); and (4) defend the prediction on the basis of parallels between the problem situation, the proposed solution, and the identified historical event(s).

Nature of Tasks:

Students will be given a description of a real or fictitious problem-situation in which a course of action is be-

Sample Task:

Read the fictitious situation described in the box, then follow the directions below the boxed description.

War or Peace?

Nation A is a large, industrialized country whose population is almost 100,000,000. Nation A has ample natural resources, and is democratically governed. Nation A also owns two groups of territorial islands that, although quite distant, are rich in iron ore and petroleum.

Nation B is a country with far fewer natural resources and a population of only 40,000,000. Nation B is about one-third as large as Nation A. Although much less industrialized than Nation A, Nation B is as technologically advanced as Nation A. Nation B is governed by a three-member council of generals.

Recently, without any advance warning, Nation A was ruthlessly attacked by Nation B. As a consequence of this attack, more than half of Nation A's military equipment was destroyed. After its highly successful surprise attack, Nation B's rulers have proposed a "peace agreement" calling for Nation A to turn over its two groups of islands to Nation B. If the islands are not conceded by Nation A, Nation B's rulers have threatened all-out war.

Nation A's elected leaders are fearful of the consequences of the threatened war because their military equipment is now much weaker than that of Nation B. Nation A's leaders are faced with a choice between (1) peace obtained by giving up the islands or (2) war with a militarily stronger nation.

Nation A's leaders decide to declare that a state of war exists with Nation B. They believe that, even though Nation B is now stronger, in the long term Nation A will win the war because of its greater industrial capability and richer natural resources.

Directions:

Compose a well-written essay on the pages provided. In that essay, drawing on your knowledge of U.S. history, select one or more important historical events that are especially relevant to the fictitious situation described above.

Then justify the relevance of your selection(s). Next, make a reasonable history-based prediction about the likely consequences of the decision by Nation A's leaders to go to war. Finally, defend your prediction on the basis of the historical event(s) you identified.

BOX 11.2 A Skill-Focused Rubric

The quality of students' response to any task will be evaluated according to three evaluative criteria, namely, (1) the selection and justification of relevant historical events, (2) the quality and defensibility of the history-based prediction regarding the proposed problem solution's consequences, and (3) the written presentation of the analysis. Each of these criteria will be described in terms of the key elements constituting a criterion. Four levels of quality (Distinguished: 4 points, Proficient: 3 points, Apprentice: 2 points, and Novice: 1 point) will be described for each criterion according to that criterion's key elements. A zero will be given to students who make no response or whose response is illegible or in a foreign language. A single overall score will be assigned to a student's response.

Evaluative Criterion One: Historical Event Selection/Justification

(identifying relevant historical events,
then justifying those events effectively)

Key Elements:

Event Selection: Choosing one or more appropriate events from the *U.S. History Timeline: Major Events,* that is, those events sufficiently parallel to the described problem-situation and the proposed solution to permit a *defensible prediction regarding the proposed solution's likely consequences. (The appropriately relevant historical event(s) for each task will be determined by the examiners.)*

U.S. History Timeline
Major Events

(For 11th-Grade American History)

Constitution	Depression
Territorial Expansion	New Deal
Civil War	World War II
Reconstruction	Cold War
Industrial Revolution	Civil Rights
Imperialism	Viet Nam
World War I	Communication Revolution

(A different timeline would be used at lower grade levels.)

Event Justification: Supporting the relevance of the historical event(s) selected to the proposed solution

by identifying features of the historical event and the proposed solution that are sufficiently similar to warrant a history-based prediction about the proposed solution's consequences.

Quality Levels:

Distinguished (4 points):   The selection of historical events is completely accurate, that is, all appropriate historical events are selected while no inappropriate events are selected. The selection of all those events is well justified.

Proficient (3 points):   The selection of historical events is satisfactorily accurate, that is, at least one appropriate historical event is selected and any inappropriate historical events selected are justified at least adequately. In addition, all appropriate historical events are justified at least adequately.

Apprentice (2 points):   Not all appropriate historical events are selected, but those inappropriate events selected are justified at least adequately.

Novice (1 point):   No appropriate historical events are selected, and those inappropriate events selected are inadequately justified.

Evaluative Criterion Two: Prediction Defensibility

(making a sound history-based prediction
and defending it strongly)

Key Elements:

- **Prediction Quality:**   Predicting the consequences of the proposed solution in a manner that is reasonably derivative from the historical event(s) selected.

- **Strength of Defense:**   Defending the history-based prediction by identifying those features of any selected historical events that bear on the likelihood of the prediction's accuracy.

Quality Levels:

Distinguished (4 points):   The prediction of the proposed solution's consequences is reasonably based on the historical event(s) selected and is strongly defended by the citation of pertinent aspects of the historical event(s) selected.

(continued)

BOX 11.2 *(Continued)*

Proficient (3 points): The prediction of the proposed solution's consequences is adequately based on the historical event(s) selected and is at least adequately defended by pertinent aspects of the historical event(s) selected.

Apprentice (2 points): *Either* the prediction of the proposed solution's consequences is adequately based on the historical event(s) but inadequately defended *or* the prediction is inadequate even though its historically based justification is strong.

Novice (1 point): The prediction of the proposed solution's consequences is inadequate and the defense of the prediction is only adequate or worse.

Evaluative Criterion Three: Written Communication

(communicating effectively in writing)

Key Elements:

● *Organization:* Structuring the essay appropriately.

● *Mechanics:* Employing suitable spelling, punctuation, and grammar.
● *Voice:* Incorporating effective usage and word choice.

Quality Levels:

Distinguished (4 points): All three key elements are well developed.

Proficient (3 points): All three key elements are at least adequately developed.

Apprentice (2 points): Only one or two key elements are adequately developed.

Novice (1 point): No key elements are adequately developed.

Overall Score:

Derived analytically or holistically, each student should be assigned an overall score of 0–4.

As you reviewed the performance test, Using History's Lessons, and its accompanying rubric, I hope you noted the effort on the part of the rubric's architects to identify evaluative criteria that they regarded as teachable. In this instance, each of the three evaluative criteria are further subdivided into two or three key elements that it was thought could be addressed instructionally by teachers.

Note also that, as this skill is conceptualized, the developers of the scoring rubric want to focus not only on whether students can apply the historical knowledge they possess (the first two evaluative criteria), but also whether they can display this ability in the form of a well-written composition (the third evaluative criterion). This represented an attempt on the part of the rubric's designers to integrate a social studies and language arts skill. That integration is, clearly, the rubric-developer's choice. Think of all the power you have when you whomp up a rubric for an important test! Imagine, for a moment, that a district's history teachers were really trying to promote the skill measured by this performance assessment. Do you think it would be "history instruction as usual" in those teachers' classes?

Applying a Rubric's Evaluative Criteria

Once teachers have selected their rubric's evaluative criteria, they then need to apply them reliably in the judgment of students' responses. If the nature of the performance-test task calls for students to create some sort of *product*, such a written report of an experiment carried out in a biology class, then teachers at their leisure can rate the product's quality in relation to the evaluative criteria. For example, if the teacher had decided to use three criteria in evaluating students' reports of biology experiments, and could award from zero to four points for each evaluative criterion, then the teacher could leisurely assign from zero to twelve points for each written report. The more clearly the teacher understands what each evaluative criterion is, and what it means to award a different number of points on whatever scale has been selected, the more accurate the teacher's scores will be. Performance tests that yield student products are easier to rate because teachers can rate students' responses when they're in the mood.

It is often the case with performance tests, however, that the student's performance takes the form of some kind of *behavior*. With such performance tests, it will usually be necessary for teachers to observe the behavior as it takes place. To illustrate, suppose that an elementary school teacher has fifth-grade students carry out fairly elaborate social studies projects that are to culminate in 15-minute oral reports to classmates. Unless the teacher has the equipment to make videotape recordings of students' oral presentations, the teacher will have to observe the oral reports and make judgments about the quality of a student's performance as it occurs. As was true when scores were given to student products, in making judgments about students' behavior, teachers will apply whatever evaluative criteria they've chosen and try to assign an appropriate number of points on the scales being used.

For some observations, teachers will find it sensible to make instant, on-the-spot quality judgments. For instance, if a teacher is judging students' social studies reports on the basis of (1) content, (2) organization, and (3) presentation, the teacher might make observation-based judgments on each of those three evaluative criteria as soon as a report is finished. In other cases, the teacher's observations might incorporate a delayed evaluative approach. For instance, let's say that a teacher is working with students in a speech class on the elimination of "filler words and sounds," two of the most prominent of which are starting a sentence with *well*, or injecting frequent *uhs* into a presentation. In the nonevaluative phase of the observation, the teacher could simply *count* the number of *wells* or *uhs* uttered by a student. Then, at a later time, the teacher could decide on a point allocation for the criterion "avoids filler words and sounds." Putting it another way, systematic observations may be set up so that the teacher makes immediate or delayed awards of points for the evaluative criteria chosen. If the evaluative criteria involve qualitative factors that must be appraised more judgmentally, then on-the-spot evaluations and point assignments are typically the way to go. If the criteria involve more quantitative factors, then a "count now and judge later" approach usually works better.

Error Sources in Judging Student Performances

When scoring student performances, there are three common sources of error that can contribute to inaccurate inferences. First, there is the *scoring scale* in the rubric. Second, there are the *scorers* themselves, who may bring a number of bothersome biases to the enterprise. Finally, there are errors in the *scoring procedure*, that is, the process by which the scorers employ the rubric.

Scoring-Instrument Flaws

The major defect with most scoring instruments is the lack of descriptive rigor with which the criteria to be used are described. Given this lack of rigor, ambiguity exists in the interpretations that scorers make about what the scoring criteria mean. This typically leads to a set of unreliable ratings. For example, if teachers are to rate students on the extent to which students are "controlling," some teachers may view this as a positive quality, and some may view it as a negative quality. Clearly, an inadequately clarified scoring form can lead to all sorts of noise in the scores provided by teachers.

Procedural Weaknesses

Among common problems with scoring students' responses to performance tests, you'll usually encounter demands on teachers to rate too many qualities. Overwhelmed scorers are scorers rendered ineffectual. Teachers who opt for a large number of evaluative criteria are teachers who have made a decisively inept opt. Care should be taken that no more than four or five criteria are employed in evaluations of students' responses to your performance assessments. Generally speaking, the fewer the rubric's evaluative criteria, the better.

Personal Bias Problems

If you recall Chapter 6's consideration of bias, you'll remember that absence-of-bias is clearly a desirable commodity. Teachers, albeit unintentionally, are frequently biased in the way they score students' responses. Several kinds of *personal bias* errors are often encountered when teachers score students' constructed responses. The first of these, known as *generosity error*, occurs when a teacher's bias leads to higher ratings than are warranted. Teachers with a proclivity toward generosity errors see good even where no good exists. At the other extreme, some teachers display *severity errors*. A severity error, of course, is a tendency to underrate the quality of a student's work. When a pupil's product deserves a *good*, a teacher suffering from this personal bias error will award it only an *average* or even a *below average*.

Another sort of personal bias error is known as *central-tendency error*. This describes a tendency for teachers to view everything as being "in the middle of the scale." Very high or very low ratings are avoided by such folks. They prefer the warm fuzziness of the mean or the median. They tend to regard midpoint ratings as inoffensive, consequently dispense midpoint ratings almost thoughtlessly.

A particularly frequent error arises when a teacher's overall impression of a student influences how the teacher rates the student with respect to an individual evaluative criterion. This error is known as *halo effect*. If a teacher has a favorable attitude toward a student, that student will get a host of favorable ratings (deserved or not) on a number of individual evaluative criteria. Similarly, if a teacher has an unfavorable attitude toward a student, the student will get a pile of unfavorable ratings on all sorts of separate evaluative criteria.

One way to minimize halo effect, at least a bit, is to occasionally reverse the order of the high and low positions on the scoring scale so that the teacher cannot *unthinkingly*

Halo Effect

The error of allowing one's overall impression of a student to influence criterion-by-criterion evaluations.

mark a whole string of positives (or negatives). What educational leaders really need to remember is that halo effect is always lurking in the wings (or, if you think of halos and angelic folks more traditionally, lurking in the clouds). Try to ensure that a student's responses are judged on each evaluative criterion using *that* specific criterion, not a contaminated general impression of the student's ability.

Portfolio Assessment

Portfolio Assessment

A systematic appraisal of students' collected work samples.

A portfolio is a systematic collection of one's work. In education, portfolios refer to systematic collections of students' work. Portfolios are applicable to assessing students' work in a variety of subject areas. Although the use of portfolios in education has been a relatively recent phenomenon, portfolios have been widely used in a number of other fields for many years. Portfolios, in fact, constitute the chief method by which certain professionals display their skills and accomplishments. For example, portfolios are traditionally used for that purpose by photographers, artists, journalists, models, architects, and so on. An important feature of portfolios is that they must be updated as a person's achievements and skills grow.

Portfolios have been warmly embraced by those educators who regard traditional assessment with less than enthusiasm. In Box 11.3, for example, a chart presented by Tierney, Carter, and Desai (1991) indicates what those three advocates of portfolios believe are the differences between assessment using portfolios and assessment based on more traditional testing approaches.

BOX 11.3 Differences in Assessment Outcomes Between Portfolio and Standardized Testing Practices

PORTFOLIO

- Represents the range of reading and writing students are engaged in
- Engages students in assessing their progress and/or accomplishments and establishing ongoing learning goals
- Measures each student's achievement while allowing for individual differences between students
- Represents a collaborative approach to assessment
- Has a goal of student self-assessment
- Addresses improvement, effort, and achievement
- Links assessment and teaching to learning

TESTING

- Assesses students across a limited range of reading and writing assignments that may not match what students do.
- Mechanically scored or scored by teachers who have little input
- Assesses all students on the same dimensions
- Assessment process is not collaborative
- Students assessment is not a goal
- Addresses achievement only
- Separates learning, testing, and teaching

Source: Material from *Portfolio Assessment in the Reading-Writing Classroom,* by Robert L. Tierney, Mark A. Carter, and Laura E. Desai, published by Christopher Gordon Publishers. Used with permission of the publisher.

Classroom Use

Efforts to apply portfolio assessment in large-scale settings, such as in statewide testing, have not proven to be especially successful. Either the scoring of students' portfolios is insufficiently reliable or the costs of scoring are too high. Proponents of portfolio assessment typically believe that the real payoffs for such assessment approaches lie in an individual teacher's classroom because the relationship between instruction and assessment will be strengthened as a consequence of students' continuing accumulation of work products in their portfolios. Ideally, teachers who adopt portfolios in their classrooms will make the ongoing collection and appraisal of students' work a central focus of the instructional program rather than a peripheral activity whereby students occasionally gather up their work to convince a teacher's supervisors or the students' parents that good things have been going on in class.

Here's a description of how an elementary teacher might use portfolios to assess students' progress in social studies, language arts, and mathematics. The teacher, let's call him Fenimore Pholio, asks students to keep three portfolios, one in each of the subject fields. In each portfolio the students are to place their early and revised work products. The work products are always dated so that Mr. Pholio, as well as the students themselves, can see what kinds of differences in quality take place over time. For example, if effective instruction is being provided, there should be discernible improvement in the caliber of students' written compositions, solutions to mathematics problems, and analyses of social issues.

Three or four times per semester, Mr. Pholio holds 15- to 20-minute portfolio conferences with each student about the three different portfolios. The other, nonconferencing students take part in small-group and independent learning activities while the portfolio conferences are conducted. During a conference, the participating student plays an active role in evaluating his or her own work. Toward the close of the school year, students select from their regular portfolios a series of work products that not only represents their best final versions, but also indicates how those final version products were created. These selections are placed in a display portfolio that is then featured at a spring open-school session designed for parents. Parents who visit the school are urged to take their children's display portfolios home. Mr. Pholio also sends home portfolios to parents who were unable to attend the open-school event.

There are, of course, many other ways to use portfolios effectively in a classroom. Fenimore Pholio, our "phictitious" teacher, employed a fairly common approach, but a variety of alternative procedures could also work quite nicely. The major consideration is that the teacher uses portfolio *assessment* as an integral aspect of the *instructional* process. Because portfolios can be tailored to a specific student's evolving growth, the diagnostic value of portfolios for teachers is considerable.

Self-evaluation as a goal. Most seasoned users of portfolio assessment contend that the real payoff from proper portfolio assessment is that students' *self-evaluation* capabilities are enhanced. Thus, during portfolio conferences the teacher encourages students to come up with personal appraisals of their own work. The conference, then, becomes far more than merely an opportunity for the teacher to dispense an "oral report card." On the contrary, students' self-evaluation skills are nurtured not only during portfolio conferences, but throughout the entire school year. For that reason, many portfolio advocates prefer the use of *working* portfolios instead of *showcase* portfolios because these educators believe that self-evaluation is nurtured more readily in connection with ongoing reviews of products that are not intended to impress external viewers.

For self-evaluation purposes, it is particularly useful to be able to compare earlier work with later work. Fortunately, even if a teacher's instruction is downright abysmal, students grow older and, as a consequence of maturation, usually tend to get better at what they do in school. If a student is required to review three versions of his or her written composition, namely, a first draft, a second draft, and a final draft, self-evaluation can be fostered by encouraging the student to make comparative judgments of the three compositions based on a rubric's evaluative criteria. As anyone who has done much writing knows, written efforts tend to get better with time and revision. Contrasts of later versions with earlier versions can prove illuminating from a self-appraisal perspective.

Guidelines for Application

Although there are numerous ways to install and sustain portfolios in a classroom, teachers probably need to consider the following:

1. *Make sure students "own" their portfolios.* In order for portfolios to really represent a student's evolving work, and to foster the kind of self-evaluation that is so crucial if portfolios are to be truly educational, students must perceive portfolios to be collections of their own work and not merely temporary receptacles for products that the teacher ultimately grades. Teachers will probably want to introduce the notion of portfolio assessment to their students (assuming that portfolio assessment isn't already a school-wide operation and that the teacher's students aren't already familiar with the use of portfolios) by explaining the distinctive functions of portfolios in the classroom.

2. *Decide on what kinds of work samples to collect.* There are various kinds of work samples that can be included in a portfolio. Obviously, such products will vary from subject to subject. In general, a wide variety of work products is preferable to a limited range. Ideally, teacher and students can collaboratively determine what goes in the portfolio.

3. *Collect and store work samples.* Students then need to collect the designated work samples as they are created, place them in a suitable container (a folder or notebook, for example), then store the container in a file cabinet, storage box, or some suitably safe location. Teachers may need to work individually with their students to help them decide whether particular products should be placed in their portfolios.

4. *Select evaluative criteria by which to evaluate portfolio work samples.* Working collaboratively with students, teachers carve out a set of evaluative criteria by which the teacher and students can judge the quality of their portfolio products. In other words, a collaboratively developed *portfolio-appraisal rubric* is created. Because of the likely diversity of products in different students' portfolios, the identification of evaluative criteria in such rubrics will not be a simple task. Yet, unless at least rudimentary evaluative criteria are isolated, students will find it difficult to evaluate their own efforts and, thereafter, to strive for improvement.

5. *Require students to evaluate continually their own portfolio products.* Using the agreed-on rubric, teachers should be sure that their students try to evaluate their own work. Students can be directed to evaluate their work products holistically, analytically, or using a combination of both approaches. Such self-evaluations can be made routine by requiring each student to complete brief evaluation slips or 3 x 5-inch cards on which they identify the major strengths and weaknesses of a given product, then suggest how the product could be improved. Teachers should be sure to have students date such self-evaluation sheets so the students can keep track of modifications in their self-evaluation skills. Each completed self-evaluation sheet should be stapled or paper-clipped to the work product being evaluated.

6. *Schedule and conduct portfolio conferences.* Portfolio conferences take time. Yet, these interchange sessions between teachers and students regarding students' work are really pivotal in making sure that portfolio assessment fulfills its potential. The conference should not only evaluate students' work products, but should also help students improve their self-evaluation abilities. Teachers should try to hold as many of these conferences as they can. In order to make the conferences time-efficient, teachers should have students prepare for the conferences so that the teacher can start right in on the topics of most concern to the teacher and the student. The rubric that is to be used in appraising students' work samples is, of course, prominently used during portfolio conferences.

7. *Involve parents in the portfolio assessment process.* Early in the school year, teachers must make sure students' parents understand what the nature of the portfolio assessment process is that the teacher has devised. Insofar as is practical, teachers should encourage students' parents/guardians periodically to review their children's work samples as well as their children's self-evaluations of those work samples. And this means, of course, that parents have received a copy of the portfolio-appraisal rubric. The more active that parents become in reviewing their children's work, the stronger the message to the child that the portfolio activity is really worthwhile. If teachers wish, they may have students select their best work for a showcase portfolio or, instead, simply use the students' working portfolios.

These seven steps reflect only the main-line activities that teachers might engage in when creating assessment programs in their classrooms. There are obviously all sorts of variations and embellishments that are possible.

The Weaknesses of Portfolio Assessment

Educational leaders need to keep in mind that portfolio assessment's greatest strength is that it can be tailored to the individual student's needs, interests, and abilities. Yet, portfolio assessment suffers from the drawback faced by all constructed-response measurement. Students' constructed responses are genuinely tough to evaluate, particularly when those responses vary from student to student.

It is quite difficult to come up with consistent evaluations of different students' portfolios. Sometimes the rubrics devised by teachers for use in evaluating portfolios are so terse and so general as to be almost useless. It is difficult to devise rubrics that embody just the right level of specificity. Generally speaking, most teachers are so busy that they don't have time to create elaborate rubrics. Accordingly, many teachers (and students) find themselves judging portfolios using fairly broad-brush evaluative criteria. Such broad criteria tend to be interpreted differently by different people.

Another problem with portfolio assessment is that it takes time, loads of time, to carry out properly. Even if teachers are very efficient in reviewing students' portfolios, they'll still have to devote many hours both in class (during portfolio conferences) and outside of class (if teachers also want to review students' portfolios by themselves). Proponents of portfolios are convinced that the quality of portfolio assessment is worth the time such assessment takes. Educational leaders need to be prepared for the required investment of time if teachers decide to follow the portfolio-assessment path.

Clearly, the role of rubrics in connection with portfolio assessment is just as pivotal as was the case with performance assessment. Well-conceived rubrics—devised with instructional decision-making in mind—can make portfolio assessment an approach that leads to high quality education. Portfolio assessment without such rubrics may be little more than a systematic scheme to store students' work.

Chapter Wrap-Up

For our chapter summary, as usual, let's hearken back to the chapter's guiding questions. (Incidentally, is it possible to hearken forward?)

● How can performance assessment be used to improve educational quality?

Although there is meaningful disagreement about the kinds of measurement approaches that should properly be considered performance assessments, most specialists agree that a performance test presents a demanding skill-based task to a student, then asks the student to construct a response to that task. Performance assessments became popular, according to Mehrens, because of educators' disenchantment with traditional selected-response tests, the influence of cognitive psychology, and as a reaction against the negative influence of conventional tests.

The skills to be assessed via performance tests should be both powerful and teachable. The tasks selected to represent students' mastery of a skill should allow educators to arrive at a reasonably valid inference about students' skill-mastery, although the small number of tasks that typically constitute a performance test sometimes makes it difficult to arrive at a valid interpretation of students' generalized skill-mastery.

● What are the qualities of rubrics that contribute to improved educational quality?

The three essential components of a rubric are: (1) the evaluative criteria employed to appraise the quality of students' responses, (2) quality definitions reflecting different levels of excellence associated with each evaluative criterion, and (3) a scoring strategy indicating whether the rubric's evaluative criteria are to be applied analytically or holistically.

Three types of instructionally unhelpful rubrics were described in the chapter. Task-specific rubrics, the first of these, are suitable for evaluating students' responses to a particular task, not to the class of tasks represented by the performance assessment. A second kind of instructionally unhelpful rubric is one that is so general it offers teachers little guidance in instructional planning. Finally, rubrics that are too detailed and, as a consequence, too lengthy, will typically be regarded as onerous by busy teachers.

A skill-focused rubric, in contrast, can be particularly helpful to teachers as they plan their instruction. Skill-focused rubrics contain a small number of evaluative criteria, pithily labeled, that are applicable to the scoring of students' responses to all tasks representing the skill that's being assessed. Each evaluative criterion must be capable of being addressed instructionally. Finally, a skill-focused rubric should not be so lengthy that teachers will be reluctant to use it. A demanding social studies skill, "Using History's Lessons," was provided to illustrate what a skill-focused rubric looks like.

When educators are applying a rubric's evaluative criteria, several sources of potential error may crop up. Among these are instrument defects, procedural weaknesses, and biases on the part of the rubric-user. Rubric-user biases stem from generosity errors, severity errors, central-tendency errors, and halo effect.

● How can portfolio assessment contribute to improved educational quality?

Portfolios, as employed in educational assessment, are collections of student work evaluated according to the sorts of evaluative criteria that one would employ in a scoring rubric for performance tests. Portfolios are especially useful in promoting students' ability to evaluate their own work. Portfolios can be used in various subject areas.

The following guidelines for classroom portfolio assessment were offered for teachers who wish to employ this approach: (1) ensure student ownership of the portfolios, (2) determine the kinds of work samples to collect, (3) collect and store work samples, (4) identify evaluative criteria, (5) require students' self-evaluation of their work, (6) conduct portfolio conferences, and (7) involve parents in the assessment process.

Portfolios have not proven particularly useful in large-scale assessments because of scorer unreliability and excessive costs. In the classroom, it was pointed out that the implementation of a portfolio assessment system is almost always quite time-consuming. Educational leaders will need to help teachers determine if the instructional dividends of portfolio assessment are worth the time it requires. Many teachers who are now using portfolio assessment swear by it. Some teachers, former portfolio users, swear at it.

Practice Exercises

For the following five practice items, decide whether the *assessment domain* identified would, based on the factors identified in the chapter, be suitable for a classroom teacher to measure using a performance assessment. For each assessment domain, indicate *Yes* or *No*, then give the reason for your choice.

1. *Assessment Domain.* The student's ability to supply the meaning of 200 words that are "not seen frequently, but are important" according to a linguistic authority.

   Yes or *No* and why? _____

   _____

2. *Assessment Domain.* The student's skill in properly punctuating simple sentences.

   Yes or *No* and why? _____

   _____

3. *Assessment Domain.* The student's skill in employing the scientific method when carrying out investigative projects in a chemistry class.

   Yes or *No* and why? _____

   _____

4. *Assessment Domain.* The student's positive attitude toward the study of history.

   Yes or *No* and why? _____

   _____

5. *Assessment Domain.* The student's skill in writing an evocative descriptive essay regarding an important event in the student's life.

   Yes or *No* and why? _____

   _____

For the next three practice items, you'll need to imagine that you're an instructional supervisor who has visited an elementary teacher's classroom to offer improvement tips. For purposes of these three practice items, assume the teacher's class was visited on the previous day by two local firefighters who talked to students for an hour about home fire-escape plans. Today, as you observe the class, the teacher asks students to write a narrative essay describing what happened during the previous day's visit by the firefighters. The teacher plans to evaluate student's essays using a rubric with four evaluative criteria, one of which is the essay's *organization.*

Now, consider each of the following three *potential* evaluative criteria for *organization* and indicate whether the criterion would be best suited for (a) a task-specific rubric, (b) an excessively general rubric, or (c) a skill-focused rubric.

6. *An Evaluative Criterion for Organization:*
   "Superior essays will (1) commence with a recounting of the particular rationale for home fire-escape plans that the local firefighters provided, then (2) follow up with a description of the six elements in home-safety plans in the order that those elements were presented, and (3) conclude by citing at least three of the

life–death safety statistics the firefighters provided at the close of their visit. Departures from these three organizational elements will result in lower evaluations of essays."

Is this evaluative criterion best suited for a rubric that is (a) task-specific, (b) excessively general, or (c) skill-focused?

7. *An Evaluative Criterion for Organization:*
   "Superior essays are those in which the essay's content has been arranged in a genuinely excellent manner whereas inferior essays are those that display altogether inadequate organization. An adequate essay is one that represents a lower organizational quality than a superior essay, but a higher organizational quality than an inferior essay."

Is this evaluative criterion best suited for a rubric that is (a) task-specific, (b) excessively general, or (c) skill-focused?

8. *An Evaluative Criterion for Organization:*
   "Two aspects of organization will be employed in the appraisal of students' narrative essays, namely, overall structure and sequence. To earn maximum credit, an essay must embody an overall structure containing an introduction, a body, and a conclusion. The content of the body of the essay must be sequenced in a reasonable manner, for instance, in a chronological, logical, or order-of-importance sequence."

Is this evaluative criterion best suited for a rubric that is (a) task-specific, (b) excessively general, or (c) skill-focused?

9. This next practice exercise is important. It is also taxing and lengthy, but worth the effort I hope you'll give to it. It calls for you to reconsider the illustrative social studies performance test and accompanying rubric given in the chapter, "Using History's Lessons," on pages 294–296. Then, in an effort to help a teacher promote students' mastery of that skill, please identify in writing (1) a set of two or more

general instructional suggestions that would apply to the promotion of *any* similar high-level cognitive skill, and (2) a set of four or more *specific* instructional suggestions that would apply directly to the teaching of this *particular* skill.

In other words, put on your instructional hat and offer teachers some tips about how they might promote students' mastery of similar cognitive skills (your two or more general suggestions) and this particular cognitive skill (your four or more specific suggestions). Good luck.

10. For this chapter's final practice exercise, your task will be to read a scenario about a fictitious teacher who is attempting to employ portfolio assessment in her classroom. You are to determine if any of the chapter's seven portfolio-assessment guidelines provided on pages 301–302 have been *violated*. It's okay if you look those guidelines over before tackling the exercise. If you wish to tough it out without review, who am I to question bravery?

Having decided to adopt a portfolio assessment approach for the composition segment of her junior high school English classes, Flora Morales introduces her students to the new assessment scheme by asking a commercial artist friend of hers to speak to each class. The artist brings his own portfolio and shows the students how the portfolio allows prospective clients to judge his work. Ms. Morales tells her students that her friend's portfolio is called a "showcase portfolio" and that students will be preparing both a showcase portfolio to involve their parents in periodically reviewing work products, and also a "working portfolio" to keep track of *all* of their composition drafts and final products. Ms. Morales and her friend emphasize that both kinds of portfolios must be "owned" by the students, not the teacher.

Because all of their drafts and final versions are to be collected, students simply place copies of all such products in folders and, when finished, in a designated file drawer. Early in the academic year, Ms. Morales works with each of her classes to decide collaboratively on the criteria to be used in judging the composition efforts for a given class. Although there are slight differences in the criteria decided on for each class, the criteria for all classes are fairly similar.

Ms. Morales makes sure to review all students' portfolios at least once per month. Typically, she devotes one preparation period per day to a different class's portfolios. Because the portfolios are readily available in a file cabinet in her classroom, Ms. Morales finds it convenient and time-efficient to evaluate students' progress in this manner. She provides a brief evaluation (dated) for students to consider when they work with their portfolios.

At least twice per term, Ms. Morales selects what she considers to be students' best finished work from their working portfolios. She places such work products in a showcase portfolio. Students are directed to take these showcase portfolios home to let their families see what kinds of compositions they have been creating. Parents are enthusiastic about this practice. A number of parents have told the school principal that Ms. Morales' "take-home" portfolio system is the way they would like to see other aspects of their children's performances evaluated.

Now, please critique Ms. Morales' efforts in relation to the seven guidelines for portfolio assessment supplied in the chapter. Which, in any way, were violated or missing?

Answers to Practice Exercises

1. The answer to this practice item ought to be *No*. This assessment domain describes a body of knowledge more readily assessable via selected-response items or, perhaps, short-answer constructed-response items.

2. Again, your response ought to be negative. The skill captured in the assessment domain is fairly low level. If teachers were to measure such small-scope skills with performance assessments, they'd be devoting too much time to assessment.

3. This is an assessment domain that seems to satisfy the considerations set forth in the chapter. It is a significant, teachable skill. For chemistry teachers, this skill should be a powerful one, hence worth the assessment time. Your answer should have been *Yes*.

4. This assessment domain is in the affective arena, an arena not readily amenable to assessment via performance tests. In Chapter 13 you'll learn about how to measure students' affect. It won't be by performance assessments. You should have answered *No*.

5. Although there would need to be some clarification given of what's involved in an "evocative descriptive essay," this looks like an assessment domain ripe for performance testing. A *Yes* answer would be a winner.

6. This evaluative criterion is best suited for a task-specific rubric. Can you see how a teacher would find it senseless to use this rubric to teach students how to organize narrative essays? After all, how often are students going to be in a class visited by firefolk?

7. This evaluative criterion is far too nebulous, hence suited only for an excessively general rubric. This kind of rubric, obviously, would provide little clarity to help teachers in their instructional planning.

8. This evaluative criterion would live "happily ever after" in a skill-focused rubric. The two pivotal features of a well-organized narrative essay are identified, namely, overall structure and sequence. Each of these is further explained. This evaluative criterion could be addressed instructionally by teachers.

9. It is, of course, impossible to foresee what general or specific instructional suggestions you might have come up with. But to supply you with some feedback, here are illustrative responses to this exercise.

10. Ms. Morales's approach to portfolio assessment had much to commend it. Indeed, if the approach is really working, she probably shouldn't tinker with it. There were, however, two ingredients that Ms. Morales overlooked that some proponents of portfolio assessment consider important. First, she didn't push students very hard in the direction of self-evaluation. Second, she didn't hold any one-on-one portfolio conferences. During such conferences, of course, Ms. Morales could nurture students' self-evaluation skills. For a first try at portfolio assessment, however, our fictitious Ms. Morales did a rather nifty job.

Illustrative General Suggestions

Reaping a Rubric's Dividends

The first general suggestion springs from the nature of the rubric itself. The rubric focuses on evaluative criteria that are employed to judge the quality of students' responses to a task. These evaluative criteria were specifically formulated so that they would be instructionally addressable. Consequently, you should devote sufficient time to become familiar with the rubric so that you recognize all of its important features. Look over the prescored students' responses to make sure you understand what it is that distinguishes higher quality responses from lower quality responses.

And if teachers can benefit from using the rubric, what about students? If a rubric has been constructed with instruction in mind (as is true in this case), then both teachers *and* students can profit from the rubric. It may be necessary, of course, to provide your students with a reworded, age-appropriate version of the rubric so that the evaluative criteria are described in student-friendly language. You can decide whether such a revision is needed. But as soon as your students are ready, you'll find that providing them with some form of the rubric will make it possible for those students to engage in meaningful evaluations of their own efforts. Such self-evaluation, of course, can be especially helpful in skill-building.

Task Analysis

One immediate benefit of teachers' understanding a to-be-taught skill is that they can then carry out more effective task analyses. Simply put, you need to decide if there is any enabling knowledge or skill that must be mastered by your students before they attain skill mastery. If you identify such knowledge or skills, then you'll need to promote them during instruction, usually rather early during instruction.

Direct Instruction's Applicability

During the past few decades, U.S. educators have identified an impressive collection of effective, research-based instructional procedures. You should employ as many of these proven instructional procedures as you believe appropriate. For instance, after describing the nature of the skill to your students and getting them to understand its importance (to them), it is usually helpful for you or selected students to model the skill. And when students un-

derstand what is being sought of them, it is often helpful to give them opportunities to discriminate between weak and strong illustrative responses. As soon as your students are ready, the provision of guided practice followed by independent practice will usually move students toward skill mastery. Such practice activities, guided or independent, will be more effective if the rubric is consistently used by you and your students.

In addition to conventional teacher-directed activities, you will also find such instructional variations as cooperative learning and peer critiquing can prove useful in promoting this skill. What you need to recognize is that the vast majority of what you know about instructional procedures will be highly relevant in promoting your students' mastery of an eminently teachable skill.

A Final Caution

Really important skills can usually be displayed in a variety of ways. Ideally, well-mastered skills will be generalizable, that is, applicable in many situations. Beware of promoting your students' mastery of this skill so that the *only* way the skill can be applied by students is in carrying out the particular types of tasks identified here. To avoid this, be sure to give students a variety of practice opportunities, only some of which are of the type defined by the tasks identified here.

Illustrative Specific Suggestions

1. Make sure that the students (and you) understand that this skill requires a distinctive way of thinking about history.

To display mastery of the skill, your students must (1) analyze a current-day problem situation and proposed solution so that they can (2) *select* and *justify* relevant historical events, then (3) *predict* the proposed solution's consequences and *defend* that prediction. This three-step sequence, analyze, select/justify, and predict/defend should offer a framework for the instruction you provide for this skill.

2. Because this skill is intended to help students apply history's lessons to their own postschool lives, you'll need to get students to start viewing historical events not merely from the perspective of "what happened," but from the perspective of "what lessons can we draw from this historical event." Not all historical events, of course, yield lessons for the future. Much of history is so dependent on the actions of unique individuals, or is so complex, that it is difficult to identify any cause–effect generalizations that would be applicable to the future. But these cause–effect generalizations based on one or more historical events are often present if we look for them. Encourage your students to be on the lookout for such history-based lessons routinely. Help them see the difference between historical events that yield lessons for the future and historical events that don't.

3. Familiarize students with time lines and how to use them. Make sure your students know that, for purposes of measuring this skill, the 14-event time line provided in the rubric cites all "eligible" major events in U.S. history. Each major event, of course, embraces a number of historical occurrences from which historical lessons might be drawn.

4. Frequently have students consider a current problem situation and see if any events in U.S. history are sufficiently relevant so that reasonable predictions about current-day consequences can be made. It is especially valuable if the current problems are seen by students as relevant to their own lives. You are encouraging students to routinely regard today's problems in light of relevant historical occurrences.

5. As soon as students have learned how they are supposed to respond to the tasks that assess their mastery of this skill, give them guided and, later, independent practice in responding to such tasks. You may need to generate your own practice tasks if such tasks are not available. For one guided practice activity, you might want to use the sample task provided with this skill's rubric.

6. Because written communication is an evaluative criterion for judging students' responses, make sure you give students practice in writing essays of the sort called for in this skill's tasks. Then help them evaluate their own essays on the basis of that criterion's three key elements: organization, mechanics, and voice.

7. Make sure that students thoroughly understand the rubric's three criteria and each criterion's key elements. Have students critique each others' responses to practice tasks on the basis of the rubric.

8. Post the rubric and the time line prominently in your classroom. You may choose, of course, to remove these materials when students are assessed on their mastery of this skill. What we want, of course, is for students to routinely use this skill in postschool life as they judge the wisdom of problem solutions they encounter. When that time comes, they will not be able to rely on crutches such as posted rubrics or time lines.

9. Teach students any special terminology associated with this skill, for example, *predict, justify, defend,* and so on.
10. Promote students' knowledge of U.S. history so they have a basis for draw

ing history-based lessons. Ideally, as you cover the necessary segments of U.S. history, you should stress the importance of drawing cause–effect lessons that can guide today's citizens.

DISCUSSION QUESTIONS

1. If you were an educational leader who was trying to guide teachers in the identification of skills to be assessed via performance tests, what would you say to them?
2. What do you think is the greatest virtue of performance assessment? How about its greater vice?
3. How do you think educators might attempt to solve the lack of generalizability that occurs because performance assessments present so few tasks to students?
4. Why do you think there are so many task-specific rubrics in educational circulation these days? What about excessively general rubrics: Why are there so many of those?
5. What do you think is the most difficult obstacle in using a skill-specific rubric for purposes of instructional improvement?
6. What do you personally believe is the most important strength of portfolio assessment? What about the most important weakness of this form of assessment?
7. How can the substantial time demands of portfolio assessment be effectively addressed by classroom teachers?

SUGGESTIONS FOR ADDITIONAL READING

Blum, Robert E., and Judith Arter (Eds.). *A Handbook for Student Performance Assessment in an Era of Restructuring.* Alexandria, VA: Association for Supervision and Curriculum Development, 1996.

Cole, Donna J., Charles W. Ryan, and Fran Kick. *Portfolios across the Curriculum and Beyond.* Thousand Oaks, CA: Corwin Press, 1995.

Danielson, Charlotte. *A Collection of Performance Tasks and Rubrics: Middle School Mathematics.* Larchmont, NY: Eye on Education, 1997.

Danielson, Charlotte. *A Collection of Performance Tasks and Rubrics: Upper Elementary School Mathematics.* Larchmont, NY: Eye on Education, 1997.

Danielson, Charlotte, and Leslye Abrutyn. *An Introduction to Using Portfolios in the Classroom* (Stock #197171M48). Alexandria, VA: Association for Supervision and Curriculum Development, 1997.

Educators in Connecticut's Pomperaug Regional School District 15. *A Teacher's Guide to Performance-Based Learning and Assessment* (Stock #196021M48). Alexandria, VA: Association for Supervision and Curriculum Development, 1996.

Hebert, Elizabeth A. "Lessons Learned About Student Portfolios." *Phi Delta Kappan,* 79, 8 (April 1998): 583–585.

Mehrens, William A. "Using Performance Assessment for Accountability Purposes." *Educational Measurement: Issues and Practice, 11,* 1 (Spring 1992): 3–9.

Mehrens, William A., W. James Popham, and Joseph M. Ryan. "How to Prepare Students for Performance Assessments." *Educational Measurement: Issues and Practice, 17,* 1 (Spring 1998): 18–22.

Northwest Regional Educational Laboratory. *Bibliography of Assessment Alternatives: Social Studies.* Portland, OR: Author, 1997.

Spandel, Vicki. *Dear Parent: A Handbook for Parents of 6-Trait Writing Students.* Portland, OR: Northwest Regional Educational Laboratory, 1997.

Stecher, Brian M., and Stephen P. Klein. "The Cost of Science Performance Assessments in Large-Scale Testing Programs." *Educational Evaluation and Policy Analysis, 19,* 1 (Spring 1997): 1–14.

AND FOR THOSE WHO TIRE OF READING

Pollock, Jane. *Designing Authentic Tasks and Scoring Rubrics* (Audiotape: Stock #295238S62). Alexandria, VA: Association for Supervision and Curriculum Development, 1997.

Popham, W. James. *A Parent's Guide to Performance Assessment* (Videotape #ETVT-26). Los Angeles: IOX Assessment Associates.

Popham, W. James. *Performance Assessment: How Authentic Must It Be?* (Videotape #ETVT-27). Los Angeles: IOX Assessment Associates.

Popham, W. James. *Portfolios and Language Arts: A First Look* (Videotape #RDVT-38). Los Angeles: IOX Assessment Associates.

Popham, W. James. *Portfolio Conferences: What They Are and Why They Are Important* (Videotape #RDVT-39). Los Angeles: IOX Assessment Associates.

Popham, W. James. *The Role of Rubrics in Classroom Assessment* (Videotape #ETVT-18). Los Angeles: IOX Assessment Associates.

Wiggins, Grant, and Richard Stiggins. "Tape 3—Performance Assessments" (Videotape: Stock #614237S62) in *Redesigning Assessment Series.* Alexandria, VA: Association for Supervision and Curriculum Development, 1992.

Wiggins, Grant, and Richard Stiggins. "Tape 2—Portfolios" (Videotape: Stock #614237S62) in *Redesigning Assessment Series.* Alexandria, VA: Association for Supervision and Curriculum Development, 1992.

ENDNOTE

1. This chapter's treatment of rubrics is adapted from an October 1997 essay I published ("What's Wrong—and What's Right—with Rubrics") in *Educational Leadership, 55,* 2, with permission from the publishers. All rights reserved.

12 Improving Test Items

- What are the most common approaches to item improvement?
  Judgmental
  Empirical

- How can judgmental procedures be employed to improve test items?
  Nonstudent Reviewers
  Student Reviewers

- What kinds of empirical procedures can be used to improve test items?
  Difficulty Indices
  Discrimination Indices
  Distractor Analysis

eophyte authors suffer from the common misconception that really seasoned writers can instantly dash off prose or poetry that rarely needs revision. Inexperienced writers of educational tests also tend to believe that their first-draft items should equal their last-draft items.

A useful pilgrimage for such novices would be a visit to the British Museum. In the authors' room of that fabulous museum, the manuscripts of writers such as Keats, Wordsworth, and Byron are on display. It is initially surprising, but then highly comforting, to see that even these literary giants revised, and revised, and revised their efforts. Visitors to the museum can see the often lengthy chain of drafts that precede the final poem or essay as these revered writers fussed over their work.

Well, if Keats and Milton were willing to shape up their writing, then item revision should not be considered beneath the dignity of any item-writer, whether a veteran or a beginner. This chapter describes ways of transforming early-version test items into a form that, though a bit less lustrous than a Shakespearean sonnet, is markedly superior to an item-writer's initial efforts.

Empirical and Judgmental Techniques

In considering the possible approaches to salvaging a flawed test item, it is helpful to isolate two fairly distinctive improvement strategies. The first of these is a *judgmental* approach in which the dominant reliance is on the human judgment that individuals render when they inspect, then weigh the merits of particular test items. Such judgmental strategies (*a priori* strategies, if you're feeling in the mood for a little ritzy Latin) can range in rigor and sophistication from a rather casual review of items to a highly sophisticated, multidimensional review. You'll often see classroom teachers relying on their own instincts as they endeavor to sharpen up their tests. These efforts would be a good example of an unsystematic use of a judgmental item-improvement approach.

A second approach to item improvement can be characterized as an *empirical* (or, if you're still in need of a little dead language suaveness, *a posteriori*) method. In contrast to judgmental methods of item improvement, which rely only on someone's judging the quality of test items, empirical schemes for item improvement require you to try the items out on honest-to-goodness students, gather data regarding how the students performed on the items, then analyze the data in various ways to help isolate possibly defective items.

Empirical Item Improvement

Improving an item's quality based on students' performance on the item.

It is important to note that, if you employ empirical item-improvement techniques, you are focusing on *student*-response data, that is, students' actual responses to the test items. You are not looking at just any old data. Merely because you're playing around with data, however, does not make that item-improvement approach empirical instead of judgmental. The data are not student-response data, but only data derived from judges.

Incidentally, although in practice you'll often find more applications of empirical item-improvement methods to selected-response items, constructed-response items can also be improved by judgmental, as well as empirical, techniques.

Although these two item-improvement strategies will be considered separately here, almost no respectable measurement specialist would recommend that you rely exclusively on either a judgmental or an empirical approach. More often than not, if resources permit, both strategies should be employed. In large-scale assessment, the use of empirical item-improvement schemes usually precedes the application of judgmental strategies. Test items are tried out, the results of the tryout are subjected to one or more statistical analyses, and these analyses are made available to individuals who then judge the items. Those judgments are, therefore, abetted by the results of the empirical item analyses.

Even busy classroom teachers, if they can somehow snag an extra hour or two every month or so, can employ both empirical and judgmental schemes to improve their tests. However, if time pressures or financial resources preclude the use of a combined empirical–judgmental approach to item improvement, it is better to use only one of the approaches than to avoid item improvement altogether. Educational test items usually need revision.

It is interesting to realize that in the past several decades the choice between judgmental and empirical item-improvement strategies has been almost perfectly correlated with the *size* of the test-development effort. In large-scale test-development projects, such as those involving the construction of nationally standardized achievement or aptitude tests, the major emphasis has been on empirical item-improvement procedures. Test items have been tried out, often with thousands of students. Results of these tryouts have then been subjected to all the exotic machinations that today's computers permit. Analyses of these empirical results have then guided the revision of the test items.

On the other hand, the sorts of small-scale test-refinement efforts that go on in a teacher's classroom have almost always emphasized a judgmental strategy. Classroom teachers, either because they are already too busy or because they aren't familiar with empirical item-improvement methods, have traditionally relied on judgmental techniques to revise their tests. In the typical case, Mrs. Jones will review the final exam she used in last year's algebra class in order to judge which items are in need of revision or replacement. Although there are a few cases in which classroom teachers have employed empirical test-improvement schemes, these are certainly exceptions.

Norm- and Criterion-Referenced Interpretations

Throughout your current text-guided trip through assessmentville, it has been emphasized that there are situations in which it doesn't make any substantial difference whether educators are focusing on norm-referenced or criterion-referenced interpretations of students' test performances. In some cases, however, the distinction between norm- and criterion-referenced inferences is quite significant. Such is the case with respect to item improvement. You'll find that with norm-referenced interpretations there is greater reliance on empirical methods and with criterion-referenced interpretations there is more attention given to judgmental methods. Why is this so?

Well, if you'll recall Chapter 2's discussion of criterion-referenced interpretations, you'll remember how important it is to come up with a clear description of the assessment domain, and then generate items that are deemed congruent with the assessment domain's boundaries. These are tasks that must be performed *judgmentally*. Indeed, in determining the degree to which a test's assessment domain has been satisfactorily described, there is no sensible alternative to human judgment.

Moreover, because the determination of a test's (1) assessment domain clarity and (2) congruence of the test's items with its assessment domain are activities that *precede* the administration of tests to students, it is apparent that when criterion-referenced inferences are sought, you'll often be emphasizing judgmental approaches.

For norm-referenced interpretations, however, you'll need to focus on the efficiency of the instrument in detecting differences among students so that you can defensibly contrast students' performances against one another. This being the case, it is evident that you'll pick up your best insights regarding the refinement of items by actually trying out the test items with students, then seeing how well the items contribute to the detection of performance differences among those students. Thus, for tests aimed at norm-referenced interpretations, there is usually a greater reliance on empirical methods in the improvement of test items.

Naturally enough, because the last half century of educational measurement saw measurement buffs stressing empirical item-improvement approaches, it is not surprising that our technical tool kit of empirical item-improvement techniques is far better stocked than is the case with judgmentally based techniques. However, as will become apparent later in the chapter, there are certainly instances when test items, irrespective of the test's focus on norm- or criterion-referenced interpretations, would be substantially benefited from the application of judgmental-improvement *and* empirical-improvement procedures.

Judgmental Improvement of Test Items

There are several sources of judgmental data by which teachers can improve test items. First, of course, teachers can supply judgmental data themselves. A teacher who writes a test item can subsequently review that item according to all sorts of criteria. If teachers themselves are to be used in supplying such judgments, then, just as authors frequently find it helpful to set aside manuscripts for a time prior to revision, it is often beneficial for teachers to wait a week or so before reviewing their own items. After the immediacy of creation has worn off, it is often more likely that parents can discern flaws in their progeny. Teachers are no different.

In addition to those who actually authored the items, it is possible to assemble independent judges who, though conversant with the subject matter, have no proprietary interests in particular items. Because of their lack of partisanship, independent reviewers are particularly valuable in the implementation of an effective judgmental item-improvement operation. External reviewers can do more than merely spot defective items; they can proffer remedies for those items. A teacher's colleagues would fit this prescription nicely. Perhaps there could be a bit of item-review trading.

Finally, students themselves can judge item quality. For example, students can be asked to comment if they find items ambiguous, misleading, too hard, too easy, and so on. It is difficult, however, for a student simultaneously to play the role of test taker and test critic. Care should be taken, therefore, to establish review procedures so that students' desires to do well on a test will not incline them to malign all items they missed.

Nonstudent Reviewers

Well, now that you know *who* might be doing the judging, *what* should they be looking for in their reviews? Let's look first at the sorts of review foci that might be employed by teachers themselves or external reviewers. Later on, you'll consider a somewhat different approach for getting the reactions of students.

The actual dimensions that serve as the basis for the review vary, of course, depending on the purposes of the examination. However, generally speaking, the following sorts of considerations serve as the heart of most item-review judgment schemes:

1. Is the item congruent with its assessment domain?
2. Are there violations of standard item-writing guidelines?
3. Is the content of the item accurate?
4. Is the item ethnically, socioeconomically, or otherwise biased?

Each of these questions, perhaps rephrased more specifically in accord with the particular purposes of the test, could serve as a bit of general guidance for item reviewers Alternatively, if one prefers something a mite more systematic, an item-review form could be devised in which the reviewers would actually need to respond in writing to such questions, item by item. If a defect is noted in any item, the reviewers might be asked to supply suggestions regarding possible improvements. Let's briefly consider each of the four questions just cited.

Assessment domain congruence. To judge whether an item is congruent with the assessment domain from whence it supposedly sprang, judges obviously have to consider both the assessment domain and the items themselves. In the case of tests focused on norm-referenced interpretations, assessment domain descriptions are often less detailed than is true with tests focused on criterion-referenced interpretations.

Reviewers of items from tests aimed at criterion-referenced inferences will have to be highly attentive to the ingredients of a described assessment domain because, with such absolute interpretations, item congruence is especially important. For such tests, Berk (1978) stressed that:

> It cannot be overemphasized how crucial this characteristic is to the effectiveness of the total test and the usefulness of the results. Irrespective of all other characteristics, *an item that is not congruent with its objective should not be included on the test.* (italics in original)[1]

One scheme for checking on the quality of the item reviewers themselves (if they are other than the teacher) is to toss in a few deliberately incongruent items to detect whether reviewers are at least spotting such clearly incongruent items. Reviewers who fail to spot such "lemon" items should have their judgments disregarded.

Adherence to item-writing guidelines. With respect to the violation of the sorts of item-writing rules that I described in previous chapters, a reviewer of items obviously needs to be familiar with a wide range of such rules. For example, if an item reviewer runs across a multiple-choice item in which the wrong-answer distractors are all short, while the correct answer is long, then that problem needs to be noted. There can, of course, be deficiencies in test items other than violations of the customary item-writing guidelines. Reviewers of test items will have to keep their wits about them in order to detect such flaws.

Content accuracy. If test items deal at all with academic content, such as achievement tests in history, language arts, or biology, then it is obviously important to have the content in those items be accurate. For example, if the correct answer to a test item in a grammar exam erroneously indicates "relative pronouns that modify gerunds should be in the objective, not possessive case," then a skillful item reviewer should spot that content error. It is true, of course, that not too many people realize (or care about) the appropriate case of pronouns that modify gerunds. Yet think what terrific item reviewers you have if they can see that the *him* in the following math item should be *his*.

A grammatically flawed arithmetic item

Jill always admired John's speed in going to the store. Each week he went to the store three times and took only twenty minutes each time. How much *total time* was involved in him going to the store?

If your item reviewers can detect such nuances, then they'll surely be able to weed out more blatant shortcomings.

Absence of bias. In Chapter 6 considerable time was spent in describing the ways in which tests can be biased. Item reviewers should be alert for blatant and subtle biases in items, whether racist, sexist, religious, gender, or socioeconomic. If, for example, a test item describes "Mrs. Gomez, a servant," then some Hispanic Americans may, with justification, be offended if it appears that Spanish-speaking people are destined to occupy positions of servitude. To remedy such an item, either transform Mrs. Gomez to Mrs. Green or, more aggressively, elevate Mrs. Gomez to the status of a corporate executive. When using judges to review test items, be sure to alert them to the necessity of monitoring items for possible bias.

To recapitulate, the use of judges to review test items, whether those judges are teachers themselves or outside reviewers, can definitely improve test items. Judgmental review of items can be carried out informally or rather systematically. Informal reviews are doubtlessly better than no reviews at all. Formal, systematic reviews are even better. Devising a scheme whereby both item writers *and* external reviewers appraise items would be particularly effective.

As indicated previously, judgmental item-refinement procedures can be used to augment the quality of both selected-response and constructed-response sorts of items. All too often you'll see measurement specialists giving item-improvement attention to selected-response test items (particularly of the multiple-choice species), yet spending no time on the improvement of, for instance, essay items. Well, essay items need their share of item-improvement attention, too. Judgmental techniques can be particularly effective in improving constructed-response items.

Student Judgment

When teachers set out to improve test items, a rich source of data is often overlooked because they typically fail to secure advice from students. Yet, because students have experienced test items in a most meaningful manner, more or less as an executionee experiences a firing squad, student judgment can provide useful insights regarding particular items and, for that matter, other features of the test such as its directions and the time allowed for completing the test.

As noted before, the kinds of data secured from students will vary, depending on the type of test being used, but questions such as the following can usually be addressed with profit to students after they have completed an examination:

Item-Improvement Questionnaire for Students

1. If any of the items seemed confusing, which ones were they?

2. Did you think any items had more than one correct answer? If so, which ones?

3. Did you think any items had *no* correct answers? If so, which ones?

4. Were there words in any items that confused you? If so, which ones?

5. Were the directions for the test, or for particular subsections of the test, unclear? If so, which ones?

It is important to let students finish a test prior to their engaging in such a judgmental exercise. (Note the use of the possessive pronoun modifying the gerund *engaging*. You are, obviously, reading some grammatically top-drawer stuff here.) If students are asked to *simultaneously* play the roles of test takers and test improvers, they'll probably botch both tasks. No student should be expected to serve these two functions, at least at the same time.

Simply give students the test as usual, collect their answer sheets or test booklets, and provide them with new, blank booklets. *Then*, distribute a questionnaire, such as the five-item one provided above. In other words, ask them to play students, and item reviewers, but to play these roles consecutively, not simultaneously.

Now, how do teachers treat students' reactions to test items? Let's say a few students come up with a violent castigation of one of a teacher's favorite items. Does the teacher automatically buckle by scrapping or revising the item? Of course not; teachers are made of sterner stuff. Perhaps the students were miffed about the item because they didn't know how to answer it. One of the best ways for students to escape responsibility for a dismal test performance is to assail the test itself. Teachers should anticipate a certain amount of carping from low-scoring students.

However, after allowing for a reasonable degree of complaining, student reactions can sometimes provide useful insights for teachers as well as test developers from high-powered testing agencies. To overlook students as a source of judgmental test-improvement information, for either selected-response or constructed-response items, would be a serious error.

Overall Item Judgments

In this chapter we've focused chiefly on *item* improvement. There is also virtue in considering a test's items *in the aggregate*. It is often useful to ask reviewers (students or other teachers) to consider an entire set of items in order to render overall judgments regarding these items. For example, although there may be no discernible gender bias in any single item, when all items are reviewed as a group, such a bias may be discovered. To illustrate, imagine that over 80 percent of a test's items included the use of males and that in those items the vast majority of males were depicted positively. Contrarily, in the 20 percent of the items that dealt with females, those females were represented negatively. Although such an image might not be perceived when the items were judged one at a time, a reviewer asked to make overall judgments about the test's items would be better able to isolate such shortcomings in the test.

Empirical Improvement of Test Items

Let's turn now to the use of student-response data in the improvement of test items. Numerous empirical item-improvement techniques have been devised over the years, particularly for tests that focus on norm-referenced interpretations. Let's consider these more traditional item-analysis procedures first, turning later to a few more recent wrinkles for improving items on tests that are supposed to yield criterion-referenced interpretations.

Educational Leaders
Look at Assessment

Wanted: Assessment Skills

Dr. Warren H. Gemmill
Assistant Superintendent
Saratoga Springs City School District
Saratoga Springs, New York

The value of a teacher's formal and informal observations regarding students' performance and achievements is difficult to calculate. I personally have always believed that the direct provider of instruction is in a pivotal position regarding assessment of student progress. The mandatory involvement of the classroom teacher in consideration of goals and objectives to be included in the Individual Educational Plan of a child identified as having educational disabilities is testimony to this fact.

On occasion, it is surprising how dramatically the results of "objective" measures (for example, standardized achievement tests) differ in comparison with the evaluation by a teacher of the same student's performance. Most practicing building administrators have had the experience of a teacher's expressing extreme surprise over a child's stellar or lackluster performance on a standardized test being so different from the child's routine class performance. Clearly, there are several possible explanations for poor performance. It may, for example, simply be the result of a child's personal or emotional health that day. Strong performance is more difficult, but not impossible to explain. Examples might include the child who is highly distracted or bored within the classroom setting. The same child, when focused on a single task without distraction, is able to produce achievement at a higher level than the child would normally demonstrate within the classroom setting.

One aspect of student assessment that could be strengthened by many classroom teachers is the area of validity. I have had the experience of teachers' assessing student performance on the basis of an instrument that was not well linked to the learning in question. An example of this occurred when a teacher conscientiously developed a screening test for students' necessity to participate in a state minimum competency testing program. I reviewed the proposed instrument, and found that the tasks being tested weren't the same tasks as those tested in the state assessment. Once this was brought to the teacher's attention, the screening instrument was revised, and the second version corresponded much more closely to the state examination. I continue to believe that this teacher was not irresponsible in developing the first test. Rather, the teacher focused on items that more closely reflected the total instructional program for that school year instead of the tasks that were specifically included on the state examination. On the basis of that experience, and many similar ones, I would strongly advocate that a course in test-construction and measurement be a part of each teacher's preparatory program. ●

Difficulty Indices

One useful index of an item's quality is its difficulty. The most commonly employed item-difficulty index (already encountered in Chapter 5), often referred to these days simply as a *p value*, is calculated as follows:

$$\text{Difficulty } p = \frac{R}{T}$$

Where R = the number of students responding correctly (right) to an item.
Where T = the total number of students responding to the item.

To illustrate, if fifty students answered an item, and only thirty-seven of them answered it correctly, then the p value for that item's difficulty would be

$$\text{Difficulty } p = \frac{37}{50} = .74$$

It should be clear that such p values can range from 0 to 1.00, with higher p values indicating items that more students answer correctly. For example, an item with a p value of .98 would be one that was answered correctly by almost all students. Similarly, an item with a p value of .15 would be one that most students missed.

The p value of an item should be viewed in relationship to the student's chance probability of getting the correct response. For example, if a binary-choice item is involved, then on the basis of chance alone students should be able to produce a p value of .50. On a four-option multiple-choice test, a .25 p by chance alone would be expected.

Sometimes slight variations of the basic item-difficulty formula are used so that, for example, you'll find a difficulty index from which the decimal point has been dumped:

$$\text{Difficulty} = \frac{\text{right}}{\text{total}} \times 100$$

In this instance, of course, multiplying by 100 the ratio between correct and total item responses gets rid of the decimal point so that difficulty indices range from 0 to 100. Other folks may prefer to use percentages, so that an item's difficulty value can range from zero percent to 100 percent. However, in all of these indices, what is being isolated is the proportion of total student responses that are correct. As you will see, item p values can prove most serviceable in empirically shaping up the items.

A note of caution should be registered at this point, because measurement people sometimes err by referring to items with high p values, of .80 and above, as "easy" items, while items with low p values, of .20 and below, are described as "difficult" items. Those assertions may or may not be accurate. Even though people typically refer to an item's p value as its *difficulty* index, the actual ease or difficulty of an item is almost always tied to the instructional program surrounding it.

Let's say you are whipping up a new test of verbal aptitude, and you administer your test to a host of students who are unfamiliar with its contents. In such a situation it probably makes sense to think of high p value items as easy and low p value items as tough. However, there are other situations.

Suppose you are teaching a course in physiology at a medical school and have produced a test that, if taken by the typical person off the street, would prove a terror. On all items, those students who were not studying medicine would almost always miss an item asking for "the location of the oblagatum." However, if you're a skillful teacher, let's say the end-of-course p value for that item is .95. Does such a p value really indicate that the item is intrinsically "easy," or does it mean that a well-taught group of examinees will answer it correctly?

Suppose that, down the hall, a colleague of yours is teaching the same course to another group of students. Because your colleague is a dull-witted person and an ineffectual instructor, only 48 percent of the students in his class answer the oblagatum item correctly. Isn't that even more reason to believe that the item isn't easy at all? Thus, when considering items with high *p* values, be a bit reluctant to characterize those items automatically as *easy*.

Discrimination Indices

For tests constructed chiefly to yield norm-referenced interpretations, one of the most powerful indicators of an item's quality is the *item discrimination index*. In brief, an item discrimination index typically indicates how frequently an item is answered correctly by those who perform well on the total test and how frequently an item is answered incorrectly by those who perform poorly on the total test. An item discrimination index reflects the relationship between students' responses on the total test and their responses on a particular test item. Indeed, one approach to computing an item-analysis statistic is to calculate a point biserial correlation coefficient between (1) the *continuous variable* of total test score and (2) the *dichotomous variable* of performance on a particular item, that is, correct or incorrect.

When I was a graduate student many years ago and encountered the topic of item discrimination indices, I thought that there was only *one* way to tell how well an item discriminated. Since that time, I've discovered that there is no single, sanctified approach to the detection of an item's discriminating efficiency. Earlier in the text (Chapter 7) you considered item-response theory approaches to the creation of scale scores. Most of those IRT schemes are accompanied by their own indicators of test-item discrimination. There are, indeed, many different indicators that can serve educators well because, in all instances, an item discrimination index is nothing more than a "red flag" that indicates there *may* be a flaw in an item.

In essence, a *positively discriminating item* indicates that an item is answered correctly more often by those who score well on the total test than by those who score poorly on the total test. A *negatively discriminating item* is answered correctly more often by those who score poorly on the total test than by those who score well on the total test. A *nondiscriminating item* is one for which there's no appreciable difference in the correct response proportions of those who score well or poorly on the total test. This set of relationships is summarized in the following chart (remember that the *caret* signs, < and >, signify *less than* and *more than*.)

Item Discrimination Index

Numerical indicators contrasting how high-scorers and low-scorers perform on a test item.

TYPE OF ITEM	PROPORTION OF CORRECT RESPONSES ON TOTAL TEST
Positive Discriminator	High Scorers > Low Scorers
Negative Discriminator	High Scorers < Low Scorers
Nondiscriminator	High Scorers = Low Scorers

Now, how does one go about computing an item's discrimination index? Well, the following procedure can be employed for both the analysis of classroom tests as well as the analysis of more elaborate examinations. When there are differences between the procedures that one might use for classroom or other exams, these will be noted.

1. *Order the test papers from high to low by total score.* Place the paper having the highest total score on top, and continue with the next highest total score sequentially until the paper with the lowest score is placed on the bottom.

2. *Divide the papers into a high group and low group with an equal number of papers in each group.* For classroom tests it is common to split the groups into upper and lower halves. If there is an odd number of papers, then simply set aside one of the middle papers so that the number of papers in the high and low groups will be the same. If there are several papers with identical scores at the middle of the distribution, then randomly assign them to the high or low distributions so that the number of papers in the two groups is identical.

For more substantial item analyses, it is recommended that the high and low groups be determined by selecting the upper and lower 27 percent of the papers. Over a half century ago, Kelley (1939) demonstrated that these percentages maximized the discrimination efficiency of the analysis while still providing high and low groups of sufficient size to be reliable.[2]

For the analysis of classroom tests, it makes little difference whether teachers employ high and low groups of 25 or 33 percent. The use of 50 percent groups has the advantage of providing enough papers to permit reliable estimates of upper and lower group performances.

3. *Calculate a p value for each of the high and low groups.* Determine the number of students in the high group who answered the item correctly, then divide this number by the number of students in the high group. This provides p_h, that is, the mean p value for the high group. Repeat the process for the low group to obtain p_l, that is, the mean p value for the low group.

4. *Subtract p_l from p_h to obtain each item's discrimination index (D).* In essence, then

$$D = p_h - p_l$$

Remember, the size of D will vary somewhat depending on which percentages of the group papers are used in the high and low groups.

Suppose you are working with a classroom teacher who is in the midst of conducting an item analysis of her midterm exam items. Let's say she split her class of thirty youngsters' papers into two equal upper- and lower-half papers. All fifteen students in the high group answered item 31 correctly, but only five of the fifteen students in the low group answered it correctly. The item discrimination index for item 31 on that teacher's test would be $1.00 - .33 = .67$.

Now, how large should an item's discrimination index be in order for one to consider the item acceptable? Using the upper and lower 27 percentages to calculate the discrimination index, Ebel[3] offered experienced-based guidelines for indicating the quality of items in tests aimed at norm-referenced interpretations. Ebel's discrimination index values can serve as reasonable approximations when teachers are reviewing items from their own classroom tests.

DISCRIMINATION INDEX	ITEM EVALUATION
.40 and above	Very good items
.30–.39	Reasonably good but possibly subject to improvement
.20–.29	Marginal items, usually needing and being subject to improvement
.19 and below	Poor items, to be rejected or improved by revision

The influence of difficulty levels. A review of the procedures for determining an item's discrimination index will suggest that an item's ability to discriminate is highly related to its overall difficulty index. For example, an item that is answered correctly by all students has a total p value of 1.00. Similarly, for that item, the p_h and p_l are also 1.00. Hence, the item's discrimination index is zero $(1.00 - 1.00 = 0)$. A similar result would ensue for items in which the overall p value was zero, that is, items that no student answered correctly.

With items that have very high or very low p values, it is thus less likely that substantial discrimination indices can be secured. Later in the chapter you will see that this situation has prompted educators, who hope that almost all postinstruction responses will be correct, to search for alternative ways to calculate indices of item quality.

Distractor Analysis

For an item that, perhaps on the basis of its p value or its discrimination index, appears to be in need of revision, it is necessary to look deeper. In the case of multiple-choice items, teachers can gain further insights by carrying out a *distractor analysis* in which they see how the high and low groups are responding to the item's distractors.

Presented next is a typical setup for conducting a distractor analysis for a multiple-choice item. Note that the asterisk indicates that choice B is the correct answer to this item. For this item the difficulty index (p) was .50, and the discrimination index was $-.33$. An inspection of the distractors reveals that there appears to be something in alternative D that is tempting the students in the high group. Indeed, while over half of the high group opts for choice D, not a single student in the low group went for choice D. Alternative D needs to be reviewed carefully.

ITEM NO. 7			ALTERNATIVES			
(p = .50, D = −.33)	A	B*	C	D	Omit
Upper 16 students	2	5	0	8	1
Lower 15 students	4	10	0	0	1

Note also that alternative C is doing nothing at all for the item. No student selected choice C. In addition to reviewing choice D, therefore, choice C should be made a bit more appealing. It is possible, of course, particularly if this is a best-answer type of multiple choice item, alternative B, the correct answer, needs a bit of massaging as well.

For multiple-choice items in particular, but also for matching items, a more intensive analysis of student responses to individual distractors can frequently be illuminating. In the same vein, careful scrutiny of students' responses to essay and short-answer items can typically supply useful insights for revision purposes.

When the Assessment Focus is on Criterion-Referenced Interpretations

As indicated earlier, when educators use tests aimed at criterion-referenced interpretations, there are situations in which those educators hope that most students will score well on tests. In such instances, because the p values of both high and low students would approach 1.0, traditional item-analysis approaches are destined to yield low discrimination indices. Accordingly, some alternative approaches to item analysis for tests have been devised in recent years.

There are two general item-analysis schemes that have been employed thus far, depending on the kinds of criterion groups available. The first approach involves the administration of the test to *the same group of students* both prior to and following instruction. A disadvantage of this approach is that one must wait for instruction to be completed before securing the item-analysis data. Another problem is that the pretest may be *reactive*, in the sense that its administration sensitizes students to certain items so that the students' posttest performance is actually a function of the instruction plus the pretest's administration.

The second approach is to locate two *different groups of students*, one of whom has already been instructed and one of whom hasn't. By comparing the performance on items of instructed and uninstructed students, it is possible to pick up some useful clues regarding item quality. This approach has the advantage of avoiding the delay associated with pretesting and posttesting the same group of students and also of avoiding the possibility of a reactive pretest. Its drawback, however, is that the "item-improver" must rely on human judgment in the selection of the "instructed" and "uninstructed" groups. The two groups should be identical in all other relevant respects, for example, in intellectual ability and socioeconomic status, but different with respect to whether or not they have been instructed. The isolation of two such groups sounds easier than it usually is.

Pretest–posttest differences. Adopting the initial strategy of testing the same groups of students prior to and after instruction, we can use an item discrimination index derived by Cox and Vargas.[4] This index is calculated as follows:

$$D_{ppd} = p_{post} - p_{pre}$$

where p_{post} = proportion of students answering the item correctly on posttest.
p_{pre} = proportion of students answering the item correctly on pretest.

The value of D_{ppd} (discrimination based on the pretest–posttest difference) can range from -1.00 to $+1.00$, with high positive values indicating that an item is apparently sensitive to instruction.

For example, if 41 percent of the students answered item 27 correctly in the pretest and 84 percent answered it correctly on the posttest, then item 27's D_{ppd} would be

State Testing Needs Improvement, Study Finds

by Millicent Lawton

Vermont is the only state with a system of measuring student achievement that is good enough to be copied by others, a testing watchdog group has concluded.

Most states do too much testing using multiple-choice exams that don't encourage students to think critically, concludes the report due out this week from the National Center for Fair & Open Testing, or FairTest, in Cambridge, Mass.

About one-third of the states need "a complete overhaul" of their systems of testing students, says the study. Another 17 states need "many major improvements." And in two-thirds of the nation, "testing systems often impede, rather than enhance, genuine education reform," the report asserts.

"What we found," said Monty Neill, FairTest's associate director, "is most state-assessment programs are not actually set up to support high-quality student learning."

If the movement to hold all students to high academic standards is to succeed, he said, tests have to improve. "Assessments must do more than measure—primarily—recall and rote application."

But the picture is not totally bleak, he said, because the remaining one-third of states "are making pretty good progress." Ten years ago, Mr. Neill said, "we might not have found any. .."

What's your reaction?

Excerpted, with permission, from *Education Week*, September 3, 1997

.84 − .41 = .43. A high positive value would indicate that the item is apparently sensitive to the instructional treatment. Items with low or negative D_{ppd} values would be earmarked for further analysis because they are not behaving the way one would expect them to behave.

Uninstructed *versus* instructed group differences. If the item-improver uses two groups, that is, an instructed and an uninstructed group, one of the more straightforward item discrimination indices is D_{uigd} (discrimination based on uninstructed *versus* instructed group differences).[5] This index is calculated as follows:

$$D_{uigd} = p_i - p_u$$

where p_i = proportion of instructed students answering an item correctly.

p_u = proportion of uninstructed students answering an item correctly.

This index can also range in value from −1.00 to +1.00. To illustrate its computation, if an instructed group of students scored 91 percent correct on a particular item, while that same item was answered correctly by only 55 percent of an uninstructed group, then D_{uigd} would be .91 − .55 = .36. Interpretations of D_{uigd} are similar to those used with D_{ppd}.

Once Improved, the Number of Items

Suppose, as an educational leader, you are assisting several teachers who are working to develop a districtwide test. The teachers have tried out a set of preliminary items for purposes of improving them. After employing all of the delightful empirical and judgmental techniques you've just read about for the improvement of their items, the teachers might have produced a pretty defensible batch of items. The next question is, "How many test items should they actually use in creating the final version of their test?"

This is obviously an important question, because if teachers use too few items in the test, they don't get an accurate fix on the students' status with respect to the assessment domain they're measuring. If teachers use too many items, there is lost economy on two counts: the unnecessary items they've produced and the unnecessary time taken from students as they wade through superfluous items. For one thing, there are situations in which teachers may set very stringent minimum levels of required learner proficiency—for example, demanding that the learner score 95 percent or better on a test. There are other situations in which teachers set very relaxed standards of requisite minimum proficiency, such as 50 percent. The level of proficiency teachers establish can influence the number of items needed in a test.

There is also the problem of making the wrong decision on the basis of the test results. Let's say the teacher is using tests in an instructional setting to monitor the progress of students as they move through a course. At various points in the course, each student must complete a test in order to establish whether he or she has mastered the skills taught during that part of the course. If the teacher makes an error in judging the student's mastery, which kind of error is more serious? In other words, is it worse to advance students (*false positives*) who have not mastered material to the next course unit or is it worse to hold back students (*false negatives*) who have actually mastered necessary skills? Of course, there may be no difference in real-life consequences associated with these two kinds of mistakes, but quite often there is. The relative gravity of making either kind of decision error is usually referred to as *loss ratio*. Not surprisingly, the relative gravity of these two kinds of decision errors can influence the number of items needed in a test.

In addition, there is the matter of students' actual level of functioning. If a teacher is testing a group of students whose average competency with respect to the test is about 95 percent, the teacher can use a different number of test items than if the teacher is testing a group of students whose average competency is about 20 percent.

All three of these factors unfortunately operate to confuse the situation so that no one can spin out a simple answer to the question of how many items. As always, you find that the world is more complex than it you might want it to be.

If the stakes associated with a test are really high, as might be the case when an exam is being used to grant a high school diploma to students, educators will not want to create tests too short to do a good job. If, on the other hand, the test is only one of several quizzes used as part of a first-year algebra course, a more relaxed approach to the test-length question may be in order. As you can see, deciding on an acceptable minimum for test length is a long way from being simple.

Final Thoughts on Item Improvement

Because of the heightened consequences associated with educational tests in recent years, the items for many high-stakes examinations have been subjected to a series of serious item-improvement activities. For example, fairly elaborate field tests of under-development items have been carried out for most state-level and nationally standardized

News in Brief: A National Roundup

Ohio Tests Ruled Public

Ohio's graduation test is a public record, the state supreme court has ruled, and it must be released to those who ask to see copies of the exams that have already been administered to students.

Tests "should not be enshrouded in a cloak of secrecy, isolated from the scrutiny and oversight of the general public, concerned parents, and students themselves," wrote Justice F. E. Sweeney for the 4–3 majority.

The April 29 decision represents a victory for Hollie Rea and her father, Stephen Rea. As a high school senior in 1995, Ms. Rea took the 12th grade Ohio Proficiency Test and the Ohio Vocational Competency Assessment. Afterward, she and her father were told they could review the tests only if they signed an agreement not to disclose the exams' contents. They refused and filed suit in 1996.

What's your reaction?

Reprinted, with permission, from *Education Week*, May 13, 1998

---

achievement tests. Indeed, developers of such high-stakes tests have almost ritualistically subjected all test items to a large-scale field test so that the various indices of item quality that I've described in the chapter can be produced.

Field-test data, however, vary substantially in their quality depending on (1) the similarity of the field-test students to the actual students who will ultimately be tested and (2) the seriousness with which the field-test students respond to the field-test's items. If either or both of these conditions are violated, then the field test's results will often lead to poor item-improvement decisions. For example, if a statewide competency test is to be used at the *end* of an academic year, but its items are field-tested at the *start* of an academic year, the field-test data may yield flawed inferences regarding item quality. Similarly, although young children tend to regard all tests as serious because such tests are being administered by "grown-ups," older students do not regard all tests with equal deference. Suppose, for instance, that you wish to give a *noncounting* field test to a group of high school seniors several months before graduation. How seriously do you think those seniors would take the field test? If you think that the graduating seniors would be serious about such a field test, you'd better do a bit of recalling about your own high school days.

Field testers who attempt to improve test items for high-stakes tests must be able to locate *appropriate and appropriately motivated* students if they wish to use empirical techniques to improve test items. Otherwise, it would be preferable to rely exclusively on judgmentally based improvement schemes.

Chapter Wrap-Up

Let's improve your recollection of what was in this improvement-focused chapter by providing a brief summary organized as usual around the chapter's guiding questions. If you don't think my summary is all that hot, improve it! After all, improvement seems to be fashionable these days.

What are the most common approaches to item improvement?

Two major strategies have been employed to improve test items. Judgmental approaches rely on individuals' registering their best judgments about item quality. Empirical approaches are based on analyses of students' actual responses to test items. When tests are primarily designed to yield criterion-referenced inferences, greater attention is usually given to judgmental item-improvement approaches. When tests are intended chiefly for the provision of norm-referenced inferences, one tends to see more reliance on empirical item-improvement strategies. The two item-improvement strategies, that is, judgmental and empirical, are applicable to both selected-response and constructed-response items.

How can judgmental procedures be employed to improve test items?

When teachers evaluate their own tests' items judgmentally, or when external reviewers are called on to render judgment regarding test items, four foci for those reviews were recommended. It was suggested that each item be scrutinized according to its (1) congruence with the test's assessment domain, (2) adherence to the tenets of good item-writing, (3) content accuracy, and (4) the absence of bias.

Students can also provide excellent insights regarding how to improve test items. If students are asked to supply item-improvement judgments, however, they should be requested to do so after finishing an assessment, not while they are in the process of completing the assessment.

What kinds of empirical procedures can be used to improve test items?

One of the most widely used indices of item quality is an item's p value. A p value is simply the proportion of students who answered the item correctly. Although p values are referred to as "difficulty" indices, a high p value does not automatically indicate that an item is easy. Rather, students may have been effectively taught to master a difficult skill or body of knowledge. Items with low p values may indicate that (1) the item is difficult, (2) the item's content has been taught poorly or even in a confusing manner, or (3) the item is itself confusing or otherwise defective.

Discrimination indices indicate the relationship between students' performances on an individual item and their performances on the total test. If a test item is a positive discriminator, the students who answer the item correctly tend to do well on the total test. A negative discriminator indicates the opposite. When an item is a nondiscriminator, this indicates that there is little difference between the total test performance of those who answer the item correctly and those who answer it incorrectly.

Procedures were described to compute discrimination indices for tests aimed at norm-referenced inferences as well as for tests aimed at criterion-referenced inferences. For the former, a single administration of a test is all that is required. For the latter, two administrations of the test (postinstruction-*versus*-preinstruction or an instructed-group-versus-uninstructed group) are typically required.

Distractor analysis is a useful procedure for determining the adequacy of the individual options in multiple-choice tests or in matching tests. Procedural guidelines and examples of all the foregoing item-improvement techniques were provided in the chapter.

Practice Exercises

Part A

Decide whether each of the item-improvement procedures sketched in the following five items is predominantly an *empirical* or a *judgmental* item-improvement strategy.

1. The test items on a test are improved on the basis of the D_{ppd} item-analysis statistic.
2. Items on a test are analyzed using the upper and lower 27 percents of the score distribution in order to detect negatively discriminating and nondiscriminating items.
3. English teachers in Washington High School routinely share their end-of-year examinations so that the exams can be critiqued by colleagues.
4. Using a costly and sophisticated item-refinement approach, a commercial testing firm hires a minimum of ten item reviewers to rate (1) the congruence of teach item with its assessment domain and (2) the content accuracy of each item. The mean ratings of reviewers (on a five-point scale) are calculated. Items failing to achieve a mean rating on each criterion of 2.5 or higher are revised.
5. A group of item analysts judge the quality of items based on the extent to which an item's p value from a field trial is within the general range of p values for the total set of items.

Part B

Assume that you are in the process of revising a series of items and secure the following sets of information. Review each solution, and decide whether you would revise the item.

6. Item 17 on a classroom test of mathematics skill has an after-instruction p value of .93 and an item discrimination index based on a point biserial correlation coefficient (of item scores versus total test scores) of .12. Should this item be revised?
7. An item on a national academic aptitude test has a p value of .26 and a discrimination index of .10. Is it likely that the item should be revised?
8. Although judged incongruent with its test-item specifications by three independent reviewers, item 47 on a test of history has a p value of .52 and a discrimination index of .49. Is it likely that item 47 should be altered?
9. Here is the distractor analysis for a multiple-choice item on a test of secondary school students' reading abilities. Review the data, then suggest what sorts of changes, if any, you would urge for the item.

ITEM 14	A	B	C*	D	E	OMIT
(p = .69) (D = .15)						
Upper 27%	1	0	15	0	4	0
Lower 27%	3	0	12	3	1	1

* = correct answer

10. An item on a twenty-item test of a physical competency has a p value fully .30 lower than the p values on all other items. Should this item most likely be revised?

Answers to Practice Exercises

1. Empirical
2. Empirical
3. Judgmental
4. Even though there are some data involved in this example, even data for which one can compute honest-to-goodness means, this still illustrates a judgmental approach to item improvement.
5. Empirical, although the item analysts *judged* the empirically derived p values. Even with

empirical item-analysis schemes someone ultimately has to judge "how good is good enough." However, in empirical schemes these judgments are focused on student-response data, such as you see in this example.

6. Well, this information certainly doesn't indicate that the item *must* be revised. It is perfectly acceptable for items on a test, particularly those on which the p values are high, to display low discriminating efficiency. While the item might warrant a bit closer look, there's nothing in the statistical data to cause alarm.

7. For items on an academic aptitude test that is almost certainly intended to yield norm-referenced interpretations, items of this sort should most likely be revised.

8. Absolutely. The test's developers must make certain that an item is consistent with its test-item specifications or it will be difficult to make sense out of students' test scores. All the empirical indicators notwithstanding, item 47 needs some reworking.

9. Because the value of D is only .15, the item certainly seems to be in need of revision. As one reviews the distractor analysis, it appears that choice E is attracting too many of the students in the high group and too few of the students in the low group. Hence, choice E should be scrutinized further. In addition, choice B is snagging no one. It, too, should be reviewed carefully. As always, these item statistics should be guides, not absolute rules. An inspection of the nature of the other alternatives will determine whether, and how, alterations should be made.

10. It's difficult to tell. If the assessment domain being measured is a fairly broad one, then the presence of a deviant p value does not indicate automatically that the item needs to be revised.

DISCUSSION QUESTIONS

1. If you, as an educational leader, were *obliged* to choose between empirical or judgmental approaches to item improvement for an under-development districtwide exam, which would you choose and why?
2. How do you think one item's p value should be most effectively used in item analyses?
3. What sorts of item-improvement techniques can classroom teachers realistically be expected to conduct for their own tests? With what sorts of classroom tests would you expect teachers to engage in item-improvement activities?
4. Can you think of an explicit procedure for reviewing essay items that is analogous to the distractor-analysis schemes used with multiple-choice tests?
5. Under what circumstances, if any, might a nondiscriminating test item be considered an acceptable item?
6. Are there circumstances under which a negatively discriminating item might be acceptable? If so, what are these circumstances?

SUGGESTIONS FOR ADDITIONAL READING

Airasian, Peter W. *Classroom Assessment* (3rd ed.). New York: McGraw-Hill, 1994.

Berk, Ronald A. "Conducting the Item Analysis." In Ronald Berk (Ed.), *A Guide to Criterion-Referenced Test Construction*. Baltimore: Johns Hopkins University Press, 1984.

Berk, Ronald A. "A Consumer's Guide to Criterion-Referenced Test Item Statistics." *National Council on Measurement in Education, 9,* 1 (Winter 1978): 8.

Bryant, Deborah, and Mark Driscoll. *Exploring Classroom Assessment in Mathematics: A Guide for Professional Development.* Reston, VA: National Council of Teachers of Mathematics, 1998.

Carey, Lou M. *Measuring and Evaluating School Learning.* Boston: Allyn & Bacon, 1988.

Cunningham, George K. *Assessment in the Classroom: Constructing and Interpreting Tests.* Washington, DC: Falmer Press, 1998.

Downing, Steven M., and Thomas M. Haladyna. "Test Item Development: Validity Evidence from Quality Assurance Procedures." *Applied Measurement in Education, 10,* 1 (1997): 61–82.

Ebel, R. L., and D. A. Frisbie. *Essentials of Educational Measurement,* pp. 267–286, 288–299, 301–315. Englewood Cliffs, NJ: Prentice-Hall, 1986.

Gay, L. R. *Educational Evaluation and Measurement: Competencies for Analysis and Application* (2nd ed.). Columbus, OH: Charles E. Merrill, 1985.

Hambleton, Ronald K. "Principles and Selected Applications of Item-Response Theory." In Robert L. Linn (Ed.), *Educational Measurement* (3rd ed.). New York: Macmillan, 1989.

Linn, Robert L., and Norman E. Gronlund. *Measurement and Assessment in Teaching* (7th ed.). Upper Saddle River, NJ: Prentice-Hall, 1995.

AND FOR THOSE WHO TIRE OF READING

Hunter, Madeline. *Teaching and Testing: A Conversation with Madeline Hunter* (Videotape #ETVT-36). Los Angeles: IOX Assessment Associates.

ENDNOTES

1. Ronald A. Berk, "Criterion-Referenced Test Item Analysis and Validation" (Paper presented at the first annual Johns Hopkins University National Symposium on Educational Research, Washington, D.C., October 1978), p. 18.
2. T. L. Kelley, "The Selection of Upper and Lower Groups for the Validation of Test Items," *Journal of Educational Psychology,* (1939), *30,* 1, 17–24.
3. Robert L. Ebel, *Essentials of Educational Measurement,* 3rd ed. (Englewood Cliffs, NJ: Prentice-Hall, 1979), p. 267.
4. R. C. Cox and J. S. Vargas, "A Comparison of Item Selection Techniques for Norm-Referenced and Criterion-Referenced Tests" (Paper presented at the annual meeting of the National Council on Measurement in Education, Chicago, Ill., February 1966).
5. L. Levin and F. Marton, *Provteori och provkonstruktuon* (Stockholm: Almquist and Wiksell, 1971)

13 Creating Affective Measures

chapter

If all possible situations were listed for which educators need measurement devices, most of those situations could be handled quite conveniently by cognitive tests. Tests of cognitive aptitude or tests of cognitive achievement pretty well satisfy the chief assessment needs of most teachers and administrators. However, of course, there are other specialists roaming the educational landscape. Counselors and school psychologists, for example, have assessment requirements that extend well beyond the confines of the cognitive domain. Most often those assessment needs extend into the affective realm. But there are also many instances in which classroom teachers should be using affective assessment devices. In this chapter you're going to consider how one should go about developing affective assessment instruments.

The Cognitive, Affective, and Psychomotor Domains

Before turning to a discussion of affective measures, however, I need to do a bit of term clarifying. These distinctions were initially drawn in Chapter 2, but are especially germane to what's going to be tussled with in this chapter. (If you already know all this stuff, read rapidly!) A *cognitive* measure is one that deals chiefly with the student's intellectual abilities or achievements. A test of a student's academic aptitude, for example, would constitute a commonly encountered cognitive measure.

A *psychomotor* measure deals chiefly with the student's small-muscle or large-muscle physical skills or aptitudes. For instance, tests of someone's typing ability or skill in skiing would be examples of psychomotor assessments.

Affective measures focus on the student's attitudes, values, interests, and feelings. For example, a measure of children's self-concepts as learners, that is, the manner in which the children view themselves as students, would be an example of an affective measure.

It is important to qualify such assertions by saying, for instance, that a psychomotor assessment device deals *primarily* (not exclusively) with physical skills. For most testing devices, a student responds to some extent with all three types of behavior. To illustrate, a student fills out an attitude inventory (*affective*) by using a pencil to make marks on an answer sheet (*psychomotor*) that requires the intellectual skill (*cognitive*) to place responses for item number six alongside answer space number six on the answer sheet. Yet, because the responses are intended to permit inferences about students' affective status, the instrument is classified as affective.

Educators have, for centuries, attended to these three domains of learner behavior. Moreover, many educators in church schools or in synagogue schools have probably focused on a *spiritual* domain as well. The point is, of course, that for analytic purposes educators can slice up learner outcomes in many different ways.

However, those who do the best slicing job typically get their personal way of carving up the world accepted. Thus, when in 1956 Benjamin S. Bloom and his colleagues published the widely known *Taxonomy of Educational Objectives, Handbook I: The Cognitive Domain*, no further slicing was requisite.[1] In that important volume, Bloom and his coworkers set forth the main elements of the cognitive, affective, and psychomotor domains. In addition, a hierarchical division of learner behaviors in the cognitive domain was provided. That hierarchy started off with low-level, memory behavior (*knowledge*) and ended up with high-level, cognitive skills such as *synthesis* and *evaluation*.

Because the various levels of the cognitive domain might sometimes be needed in connection with the creation of tests, they will briefly be described. It should be noted, however, that whereas the three major divisions of the taxonomies have been widely accepted (cognitive, affective, and psychomotor), the particular levels within each domain have never been used to any appreciable extent by educators. Nevertheless, because you surely want to be a superinformed educational leader, here are the cognitive domain's six levels.

Knowledge. Knowledge involves the recall of specifics or universals, the recall of methods and processes, or the recall of a pattern, structure, or setting. It will be noted that the essential attribute at this level is recall. For assessment purposes, a recall situation involves little more than "bringing to mind" appropriate material.

Comprehension. This level represents the lowest form of understanding and refers to a kind of apprehension that indicates that a student knows what is being communicated and can make use of the material or idea without necessarily relating it to other material or seeing it in its fullest implications.

Application. Application involves the use of abstractions in particular or concrete situations. The abstractions used may be in the form of procedures, general ideas, or generalized methods. They may also be ideas, technical principles, or theories that must be remembered and applied.

Analysis. Analysis involves the breakdown of a communication into its constituent parts so that the relative hierarchy within that communication is made clear, that the relations between the expressed ideas are made explicit, or both. Such analyses are intended to clarify the communication, to indicate how it is organized, and the way in which the communication manages to convey its effects, as well as its basis and arrangement.

Synthesis. Synthesis represents the combining of elements and parts so that they form a whole. This operation involves the process of working with pieces, parts, elements, and so on and arranging them so as to constitute a pattern or structure not clearly present before.

Evaluation. Evaluation requires judgments about the value of material and methods for given purposes. Quantitative and qualitative judgments are made about the extent to which material and methods satisfy criteria. The criteria employed may be those determined by learners or those given to them.

Most of these levels have been broken down into various subcategories. For example, under *evaluation* there are two categories that deal with "judgments in terms of internal evidence" and "judgments in terms of external criteria." The knowledge category has twelve separate subdivisions.

The 1956 *Taxonomy* languished almost unnoticed for several years after its initial publication. However, in the early sixties the nation's intense interest in instructional objectives altered that situation dramatically. Sales of the *Taxonomy* started to soar, and educators nationwide started spouting phrases such as "affective objectives" and "cognitive objectives" with ease. The cognitive, affective, and psychomotor domains became household notions for most school people during the sixties.

In 1964 David R. Krathwohl and his colleagues extended Bloom's pioneering efforts by publishing a second taxonomy of objectives, but this time one that concentrated on the affective domain.[2] As with the cognitive taxonomy, Krathwohl and his collaborators attempted to subdivide the affective realm into relatively distinct divisions. Five different levels of affective objectives were described in the affective taxonomy:

Receiving (Attending). The first level of the affective domain is concerned with the student's sensitivity to the existence of certain phenomena and stimuli, that is, with his or her willingness to receive or to attend to them. This category is divided into three subdivisions that indicate three different levels of attending to phenomena—namely, awareness of the phenomena, willingness to receive phenomena, and controlled or selected attention to phenomena.

Responding. At this level one is concerned with responses that go beyond merely attending to phenomena. Students are sufficiently motivated that they are not just "willing to attend" but are actively attending.

Valuing. This category reflects the student's holding of a particular value. Students display behavior with sufficient consistency in appropriate situations that the are perceived as holding this value.

Organization. As students successively internalize values, they encounter situations in which more than one value is relevant. This requires the necessity of organizing their values into a system such that certain values exercise greater control.

Characterization by a Value or Value Complex. At this highest level of the affective taxonomy, internalization has taken place in an individual's value hierarchy to the extent that he or she can be characterized as holding a particular value or set of values.

Arriving as it did on the heels of increased educator fascination with instructional objectives, the affective taxonomy stimulated a fair amount of interest among educators. But, sadly, although there was a solid pile of rhetoric tossed about regarding "the fundamental importance of the affective realm," educators saw the emergence of few actual assessment devices that attempted to tap affective outcomes.

In part, the dearth of measures to assess students' affective status is due to the considerable difficulty in devising defensible instruments. As you will see in this chapter, it is awfully hard to create a satisfactory instrument that assesses the elusive kinds of quarries to be pursued in the affective domain.

A Closer Look at Affect

When individuals are asked to define what they mean by the term *affective*, they typically offer examples instead of definitions. They'll say something like, "Affective variables are nonintellectual attributes, such as one's attitudes, interests and values." In a sense, they define *affect* by saying what it *isn't*, namely, that it isn't intellectual behavior. However, it is possible to define affective variables more precisely by noting how affective measures are actually used. If you think about it just a bit, you'll realize that educators assess students' affective status—for example, by using some kind of self-report attitudinal inventory—not really to find out how those students score on the inventory. No, instead educators want to use those scores on the inventory to get a fix on how the students will respond *in the future* to similar, but typically more realistic, stimulus situations. In other words, because educators interpret responses to their affective measure as predictors of students' future acts, it is sensible to conceive of affective measures as attempts to assess the students' dispositions with respect to their future behaviors. When teachers try to measure children's attitudes toward the democratic process, those teachers are really trying to find out how their students will be likely to act toward the democratic system when they grow up. Teachers see whether children currently enjoy art and music so that the teachers can predict whether those children will derive pleasure from art and music later in life.

Many psychologists have spent their entire professional lives trying to draw subtle and defensible distinctions among such constructs as attitudes and values. Some specialists believe, for instance, that an attitude consists of an individual's *set* (or tendency to behave) toward a fairly limited class of objects, such as when certain people are annoyed by small, nervous, and fidgety dogs. In contrast, a value consists of a person's set toward a much broader class of objects, such as when a person holds the value of human life in such high esteem that all nonhuman life is expendable, including small, fidgety dogs as well as big, docile ones.

There are several exceptions to the general rule that affective measures are future oriented, such as when teachers want to assess students' current attitudes toward school because they want to alter any situation contributing to negative attitudes. Most of the time, however, educators are trying to isolate some current behavior that will be predictive of students' future behaviors. The affective disposition itself can never be captured. Educators must infer the students' status with respect to that attitude by devising a current situation in which the student's affective state will be revealed, allowing educators to predict the students' future behaviors in situations governed by the affective disposition being assessed.

The predictive rationale underlying affective assessment is displayed graphically in Figure 13.1, where it can be seen that by assessing students' current affective status, educators make inferences about students' future behavior.

Although measures in the cognitive domain attempt to find out what students *can* do intellectually, and measures in the psychomotor domain attempt to find out what students

FIGURE 13.1.

The relationship between current affect and future behavior whereby students' currently assessed affective status yields predictive inferences about students' future behavior

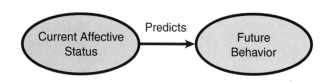

can do physically, measures in the affective domain attempt to find out what students *will* do in the future. Cognitive and psychomotor assessments generally deal with ability assessment. Affective assessments generally deal with dispositional assessment.

With cognitive measures there is a handy "number correct" that teachers can use as a reflection of students' performances. Affective measuring devices, unfortunately, often don't lend themselves to readily discernible scoring schemes. On occasions the test developer must engage in a good deal of exotic analytic work in order to come up with a defensible scoring key. Sometimes the scoring approaches are apparent from the nature of the items employed. For instance, suppose teachers were asking children to register the extent of their agreement on a five-point scale—strongly agree to strongly disagree—with statements about school, some of which are positive and some of which are negative. If the youngsters agree with a positive item, then they get a plus score. If they agree with a negative item, then they get a minus score. Similarly, if they disagree with a negative statement, they get a plus; whereas if they disagree with a positive statement, they get a minus.

The real task, in this example, is to decide what constitutes a reasonably positive attitude toward school. Very frequently, educators are looking for shifts in affective responses, such as promoting students' *more* positive attitudes toward school. In such cases, a pretest–posttest contrast of affective scores often proves useful.

If the affective measure is a totally new one, and no pretest-posttest strategy is being employed, it is almost certain that educators must gather a fair amount of real data before reaching a tentative, a very tentative, decision regarding what kinds of expectations to have for an affective measure.

Biased toward Affect

As you saw in Chapter 6, assessment biases should be expunged. But not all biases are bad. I have a few that I think are altogether laudable. One of them concerns the importance of affective assessment.

I want to get my own bias regarding affective assessment's importance out in the open so you don't think I'm trying to influence you covertly. I personally regard affective variables as far more significant than cognitive variables. How many times, for example, have you seen people who weren't all that "gifted" intellectually still succeed because they were highly motivated and hardworking? Conversely, how many times have you seen truly able people simply veer away from challenges because they did not consider themselves worthy? Day in and day out, you can see the enormous impact that people's affective status has on their behavior. Affect is every bit as important in school.

Have you ever seen a group of kindergarten students scurry off to school, loaded with enthusiasm and gumption, only to encounter those same students a few years later and see that a fair number have become disenchanted with school and are down on themselves? Well, I have. And what's going on with such children is surely taking place in the affective realm. When most kindergartners start school, they are enthused about school and themselves. However, after failing to measure up for a year or two, many of those formerly upbeat children begin to carry around decisively lowered self-concepts. They've tried and been found wanting. Such negative attitudes about self and school will typically influence all of a child's subsequent education. Yet, because few teachers try to assess their students' affective status formally, most teachers don't know what their students' attitudes and values really are. That situation, I believe, needs to be changed. If it's going to be changed, educational leaders will have to do the changing.

Stimulating Affectively Oriented Instruction

Suppose there were no such thing as externally imposed "educational accountability" whereby students' performances on high-stakes tests serve as indicators of educational effectiveness. I think that what's on achievement tests would still influence what teachers teach. When I was a high school teacher, I knew what kinds of items I had on my final exams. (That is, I knew in the second year of teaching, after I'd whipped out my first-year final exams only minutes before my students needed to take those exams.) Because I wanted my students to do well on my final exams, I made reasonably sure that I spent at least some instructional time on the content covered by the final examinations.

It's the same with affective assessment. Let's say a teacher has installed a pretest–posttest evaluation design to assess any meaningful changes in students' responses to an attitude inventory regarding how much they are interested in the subject the teacher is teaching. The teacher's recognition that there will be a formal pretest–posttest assessment of students' subject-matter interest will, as surely as school busses run late, influence the teacher to provide instruction so that his or her students will, in fact, become more positive about the subject being taught.

The presence of affective postinstruction measurement will, in the same way, incline teachers to include affectively focused activities in the instruction. In a sense, teachers are saying to themselves that affective outcomes are *important*, that is, important enough to assess formally. Teachers can be assured that what's important enough to be assessed, even if it's measured in their classroom and nowhere else in the world, is likely to influence their instruction. As I confessed earlier, I think that affectively focused instruction deals with the kinds of outcomes that are among the most important ones educators should be promoting.

Moreover, besides serving as one of the teacher's instructional targets, affective assessment devices, if administered regularly, help teachers determine if modifications in the instructional program are warranted. For example, let's say that a physics teacher, Mr. Hull, wants to get a fix on how enthused his students are about continuing their study of physics in college. Ideally, Mr. Hull would like a fair number of his students to get fairly ecstatic over the raptures of future physics coursework. Suppose that each month he employed a brief self-report attitudinal inventory focused on the likelihood of students' pursuing future physics instruction. For illustrative purposes, let's assume that in September about 60 percent of Mr. Hull's students registered an interest in taking college physics courses and that in October about 65 percent indicated such an interest. In November, however, interest in taking future physics courses nose-dived so that only 25 percent of his students signified any interest in enrolling in college physics courses. This is a clear message to Mr. Hull that something went on in late October or early November that really turned off his budding physicists. A review of Mr. Hull's instructional program during that period, and some serious effort on his part to generate more interest in postsecondary physics, would seem necessary. As you can see, periodic monitoring of students' affective status can assist teachers in seeing what sorts of shifts in their instructional program might be needed.

In review, there are a number of reasons that classroom teachers should devote at least a segment of their assessment program to the measurement of students' affect. If you don't believe that your students' attitudes and values are important, of course, you'll not agree with the views I've expressed. But if you do think that student affect is significant, you'll want to learn what kinds of affective variables to assess, and how to assess them. That's coming up shortly.

Detractors of Affect

In fairness, I must point out that a good many citizens do not share my view regarding the importance of affective educational assessment. Particularly in the past few years, the nation has seen the emergence of a vocal group of individuals who have taken strong positions against the school's offering anything other than traditional academic (cognitive) education. Usually representing religious or conservative constituencies, these critics have argued that it is the job of the family and church to promote values in children, and that any attempt by the schools to systematically modify students' attitudes or values should cease.

In several states there have been heated attacks on "outcomes-based education" (an approach to education in which heightened attention is given to the cognitive and affective consequences of an educational program rather than the procedures employed to deliver the program). A major argument voiced by those who argue against outcomes-based education is that it may foster attitudes and values that are unacceptable to certain stakeholders.

If any instructional attention to affective outcomes is to be given in the schools, I believe it must be focused only on those affective consequences that would be near-universally approved. For example, I regard the promotion of students' *positive attitudes toward learning* as an affective aspiration that almost everyone would support. Similarly, I can't really imagine that there are too many people who wouldn't want the schools to nurture *students' self-esteem*. Yet, I would hate to see educators dabbling with any controversial attitudes or values, that is, those that a meaningful number of parents wouldn't want their children to possess.

If you, as an educational leader, decide to advocate the use of some assessment/instruction to affective targets, you'll clearly need to consider carefully the legitimacy of the targets you select. And even if you do so, you should recognize that there will be some well-meaning individuals who may disapprove of such affective education regardless of the circumspection with which you select your affective objectives (Droegemueller 1993).

What Affective Variables to Assess?

Educational leaders who wish to encourage the assessment of affect will find that one of their most challenging assignments is to help teachers isolate genuinely defensible affective variables to assess. And, of course, affective variables that are assessed will, almost always, become affective variables that receive at least some instructional attention. Let's consider possible attitudinal variables and value variables that might be adopted.

Attitudinal Variables

Numerous attitudinal variables can serve as defensible educational targets. Here are a few of the attitudes that are most commonly endorsed by thoughtful educators as reasonable attitudinal targets:

- *Positive Attitudes toward Learning.* Students should regard positively the act of learning. Students who are positive today about learning will tend to be tomorrow's learners.
- *Positive Attitude toward Self.* Self-esteem is the attitude on which most people's personal worlds turn. Although, in many instances, children's self-esteem is probably influenced more by parents and nonschool events than by teachers, what happens in the classroom can have a significant impact on children's self-esteem.
- *Positive Attitudes toward Subjects.* Students should regard the subject matter taught, for example, mathematics, more positively at the end of instruction than they did when instruction began. At the very least, students should be no more negative toward the subjects being taught as a consequence of instruction.
- *Positive Attitude toward Self as a Learner.* Self-esteem as a learner is an affective variable over which educators have substantial influence. If students believe they are capable of learning, they will tend to learn.

There are numerous other subject-specific kinds of attitudes that teachers will want to foster. For example, many teachers who deal with language arts will want to enhance students' heightened confidence as writers, that is, students' more positive attitudes toward their own composition capabilities. Science teachers may want to foster students' curiosity. Health education teachers will wish to promote students' accurate perceptions about their vulnerability to health risks such as drugs or sexually transmitted diseases. Depending on particular teachers' instructional responsibilities, they'll usually discover that there are several attitudinal assessment contenders that they'll want to consider for their classes.

Value Variables

There are all sorts of values to which people subscribe that the schools should have nothing to do with. Most educators agree that political values and religious values, for example, should not be dealt with instructionally in the schools. Whether students turn out to be liberals or conservatives is really none of the teacher's business. And, historically, there's been a long tradition of separating church and state. Teachers, therefore, certainly shouldn't be advocating the acceptance of particular religions or the rejection of others. Well, then, what sorts of values are sufficiently meritorious and noncontroversial so that they could serve as the targets for classroom attention? Here are a few to consider:

- *Integrity.* Students should firmly adhere to their own code of values, for example, moral or artistic.
- *Justice.* Students should subscribe to the view that all citizens should be the recipients of equal justice from governmental law enforcement agencies.

- *Honesty.* Students should learn to value honesty in their dealings with others.
- *Freedom.* Students should believe that democratic nations must provide the maximum level of freedom to its citizens.

Although these kinds of values may seem to be little more than lofty, mother-pie and apple-hood endorsements of goodness, educators may still wish to consider them and similar values for potential affective assessment. If there really are significant values that teachers would like their students to embrace, and if those values fall properly in the sphere of what the schools should be about, then the possibility of including such values in a classroom or schoolwide assessment program may have real appeal. A number of school districts have recently embarked on serious "character education" programs that are intended to impart such student values as honesty and compassion.

Be sure not to try to assess too many affective variables. Educational leaders will be surprised how quickly teachers can become overwhelmed with the time required to gather such data, and the time needed to make sense of the data teachers collect. This is another "less is more" setting in which educational leaders should encourage teachers to get a fix on only a few of the affective dimensions the teachers regard as most important for their students.

Isolating the Affective Variable

For educators wishing to develop an affective measure, the initial task involves isolating some current student behavior that will reflect that more general affective disposition in which those educators are interested. At this very early stage, educators need to consider alternative ways of measuring the more general attribute they're trying to assess. The first step, therefore, calls for the creation of a variety of potential assessment schemes for review.

In several previous affective-measurement projects, my colleagues and I have had some success with a straightforward, four-step strategy for isolating possible affective-assessment approaches. Here are its chief features.

In step one, we try to discuss the general nature of the affective variable we're dealing with so we understand it better. Then we try to imagine what an individual would be like who possessed (in a positive way) that affective variable in a thoroughgoing manner. For instance, if we were trying to measure an individual's attitudes toward participatory athletics, we might think of a hypothetical *attribute-possessor* who lived and died just to get into the next game of softball, tennis, jai alai, golf, and so on. We then tuck this totally fictitious individual away for a while in the corner of our fantasy world.

Step two calls for the creation of a fictitious counterpart to the imaginary individual we conjured up in step one. Now we create a hypothetical *attribute-nonpossessor* who is either neutral toward participatory sports or finds them downright repugnant. This sort of person might watch a tennis match in person or on television but would never actually trot out on a court. Moreover, the idea of taking part in a sweaty, dusty, softball game would be dreadfully disgusting. This second fictitious person we also send flying around our heads in a holding pattern.

Now, in step three we attempt to think of many difference-producing situations, that is, situations in which our two hypothetical people would behave in a substantially different fashion. Maybe we'll come up with paper-and-pencil inventories, actually observe behaviors in natural settings, observe behaviors in artificial settings, or analyze products that might be generated in stress-free or stress-laden settings. Here is where we engage in no-holds-barred and nonpunitive brainstorming, preferably with a fair number of colleagues, so we get all sorts of ideas out on the table, the simple-minded, the exotic, the super. Just let the ideas reel off and we record them; we sort out the winners from the losers later on. Often, at the end of step three, we have upwards of a dozen or more potential measurement approaches.

In step four, we survey the numerous measurement ideas, for that's what they really are, seeds of measurement approaches, generated in step three. We pick out the ones that are both likely to yield valid inferences and are also practicable. Practicality considerations should only be raised at this point, not in step three, because practicality is such a stultifying notion that we might lose some potentially valuable ideas. However, if a proposed scheme is too costly, takes too much student time, or requires too much teacher time, it just may not be sufficiently practical to employ.

Socially Desirable Response

Responses of students that do not represent the students' actual affect but, instead, how they think they *should* respond.

Valid inferences, of course, are a crucial commodity in any measurement setting, and we want to be as sure as we can that we have at least a reasonable strategy for coming up with valid inferences. Ideally, we could select several substantially different ways of trying to isolate the affective variable we're going after with the hope that each of our different measures would snare a somewhat different facet of the affective attribute. Thus, we would, in effect, triangulate in on the attribute more effectively. Because it's highly unlikely that a single affective measuring device will ever satisfactorily measure a significant affective variable all by itself, the use of multiple affective measuring devices (with similar missions) is strongly recommended. However, if you're short on resources, one affective measure is surely better than none at all.

When developing affective measures, it is particularly important to eliminate any cues that might prompt the student to supply a *socially desirable* response. Measuring devices that fail to eliminate such cues are destined to yield invalid inferences. If students sense how they *should* respond—that is, how they think others would like them to respond—they often supply such responses instead of the ones they really might give without such influence. Clearly, the resulting data will be misleading.

To illustrate, returning to our little four-step strategy for a moment, suppose we were trying to create measures of children's attitudes toward the school's instructional program. Now in step three, one of the suggestions was that a teacher ask pupils to raise their hands if they like the way they're being taught. We leave this inane suggestion in the eligible pool until step four when we quickly expunge it because it's cluttered by cues as to social desirability. Surely when a teacher asks pupils to raise their hands if they like the class, a good many youngsters will send fingers flying skyward because they don't want to hurt the teacher's feelings or, perhaps, because they fear potential grading recriminations. In any event, the social desirability cue would completely compromise the validity of inferences drawn from such an assessment approach.

In step four we look hard at any cues to social desirability as well as any other factors, conceptual or procedural, that might influence a measurement scheme's capability of yielding valid inferences. Having done so, we can rank a few affective measurement schemes in order of their merits and try to create several measures if our resources permit.

"There's just one problem with our affective measuring devices—the kids keep getting tangled."

Opting for Self-Report Inventories

You are an educational leader, or an educational leader-in-training. You are not a specialist in affective assessment. You do not need to know all of the conceptual and procedural complexities that vex affective assessors. If you did want to delve into that realm of assessment exotica, you'd probably have no time left over to do much educational leading. Educational leaders need to lead, not lurk around looking into affective assessment. Accordingly, instead of laying out a plethora of affective assessment options for you, then describing why one of them is the hands-down winner in the affective assessment sweepstakes, I'm going to cut to the chase and identify, absent any foreplay, the assessment strategy that educational leaders ought to advocate. Put simply, the affective strategy that should be adopted is the use of truly anonymous self-report inventories along the lines originated more than a half century ago by Likert (1932).

The assessment of affect can be carried out at varying levels of complexity and sophistication. To illustrate, in psychological experiments designed to get a fix on children's honesty, researchers have utilized trained accomplices who create elaborate situations in which a child can or cannot cheat, then the researchers observe the child's behavior through one-way mirrors in order to draw inferences about the child's tendencies to be honest or dishonest in situations in which the attractiveness of the temptations vary. I know few educators who have the time or inclination to engage in very elaborate assessment of students' affective status, although I suspect that some teachers would know how to use one-way mirrors advantageously.

As a practical matter, the classroom assessment of student affect must be relatively easy to pull off, or it simply isn't going to happen. Teachers are too busy to carry out the galaxy of responsibilities that they face each day. That's why, as I just indicated, I'm only going to set out for you a single, readily accomplishable procedure to assess students' attitudes and values. If you wish to consider more elaborate and time-demanding ways of measuring your students' affect, there are several excellent volumes cited at the end of the chapter. The classic volumes by Anderson (1981) and by Webb and others (1981), though a mite dated, are particularly thought-provoking.

Self-Reports

Self-Report Inventories

Assessment tools, often completed anonymously, wherein students' responses reveal their views, behaviors, and so on.

Educators can get a decent fix on students' affective status by asking them to complete self-report assessment devices. If teachers set up the assessment situation so that students can respond in a truly anonymous fashion, the data derived from self-report instruments can really be useful. Just as importantly, the use of straightforward self-report devices won't be so onerous that teachers become disenchanted with such measurement. Anderson (1981) has provided a compelling argument in favor of self-report affective measurement by educators. If you really have trouble accepting the proposition that self-report assessment is the measurement scheme to use when assessing students' affective status, you might want to review the reasons that Anderson put forth when he arrived at his advocacy of self-report affective assessment in schools.

Likert Inventories

Because of its ready applicability to a variety of affective assessment targets, the approach to attitudinal measurement introduced many years ago by Likert (1932) is the most widely used. Likert inventories will handle almost all of an educator's affective assessment requirements, hence that approach is the only one you'll be learning about here. It is, by all odds, the most serviceable affective measurement strategy you'll encounter.

Likert Inventories

Affective assessment devices organized around someone's self-reported degree of agreement with presented statements.

You've probably responded to Likert inventories many times in your life. They consist of a series of statements to which you register your agreement or disagreement. For example, you are given a statement such as "Reading this book about educational measurement represents one of the finest professional experiences of my career." You then choose from a set of options to decide whether you agree/disagree with the statement. The usual options, at least for adults, are *Strongly Agree, Agree, Uncertain, Disagree, Strongly Disagree.* (I am altogether confident that you would have opted for the *Strongly Agree* response regarding the previous illustrative statement about this measurement book's impact on your professional life.)

Depending on the age of the students being assessed, it may be necessary to make adjustments in the statements used and in the number and/or phrasing of the response options. With very young children, for example, educators might need to use brief statements containing very simple words. Teachers might even have to read the statements aloud. And while older students might be able to handle the five-choice agreement scale described earlier, for younger students it may be necessary to drop down to three response options (for instance, *Agree, Don't Know,* and *Disagree*), or even two response options (perhaps *Yes* or *No*). Classroom teachers are usually the best judges of the language level that should be used with the students. In general, err in the direction of less-demanding rather than more-demanding language.

How to Build a Likert Inventory

Here are eight steps educators should follow to create a Likert inventory.

1. *Choose the affective variable to be assessed.* Decide what attitude or value is to be assessed, then try to get as clearheaded as possible about what the affective variable really means.
2. *Generate a series of favorable and unfavorable statements regarding the affective variable.* For example, if you were interested in students' attitudes regarding reading, you might construct a positive statement such as "I like to read on my own when I have free time" or a negative statement such as "People who read for fun are dull." Try to generate a few more statements than you ultimately plan to use. For students in secondary schools, a 10-item Likert inventory takes little time to complete. For students at lower grades, you'd probably want to use fewer items, for instance, five or six. Try to construct an approximately equal number of positive and negative statements.
3. *Get several people to classify each statement as positive or negative.* Snare a few colleagues or family members to look at your generated statements and classify each statement as positive or negative. Toss out any statement that isn't unanimously classified as positive or negative.
4. *Decide on the number and phrasing of the response options for each statement.* The original Likert inventory had the following five options: SD = Strongly Disagree, D = Disagree, NS = Not Sure, A = Agree, and SA = Strongly Agree. As noted, for younger children you should employ fewer and, possibly, more simple options.
5. *Prepare the self-report inventory giving students directions regarding how to respond and stipulating that the inventory must be completed anonymously.* If students haven't previously completed such inventories, they'll need clear directions. It is helpful to include an illustration or two of how students might respond. Sample statements about generally known topics, for example, foods or movies, work well for such illustrations.
6. *Administer the inventory either to the target students or, if possible (as a tryout), to other students.* If another teacher is willing, it is useful to try out the inventory with students similar to those for whom it is ultimately intended. Based on the responses of those students, the inventory can then be improved before giving it to the intended students. If teachers must use their own students, the inventory can still be improved for use later in the year with the same students or, perhaps, next year with another set of students.
7. *Score the inventories.* Assign points for each student's response to each item based on the *direction* of the statement. For instance, if you are using five response options, you would give five points to *Strongly Agree* responses to *positive* statements and also five points to *Strongly Disagree* responses to *negative* statements. Thus, for a 10-item inventory the scores could ranges from 10 to 50. Generally speaking, the higher the score, the more appropriate students' affective status appears to be.

8. *Identify and eliminate statements that fail to function in accord with the other statements.* If you know how to compute correlation coefficients, simply compute the correlation between students' responses to each item (1, 2, 3, 4, or 5, for example) and their total scores on the inventory (10 to 50). Eliminate those statements whose correlations to the total score are not statistically significant. (This is referred to as "Likert's criterion of internal consistency.") If you don't know how to compute correlation coefficients, simply "eyeball" students' responses and try to detect statements to which students are responding differently than to the rest of the statements. Dump those statements. (This is referred to as "Likert's criterion of internal consistency for people who don't know squat about computing correlations.") Then rescore the inventories without the rejected items.

It's really just that simple to bang out a Likert inventory for assessing student affect. For each affective variable, educators need a different inventory (or at least a different subset of items). Educators can certainly measure several affective variables with different sets of items on the same inventory. For instance, you might want to measure four distinctive affective variables by combining four subsets of five Likert statements into a single, 20-item inventory. The more experience that teachers have in creating Likert inventories, the easier it gets. After a short while, most teachers really become quite skilled in whipping out such affective assessment devices.

Anonymity's Paramount Importance

Anonymity Enhancement Procedures

Steps a teacher takes so students will accurately perceive their affective responses to be untraceable.

For educators to draw accurate inferences about students' affective state based on their responses to self-report inventories, *it is clearly necessary for students to respond truthfully* to the self-report affective inventories. Unfortunately, many students tend to provide *socially desirable* responses to affective self-report devices. In other words, many students are inclined to respond in the way that they think teachers want them to respond. Students are particularly apt to provide socially desirable responses if they believe the teacher can trace their responses. Consequently, to increase the likelihood that students will respond honestly to affective inventories, it is imperative that teachers not only make sure all students' responses are anonymous, but also that teachers employ as many procedures as possible so most students regard their responses as truly untraceable.

Among the simpler but effective *anonymity enhancement procedures* teachers might want to consider are these:

1. *Directions.* Make sure the directions for affective inventories stress the importance of honest answers and that students are not to put their names or any other written remarks on their inventories.

2. *Response restrictions.* Set up affective inventories so that the *only* form of student response is to be check marks, circling of preferred answers, and so on. Prohibit students from writing any words whatsoever on their inventories. Because students believe that the teacher may figure out who supplied which inventory by recognizing students' handwriting, don't permit *any* handwriting whatsoever on affective inventories. (If teachers feel compelled to allow students to write out comments, a separate comment sheet—collected separately—can be employed.)

3. *Collection.* Install a procedure whereby students deposit their completed inventories in a collection box or, instead, have a student (not one thought to be the teacher's "pet") collect the completed inventories. Announce *before* students start to fill out the inventories that one of these collection methods will be employed.

As you can see, educators must try to make sure students really don't think there's any way to trace their responses back to them. Even under those circumstances, this doesn't ensure that students will respond truthfully. However, well conceived anonymity-enhancement techniques increase the odds that students will respond honestly.

Individual and Group Affective Assessment

In the case of cognitive and psychomotor tests, educators typically use the test results to make decisions about individuals. For instance, college professors decide whether or not to admit Lee Smith to a graduate school on the basis of Lee's score on an academic aptitude test. Alternatively, choosing another common example, a geometry teacher reaches a decision about Sally's final grade in geometry on the basis of Sally's performance on the end-of-course test.

Cognitive test results are thus employed to make decisions about *individuals*. Cognitive test results are also used to make decisions about *programs*, such as the effectiveness of a particular instructional program. Educational evaluators might see, for instance, whether the pretest–posttest gains in student achievement after a special reading instruction program were sufficient.

In the case of affective measures, there are only a few instances in which educators use test results to make decisions about individuals. Almost all of these occur in connection with educational counseling, such as when counselors attempt to isolate an individual's vocational interests for purposes of career counseling. There are also instances in which a school psychologist needs to pick up some affective information on a student's emotional status for counseling purposes. With any affective measure that will be used for making decisions about *individuals*, those measures need to permit the traditional sorts of score-based inferences that educators have always sought for cognitive tests.

However, with most affective tests in education, there are no individual decisions at issue. Instead, these measures are employed to make *decisions about instructional programs*, not about particular students. As a consequence, substantially different validity evidence requirements exist for such measures. For instance, when educators employ the results of students' scores on an attitude test regarding environmental pollution to evaluate the effectiveness of a schoolwide antipollution campaign, the educators will make decisions about the campaign, not particular students.

Because many affective-assessment results are never used for purposes of individual decision-making, it follows that those assessment devices need not yield valid inferences for individual students. If the inventories can be employed to make sensible decisions about *groups* of students, as is the case when educators need to evaluate programs, then those inventories will be quite serviceable for our needs.

Let's see how this kind of situation might occur. Suppose you and your colleagues had put together a really oblique questionnaire that you believed would work beautifully for the vast majority of your students but that might mislead a small number of them. What should you do? The answer is simple if you're only evaluating a program and not students, as is frequently the case when educators assess affect. For your purposes, a questionnaire that yields valid inferences for *groups* of students will do the job nicely because the aberrant responses of a few students will be overwhelmed by the responses of majority. In other words, even if a super-anonymous Likert inventory is used with students, there are still some students who will respond dishonestly in an effort to "butter up" the teacher or, in an act of vengeance, to "batter down" the teacher. If you consider the mean (or median) score for the *entire* group, however, these dishonest outlyer responses will usually tend to be canceled out. (If there are too many of those responses, they certainly aren't "outlyers.")

Chapter Wrap-Up

As is customary, the chapter summary will be connected to the chapter's guiding questions. In the interest of succinctness, I shall endeavor to be inordinately pith-prone in my summarization.

What is the affective domain?

The *affective* domain deals with students' attitudes, interests, and values. It can be contrasted with the *cognitive* domain's focus on students' intellectual activities and the *psychomotor* domain's focus on small-muscle and large-muscle skills. Educators assess students' current affective status as a way of predicting students' future behaviors, behaviors likely to be influenced by students' attitudes, values, or interests.

Is affective assessment important?

I contended in the chapter that affective variables were, in the long term, even more important than cognitive variables because children's affect can be so influential in shaping their behaviors. Deeply held concerns, however, have been voiced about affective assessment by critics who would prefer that the schools focus exclusively on the "3Rs" rather than any attitudes or values that, in the view of these critics, should be dealt with by families and religious entities—not by the schools.

What affective variables should be assessed?

Because of the concern that affective education should not be carried out in the schools, any affective assessment that takes place should deal only with those affective variables likely to be near-universally approved by members of the community in which the schools are located. Examples of acceptable attitudinal assessment targets (for example, positive attitudes toward subjects) and acceptable value-focused assessment targets (for example, honesty) were presented.

How should affective variables be assessed?

Likert self-report inventories were recommended as the most efficient assessment instruments likely to yield valid inferences about students' affective status. An eight-step procedure for developing a Likert-type affective self-report inventory was described. In order that students' responses lead to valid inferences, however, it was stressed that anonymity was an indispensable consideration. Several anonymity techniques were presented in an effort to forestall students' tendencies to provide socially desirable rather than honest responses.

● **What kinds of inferences should be drawn from the use of self-report affective assessment?**

Because in supplying responses to self-report affective inventories some students will give false responses, it is impossible to make valid inferences about *individuals* based on such assessment instruments. Rather, teachers should use affective assessment instruments, for example, anonymously completed self-report Likert inventories, to draw *group-focused* inferences about a collection of students. By using group means or medians, the influence of outlier students tends to be canceled out. Thus, reasonable confidence can be placed in a group-focused inference based on the use of a properly constructed affective self-report inventory.

Practice Exercises

For this chapter's practice exercises, you'll be presented with four descriptions of fictitious teachers engaged in some form of affective assessment. Based on what you've read in the chapter, critique the actions of the teachers described in the following vignettes.

Vignette One

Milton Morehead has recently returned from a full-year, half-pay sabbatical leave from his position as a high school social studies teacher. During the year, Milton spent a full six months with an isolated Amazonian tribe in the Brazilian rain forests. Although the experience was physically demanding, Milton found the tribe's "spiritual simplicity" to be the most exciting part of his South American adventure.

This school year, he plans to incorporate important tenets of the tribe's spiritual values in his own teaching. He has even gone so far as to develop a 15-item Likert self-report inventory that he plans to administer to all of his classes on a pretest–posttest basis. The inventory contains statements such as, "For my own peace of mind and personal

tranquility, I realize that a higher being is everywhere around me." Milton is truly excited about giving the affective pretest to his students so he can use their responses to focus his instructional efforts more accurately.

What do you think of Milton's affective assessment plans?

Vignette Two

Having read a chapter such as the one you've just about finished, Paul Panini has jumped into affective assessment with both feet. He measures his third-grade students' attitudes toward reading, writing, mathematics, science, and social studies every month. Paul's students are asked to complete the following sentence for each of the five subjects: "My current opinion of (*name of subject*) is:

_____

_____

_____

The monthly affective assessment takes only about 10 minutes. Paul has identified certain students who have particularly negative reactions toward particular subject areas. He intends to work individually with these students in an attempt to foster more positive attitudes.

What do you think of Paul's affective assessment efforts?

Vignette Three

After choosing to employ a Likert inventory for her affective assessments, Melinda Miles, an English teacher, decided to focus on her students' confidence as writers. She then authored 10 positive statements such as "When I have to write something, I know I can," and 10 negative statements such as "If I'm called on to do a written report, I really panic." Melinda mixed up the order of the 20 statements, then asked three other English teachers to classify each statement as positive or negative. Because three supposedly negative statements and two supposedly positive statements were classified divergently by her three coworkers, Melinda tossed out those five statements.

She decided to use a five-point response scale: *strongly agree, agree, uncertain, disagree,* and *strongly disagree.* Melinda then developed directions for her inventory, which she entitled "You and Composition." The directions explained the response procedures and made it clear that there were no right or wrong answers. The directions also indicated that students were to respond anonymously and to deposit their completed inventories in a specially provided collection box. Because she had mixed up the 15 remaining statements (8 positive and 7 neg-

ative), she made sure that her scoring key coincided with the proper positive and negative statements.

One of the other English teachers in her school offered Melinda the opportunity to try out her under-development affective assessment instrument to see how it worked. Melinda jumped at the chance and administered the inventory to 31 of the other teacher's students. In looking over the results, Melinda identified 2 negative and 3 positive statements that didn't seem to function like the rest of the statements. Accordingly, she dropped those statements and ended up with a 10-item Likert inventory that she intends to use with her class both before she gets into a major unit on composition and, a month later, when the unit has been completed.

What do you think of Melinda's efforts to create a Likert inventory?

Vignette Four

Woodshop teacher Bill Bartlett is immensely interested in affect. Because fewer and fewer students are signing up for his woodshop classes, Bill tries to promote subject-approaching tendencies on the part of his students. "I want my students, boys and girls alike, to become truly enthralled with the feel of sawdust in their pockets and the sound of other students using the woodshop's lathe." Bill spends at least five minutes per week jotting down in his notebook the behaviors that indicate to him certain students are responding positively to woodshop activities.

What do you think of Bill's method of getting a fix on his students' attitudes?

Answers to Practice Exercises

Vignette One

Although Milton seems to have the hang of affective assessment, he is focused on an affective variable that would almost certainly be disapproved by many of his students' parents. Milton is about to dabble in the spiritual side of his students' belief systems. Milton shouldn't.

Vignette Two

Paul went wrong on a monthly basis. By requiring students to write out their responses, anonymity was blown. It's not even clear that students weren't supposed to put their names on their responses. In addition, Paul appears to be making individually focused inferences about how much certain subjects are liked. At best, even if he cleaned up his measurement act, Paul should only draw group-focused inferences. Paul's affective assessment efforts were not awe-inspiring.

Vignette Three

Melinda was pretty much on target the whole way through. Indeed, she so compliantly adhered to the eight steps suggested on pages 346–347 for creating Likert inventories that you might conclude she had read and/or memorized the chapter.

Vignette Four

Certain teachers can make extremely insightful judgments about students' unobservable affective status based on particular observable acts of students. Unfortunately, there are probably just as many teachers who are likely to make the wrong inferences about students' affect based on observed behaviors. One of the more vexing difficulties to be coped with when using observation-based assessments of affect is the universal truth that most people see what they want to see in a given situation. Teachers are no different. Thus, although we're glad to see Bill's attentiveness to affect, his assessment approach leaves a load to be desired.

DISCUSSION QUESTIONS

1. What do you think the role of an educational leader should be in encouraging or discouraging teachers to promote affective outcomes and to assess students' attainment of those outcomes?
2. Many citizens are opposed to having the schools engage in any kind of systematic instructional effort to influence students' attitudes or values. What do you suppose might be the reasons for their resistance to affective instruction and, most probably, to affective assessment as well?
3. If you were working with a classroom teacher who was limited to only two affective variables to assess, could you help the teacher identify two such affective variables that should be assessed irrespective of the subject matter involved?
4. Why do you think that one finds affective measures used so infrequently in the schools?
5. If you were asked to summarize for a high school faculty the ethical principles you believed important in the assessment of affect, what would you say?
6. Although the chapter suggested that group-focused inferences should be made from affective assessment devices, can you think of any defensible ways that teachers could get a decent fix on an individual student's attitudes and values? If so, how?

SUGGESTIONS FOR ADDITIONAL READING

Anderson, Lorin W. *Assessing Affective Characteristics in the School.* Boston: Allyn & Bacon, 1981.

Cox, James. *Your Opinion, Please! How to Build the Best Questionnaires in the Field of Education.* Thousand Oaks, CA: Corwin Press, 1996.

Droegemueller, Lee. *The New Religious Right.* Paper presented to Education Policy Fellows, Arizona State University, April 9, 1993.

Kohn, Alfie. "How Not to Teach Values: A Critical Look at Character Education." *Phi Delta Kappan, 78,* 6 (February 1997): 428–439.

Likert, R. "A Technique for the Measurement of Attitudes." *Archives of Psychology 140,* 1932.

Popham, W. James. "Education Assessment's Lurking Lacuna: The Measurement of Affect." *Education and Urban Society, 26,* 4 (August 1994): 404–416.

Popham, W. James. "Using Participant-Satisfaction Forms to Evaluate Staff Development Programs." *NASSP Bulletin, 81,* 586 (February 1997): 112–116.

Webb, Eugene J., Donald T. Campbell, Richard D. Schwartz, Lee Sechreat, and Janet Belew Grove. *Nonreactive Measures in the Social Sciences* (2nd ed.). Boston: Houghton Mifflin, 1981.

AND FOR THOSE WHO TIRE OF READING

Popham, W. James. *Improving Instruction: Start with Student Attitudes* (Videotape #ETVT-19). Los Angeles: IOX Assessment Associates.

Popham, W. James. *Assessing Student Attitudes: A Key to Increasing Achievement* (Videotape #ETVT-20). Los Angeles: IOX Assessment Associates.

ENDNOTES

1. B. S. Bloom, ed., and others, *Taxonomy of Educational Objectives, Handbook I: The Cognitive Domain* (New York: D. McKay, 1956).
2. D. R. Krathwohl, B. S. Bloom, and B. B. Masia, *Taxonomy of Educational Objectives, Handbook II: The Affective Domain* (New York: D. McKay, 1964).

Using
Educational
Tests

Two chapters to go! In this final section of the book, you'll be dealing with two related but different topics, both of which bear directly on the *use* of test results.

In Chapter 14, you'll learn how to administer and score educational assessment devices. The chapter also deals with the setting of performance standards and with teachers' assignment of grades for students. Chapter 14, in other words, deals with several somewhat heterogeneous topics related to test usage.

In Chapter 15, however, there is just one focus, and it's on the misuse of standardized achievement tests as indicators of educational quality. Chapter 15 supplies you with sufficient explanations and illustrative items so that, if you read the chapter thoughtfully, you ought to be able to explain to anyone—educator or layperson—why such tests should not be used to evaluate the quality of schooling. It's an important issue. That's one reason I saved it for last.

part four

Administering Educational Tests and Using the Results

Administering Educational Assessments

It's time to tussle with the practicalities of educational assessment, that is, to address the problems associated with assembly, administration, and scoring of tests. Such practicalities, of course, are tremendously important because, even if educators possess a test that yields remarkably reliable scores from which astonishingly valid inferences can be drawn, an ill-conceived administration of the test can yield meaningless student responses.

For instance, let's say educators administered a psychometrically super test under truly adverse physical conditions, for example, in an insufficiently ventilated, poorly lighted, overheated, and noisy school auditorium. Not surprisingly, any sensible clod could anticipate many distortions in the responses of the students, that is, those students who did not swoon during the test-taking period.

Although the situation just cited may seem somewhat far-fetched and you would think that few educators would make such egregious errors in the selection of a test setting, there are more subtle, but nevertheless significant, practical errors that educational leaders routinely make as they ready tests, dispense them, and try to make sense out of their results. By being alert to such potential mistakes, educators can help others avoid such errors. Thus, because this text is intended to make you an educational leader who is a flawless and facile user of educational tests, prepare to plunge into the practical complexities of test administration.

Selecting or Constructing the Test

The basic choice facing most educators who need tests is "buy 'em or build 'em." Buying tests, of course, costs money. Building tests, at first blush, sounds less expensive. After all, most schools are staffed by a host of able teacher types who could surely create a clever test or two. However, distressingly, local construction of tests usually turns out to be an assessment disaster, and badly built tests can prove far more *educationally* expensive than is typically thought.

For example, suppose that a school district's staff builds its own basic-skills achievement tests and uses student performance on these tests to inform citizens of the school's effectiveness. Let's say the tests turn out to be pretty shabby and, as a consequence, students' performance levels fail to rise in spite of valiant efforts by teachers to boost test scores. The public, dismayed at apparent ineffectiveness on the part of the schools, registers its dissatisfaction by defeating all subsequent school bond elections. The resulting loss in revenue to the district dramatically exceeds the funds that would have been required to buy an appropriate off-the-shelf test from a commercial publisher or even to have a test custom-built by an outside contractor.

Ordinarily, in most districts you'll not find a sufficiently large number of teachers or district personnel who are interested in developing assessments. Teachers become teachers to teach, not to build tests. It's not that teachers are insufficiently talented to build tests. Given suitable leadership and time, teachers could certainly build solid educational assessments. But, in my experience, the most able classroom teachers usually want to get back to their students rather than spend time in constructing tests. Test construction, they think, is the job of test constructors. For classroom tests, of course, teachers are ordinarily willing to do their own test development. They regard the creation of class-room tests as part of a teacher's responsibilities.

Those who must decide whether the tests will be constructed locally and/or pur-chased will need to weigh all sorts of factors such as cost, the congruence of the com-mercial test's mission with the needs of the local schools, the absence of cultural bias in the commercial test, and so on. Let's assume that the tests have been acquired or con-structed. Now you need to get ready to administer them.

Separate Response Sheets

In getting ready to use an educational test, one of the first matters to decide is, "Where will students respond?" For selected-response and short-answer tests, students can sup-ply their answers by either marking on the test itself or on a separate answer sheet. There are economic advantages associated with the use of separate answer sheets, because the test booklet itself can be reused. In addition, separate answer sheets are typically easier to score because the scorer does not have to leaf through a series of pages in the test it-self. Besides that, the costs of electronic scanning machines that can be used to process scannable answer sheets have been dropping in recent years, thereby making such scor-ing machines more accessible to teachers and administrators.

However, there is some evidence that first- and second-grade children's scores are lower when separate answer sheets are employed.[1] Apparently, it is distracting for younger children to transfer their responses from the test booklet to a separate answer sheet. In middle and later grades it would seem prudent to employ separate answer sheets with tests. Accordingly, of course, the directions to the student should make it clear that a separate answer sheet is to be used.

Effective Test Directions

Given the considerable energy that teachers devote to the construction of test items, it is always a bit surprising to see how casually most teachers approach the task of devising di-rections for a test. Indeed, in some cases no directions at all are prepared, supposedly on the assumption that an alert student should be able to figure out what's called for by the items. Well, as experienced teachers know, not all students are alert. In fact, some students appear to have completed advanced training programs in anti-alertness.

It is important, therefore, for teachers to fashion decent directions for their tests be-cause, without those directions, many students will flounder on the assessment due to confusion regarding the task at hand. A good set of directions for a test will include the following six kinds of information:

1. The test's purpose
2. Time allowance
3. The basis for responding
4. Method of recording responses
5. Appropriateness of guessing
6. Differential scoring weights

The nature of the directions, particularly for classroom tests, will depend on such factors as the students' familiarity with the types of items on the test. To illustrate, if Mrs. Thomas has been dishing out weekly multiple-choice vocabulary quizzes in her English class for the last fifteen weeks, her students will doubtlessly need little guidance about how to answer the questions on this week's quiz. Suppose, on the other hand, that Mr. Gale is introducing an exotic new type of interpretive exercise in which his students must first make sense out of a complicated map *and* a complicated graph, *then* respond to a series of matching items. Under such circumstances, a detailed set of test directions is definitely needed for Mr. Gale's innovative assessment approach.

The Test's Purpose

Although for many tests it is apparent what the intent of the test is, for some tests the purpose is more opaque. As a general rule, because it usually takes no more than a single sentence to do so, it is a good idea to include in the test directions a statement that describes the intended mission of the test.

Time Allowance

Directions should indicate how much time is being allowed for the total test. It is also helpful to suggest to students how they should allocate their time during an examination. If, for example, there" are several sections on the exam, then the directions should estimate how much time should be spent on each section.

For tests consisting of essay questions, it is useful to provide question-by-question guidelines regarding appropriate time expenditures. At UCLA's Graduate School of Education, for example, doctoral qualifying examinations used to consist of six questions, each of which was to be answered in about one hour by doctoral candidates. Even with a reminder alongside each question that it was a "one-hour" question, some students would invariably use up too much of their time in responding to early items. Without such reminders, some students might never get beyond the first question. (Doctoral candidates are a decidedly verbose crew.)

The Basis for Responding

In some instances, such as with multiple-choice tests, all the directions need do is to indicate that students "should select the best alternative for each item." If possibilities for confusion are present, such as might be encountered with matching items for which students would be uncertain as to whether responses can be used more than once, then such matters need to be clarified in the directions. In particular, essay questions should provide students with cues regarding what their responses should stress, for example, particular facts or a synthesis of such facts.

For very young children it is frequently helpful to provide a sample test question that shows how a response should be made. Many nationally standardized examinations, in recognition of the value of a good model, routinely provide such sample questions and oblige the test administrator to show students how the sample items should be completed. Most standardized achievement tests also provide relatively brief practice exams so that students, prior to taking the standardized test, will become familiar with the format of its items.

Method of Recording Responses

As indicated earlier, if separate response sheets are used with the assessment instrument, students may need to be given directions about how to use the response sheets. If the answer sheets are to be scored by machine, it may be necessary to indicate precisely how the sheets are to be filled out. For example, many machine-scorable response forms consist of circles (or "bubbles") that must be darkened by examinees. Indeed, a new verb has been created by the educational testing industry during the past few decades, because test directions routinely inform students that they are "to *bubble* in the correct answer for each item."

Appropriateness of Guessing

Later in the chapter you'll learn the pros and cons of employing correction-for-guessing procedures. If there is any special guidance that students should have regarding whether guessing is appropriate, the test's directions are an eminently suitable place for such guidance. However, with respect to the wisdom of employing guessing-correction formulae, please hold off for a bit in making your judgment.

Differential Scoring Weights

Differential Scoring Weights

Assignment of different values for students' responses to various items on a test.

Teachers will sometimes decide that because certain items are more significant, those items should be assigned double or even triple weighting. For instance, instead of giving every item one point, these special items might receive two or three points. Similarly, errors on such items carry heavier penalties.

Although differential weighting of items makes intuitive sense, this process rarely raises or lowers students' overall rankings to any appreciable extent. Differential weights generally do not improve or lower a test's reliability or the validity of inferences drawn from its use. This process usually makes little difference in the way that students are ultimately ranked.

Even though differential weighting of items may make little difference in the rankings of students, it may substantially influence students' study efforts if they are aware that certain kinds of items will receive heavier weighting on major exams. Accordingly, because the quality of the exam is not affected adversely, teachers may wish to use differential weighting as a helpful emphasis guide for students. Although differential weighting may have no *assessment* impact, it may have a decisive *instructional* impact. If responses to certain items in a test are to be weighted differentially, that information should most certainly be in the test's directions.

The Actual Administration

The two main factors to consider when administering a test are (1) the physical setting in which the testing takes place, and (2) the nature of the test administrator's interaction with the students. If either the physical setting or the test administrator's instructions are unsatisfactory, students may end up with lower (or higher) scores than they deserve.

New Fla. Assessment Suffers Glitch

About 11,500 Florida 5th and 10th graders are still waiting to find out how they did on a January statewide exam, after a technical glitch caused mistakes on their test results.

The errors affected about 2 percent of the 550,000 students who took the exam, which is based on the state's new learning standards. The test will eventually be required for graduation and promotion. It was being offered statewide for the first time.

Brewser Brown, a spokesman for the Florida education department, said test-scanning equipment randomly misread answers. But the errors appear to have been made on questions that were correctly answered by students, which means that scores will go up.

The company that published the test, CTB/McGraw-Hill, is working on the problem. "They're trying to get scores to parents as soon as possible," Mr. Brown said.

What's your reaction?

Reprinted, with permission, from *Education Week*, May 27, 1998

The Physical Setting

When most of us think about the ideal assessment room, particularly for important tests, our minds usually conjure up a delightful, well-lighted, properly ventilated classroom or cafeteria with ample work space for each student. More often than not, of course, students are obliged to complete tests in their regular classrooms. Accordingly, teachers should strive to make certain that their classrooms possess all the virtues of an ideal testing room.

It is customary for test manuals of commercially distributed tests to urge that examinations take place in well-lighted rooms where desks or tables provide students with adequate work space. Interestingly, at least one investigation suggests that pupils can adapt quite satisfactorily to less than optimum conditions of this sort. In a study of testing conditions, Ingle and DeAmico found that students who took standardized tests in a poorly lighted auditorium using lapboards, instead of desks, performed as well on the tests as did youngsters who took the tests in well-lighted classrooms with adequate work space.[2]

However, even though children might be able to take tests on lapboards in darkness, that doesn't mean educators should oblige them to do so. No, it just makes common sense to provide students with decent lighting, reasonable work space, an acceptable room temperature, and adequate ventilation.

Teachers should also be attentive to the number and magnitude of auditory distractions that may arise during a testing period. Not all students are bothered by loud noises, but some are. I used to teach in a small high school on the ground-floor next to an expansive front lawn. It seemed that the school's custodian (who was also its gardener, mechanic, plumber, and painter) had access to special information regarding my exam schedule, for he invariably chose my exam day to mow the lawn. It would have been all right had he used a small lawn mower and finished the job quickly. However, our school's congenial custodian had rigged up an adapted tractor engine with the lawn mower. That engine, when running, sounded like the first stage of a space rocket. Furthermore, he kept going back and forth, back and forth, apparently wishing to give every blade of grass its fair share of shearing. Both my students and I suffered as a consequence of these mower-marred exam periods.

The Test Administrator's Behavior

In most instances, the test administrator for educational test will be the teacher. Certainly, teachers will administer their own classroom tests. However, whether special test administrators or typical classroom teachers are dishing out the tests, there are a few guidelines that should be attended to when directing a testing session. If you are an educational leader who's trying to help teachers administer tests properly, you might wish to bring the following guidelines to your colleagues' attention.

Avoid verbal or nonverbal behaviors that are likely to make students anxious.
Do not assert that the test is a "crucial" one or that evil will befall all those who fail it. Don't pace back and forth in the front of the testing room, looking up frequently at the clock. Don't "hover" over students, observing them with intensity as they make their answers.

Instead, try to reassure students that the purpose of the test is to help them, either to learn or to guide instructional decisions. Let them know that the time limits are adequate (assuming they are). In fact, the teacher should deliberately try to *allay* anxiety, not foster it. Studies reveal that there are certain students who become so anxious during testing sessions that the quality of their performance is substantially reduced. Even an adroit test administrator will not be able to transform some nervous students into tranquil test-takers. However, teachers may be able to at least keep such students' anxieties within reasonable limits.

Don't talk unnecessarily before the test, and never talk during the test. Some teachers get carried away with the significance of an assessment occasion, and jabber on endlessly before actually dispensing the tests. Students are ready, but their time is being used up by a long-winded teacher. Similarly, some teachers choose the moments prior to exams to comment about last week's activities or this week's assignments. Such diatribes probably won't be well attended to by students, and they certainly will annoy the students who are eager to get going on the test.

After the exam begins, teachers sometimes interrupt for one reason or another to make announcements. Such interruptions should be avoided unless critically important (such as, for example, when a mistake in a test item has been discovered or the school is on fire). Some insensitive teachers will carry on a loud conversation with a student during the examination. Teachers should sharpen their whispering skills.

While on the subject of interruptions, try vigorously to reduce external interruptions. One helpful way that teachers can do so in a room is to post a sign outside the door that says something like "Test in Session—Do Not Disturb." Some teachers, frustrated by excessive interruptions during their regular teaching schedules, may be inclined to post such signs on a daily basis whether or not there's a test taking place.

Monitor for possible cheating, taking steps to discourage such behaviors. Teachers have to cope with the possibility of student dishonesty during examinations. By attentive proctoring, that is, alert surveillance, much potential cheating can be forestalled. Alternate forms of the test can also be employed to discourage students from casual copying of the marks on others' answer sheets.

Do not give hints to students about individual test items. Certain students are more willing to ask about test items than are others. Perhaps they are cunning, merely outgoing, or caught up in a continuing quest for cognitive insight. However, an experienced teacher will tell you that during an exam it usually turns out to be the same few students who approach the teacher with queries, such as, "On item 22, did you mean . . . ?"

Now it is perfectly reasonable to clarify ambiguous test items, if that is the kind of clarification needed. However, some astute students are really trying to secure hints as to the correct answer. Yet teachers, wanting to be nice folks, sometimes succumb to these entreaties by dispensing little bits of information that lead directly to the correct response.

However, teachers should play the proctoring game with evenhandedness. They should not reward a few aggressive students by giving them special information while withholding that information from less aggressive, but no less deserving, students. Teacher should avoid giving hints on test items, even if they're strongly tempted to do so.

When administering a standardized test, teachers must follow the directions explicitly. So far the discussion of test-administration practices has dealt with the kinds of tests that could be teacher-made *or* distributed by commercial firms. When using standardized tests, such as, for example, the *Iowa Tests of Basic Skills*, there are always

Assessing All Not Easy, Research Group Warns

Under the Individuals with Disabilities Education Act amendments of 1997, states and districts must include disabled students in general state and districtwide assessments and report their results with the rest of the students. That change earned widespread praise from educators and disability-rights advocates.

But now, the National Center on Educational Outcomes is warning that measuring the educational progress of students with disabilities may be more difficult than expected.

Problems will arise because of different interpretations of the IDEA assessment language and its requirements, the University of Minnesota-based federally funded research center says in a recent report. Different states have varying guidelines for such terms as "accommodations," "alternate assessments," and "disaggregated scores."

In addition, states are taking divergent approaches to designing assessments and accountability systems, and some are further along in the process than others.

The center calls on the U.S. Department of Education to write clear definitions and guidelines on the new IDEA requirements, and to research and create model demonstration projects for alternative assessments. It also recommends that teachers receive adequate professional development to administer tests. . . .

What's your reaction?

Excerpted, with permission, from *Education Week,* July 8, 1998

directions provided for test administrators. These directions include not only how much time to allow for the test and its subparts but often the explicit words to be read aloud when explaining how the test is to be completed.

Because the entire conception of a standardized test is premised on the extent to which it is administered, scored, and interpreted in a *standardized* manner, teachers must adhere religiously to the directions provided (unless that violates the separation between church and state).

Scoring the Tests

It would be nice if tests would score themselves. Scoring tests is so boring. However, distressingly, that little innovation is not yet at hand. Hence, educators will need to face the problem of how to score tests after students have completed them.

Hand Scoring

In classrooms, the bulk of tests are scored by hand, usually the teacher's. In a few cases teachers can have students exchange papers and score each other's test, but because of the possibility of "mutual kindness" by pairs of students, this practice is rarely recommended for important examinations.

If tests must be hand-scored, it is important to devise the most efficient method of scoring. For example, if short-answer tests are to be scored, it usually helps the teacher to write out a numbered list of the correct answers and have the list at hand during the scoring.

For selected-response answers, particularly those made on a separate response sheet, it is often effective to use a scoring stencil (or template) in which holes have been punched out over the correct answers. The teacher simply scores a student's answer sheet, marks with a colored pencil any missing answers, then totals the score. (A quick glance at the answer sheet to see that students weren't filling in too many responses is also recommended.) By returning the answer sheets to students (with errors marked in colored pencil), they can determine not only how many but what sorts of errors they made.

Electronic Scoring

For large-scale test scoring, there is no substitute for a well-trained, electronically powered machine. In this era of ever-increasing advances in electronics, recent years have seen a number of improvements in the computer scoring of tests. Most of these involve the use of some sort of optical scanning equipment that can be used to "read" a student's response sheet, then pump out a record of correct and incorrect answers. Sophisticated test-scoring machines will also produce a series of subscores, error patterns, and so on.

Electronic scanning machines can be used to score single-response sheets as well as test booklets on which younger students write directly. The major variable in the cost of optical scanning machines is the number of sheets that can be processed in a given period of time. Whereas a machine that can score 1,000 sheets an hour might cost a substantial amount, a machine that can score 6,000 sheets per hour might cost two or three times that amount. Currently, low-cost models suitable for use in schools and in classrooms are being widely marketed. Educators can expect continuing increases in the efficiency of such machines and, hopefully, a reduction in their cost. Researchers are even reporting favorable results with computers that scan and score students' essay responses. And machine-scored, short-answer test items will soon be commonplace if the advances in electronic "scanning" capabilities continue to emerge.

Most large school districts now own their own electronic test-scoring equipment, so teachers in such districts will often find themselves administering tests that will be machine-scored at the district office. One of the major impediments to effective use of electronic scoring is the extensive turnaround time that sometimes delays a teacher's receiving test results until well after the test was administered. Such delays, of course, render test results fairly useless for instructional purposes. The in-school or in-classroom models now available will circumvent that difficulty.

For districts that do not possess their own test-scoring machines, there are increasing numbers of scoring services available. Typically, these scoring services can accommodate mailed-in batches of answer sheets and, depending on priorities and costs, provide fairly rapid turnarounds. Some school districts and universities are even providing such test-scoring services at a nominal cost to other users.

Correcting for Guessing

Because it is feared that, if there are no penalties associated with guessing, some students might "blind guess" their way to unwarrantedly high scores, *correction-for-guessing* formulae are sometimes recommended for use in calculating a student's score on a test that uses many selected-response items. The usual formula for this purpose is

$$\text{Score} = R - \frac{W}{n-1}$$

where R = number right
W = number wrong
n = number of alternatives

Thus, for a test consisting of binary-choice items the formula would be

$$\text{Score} = R - \frac{W}{2-1} = R - W$$

For multiple-choice items the formula would be different, depending on the number of options on the items.

Guessing-Correction Formulae

Procedures intended to penalize students whose responses reflect excessive guessing.

$$\text{For 3 alternatives, Score} = R - \frac{W}{2}$$

$$\text{For 4 alternatives, Score} = R - \frac{W}{3}$$

$$\text{For 5 alternatives, Score} = R - \frac{W}{4}$$

Items that are omitted by the student are not counted as wrong.

To illustrate the use of the correction-for-guessing formula, let's consider the case of a student who completes a fifty-item multiple-choice exam on which each item has four alternatives. The student answers twenty-seven items correctly, misses eighteen, and does not respond at all to five items. If the teacher were scoring the student's paper only by number correct, then the student would get a score of 27. If, however, the teacher applies our correction-for-guessing formula, then the scoring would take place as follows:

$$\text{Score} = 27 - \frac{18}{3} = 21$$

There are two fairly distinctive settings in which the correction-for-guessing formula might be applied. The first of these involves unspeeded tests, that is, tests for which most students have ample time to complete the test. The second, not surprisingly, involves speeded tests, that is, tests for which it is not thought that most students will be able to finish. To oversimplify, with speeded tests there appears to be some value in correcting for guessing, because such a correction (if announced in advance) can deter slower students from answering the final test questions on the basis of wild guessing.

Speeded Tests

Examinations of sufficient length that it is thought all students cannot finish in the time allowed.

For unspeeded tests, most measurement specialists advise against the use of correction-for-guessing formulae. Considerable research suggests that there is little advantage in using such corrections.[3] In general, scores that have been corrected for guessing will rank students in approximately the same relative positions as will uncorrected scores. In other words, in spite of the fact that their scores have been subjected to dia-

bolical correction schemes, students usually end up with scores that rank them in essentially the same way as would have been the case without any correction schemes.

For classroom tests, therefore, it is usually inappropriate to correct for guessing unless the test is speeded to the point that many students will be unable to complete all of its items. Under any circumstances, as suggested before, the test's directions should make clear whether any penalties will be applied. It is generally good advice to suggest that students employ *informed guesses* if they are uncertain but have some sort of idea of an item's correct answer. For speeded tests it is helpful to urge students to work rapidly so they can complete as many items as possible (rather than suggesting they complete the test's final items by random marking of the answer sheet).

Recording Test Results

Once tests have been scored, results must be recorded in such a way that they can be both stored and retrieved efficiently. This sounds more routine and simpler than it actually is.

For instance, in any sort of large educational operation, such as a school district with several thousand pupils, the data storage space requirements are considerable. In addition, if someone wants access to a certain pupil's records, how will those records be plucked from the tens of thousands of student records that will accumulate even over a short span of years?

In recent years, these records have increasingly been maintained by means of electronic computers, particularly the low-cost microcomputers that have become a standard fixture in most schools and school districts. Some larger districts, in fact, currently maintain all pertinent records in a district-operated student data file. Some of these computer-based data retrieval systems have all sorts of nifty features associated with them, such as procedures for printing up special letters that inform parents of their children's progress on a subtest-by-subtest basis.

There is a decided tension existing between our wish to make records of student test scores available to those who need to use them and, simultaneously, to prevent those records from being seen by those who have no business with them. It should be clear that we don't want every Tom, Dick, and Harriet browsing through records of students' test scores. The trick is to set up a storage and retrieval system that provides requested data to authorized personnel while making certain that no unauthorized individuals can penetrate the retrieval system.

Test Security

Should tests be kept from students after the tests have been used, or should the test be returned to students in order to gain the instructional dividends that might accompany such an act? Although there is a division of opinion on this issue, it is my view that educators should *not* turn over important examinations to students because by that act the teacher is thereafter unable to use those exams again.

It's not that I don't want students to learn well. On the contrary, I've spent most of my career messing around with methods of making students learn more, faster. However, teachers can construct only so many decent test items before they run out of ideas. If, after generating two terrific exams in successive years, a drained teacher must then turn out a series of mediocre exams for years to come, think of the students who will be mismeasured.

No, teachers should devise the very best test items they can, refine them, then guard them with the diligence of James Bond (aka Agent 007). By maintaining secure tests, over the years a teacher will be able to build a file of increasingly fine test items to use in future exams. Items can be stored along with results, for example, item-analysis data, p values, and (in the case of multiple-choice items) distractor analyses from previous exams. By having more than the items needed for a given exam, the teacher will be able to select enough items from the item file to create different forms of the test each year, term, and so on.

For less important tests, such as weekly quizzes or easily generated tests, little is lost by turning over the test itself to the students. Tests of this sort can usually be churned out without much difficulty.

Some states have installed so-called truth-in-testing laws that oblige testing organizations to release, annually, copies of the actual tests used. These laws generally apply to high-stakes achievement tests or, sometimes, to various sorts of admission tests. Although testing organizations have fought vigorously against such legislation, certain states have nonetheless enacted such requirements. It is too early to tell what the impact of truth-in-testing laws will be. I believe that a mechanism must be established whereby tests are reviewed to make sure that defective items have not been included in a test (thereby leading to inaccurate scores for some students). However, an annual review of test forms, under

Educational Leaders Look at Assessment

"Reliable" Grading

Lynn Winters
Assistant Superintendent
Research, Planning & Evaluation
Long Beach Unified School District
Long Beach, California

Consistency in classroom testing does not mean that "A" students are always "A" students and "F" students are always "F"; it means that the kind and quality of performance required for an "A" or an "F" remain the same. It is the opposite of grading on the curve, but a little more complicated than just setting a consistent passing score on each exam. Not all classroom tests will have the same number of items, or the same percent correct score for "passing," but the expectation for what constitutes acceptable performance should be comparable across assessments. For example, on a 20-item history quiz of fairly easily remembered facts, the passing score might be 80%. On another 20-item quiz assessing complex concepts about causes of the depression and problems in the world financial markets, the passing score might be 60%. If the passing score were set at some arbitrary percent, most commonly 70%, student performance on the two quizzes might actually be inconsistent. If the passing score for both quizzes were 70%, students who "failed" the history-fact quiz (scored below 70% correct) and passed the economics quiz (scored above 70%) might actually have a deeper understanding of history than students who passed the facts quiz but failed the economics quiz. The different passing scores represent differences in the complexity and importance of the material being assessed. The different scores represent an attempt to "equate" assessments so that we aren't failing students who know the material well and passing students with a superficial understanding of content. ●

security-monitored conditions, by a qualified group of reviewers, would accomplish that mission satisfactorily. I believe the long-term effects of requiring that tests be released annually will be detrimental. For instance, not only will high-quality items become "insecure," hence, will be unable to be used again, but test publishers will be inclined to devote less effort to creating first-rate test items because the publishers will know that such items will be able to be used only once. Thus, the quality of such high-stakes tests will, over time seriously drop.

Setting Performance Standards

Today, more than at any previous time in the history of education, classroom teachers and school administrators are being obliged to set explicit performance standards for students. Educators have recently been asked, and sometimes required by law, to specify a precise level of performance below which a student will be considered deficient. Because few educators have seriously wrestled with the problems of setting standards and because so many educators must now do so, let's consider how to come up with an answer to the question: "How good is good enough?"

What a Performance Standard Is

Because the topic of concern in the following paragraphs is performance standards, and how to set them, it seems only reasonable to spend a few sentences attempting to clarify the expression, *performance standard*. The interpretation that most of us ascribe to *standard* is the following definition offered by the *Oxford English Dictionary*:

> A definite level of excellence, attainment, wealth, or the like, or a definite degree of any quality, viewed as a prescribed object of endeavour or as the measure of what is adequate for some purpose.

When people apply such an interpretation to education, and to student performance, they're clearly talking about a "measure of what (student performance) is adequate for some purpose." However, when educators are forced to set *measurable* performance standards, rather than talk about them, the game's stakes instantly skyrocket. And that, of course, is the situation today because legislative bodies, and the public in general, are demanding that educators describe measurable performance standards for students, typically in connection with state-established *assessments*.

In situations in which educators have merely been admonished to set general (and by implication, not necessarily measurable) performance standards, one can detect markedly increased tranquility in the educational establishment. Unmeasurable standards need be little more than rhetoric. However, when educators have actually been forced to measure students' mastery of performance standards, anxiety indices rise and a quest for sensible standard-setting procedures commences.

Cut-Score

A performance standard, that is, an acceptable level of student performance.

It is important to recognize that performance standards, in the sense that this phrase is used here, apply to an *individual*, not a group of individuals. There are many instances in which educators use a group's performance to help them make decisions, for instance, when a teacher decides whether to revise an instructional procedure for a group of students. However, the types of standard-setting dilemmas often facing educators are clearly focused on individual students, for example, "Should John Jasper receive a high school diploma or should Millicent Muggins be advanced to the next grade?" In some settings, a performance standard, that is, an acceptable level of student performance, is also referred to as a "cut-score."

On a similar note, today's preoccupation with standards is almost exclusively associated with performance in the cognitive domain, only occasionally in the psychomotor domain, and never in the affective domain. Although we might set some *group* standards in the affective domain, educators never set minimum requisites (for example, regarding a pupil's attitudes toward school) which, if not satisfied, would result in an adverse decision regarding an individual student. No, our concern here is chiefly with the establishment of performance standards in the cognitive domain. While the strategies to be described pertain to psychomotor skills as well, all of our examples will be drawn from cognitive pupil behavior.

A Camouflaged Problem

Although educators have perennially been obliged to decide when a student "passed a test" or "passed a course," this obligation was discharged in private, behind closed classroom doors. When students were asked to pass competency tests as a precursor to high school graduation, however, the issue of what it means to *pass* competency tests clearly began to receive spotlight attention. Yet, unlike some problems that, when illuminated, become less vexing, the highlighting of educators standard-setting shortcomings has not been accompanied by the emergence of sure-fire solution strategies.

Putting it simply, educators have always faced decisions about whether students' performances were good enough to pass the students, but those decisions were typically made individually and privately. Now, educators are being called on to deal *openly* with the question of performance standards. Moreover, instead of setting a passing level for each teacher's class, so that it impacts on only a limited set of student grades, educators are currently being asked to set passing levels for large collections of students, such as all seniors in a school district or even an entire state.

When teachers were struggling with the passing-standards problem in private, they could take solace in the fact that, if some students were penalized because of the too-stringent standards in one teacher's class, those students would most likely benefit from another teacher's more relaxed grading standards. Most of us remember classes in which our final grades seemed unwarrantedly low or, conversely, charitably high. Thus, educators could console themselves with the recognition that grading inequities tended to cancel out over the long haul.

However, with competency testing programs that are linked to important contingencies for students, such as high school graduation tests, such "over-the-long-haul" compensation is unavailable to the student. If an excessively stringent passing standard is set on a districtwide high school graduation test, many students will be penalized irrevocably. There won't be numerous other opportunities whereby this error will be rectified because of an unduly relaxed passing standard. Clearly, errors in setting an excessively high passing score on a high-stakes competency test can have lasting consequences for many people, not just the students who are inequitably failed, but also for their families and friends.

The flip side of that argument, of course, is that if we set standards that are too low, society is ultimately the loser. It is generally conceded that one strong motive underlying the enactment of state-level competency testing programs was to halt, both in the public's perception and in fact, a devaluation of the high school diploma. Clearly, if performance standards are set too low, the devaluation of high school diplomas will have been accelerated, not impeded.

It is apparent that educators have been historically plagued by the problem of how to set defensible passing standards but have thus far been unsuccessful in producing sensible solution strategies. Further, because passing standards were generally established in private by individual teachers, no large-scale attention has been given to this issue. The setting of standards has been a major, but well-camouflaged educational problem for centuries. That problem is now decisively out of the closet.

The Arbitrariness Bugbear

It has been contended by some (for example, Glass, in 1977) that the act of setting a performance standard is *by its very nature* so arbitrary, mindless, and capricious that educators ought not to engage in the enterprise. However, such critics unwarrantedly equate caprice with human judgment. Admittedly, when human beings apply their judgmental powers to the solution of problems, mistakes will be made. However, the fact that judgmental errors are possible should not send educators scurrying from such tasks as the setting of standards. Judges and juries are capable of error, yet they do the best job they can. Similarly, educators are now faced with the necessity of establishing performance standards, and they, too, must do the best job they can.

That educational performance standards need to be set in order for instructional decisions to be made is indisputable. That those standards will, in the final analysis, be set judgmentally is equally indisputable. However, that all judgmental standards must be arbitrary is decidedly disputable.

Approaching the standard-setting task seriously, taking full cognizance of available data and the preferences of concerned constituencies, need not result in an enterprise that is arbitrary and capricious. On the contrary, the act of standard-setting can reflect the very finest form of judgmental decision-making.

Key Considerations

Although there are a number of step-by-step procedures now available if an educational leader needs to set a performance standard, and a review of the references at the chapter's conclusion will point you toward many of them, there are several general considerations to which educational leaders who are would-be standard setters should attend.

Revisability. Because of the obvious reliance on human judgment in the setting of performance standards, everyone involved in a standard-setting enterprise should, early on, alert the world to the tentativeness of the standards being established. Standard setters should concede without debate that they may, in all likelihood *will*, make mistakes in the establishment of performance standards. That being the case, the expectation should be established that performance standards, once established, will be continually reviewed and, probably, revised.

With regard to revisability, it will typically be easier to raise than to lower widely publicized performance standards. Suppose, for example, that a state sets its high school graduation performance standards for a given mathematics test at the 80 percent correct level, then discovers that two-thirds of the state's youngsters can't pass the test at that level. There will be far more loss of public confidence if the state's educators "lower their standards" to the 75 percent level than if they had set an initial level at 70 percent and, after a year or so, "raised their standards" to 75 percent. There is a danger, of course, in playing it so safe at the outset that the initially set standards are far too low, thus inviting ridicule. Nevertheless, standard setters should be aware that it's decidedly easier to adjust standards up than down.

Quantitative quicksands. Most educators would like to have a compact, portable, and perfectly reliable standard-setting machine that, with a crank or two, would spit out a simply splendid performance standard. However, although nearly all educators recognize the folly of looking for such a magic standard-setting machine, there are many educators who will settle for the next best thing: a *quantitative* standard-setting procedure. Most people just love quantitative decision schemes. They reverently genuflect in the face of numerically sophisticated formulae because such quantitative schemes smack of genuine authoritativeness. After all, if it has numbers in it, can precision be far removed?

Yet, in spite of many folks' commitment to number magic, even a quantitative standard-setting approach just brimming with numbers and symbols must be appraised as rigorously as any nonquantitative scheme. Later, if you consider any of these quantitatively oriented standard-setting schemes, you will discover that, in all of them, there are key points where

human judgment operates. Thus, even though a standard-setting scheme appears to be exclusively quantitative, and thereby to have dodged that messy commodity known as human judgment, one invariably finds that judgmental operations have been slipped into the procedures. For standard setting, educators won't be able to escape the necessity of making some tough judgments, all the numbers in the universe notwithstanding.

Experience-based standards.   There have been several recent reports of states or major school systems that have attempted to set performance standards in the absence of *any* data regarding how students will actually perform on the tests being used. This is foolhardy. Preferably, standards would be set only after there has been a thoroughgoing tryout of the tests with the kinds of pupils for whom they are ultimately intended. At the very least, a sample of student performance should be gathered to guide standard setters in their efforts to isolate realistic expectations. Ideally, performance standards should not be set until after a test has actually been administered in an "it really counts" setting.

Time requirements.   There are so many time-consuming activities associated with the educational programs for which performance standards are required that educators sometimes try to race by the standard-setting phase of the program. "After all," they naively assume, "all we have to do is choose a few percentages."

Well, badly set performance standards can surely be set in a hurry, but decent ones rarely can. It takes plenty of relevant data, and time for reflection, if performance standards are to be set properly. For example, if local citizens have a stake in the decision at hand, such as setting high school graduation standards for a competency testing program, those citizens should be given ample opportunity to develop the meaningful sort of local "ownership" that in the long run will result in acceptance of the program *and its standards*. All relevant stakeholders should have an opportunity to offer their opinions about performance standards. Attempting to rush the process will make the program's failure likely.

Grading

Teachers have been graders for almost as long as there have been teachers. When archaeologists find fragments of pottery from ancient Assyria with only single letters on them, the initial hypothesis should be that an Assyrian instructor was dishing out end-of-course grades, probably using a norm-referenced interpretive framework.

The reasons that grades are necessary, of course, are numerous. In general, people need to know how students performed in school and in particular courses. Included in the individuals who have a legitimate use for grades are students themselves, students' parents, persons involved directly with the education of students (that is, teachers, counselors, and administrators), prospective employers, and college admission officials. Each of these groups has a high priority reason for wanting to know how Melanie performed in her eleventh-grade English class. Educational leaders must devise schemes for supplying all such individuals with reasonable estimates of how well Melanie really did in the class, and that, obviously, tosses them right in the middle of grading.

Arguments to Abolish Grading

Lest it be assumed that there is universal support for the awarding of grades in school, you should know that there are plenty of individuals who have mounted strong, emotional arguments for the abolition of grades.[4] Proposals to do away with grades were actually proffered over a half century ago.[5]

Although our systems for grading are fraught with frailties, to abandon them would be perilous. Indeed, as Moynihan observed when he stressed the value of the grading system as a democratic vehicle by which persons born to modest or lowly circumstances can be recognized for their worth:

> I have not the least doubt that this system is crude, that it is often cruel, and that it measures only a limited number of things. Yet it measures valid things, by and large. To do away with such systems of accreditation may seem like an egalitarian act, but in fact it would be just the opposite. We would be back to a world in which social connections and privilege count for much more than any of us, I believe, would like. If what you know doesn't count, in the competitions of life, who you know will determine the outcomes.[6]

The fact that an enterprise has imperfect aspects should not incline us to abandon that enterprise in its entirety. Our task should be to strengthen the quality of our grading systems, not chuck them out.

Reliance on Test Results

Teachers exercise power when they dispense students' grades. One of the most serious defects of the grading enterprise is that teachers often exercise this power cavalierly. High grades are given to students who court the teacher's favor. Low grades are given to class cutups, no matter how much they know about the course content. Far too many teachers use grades as an omnipurpose tool for rewarding or rebuking students on other than academic grounds. However, just because something *is* done, does not mean that it *should* be done.

One effective way of discouraging teachers from using petty personality differences with students as a factor in grading is to rely heavily, perhaps exclusively, on the results of educational tests in deciding what grade the student should receive. As usual, when I refer to students' educational tests in this context, I'm thinking about the whole gamut of assessment devices I have discussed in this text, such as observations of classroom performance and ratings of students' oral presentations. I certainly do not mean only the teacher's end-of-unit or end-of-course written examinations.

By relying on documented evidence of this sort (typically compiled in the teacher's gradebook), teachers will be less likely to succumb to uncontrolled subjectivity. Mabel will be less apt to get a high grade chiefly because "she is always so neat, punctual, and well-balanced." Mary Jane will be less likely to pick up a low grade because "at least once per week she is horrible, disrupting class with her unruly behavior."

By relying on a systematically amassed set of test scores, project ratings, and classroom observations, teachers will more likely be able to use grades as the indicators most people believe them to be, namely, as an accurate indication of the student's academic performance in a class.

There should, of course, be a way for teachers to register their reactions to the positive and negative qualities of students. If Mabel is an angel and Mary Jane is a scurrilous child, these points can be made in a grading system that also allows teachers to enter comments regarding the pupil's sociopersonal development. However, such factors should not be unthinkingly merged with grades that supposedly reflect academic attainments. By rooting grades in students' test results, teachers can more readily move in the direction of defensible grading.

Conventional Grading Systems

The most widely employed system of grading is the use of a single letter grade (*A, B, C, D,* or *F*) to describe a student's performance. Sometimes teachers will be permitted to employ a plus or minus in connection with such letter grades, so that students can get a *C*+ or an *A*–. By so doing, of course, teachers move from a five-point scale (the five letter grades) to a fifteen-point scale (the five letter grades as well as a plus and minus variant of each).

Because most teachers grew up in settings in which traditional single-letter grades were awarded, it is not surprising that teachers persist in using such grades themselves. We do what we know. However, even within the confines of a traditional grading system, there are substantially different ways of determining who gets an *A* or who gets a *C*. Let's consider the most common of these.

Relative grading. In *relative grading,* the focus is on giving grades to students on the basis of their performances in relationship to each other. To award a grade to a student on the basis of how that student stacks up with other students is by all odds the most common way of granting grades. There is the problem, however, of deciding which group will be used as the reference (or comparison) group for the student. For instance, is it only this term's classroomful of students, or is it perhaps an inferred district or national sample of such students? More often than not, the comparison group employed to make grading decisions is "the group existing in the teacher's head." In other words, most teachers carry around a mental image of how well students typically perform on the kinds of tasks encountered in their classes. It is this experience-based conception of the typical student against which relative comparisons are usually made. Such notions of the typical student are often accumulated by teachers over a period of many years.

Clearly, it is more equitable for teachers to use a generalized notion of typical student performance than to reference grades directly to a particular classroom's students. For example, suppose that the bulk of this year's class is academically deficient. If grades are assigned on the basis of this year's inferior class, then even a weak student might end up with an *A* because, *in comparison to the rest of this class,* the student appears to be strong. Contrarily, if the class turns out to be flooded with near geniuses, then pity the poor pupil who will get an *F* because of a poor relative standing.

If teachers call on their experience to form a more generalized estimate of a reference group, such injustices are less likely. The larger the reference group, the more defensible the assignment of grades on a relative basis.

The system of assigning grades on a relative basis is sometimes referred to as "grading on the curve." However, grading on the curve does not mean that a teacher is obliged to force a class grading distribution into a normal curve in which a certain proportion (for example, 5 to 7 percent) of the class must get *F*s and a similar proportion *A*s. More commonly, grading on the curve merely means that the teacher is using the relative performances of that year's class in the calculation of grades.

If a teacher truly graded according to the normal curve and allocated proportions of high and low grades on the basis of the normal curve's properties, such a grading scheme would be truly reprehensible. Procrustean grading proclivities of that sort should definitely be expunged.[7]

Absolute grading. Well, if there is a *relative* approach to grading that is essentially *norm-referenced*, it would seem to follow that there should be an *absolute grading* approach that is *criterion-referenced*, in nature. And there is, more or less.

As was noted earlier, the problem of determining "how good is good enough" can get genuinely annoying. To come up with reasonable expectations for students, that is, to decide what levels of student performance are required for an *A*, *B*, and so on, will almost always involve the grader's reliance on some sorts of comparative data. Without a rough idea about how the student population in general behaves, educators are in a bind when it comes to deciding on grading levels. Thus, when a teacher describes a set of skills or a body of knowledge that the teacher expects students to master in order to achieve a certain grade, the teacher's decisions are invariably influenced by normative considerations.

However, even though teachers may arrive at a set of grading standards by means of normative comparisons, what they do with those standards *at that point* helps distinguish between absolute and relative grading standards. Graders who are relativists will be markedly influenced by the performance of this year's crop of students. Graders who are absolutists tend to be less influenced by the performance of current students. In other words, when a criterion-referenced grader has chosen mastery of particular skills as a requisite for certain grades, then students must either master those skills or expect a lower grade. There's much less bending once an absolutist grader has decided on standards for grading.

Achievement based on aptitude. I once learned that, according to Aristotle, achieved potential constituted a metaphysical good. Being particularly enamored of Aristotle's insights (and Greek food), I always remembered that. When I became a high school teacher and grading requirements rolled around for the first time, I tried to carry out my task in a somewhat Aristotelian manner. That is, I attempted to judge my students' academic attainments in relationship to their intellectual potential.

My plan did not prosper. I really had no clear idea of what my students' intellectual potentials truly were. No doubt Aristotle could have discerned what his students would be capable of performing, but I certainly could not.

The chief difficulty associated with grading students' achievement on the basis of their aptitudes is that teachers have inadequate bases on which to make accurate estimates of their students' potentials. It is because teachers miss one of the key pieces of the puzzle that Stanley and Hopkins assert "achievement in relation to aptitude is an untenable basis for marking, despite the obvious appeal that the idea has for many educators."[8]

Student growth. In a related grading approach, some teachers find the notion of student growth an appealing idea to serve as the foundation of a grading method. At first blush, it would seem to make sense if we award students who make the best strides in achievement. For example, if Johnny scores only 20 percent correct on a pretest at the first of the term but scores 85 percent correct on an equivalent form of that test when the term is over, then Johnny has experienced a gain of 65 percent. Joe, on the other hand, ends up with a perfect score on the test, but his pretest score was already 90 percent correct. Hence, Joe only gained 10 percent. Surely Johnny's 65 percent jump is more worthy of a high grade than Joe's meager 10 percent increase. But wait a minute. If we only look at the final exam results, Joe scored 100 percent correct and John only scored 85 percent correct. Is it really fair to give Johnny an *A* and give Joe a *B* or *C*?

If this sort of dilemma were not enough, and it ought to be, there is the reliability of gain scores themselves. Harris has shown that, even with well-honed testing devices, gain scores are highly unreliable.[9] With the sorts of tests that most teachers are obliged to use, unreliability multiplies exponentially. In fact, basing grades on pupil growth poses even more formidable problems than using achievement based on aptitude. Basing grades on student growth is not a defensible scheme.

Pass–Fail Grading Systems

During the seventies and eighties, the use of *pass–fail* grading procedures became rather popular at a number of colleges and universities. In part, the initiation of pass–fail grading was due to the same factors that led to the well-documented *grade–inflation* of that period in which the grade point averages of college students rose substantially. Because it is most difficult to conclude that during the seventies and eighties college students became dramatically more intelligent, one assumes that college professors became more lenient in their grading practices. Pass–fail grading systems, some contend, were installed as an antidote to grade inflation. Irrespective of its origins, a pass–fail grading system now constitutes another alternative that teachers, grades K through postgraduate, can consider.

At the college level, a pass–fail scheme is applied to a total course. For example, students may sign up for specified courses (or, in some colleges, for any course) so that they receive no letter grade, only a pass or a fail. In general, of course, students who select a pass–fail option reduce the likelihood of receiving a low grade (for instance, a *C* or *D*). Moreover, because results of pass-fail courses do not count on the student's grade point average, it is much safer to take difficult courses on a pass-fail basis.

But how about elementary or secondary schools? Can pass-fail systems be used there? Yes, they can, but usually not in the same way as is seen at the college level, that is, not as a total course grade. Instead, educators have seen the emergence of grading systems in some public schools whereby students receive pass-fail marks, but on a skill-by-skill (or objective-by-objective) basis.

To illustrate, some school districts have isolated a number of content standards (in reading, writing, and mathematics) that it is assumed a competent student should possess.

Test Coaching Alleged in Ky.

The Kentucky education department is investigating allegations that teachers at the 800-student Louisa Elementary School in Lawrence County improperly prepped 4th graders for a state achievement test.

The 4th grade teachers are accused of coaching students on the exam questions and helping them with the writing portion of the test, according to the *Lexington Herald–Leader* newspaper.

The school's scores on the test—the Kentucky Instructional Results Information System—have risen dramatically in the past couple of years.

The education department has used 4th graders' KIRIS test scores to rate elementary schools since 1991. Employees at schools with rising scores receive substantial cash bonuses.

Department officials said they will not comment on the specifics of the case until the investigation is complete. Lawrence County school officials did not return phone calls last week.

What's your reaction?

Reprinted, with permission, from *Education Week*, June 11, 1997

However, rather than testing the student's mastery of these content standards and then awarding a letter grade based on the student's overall prowess, mastery versus nonmastery is determined, on a standard-by-standard basis. In essence, a number of pass-fail decisions are made, content standard by content standard. Typically, a final decision is made about each student with respect to high school graduation or between-grade promotions by summing the number of pass-fail decisions per content standard.

Report Cards and Supplementary Reporting Schemes

When my father was growing up, the report cards used in the schools were rather rudimentary. I ran across his old report cards sometime ago while cleaning out a drawer. The cards had been saved by his mother and by my mother. In view of my dad's rather poor performance in mathematics classes, perhaps the cards should have been "lost." However, the report cards of the twenties were rather lean in what they reported. At the high school level, in each course he received an *E* (Excellent, above 90), a *G* (Good, 80 to 90), an *F* (Fair, 70 to 80), or a *U* (Unsatisfactory, below 70). At the elementary school level, the report cards were even more global, with the same four-letter grading scheme being applied to only three dimensions, namely, "scholarship, deportment, and application." I must confess that I don't know how my father ever pulled a *fair* in application at Sunnyside Elementary School in the third grade. He always seemed to apply himself rather well.

In Figure 14.1 I've included a copy of my father's third-grade report card, and in Figure 14.2 one of his high school report cards. The attentive reader will note that he was advanced to the fourth grade "on trial." I am pleased to report that he made it.

While yesteryear's report cards were succinct, some of today's report cards often resemble a set of convoluted income tax forms. In the eighties my children brought home report cards dealing with so many dimensions that two evenings of diligent reading, and with a paid consultant, were required to figure them out. Instead of grading only academic progress on a subject-by-subject basis, each of the academic subjects was broken down in considerable detail. There were, for example, four distinct grades associated with

FIGURE 14.1.

A 1919 elementary school report card of the father of a measurement textbook writer.

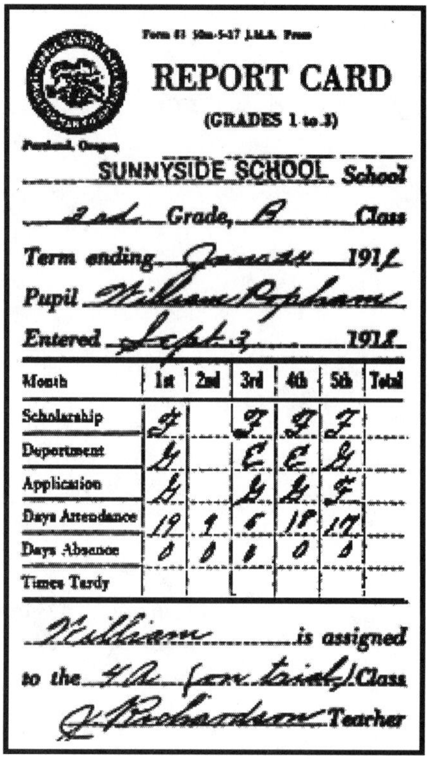

REPORT CARD

(GRADES 1 to 3)

Portland, Oregon

SUNNYSIDE SCHOOL School

2nd Grade, B Class

Term ending January 1919

Pupil William Popham

Entered Sept. 3 1918

Month	1st	2nd	3rd	4th	5th	Total
Scholarship	F		F	F	F	
Deportment	G		E	E	G	
Application	G		G	G	F	
Days Attendance	19	1	6	18	17	
Days Absence	0	0	1	0	0	
Times Tardy						

William is assigned to the 4A (on trial) Class

J. Richardson Teacher

different skills in reading. Moreover, when it came to nonacademic behavior, designers of these more recent report cards really went wild. It seems that I not only had a grade report on my son, but almost a complete psychosocial clinical report. I marvel at (or sympathize with) teachers who have the patience to fill out these near-endless sets of student evaluations. Apparently, some educators adore elaborate *multidimensional report cards* that provide pupils and parents with ample information about all important aspects of a student's accomplishments. Personally, I lean toward lean.

Letters to parents. To supplement final report cards, some teachers rely on the use of less formal letters to parents in which the unique strengths and weaknesses of each pupil can be described. Given the distinctiveness of each child, such letters provide teachers with an opportunity to be as particularized as they wish in communicating with parents about a child's special potentials, shortcomings, and so on.

The major drawback with such letter reports is the enormous time it takes to prepare a letter for each child. A few school districts with access to adequate clerical–stenographic resources have provided teachers with dictating equipment so that such report letters can be dictated, then transcribed by secretarial personnel. However, most don't.

As indicated earlier, some school districts also have access to fairly sophisticated computer equipment that can be programmed to provide parents with the sort of individual-

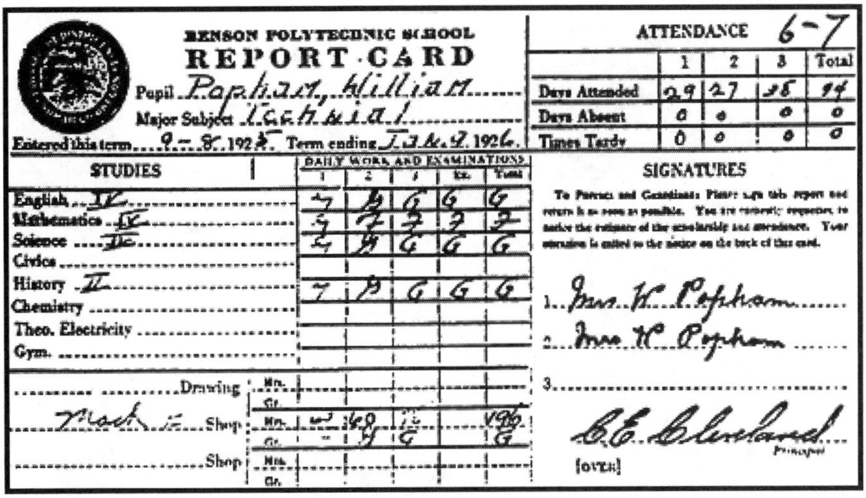

FIGURE 14.2.

A 1926 high school report card of the father of a measurement textbook writer.

ized pupil-progress information available in multidimensional teacher-prepared report cards.

Parent–teacher conferences. Particularly in the early elementary grades, another supplement to the standardized report card is the parent–teacher conference. In such conferences teachers have a more extended opportunity to describe a child's progress, or lack of it, on a face-to-face basis with the pupil's parents. As with letters to parents, such supplementary reporting activities can be highly useful but extremely time-consuming.

Not only is there the actual time the teachers must spend in the conferences themselves, but there's also the time spent in arranging the conferences. Besides that, some parents aren't so eager to know how their children are progressing that they're willing to make a special trip to school. Accordingly, for some students, teachers will be unable to arrange conferences with the parents. In spite of the practical difficulties associated with parent–teacher conferences about grades, many teachers euphorically endorse them. For the lower elementary grades, a parent conference appears to have sufficient dividends that educational leaders can anticipate its continued use as a grade-reporting procedure.

Imprecision, Grading, and Guilt

Anyone who grew up under the influence of some sort of religious training ought to be beset occasionally by *guilt.* Guilt, or so it seems, is one of those universal human characteristics that, given the right (wrong) kind of early assistance, really blossoms full-blown in adulthood. Many teachers, realizing that the dispensation of grades is a nonscientific and intuitive enterprise, often suffer guilt pangs during and after the grading process.

How do we defend, for example, the decisions we make about borderline cases? Oh, it's always easy and usually satisfying to award *A*s to outstanding students. It's even easy

and sometimes satisfying to toss an *F* at a student who didn't try during a course and failed every single exam. But how about all those in-betweeners? Can the teacher always make the right grading decision with such students? The answer is, distressingly, *no*.

Teachers must anticipate that they'll mess up more than a few grades. However, thank heaven, over the long haul, students who get shortchanged in one course will be benefitted in another. This point was made earlier in this chapter. Teachers, in recognition that they're working with an imprecise, value-laden operation that is subject to all sorts of human error, should do the best grading job they can, then shed any guilt.

Chapter Wrap-Up

This was a practicality-focused chapter, so let's have a cut-and-dried practical wrap up based, as always, on the chapter's guiding questions.

What should be considered when teachers administer tests?

An important choice-point arises early on when educators are trying to decide whether to purchase tests or to construct tests themselves. Although district level tests could be developed by a district's teachers, in most instances the most talented of those teachers would rather be teaching than building tests. If tests are purchased, care must be taken to see that the tests are genuinely consonant with the district's instructional emphases.

Effective test directions should contain sufficient information regarding (1) the test's purpose, (2) time allowance, (3) the basis for responding, (4) the method that students are to use when making their responses, (5) the appropriateness of guessing, and (6) any differential scoring weights that are to be used in evaluating students' performances.

When educational assessments are actually administered, the physical setting must be made as conducive as possible to the promotion of optimal student test performance, whether for high-stakes tests or for teachers' classroom tests. When administering the test, teachers should (1) avoid behaviors that are apt to make students anxious, (2) refrain from excessive talk prior to the test and never talk during the test, (3) monitor for possible cheating, and (4) avoid giving students hints about individual test items. If teachers are administering a standardized test, then the administrative procedures for such testing should be assiduously followed.

How should educational tests be scored?

Although some teachers have aides who can help them score tests, and some teachers have access to electronic scoring devices, most classroom tests are still hand-scored by teachers. The remarkable advances in electronic scoring of students' responses, however, makes it possible for educational leaders to contemplate a near-future time when much scoring of tests, certainly of the selected-response variety and even of short-answer items, will be accomplished with the aid of computers.

For selected-response tests, correction for guessing formulae can be employed, but these scoring adjustments were recommended only for speeded tests. Few teachers employ genuinely speeded tests, in other words, tests that most students won't have time to finish. For nonspeeded tests, students' performance ranks remain relatively unchanged whether or not a correction-for-guessing formula is employed. Accordingly, for most classroom tests, a correction-for-guessing formula is unnecessary.

How should performance standards be set?

Increasing pressures on educators to set measurable performance standards for students' test performances has, during recent decades, directed substantial attention to the establishment of defensible passing levels (cut-scores) for educational assessments. Although performance standards must, ultimately, be based on human judgments, there is no inherent need for standard-setting to be capricious or arbitrary.

Based on substantial experience in the 1980s and 1990s, several general considerations for sensible standard-setting were identified in the chapter. First, performance standards should be subject to revision because, given their judgmental roots, it is often the case that changes on standards will be needed. From a practical public relations perspective, it is easier to raise standards than to lower them. Second, it was pointed out that there are no quantitative, judgment-free systems available for the generation of performance standards despite the appeal of quantitatively oriented decision-making models. A third general consideration focused on the need to collect real performance data from students under actual "it counts" assessment auditions before arriving at performance standards. Finally, because of the impact of the assessment enterprise, it was suggested that sufficient time be allowed for standard-setting so that all concerned constituencies can offer their views regarding appropriate performance levels.

● **How can educational leaders help teachers grade students more defensibly?**

One way that educational leaders can assist teachers in arriving at defensible grading approaches is to familiarize teachers with the available alternatives. In this chapter, the following student-grading approaches were described: (1) relative grading, (2) absolute grading, (3) aptitude-based grading, (4) growth-based grading, and (5) pass–fail grading. The relative merits of report cards, letters to parents, and parent–teacher conferences were also considered.

Because of the inherent imprecision associated with teachers' grade-giving, a plea was made for teachers not to experience guilt associated with the grading of students. Over the long haul, students who receive an unwarranted low grade in one teacher's class are apt to get an unwarranted high grade in another teacher's class. Grading errors are often self-canceling.

Practice Exercises

For this chapter, the end-of-chapter merriment will be organized around items of the multiple binary-choice variety. Read each boxed vignette presented below, then respond with a highly motivated *True* or *False* to the three items following it.

Dora Dalrymple's Exam Directions

At the beginning of the final examination for her eleventh-grade American Government course, Mrs. Dalrymple provided the following directions. Look over what she wrote.

Directions: *As you know, your performance on this 10-section final examination will determine approximately 50 percent of your course grade. You'll have the full 55 minutes of class time to complete the exam. Write directly on the test booklet in the spaces provided. Use your best judgment, but do not guess on the multiple-choice items. (Leave them blank if you don't know.) For the multiple-choice and right-wrong items, choose the* best *answer. Do your best!*

---

1. Dora's directions contained all of the six kinds of information recommended in the chapter. (*True* or *False?*)

2. The directions supplied adequate guidance regarding how students were supposed to make their responses. (*True* or *False?*)

3. Given these directions, it is certain that no student will guess the answers to Mrs. Dalrymple's multiple-choice items. (*True* or *False?*)

Pumpkin Pressure

In the school district in which Martha Milton teaches fourth grade, a high-stakes standardized achievement test is given at the close of fifth grade. Accordingly, Martha tries to get her fourth-graders ready for the kind of examination hurdle they'll face in the fifth grade. Whenever Martha tests her students, even if it's a relatively unimportant weekly quiz, she adopts a stern demeanor with the class and usually says, "Okay, my little pumpkins, it's pressure time!" She paces back and forth, in front of the class, announcing every five minutes how much testing time remains. Some students' parents complain, but Martha responds by saying, "This is getting my little pumpkins ready for the real world."

4. Martha did *not* adhere to the chapter's initial guideline for test administrators regarding anxiety-induction. (*True* or *False?*)

5. Given her general approach to preparing her fourth-graders for assessment adventures in the next grade, it's likely that Martha did not discourage cheating. (*True* or *False?*)

6. Martha is likely to have given students hints about how to answer individual test items. (*True* or *False?*)

Guessers, on Guard

Clyde Cory uses only selected-response tests on his classroom assessments. Although none of his tests are speeded, and although he gives students ample time for all tests, Clyde always corrects students' responses for guessing. Here's an illustration of how Clyde does so on his midterm exam:

> *Jimmy Joseph answered 21 of the exam's 25 binary-choice items correctly and missed 4. Clyde computed a score of 19 for Jimmy on the binary-choice items.*

> *Sandra Selvin answered all but 4 of the exam's 40 five-option multiple-choice items correctly. She was wrong on the others. Clyde gave Sandra a score of 35 on this part of the exam.*

His students are comfortable with Clyde's guessing-correction scheme for scoring their test performances.

---

7. Clyde computed Jimmy's score for the binary-choice items accurately according to the chapter's correction-for-guessing formula. (*True* or *False?*)

8. Turning to Sandra's score on the multiple-choice items, Clyde used the chapter's correction for guessing formula correctly. (*True* or *False?*)

9. Clyde did *not* follow the chapter's recommendation regarding the use of a correction-for-guessing formula with unspeeded tests. (*True* or *False?*)

Set Standards and Sigh

The Assistant Superintendent at Strive-a-While School District, Larry Lofton, has been asked to coordinate the district's efforts to establish a "cut-score" for the district's new high school graduation test. Here's how Dr. Lofton addressed the topic in a recent memorandum to all district teachers:

"As all of you know, this is the first year when we'll be denying district diplomas to students who fail to pass the graduation test. Although we've not yet given the test to any of our students, the test's publishers assure me that a score of at least 70 percent correct 'should be readily attainable by any reasonably competent high school graduate.'

"Accordingly, after giving considerable thought to this issue over the weekend, I'm going to establish a passing rate of 75 percent correct to show our parents that we really mean business. If too many students fail to reach that level, we can always drop the standard somewhat at a later point. I hope you'll join me in supporting this demanding cut-score."

---

10. Dr. Lofton's approach to standard-setting was consistent with most of the recommendations offered in the chapter. (*True* or *False?*)

11. The proposal by Dr. Lofton to lower the 75 percent cut-score if too many students failed to pass was not consonant with the chapter's recommendations. (*True* or *False?*)

12. A weekend's deliberations over the cut-score issue by Dr. Lofton represented a sufficient time commitment to the task. (*True* or *False?*)

Answers to Practice Exercises

1. *False.* (Dora's directions left out information about differential scoring weights. Students won't know if the exam's 10 sections are equal in importance.)
2. *True.*
3. *False.* (If you answered *True*, get real!)
4. *True.*
5. *False.* (We can't know for sure, of course, whether Martha did or didn't discourage cheating. But please consider the weakness of this binary-choice item wherein you are asked to render a true–false judgment about a teacher's *failure* to implement a *negative* guideline about *not* cheating. Educational leaders should not allow teachers to use such ghastly items.)
6. *False.* (At least, knowing Martha, it seems unlikely.)
7. *False.* (Jimmy should have been scored on a Right minus Wrong basis, so he would have ended up a binary-choice score of 17.)
8. *True.* (Did Clyde just get lucky this time?)
9. *True.*
10. *False.* (by a wide margin)
11. *True.* (It is, as suggested, easier to boost standards than lower them.)
12. *False.* (Maybe *two* weekends?)

DISCUSSION QUESTIONS

1. If you were asked to defend the proposition that test results and tests should be returned to students after all exams, how would you defend your case?
2. If you were in charge of setting a performance standard for a high-stakes educational assessment, how would you go about doing so?
3. If you were a school superintendent describing to your district's school board what an "Appropriate District Grading Policy" should be, what would you say to the board?
4. In what ways can student test anxiety be reduced by classroom teachers?
5. What is your opinion of truth-in-testing laws that require the release of test forms once those forms have been administered?
6. If you were a school principal working with your school's teachers, how would you recommend dealing with instances of cheating on exams?
7. What is your view about the "arbitrariness of standard-setting?" Do you think all performance standards, in the final analysis, are arbitrary?

SUGGESTIONS FOR ADDITIONAL READING

Green, Bert F. *Setting Performance Standards: Content, Goals, and Individual Differences.* In William H. Angoff Memorial Lecture Series (ED 401 318). Princeton, NJ: Educational Testing Service, April 1996.

Guskey, Thomas R. (Ed.). *Communicating Student Learning: 1996 ASCD Yearbook.* Alexandria, VA: Association for Supervision and Curriculum Development, 1996.

Impara, James C., and Barbara S. Plake. "Standard Setting: An Alternative Approach." *Journal of Educational Measurement, 34,* 4 (Winter 1997): 353–366.

Impara, James C., and Barbara S. Plake. "Teachers' Ability to Estimate Item Difficulty: A Test of the Assumptions in the Angoff Standard Setting Method." *Journal of Educational Measurement, 35,* 1 (Spring 1998): 69–81.

Krumboltz, John D., and Christine J. Yeh. "Competitive Grading Sabotages Good Teaching." *Phi Delta Kappan, 78,* 4 (December 1996): 324–326.

Niyogi, Nivedita S. *The Intersection of Instruction and Assessment: The Classroom, A Policy Issue Perspective (Policy Information Center Publications* Catalog, ED 388 724). Princeton, NJ: Educational Testing Service, March 1995.

Shepard, Lorrie A., Roberta J. Flexer, Elfrieda H. Hiebert, Scott F. Marion, Vicky Mayfield, and Timothy J. Weston. "Effects of Introducing Classroom Performance Assessments on Student Learning." *Educational Measurement: Issues and Practice, 15,* 3 (Fall 1996): 7–18.

Smith, Mary Ann. "The National Writing Project after 22 Years." *Phi Delta Kappan, 77,* 10 (June 1996): 688–692.

Tchudi, Stephen (Ed.). *Alternatives to Grading Student Writing.* Urbana, IL: National Council of Teachers of English, 1997.

AND FOR THOSE WHO TIRE OF READING

Association for Supervision and Curriculum Development. *ASCD Conference on Teaching & Learning: Assessment* (Videotape: Stock #496274S62). Alexandria, VA: Author, 1996.

Association for Supervision and Curriculum Development. *Reporting Student Progress* (Videotape: Stock #495249S62). Alexandria, VA: Author, 1995.

Association for Supervision and Curriculum Development. *Reporting Student Progress* (Videotape: Stock #495249T87). Alexandria, VA: Author, 1996.

Guskey, Tom, and David Johnson. *Alternative Ways to Document and Communicate Student Learning (Audiotape:* Stock #296211S62). Alexandria, VA: Association for Supervision and Curriculum Development, 1996.

Popham, W. James. *Improving INSTRUCTION through Classroom Assessment* (Videotape #ETVT-25). Los Angeles: IOX Assessment Associates.

Popham, W. James. *Making the Grade: Helping Parents Understand What's Important* (Videotape #ETVT-22). Los Angeles: IOX Assessment Associates.

Popham, W. James. *Test Preparation Practices: What's Appropriate and What's Not* (Videotape #ETVT-31). Los Angeles: IOX Assessment Associates.

ENDNOTES

1. V. M. Cashen and G. C. Ramseyer, "The Use of Separate Answer Sheets by Primary Age Children," *Journal of Educational Measurement, 6* (1969), 155–158.
2. B. Ingle and G. DeAmico, "Effects of Physical Conditions of the Test Room on Standardized Achievement Test Scores," *Journal of Educational Measurement, 6* (1969), 237–240.
3. For example, see G. L. Rowley and R. Traub, "Formula Scoring, Number-Right Scoring, and Test Taking Strategy," *Journal of Educational Measurement, 14* (1977), 15–22.
4. See, for example, W. Glasser, *Schools Without Failure* (New York: Harper & Row, 1969), or J. Holt, *How Children Fail* (New York: Pitman, 1968).

5. H. M. Dadourian, "Are Examinations Worth the Price?" *School and Society*, *21* (1925), 442–443.
6. P. Moynihan, "Seek Parity of Educational Achievement, Moynihan Urges," *Report on Educational Research*, *3*, 5 (March 3, 1971), 4.
7. Procrustes was a fabled Greek giant who stretched short captives or lopped off parts of tall captives to make them fit his uni-sized iron beds. One must view Procrustes's standards as somewhat absolute.
8. J. C. Stanley and K. D. Hopkins, *Educational and Psychological Measurement and Evaluation*, 5th ed. (Englewood Cliffs, NJ: Prentice-Hall, 1972).
9. C. W. Harris, Ed., *Problems in Measuring Change* (Madison, WI: University of Wisconsin Press, 1963).

Standardized Achievement Tests: Marvelous Measures— Often Misused

You are, at this very moment, starting to travel the final chapter of your trip through educational assessmentland. There is, as you already know, an optional appendix about statistical stuff that stands between you and the index. But you've either already dipped into that statistical stew or you have decided you have no use for it. Then, of course, there's the index itself. But no author really tries to get much accomplished via an index. An index is so unrelentingly alphabetical.

Although this book about educational measurement was decidedly short of a compelling storyline, I'd be downright dim-witted to close out a text for educational leaders by addressing a trivial topic. This is, obviously, my last chance to chat with you about the important mysteries of educational measurement.

And that's why I've chosen the closeout topic of standardized achievement tests. Today's educational leaders, you see, are often evaluated almost exclusively on the basis of students' scores on standardized achievement tests. If you're a school principal and your students earn low scores on such tests, you are invariably regarded as an instructional loser. If you're a superintendent and your district's students score high on standardized achievement tests, you are thought to be in charge of an effective educational enterprise. But these sorts of judgments about an educational leader's competence, because they're based on students' standardized test scores, are often wrong. And you, as an educational leader, or an educational leader-in-training, *must* understand why.

So I've saved this important topic for last. I want you to understand, inside and out, why standardized achievement tests should not be used to determine the effectiveness of education. I want you to understand this, because there's a strong likelihood that you'll find yourself in situations in which standardized achievement tests are trotted out as the definitive indicator of educational quality. They're not. Every educational leader needs to know *why*. And you need to be able to explain *why* to others.

So there's no doubt about this chapter's focus, I'll be referring to the nationally standardized *achievement* tests that are used throughout the land. Technically, of course, a standardized test is any test that's administered, scored, and interpreted in a standard, predetermined fashion. But I'm referring specifically to the national achievement tests distributed by the three major commercial test publishers. As this book was written, there were five such tests: the *California Achievement Tests*, *Comprehensive Tests of Basic Skills*, *Iowa Tests of Basic Skills*, *Metropolitan Achievement Tests*, and *Stanford Achievement Tests*.

The chapter will not deal with standardized *aptitude* tests such as the *SAT* (Scholastic Assessment Test) or the *ACT Assessment*, both of which are widely used academic aptitude tests that are employed to forecast how well high school students will perform in college. Although there have been a few misguided attempts to evaluate schools on the basis of students' scores on academic aptitude tests, such evaluative efforts are usually dismissed, with good reason. No, this chapter will deal exclusively with standardized *achievement* tests.

Standardized Test

Any test administered, scored, and interpreted in a standard, predetermined manner.

The Problem's Antecedents

Years ago, I was a public school teacher in Oregon. (It was not so many years ago that Oregon was still a territory instead of a state, but it was a long time ago.) We used standardized achievement tests in those days, even that far back. In the district where I taught, nationally standardized achievement tests were administered to students at three grade levels.

Although students in the district were obliged, in those three grades, to take standardized achievement tests, there really wasn't all that much use made of the results. Students' test results were placed into students' cumulative record folders, and that was it. A few teachers, I suspect, referred to those test scores. Most of us didn't. No one ever asserted that the quality of students' test performances indicated whether my fellow teachers and I were doing a good instructional job. A possible relationship between children's standardized test performances and teachers' instructional quality was never even considered. How did all this change?

Data for Doubters

There have always been critics of the schools. The ability of certain parents to carp about their children's schooling, it sometimes seems, distinguishes humankind from the other animal species. But, by and large, in the middle of the twentieth century, people in the United States were pretty happy with their public schools. Public schools, it appeared to most citizens, represented an educational avenue whereby even children of low social circumstances could elevate themselves. The U.S. public school system was regarded by most of the nation's citizens as a shining example of democracy in action. Public schools were seen as a potent force to make the United States great.

But then, sometime during the 1970s, growing numbers of thoughtful citizens began to register dissatisfaction with the nation's public schools. Newspapers started to carry stories about high school graduates who couldn't (1) fill out a job-application form, (2) comprehend what they had read, or (3) write anything more complicated than a grocery list. Increasing numbers of taxpayers began to question whether the dollars being spent on schools were being well spent.

No longer were parents assuaged by the reassurances of educational leaders that "all is well in your children's schools." What these doubting parents wanted was *evidence* that their children were really learning. And it was in the midst of such increasing incredulity about school quality that legislators in many states began to enact "minimum competency" testing programs to assure citizens that students who completed a high school education could at least comprehend the meaning of brief written passages or would be able to perform simple mathematical calculations.

In some cases, if students failed to pass these statewide tests, a high school diploma was denied. In other instances, a "second-class" diploma was awarded to those who failed to demonstrate the basic skills measured by these tests. But whatever the sanctions that were linked to these typically undemanding competency tests, it was clear that students who did not pass the tests were performing less well than they ought to be performing. And who was to blame for such inadequate performances? In most instances, the answer was quick and loud—U.S. educators. The era of *educational accountability* had arrived, and the measuring tool by which educators' quality was to be judged was to be a *test* of students' knowledge and skills.

Most of the early versions of state-level competency tests were developed within each state. In many instances, the state's education department entered into a contract with a test development agency to create a customized test that assessed students' mastery of whatever the state's educators regarded as suitable minimum competencies. In only a few states were "off-the-shelf" standardized achievement tests employed for minimum competency testing programs.

But, irrespective of the kind of test being used, and the fact that unsuccessful students often experienced some sort of penalty, the competency tests of the 1970s were, in large measure, aimed directly at educators. State legislators wanted *evidence* that the state's school dollars were being properly spent. Although a superficial review of the many statewide testing laws of that era suggests that students were the target of the new laws, closer scrutiny reveals that the *student-* testing laws of that era were thinly masked mechanisms for holding *educators* accountable. Those who doubted that the schools were doing a good job were clearly demanding evidence of educational effectiveness. And minimum competency tests were going to supply that evidence.

It was in this "evidence-via-tests" spirit that a number of state policymakers meaningfully expanded their state's use of nationally standardized achievement tests. These tests were thought by state legislators to supply the sort of evidence that would permit judgments about "how our state's students stack up against students elsewhere." In most instances, state legislators provided increased funds for more frequent use of standardized achievement tests at designated grade levels. Some state laws went so far as to specify the particular standardized achievement test that was to be used.

Newspaper-Generated Competitiveness

When I was a high school teacher, I doubt if most newspaper reporters even knew what a standardized achievement test was, much less that students in school sometimes completed such tests. But as more and more states required their students to complete nationally standardized achievement tests, a newspaper editor's dream came galloping into the newsroom. Newspapers could *rank* the state's schools according to their students' test performances. In some states where a single standardized achievement test was used for the entire state (for instance, in Arizona), it was possible for newspapers to publish school-by-school rankings for the entire state. In other states, where different districts were allowed to choose their own standardized achievement tests (for instance, in Florida), schools could be ranked within a district or county.

But whether statewide or districtwide, rankings were rankings. From a newspaper editor's perspective, test rankings were an outright blessing. For one thing, test rankings cost nothing to obtain. As public documents, the rankings were readily available. Most importantly, however, with rankings, there are winners and, thankfully for newspapers, *there are losers.* Newspapers routinely began to carry test-score rankings of schools and/or districts with the clear message to the newspaper's readers: "high-ranked schools are good; low-ranked schools are bad." It's surprising that the stories about schools' test rankings did not appear in most newspapers' sports sections!

But when these newspaper accounts of school's test-score rankings began to appear annually, usually in late spring or early summer, a public perception began to form, namely, that a school's test scores *equaled* that school's educational effectiveness. And even though some members of the educational community might have experienced misgivings

Educational Leaders
Look at Assessment

Sanity and Standardized Tests

Sheryl L. Frascht
School Improvement Liaison
DoDDS–Brussels District
Belgium

As a first year teacher determined to make a positive educational difference in the lives of her students, I approached all directives from my administration quite seriously. I was teaching in a district that put a great deal of emphasis on standardized test results. I had been told that it was my job to be sure that we saw "good" results by all students.

I didn't have a clue how to achieve "good" results by all students, but I spent hours pouring over previous years' reports. I studied the content that the test focused on and I tried to map out a plan for the year that would be sure to teach all the skills that students would be asked to demonstrate. I would have until the first of March to get it all in their heads and then I would just have to hope that it came back out when required.

What pressure I felt. The diversity of questions on the test meant that I certainly had my work cut out for me. And work I did! And then it was the payoff day. I anxiously watched as students gave the test their all. I even went so far as to review their answers before I packed the tests up. This didn't relieve my anxiety, but only increased it as I didn't see the performance I had expected.

Results came and I spent hours pouring over them. Although I had never really known what the expectation "good" meant in reference to the scores, I was pretty sure I hadn't met that expectation. Student scores were similar and sometimes identical to the scores of the previous year. How could all of the effort I put into teaching during the year apparently yield so little? Depression set in and I began to question my calling to the profession of education. Maybe I wasn't cut out for this after all.

All summer long I reran the tape of the year through my mind. What was intended to be reflective became a game of second-guessing. I was driving myself crazy!

In an effort to save my sanity, I had to come to terms with standardized tests and their purpose. Were they truly a measure of what I had done all year long? If students didn't score high, did that mean I had taught them nothing? And if they did do well, could I take credit for that? What I did know was I was unsure about what standardized tests measured and how to use that information effectively. I also knew the school system I worked with demanded that these scores be used as a yearly measure of student achievement.

I wish I had a happy ending to this story. But the truth is that the conflict I felt then was never resolved. For years I have struggled to develop a clearer understanding of the true purpose of standardized tests. What I do know, however, is that students in my classroom do learn and I can prove that through assessments that *I* create. ●

about what was going on, the education profession itself was remarkably silent regarding the growing perception that students' standardized test scores reflected a school staff's effectiveness. Because acquiescence on the part of educators, at least in the view of educational policymakers, appeared to support the contention that students' test scores provided a suitable index of educational effectiveness, this perception became almost uniformly accepted, even by educators.

In most settings where a state-developed competency test was being used, it was often the case that a nationally standardized achievement test was also administered to the state's students, typically at several grade levels. And in those situations, because of the public's fears that the state's students were only doing well on a locally developed test, and might not compare favorably to students across the nation, the public usually gave greater credence to scores on the nationally standardized achievement test than to scores on the state-developed competency test.

After all, the nationally standardized achievement test was *national*. It was published by a reputable measurement agency, and it was accompanied by technical manuals simply brimming with psychometrically impressive numbers. It's no surprise, in retrospect, that nationally standardized achievement tests came to be regarded in the 1980s and 1990s as the definitive yardstick by which to gauge the effectiveness of any educational enterprise. And, once more, this increasingly prevalent perception was not challenged by educators. As a consequence, students' scores on standardized achievement tests have become almost universally accepted as the best way of judging schools. And that perception is held by legislators, members of school boards, the public, and most educators.

Why No Protests?

Why did U.S. educators so meekly accede to the notion that their competence ought to be evaluated on the basis of students' scores on standardized achievement tests? I'm not sure I have the answer to that question, but I think they accepted the notion that standardized achievement tests represented the appropriate tool for evaluating education for the simple reason that *they didn't know any better*.

I suggest that the vast majority of today's educators know almost nothing about the innards of standardized achievement tests. Even the teachers who are annually obliged to administer such tests rarely scrutinize those assessment instruments with this question in mind: "Should students' performances on this test serve as an indication of my instructional effectiveness?" Because of the widespread ignorance regarding the nature of standardized achievement tests, too many educators simply acquiesced to the prevalent perception that high student test scores indicated good schooling and low student test scores indicated the opposite.

Although many current educators might have the feeling, often ill-defined, that standardized achievement tests are not the right tool to determine their educational effectiveness, they can't say why. And, in the absence of solid reasons, it's tough to take on the distributors of widely used, well-established national achievement tests—some of which have been revised more times than the dictionary. So, most educational doubters simply rolled over and deferred to those who contended that the quality of schooling should be judged chiefly on the basis of students' standardized test scores.

If you're following this logic trail, you probably have guessed that I'm not going to be endorsing the use of students' scores on standardized tests as an appropriate way to evaluate the quality of education. Neither should you. I'm hoping that you'll master the contents of this concluding chapter so well that, as an educational leader, you'll be able to educate your colleagues, and members of other key constituencies, about the appropriate and inappropriate uses of standardized achievement tests. As the chapter's title suggests, those tests really are marvelous measuring instruments. Unfortunately, the educational community has allowed those tests to be *misused* as indicators of educational quality. Hopefully, as an educational leader, you can help change that.

Let me get a couple of disclaimers on the table right away. I am *not* suggesting that students' measured achievement is an inappropriate way to judge educational quality. I think that students' learning is the most important consideration in determining educational quality. We simply have to measure it more appropriately. Later on in the chapter, I'll suggest how.

Second, I am *not* suggesting that our schools are so solidly successful that no improvements are warranted. On the contrary, I believe that schools in the United States are in need of ample upgrading. It's just that when educational quality is determined on the basis of the wrong assessment evidence, such improvements are less likely.

Okay, I've suggested that standardized achievement tests are super assessment tools. Let's take a look at what those supertests do, in fact, measure.

What Standardized Achievement Tests Measure

The Central Assessment-Based Inference

The folks who create standardized achievement tests are terrifically talented. What they are trying to do is create assessment tools that permit someone to make a valid inference about the knowledge and/or skills that a given student possesses in a particular content area such as mathematics. More precisely, that inference is to be a norm-referenced one so that a student's relative knowledge and/or skills can be compared with the knowledge and/or skills possessed by a national sample of students at the same age or grade level.

Such relative inferences about a student's status with respect to the mastery of knowledge and/or skills in a particular subject area can be enormously informative to both parents and educators. For example, think about the parents who discover that their fourth-grade child is performing really well in both language arts (a 94th percentile) and mathematics (an 89th percentile), but rather poorly in both science (a 39th percentile) and social studies (a 26th percentile). That sort of information, because it illuminates a child's strengths and weaknesses, can be helpful to the parents not only in dealing with their child's teacher, but also in deciding what sorts of at-home assistance they can supply to help the child. Similarly, if teachers know how their students compare to other students across the nation, such information can be used to devise appropriate classroom instruction.

Hefty Content Domains

But there's a substantial amount of stuff that children at any grade level are likely to know. The breadth of that stuff (AKA knowledge and/or skills) is represented in Figure 15.1, in which it's referred to as "a content domain." Think of a child (real or imaginary) at a grade level of your choice, and pick any one of the following four content areas: language arts, mathematics, social studies, or science. Then think about *all* the knowledge that the child

FIGURE 15.1.

The complete array of knowledge and/or skill represented by a standardized achievement test.

is likely to know in that content area. Next, think about *all* the skills that the child is likely to possess in that content area.

Put that knowledge and those skills together, and you'll see that the content domain represented in Figure 15.1 covers a hefty chunk of content. It is the student's status with respect to that considerable chunk of content about which a norm-referenced inference is made.

The substantial size of the content domain that a standardized achievement test is supposed to represent poses difficulties for the developers of such tests. If a test actually covered *all* the knowledge and skills in the domain, it would be far too long. Students would need to sign up for month-long marathon assessments. No one would sit still for such assessment idiocy, neither teachers nor parents. Students, of course, rarely sit squirm-free still for any test longer than a five-minute quiz.

So, standardized achievement tests often need to accomplish their measurement mission with a far smaller collection of test items than might otherwise be employed if testing time were not an issue. Consider Figure 15.2 in which you'll see that the way out of this assessment bind is to *sample* the knowledge and/or skills in the content domain. Notice that the X-marks represent test items, and that there are exactly 40 test items represented. (You can count them if you think I'm fibbing.) Frequently, standardized achievement tests try to do their assessment job with only 40–50 items per subject field, sometimes fewer.

Striving for Accurate Differentiation

All right, the task for those developing standardized achievement tests is to create an assessment instrument that, with a relative handful of items, yields valid norm-referenced interpretations of a student's status regarding a substantial chunk of content. And that's where standardized test developers hearken back to World War I's *Army Alpha* test that you read about in Chapter 1. Although the *Alpha* was an aptitude test rather than an achievement test, its measurement mission was to discriminate among prospective officer candidates by differentiating on the basis of servicemen's ability to answer various sorts of paper-and-pencil items.

FIGURE 15.2.

How the test items in a standardized achievement test sample a content domain.

The *Army Alpha's* architects, just like the architects of today's standardized achievement tests, had little actual testing time available to them. (There was a war to be fought.) Accordingly, the *Alpha's* developers tried to include those items that most effectively discriminated among examinees. Recall in Chapter 12 how an item's discriminating efficiency was calculated, that is, a positively discriminating item is most often answered correctly by students who perform well on the total test and is answered incorrectly most often by students who perform poorly on the total test.

Well, using that *Alpha*-based approach, today's developers of standardized achievement tests try to make sure that the limited number of test items they have at their disposal do, indeed, a good job of discriminating among students. Items that do the best job of discriminating among students are those that are answered correctly by roughly half of the students. In other words, for optimal discrimination purposes, the items on a standardized achievement test should have p values of somewhere between .40 and .60. Items that are answered correctly by too many students, say, items with p values of .85 or above, or by too few students, say, items with p values of .15 or below, do not do a good job in discriminating among students.

Accordingly, such high-p-value items or low-p-value items are avoided by developers of standardized achievement tests. For example, if it appears that too many students are apt to answer a given test item correctly, it is unlikely that the item will ever be put onto the test in the first place. And if it turns out that any item on a standardized test is being answered correctly by too many students (for example, a p-value of .85 and above), then it is almost certain such a *nondiscriminating item* will be removed when the test is revised.

Educationally Useful Inferences

As a consequence of carefully sampling from a content domain, and concentrating on items that discriminate optimally among students, the creators of standardized achievement tests have produced assessment tools that do a great job of providing relative comparisons of a student's content-domain mastery with that of students throughout the nation. Assuming that the national norm group (on which those normative comparisons are based) is genuinely representative of the nation at large, then educators and parents can make useful inferences about students.

One of the most useful of those inferences typically deals with students' relative strengths and weaknesses across subject areas, such as when parents find that their daughter sparkles in mathematics, but sinks in science. It's also possible to identify students' relative strengths and weaknesses *within* a given subject area if there are enough items on the test to do so. For instance, if a 45-item standardized test in mathematics allocates 15 items to "basic computation," 15 items to "geometry," and 15 items to "algebra," it might be possible to get a rough idea of a student's relative strengths and weaknesses in those three realms of mathematics. More often than not, however, there are too few items on standardized achievement tests to allow meaningful within-subject comparisons of students' strengths and weaknesses. But if the number of items is sufficiently large, then students' within-content strengths and weaknesses of students can be identified.

A second kind of useful inference that can be based on standardized achievement tests revolves around a student's growth over time in different subject areas. For example,

Educational Leaders
Look at Assessment

Migraine Moments

Jo-Ann Harunaga
Technology Coordinator
Kapaa Elementary
Kapaa, Hawaii

One thing has never changed in my 25 years of teaching. Each September, eager with anticipation of a new school year, teachers are greeted with the results of last spring's standardized achievement test scores. The results are always the same—rotten. Instant depression!

The children at my school come from a poor community. Over half of the student population qualifies for a free or reduced-price lunch and, as a result, the school is designated as Title I. Year after year, our test results on the Stanford Achievement Tests are always at the bottom. When the test results are published in the local newspaper, citizens think our school is one of the worst on the island. And, most parents wonder how teachers are spending their time in the classroom. Indeed, the low scores occasionally make me question my own effectiveness as a teacher.

Although teachers work incredibly hard to increase student achievement, our standardized achievement test scores never really change. One year I had the lowest fourth grade reading group to work with. Two Title I reading teachers and I worked as a team. Rather than send kids out to Title I remedial reading classes, these teachers joined me in the classroom. This helped bring the teacher-student ratio, for reading instruction, to one teacher for every eight students.

In addition to using the basal reading program, students wrote and performed plays, did research projects, wrote and performed songs, created puppet shows, and "published" their own books. It was a literacy-rich learning environment. My colleagues and I were thrilled by the tremendous progress these kids made, and thought the small teacher–student ratio really worked to help kids who were behind in reading.

Imagine how we felt when our standardized achievement test results came back and, despite all the work, the scores were still very low. What were we to think? Three certified teachers who (along with the students) had worked diligently to raise reading scores. We knew our students had learned a great deal. We could see it in their work and in their new enthusiasm for reading. But, according to the test results, we had failed. When teachers keep knocking their heads against a wall, is it any wonder they leave school with a headache? ●

let's say a child is given a standardized achievement test every third year and we see that the child's percentile performances in most subjects are relatively similar at each testing, but that the child's percentiles in mathematics appear to drop dramatically at each subsequent testing. That's useful information for educators and parents.

Unfortunately, both educators and parents often ascribe far too much precision and accuracy to students' scores on standardized achievement tests. As I noted in Chapter 3, when I described reliability, there are a number of factors that might cause students' scores to flop about a bit. Merely because standardized achievement test scores are reported in *numbers* (sometimes even with decimals!) should not incline anyone to attribute unwarranted precision to those scores. Standardized achievement test scores should be regarded as rough approximations of a student's status with respect to the content domain represented by the test.

The Tool-User's Fault

To sum up so far, standardized achievement tests do a wonderful job of supplying the evidence needed to make norm-referenced interpretations of students' knowledge and/or skills in relationship to those of students nationally. The educational usefulness of those interpretations is considerable, both to educators and to parents. Given the size of the content domains to be represented and the limited number of items that the test-developers have at their disposal, standardized achievement tests are really quite remarkable. They do what they are supposed to do.

But standardized achievement tests should not be used to evaluate the quality of education. That's not what they are supposed to do. Every educational leader needs to know why.

Measuring Temperature with a Tablespoon

Right Test, Wrong Inference

There are several important reasons that standardized achievement tests should not be used to judge the quality of education. The overarching reason that students' scores on these tests do not provide an accurate index of educational effectiveness is that any *inference about educational quality* based on students' standardized achievement test performances is apt to be *invalid.* As I told you in Chapter 4, it is not the standardized achievement tests that are, themselves, invalid. Rather, it's the second-level inference about educational quality that's wrongheaded.

Think back about the chief function of a standardized achievement test described on page 395. That function is to permit inferences about the knowledge and/or skills students possess, in a given content area, in relationship to the knowledge and/or skills possessed by other students throughout the nation. When standardized achievement tests are used in order to make such inferences, the tests are yielding altogether valid inferences. Even though, as was pointed out earlier in the chapter, the content coverage of standardized tests is often fairly skimpy—when you think about the total content domain of knowledge and/or skills that the tests represent—score-based inferences reflecting this basic measurement function typically ooze validity.

For example, if Leonard Larsen, a super-smart sixth-grader, gets a 98th percentile score on the social studies portion of a nationally standardized achievement test, it is valid to infer that "Leonard's current mastery of the knowledge and/or skills represented by the test is superior to almost all of the students in the nation." Let's grant that Leonard's score may not be a *perfect* representation of his knowledge and/or skills, and that the normative sample being used to calculate his percentile may not be *perfectly* representative of the nation's students. Even so, the inference that Leonard nearly topped out on his test is essentially valid.

Similarly, suppose a school principal received the average percentile performance of his tenth-grade students on a standardized achievement test in mathematics and discovered that they had, as a group, scored at the 24th percentile. It would be a valid inference to assert that, "In comparison to students throughout the nation, our school's tenth-graders are being outperformed in mathematics by roughly three-fourths of the nation's students."

Both the inference about Leonard Larsen and the inference about the school's tenth-graders are consonant with the chief purpose of standardized achievement tests. But let's extend those inferences a mite and note how quickly invalidity scurries onto the scene.

Suppose someone looked at the 24th-percentile mathematics scores for a school's tenth-graders and came up with the following second-level inference: "Because the standardized test shows that the school's tenth-graders are performing poorly in mathematics, it follows that the school's mathematics instruction is ineffective." That inference is invalid.

Even worse, suppose a school principal looked at Leonard Larsen's high score on the social studies section of a standardized achievement test and made the following second-level inference: "Leonard's sixth-grade teacher is remarkably skilled in providing social studies instruction; after all, Leonard was outperformed on the test by only 2 percent of the sixth-grade students in the nation!" This inference, too, is invalid. An inference about a teacher's instructional competence, even if *all* the teacher's students had scored well on the social studies standardized achievement test, might be equally invalid.

When standardized achievement tests are employed to ascertain educational quality, it really is like measuring temperature with a tablespoon. Tablespoons have a different measurement mission than indicating how hot or cold something is. Standardized achievement tests also have a different measurement mission than indicating how good or bad a school is. Standardized achievement tests should be used to make the comparative interpretations that they were intended to provide. They should not be used to judge educational quality. Let's look at three significant reasons it is thoroughly invalid to base inferences about the caliber of education on standardized achievement test scores.

Testing–Teaching Mismatches

A profit motivation. The companies that build and sell standardized achievement tests are all owned by larger corporations. These corporations, as is the case with all for-profit corporations, attempt to produce revenues for the corporation's shareholders. Accordingly, these for-profit companies, if they're going to live up to their name, try to make a profit.

A distinction should be drawn between the for-profit companies that distribute nationally standardized achievement tests and the not-for-profit assessment agencies, such as the Educational Testing Service, that build and distribute standardized aptitude tests. Although the officials of both kinds of measurement organization would like to see their assessment instruments widely used, there is more palpable profit-motivated pressure on those who build and distribute standardized achievement tests for profit-making firms.

Curricular diversity. All right, recognizing that there is substantial pressure to sell standardized achievement tests, those who must market those tests encounter a dilemma

**Testing–
Teaching
Mismatches**

When the content measured by a test is not congruent with the content taught.

that arises from the considerable curricular diversity present in the United States. Because different states often choose somewhat different educational objectives (or, as they are frequently called these days, *content standards*), there's the need to build standardized achievement tests that are properly aligned with, in some instances, educators' meaningfully different curricular preferences. The problem becomes even more exacerbated in states where different counties or different school districts can exercise a bit of localized curricular decision-making.

It is true, of course, that at a very general level, there's reasonable similarity in the goals educators pursue in different settings. For instance, you can be sure that in all schools there'll be attention given to language arts, mathematics, and so on. But that's at a *general* level. When you start breaking down mathematics (for instance, into what's actually going to be taught), then there are substantial differences among states and school districts. At the level where it really makes a difference to instruction—in other words, *in the classroom*—there are significant differences in the educational objectives sought. And that presents a problem to those who must sell standardized achievement tests.

In view of the nation's substantial curricular diversity, those who build standardized achievement tests are obligated to create a series of "one-size-fits-all" assessment tools. But, as most of us know from attempting to wear one-size-fits-all garments, there are instances in which one size really can't fit all. That's the situation with nationally standardized achievement tests.

The designers of these tests do the best job they can in selecting test items that are likely to measure all of the knowledge and skills (in the content area being tested) that the nation's educators regard as important. But the test developers can't really pull it off. Thus, there will always be a good many items on standardized achievement tests that are not aligned with what's emphasized instructionally in a particular setting.

A landmark study. To illustrate the seriousness of the mismatch that can occur between what's taught locally and what's tested via standardized achievement tests, you ought to know about an important study at Michigan State University reported in 1983 by Freeman and his colleagues (Freeman, D. et al., 1983). These researchers selected five nationally standardized achievement tests in mathematics and studied their content for students in grades 4–6. Then, operating on the very reasonable assumption that what goes on instructionally in classrooms is often influenced by what's in the textbooks that children use, four widely used textbooks for grades 4–6 were also studied. Employing rigorous review procedures, the researchers identified the items in the standardized achievement test that had *not* received meaningful instructional attention in the textbooks. What they arrived at was the disquieting conclusion that between 50 percent and 80 percent of what was measured on the tests was *not* suitably addressed in the textbooks. As the Michigan State researchers put it, "the proportion of topics presented on a standardized test that received more than cursory treatment in each textbook was never higher than 50 percent" (Freeman, D. et al., 1983, p. 509).

Well, if the content of standardized tests is not satisfactorily addressed in widely used textbooks, isn't it likely that in a particular educational setting there will be topics covered in the test that aren't addressed instructionally in that setting? Suppose, for example, that you were the assistant superintendent for instruction in a district where your language arts teachers have emphasized the role of graphic organizers (for example, web charts or Venn diagrams) to help students both plan their written compositions and better comprehend what they have read. *Substantial* instructional time is spent in your district on graphic organizers, and the district's students really seemed to have mastered that topic.

But suppose your state has selected a standardized achievement test in which that topic is not addressed by even one test item. (Remember, standardized achievement test developers have only a few items they must use in trying to represent very substantial content domains.) Now, when your district's standardized achievement test scores are announced in the local newspaper, you see that the students' language arts scores aren't all that super. But a skill that your teachers really regarded as important wasn't even tested. How wonderful do you think you'd feel about your district's so-so language arts performance when one of your district's language arts emphases wasn't even assessed?

Unrecognized mismatches. Unfortunately, because most educators are not genuinely familiar with the ingredients of standardized achievement tests, educators often assume that if a standardized achievement test asserts it is assessing "children's reading composition capabilities," then it's likely that the test meshes with the way reading is being taught locally. More often than not (remembering the Michigan State University study), the assumed match between what's tested and what's taught will not be warranted.

If you spend much time with the descriptive materials presented in the manuals accompanying standardized achievement tests, you'll find that the descriptors for what's tested are often fairly general. Those descriptors need to be general, remember, to make the tests acceptable to a nation of educators whose curricular preferences vary. But such general descriptions of what's tested often permit assumptions of teaching–testing alignments that are way off the mark. The mismatches between what's taught and what's tested are there, but they're not recognized. And such mismatches, recognized or not, will often lead to spurious conclusions about the effectiveness of education in a given setting. *Those conclusions will be spurious if students' scores on standardized achievement tests are used as the indicator of educational effectiveness.* And that's the first reason that standardized achievement tests should not be used to determine the effectiveness of a state, a district, a school, or a teacher. There's almost certain to be a significant mismatch between what's being taught and what's being tested.

A Psychometric Tendency to Eliminate Important Test Items

The quest for score variance. A second reason that standardized achievement tests should not be used to evaluate educational quality arises directly from the requirement that these tests permit meaningful comparisons among students, using only a small collection of items. To illustrate, suppose you were in charge of developing a new 50-item standardized achievement test in Subject *X*. Because you would want to make it possible for your new test to discriminate sensitively among future test-takers on the basis of their mastery of Subject X (so it can be determined that Millie Murphy scores at the 87th percentile and Mario Mercato scores at the 88th percentile), it would be important for your 50-item assessment tool to spread out students' scores. You can't have most of the

In the News

A New Accountability Player: The Local Newspaper

by Lynn Olson

This spring, the *Detroit Free Press* announced that it would no longer rank schools and districts based simply on scores from statewide tests.

The newspaper reached its verdict after conducting a six-month computer analysis of results from the Michigan Educational Assessment Program. It found that poverty and other factors outside a school's control were so strongly linked to test scores that it made straight-up comparisons "inevitably flawed" and "mostly meaningless."

"I think we realized, with some embarrassment, that we never had any business ranking districts based on MEAP scores," said Tracy Van Moorlehem, the paper's K–12 education reporter. "It's just not fair, nor really particularly accurate."

Instead, the *Free Press* vowed that from now on it will produce a more nuanced picture of how well Michigan's schools are doing given the challenges they face. With that commitment, the Motor City daily joins a growing number of other newspapers that are investing heavily in time and resources on special reports on education that go far beyond the mere reporting of test scores.

Many, like the *Free Press*, are using sophisticated computer techniques to delve into educational data. The *Charlotte Observer* in North Carolina, the *Arkansas Democrat Gazette* in Little Rock, *The Seattle Times*, and *The Philadelphia Inquirer,* to name a few, now produce regional report cards on schools.

The newspapers' reports often surpass the documents produced by states and districts in their level of detail, sophistication, and accessibility, and most are available on the World Wide Web. . . .

What's your reaction?

Excerpted, with permission, from *Education Week*, June 17, 1998

---

students who take the 50-item test getting very high scores of, say, 48 or 49 items correct. Too many scores all lumped together will not allow the fine-grained comparisons that are at the heart of the norm-referenced assessment strategy first adopted by creators of the *Army Alpha* and adhered to thereafter by the creators of standardized achievement tests.

It is a good assessment strategy if the aim of a test is to provide relative comparisons among students. The more spread out that students' test scores are, the more sensitively such comparisons can be made. Accordingly, if you really want your new 50-item test to do a good job in permitting comparisons among students, you'll need to have a test that produces substantial *score variance* among test-takers. In other words, you need a test on which students will earn diverse scores so that the resulting score distributions are quite *heterogeneous*, not *homogeneous*.

Score Variance

The degree to which students' scores are diverse, that is, spread out.

Items that boost score variance. A test *item* that does the best job in spreading out students' total test scores is, as noted earlier, a test item that's answered correctly by about half the students. Items that have *p* values of, for example, .40 to .60, do a solid job in spreading out the scores of test-takers.

Items that are answered correctly by very large numbers of students, on the other hand, do not carry their weight when it comes to spreading out students' test scores. As a consequence, items with extremely high or extremely low *p* values are not usually included when standardized achievement tests are initially constructed. A test item with a

p value of .90 is, from the perspective of a test's efficiency in providing *comparative* interpretations, being answered correctly by too many students.

Test items with high *p* values, therefore, usually don't make it past the final cut when a standardized achievement test is first developed, and such high *p* value items will most likely be jettisoned when the test is revised every half-dozen years or so. As a result, the vast majority of the items on standardized achievement tests are "middle difficulty" items. Items with high *p* values tend to be excised from standardized achievement tests.

Standardized achievement testing's Catch-22. As a consequence of the quest for score variance in a standardized achievement test, items on which students perform well are often excluded from the test. Items on which students perform well, however, often cover the content that, *because of the content's importance,* teachers stress. Thus, the better the job that teachers do in teaching important knowledge and/or skills, the less likely it is that there will be items on a standardized achievement test measuring such knowledge and/or skills.

It's not that every single high *p* value item is ritualistically made to walk the testmaker's gangplank. A few such items slip through. But not many. If you were eager for a standardized achievement test to do its comparative assessment job well, you simply couldn't allow the inclusion of many high *p* value items.

What this means, of course, is that much of the most important content teachers emphasize instructionally will not be measured by the items on standardized achievement tests. To evaluate teachers' instructional effectiveness using assessment tools that deliberately avoid important content is fundamentally foolish.

Another need for score variance.   There's a second reason that the developers of standardized achievement tests struggle so vigorously to produce tests that yield score variance. Think back, if you are willing, to my treatment of reliability in Chapter 5. For any kind of reliability index, the more score variance that there is, the better will be the reliability result. To illustrate, if you're calculating an internal consistency reliability coefficient, you'll almost always get a higher coefficient if there is more score variance among students. The more the score variance, in general, the better the test's reliability indicators.

Now, recall that standardized achievement tests are produced by test companies that need to sell tests. Often, when competing with other test-producing companies to see whose test will be adopted by a given state or school district, marketing officials of those companies will present their tests in as favorable a light as possible. It's only natural. That's what marketing folks do.

If a prospective test purchaser is choosing between two standardized achievement tests, and the tests are seen as equal on all other counts, then the test that has the higher reliability coefficients will typically be chosen. High reliability coefficients, in many instances, can thus be a sales clincher. Is it any wonder that the original developers and subsequent revisers of standardized achievement tests revere substantial score variance? (A potential commandment for employees of for-profit testing companies might well be, "Thou shall not covet thy competitor's high reliability coefficients.")

That quest for ample score variance, as we have seen, introduces a subtle psychometric pressure to dump items with high p values. Yet, that sort of item-dumping leads to the likelihood that many important topics teachers teach will be unassessed by standardized achievement tests.

If you're a district educational leader whose instruction is being panned because of students' low scores on standardized achievement tests—and you know that the most important things being taught by your district's teachers are not even measured by those tests—how placid should you be when your education is being evaluated by standardized tests? And that's the second reason standardized achievement tests should not be used to evaluate educational quality. Those tests often don't assess important content.

Confounded Causation

The third reason that students' performances on standardized achievement tests should not be used to evaluate educational quality is especially compelling. In a nutshell, this is the problem: Because students' performances on standardized achievement tests are heavily influenced by three different causative factors, only one of which is linked to instructional quality, to assert that low or high test scores are caused by the quality of instruction is illogical.

In order for you to understand this confounded causation problem clearly, I'll be asking you to look at the kinds of test items that appear on standardized achievement tests. I can pound away at the "theoretical" reasons standardized achievement tests should not be used to measure educational quality, but you'll never be convinced until you spend time with the test items themselves. Remember, students' test scores are based on how well students do on the test's items. To get a really solid idea of what's in standardized tests, you need to grub around with the items themselves. Later on, I'll give you a simple appraisal scheme you can use when judging the quality of those items.

To give you a true sense of the kinds of items you'll encounter in actual standardized achievement tests, but so I don't break test security by reproducing actual test items, the illustrative items you'll be encountering from this point forward in the chapter are mildly massaged versions of actual test items that you'll currently find in the operational forms of standardized achievement tests. I've altered the items' content slightly, without altering the essence of what the item is trying to measure. The central core of each item is equivalent to the actual item on which it is based. (Besides that, by massaging the items sufficiently, I didn't have to go to the trouble of getting permission to reproduce copyrighted items from the test publishers. I hate to mess around with such permissions!)

All right, let's get back to the problem of confounded causation. It revolves around three factors that contribute to students' scores on standardized achievement tests: (1) what's taught in school, (2) a student's native intellectual ability, and (3) a student's out-of-school learning. We'll look at each factor in turn.

What's taught in school. Some of the items of standardized achievement tests measure the knowledge or skills that students learn in school. Especially in certain subject areas, such as mathematics, children learn in school most of what they know about a subject. Few parents spend much time in teaching their children about the intricacies of algebra or how to prove an algebraic theorem.

So, if you look over the items in any standardized achievement test, you'll find a fair number of items similar to the mathematics item presented in Figure 15.3 and the language arts item presented in Figure 15.4. Both items are mildly modified versions of items appearing in a standardized achievement test intended for third-grade children.

The mathematics item presented in Figure 15.3 would help teachers arrive at a valid inference about third-graders' abilities to choose number sentences that coincide with verbal representations of subtraction problems. Or, along with other similar items dealing with addition, multiplication, and division, this item would contribute to a valid inference about a student's ability to choose appropriate number sentences for a variety of basic computation problems presented in verbal form.

In the language arts item in Figure 15.4, you see an item that would help teachers make a valid interpretation specifically about third-graders' ability to employ an apos-

FIGURE 15.3.

A third-grade standardized achievement test item in mathematics

Sally had 14 pears. Then she gave away 6. Which of the number sentences below can you use to find out how many pears Sally has left?

A. $14 + 6 = \square$		C. $\square - 6 = 14$	
B. $6 + 14 = \square$		D. $14 - 6 = \square$	

FIGURE 15.4.

A third-grade standardized achievement test item in language arts.

Directions: Read the sentence. Look at the underlined word carefully. If there is no error, mark the *A* answer space for correct. If there is an error, mark the answer space that corrects the error.

● <u>Wev'e</u> already eaten our breakfast.

A. Correct		C. Weve'
B. We've		D. Weve

trophe correctly. Or, as you saw in the case of the earlier number-sentence item in Figure 15.3, if there were various sorts of items dealing with punctuation, a valid interpretation could be made about students' punctuation skills.

Because both of these illustrative items measure what has been taught in school, it certainly seems reasonable to applaud educators if they've helped students do well on such items or to become distressed with educators whose students can't answer such items correctly.

There is the sampling problem previously alluded to, of course, and that is the difficulty the developers of standardized achievement tests face in trying to measure large content domains with relatively few items. For example, the language arts item in Figure 15.4 came from a standardized achievement test that included only forty-five language arts items for third-graders. It's impossible to measure *well* the full range of third-grade mathematics or language arts content if you only have a limited number of items to do so.

However, if the only kinds of items in standardized achievement tests measured what actually had been taught in school, I wouldn't be so negative about using standardized achievement tests to determine educational quality. As you'll soon see, however, there are other kinds of items hiding in standardized achievement tests.

A student's native intellectual ability. I wish I believed that all children were born with identical intellectual abilities; I don't. Some kids were luckier at gene pool time. Some kids, from birth, will find it easier to mess around with mathematics than will other kids. Some children, from birth, will have an easier time with verbal matters than will others. If children came into the world having inherited *identical* intellectual abilities, teachers' pedagogical problems would be far simpler. At least on intellectual grounds, the playing field for students would be perfectly level.

Recent thinking among many leading educators (see Gardner, 1994) suggests that there are various forms of "intelligence," not just one. A child who is born with less aptitude for dealing with quantitative or verbal tasks, therefore, might possess greater "interpersonal" or "intrapersonal" intelligence. But when it comes to the kinds of items that are most commonly found on standardized achievement tests, there are meaningful differences in children's innate abilities to respond correctly. And some items on standardized achievement tests are aimed directly at measuring such native intellectual ability.

Consider, for example, the items in Figures 15.5 and 15.6. I believe that both of the items attempt to measure a child's ability "to figure out" what the right answer is. I don't think either item measures what's taught in school. The items measure what students come to school with, not what they learn there.

FIGURE 15.5.

A sixth-grade standardized achievement test item in social studies.

If someone really wants to conserve resources, one good way to do so is to:

A. leave lights on even if they are not needed.
B. wash small loads instead of large loads in a clothes-washing machine.
C. write on both sides of a piece of paper.
D. place used newspapers in the garbage.

In Figure 15.5's social studies item for sixth-graders, look carefully at the four answer options. Read each option and see if it might be correct. A "smart" student, I contend, can figure out that Choices A, B, and D really would not "conserve resources" all that well, hence Choice C is the winning option. Brighter kids will have a better time with this item than their less bright classmates.

In Figure 15.6 you see a science item (although what this sort of item has to do with *science* frankly eludes me). Again, a reasonably bright fourth-grader shouldn't have all that much trouble in figuring out that the lion in Scene A's lower left-hand corner did a bit of

Scene A

Scene B

• **Which of the animals has moved the most from Scene A to Scene B?**

A. tiger   C. chipmunk

B. lion   D. pig

FIGURE 15.6.

A fourth-grade standardized achievement test item in science.

trotting to end up in Scene A's lower right-hand corner. All the other animals remain, statuelike, in the same place. Brighter students will do better on this item.

But why, you might be thinking, do developers of standardized tests include such items on their tests? The answer is all too simple. These sorts of items, because they tap innate intellectual skills that are not readily modifiable in school, do a wonderful job in spreading out test-takers' scores. The quest for score variance, coupled with the limitation of having few items to use in assessing students, makes such items very appealing to those who construct standardized achievement tests.

But items that primarily measure differences in students' inborn intellectual abilities obviously do not contribute to valid inferences about "how well children have been taught." Would we like all children to be able to do well on such "native smarts" items? Of course, we would. But to use such items to arrive at a judgment about educational effectiveness is unsound.

Out-of-school learning. The most troubling items to be found on standardized achievement tests assess what students have learned outside of school. Unfortunately, you'll find more of these items on standardized achievement tests than you'd suspect. If children come from advantaged families in which there are stimulus-rich environments, then those children are more apt to succeed on more items in standardized achievement test items than will other children whose environments don't mesh as well with what the tests measure. Hopefully, the items in Figures 15.7 and 15.8 will make it clear to you what's actually being assessed by a number of items on standardized achievement tests.

In Figure 15.7 you'll find a sixth-grade science item that first tells students what an attribute of a fruit is (namely, that it contains seeds). Then the student must identify what "is not a fruit" by selecting the option without seeds. As any child *who has encountered celery* knows, celery is a seed-free plant. The right answer, then, for those who have coped with celery's sometimes annoying strings (but never its seeds) is clearly Choice D.

But what if, when you were a youngster, your folks didn't have the money to buy celery at the store? What if your circumstances simply did not give you the chance to have meaningful interactions with celery stalks by the time you hit the sixth grade? How well do you think you'd do in correctly answering the item in Figure 15.7? Let's muddy the picture a mite more, and ask how well you'd do if you didn't know pumpkins were seed-carrying spheres? Clearly, if children know about pumpkins and celery, they'll do better on the item in Figure 15.7 than will those children who only know about apples and oranges. That's how children's *socioeconomic status* gets mixed up with their performances on standardized achievement tests.

The higher your family's socioeconomic status is, the more likely you are to do well on a number of the test items that you'll encounter in a standardized achievement test. The

FIGURE 15.7.

A sixth-grade standardized achievement test item in science.

● A plant's fruit always contains seeds. Which of the items below is not a fruit?

A. orange	C. apple
B. pumpkin	D. celery

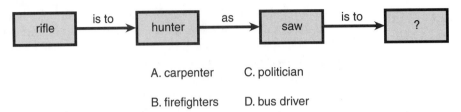

FIGURE 15.8.

A fourth-grade standardized achievement test item in social studies.

item in Figure 15.8 provides a vivid sample of the role a child's socioeconomic status can have in how the child will perform on certain items in standardized achievement tests.

In Figure 15.8's social studies item for fourth-graders, you'll see the kind of analogy item that standardized test developers have been using for eons. In fact, the *Army Alpha* contained its fair share of such items. If you study the item carefully, you'll see that the first half of the analogy, "rifle is to hunter," sets the nature of the relationship being sought in the analogy's second half. What's described in the analogy's first half is a distinctive device employed by a particular category of individuals. And, because a "saw" starts out the analogy's second half, the correct answer will be "carpenters." Carpenters use saws, whereas firefighters, bus drivers, and politicians don't. (Although, I am told, certain politicians sometimes "cut a deal.")

So, if a child's socioeconomic background allows the child to know about the tools that carpenters use, then the child is going to do better on the item in Figure 15.8 than will a child who doesn't know what carpenters do (or what they do it with). If children come from families in which television programs dealing with home remodeling are watched regularly or there are magazines dealing with such topics, then those children are going to be better off when responding to an item such as Figure 15.8's verbal analogy item. Those advantaged children will do better because they come from a stimulus-rich environment, not a deprived environment. The more books, magazines, and TV programs in a child's home, and the more leisure time that the child's parents have to spend with him or her in using those resources, the more likely that the child will do well on such verbal analogy items.

Moreover, I doubt if many fourth-grade teachers actually spend any social studies instructional time teaching children how to answer this formal type of verbal analogy problem. They really shouldn't be doing so. How often, in real life, do people ever encounter this specific kind of "fill-in-the-box" verbal analogy problem? I'd say the answer is *never*. These analogy items may be wonderful for discriminating among students (unfortunately, I'd say, the discriminations are often based on socioeconomic background), but the items don't measure student's mastery of a skill or knowledge worth promoting.

And how would a teacher get children ready to do well on Figure 15.8's item? Well, the teacher could isolate the 100 or 200 most common vocations that can be used to categorize people, then help children memorize the most important implements associated with each vocation. What a dumb thing to do!

Suppose you're a principal of a school in which most students come from low socio-economic situations. How are your students likely to perform on standardized achievement tests if a substantial number of the test's items really measure the stimulus-richness of your students' backgrounds? That's right, your students are not apt to earn very high scores. Does that mean your school's teachers are doing a poor instructional job? Of course not.

Conversely, let's imagine you're a principal in an affluent school whose students tend to be the progeny of upper-class, well-educated parents. Each spring, your students' scores on standardized achievement tests are dazzlingly high. Does this mean your school's teachers are doing a super instructional job? Of course not.

It's been said that if you want to predict how well a school's students will perform on standardized achievement tests, simply determine the average parental income level for the school. If the income level is high, then test scores are likely to be high as well. If parental income is low, then look out for low scores on standardized achievement tests.

One of the chief reasons that children's socioeconomic status is so highly correlated with standardized test scores is that there are many items on standardized achievement tests really focused on assessing knowledge and/or skills learned outside of school, knowledge and/or skills more likely to be learned in some socioeconomic settings than in others.

Again, you might ask, why on earth would standardized achievement test developers place such items on their tests? As usual, the answer is consistent with the dominant measurement mission of those tests, namely, to spread out students' test scores so that accurate and fine-grained norm-referenced interpretations can be made. Because there is substantial variation in children's socioeconomic situations, items that revolve around such variations are efficient in producing among-student variations in test scores.

Three potential causes: Which one is it? You've just concluded a review of three important factors that can influence students' scores on standardized achievement tests. One of these factors was directly linked to educational quality. But two factors weren't. It all depends, of course, on how many items of each sort you'll encounter in a *particular* standardized achievement test.

Take a look at Figure 15.9, in which you'll see fictitious distributions of test items on two 45-item imaginary standardized achievement tests. For Fictitious Test A, the vast majority of the test's items revolve around what was taught in school. Inferences about instructional effectiveness would make far more sense using that test rather than Fictitious Test B, in which more than half of the items are focused on the measurement of things not taught in school.

	NUMBER OF TEST ITEMS	
ASSESSMENT FOCUS OF ITEM	**FICTITIOUS TEST A**	**FICTITIOUS TEST B**
Assesses What's Taught in School	38	20
Assesses Native Ability	3	13
Assesses Out-of-School Learning	4	12

FIGURE 15.9.

Two distributions of test items on fictitious standardized achievement tests according to an item's dominant assessment focus.

If you're an educational leader whose school hasn't made much progress on a standardized test akin to Fictitious Test B, you really can't tell which of the three potential causes is most influential. The poor progress might be due to one, two, or even three of the factors being assessed by the test. And always remember, of course, that standardized achievement tests, of necessity, represent a pretty small sample of the content domains they are trying to represent.

What's an Educational Leader to Do about Standardized Achievement Tests?

All right, I've described a situation that, from the perspective of an educational leader, looks pretty bleak. What, if anything, can be done? I want to suggest a three-pronged attack on the problem. First off, I think *you* need to learn more about the viscera of standardized achievement tests. Second, I think *you* need to carry out an effective educational campaign so that (1) your educational colleagues, (2) parents of children in school, and (3) educational policymakers understand what the evaluative shortcomings of standardized achievement tests really are. Finally, I think *you* need to set up arrangements whereby a more appropriate form of assessment-based evidence of educational effectiveness is at hand. Let me deal, briefly, with each of these tasks for you. (It's always easy to inform other folks about what they should be doing. In self-defense, I need to point out that I've been trying personally to follow this three-step prescription myself. I hope you'll join in.)

Learning about Standardized Achievement Tests

Far too many educators haven't really studied the items on standardized achievement tests since the time that they were, as students in school, obliged to respond to those items. But the inferences that are based on students' test performances rest on nothing more than an aggregated sum of students' item-by-item responses. What educational leaders need to do is spend some "quality time" with standardized achievement tests, scrutinizing the test items one at a time. If you do attempt to review the items in a standardized achievement test, you'll find a set of four questions in the review form in Figure 15.10 that can help focus your efforts.

Notice that there are three questions in the review form that deal with the three score-influencing factors that were just treated. An additional question (the first of the four), asks you to think about whether the item really assesses a worthwhile skill. You'll sometimes find items on standardized achievement tests that deal with fairly insignificant content. In the practice exercises at the close of this final chapter (does that mean they are *terminal* exercises?), you'll have an opportunity to use the review form in Figure 15.10. What I hope you'll do, however, after you've put this book aside and only have sweet dreams about it, is to get hold of an actual standardized achievement test (ideally, one that's currently being used), then review the test's items using an approach similar to that embodied in Figure 15.10's review form.

A REVIEW FORM FOR JUDGING ITEMS FROM
STANDARDIZED ACHIEVEMENT TESTS

Directions: For all items reviewed, supply a Yes (Y) or No (N) answer to each of the four questions listed below.

Important Content?	Is the knowledge and/or skill measured by this item genuinely *important* for students either in school or after they leave school?
Taught in School?	Typically, is the knowledge and/or skill measured by this item actually *taught* in school?
Absence of Innate Ability Influence?	Will students' likelihood of answering this item correctly be relatively *uninfluenced* by their innate intellectual abilities?
Absence of SES Influence?	Will students' likelihood of answering this item correctly be relatively *uninfluenced* by their socioeconomic status (SES)?

ITEM NUMBER	IMPORTANT CONTENT?		TAUGHT IN SCHOOL?		ABSENCE OF INNATE ABILITY INFLUENCE?		ABSENCE OF SES INFLUENCE?	
____	Y	N	Y	N	Y	N	Y	N
____	Y	N	Y	N	Y	N	Y	N
____	Y	N	Y	N	Y	N	Y	N
____	Y	N	Y	N	Y	N	Y	N
____	Y	N	Y	N	Y	N	Y	N
____	Y	N	Y	N	Y	N	Y	N
____	Y	N	Y	N	Y	N	Y	N
etc.	etc.		etc.		etc.		etc.	

FIGURE 15.10.

A four-question form for reviewing items on standardized achievement tests.

Spreading the Word

Most educators, and almost all parents and school board members, think that schools should be rated on the basis of their students' scores on standardized achievement tests. Those people need to be educated. It is the responsibility of educational leaders to do that educating. If you've mastered the contents of this chapter, you really ought to be in a good position to do just that. And if you haven't mastered the chapter's contents, go back and read it again, but much more slowly.

If you do try to explain to the public, to parents, or to policymakers why it is that standardized test scores will probably provide a misleading picture of educational quality, be sure to indicate that you're not simply running away from the need to be held accountable. No, you must be willing to identify other, more credible evidence of student achievement. I'll offer a suggestion or two along those lines as the final point in the chapter.

In the end-of-chapter practice exercises, you'll be asked to prepare a written explanation to one of three audiences (teachers, parents, or the media) about why standardized achievement tests should not be used to judge educational quality. I hope you'll undertake that practice exercise seriously, because, as an educational leader, you really do need to know how to explain to others, in writing or aloud, why students' scores on standardized tests typically yield a misleading indication of educational quality.

Coming Up with Other Evidence

If you're going to argue against standardized achievement tests as a source of educational evidence for determining school quality, and you still are willing to be held educationally accountable, then you'll need to ante up some other form of evidence to show the world that you really are doing a good educational job.

I recommend that you attempt to assess students' mastery of genuinely significant cognitive skills, such as their ability to write effective compositions, their ability to use historical lessons to make cogent analyses of current problems, and their ability to solve high-level mathematical problems.

If the skills selected (1) measure really important cognitive outcomes, (2) are seen by parents and policymakers to be genuinely significant, and (3) can be addressed instructionally by competent teachers, then the assembly of a set of pretest-to-posttest evidence showing substantial student growth in such skills can be truly persuasive.

What teachers need are assessment instruments that measure truly worthwhile skills or significant bodies of knowledge. Then teachers need to show the world that they can instruct children so those children make striking pre-instruction to postinstruction progress.

Problems with a Simple Pretest–Posttest Model.   One of the most intuitively appealing ways of determining how much students have learned is to pretest them prior to instruction, then provide instruction, and posttest them when instruction is finished. This classic pretest–posttest is shown in Figure 15.11.

A problem with the pretest–posttest model is that, if the same test is used prior to and following instruction, the pretest may sufficiently sensitize students to what's important so that they devote atypical attention (during instruction) to what was covered on

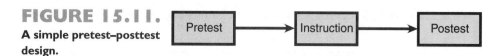

FIGURE 15.11.
A simple pretest–posttest design.

the pretest. This is referred to as the "reactive" effect of pretesting. It was discussed in Chapter 13 regarding the assessment of affect. Reactive pretesting tends to confound a teacher's estimate of how much students have learned because high posttest performances may have occurred simply because students knew "what was coming."

Sometimes, the problem of reactivity is dealt with when teachers use a different pretest and posttest. But, as a practical matter, it is impossible for teachers to create (or find) two truly equidifficult test forms. Unfortunately, therefore, if the posttest is easier than the pretest, the students' "growth" may simply be a function of the disparity in the two tests' difficulty levels. Or, conversely, a tougher posttest may lead to the erroneous conclusion that a skilled teacher has had no impact on students.

The split-and-switch model. To circumvent these problems, teachers can use the split-and-switch variation of the pretest–posttest model presented that is portrayed graphically in Figure 15.12. The split-and-switch data-gathering design relies on the assumption

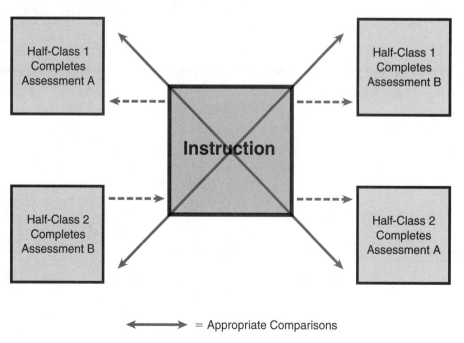

FIGURE 15.12.
A split-and-switch version of the pretest–posttest design.

The Daily News

EDUCATIONAL ASSESSOR BURNED AT STAKE!

While sizzling, evaluated quality of flames using a 5-point holistic rubric

Yesterday, educational assessors were generally considered to be members of the education profession. Granted, educational assessors deal with a very specialized aspect of the educational enterprise, namely, measuring students' cognitive, affective, or psychomotor status. Nevertheless, educational assessors don't measure the tensile strength of steel cables or the distance between Earth and Jupiter. Almost without exception, educational assessors measure students. And, if the adjective *educational* signifies anything, the

assessing done by educational assessors ought to have a direct bearing on education. Yet, I believe that large scale assessors are deliberately distancing themselves from the central mission that guides the profession to which they belong. The central mission of education is the education of children. To the extent that the large-scale-assessment community remains seemingly oblivious of education's central mission, then I think that large-scale assessment is headed in a dysfunctional direction.

The fundamental function of almost all educational assessment is to measure students so that we can make assessment-based inferences about their status with respect to educationally relevant cognitive, affective, or psychomotor domains. There are varied uses to which these assessment-based inferences can be put, but I believe the two most important uses of large-scale assessment-based inferences are the following: *Educational Accountability*, that is, the accumulation of evidence to help determine if educational expenditures are achieving the intend

---

that a sample of roughly half the teacher's students will provide a reasonable approximation of how well the whole class would have scored on a test. Because Form A pretest and posttest responses are to be compared, but different students are completing the tests, the forms are identical in difficulty. Yet, there is no pretest reactivity (because the students taking the posttest, Form A, for example, have never seen that test form previously). The teacher, in essence, has two replications (the Form A contrast and the Form B contrast) to see how much students have learned.

Steps in carrying out the split-and-switch model. For educational leaders who wish to use this data-gathering approach, the following steps should be taken:

1. You will need two forms (A and B) of a test. The test can be a traditional selected-response test or a more elaborate constructed-response performance test complete with a rubric). Ideally, the two test forms should both measure a student's mastery of

an important skill or knowledge domain and should be at least *approximately* equivalent in difficulty. Label one form as Form A and another as Form B.

2. For the pretest, half of a class should receive one form and the other half of a class should receive the other form. It is suggested that you simply count the number of students, for example, 30, then go down your alphabetical class list so that the first-listed 15 students receive one form and the other students receive the second form.

3. Be sure to use the same kind of paper on test forms for both the pretest and posttest so that either you (or, if you prefer, a colleague) can subsequently "blind-score" the tests without knowing which responses were made as pretests or posttests. Direct your students, at both pretest and posttest, to put their names on their responses but *not* to put a date on their responses. Ideally, ask them to put their names on the *back* of the last page of the test form.

4. Next, using a code that only you know, mark each pretest response unobtrusively (for instance, on the back of the last page) so that, *after* the papers have been scored, they can be identified as pretests. (You might use a group of numbers that appear to be random, but you know that the next-to-the-last number is always even.) Posttests, of course, would have a different coding scheme so that, for instance, the second number in the sequence was always odd. Any coding scheme will work as long as you can tell how to separate pretest and posttest responses after they have been scored.

5. Encourage students to do well on both the pretest and the posttest by stressing, in your own words, the significance of the tests. For the pretest, you may want to provide some small grade or similar incentive for students' participation. Ideally, the students' motivation levels should be the same for both the pretest and the posttest.

6. Teach as effectively as you can toward the skill or body of knowledge being assessed via the test forms. *Do not teach toward the particular tasks being used for pre- and posttests.* Teachers want to promote increases in students' skill or knowledge, not students' familiarity with a given test's particulars. If you teach toward the test forms, an inaccurate picture of students' growth will be the result.

7. At posttest time, reverse the tasks taken at pretest so that all students will be responding to different tasks. For instance, using Form A and Form B, make sure the students who completed Form A at pretest time get form B at posttest time (and vice versa).

8. When the posttests have been collected, split them into Forms A and B. Then code the posttests so they can be distinguished from the pretests.

9. Next, mix the Form A pretests and posttests together; thereafter do the same for Form B. When the tests are scored, the scorer must not know whether a pretest or posttest is being scored.

10. You may wish to score each set of tests (Form A, then Form B) yourself, or you may wish to call on a colleague to supply truly nonpartisan scoring.

11. After the tasks in a form have all been scored, using your coding system, separate students' responses into pretests and posttests. Then, for number-correct tests, compute the average pretest and posttest scores for the pretests and for the posttests. For skill-determining performance tests, calculate the percentage of papers assigned to

different rubric-defined quality categories. Repeat the process for the other form. Compare students' pretest and posttest performances.

12. If you intend to use the students' responses for grading purposes, make certain that the two test forms are approximately equal in difficulty. If not, take any difficulty differences into consideration when grading.

Other evidence needed. Remember, if you're an educational leader who chooses to reject standardized achievement test scores as indicators of instructional effectiveness, you need to come up with some *believable* evidence to fill that void. If you really want the evidence of student progress measured via the split-and-switch design to be taken seriously, you should make sure that at least some of the students' mixed-together pretests and posttests are blind-scored by nonpartisans. This could mean district-level educators or, ideally, parent volunteers.

One of the attractive features of the split-and-switch data-gathering design is that you don't need to have test-scorers who bring identical scoring standards to the enterprise. To illustrate, suppose Mother Mahoney and Father Franklin are two parent-volunteer scorers. Mother M. is a "tough" scorer while Father F. is a "softy." Because Mother M. will be stringent as she scores *both* the mixed-together pretests and posttests, her stringency will come crashing down on students in an evenhanded manner. The same is true for Father F.'s marshmallow standards. He'll score the pretests as softly as he'll score the posttests. Consequently, when the pretests and posttests have been sorted out, irrespective of who supplied the scores, the same scoring standards will have been applied to both.

The fundamental point is this: If, as an educational leader, you accept the position that standardized achievement test scores should not be used to measure the quality of schooling, then you really *must* provide other, credible evidence that can be used to ascertain the quality of schooling. Nonpartisan evidence regarding educators' pretest-to-posttest promotion of undeniably important skills or knowledge just might do the trick.

Chapter Wrap-Up

Okay, one last chapter wrap-up awaits you. As has been our custom (traditions can spring up almost overnight), this summary will be organized around Chapter 15's guiding questions. (A guiding question is supposed to *guide*, isn't it?)

● **Why did the public start using students' standardized achievement scores to evaluate educational quality?**

The public turned to test results looking for meaningful evidence of educational quality. As increasing incredulity on the part of citizens arose regarding the quality of schooling, more and more parents and policymakers turned to what they regarded as technically solid, nationally sanctioned measuring tools, that is, the standardized achievement tests that had, for years, been published by many of the nation's leading measurement organizations.

The publication by newspapers of district-by-district and school-by-school rankings according to students' standardized test scores clearly increased the inclination of people to equate high scores with good schools and low scores with poor schools. In recent years, the identification of schools with low test scores as "targeted" or "failing" schools has escalated dramatically.

It was suggested in the chapter that educators' silence on this issue made a significant contribution to the growing public perception that scores on nationally standardized achievement tests should be regarded as the most important factor in judging schools. The reason for educators' silence, it was suggested, was widespread ignorance among educators regarding how standardized achievement tests should and should not be used.

What do standardized achievement tests measure?

The central assessment-based inference that hinges on a standardized achievement test regards the comparison of the test-taker's knowledge and/or skills with that of a national sample of students at the same age/grade level. Because the content domains (of skills and/or knowledge) represented by standardized achievement tests are very substantial, and there are often relatively few items on a standardized achievement test per subject area, the content domains being measured are represented by a sampling procedure. Because the assessment focus of standardized achievement tests is on norm-referenced interpretations (that is, allowing a student's score to be contrasted with the performance of a national norm group), it is important for standardized achievement tests to yield a substantial amount of variation in the scores earned by test-takers.

Why shouldn't standardized achievement tests be used to judge educational quality?

Although standardized achievement tests do a wonderful job of permitting the norm-referenced interpretations they were intended to permit, ascribing high educational quality to schools with high test scores and ascribing low educational quality to schools with low test scores is unsound.

Three reasons that erode the validity of any inferences about educational quality based on students' standardized achievement test scores were identified. First, there are substantial mismatches between what's tested on these instruments and what's taught in a particular school. In an important investigation carried out at Michigan State University, researchers found that more than half of the content covered in standardized achievement tests never received more than cursory treatment in widely used textbooks (and, by implication, in the classrooms where those textbooks were used).

The second problem with using standardized achievement tests to rate educational quality is a technical tendency to remove items from these tests that cover the most important content teachers teach. This difficulty arises because of the need for a standardized achievement test's items to contribute to substantial score-variance among students. Items answered correctly by too many students, that is, items with high p values, do not do their share in spreading out test-takers' scores. Accordingly, such high p value items are rarely put into standardized achievement tests in the first place, and are almost certainly removed from a test when the test is revised. But items on which students perform well often cover the content that teachers believe important enough to spend substantial time teaching. Yet, those are the very items that are usually excised from the final version of a standardized achievement test. Quite often, therefore, the most important content that's taught by teachers is not assessed by the items on standardized achievement tests.

The final shortcoming of standardized achievement tests—insofar as they can be used to evaluate educational quality—is that it is impossible to sort out the contribution to students' test scores of three different potentially causative factors. An inspection of the items on standardized achievement tests indicates that those items are chiefly aimed at measuring (1) what has been taught in school, (2) students' innate intellectual abilities, or (3) what the student has learned outside of school, the latter being heavily influenced by the socioeconomic stratum in which the child has been raised. Because only one of these three factors reflects on the quality of education, it is illogical to base estimates of educational effectiveness on students' performances on standardized achievement tests.

● What's an educational leader to do about standardized achievement tests?

It was suggested that educational leaders (1) learn more about standardized achievement tests, particularly the items themselves, (2) educate all relevant constituencies about why it is that standardized achievement tests—wonderful assessment tools when used properly—are not suitable for determining educational quality, and (3) produce alternative test-based evidence that reflects more accurately on the quality of educators' efforts. A series of step-by-step suggestions and a data-gathering design for collecting such evidence was provided.

Practice Exercises

Part One

There are two kinds of practice activities that I hope you'll tackle to close out the chapter. First off, I want you to review several standardized achieve-

ment test items using the review form that was presented in Figure 15.10 on page 413. Familiarize yourself with the four questions that the form presents, then answer each of those questions for the five items that follow the review form.

ITEM NUMBER	IMPORTANT CONTENT?		TAUGHT IN SCHOOL?		ABSENCE OF INNATE ABILITY INFLUENCE?		ABSENCE OF SES INFLUENCE?	
1	Y	N	Y	N	Y	N	Y	N
2	Y	N	Y	N	Y	N	Y	N
3	Y	N	Y	N	Y	N	Y	N
4	Y	N	Y	N	Y	N	Y	N
5	Y	N	Y	N	Y	N	Y	N

ITEM 1
A 6th-Grade Science Item

A 6th-Grade Science Item

- If you wanted to find out if another planet had mountains or rivers, which of these tools should you use?

binoculars

telescope

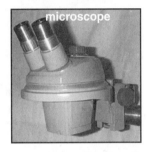

microscope

camera

ITEM 2
A 7th-Grade Mathematics Item

A 7th-Grade Mathematics Item

- Larry wants the total of the numbers in Circle A to be equal to the total of the numbers in Circle B. Which two number tiles should he trade?

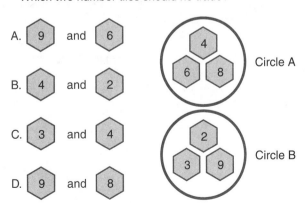

A. 9 and 6

B. 4 and 2

C. 3 and 4

D. 9 and 8

Circle A

4
6   8

Circle B

2
3   9

ITEM 3
A 3rd-Grade Language Arts Item

● Which of the following word groups is in alphabetical order?
A. had, hunger, home
B. hunger, home, had
C. had, home, hunger
D. home, had, hunger

ITEM 4
A 6th-Grade Social Studies Item

● Of the following inventions, which helps farmers in the production of food?

A. flashlight		C. plow	
B. television		D. radio	

ITEM 5
A 6th-Grade Mathematics Item

● Charlie walked 8 blocks in one-half hour. At that rate, how many blocks would he walk in one hour?

A. 4 blocks		C. 10 and 1/2 blocks
B. 16 blocks		D. 8 blocks

Part Two

To close out the exercises, I want you to choose one of the following audiences: (1) parents, (2) teachers, or (3) representatives of the media. Then, write a brief persuasive essay that will convince members of that audience they should not support the use of standardized achievement tests to evaluate educational quality. This will give you an opportunity to organize your own thinking regarding how an educational leader ought to spread the word regarding the shortcomings of standardized achievement tests for evaluating educational quality.

In the Answer to Practice Exercises, I've written one of these essays myself. See how your effort compares with mine. If you chose a different audience, see whether the differences between our approaches were major or minor.

Answers to Practice Exercises

Part One

Presented below is the four-question review form with the Yes and No answers that I said I would supply. It's unlikely that you'd fill out the form exactly as I would. There are too many close calls. After supplying the completed form, I'll provide a brief comment regarding each item.

ITEM NUMBER	IMPORTANT CONTENT?		TAUGHT IN SCHOOL?		ABSENCE OF INNATE ABILITY INFLUENCE?		ABSENCE OF SES INFLUENCE?	
1	Y	(N)	Y	(N)	(Y)	N	Y	(N)
2	Y	(N)	Y	(N)	Y	(N)	(Y)	N
3	(Y)	N	(Y)	N	(Y)	N	Y	(N)
4	(Y)	N	Y	(N)	(Y)	N	(Y)	N
5	(Y)	N	(Y)	N	(Y)	N	(Y)	N

Comments:

Item 1: I'm not sure how important this item's content is or whether it's likely to be taught. I think it's most serious drawback is the probability of a strong SES influence. Children from affluent homes where there actually are telescopes, or where TV programs about astronomy are often seen, will usually do better in this item than will children from less stimulus-rich homes.

Item 2: Again, I'm not sure how important this kind of tile-juggling is or whether it's likely to be taught. But I do think that kids who got lucky at genepool time will do better on this item than will those whose innate ability isn't all that high.

Item 3: I think this item deals with an important skill (alphabetizing) that third graders ought to ac-quire. Assuming there were enough items of this type to get a decent fix on a child's alphabetizing prowess, the item looks fine to me.

Item 4: I suppose this item taps worthwhile content. We'd all like children to be able to answer the item correctly. I fear its link to students' socioeconomic status is its greatest defect. Children from stimulus-rich environments will do better on this item, especially if the item's content is not taught in school.

Item 5: This item seems to pass muster with respect to all four questions.

Part Two

I chose parents as my target audience. See what you think of the essay that starts on the next page.

SUGGESTIONS FOR ADDITIONAL READING

Freeman, Donald J., Therese M. Kuhs, Andrew C. Porter, Robert E. Floden, William H. Schmidt, and John R. Schwille. "Do Textbooks and Tests Define a National Curriculum in Elementary School Mathematics?" *Elementary School Journal, 83*, 5 (1984): 501–513.

Gardner, H. "Multiple Intelligences: The Theory in Practice." *Teachers College Record, 95*, 4 (1994): 576–583.

Popham, W. James. "The Instructional Consequences of Criterion-Referenced Clarity." *Educational Measurement: Issues and Practice, 13*, 4 (Winter 1994): 15–18, 30.

AND FOR THOSE WHO TIRE OF READING

Farr, Roger C., and W. James Popham. *Standardized Tests Should Not Be Used to Evaluate Educational Quality: A Debate* (An Audiotape). Presented at the annual meeting of the American Educational Research Association, San Diego, CA, April 13–17, 1998.

Popham, W. James. *Criterion-Referenced Measurement: Today's Alternative to Traditional Testing* (Videotape #ETVT-35). Los Angeles: IOX Assessment Associates.

Popham, W. James. *Norm-Referenced Tests: Uses and Misuses* (Videotape #ETVT-32). Los Angeles: IOX Assessment Associates.

Popham, W. James. *A Parent's Guide to Standardized Tests* (Videotape #ETVT-34). Los Angeles: IOX Assessment Associates.

Don't Judge Your Child's School By Its Standardized Test Scores!

By W. James Popham

Parents have a right to know whether their children's schools are doing a good job. Because parents want the best for their offspring, it's only natural that they want their children to be well educated.

In order to reach a conclusion about the effectiveness of schools, many parents now rely on the standardized test scores earned by a school's students. If a school's scores are high, the school is regarded as effective. If a school's scores are low, the opposite judgment is reached. This perspective is fueled by newspapers' test-score rankings of schools.

Yet, despite the widespread use of standardized test scores as the chief yardstick by which to judge a school's success, parents will be misled if they use that yardstick. Standardized test scores do *not* provide an accurate picture of a school's effectiveness. Let's see why.

What Is a Standardized Test?

Technically, a standardized test is any examination that's administered and scored in a predetermined, standard manner. There are two major kinds of standardized tests, *aptitude* tests and *achievement* tests.

Standardized *aptitude* tests predict how well students are likely to perform in some subsequent educational setting. The most common examples of these are the SAT (*Scholastic Assessment Test*) and the *ACT Assessment*, both of which attempt to forecast how well high school students will perform in college.

But what most parents rely on when they evaluate a school's effectiveness are students' scores on standardized *achievement* tests. Nationally, there are five such tests in use, namely, the *California Achievement Tests, Comprehensive Tests of Basic Skills, Iowa Tests of Basic Skills, Metropolitan Achievement Tests,* and *Stanford Achievement Tests.*

A Standardized Test's Mission

The overriding purpose of a standardized achievement test is to permit comparisons among students. To do so, a standardized achievement test is initially administered to a nationally representative sample of students. Scores of

these students, known as the test's *norm group,* provide a comparative scale by which the scores of future test-takers are interpreted. So, when Mom hears that "Johnny scored at the 85th percentile" on such a test, this means that Johnny's score was better than scores of 85 percent of the students in the norm group.

Standardized achievement tests usually cover four subject areas: mathematics, language arts, social studies, and science. The mission of such tests is to allow comparisons among students with respect to the knowledge and skills they possess. In science, for example, such a comparison would be based on how a student's test performance stacks up to the test performances of students in the norm group.

In order to make these comparisons properly, standardized achievement tests must "spread out" students' scores. If too many students earn similar scores, it is difficult to make fine-grained comparisons among those students. An underlying tenet of standardized testing, therefore, is that students' scores must be substantially spread out.

Three Shortcomings

There are three key reasons that parents shouldn't judge schools using standardized test scores. The first of these is the enormous, and usually unrecognized *mismatch between what's tested and what's taught.* Because of the considerable curricular diversity in this nation, what's taught in different school districts often varies substantially. Test companies do their best to accommodate these curricular differences by making their content-coverage very general. Yet, in many instances as much as 50–65 percent of what's tested is not even taught in schools—or is even supposed to be taught. It's obvious that parents should not be judging schools on the basis of tests that don't measure what our schools ought to be teaching. That's strike one.

A second difficulty with standardized tests is that *they fail to measure the most important things teachers teach.* This problem stems from the need of these tests to produce a sufficient spread of scores. Test items that do the best job of spreading out students' scores are those items that are answered correctly by about half of the test-takers. Test items that are answered by large proportions of students, for instance, 80–90 percent, are usually not put in standardized tests in the first place, and will most likely be eliminated when the tests are revised.

But here's the snag. Typically, the items on which many students score well actually cover the most important content that teachers try to teach. Yet, the more effectively teachers teach such content, the better students will perform on items dealing with that content. As a consequence, the test items covering that content will often be discarded. In short, if teachers do a great job in promoting students' mastery of important knowledge and skills, it is unlikely that this content will be measured on a standardized achievement test. That's strike two.

A final problem with using students' standardized achievement test scores to judge a school staff's success is that *teachers' familiarity with a test's content can, over time, artificially inflate students' test scores*. Here's how this arises. These tests are often re-used in a school district for quite some time, often as long as 5–10 years. Teachers themselves administer these tests each year. In many instances, teachers are directed by test publishers to first "take" the standardized test themselves so they'll be familiar with the test when they administer it.

Let's say you are an elementary teacher who, each year, gives your students an end-of-school-year standardized achievement test on which there are two items dealing with "the origins of the steam engine." After a year or two of administering the test, don't you think you might want to teach your future students about the ancestry of steam engines? It's not that you're trying to teach students how to respond to the test's two steam-engine items. Instead, you might reason that if the developers of a "national" test believe the origins of steam engines are so significant, perhaps you should be spending a bit of classroom time on that important topic.

Over time, therefore, students' scores on standardized achievement tests almost always get better. And these increases in test scores take place even if not one teacher in a school is improperly "teaching to the test items." Such increases in students' scores often reflect teacher familiarity with test content rather than genuine rises in student accomplishments. But artificial improvements in students' test performances, of course, will mislead parents who may think "all is well" when it really isn't. And that's strike three.

What Do These Tests Measure?

Standardized achievement tests, consistent with their mission to compare students, are designed to permit individual students' performances to be contrasted with the performances of a norm group. By doing so, relative comparisons can be made among students with regard to their mastery of a very small sample of content. Sometimes

there are only 40 items on a standardized achievement test. Those items are intended to represent a huge domain of content (for example, the mathematical skills and knowledge possessed by a typical eighth-grader).

But performances on standardized achievement tests are most influenced by (1) students' genetically transmitted intellectual abilities and (2) the extent to which students were raised in a stimulus-rich environment. If students in a school are socioeconomically well off, the school's test scores invariably will be high. The opposite is also true. Indeed, if you want to predict how well a school's students will perform on a standardized achievement test, simply find out what the school's average parental income is.

Given these testing realities, it is clearly inappropriate for parents to judge a school staff's effectiveness on the basis of students' standardized achievement test scores. A school's teachers and administrators can be doing a superb instructional job, but their school's standardized test scores may not be all that high. Conversely, even if an affluent school's students score well on standardized achievement tests, that does not *necessarily* signify that the school's educators are all that effective. Standardized tests measure what students come to school with, not what they learn there.

What's a Parent To Do?

As indicated at the outset of this analysis, parents have a right to know whether their children's schools are doing a good job. Fortunately, there are a number of legitimate sources of *evidence* that parents can consider when reaching a judgment about a school staff's effectiveness.

For example, parents should review students' growth, over time, on a variety of demanding teacher-made tests as well as on attitudinal inventories assessing such things as students' interest in learning or their enjoyment of reading.

There are many other factors related to school quality, such as a school's absenteeism rates. All of these sorts of indicators, in concert with a wide range of evidence regarding students' increased knowledge and skills, can provide parents with a defensible idea about a school's effectiveness—an estimate far more meaningful than the distorted picture provided by standardized achievement tests.

W. James Popham is an emeritus professor in the UCLA Graduate School of Education and Information Studies. A former president of the American Educational Research Association, Dr. Popham is the author of more than 20 books, many of which are devoted to educational testing.
This essay may be duplicated.

APPENDIX

Statistical Concepts Needed to Evaluate and Use Educational Tests

For most educators, mere contemplation of the term *statistics* conjures up images akin to bubonic plague and the abolition of tenure. Far too many educators, even those who do not consider themselves numerically deficient, are intimidated by any sort of statistical monkey business. It is assumed that sense can be made out of educational statistics only by those who are members of a rather exclusive quantitative cult.

However, such an approach to educational statistics is not only shortsighted but decisively dumb. At the level of statistical analysis needed by those who work with educational measurement, there is no legitimate reason for anyone to be intimidated by statistics.

In this appendix, for example, a variety of statistical procedures are explained. All of them involve numbers. Some of them *at first glance* appear pretty complicated and difficult to understand. *None* of them is. In fact, here is a promise from author to reader: If you complete this appendix carefully, with the well-warranted conviction that you can master all of the statistical concepts treated herein, *you will.*[1]

Enough of this pre-appendix pep talk. It must be noted that some readers will already be conversant with the rudimentary sorts of statistical procedures to be dealt with in this appendix. Those folks certainly don't need to relearn what they've already mastered. For such readers a quick leaf-through of the appendix headings is recommended. Pause only if you find something unfamiliar or if you need a bit of review.

The increasingly widespread use of pocket calculators (many of which perform fairly sophisticated statistical highjinks) and computers (many of which outthink their operators) dramatically reduces the likelihood that you will ever need to compute *by hand* some of the statistical indicators we'll be considering in this appendix. Nonetheless, I'm going to ask those who read this appendix to do a bit of hand-calculating with super-simple examples because I want you to see where these statistical quantities come from. If you regard statistics as an awesome mystery controlled somehow by electronic instruments, you'll not be all that comfortable in using statistics. Today's educational leaders dare not be put off by elementary statistical notions. You must have at least an *intuitive* understanding of the procedures I'm about to treat. Let's start building that intuitive understanding.

Function of Statistics

You should begin your consideration of statistics by recalling why you are playing around with such notions at all. Remember, in Part Two you acquired an idea about how to *evaluate* educational tests. In evaluating an educational measuring instrument, it seems quite obvious that you'll need to know something about students' performances. In fact, a good many of the schemes educators employ to appraise educational tests depend quite directly on having a good idea about how students actually score on a test.

Well, what are your options in discovering how students perform on a test? Let's say you administered a fifty-item vocabulary test to five students in a third-grade teacher's high-performance reading group and found that each student achieved the following number of items correct: (Joe, 42; Raul, 43; Mary, 36; Clyde, 35; José, 32). With only five students to report, you could easily reel off all five third-graders' individual scores, and you could make some sense of what those scores meant.

However, let's say you're dealing with a class of thirty-five third-graders. Alternatively, imagine you're working at the senior high level with five different tenth-grade English classes of twenty-five to thirty-five students per class. In such instances, if you tried to make sense out of individually reported test performances, you would be quite unable to do so. With more than a hundred, or even with more than a handful, it is next to impossible to draw any meaningful conclusions about students' scores that are reported on a one-by-one basis.

To cope with this problem, people who were fairly skilled with numbers, that is, who knew more than their multiplication tables, came up with some economical ways of describing sets of data such as students' test scores. Some of these statistical techniques were borrowed from other fields, particularly agriculture, in which similar needs existed for precise, yet pithy descriptive schemes.

By taking a large number of diverse test scores and subjecting them to some fairly routine sorts of mathematical computations, statisticians have made it possible to depict accurately and economically how groups of students perform on tests. Furthermore, because these statistical descriptive techniques have become widely used during the past half century or so, a series of conventional expectations have been created among measurement people regarding these statistical indicators.

I can illustrate this last point in the case of the statistical procedures employed to estimate a test's reliability, that is, the consistency with which the test measures. One way of determining a test's reliability is to give the test to a group of students, wait a week or two, then readminister the test to the same students in order to see how each individual's scores compare on the two testing occasions. The statistical technique used to gauge the relationship between examinees' scores on the two test administrations is called the *correlation coefficient*. By producing only a single numerical value, the correlation coefficient provides educators with a useful summary of the degree to which students' performances on the two testing occasions were similar. Indeed, when applied in such instances, the resulting correlation coefficient is referred to as a *reliability coefficient*.

Because folks have employed this statistical technique over many years, measurement people have arrived at a fairly realistic set of expectations regarding the appropriate size that a reliability coefficient will *typically* be if a test is going to be considered sufficiently reliable. Those sorts of expectations would have been impossible to come up with had people been forced to rely on the imprecise conclusions that might be drawn from decades of reporting one-score-at-a-time retest results.

Thus, for economy of description and to aid educators in the establishment of conventional expectations regarding various aspects of measurement, statistics have proven a valuable tool for the measurement specialist. Statistical procedures, as you might suspect, can be fairly straightforward, or they can be rather exotic. There are statisticians around who actually seem to thrive on the extent to which they can make themselves obscure by means of numerical incantations and formulae that resemble Mayan hieroglyphs.[2] Thankfully, however, you'll not have to deal with such sophisticated statistical machinations in this appendix. The sorts of statistical tools needed to evaluate educational tests are alarmingly sensible and, with just a smidgen of effort, even understandable.

With your latent anxieties hopefully allayed, I can turn now to a consideration of the techniques employed to describe educational test performances. You'll warm up with some common, nonstatistical descriptive techniques, then seductively and painlessly make friends with statistical descriptive techniques.

Frequency Distributions

When educators administer a test in most situations, they find that students get all sorts of scores. Irrespective of whether it's an attitude inventory or an achievement test, and probably because of inborn perversity, students seem driven to come up with different scores. Just think of how simple it could be if a teacher dished out a 100-item final exam, then found that all students had earned a score of 93 correct. However, the world is not simple and, more often than not, educators will have to cope with sets of scores, such as those presented in Table A.1, which show that, on a fifty-item end-of-semester exam, twenty-five students displayed predictable diversity. Student nine (Cora Snively, as usual)

TABLE A.1	Scores of 25 Students on a 50-Item End-of-Semester Exam		
STUDENT	**SCORE**	**STUDENT**	**SCORE**
1	33	14	35
2	35	15	42
3	36	16	47
4	26	17	33
5	38	18	19
6	38	19	36
7	29	20	29
8	36	21	38
9	50	22	31
10	25	23	43
11	42	24	30
12	35	25	38
13	43		

earned the top score of 50 correct, while student eighteen (poor Peter Coogin again) messed up by getting only 19 correct. The rest of the group's scores are scattered all over the place between those two extreme scores.

Although it's possible to look over a set of test scores, such as those in Table A.1 and make some sense out of them, it is sometimes more useful to set up the scores in a frequency distribution, similar to that seen in Table A.2 in which, instead of organizing the results according to students (as in Table A.1), you use the obtained test scores as the organizing scheme. At the left of Table A.2 in descending order, I've listed the scores that the class obtained, from Cora's 50 to Peter's 19, then listed the frequency (number of times) that each such score occurred. In the column immediately to the left of the frequency column, I have also listed the *cumulative frequencies* (by adding them up from the bottom). In the next column to the right I have presented the *cumulative percentages*. Because there are exactly twenty-five students, each student equals 4 percent, thus simplifying the computation of the cumulative percentage column.

By analyzing a set of test scores presented as in Table A.2, you can certainly make more sense out of the scores than if you had to work only with scores arrayed as in Table A.1. In particular, you can more readily see how the scores cluster (by viewing the frequency column) and how they accumulate as they get larger (by viewing the cumulative frequency and cumulative percentage columns).

TABLE A.2   **Frequency Distribution of 25 Students' Scores on a 50-Item End-of-Semester Exam**

EXAM SCORE	FREQUENCY (f)	CUMULATIVE (f)	CUMULATIVE %
50	1	25	100
47	1	24	96
43	2	23	92
42	2	21	84
38	4	19	76
36	3	15	60
35	3	12	48
33	2	9	36
31	1	7	28
30	1	6	24
29	2	5	20
26	1	3	12
25	1	2	8
19	1	1	4

However, let's suppose that, instead of working with only twenty-five scores and a test with only a 50-point range of possible scores, you were trying to make sense out of a huge set of test scores, say for a total school district, and had to work with a test that had a 150-point range of possible scores. In such situations it is sometimes helpful to set up frequency distributions in such a way that you use *class intervals*, instead of actual scores. This cuts down immensely on the size of the frequency distribution table yet still provides a decent idea of what the test scores are like.

In Table A.3 you'll see a frequency distribution in which class intervals of five points have been employed in setting up the table. You'll still have the same twenty-five test scores that you were using before, but now you can't tell exactly where Cora Snively's score is. You can still spot Peter Coogin's dismal 19 because his score happens to be the only one in the 16 to 20 class interval.

There are some new wrinkles in Table A.3 that warrant a bit of explanation. Notice that, in the second column, that is, the one to the right of the class-interval column, there are intervals identified by their *theoretical limits*. You can see that these theoretical limits extend 0.5 above and 0.5 below the class intervals. It may help to think of each class interval as extending halfway to the intervals below and above it. For example, let's say that students' test scores were reported in decimals, as they sometimes are. Would you put a score of 45.9 in the 46 to 50 interval or the 41 to 45 interval? Hopefully, you can see that a score of 45.9 ought to go in the 46 to 50 interval because it's closer to 46 than to 45. Theoretically, even a single score, such as 27, extends plus or minus 0.5 of itself and, thus, consists technically of an interval between 26.5 and 27.5.

The midpoint of each class interval is presented in the third column. Midpoints can be used as a convenient way to describe an interval. The last three columns, identical to those in Table A.2 represent frequencies (f = the number of scores in each interval), cumulative frequencies, and cumulative percentages. When you use a frequency distribution with class intervals, of course, you lose some of the precision of the individual scores

TABLE A.3 Class-Interval Frequency Distribution of 25 Students' Scores on a 50-Item End-of-Semester Exam

CLASS INTERVAL	THEORETICAL LIMITS	MIDPOINT	f	CUM f	CUM. %
46–50	45.5–50.5	48	2	25	100
41–45	40.5–45.5	43	4	23	92
36–40	35.5–40.5	38	7	19	76
31–35	30.5–35.5	33	6	12	48
26–30	25.5–.30.5	28	4	6	24
21–25	20.5–25.5	23	1	2	8
16–20	15.5–20.5	18	1	1	4

because they are dumped somewhat unceremoniously into their respective class intervals. For instance, let's say you had a five-point class interval from 27 to 32 (theoretically, of course, from 26.5 to 32.5) and found that there were ten frequencies falling in that interval. You have no idea whether all ten frequencies were at 27, 32, or whether they were spread out more evenly. This illustrates a general principle in the use of statistics, namely, that sometimes there are procedures used that sacrifice a degree of accuracy in order to pick up other dividends, such as simplicity of reporting.

If you intend to use a class-interval frequency distribution to report a set of test scores, you'll probably find it useful to have somewhere between ten and twenty intervals. It helps if you employ intervals with an odd number of scores, for example, 3, 5, 7, and so on, so that the midpoint of the interval is a whole number, instead of a decimal number. This feature turns out to be useful for certain kinds of computation and for displaying the data graphically. Soon, you'll consider some of the more common of the graphic display schemes.

As more and more educators have access to electronic calculators and computers that, with the press of a button or two, can send a swarm of test scores swirling through a preprogrammed set of statistical gyrations, the use of class-interval schemes to report or analyze data has diminished considerably. After all, why muck around with class intervals that, in a very real sense, abandon the precision of actual test scores by dumping different scores into the same class-interval receptacle? However, because educational leaders occasionally run into class-interval reporting and/or analysis schemes, I wanted you to have at least a nodding acquaintance with such schemes.

Graphic Displays

It is alleged that Confucius once opined, "one picture is worth a thousand words." Now if certain statisticians were to render that adage, it would probably come out something like this: "One graphic illustrative representation is worth a series of verbal symbols numbering 10 to the third power." Regardless of how the notion is phrased, it's clear that pictorial display techniques represent potent ways to describe a set of test scores. Let's take a look at two of the more popular graphic display schemes.

Histograms

A *histogram* (*histo*[ry] + *gram*) is often referred to as a *bar graph* because columns or bars are employed to represent the frequency with which particular scores, or scores in class intervals, occur. You can represent the data in Table A.3 by constructing a histogram, such as is seen in Figure A.1. Note that, because you are working with class intervals, the designations along the base line are the points that separate the theoretical limits of the class intervals.

Notice that, in a histogram, the concept of *area* is used to represent frequency of test scores. For instance, the little rectangle at the Iowa left-hand corner of the histogram is poor old Peter Coogin's score of 19 correct. In the column at the far right, we have half of that bar represented by snippy little Cora Snively who invariably snags the top score

FIGURE A.1.

Histogram of 25 students' scores on a 50-item end-of-semester examination.

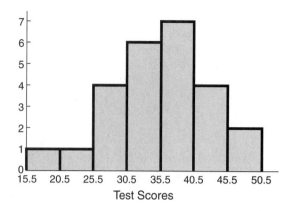

Test Scores

on any test. The reader's attention has been frequently pointed toward Peter and Cora because as you put our test scores through ever more labyrinthian analyses, it is easy to forget that the numbers you're massaging came from real people (in education, most often they're little real people) and are not merely numerical abstractions.

Histograms constitute an excellent way of communicating test-score performances of students to audiences not well versed in statistics. For example, if an educator is trying to describe a set of test scores to a lay audience, a histogram is often a happy choice. The performance of two or more groups, such as students taught by means of different instructional procedures, can be represented in histograms merely by using adjacent columns of different colors or shadings. Modestly priced computers now dispense snazzy multicolored histograms and similar displays.

Frequency Polygons

Another way to depict a set of test data graphically, again using *area* as the key concept, is the *frequency polygon*. Remember that in a histogram the frequency of scores were represented by columns. In a frequency polygon, you simply connect the midpoints at the top of each column with a single line, thus forming a polygon (many-sided figure), such as that seen in Figure A.2.

In that frequency polygon you have represented the same set of data with which you've been working in this appendix. As with the histogram, the area under the line represents the frequency with which certain scores occur.

Notice that on the base line of the frequency polygon in Figure A.2, I have used the midpoints of the class intervals to represent score frequencies. Note also that the polygon starts at the left with zero frequencies and concludes at the right with zero frequencies. Indeed, because I'm using a fifty-point exam, not even Cora Snively could earn a score of 53. The 53 point on the base line is merely the midpoint of the next class interval above the highest scores.

Smoothing the curve. In many instances a set of scores, such as those seen in Figure A.2, will be represented by a smoothed-out curve line, as seen in Figure A.3. All I've done

FIGURE A.2.

Frequency polygon of 25 students' scores on a 50-item end-of-semester examination.

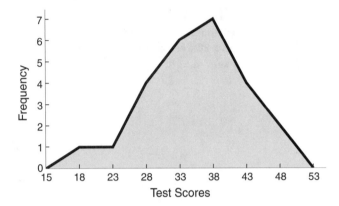

in Figure A.3 is to bend the frequency polygon's line so it's a mite more aesthetically pleasing. As before, the area under the curve line represents the cumulative percent frequency of scores. The height of the curve at any point represents frequencies.

Because curves similar to that in Figure A.3 are often used to represent test-score distributions, you should be familiar with a few of the more common shapes that those distributions take. In Figures A.4, A.5, and A.6, you'll see three distribution curves that pop up quite often in the reporting of test scores.

In Figure A.4 there is a symmetrical, bell-shaped curve represented, that is, with an equal number of high and low scores at equidistant points from the center of the curve. In this case the curve is also distributed in a normal shape. In Chapter 8 the virtues of normal curves are extolled because educators can do all sorts of interesting things with normally shaped distributions. For the time being, however, merely note that if a symmetrical curve tends to look like the bell-shaped distribution in Figure A.4, you can describe it as a normal curve or a normally shaped distribution.

In Figures A.5 and A.6 you will see curves representing what are referred to as *skewed* distributions. In Middle English the term *skewen* meant 'escape' and, in a way, the tails

FIGURE A.3.

A smooth distribution curve representing test scores.

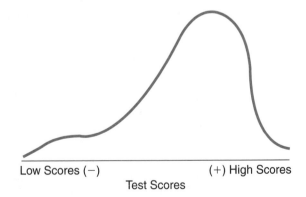

FIGURE A.4.

A symmetrical, normal distribution.

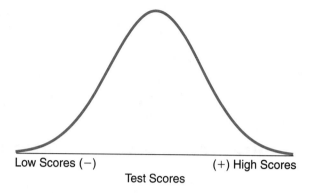

Low Scores (−)   (+) High Scores
Test Scores

FIGURE A.5.

A positively skewed distribution.

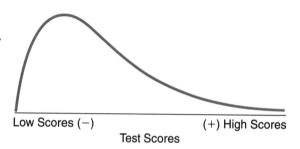

Low Scores (−)   (+) High Scores
Test Scores

FIGURE A.6.

A negatively skewed distribution.

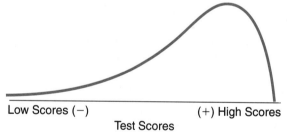

Low Scores (−)   (+) High Scores
Test Scores

of the curves in Figures A.5 and A.6 appear to be bent on escape from the rest of the distribution.

In a negatively skewed curve, the long tail of the curve is to the left, that is, toward the lower (or negative) scores. In a positively skewed curve, the long tail of the curve is to the right, that is, toward the higher (or positive) scores. Here's a little thought problem. Suppose you were a teacher who wanted to design a super instructional unit so that many of your pupils scored well on the end-of-unit test and very few scored badly. Would you want scores on the end-of-unit test to be normal, negatively skewed, or positively skewed? (Pause for a moment, and consider your answer.) If you answered anything other than negatively skewed, restudy Figures A.4 to A.6.

So far you've seen that graphic display techniques serve as rather decent devices to depict a set of data. Unfortunately, they're almost indecent when it comes to comparing different sets of data. Do you think you can say that "in relationship to another curve, one distribution curve was somewhat fatter near the middle but had a much cuter bump on the left?" No, to carry out meaningful comparisons among sets of test scores, you'll need other tools. The most common of those tools are referred to as *indicators of central tendency* and *indicators of variability*.

Indicators of Central Tendency

If you want to describe a set of test scores to someone, there are at minimum two basic ingredients that you'd need to convey. One of these notions concerns the way that the distribution of scores is *spread out*, that is, how variable or dispersed the test scores are. I will consider such indicators of variability shortly. Another descriptive ingredient that helps convey the nature of a set of test scores to someone is one in which the test scores tend to be *centered*, that is, where the bulk of the scores pile up. If you can characterize a data distribution's central tendency and variability with a few numbers, you've gone a long way toward rendering a useful description of that distribution. The three most common indicators of central tendency are the *mean*, the *median*, and the *mode*. I'll consider each of these in turn.

The Mean

The most frequently used index of a distribution's central tendency is the mean. The mean is simply an arithmetic average of all the scores in a distribution. It is computed by summing all the scores, then dividing that sum by the number of scores in the distribution. The formula for the mean is seen below. Incidentally, for any formula presented in this appendix, there'll be the formula, an explanation of its symbols, and an *in-words-only* representation of the same formula.

$$\overline{X} = \frac{\Sigma X}{n}$$

where = the mean
X = a raw score
Σ = the sum of the raw scores
n = the number of raw scores

or, in other words:

The *mean* = all of the raw scores added together, then divided by the number of raw scores.

When people talk about an "average score" or "average height," they often are thinking of a mean. Because the mean is computed by using every score in the distribution, it is an extremely representative measure. Its strength, however, is also its weakness, because several atypically high or atypically low scores can really distort the value of the mean.

For example, let's assume that you're testing a group of 100 high school seniors with a ninety-five-item examination covering the fundamental facts of government. You want to secure a decent idea of how much information the 100 seniors possess about the way that their country is governed. You plan to present the results of this examination to the district's school board to help board members make a decision regarding whether the study of government should receive a larger share of the district's instructional time.

Now imagine that most of the 100 seniors answer between sixty and eighty items correctly, thus reflecting a fair degree of conversance with what's going on in government. However, imagine also that ten of the brighter seniors got together before the exam and decided as a prank to "play it dumb," that is, they deliberately tried to answer the questions incorrectly. Instead of ending up with a mean of, for instance, 70.3 items correct (which would have been the case if the ten pranksters had played it straight), the resulting mean might turn out to be only 63.5. Such a misleading mean can result whenever there are a few very atypical scores.

For instance, if you're computing the average income of several hundred typical folks, then add in the yearly income of just one multimillionaire, it will really inflate the mean. Thus, although the mean is a stable and sensitive index of central tendency, and to be preferred in most instances, you must be attentive to the impact of aberrant scores on the mean.

The Median

The second most frequently used index of central tendency is the median. The median of a distribution of test scores is that point that divides the scores into two equal halves. For example, the median of the following set of such scores—10, 9, 9, 8, 7, 6, 5—would be 8 because 8 is the score point that divides the set of scores into two equal halves.

Now consider the following set of scores: 8, 7, 7, 6, 5, 4, 4, 3. What would the median be for this score distribution? Well, remembering that a single score theoretically extends 0.5 above and 0.5 below that score, the median for this set of eight scores would be 5.5. This illustrates that the median need not be an actually occurring score, only a *point* that splits the distribution into two equal parts.

One advantage of the median as a measure of central tendency is that it is not unduly affected by atypically large or small scores. Unlike the mean, which gets jolted around because of hyper-high or hyper-low scores, the median treats each of these wild scores as "merely another score," no more or less important than any other score. For example, remember that the median was 8 for the following set of seven scores: 10, 9, 9, 8, 7, 6, 5. Well, the median would still be 8 for the following set of seven scores: 521, 9, 9, 8, 7, 6, 5. You would have to concede, of course, that if you're dealing with a ten-point test, the person with a score of 521 is apparently pretty bright. However, note that such a wildly high score fails to alter the median one whit (or even a half-whit).

As with the mean, it is the strength of the median that is also its weakness. The median fails to reflect the magnitude of the impact of every score in the distribution, even when certain of those scores are very high or very low. Thus, although the median would not be *unduly* influenced by the score of 521 in the previous example, it would not be influenced *at all* by the magnitude of that score.

The Mode

The mode of a distribution of scores is simply the most frequently occurring score in the distribution. With most reasonably large sets of test scores, the mode will occur somewhere near the middle of the distribution, so it can also serve as an index of the distribution's central tendency. There are some cases in which a distribution has two or even three most frequently occurring scores. In such cases, statisticians refer to *bimodal* or *trimodal* distributions.

Because the mode takes account of even fewer data than the median, and much fewer than the mean, it is not used often in describing a distribution's central tendency. In a few instances educational leaders may be interested in what test score most of the students earned, but such situations arise fairly infrequently.

Relationships among central tendency measures. In a normally shaped distribution of scores, the mean, median, and mode are identical. Merely think about a bell-shaped symmetrical curve for a moment, and you'll realize that the value of all of these three indicators will coincide. With skewed distributions, however, there will be the relationships depicted in Figure A.7 in which you see that in skewed distributions the mean is closer to the tail of the distribution, the median is next closest to the tail, but the mode is farthest from the tail.

You have now considered three different indicators of a score distribution's central tendency, that is, the mean, median, and mode. Quite often, particularly when the score distribution is symmetrical, only one of these indicators is used to describe how the distribution's scores tend to center. In such instances, that indicator is usually the mean. When there is a substantial difference between the numerical values of the mean and the median (which, as you have seen, arises when a score distribution is skewed), it is a good idea to describe the distribution's central tendency by supplying both the mean and the median. If you're feeling generous, toss in the mode as well.

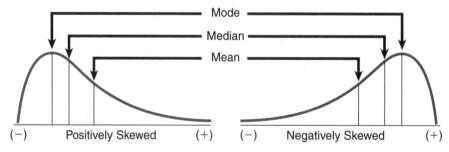

FIGURE A.7.

Relationship of the mean, median, and mode in positively and negatively skewed distributions.

Indicators of Variability

In addition to letting people know how a set of scores tends to center, you need to let them know how variable the scores in the distribution are. Putting it another way, people need to know how spread out the scores are.

Consider Figure A.8 in which two sets of scores with identical means are presented. The distribution at the left is spread out considerably, with a good many very high and very low scores, while the distribution at the right has few extreme scores. Even though the means are the same, the left-distribution's scores are more variable than the right-distribution's scores, with the result that the distribution at the right is decisively more scrunched. (The adjective *scrunched*, incidentally, is not a technically respectable statistical descriptor.)

As a further aside, it must be regrettably noted that, while statisticians have come up with some remarkably precise descriptive techniques, most of these techniques are inordinately bland. You'll hear distributions described by their means and medians but never by their more subtle dimensions. When, for example, have you ever heard a set of test scores being described as *cuddly* or *aloof?* The time has come for statisticians to embellish their descriptive repertoire by providing something other than their austere indicators of central tendency and variability. However, until they do, we're stuck with what we have. Hence, let's return to our interrupted discourse on the virtues of variability.

As you can see from Figure A.8 it is possible for two sets of test scores to have completely identical central tendencies, yet be substantially different with respect to how divergent their test scores are. Because the two distributions in Figure A.8 are both symmetrical, not only are their means equivalent, but their medians and modes are also identical. In other words, if all you knew about these distributions were their indicators of central tendency, you would not have a very good description of the two sets of test scores. You need an indicator of the variability, that is, the *dispersion* of the scores within a distribution.

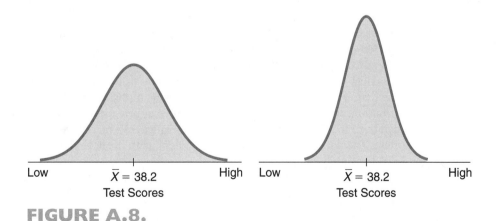

FIGURE A.8.

Two sets of test scores with equal means, yet different variabilities.

The Range

The most readily calculated index of a distribution's variability is its *range*. The range is calculated merely by subtracting the lowest score from the highest score as demonstrated in the following formula:

$$\text{Range} = X_h - X_l$$

where X_h = the highest score in the distribution
X_l = the lowest score in the distribution

or, in other words:

The *range* = the distribution's highest score minus its lowest score.

To illustrate, if you had a set of thirty-five pupils' scores on a fifty-item exam, and the lowest score was 15 while the highest score was 47, the range would be computed merely by subtracting the 15 from the 47, thus resulting in a range of 32. The simplicity of the range's computation is just about its only redeeming virtue, because there are only two scores involved in its computation. If you have an aberrantly highest and/or lowest score, the resulting range will yield a misleading indication of the distribution's overall variability.

The Standard Deviation

To circumvent the deficiencies of the range and its vulnerability to being influenced by one or two unusual scores, statisticians have devised a far more sensitive index of a distribution's variability, known as the *standard deviation*. The standard deviation offers you a way of thinking about the *average* variability of test scores that is roughly equivalent to the way people think about the *average* size of a test score when they compute the mean. In essence, the standard deviation tells you what the *average distance* from the mean is for each of the scores in a distribution. To get an idea of what that notion involves, return for a moment to Figure A.8, and note that in the distribution to the left, the individual scores in the distribution are, on average, farther from the mean of that distribution than are the scores in the distribution on the right from their mean. Accordingly, the distribution at the left ought to have a larger standard deviation, that is, a greater average distance of scores from the mean, than the distribution at the right. It does.

Let's see, now, how the standard deviation is calculated. Let me start off by observing that, if you wish, you can subtract the value of the mean from each score in the distribution, thus producing what is referred to as *deviations* from the mean. You use the symbol x to represent such a deviation. In Figure A.9 you see a set of eighteen test scores represented in a blocked-out histogram, along with the deviations of several scores from the distribution's mean of 10.0.

Remember that each of the separate blocks in the histogram stands for an individual's actual test score. To determine what the deviation score is for each test score, all you do is to subtract the mean from that score.

$$x = X - \overline{X}$$

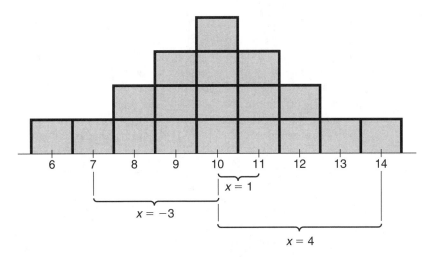

FIGURE A.9.

A histogram for 18 test scores illustrating 3 deviation scores from the distrubution's mean.

where x = a deviation from the mean
  X = a raw score
  $\overline{X}$ = mean

or, in other words:

A *deviation* from the mean = a raw score minus the score-distribution's mean.

Notice that the person who scored 14 correct has a deviation of +4.0 while the person who scored only 7 has a deviation of −3.0. An easy way to picture deviation scores is to conceive of them as the *distance* (along the base line of a graphically represented distribution) of a score from its distribution's mean.

   To get a fix on the average distance (spread) of scores in a distribution, your first inclination might be to sum all of the deviations Σx (where the upper-case or capital sigma signifies "the sum of"), then divide by the number of scores. In such a way you would secure a sort of mean deviation score. Distressingly, however, because there are precisely enough negative deviation values to cancel out the positive deviation values, Σx always turns out to be zero. Hence, this simple-minded average of variability would turn out to be zero, because zero divided by anything equals zero. Foiled.

   However, statisticians, being nimble with numbers, added a clever wrinkle to the process by *squaring* each deviation, that is, multiplying each number times itself. If you will reach back into your past and recall any fleeting brushes with algebra you might have had, you'll recollect that a negative number multiplied by a negative number equals a positive product. Accordingly, our −3 when multiplied by itself is magically transformed into a +9.

You first square all of the deviations, then sum them to obtain a quantity (Σx^2) referred to as the sum of squared deviations. Now because you squared every deviation to get rid of the negatives, the sizes of your quantities have mushroomed. To get those score values back to where they were originally, that is, to unmushroom them, it's time for another bit of statistical sleight of hand. First, you divide the sum of squared deviations by the number of scores in the distribution (reminiscent of how you calculate a mean), then take the square root of the whole works, and, presto, you're back to the original number magnitudes but without the negatives. The formula for the standard deviation follows:

$$s = \sqrt{\frac{\Sigma x^2}{n}}$$

where s = the standard deviation
Σx^2 = the sum of squared deviations
n = the number of scores in the distribution

or, in other words:

The *standard deviation* = the square root of all the squared deviation scores, summed, then divided by the number of scores.

Different notation schemes are often employed to represent the standard deviation. For example, the letters *S.D.* are sometimes used, as is the Greek symbol σ (lower-case sigma). But whatever its symbol, always remember that the standard deviation is nothing more than an average of the spread of the scores in a distribution from the mean of that distribution. The more spread out the scores are, the larger the standard deviation. The less spread out the scores are, the smaller the standard deviation.[3]

It should add a bit of insight to the meaning of the standard deviation if you actually compute one. Please use the same scores as you saw in Figure A.9. In Table A.4 are presented the eighteen scores (column 1), their deviations (column 2), their squared deviations (column 3), and a fourth column of squared raw scores I'll discuss in a moment.

Now place the necessary quantities in the formula for the standard deviation, then compute the *s*.

$$s = \sqrt{\frac{72}{18}}$$
$$= 4$$
$$= 2$$

So your standard deviation for the set of eighteen test scores turns out to be 2.0. It is interesting to see how the addition of a few divergent test scores would affect the size of *s*. For instance, if you added a score of 0 and another of 20 to the set of eighteen scores, their contribution to the sum of squared deviations (200) actually exceeds the entire contribution of the initial eighteen scores. You would have the following results:

$$\Sigma x^2 = 72 + 100 + 100, s = \sqrt{\frac{272}{20}} = 3.7$$

TABLE A.4	A Set of Test Scores, Their Deviations, Squared Deviations, and Squares		

(1) RAW SCORES X	(2) DEVIATIONS x	(3) SQUARED DEVIATIONS x^2	(4) SQUARED RAW SCORES X^2
14	4	16	196
13	3	9	169
12	2	4	144
12	2	4	144
11	1	1	121
11	1	1	121
11	1	1	121
10	0	0	100
10	0	0	100
10	0	0	100
10	0	0	100
9	−1	1	91
9	−1	1	81
9	−1	1	81
8	−2	4	64
8	−2	4	64
7	−3	9	49
6	−4	16	36
$\Sigma X = 180$	$\Sigma x = 0$	$\Sigma x^2 = 72$	$\Sigma X^2 = 1,872$

In other words, the addition of the two widely divergent scores almost doubles the size of the original standard deviation of 2.0.

It is sometimes more convenient, particularly given today's reliance on electronic calculators, to employ the following raw score formula for the sum of squared deviations:

$$\Sigma x^2 = \Sigma X^2 - \frac{(\Sigma X)^2}{n}$$

where Σx^2 = the sum of squared deviations
ΣX^2 = the sum of squared raw scores
ΣX = the sum of raw scores
n = the number of raw scores

or, in other words:

The *sum of squared deviations* = the sum of squared raw scores less the squared sum of raw scores divided by the number of scores.

By using this raw score formula, you obtain a quantity identical to that derived by subtracting the mean from the individual raw scores, then squaring the resulting deviations. Although there's little difference in the difficulty when you're working with convenient means ($\overline{X} = 10$) and small whole numbers, such as in the present examples, when the raw scores are larger and the mean has two decimal places, this raw score formula comes in handy. Let's use it with the data in Table A.4 to see how it works.

$$\Sigma x^2 = 1,872 - \frac{(180)^2}{18}$$

$$= 1,872 - \frac{32,400}{18}$$

$$= 1,872 - 1,800$$

$$= 72$$

The 72 you obtained via the raw score formula is, of course, equivalent to the sum of squared deviations you secured by subtracting the mean from the individual raw scores, then squaring and summing those deviations. If you feel a need to discover the algebraic

equivalencies of the two formulae for the sum of squared deviations, feel free to do so. Otherwise, simply think of it as magic, magic that works!

Because of its sensitivity to raw score dispersion from the mean, the standard deviation is an excellent index of variability and, consequently, is almost universally employed to describe the spread in a set of test scores. Anticipate that if, as an educational leader, you're going to be working with many sets of test scores, you'll most likely become well acquainted with standard deviations and what they signify. As with all statistical indicators, the more you work with standard deviations, the more knowledgeable you'll be when employing them.

The Variance

Had you stopped one step before the conclusion of the standard deviation computations, that is, if you had stopped prior to taking that final square root, you would have had a quantity known as the *variance*. The variance of a distribution, just like the standard deviation of the distribution, becomes larger when there is more score variability present. However, because the numerical size of the variance is more difficult to make sense out of, at least for nonstatistical folks, it is rarely used for descriptive purposes.

Thus, of the three indicators you have seen that are sometimes used to describe a distribution's variability, namely, the range, the standard deviation, and the variance, by all odds the most frequently employed (that makes it modal) is the standard deviation.

Indicators of Relationship

Does a person who gets a high score on an academic aptitude test tend to earn good grades? If you administer Achievement Test X to students this week and readminister it to them two weeks later, how similar are their scores apt to be? Will people who display healthy self-concepts on a self-esteem inventory be likely to perform well academically? Are students' scores on academic tests decent predictors of students' postschool effectiveness?

Questions such as these are constantly being tossed around by educators, especially those who enjoy question-tossing. The answers to all such questions hinge on *the extent to which two variables are related*. Take, for instance, the initial questions about academic aptitude test scores and grades. One variable is the scores people get on the academic aptitude test; the other variable is their grades as reflected, perhaps, by their end-of-year grade point averages. To answer the question of whether a high test-scorer is apt to be a high grade-getter, you need to determine the nature of the *relationship* between the academic aptitude test scores and grades.

Graphic Representations

You can attempt to identify the nature of the relationship between two variables in a number of ways, some of them far less satisfying than others. For example, you might gather some academic aptitude test scores and grade point averages for fifty or sixty students and visually inspect them in an effort to "eye-ball" your way toward understanding. You could also place scores on a scatterplot graph, such as the one seen in Figure A.10 where a dot represents an individual's score on the two variables. Note, for instance, the dot in the lower left-hand corner of the graph. That dot represents the performance of someone who scored low on the academic aptitude test and who also received low grades. The dot in the upper right-hand corner of the cluster of dots represents the performance of someone who garnered high grades and a high academic aptitude score. Now, by visually surveying the array of dots in Figure A.10, you can get a rough sense of the manner in which the two variables are related. If individuals perform well on one variable, they tend to perform well on the other variable, and conversely. This sort of relationship is referred to as a *positive relationship*. It occurs when high performances on one variable tend to go with high performances on the other variable, low performances go with low performances, and middling performances go with middling performances.

A *negative relationship* would be reflected by a different array of plottings on a graph, such as is seen in Figure A.11 where you see that as individuals get a high score on Variable One, they tend to get low scores on Variable Two, and vice versa. The absence of any substantial relationship between two variables would turn out to be a set of score plots that are scattered, unsystematically, all over the place.

There's also something else to note in the differences of the score plot arrays in Figures A.10 and A.11. Observe the fact that the dots in Figure A.11 are more closely clustered than those in Figure A.10. This difference in the clustering of the two sets of scores relates to the *magnitude*, that is, the *strength*, of the relationship. The stronger the relationship between two variables, the less scattered the points will be. Therefore, it is apparent that the (more tightly clustered) negative relationship represented in Figure A.11 is a stronger relationship than the (less tightly clustered) positive relationship represented in Figure A.10.

FIGURE A.10.

A graphic representation of a positive relationship between students' performance on two variables.

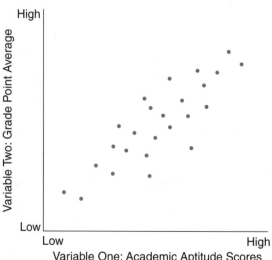

FIGURE A.11.

A graphic representation of a negative relationship between two variables.

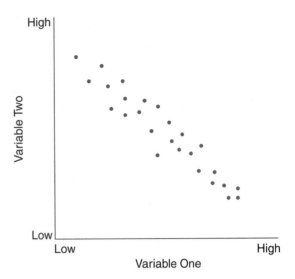

By using these graphic display techniques, you have seen that the relationship between two variables can be described according to its magnitude (strong or weak) and its *direction* (positive or negative). The graphic display techniques should also have made it clear that it's difficult to get a firm grasp on graphically displayed relationships because of the imprecision of visually derived estimates. Accordingly, with the hope that the foregoing few paragraphs provided a useful preliminary glimpse of statistical relationships, let's move on to a more precise indicator of the relationship between two variables.

The Product-Moment Correlation Coefficient

Without question, the most widely used indicator of the magnitude and direction of the relationship between two variables is the *product-moment correlation coefficient* (*r*), sometimes referred to as the Pearson correlation coefficient after its originator, the English statistician Karl Pearson.

The product-moment correlation coefficient can range in size from +1.00 to –1.00. An *r* of +1.00 (see Figure A.12A) represents a perfect positive relationship while an *r* of –1.00 (see Figure A.12B) represents a perfect negative relationship. An *r* of zero (see Figure A.12C) indicates that there is no linear relationship whatsoever between two variables. The product-moment correlation approach is used with *linearly* related data, that is, data whose scatterplots suggest a more or less straight-line relationship, not a curvilinear one (see Figure A.12). Other statistical techniques are employed to represent curvilinear relationships.

Because the product-moment correlation coefficient provides measurement specialists with a fairly precise tool to depict the magnitude and direction of a relationship, it has been widely used since the early days of the twentieth century. Quite naturally, therefore, a number of conventional expectations have grown up around the correlation coefficient. For example, if you're trying to establish the extent to which a 100-item standardized

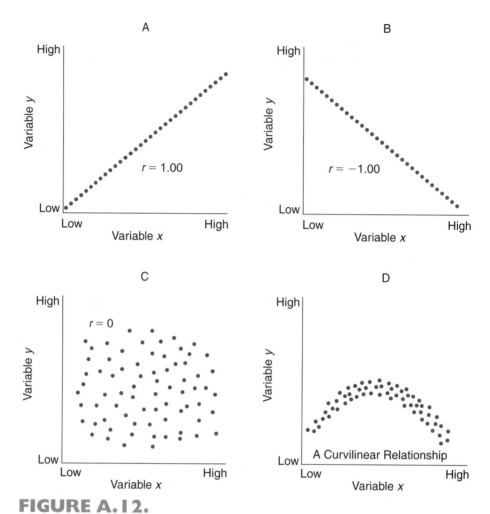

FIGURE A.12.

Scatterplots representing various relationships between two variables.

achievement test yields consistent scores on two different testing occasions, you usually expect that the resulting r will be around .80 to .90. The more you work with educational tests, the more familiar you will become with these conventional expectations.

The deviation score formula. Let's see now how you compute a Pearson product-moment correlation coefficient, and, more importantly, let's find out why this computational procedure works. You can commence your exploration of r by considering the following fundamental *deviation score formula* for the correlation coefficient:

$$r_{xy} = \frac{\Sigma_{xy}}{\sqrt{(\Sigma x^2)(\Sigma y^2)}}$$

where r_{xy} = the coefficient of correlation between Variable X and Variable Y

Σx^2 = the sum of the squared deviation scores for the x variable

Σy^2 = the sum of the squared deviations scores for the y variable

Σxy = the sum of the crossproducts, that is, the sum of an individual's deviation score on the x variable times that individual's deviation score on the y variable

or, in other words:

The *correlation coefficient* = the sum of the deviation crossproducts divided by the square root of the product of the two different sums of squared deviations.

This formula for the correlation coefficient can easily intimidate a reader, for it appears to reflect a covey of exotic little statistical quantities that bear little relationship to the realities of how one tells whether a person's score on Variable X will be like (or unlike) that person's score on Variable Y. However, as you will see by slowly analyzing that formula, you will discover that it is merely a numerical way of representing a common-sensical insight. Let's start analyzing.

You can begin by remembering that an individual's deviation score on one variable, for example, Variable X, indicates how far removed that individual's score is from the mean of the X distribution. For example, a person who scores 14 on Test X in which the mean is 10 gets an x of $+4.0$, thus indicating that the individual's raw score was four points above the mean. A similar way of representing an individual's score on Variable Y is used, so that a y deviation score of -2.0 indicates that the individual's raw score was two points below the mean of the Y distribution.

Now keep your thinking cap tightly affixed to your head as I inch toward an explanation of why an r of, say, $+.75$ signifies a situation meaningfully different than, for instance, an r of $+.52$ or $-.38$.

You have seen what a perfect positive relationship of $r = 1.00$ would look like (Figure A.12A). That relationship occurs whenever all the individuals' scores on Variable X are exactly the same distance from the mean of the X distribution as their scores are on Variable Y from the mean of the Y distribution. In other words, each individual's x deviation score is precisely the same as that individual's y deviation score. For a perfect positive relationship between two eighty-item tests, if Jasmine Jones scored twelve points above the mean in the x distribution, then Jasmine would have to score precisely twelve points above the mean of the y distribution. For Jasmine, then, you would have an x of 12 and a y of 12. Accordingly, for Jasmine you would find that $x^2 = 144$, $y^2 = 144$, and $xy = 144$.

Now just for illustration purposes, let's say you tossed Jasmine's scores into the deviation score formula for r, so that you'd come up with the following:

$$r_{xy} = \frac{\Sigma_{xy}}{\sqrt{(\Sigma x^2)(\Sigma y^2)}}$$

$$= \frac{144}{\sqrt{(144)(144)}}$$

$$= 1.0$$

If everyone in a group of 100 individuals behaved as delightfully as Jasmine, even though your numbers would be larger, the result would be the same. For example,

$$r = \frac{1,440,000}{\sqrt{(1,440,000)(1,440,000)}}$$

$$= 1.0$$

The sum of the crossproducts (deviation x times deviation y) would be *equivalent* to the two sums of squared deviations (Σx^2 and Σy^2). Thus, because the latter two sums are identical, the square root of their product would be the same as the sum of the crossproducts. Moreover, when identical quantities are divided into each other, the result is 1.0.

Now, for a moment or two, try to imagine a set of fifty or so test performances similar to Jasmine's, insofar as all students scored *exactly* the same distance above (or below) the means of the X and Y distributions. The result would be a perfect + 1.00 correlation. However, suppose that a few of those fifty students were not quite so obliging and that a few of them actually had an x of +2.0 and a y of −2.0. The xy contribution to the sum of crossproducts for each of these individuals would be a *negative* 4.0. Moreover, when you add two −4.0 contributions to your otherwise completely positive xy, the result would be a smaller sum of crossproducts. Using the previous fictitious example, you would find yourself in a situation in which the sum of the squared deviations remained the same (remember a negative number multiplied by itself yields a positive result), but the size of the crossproducts would be smaller. For example, instead of

$$r = \frac{1,440,000}{\sqrt{(1,440,000)(1,440,000)}}$$

$$= 1.0$$

you might have

$$r = \frac{1,320,000}{\sqrt{(1,440,000)(1,440,000)}}$$

$$= .92$$

Hopefully, you can begin to see that the kernel idea in Pearson's correlation approach is the extent to which an individual's deviation score on one variable matches that individual's deviation score on the other variable. In a perfect negative relationship, everyone's x score would be the same value as their y score but with the algebraic signs reversed. Jasmine Jones would have to get a y of −12 to go with her x of +12. For situations in which no discernible relationship is present, there is no systematic similarity or dissimilarity in students' x and y scores.

To get a bit of practice in the use of deviation score formulae for r, you might find it profitable to study the data presented in Table A.5 for you will compute an r with the deviation score formula using the data in the table. In particular, note the values in the three columns at the right, because the sums of these columns are t quantities you'll insert in the formula. Notice, for example, that whereas mo students' xy values are positive, Student A and Student C have negative xy values. Also observe that a student's xy value is typ-

TABLE A.5 Scores of Ten Students on Two Tests Along with the Calculations and Totals Necessary for Computation of the Deviation Score Product-Moment Correlation Coefficient Formula

STUDENT	TEST X	TEST Y	x	y	x^2	y^2	xy
a	8	3	.2	−3.1	.04	9.61	−.62
b	2	1	−5.8	−5.1	33.64	26.01	29.58
c	8	6	.2	−.1	.04	.01	−.02
d	5	3	−2.8	−3.1	7.84	9.61	8.68
e	15	14	7.2	7.9	51.84	62.41	56.88
f	11	12	3.2	5.9	10.24	34.81	18.88
g	13	9	5.2	2.9	27.04	8.41	15.08
h	6	4	−1.8	−2.1	3.24	4.41	3.78
i	4	4	−3.8	−2.1	14.44	4.41	7.98
j	6	5	−1.8	−1.1	3.24	1.21	1.98
Σ	78	61	0	0	151.6	160.9	142.2

ically larger than one of that student squared deviation values. Try to go through all ten sets of scores and attempt to see what happens when you subtract the $\overline{X}$ of 7.8 and the $\overline{Y}$ of 6.1 from their respective scores.

To compute the value of r, all you need do is plug in the necessary summation from the table as follows:

$$r = \frac{142.2}{\sqrt{(151.6)(160.9)}}$$
$$= \frac{142.2}{156.2}$$
$$= .91$$

The raw score formula. Now that you understand, hopefully, the basic logic of the product-moment correlational method of describing a relationship, you can employ another formula for r which, though far more imposing because it is simply brimming with letters and symbols, is much easier to use. It is the *raw score formula* for the product-moment correlation coefficient:

$$r_{xy} = \frac{\Sigma XY - \frac{(\Sigma X)(\Sigma Y)}{n}}{\sqrt{\left(\Sigma X^2 - \frac{(\Sigma X)^2}{n}\right)\left(\Sigma Y^2 - \frac{(\Sigma Y)^2}{n}\right)}}$$

or, in other words:

The *coefficient of* the raw score formula for the sum of crossproducts divided by the
correlation between = square root of the product of the raw score formulae for the sums
Variables X and Y of squares for variables X and Y.

If you will recall the earlier treatment of the standard deviation, I introduced (ever so politely) the raw score formula for computing the sum of the squared deviations (Σx^2). You'll recognize that the expression at the lower left of this new formula for r is the very same formula. The two other expressions in the raw score formula for r are merely the raw score equivalents of (Σy^2) and (Σxy).

You can apply the raw score formula to the same set of scores you used in the previous example with the deviation score formula. In Table A.6 those scores and the necessary quantities for the raw score product-moment correlation formula are presented. Substituting the necessary values in the raw score formula, you have

$$r_{xy} = \frac{618 - \frac{(78)(61)}{10}}{\sqrt{\left(760 - \frac{(78)^2}{10}\right)\left(533 - \frac{(61)^2}{10}\right)}}$$

$$= \frac{142.2}{156.2}$$

$$= .91$$

You will notice, of course, that because you are using the raw scores, their squares, and their crossproducts (as opposed to subtracting the two means from each of the scores), the calculations are usually more simple with the raw score formula. By working through the practice exercises at the close of this appendix you should become quite comfortable in the use of either of these two formulae.

The Rank-Order Correlation Coefficient

Another technique for estimating the magnitude and direction of the relationship between two variables is the rank-order correlation coefficient introduced by Sir Charles Spearman. (Anyone who has been knighted should be taken seriously.) Spearman's correlation coefficient (r_s) is interpreted in essentially the same way as the Pearson product-moment r; but it is generally simpler to compute. Besides its computational simplicity, it may be used with data that represent only an *ordinal scale* and not necessarily an *internal scale*.

Measurement scales. It's necessary to spend a few sentences on the kinds of scales that educational leaders work with in educational measurement because, for the first time, you must be concerned about these scales. An *interval scale* is one that allows you to believe there are actually equal intervals between equidistant points on the scale. For example, the ten-point difference between scores of 48 and 58 on a 100-item scale would be con-

	TABLE A.6	**Scores of Ten Students of Two Tests Along with the Calculations and Totals Necessary for Computation of the Raw Score Product-Moment Correlation Coefficient Formula**			
STUDENT	**TEST X**	**TEST Y**	**X²**	**Y²**	**XY**
a	8	3	64	9	24
b	2	1	4	1	2
c	8	6	64	36	48
d	5	3	25	9	15
e	15	14	225	196	210
f	11	12	121	144	132
g	13	9	169	81	117
h	6	4	36	16	24
i	4	4	16	16	16
j	6	5	36	25	30
β	78	61	760	533	618

sidered identical to the ten-point difference between scores of 88 and 98. If you are convinced that such is the case, then you have an interval scale. A *ratio scale*, incidentally, is an interval scale for which a zero point exists, such as a weight scale or a height scale in which it is possible to have a true zero. You'll encounter few ratio scales in educational measurement.

An *ordinal scale* needs no equal intervals between its points. Instead, only rank order is requisite. For instance, if a principal ranked five teachers in order of their effectiveness, this would be an example of data representing an ordinal scale. There are many situations in education in which you cannot confidently believe that equal scale intervals are present in the data; hence, educators choose to assume they're working with data on an ordinal, rather than interval, scale. The Pearson product-moment correlation coefficient requires *interval* data. The Spearman coefficient can be computed with data even if they represent only an ordinal scale.

The formula for the rank-order correlation coefficient is the following:

$$r_s = 1 - \frac{6\Sigma d^2}{n^3 - n}$$

where r_s = the rank-order correlation coefficient

n = the number of subjects

Σd^2 = the sum of the squared differences between subjects' ranks

or, in other words:

The *rank-order correlation coefficient* = six times the sum of squared differences between individuals' ranks on the two variables divided by a quantity formed by the number of individuals subtracted from the number of individuals cubed.

I can illustrate the application of the formula for r_s by using it with the data in Table A.7 where seven students' scores on two attitude inventories are presented.

$$r_s = 1 - \frac{6(8.5)}{7^3 - 7}$$

$$= .85$$

Obviously, the computation of r_s is almost fool's play in contrast to the laborious calculation of the deviation score and raw score product-moment correlation formulae.

Applications

Well, if you've survived this brief brush with numbers and notations, you have mastered the key statistical concepts that you need to evaluate and use educational tests. To solidify your grasp of the statistical notions treated in this appendix, try your hand at the appendix's practice exercises and discussion questions.

TABLE A.7 **Scores of Seven Students on Two Attitudes Inventories**

STUDENT	INVENTORY 1 SCORE	INVENTORY 1 RANK	INVENTORY 2 SCORE	INVENTORY 2 RANK	d	d²
a	124	1	62	2	−1	1
b	123	2	59	3	−1	1
c	119	3	67	1	2	4
d	117	4	57	4.5	−0.5	0.25
e	110	5	57	4.5	−0.5	0.25
f	104	6	50	7	−1	1
g	94	7	52	6	1	1
						$\Sigma d^2 = 8.5$

Practice Exercises

1. For these test scores what is the mean?
   10, 8, 7, 6, 6, 6, 6, 3, 2, 1
2. For these exam scores what is the median?
   27, 24, 23, 23, 22, 20, 19, 18, 17, 9
3. For these test scores what is the mode?
   9, 9, 9, 8, 8, 7, 6. 5, 5, 3
4. For the following set of test scores, what are the mean, median, and mode?
   47, 45, 44, 44, 43, 42, 41, 39, 28
5. What is the standard deviation of the following set of test scores?
   6, 4, 3, 2, 0
6. What is the standard deviation of the following set of exam scores?
   20, 19, 18, 18, 17, 16, 15, 14, 14, 10
7. What are the mean, median, and standard deviation for the following set of scores?

69	64	56
68	63	56
68	62	54
67	61	54
65	60	51
64	58	50
64	58	48

8. What is the product-moment correlation between the X and Y measures?

X	Y	X	Y
49	42	40	38
46	42	38	39
44	44	38	40
44	40	36	29
42	43	34	37

9. What is the product-moment r between the following pretest and posttest scores?

Student	Pretest	Posttest	Student	Pretest	Posttest
1	23	82	11	20	95
2	20	90	12	21	81
3	15	78	13	20	69
4	20	74	14	19	84
5	21	84	15	17	69
6	22	78	16	21	77
7	20	82	17	19	78
8	12	80	18	18	85
9	15	84	19	23	90
10	15	54			

10. What is the rank-order correlation coefficient between the following two sets of test scores?

Student	Test A	Test B
Joe	20	17
Tom	19	19
Ann	17	11
Lee	15	14
Jim	13	15

Answers to Practice Exercises

1. mean = 5.5
2. median = 21
3. mode = 9 (Wasn't that easy?)
4. mean = 41.4, median = 43, mode = 44
5. standard deviation = 2.0
6. standard deviation = 2.8
7. mean = 60, median = 61, standard deviation = 6.1
8. $r = .67$
9. $r = .35$
10. $r_s = .50$

DISCUSSION QUESTIONS

1. How skilled in statistics do you think that a measurement specialist should be? How about a classroom teacher? What about a school administrator, for example, a district superintendent? Why?

2. In what sorts of situations, if ever, do you think that graphic display techniques are preferable to numerical indices, such as the mean and standard deviation?

3. Do you think it is possible to describe the statistical procedures treated in this appendix so that lay citizens can understand them? Will this be necessary for citizens to understand the results of large-scale educational assessment operations?

4. Why do you suppose so many educators register fear and mild loathing when the subject of educational statistics arises? Do you think such aversion tendencies can be eliminated? If so, how?

5. Can you explain to a nonmathematician in common-sense language how to understand intuitively the meaning of the standard deviation and the correlation coefficient? How would you do it?

6. Try to think of the instances in which educational leaders might need to calculate or interpret the statistical procedures treated in this appendix. List at least a half dozen such instances.

SUGGESTIONS FOR ADDITIONAL READING

Bartz, Albert. *Basic Statistical Concepts.* Old Tappan, NJ: Prentice-Hall, 1998.

Janda, Louis. *Psychological Testing.* Boston, MA: Allyn & Bacon, 1998.

Popham, W. James, and Kenneth A. Sirotnik. *Understanding Statistics in Education.* Itasca, IL: F. E. Peacock, 1992.

Silver, N. Clayton. *Guidebook of Statistical Software for the Social & Behavioral Sciences.* Boston, MA: Allyn & Bacon, 1998.

ENDNOTES

1   The possibility of a purchase-price, money-back warranty on this promise was discussed with the text's publishers who, chuckling quietly, suggested I not tie dollars to whimsy.

2   The attentive reader will note the subtle use of the Latin plural (formulae) for formula. Anyone could have said formulas. Such niceties are intended to (1) add some needed class to this book and (2) make my three years of college Latin seem worthwhile.

3   Some statisticians, for subtle reasons beyond the scope of this text, prefer to use $n - 1$ rather than n in the denomination of the standard deviation formula. With any reasonably large sample, it makes little difference whether n or $n - 1$ is used. The principle that the standard deviation is merely an average of raw score dispersion remains unaltered.

INDEX